Staffing Organizations

Herbert G. Heneman III
University of Wisconsin-Madison

Robert L. Heneman
The Ohio State University

Timothy A. Judge
University of Iowa

Mendota House
Middleton, WI

IRWIN
Chicago • Bogotá • Buenos Aires • Caracas
London • Madrid • Mexico City • Sydney • Toronto

Publisher: Mendota House, Inc.
Marketer and Distributor: Richard D. Irwin, A Times/Mirror Higher Education Group company
Development, production, composition: Impressions, Madison, WI

Irwin Team: Robin J. Zwettler, Publisher; John E. Biernat, Sponsoring Editor; Kim Kanakes, Editorial Coordinator; Michael Campbell, Marketing Manager; Robert Lange, Production Supervisor.

Impressions team: Mary Boss, Nancy MacMiller, Meg Ulber, Megan Schliesman.

Address orders and customer service questions to:
Richard D. Irwin, Inc.
1333 Burr Ridge Parkway
Burr Ridge, IL 60521
1-800-323-4560

Address editorial correspondence to:
Herbert G. Heneman III, President
Mendota House, Inc.
5621 Mendota Drive
Middleton, WI 53562
608-233-4417

Library of Congress Cataloging-in-Publication Data

Heneman, Herbert Gerhard III (1944)
     Staffing organizations / Herbert G. Heneman III, Robert L. Heneman, Timothy A. Judge
  2nd ed.
        p.   cm.
     Includes index.
      ISBN 0-256-20806-9
     Robert L., II. Judge, Tim. III. Title
     HF5549.5.R44H46   1997
     658.3′11-dc20

96-21835
CIP

Dedication

To Susan, Renée and Jill

AUTHOR PROFILES

Herbert G. Heneman III

Herb Heneman is the Dickson-Bascom Professor in Business at the University of Wisconsin-Madison. He also serves as a participating faculty member in the Industrial Relations Research Institute. Herb has also served on the faculty at the University of Washington and The Ohio State University.

Herb's research and teaching interests are in the areas of staffing, employment law and equal employment opportunity, compensation, and union growth. He is the coauthor of four books. His research has been published in *Journal of Applied Psychology, Academy of Management Journal, Personnel Psychology, Industrial and Labor Relations Review,* and *Academy of Management Review.*

Herb is a member of the Academy of Management, and a former Chair of its Human Resources Division. He is also a member of the Industrial Relations Research Association, Society for Industrial and Organizational Psychology, Society for Human Resource Management, Employment Management Association, and the International Personnel Management Association.

Robert L. Heneman

Rob Heneman is Director of Graduate Programs in Labor and Human Resources and is an Associate Professor of Management and Human Resources in the Max M. Fisher College of Business at The Ohio State University. Rob has a Ph.D. in Labor and Industrial Relations from Michigan State University, an M.A. in Labor and Industrial Relations from the University of Illinois at Urbana-Champaign, and a B.A. in Economics and Psychology from Lake Forest College. Prior to joining The Ohio State University, Rob worked as a Human Resource Specialist for Pacific Gas and Electric Company. Rob's primary areas of research, teaching, and consulting are in performance management, compensation, and staffing. His research has been published in the *Academy of Management Journal, Personnel Psychology, Research in Personnel and Human Resources Management,* and *Journal of Business and Psychology.* His research has been funded by the Work in America Institute, American Compensation Association, State of Ohio, and Consortium for Alternative Rewards Strategies Research. He is on the editorial boards of the *Human Resource Planning Journal* and *Compensation and Benefits Review.* He has been awarded the "Outstanding Teacher Award in the MLHR Program" three times by the students at The Ohio

State University. He is the author of the book *Merit Pay: Linking Pay Increases to Performance Ratings*. He has consulted with over 45 public and private sector organizations including IBM, Time Warner, Whirlpool, The Limited, and the State of Ohio. Rob is past Division Chair, Program Chair, and Executive Committee member for the Human Resources Division of the Academy of Management.

Timothy A. Judge

Tim Judge is Associate Professor of Management and Organizations in the College of Business at the University of Iowa. Prior to receiving his Ph.D. at the University of Illinois, Tim was employed as a manager at Kohl's Department Stores. Tim also has served on the faculty at Cornell University.

Tim's primary research and teaching interests are in the areas of staffing, career systems, personality assessment, and organizational behavior. He has published articles on these topics in the *Academy of Management Journal*, *Journal of Applied Psychology*, *Organizational Behavior and Human Decision Processes*, and *Personnel Psychology*. Tim serves on the editorial boards of *Journal of Applied Psychology*, *Journal of Management*, and *Personnel Psychology*. In 1995, Tim received the Ernest J. McCormick Award for distinguished early career contributions from the Society for Industrial and Organizational Psychology.

Tim is a member of the Academy of Management, American Psychological Association, and Society for Industrial and Organizational Psychology. Tim serves on the Executive Committee of the Human Resource Division of the Academy of Management and on the Steering Committee of the Careers Division of the Academy of Management. Tim is also serving as Program Chair for the Society for Industrial and Organizational Psychology's 1998 Annual Meeting.

PREFACE TO SECOND EDITION

This revision of *Staffing Organizations* continues to be based on the staffing organizations model. The model views staffing as the process by which the individual and the organization become matched to form the employment relationship. As depicted in the model, the staffing process is a product of:

- External Influences—economic conditions, labor markets, labor unions, laws and regulations
- Support Activities—strategy and planning, job analysis, measurement
- Staffing Activities—external and internal recruitment, external and internal selection, decision making and final match
- Staffing System Management—administration and evaluation

Preparation of this revision was guided by the invaluable inputs of many individuals (see Acknowledgments). Based on their suggestions and concerns, four major changes, plus numerous topical additions and updates, were made. The first major change was to incorporate staffing strategy and planning for core and flexible workforces into Chapter 4 (Strategy and Planning). The second major change was to greatly expand the treatment of external selection techniques. This was done by expanding external selection into two chapters. Chapter 9 (External Selection I) treats initial assessment methods, and the new Chapter 10 (External Selection II) treats substantive, contingent, and discretionary assessment methods. The third major change was to create a new chapter, Chapter 14 (Staffing System Management). It deals with the administration and evaluation of staffing systems. The fourth major change was to add two ''applications'' (cases and exercises) at the end of each chapter. These may be used for class discussions, projects, and paper assignments.

The topical additions and updates are as follows:

Chapter	**Topic/Update**
1. Overview and Models	• Person/organization match
	• Examples of staffing systems
2. Economic Conditions, Labor Markets, Labor Unions	• Updated labor market statistics
	• New data on alternative employment arrangements (temporary workers, independent contractors)
	• Impacts of external forces on staffing practices
3. Laws and Regulations	• Legal terms—employer, employee, independent contractor, temporary employee, coemployment
	• EEOC definition of a disability
	• Alternative dispute resolution—EEOC
4. Strategy and Planning	• Staffing strategies
	• Core and flexible workforce
	• Choosing temporary employment agencies and independent contractors
	• Future of affirmative action plans
5. Job Analysis	• Types of jobs—traditional, evolving, flexible, idiosyncratic, team-based
	• "Other" job requirements—legal, availability, moral
6. Measurement	• Meta-analysis
7. External Recruitment	• Recruitment sources—employee referral, internships and cooperatives, seniors networks
	• On-line recruiting
	• Videos and videoconferencing
	• Process flows and record keeping
	• Transition to selection
	• Applicant reactions
8. Internal Recruitment	• Mobility paths and policies
	• Targeted recruitment
	• In-house temporary pools
	• Employee nomination
	• Glass ceiling
9. External Selection I	• Expansion on all initial assessment methods
	• New ADA guidance on preemployment inquiries

10. External Selection II	• Expansion on all substantive assessment methods • Team- and quality-based assessments • Contingent methods—drug testing, medical examinations • New ADA guidance on medical examinations
11. Internal Selection	• Updates on all assessment methods • Career concepts • Applicant reactions
12. Decision Making	• Test score banding • Applicant reactions
13. Final Match	• Job offer strategy • Orientation of new employees • Socialization of new employees
14. Staffing System Management	• New chapter

Despite all of the above changes, the core features of the first edition of *Staffing Organizations* remain in the revision. These are described in the original preface.

PREFACE

Staffing is a process and function that plays a prominent role in an organization's Human Resource Management (HRM) system. At the heart of the process is an attempt to form matches between people and jobs that will result in an effective workforce for the organization. Since staffing involves the creation of the person/job match, it is the starting point for building workforce effectiveness. Other HRM activities, such as compensation and training, follow from the initial endeavor of bringing people and jobs together via staffing.

Designing and managing successful staffing processes is a major challenge for an organization. It requires multiple tools, techniques, activities, and participants. It must occur within a complex set of external influences beyond organizational control, such as labor markets and laws and regulations. Science, past experience, and gut feel must be carefully blended together to create a process that will maximize the likelihood of successful person/job matches as the employment relationship is established. This book seeks to both describe and prescribe staffing activities that can be undertaken in order to meet the staffing challenge. To do this, several features have been incorporated into the book.

First, the book is structured around the staffing organizations model. The model identifies key influences on, and components of, staffing. These include external forces, staffing support activities such as job analysis, external and internal recruitment activities, external and internal selection activities, and employment activities that represent the end point of the person/job match.

Second, the book is written from an organizational, managerial perspective. It emphasizes the role of staffing as an HR mechanism that can further the managerial purpose of achieving organizational effectiveness. However, since research increasingly reveals that applicants are vitally affected by the organization's staffing process, the applicant's perspective is not ignored. Rather, results of this research are incorporated into suggestions for how the organization can align its staffing practices in ways that will yield positive impacts on job applicants.

Third, as a logical outgrowth of the staffing organizations model, there is a wide breadth of topical coverage. This is in contrast to most other books that focus on only a single, narrow aspect of staffing, such as recruitment or selection. Staffing is a much more inclusive process than is implied in these types of books.

Fourth, accompanying this broad scope of topical coverage is reference to a diversity of literature. These references draw upon both academic and practitioner literature from behavioral, managerial, economic, and legal sources. The references were chosen in part to provide students with a useful starting point for further pursuit of topics that interest them.

Through use of the above features, we seek to provide students and others with an appreciation for, and knowledge of, the multiple facets of staffing organizations. These facets must be designed, managed, and evaluated as components of the organization's overall staffing process. Our goal is to provide individuals with an understanding of this process and to help them function as effective practitioners within it.

ACKNOWLEDGMENTS

We have received substantial and important inputs from many people in the preparation of both the first and second editions of *Staffing Organizations*. To all of the following, we gratefully acknowledge your contributions:

Steve Abraham (Northern Iowa University)
Peter Allan (Pace University)
Richard Arvey (University of Minnesota)
James Austin (The Ohio State University)
Alison Barber (Michigan State University)
Murray Barrick (University of Iowa)
Ronald Beaulieu (Central Michigan University)
Michael Bedell (Indiana University)
Chris Berger (Purdue University)
Robyn Berkley (University of Wisconsin-Madison)
Terry Bishop (Northern Illinois University)
John Blackburn (The Ohio State University)
Donna Blancero (Arizona State University)
James Breaugh (University of Missouri-St. Louis)
Robert Bretz (University of Iowa)
Wayne Cascio (University of Colorado-Denver)
Maria Castenada (SUNY-Albany)
Russ Cunningham (Pacific Gas and Electric)
John Delery (University of Arkansas)
Mildred Doering (Syracuse University)
Lee Dyer (Cornell University)
Rebecca Ellis (California Polytechnic-San Luis Obispo)
Linda Flynn (Georgia State University)
John Fossum (University of Minnesota)
Rusty Freed (Tarleton State University)
Sally Fuller (University of Washington)
Stephen Gilliland (University of Arizona)

Dennis Huett (State of Wisconsin)
Brian Klaas (University of South Carolina)
Howard Klein (The Ohio State University)
Linda Koepp (Marquette University)
Robert Lavigna (State of Wisconsin)
Anthony Milanowski (University of Wisconsin-Madison)
Michael Mount (University of Iowa)
Brian Murray (University of Texas-San Antonio)
Raymond Noe (Michigan State University)
Judy Olian (University of Maryland)
Sara Rynes (University of Iowa)
Frank Schmidt (University of Iowa)
Mark Schmit (University of Florida)
Randall Schuler (New York University)
Donald Schwab (University of Wisconsin-Madison)
Frank Siciliano (University of Wisconsin-Madison)
Judy Strauss (Illinois Benedictine College)
Judy Van Hein (Middle Tennessee State University)
Gale Varma (Deloitte Touche)
Nila Whitfield (The Ohio State University)
Margaret Williams (Purdue University)
Bruce Wonder (Western Washington University)
Phil Young (The Ohio State University)

We also thank the following people for their excellent clerical, administrative, and editorial support: Joan Evans, Michelle Brausch Roach, Rona Velte, and Donna Wallace. Finally, we thank John Biernat, Michael Campbell, Kim Kanakes, Bob Lange, and Rob Zwettler of Richard D. Irwin, and Impressions, for their dedicated work in this collaborative undertaking.

BRIEF CONTENTS

CONTENTS

CHAPTER TEN
External Selection II

PART FIVE

STAFFING ACTIVITIES: EMPLOYMENT   **539**

CHAPTER TWELVE

Decision Making   **541**

Note To The Instructor:

Mendota House and Richard D. Irwin have combined their respective skills to bring you *Staffing Organizations* in your classroom. This text is marketed and distributed by Richard D. Irwin. For assistance in obtaining information or supplementary material please contact your Irwin sales representative or the customer services division of Irwin at 800-323-4560.

STAFFING ORGANIZATIONS MODEL

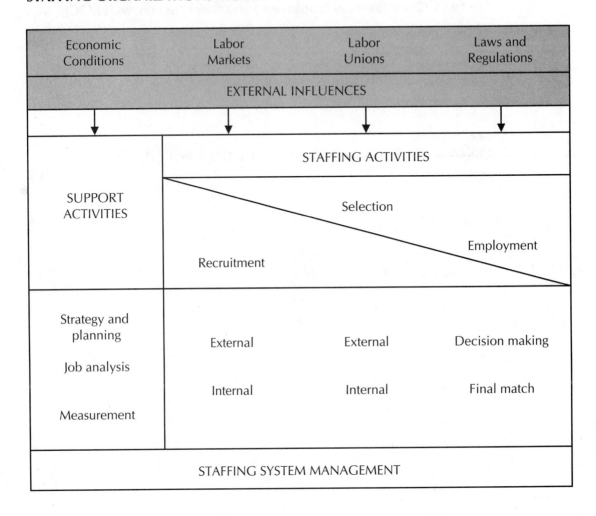

PART ONE

Staffing and External Influences

CHAPTER ONE
Overview and Models

CHAPTER TWO
Economic Conditions, Labor Markets, and Labor Unions

CHAPTER THREE
Laws and Regulations

CHAPTER ONE

Overview and Models

The Nature of Staffing
Definition of Staffing
Implications of Definition
Importance of Staffing

Staffing Models
Person/Job Match
Person/Organization Match
Staffing Components
Human Resource Management
Staffing Organizations

Staffing System Examples
Police Department
Work Team Members
State Government
Temporary Help Agency

Plan for the Book

Summary

Discussion Questions

Applications

S taffing is a critical organizational function concerned with the acquisition and deployment of the organization's workforce. This chapter begins with a formal definition of staffing, followed by a detailed examination of the implications of the definition for helping us understand staffing systems. Staffing is also looked at from three perspectives, namely strategy and planning, the human resource (HR) department, and the individual manager.

Several models are then presented to elaborate on and illustrate various facets of staffing. The first model describes the person/job match, which is the foundation of all staffing activities. Next, a model for the person/organization match is given to show how person/job matching concerns often extend beyond the confines of the target job for which the person is being considered. Then the staffing components model identifies recruitment, selection, and employment as the three key staffing activities; it also shows how both the applicant and the organization mutually interact in all of these activities. The HR management model places staffing within a broader context, showing how staffing occurs in concert with other HR activities (e.g., compensation) and is subject to important external forces (e.g., laws and regulations). Finally, the staffing organizations model pulls together all of these models and is developed to provide the basis for the structure of this book.

To bring these models to life, descriptions of several staffing systems are given. The systems involve a police department, a customer service work team, a state government, and a staffing services (temporary help agency) company. Though their staffing systems are very different in some respects, they share in common the components shown in the staffing organizations model.

Finally, the plan for the remainder of the book is presented. The overall structure of the book is shown, along with key features of each chapter.

THE NATURE OF STAFFING

Definition of Staffing

The following definition of staffing is offered and will be used throughout this book:

> Staffing is the mutual process by which the individual and the organization become matched to form the employment relationship.

This straightforward definition contains several implications, which are identified and explained next.

Implications of Definition

Organization and Individual Perspectives
Staffing is a mutual process that involves organizations seeking individuals (the traditional view of staffing) as well as individuals seeking organizations (a more

recent view). Both the organization and the individual are thus active players in the staffing process, and both organizational and individual perspectives are important to reckon with and understand.[1]

The organizational perspective emphasizes staffing as activities undertaken to further the attainment of organizational goals, such as survival, profitability, and growth. The individual perspective stresses the fact that individuals seek jobs that they will find rewarding, and that these individuals are affected by their experiences in the staffing process (e.g., how fairly they feel they have been treated by the organization).

Throughout this book, the organizational perspective is dominant. Staffing is examined primarily through an organizational lens that focuses on how staffing may contribute to organizational effectiveness. The individual perspective is not ignored, however, since individuals' experiences with the staffing system may influence the effectiveness of that system. For example, applicants who are "turned off" by aspects of the staffing process may enter the organization as less than fully committed new hires, or they may actually opt out of even joining the organization at all.

Staffing as a Process or System

Staffing is not an event such as "we hired two new sales people today." Rather, staffing is a process or system composed of a series of interrelated activities such as recruitment, selection, decision making, and job offers. Actually hiring someone is the culmination of the staffing process.

It is best to think of staffing as a process that establishes and governs the flow of applicants into the organization (external staffing) and within the organization (internal staffing). There are many steps through which applicants flow from the time they first enter the system to the time they become new hires.

The steps begin with the organization's decision to fill a vacancy, which in itself is a decision derived from strategic HR and staffing planning exercises. Usually, recruitment activities are undertaken to identify and attract applicants for the position. These blend into selection activities in which various selection techniques, such as interviews and tests, are used to assess and evaluate applicants against the requirements of the job. Results of these evaluations are then used to make decisions about which applicants to reject and which to offer a job. The final step of the staffing process is the applicant's acceptance of the job offer.

In short, applicants flow through staffing systems. The processes used in the system must be planned and managed to facilitate the making of effective person/job matches. Staffing is a generic term that encompasses these processes, be they external or internal in focus.

Forming the Employment Relationship

An emphasis on forming or entering into the employment relationship includes certain staffing decisions and excludes others. Included are hiring, promotion, and transfer decisions since all lead to the creation of a new person/job match. Excluded are decisions and actions that sever or end the employment relationship, such as voluntary quits, layoffs, and discharges. Both the organization and the individual must act positively to create a person/job match. There must be both organization selection and self-selection as part of the formation of the employment relationship. Only formation of the employment relationship is treated in this book.

Importance of Staffing

Staffing is a vital activity from the perspectives of organizational strategy, the HR department, and the individual manager. Strategically, the role of staffing is to anticipate and then fulfill the organization's workforce needs in ways that contribute to the organization's mission and objectives. Consider, for example, an organization that provides specialized automobile services such as on-demand oil and oil filter changes. Its strategic objective may be to open 25 new service units, in 5 new geographic territories, within the next two years. Its staffing systems will be expected to provide sufficient quantity and quality of new employees to staff these units. Indeed, judgments about the likely availabilies of these new employees may have contributed to the establishment of this growth objective in the first place.

The HR department normally plays a key leadership role in staffing activities for the organization. It will be responsible for the design and management of staffing systems, for the involvement of managers at critical points in these systems, and for ensuring compliance with all applicable laws and regulations. Results of a recent survey indicate these activities play a major role in an organization's HR department. The survey was conducted among a nationwide, random sample of HR department individuals who are members of the Society for Human Resource Management. The respondents were asked to indicate the percentage of their HR department's budget and time that is spent on staffing and other activities. Results of the survey are shown in Exhibit 1.1. As can be seen, staffing received the greatest percentage of budget dollars (19%) and the second greatest percentage of time spent (15%) among the HR activities.

For individual managers, having sufficient numbers and types of employees on board is necessary for the smooth and efficient operation of their work unit. Employee shortages often require disruptive adjustments, such as job reassignments or overtime for current employees. Underqualified employees present special challenges to the manager, such as a need for close supervision and training. Failure of the underqualified to achieve acceptable performance may require termination of employees, a difficult decision to make and implement.

EXHIBIT 1.1   Survey Results Regarding Staffing and Other HR Activities

In the spring of 1993, the Society for Human Resource Management (SHRM) surveyed a random sample of its members on their views about a variety of human resource activities and their satisfaction with those activities as individual HR professionals.

The first section of the questionnaire was a general overview of respondents' involvement in human resource activities. Rough estimates were obtained of the allocation of budgetary and time resources across a variety of major human resource domains. As the table below indicates, more budget dollars are devoted to staffing than any other human resource function, while the most time is spent on employee and labor relations.

	% of Budget	% of Time
Staffing	19	15
Design/administration of employee benefits programs	15	10
Employee & labor relations	13	18
Training	11	9
Design/administration of employee compensation programs	9	10
Health, safety & security	8	6
Design/administration of programs in response to government regulations	6	7
Performance appraisal	5	7
Strategic planning	4	7
Conducting other activities	10	11

Source: "Human Resource Practices and Job Satisfaction" (Executive Summary), 1993. Reprinted with the permission of the Society for Human Resource Management, Alexandria, VA.

STAFFING MODELS

Person/Job Match

At the heart of staffing organizations is the person/job match. This match seeks to align characteristics of individuals and jobs in ways that will result in desired HR outcomes. Casual comments made about applicants often reflect awareness of the importance of the person/job match. "Clark just doesn't have the interpersonal skills that it takes to be a good customer service representative." "Mary has exactly the kinds of budgeting experience this job calls for; if we hire her there won't be any downtime while she learns our systems." "Gary says he was attracted to apply for this job because of its sales commission plan; he says he likes jobs where his pay depends on how well he performs." "Diane was impressed by the amount of challenge and autonomy she will have." "Jack turned down our offer; we gave him our best shot, but he just didn't feel he could handle the long hours and amount of travel the job calls for."

Comments such as these raise four important points about the person/job match. First, jobs are characterized by their requirements (e.g., interpersonal skills, previous budgeting experiences) and embedded rewards (e.g., commission sales plan, challenge and autonomy). Second, individuals are characterized by their level of qualification (e.g., few interpersonal skills, extensive budgeting experience) and motivation (e.g., need for pay to depend on performance, need for challenge and autonomy). Third, in each of the previous examples the issue was one of the likely degree of fit or match between the characteristics of the job and the person. Fourth, there are implied consequences for every match. For example, Clark may not perform very well in his interactions with customers; retention might quickly become an issue with Jack.

These points and concepts are shown more formally through the person/job match model in Exhibit 1.2. In this model, the job has certain requirements and rewards associated with it. The person has certain qualifications, referred to as KSAOs (knowledges, skills, abilities, and other characteristics), and motivations. There is a need for a match between the person and the job. To the extent that the match is a good one, it will likely have positive impacts on HR outcomes, particularly attraction of job applicants, job performance, retention, attendance, and satisfaction.

EXHIBIT 1.2   Person/Job Match

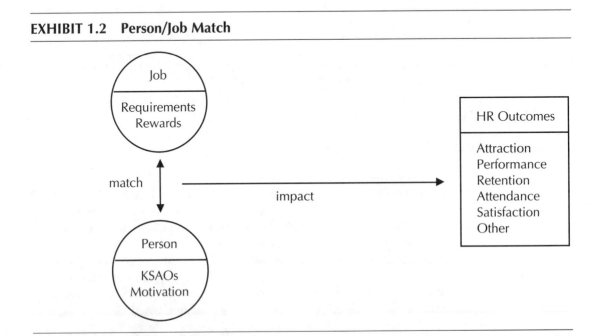

There is actually a need for a dual match to occur: job requirements to KSAOs, and job rewards to individual motivation. In and through staffing activities, there are attempts to ensure both of these. Such attempts collectively involve what will be referred to throughout this book as the matching process.

Several points pertaining to staffing need to be made about the person/job matching model. First, the concepts shown in the model are not new.[2] They have been used for decades as the dominant way of thinking about how individuals successfully adapt to their work environments. The view is that it is the positive interaction of individual and job characteristics that creates the most successful matches. Thus, a person with a given "package" of KSAOs is not equally suited to all jobs, because jobs vary in the KSAOs required. Likewise, an individual with a given set of needs or motivations will not be satisfied with all jobs, because jobs differ in the rewards they offer. Thus, in staffing, each individual must be assessed relative to the requirements and rewards of the job being filled.

Second, the model emphasizes that the matching process involves a dual match of KSAOs to requirements and motivation to rewards. Both matches require attention in staffing. For example, a staffing system may be designed to focus on the KSAOs/requirements match by carefully identifying job requirements and then thoroughly assessing applicants relative to these requirements. While such a staffing system may be one that will accurately identify the probable high performers, problems may arise with it. By ignoring or downplaying the motivation/rewards portion of the match, the organization may have difficulty getting people to accept job offers (an attraction outcome) or having new hires remain with the organization for any length of time (a retention outcome). It does little good to be able to identify the likely high performers if they cannot be induced to accept job offers or to remain with the organization.

Third, job requirements should usually be expressed in terms of both the tasks involved and the KSAOs thought necessary for performance of those tasks. Most of the time, it is difficult to establish meaningful KSAOs for a job without having first identified the job's tasks. KSAOs usually must be derived or inferred from knowledge of the tasks. An exception to this involves very basic or generic KSAOs, such as literacy and oral communication skills, that are reasonably deemed necessary for most jobs.

Fourth, job requirements often extend beyond task and KSAO requirements. For example, the job may have requirements about reporting to work on time, attendance, safety toward fellow employees and customers, and needs for travel. With such requirements, the matching of the person to them must also be considered when staffing the organization. Travel requirements of the job, for example, may involve assessing applicants' availability for, and willingness to accept, travel assignments.

Finally, the matching process can yield only so much by way of impacts on the HR outcomes. The reason for this is that these outcomes are influenced by factors outside the realm of the person/job match. Retention, for example, depends not only on how close a match there is between job rewards and individual motivation, but also on the availability of suitable job opportunities in other organizations and labor markets. As another example, Total Quality Management proponents argue that it is characteristics of the production or service system that have the biggest impact on performance outcomes, not the person/job match.[3] According to this view, the system itself establishes a baseline level of performance that individuals achieve. Variations in performance are due to anomalies of the system, rather than problems with the person/job match. These examples suggest potential limitations on the usefulness of staffing (and the person/job match) for influencing HR outcomes.

Person/Organization Match

Often the organization seeks to determine not only how well the person fits or matches the job, but also the organization. Likewise, applicants often assess how they think they might fit into the organization, in addition to how well they match the specific job's requirements and rewards. For both the organization and the applicant, therefore, there may be a concern with a person/organization match.[4]

Exhibit 1.3 shows this expanded view of the match. The focal point of staffing is the person/job match, and the job is like the bullseye of the matching target. Four other matching concerns, however, involving the broader organization, also arise in staffing. These concerns involve organizational values, new job duties, multiple jobs, and future jobs.

Organizational values are norms of desirable attitudes and behaviors for the organization's employees. Examples include honesty and integrity, achievement and hard work, fairness, and concern for fellow employees and customers. Though such values may never appear in writing, such as in a job description, the likely match of the applicant to them is judged during staffing.

New job duties represent tasks that may be added to the target job over time. Organizations desire new hires who will be able to successfully perform these new duties as they are added. In recognition of this, job descriptions often contain the catchall phrase "and other duties as assigned." These other duties are usually vague at the time of hire, and they may never materialize. Nonetheless, the organization would like to hire persons it thinks could perform these new duties. Having such people will provide the organization a degree of flexibility in getting new tasks done without having to hire additional employees to do them.

Flexibility concerns also enter into the staffing picture in terms of hiring persons who could perform multiple jobs. Small businesses, for example, often desire new hires who can wear multiple job hats, functioning as "jacks of all trades"; or, organizations experiencing rapid growth may require new employees who can handle several different job assignments, splitting their time between them on an

EXHIBIT 1.3   Person/Organization Match

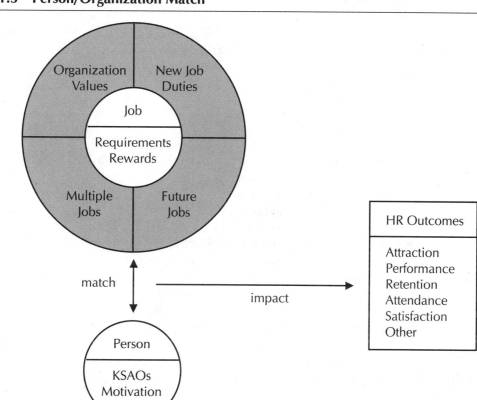

"as needed" basis. Such expectations obviously require assessments of person/organization fit.

Future jobs represent forward thinking by the organization and person as to what job assignments the person might assume beyond the initial job. Here the applicant and the organization are thinking of long-term matches over the course of transfers and promotions as the employee becomes increasingly "seasoned" for the long run.

In each of the above four cases, the matching process is expanded to include consideration of requirements and rewards beyond those of the target job as it currently exists. Though the dividing line between person/job and person/organization match is fuzzy, both types of matches are frequently of concern in staffing. Ideally, the organization's staffing systems focus first and foremost on the person/job match. This will allow the nature of the employment relationship to be specified and agreed to in concrete terms. Once these terms have been established, person/organization match possibilities can be explored during the staffing process. In this book for simplicity's sake we will use the term "person/job match" broadly to encompass both types of matches, though most of the time the usage will be in the context of the actual person/job match.

Staffing System Components

As noted, staffing encompasses managing the flows of people into and within the organization. The staffing process has several components that represent steps and activities that occur over the course of these flows. Exhibit 1.4 shows these components and the general sequence in which they occur.

As shown in the exhibit, staffing begins with a joint interaction between the applicant and the organization. The applicant seeks the organization and job opportunities within it, and the organization seeks applicants for job vacancies it has or anticipates having. Both the applicant and the organization are thus involved as "players" in the staffing process from the very start, and they remain joint participants throughout the process.

At times, the organization may be the dominant player, such as in aggressive and targeted recruiting for certain types of applicants. At other times, the applicant may be the aggressor, such as when the applicant desperately seeks employment

EXHIBIT 1.4   Staffing System Components

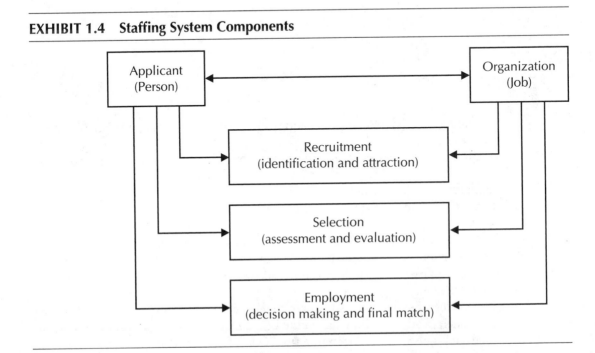

with a particular organization and will go to almost any length to land a job with it. Most of the time, staffing involves a more balanced and natural interplay between the applicant and the organization, which occurs over the course of the staffing process.

The initial stage in staffing is recruitment, which involves identification and attraction activities by both the organization and the applicant. The organization seeks to identify and attract individuals so that they become job applicants. Activities such as recruitment advertising, job fairs, use of recruiters, preparation and distribution of informational brochures, and "putting out the word" about vacancies among its own employees are undertaken. The applicant attempts to identify organizations with job opportunities through activities such as reading advertisements, contacting an employment agency, mass mailing resumes to employers, and so forth. These activities are accompanied by attempts to make one's qualifications (KSAOs and motivation) attractive to organizations, such as by personally applying for a job or preparing a carefully constructed resume that highlights significant skills and experiences.

Gradually, recruitment activities phase into the selection stage and its accompanying activities. Now, the emphasis is on assessment and evaluation. For the organization, this means the use of various selection techniques (interviews, application blanks, and so forth) to assess applicant KSAOs and motivation. Data from these assessments are then evaluated against job requirements to determine the likely degree of person/job fit. At the same time, the applicant is assessing and evaluating the job and organization. The applicant's assessment and evaluation are based on information gathered from organizational representatives (e.g., recruiter, manager with the vacancy, other employees); written information (e.g., brochures, employee handbook); informal sources (e.g., friends and relatives who are current employees); and visual inspection (e.g., a video presentation, a work-site tour). This information, along with a self-assessment of KSAOs and motivation, is evaluated against the applicant's understanding of job requirements and rewards to determine if there is likely to be a good person/job match.

The final component of staffing is employment, which involves decision-making and final match activities by the organization and the applicant. The organization must decide which applicants to reject from further consideration and which to allow to continue in the staffing process. This may involve multiple decisions over successive selection steps or hurdles. Some applicants ultimately become finalists for the job. At that point, the organization must decide to whom it will make the job offer, what will be the content of the offer, and how it will be drawn up and presented to the applicant. Upon the applicant's acceptance of the offer, the final match is complete, and the employment relationship is formally established.

For the applicant, the employment stage involves self-selection, a term that refers to decisions about whether to continue in or drop out of the staffing process. These decisions may occur anywhere along the selection process, up to and including the moment of the job offer. If the applicant continues as part of the process through the final match, the applicant has decided to be a finalist. The individual's attention now turns to a possible job offer, possible input and negotiation on its content, and making a final decision about the offer. The applicant's final decision is based on overall judgment about the likely suitability of the person/job match.

It should be noted that the staffing components apply to both external and internal staffing. While this may seem obvious in the case of external staffing, a brief elaboration may be necessary for internal staffing. In internal staffing, the applicant is a current employee, and the organization is the current employer. Job opportunities (vacancies) exist within the organization and are filled through the activities of the internal labor market. Those activities involve recruitment, selection, and employment, with the employer and employee as joint participants. For example, the employer may recruit through use of an internal job posting system. Employees who apply may be assessed and evaluated on the basis of supervisory recommendation, a formal promotability rating, and past job assignments for the employer. Decisions are made by both the employer and the employees who are applicants. Ultimately, the position will be offered to one of the applicants and, hopefully, accepted. When this happens, the final match has occurred, and a new employment relationship has been established.

Human Resource Management

Since staffing is only one of several activities that compose human resource management (HRM), its nature must be considered in the broader HRM context. A particular model of HRM, shown in Exhibit 1.5, depicts the nature of HRM and staffing's place within it. The model is discussed next.

Person/Job Match

As the model shows, the person/job match plays a central role in all of HRM. Indeed, it shows that all HR activities are directed toward creating and maintaining effective person/job matches as a way of having a positive impact on the HR outcomes.

HR Activities

Each HR activity is classified as a support or functional activity. Support activities include strategy and planning, job analysis, and measurement. These three activities are not intended to directly influence the person/job match. Rather, they serve in a supportive role, providing input to the functional activities. This suggests that they are logical prerequisites for staffing activities; their conduct should enhance the effectiveness of staffing activities.

Functional activities are undertaken to have a direct impact upon the person/job match, and thus, the HR outcomes. These activities include external staffing,

EXHIBIT 1.5   Human Resource Management Model

Economic Conditions	Labor Markets	Labor Unions	Laws and Regulations
EXTERNAL INFLUENCES			

HR ACTIVITIES

SUPPORT ACTIVITIES
  Strategy and planning
  Job analysis
  Measurement

FUNCTIONAL ACTIVITIES
  External staffing
  Internal staffing
  Training & development
  Compensation
  Labor relations
  Work environment

Job
Requirements
Rewards

Person
KSAOs
Motivation

HR OUTCOMES

Attraction
Performance
Retention
Attendance
Satisfaction
Other

Source: Adapted from H. G. Heneman, III, D. P. Schwab, J. A. Fossum, and L. Dyer, *Personnel/Human Resource Management,* fourth ed. (Homewood, IL: Irwin, 1989).

internal staffing, training and development, compensation, labor relations, and work environment (e.g., physical and environmental conditions, hours of work schedules). Each of these activities has the potential for making important and unique contributions to the matching process. For this reason, they are typically administered as separate functional areas within HRM and the HR department.

Interrelationships Among Activities

While administered separately, the functional HR activities are highly interrelated and, hence, must work in concert with each other. For example, assume that the results of HR planning lead an organization to establish a goal of hiring 20 new management trainees over the next 12 months. Achieving this goal requires co-ordination among the functional HR activities. Will the trainees be sought from outside the organization, inside, or both? What will be the qualifications desired of external and internal applicants? What starting pay level and other terms will be necessary to attract sufficient numbers of applicants? What types of training and development will the trainees receive and when? What evening and weekend work will be required?

Answers to these questions must be coordinated in ways that have functional activities all working toward attaining the common hiring goal. This is difficult in practice because decisions made in one area may have consequences in other areas. Suppose, for example, that in order to control labor costs, the compensation staff recommends that there be (a) the same starting salaries for trainees as last year, and (b) elimination of hiring bonuses that were commonly used in past years. If implemented, these recommendations could make it difficult to attract new train-ees, thus requiring new and stepped-up recruiting efforts relative to past years. Moreover, the qualifications of those recruited may be lower, necessitating revi-sions in the training and development curriculum. Finally, weekend work may have to be scaled back, or even curtailed, in order to compensate for the starting salary freeze and elimination of hiring bonus.

External Influences

At the top of Exhibit 1.5 are listed several external influences that affect HR activities, the person/job match, and HR outcomes. These influences are economic conditions, labor markets, labor unions, and laws and regulations.

Economic Conditions Economic conditions influence the overall financial health of an organization. They have a direct bearing on the numbers and types of jobs the organization has, the numbers and types of people it will need in those jobs, and the types of rewards it will be able to offer in those jobs. In the preceding management trainee example, declining economic conditions may require a goal of hiring only ten trainees, accompanied by reducing starting pay relative to last year. Such changes will obviously carry over to and have an impact upon staffing activities for the job (e.g., college recruitment may be cut back).

Labor Markets Labor markets represent the external arena in which the orga-nization seeks new employees (labor demand) and individuals offer their avail-ability (labor supply). Staffing activities are very susceptible to labor market un-dercurrents in both numerical and qualitative terms. Numerically, "tight" labor markets (strong demand relative to supply) make recruiting adequate numbers of applicants both difficult and expensive. Alternatively, "loose" labor markets (weak demand relative to supply) create a more favorable environment for identifying and attracting sufficient numbers of applicants.

The qualitative aspect of labor demand and supply refers to the types of qualifications required by jobs and provided by job applicants. In the previous management trainee example, the numerical hiring goal will be accompanied by specifying the desired KSAOs and motivation characteristics of applicants. These are also a reflection of labor demand. On the labor supply side, obtaining applicants who can meet these qualitative specifications depends upon the actual availability of people with the desired qualifications.

Labor Unions   Labor unions negotiate with the organization about the terms and conditions of employment for their members, expressed in a written labor contract. The terms and conditions typically deal with both job requirements and rewards. For job requirements, the job tasks and duties, as well as the classification of jobs into a hierarchy (for promotion and transfer purposes), may be negotiated. Actual workings of the internal labor market, such as job posting and seniority systems, are almost always negotiated. For job rewards, virtually all extrinsic job rewards are negotiated and then "locked in" for the life of the contract. Establishment and flexibility of both job requirements and rewards are thus greatly affected by the union presence.

Laws and Regulations   Laws and regulations serve to define (a) the nature of the employment relationship, and (b) the limits of permissible and impermissible HR practices, including staffing ones. The employment relationship is specified as a contractual one that is entered into by the organization and the individual. The contract is determined either collectively (as with a labor union) or individually through a job offer/acceptance process. But the nature of the employment relationship is also established legally by subsequent HR policies and practices as well. Laws and regulations specify and clarify the boundaries between permissible and impermissible HR practices. This is particularly the case with equal employment opportunity and affirmative action (EEO/AA) laws and regulations. All support and functional HR activities are strongly and vitally affected by their content and enforcement.

In summary, staffing occurs within the framework and conduct of HRM generally. HR activities, including staffing, seek to influence the person/job match and (through it) the HR outcomes. Some of these activities influence the match indirectly (support activities), while others have a more direct impact (functional activities). External influences constrain and complicate these activities. Since the organization has little control over these external influences, it must modify its staffing and other activities to meet these conditions and changes in the external environment.

Staffing Organizations

The concepts and terminology from the discussions of staffing components and staffing within HRM may be drawn together to yield the staffing organizations model as shown in Exhibit 1.6. In that model, staffing is composed of support activities, staffing activities, external influences, and staffing system management. The support activities are strategy and planning, job analysis, and measurement. Recruitment, selection, and employment form the staffing activities. External influences have an impact upon both the support and staffing activities, in the form of economic conditions, labor markets, labor unions, and laws and regulations.

EXHIBIT 1.6   Staffing Organizations Model

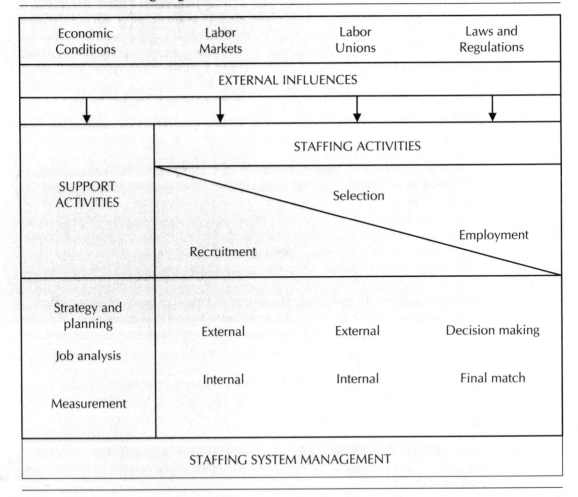

Staffing system management draws together and integrates the various staffing activities.

The staffing model requires several comments. While it does not depict the person/job match and resultant HR outcomes, these remain the central, underlying focus of staffing organizations. The support activities, staffing activities, and external influences all combine and interact to implement the matching process.

The three support activities from the HRM model are included in the staffing model. This signifies and reinforces their importance to staffing organizations. Indeed, they are the foundations upon which effective, and legally defensible, staffing practices are built for an organization.

The diagonal line in Exhibit 1.6, cutting through the three staffing activities, signifies that there is no clear line of demarcation between them. In fact, all three activities may occur at the same time. While recruitment dominates staffing activities in the early stages of the process, selection and then employment activities become more prominent as the process unfolds. However, even recruitment does not formally end until the final match has been completed and the applicant has "signed on the dotted line."

The recruitment, selection, and employment activities occur for both external and internal applicants. The fundamental purpose of these activities (identification and attraction, assessment and evaluation, decision making and final match) are identical for both external and internal staffing.

Staffing organizations requires more than recruitment and selection. Decision-making and final match activities are critical in bringing the results of recruitment and selection to fruition. Quite simply, without decision-making and final match activities, the recruitment and selection activities would yield no new hires for the organization.

External influences play prominent roles in all staffing activities. They set the external parameters and constraints within which staffing systems operate. So large and all-encompassing is their impact that external influences will be discussed prior to support and staffing activities.

Finally, staffing system management is needed to provide direction and control for these staffing system components, and to ensure that all components are attuned to the myriad external influences. The HR department figures prominently in staffing system management.

The remainder of the book is structured around and built on the staffing organizations model shown in Exhibit 1.6.

STAFFING SYSTEM EXAMPLES

Any organization with more than one member has some sort of staffing system. These systems elude easy characterization since they are tailored to suit the unique needs of each organization, its applicants, and its external influences. Despite these differences, all staffing systems share in common the elements shown in the staffing organizations model. Described below are four staffing systems that illustrate the diversity within the confines of these shared elements.

Police Department

The Madison, Wisconsin police department staffs its entry level police officer jobs periodically, under the direction of the public Police and Fire Commission (PFC). In one recent instance, vacancies for 30 positions were publicly announced and widely advertised in order to attract an applicant pool that was diverse with respect to gender and minority group membership. Police officers themselves served as active, outreaching recruiters throughout the total staffing process. This recruitment yielded 1,284 applicants. After ascertaining possession of key KSAOs (e.g., high school graduate, drivers license, no felony conviction record, vision correctable to 20/20), applicants took a written test of reading comprehension and vocabulary.

For the 900 who passed the test, written application materials were reviewed by a four-person panel of police force members. The 200 survivors then took a physical ability test (sit ups, lifting, running, and trigger pull), which 68 passed. These persons were then given a panel (group) interview, followed by a thorough background check. The 40 finalists were then individually interviewed by the Chief of Police. Those offered and accepting a job were required to pass a medical exam before being placed into an eight-month training program, followed by a regular job assignment.[5]

Work Team Members

The Delta Dental Plan in Medford, Massachusetts organized some of its service employees into a 12-member team that would manage the dental plan account with the Massachusetts Public Employees. Applicants were recruited from both inside and outside the company in order to get a mixture of employees who understood the business and who would bring fresh perspectives to the job. The HR department first administered a personality test to applicants, followed by an assessment of bilingual skills (many of the customers spoke primarily Spanish or French Creole). Applicants' interpersonal skills were assessed via interviews with HR department representatives, as well as other employees and managers. New hires were placed on the job but also received training in areas such as corporate culture, product knowledge, and statistics.[6]

State Government

Staffing for the state of Wisconsin is handled by the Division of Merit Recruitment and Selection (DMRS) within the Department of Employment Relations. Operating within state civil service laws and regulations, the DMRS provides staffing services to 40 agencies and 26 university campuses. Each year it processes 70,000 applicants, administers over 1,000 exams (e.g., written tests, work samples, interviews), and enables agencies and campuses to hire and promote 4,000 employees statewide. Applicants are recruited through both internal job postings and external vacancy announcements. Recently, the DMRS implemented several new staffing initiatives. These were intended to reduce the average time to fill vacancies (it went from 69 to 45 days), quickly hire employees into hard-to-fill vacancies, attract high quality entry-level professional employees, and advertise vacancies on-line through its JOBS (Job On-Line Bulletin System). These initiatives won the DMRS a special national award sponsored by the Ford Foundation and Harvard University.[7]

Temporary Help Agency

The Olsten Corporation is a large company in the temporary help (staffing services) industry, with over 1,200 offices nationwide and in the United Kingdom. Its core business is to provide temporary ("assignment") employees to corporate, government, and health care clients. The Columbus, Ohio office, for example, works closely with a client to develop a customized staffing plan. After identifying the client's specific needs and conducting job analysis, the Columbus office conducts a targeted recruitment program to find and attract potentially qualified job applicants. The applicants then undergo assessments of their qualifications via skills tests (e.g., word processing), background and reference checks, drug testing, and an interview. Applicants who meet the selection criteria are offered a job, and they receive an explanation of the fringe benefits and training opportunities available as an added inducement to accept the offer. Those who accept the offer become employees of Olsten, ready for assignment to the client. Olsten often provides its own on-site manager for these employees. The client pays Olsten a negotiated fee for these assignment employees and its staffing services.[8]

PLAN FOR THE BOOK

The book is divided into six parts:

1. Staffing and External Influences
2. Support Activities
3. Staffing Activities: Recruitment
4. Staffing Activities: Selection
5. Staffing Activities: Employment
6. Staffing System Management

Each chapter in these six parts begins with a brief topical outline in order to help the reader quickly discern its general contents. The "meat" of the chapter comes next. A chapter summary then reviews and highlights points from the chapter. A set of discussion questions, applications (cases and exercises), and detailed endnotes complete the chapter.

As noted, the importance of external influences is such that they are considered first in Chapter 2 (Economic Conditions, Labor Markets, and Labor Unions) and Chapter 3 (Laws and Regulations). The laws and regulations, in particular, have become so pervasive that they require special treatment. To do this, Chapter 3 reviews the basic laws affecting staffing, with an emphasis on the major federal laws and regulations pertaining to EEO/AA matters generally. Specific provisions relevant to staffing are covered in depth. Each subsequent chapter then has a separate section at its end labeled "Legal Issues" in which specific legal topics relevant to the chapter's content are discussed. This allows for a more focused discussion of legal issues, while not diverting attention from the major thrust of the book.

The endnotes at the end of each chapter are quite extensive. They are drawn from academic, practitioner, and legal sources with the goal of providing a balanced selection of references from each of these sources. Emphasis is on inclusion of recent references of high quality and easy accessibility. Too lengthy a list of references to each specific topic is avoided, with instead a sampling of only the best available included.

The applications at the end of each chapter are of two varieties. First are cases that describe a particular situation and require analysis and response. The response may be written or oral (such as in class discussion or a group presentation). Second are exercises that entail small projects and require active practice of a particular task. Through these cases and exercises the reader becomes an active participant in the learning process and is able to apply the concepts provided in each chapter.

SUMMARY

Staffing is defined as "the mutual process by which the individual and the organization become matched to form the employment relationship." This definition suggests that staffing should be viewed, using both individual and organizational perspectives, as a process undertaken by the organization to manage the occurrence of the person/job match. Several models illustrate this point.

The person/job match model indicates there is a dual need to match (a) the person's KSAOs to job requirements, and (b) the person's motivation to the job's rewards. Managing the matching process effectively results in positive impacts on HR outcomes such as attraction, performance, and retention of employees.

In the person/organization model, the person's characteristics are matched to additional factors beyond the target job. These factors are organizational values, new job duties for the target job, multiple jobs, and future jobs.

The staffing components model shows that there are three basic activities in staffing. Those activities and their fundamental purposes are recruitment (identification and attraction of applicants), selection (assessment and evaluation of applicants), and employment (decision making and final match).

The human resource management model shows staffing within the broader framework of HRM. That framework has various support activities (e.g., job analysis) and functional activities (e.g., staffing, compensation) that influence the HR outcomes through their impact upon the person/job match. Importantly, the model also identifies several external influences on the conduct of HRM activities. These influences are economic conditions, labor markets, labor unions, and laws and regulations.

The staffing organizations model shows that staffing is composed of three support activities (strategy and planning, job analysis, and measurement) and the three staffing activities (recruitment, selection, and employment). These activities occur for both external and internal staffing. Their fundamental purpose is to manage the person/job matching process. They do this, however, within the confines of the external influences previously identified, as well as staffing system management requirements.

Staffing systems, though diverse in many respects, share in common the elements from the staffing organizations model. Examples of staffing systems are provided for a police department, a work team, a state government, and a temporary help agency

The staffing organizations model serves as the structural outline for the remainder of the book. The first part treats external influences. This is followed by separate parts for support activities, recruitment, selection, employment, and staffing system management. Each chapter in these sections has a separate section labeled "Legal Issues," as well as discussion questions, applications, and endnotes.

DISCUSSION QUESTIONS

1. What would be potential problems with having a staffing process in which vacancies were filled (a) on a lottery basis from among job applicants, or (b) on a first come–first hired basis among job applicants?

2. Why is it important for the organization to view all components of staffing (recruitment, selection, employment) from the perspective of the job applicant?

3. Would it be desirable to hire people only according to the person/organization match, ignoring the person/job match?

4. What are examples of how staffing activities are influenced by training activities? Compensation activities?

APPLICATIONS

Person/Job Match for Your Own Job

Job Requirements/KSAOs

1. Think of a time on your current job, or a past job, when you were performing your work very effectively, when you were at "peak performance." Using the person/job match model, identify and write down specific examples of effective matches between your own KSAOs and job requirements that seemed to be responsible for your high level of performance. For example, maybe you were a medical claims adjuster, the job required substantial knowledge of correct reimbursements for medical procedures, and you were very knowledgeable about reimbursement schedules.

2. Now that you have identified examples of an effective person/job match, write down ways you could try using staffing activities to achieve equally effective matches for new job applicants. For example, for the medical claims adjuster job perhaps you might develop a special recruitment advertisement explaining exact claims knowledges needed, develop a knowledge test to be used as part of the selection process, and have a higher starting pay for the most knowledgeable applicants to whom you make employment offers.

Job Rewards/Motivation

1. Think of a time on your current job, or a past job, when you were extremely satisfied with the job, when you felt "it doesn't get any better than this." Using the person/job match model, identify and write down specific examples of effective matches between your own needs and job rewards that seemed responsible for this satisfaction "high." For example, on the medical claims adjuster job perhaps you received a formal letter of recognition from your boss for having the lowest error rate among all adjusters for the past six months.

2. Now that you have identified examples of an effective person/job match, identify and write down ways you could try using staffing activities to achieve equally effective matches for new job applicants. For example, for the medical claims adjuster job perhaps you could feature an employee recognition program in recruitment brochures, ask applicants interview questions about previous times they had received recognition and how they felt, and provide a job offer to applicants that guaranteed they would attend an extensive training program on reimbursement procedures during their first six months on the job.

Staffing for Your Own Job

Instructions

Consider a job you previously held, or your current job. Use the staffing components model to help you think through and describe the staffing process that lead to your getting hired for the job. Trace and describe the process (a) from your own perspective as a job applicant, and (b) from the organization's perspective. Listed below are some questions to jog your memory. Write your responses to these questions and be prepared to discuss them.

Applicant Perspective

Recruitment:

1. Why did you identify and seek out the job with this organization?
2. How did you try to make yourself attractive to the organization?

Selection:

1. How did you gather information about the job's requirements and rewards?
2. How did you judge your own KSAOs and needs relative to these requirements and rewards?

Employment:

1. Why did you decide to continue on in the staffing process, rather than drop out of it?
2. Why did you decide to accept the job offer; what were the pluses and minuses of the job?

Organization Perspective

Even if you do not know, or are unsure of, the answers to these questions, try to answer them or even guess at them.

Recruitment:

1. How did the organization identify you as a job applicant?
2. How did the organization make the job attractive to you?

Selection:

1. What techniques (application blank, interview, etc.) did the organization use to gather KSAO information about you?
2. How did the organization evaluate this information; what did it see as your strong and weak points KSAO-wise?

Employment:

1. Why did the organization decide to continue pursuing you as an applicant, rather than reject you from further consideration?
2. What was the job offer process like? Did you receive a verbal or written (or both) offer? Who gave you the offer? What was the content of the offer?

(continued)

Reactions to the Staffing Process

Now that you have described the staffing process, what are your reactions to it?

1. What were the strong or positive features of the process?
2. What were the weak points and negative features of the process?
3. What changes would you like to see made in the process, and why?

ENDNOTES

1. J. A. Breaugh, *Recruitment: Science and Practice* (Boston: PWS-Kent, 1992); R. D. Gatewood and H. S. Feild, *Human Resource Selection,* third ed. (Chicago: Dryden, 1994); S. L. Rynes, "Recruitment, Job Choice, and Post-Hire Consequences: A Call for New Research Directions," in M. D. Dunnette and L. M. Hough (eds.), *Handbook of Industrial and Organizational Psychology,* vol. 2, second ed. (Palo Alto, CA: Consulting Psychologists Press, 1991); J. P. Wanous, *Organizational Entry,* second ed. (Reading, MA: Addison-Wesley, 1992).

2. D. F. Caldwell and C. A. O'Reilly III, "Measuring Person-Job Fit with A Profile-Comparison Process," *Journal of Applied Psychology,* 1990, 75, pp. 648–657; R. V. Dawis, "Person-Environment Fit and Job Satisfaction," in C. J. Cranny, P. C. Smith, and E. F. Stone, *Job Satisfaction* (New York: Lexington, 1992), pp. 69–88; R. V. Dawis, L. H. Lofquist, and D. J. Weiss, *A Theory of Work Adjustment (A Revision),* (Minneapolis: Industrial Relations Center, University of Minnesota, 1968).

3. G. H. Dobbins, R. L. Cardy, and K. P. Carson, "Examining Fundamental Assumptions: A Contrast of Person and System Approaches to Human Resource Management," in G. R. Ferris and K. M. Rowland (eds.), *Research in Personnel and Human Resources Management* (Boston: JAI Press, 1991), pp. 1–38.

4. D. E. Bowen, G. E. Ledford, Jr., and B. R. Nathan, "Hiring for the Organization and Not the Job," *Academy of Management Executive,* 1991, 5(4), pp. 35–51; T. A. Judge and R. D. Bretz, Jr., "Effects of Work Values on Job Choice Decisions," *Journal of Applied Psychology,* 1992, 77, pp. 001–011; C. A. O'Reilly III, J. Chatman, and D. F. Caldwell, "People and Organizational Culture: A Profile Comparison Approach to Assessing Person-Organization Fit," *Academy of Management Journal,* 1991, 34, pp. 487–516; R. J. Karren and L. M. Graves, "Assessing Person-Organization Fit in Personnel Selection: Guidelines for Future Research," *International Journal of Selection and Placement,* 1994, 3, pp. 146–156; D. Cable and T. A. Judge, "The Role of Person-Organization Fit in Organizational Selection Decisions," (Cornell University: Center for Advanced Human Resource Studies, 1995); A. L. Kristof, "Person-Organization Fit: An Intergrative Review of its Conceptualizations, Measurement, and Implications," *Personnel Psychology,* 1996, 49, pp. 1–50.

5. J. Richgels, "Future Cops Face Grueling Obstacles," *The Madison (Wis.) Capital Times,* 12/29/93, p. A1

6. S. Caudron, "Team Staffing Requires New HR Role," *Personnel Journal,* 1994, 73(5), pp. 88–94.

7. Documents furnished by the Division of Merit Recruitment and Selection, Department of Employment Relations, State of Wisconsin, 1995.

8. J. Skoglind, Olsten Staffing Services, Columbus, Ohio, 1995.

CHAPTER TWO

Economic Conditions, Labor Markets, and Labor Unions

Economic Conditions
  Forces of Change
  Impacts on Staffing

Labor Markets
  Labor Demand: Quantity
  Labor Demand: Quality
  Labor Supply: Quantity
  Labor Supply: Quality
  Employment Arrangements
  Impacts on Staffing

Labor Unions
  Labor Contracts
  Contract Clauses Affecting Staffing
  Impacts on Staffing

Summary

Discussion Questions

Applications

In the previous chapter, external influences were shown to have a vital impact upon the conduct of HR activities, as well as upon the person/job match and the HR outcomes. This chapter explores in more detail the nature of the first three of these external influences (:onomic conditions, labor markets, labor unions) and how they have specific impacts on staffing activities. A similar treatment for laws and regulations is provided in the following chapter.

The first section of this chapter deals with economic conditions. It shows that these conditions have both a positive and negative impact on job growth. Job growth, in turn, affects the movement of people into jobs, among jobs, and out of jobs. Staffing activities must anticipate and manage these movements.

Job growth also directly involves labor markets. Labor markets are the mechanism by which organizational signals about job availability (labor demand) and individual signals about willingness to work (labor supply) converge and play themselves out. Both labor demand and supply involve numerical (numbers of people) and qualitative (KSAOs and motivation) aspects. This section describes the numerical and qualitative components of labor supply and demand, as well as their future trends. Also, data are given on various employment arrangements (e.g., part-time and temporary help) that are used to fulfill the organization's staffing needs. Numerous illustrations of how labor market forces impact staffing activities are provided.

The final section of this chapter shows the role of labor unions vis-à-vis organizational staffing. Labor unions negotiate and help administer labor contracts. Each contract contains the terms and conditions of employment that will govern the employment relationship between labor and management in a workplace. The terms of the contract affect job requirements and rewards, and have a direct impact upon staffing activities through clauses dealing with staffing issues. The nature of these clauses, as well as their implications for staffing the organization are detailed.

ECONOMIC CONDITIONS

Forces of Change

In Chapter 1, staffing was said to involve the managed movement of individuals. Economic conditions have a vital impact on such movement, particularly because of the influence they exert on job growth. The general nature of these relationships is shown in Exhibit 2.1.

The exhibit shows that organizations operate within, and must contend with, a multitude of general economic conditions. These include product and labor market competition (both national and international), inflation, interest rates, foreign exchange rates, and government regulations. From these forces emerge positive, neutral, or negative impacts on job growth. In response to these forces, organizations move people into (new hires), within (internal labor markets), and out of

EXHIBIT 2.1   General Economic Conditions, Job Growth, HR Movement Impacts

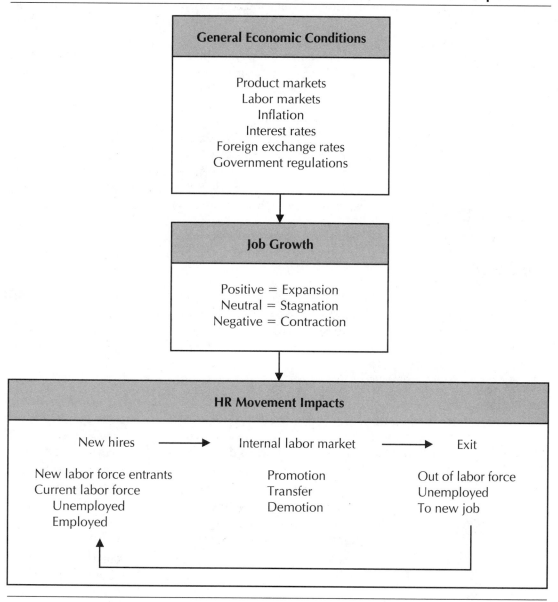

(exit) organizations. Job growth thus functions like a spigot governing the movements of people.

Consider the case of job expansion. When new jobs are created, new hire rates begin to increase for both entry-level and higher level jobs. These new hires are either new entrants into the labor force (e.g., recent college graduates) or current members of the labor force, both unemployed and employed. There will also be increased movement within organizations' internal labor markets through the operation of their promotion and transfer systems (there may also be occasional demotions). This movement will be necessitated by a combination of new jobs being created that will be filled internally, and the exit of current employees from the organization. Most likely, the departure of employees will be due to their leaving the organization to take new jobs at other organizations. Some, however, may be temporarily unemployed (while they look for new job opportunities), and others may leave the labor force entirely.

With lesser rates of job growth or actual job contraction, the movement flows are lessened. Organizations will be hiring fewer people, and job seekers will have longer job searches and fewer job opportunities to choose from. Promotion and transfer opportunities for current employees will dry up, and many employees may even experience termination through involuntary layoff or a voluntary early retirement program.

Impacts on Staffing

As economic conditions change, so must the organization's staffing activities. Job growth and its impacts on HR movement must be anticipated, planned for, accommodated, and managed. Responsibility for this will lie with the organization's HR department and staffing function, often in concert with strategic decision makers and planners.

Here are some examples of the types of staffing issues that will be wrestled with:

1. Staffing flexibility—How can we develop a rapidly fluctuating workforce to accommodate changing business conditions, and how can we obtain new employees who will be flexible in the job assignments they can perform?

2. Career paths—How can we design career routes for employees that will combine both lateral and upward movement, often on short notice?

3. New employee shortages—How will we staff units in which we anticipate shortages of qualified new employees, and should we revise our plans in light of these shortages?

4. Job rewards—What are the types of rewards most valued by employees, and how closely are our current rewards aligned with these preferences?

LABOR MARKETS

In and through labor markets organizations express specific labor preferences and requirements (labor demand) and persons express their own job preferences and requirements (labor supply). Ultimately, person/job matches occur from the interaction of the demand and supply forces. Both labor demand and supply contain quantity and quality components, as described below. The person/job matches occur in the form of a variety of possible employment arrangements that are also discussed.

Labor Demand: Quantity

Labor demand is a derived demand, meaning it is a result of consumer demands for the organization's products and services. The organization acquires and deploys its workforce in ways that will allow it to be responsive to consumer demand in a competitive manner.

To learn about labor demand, national employment statistics are collected and analyzed. They provide data about employment patterns and projections for industries, occupations, and organization size.

Industry

The national distribution of employment in 1979, 1992, and 2005 (projected) is shown in Exhibit 2.2. As can be seen, the goods-producing sector has been stagnant or declining for the past two decades, while the service sector has been expanding. This expansion is projected to continue. There are also substantial industry differences within overall sector employment patterns. For example, manufacturing employment will actually decline by 2005, while there will be substantial growth in services, retail trade, and government.

Occupation

Employment by major occupational groups is shown in Exhibit 2.3. As can be seen, in 1990, the greatest number of occupations were in administrative support and services, followed (in order) by operator, fabricator, and laborer positions; professional specializations; precision production, craft, and repairs; marketing and sales; administration and management; technicians; and agricultural, forestry, and fishing.

Projecting ahead to 2005, the data in Exhibit 2.3 indicate that occupations will have very different employment growth rates. The highest rates will be for technicians, professional specialists, and service providers. At the other extreme, there will be very low growth rates for operators, fabricators, and laborers, and for agricultural, forestry, and fishing workers.

More specific occupational projections indicate there will be major occupational "winners" and "losers." Projecting to 2005, examples of winners include home health aids (138%), computer engineers (112%), paralegals (86%), and special education teachers (74%). Some of the losers will be communication equipment operators (-28%), computer operators (-28%), typists and word processors (-16%), private household workers (-33%), and job printers (-35%).[1]

EXHIBIT 2.2   Employment Projections, by Industry

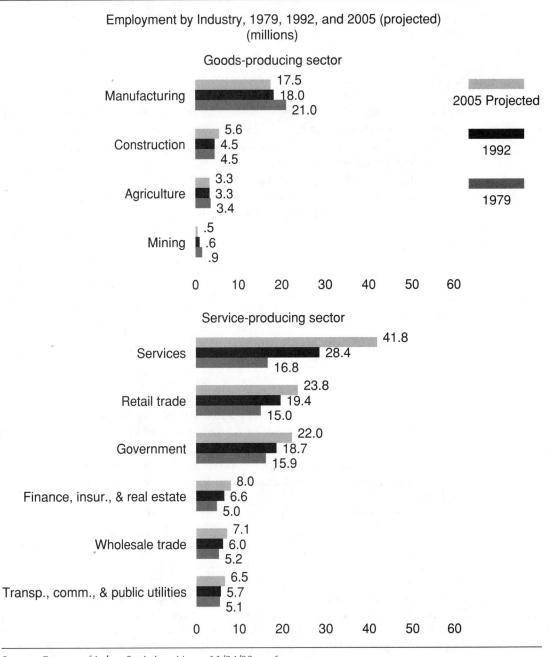

Employment by Industry, 1979, 1992, and 2005 (projected)
(millions)

Goods-producing sector

2005 Projected

1992

1979

Service-producing sector

Source: Bureau of Labor Statistics, *News*, 11/24/93, p. 6.

EXHIBIT 2.3   Employment by Major Occupational Group

Employment by major occupational group, 1992 and 2005 (projected)

(Number in thousands)

	1992		2005		Change 1992–2005	
Occupation	Number	Percent	Number	Percent	Number	Percent
Total, all occupations..................	121,099	100.0	147,482	100.0	26,383	21.8
Executive, administrative, and managerial...............................	12,066	10.0	15,195	10.3	3,129	25.9
Professional specialty	16,592	13.7	22,801	15.5	6,209	37.4
Technicians and related support	4,282	3.5	5,664	3.8	1,382	32.2
Marketing and sales	12,993	10.7	15,664	10.6	2,671	20.6
Administrative support occupations, including clerical...	22,349	18.5	25,406	17.2	3,057	13.7
Service occupations	19,358	16.0	25,820	17.5	6,462	33.4
Agricultural, forestry, fishing, and related occupations..................	3,530	2.9	3,650	2.5	120	3.4
Precision production, craft, and repair	13,580	11.2	15,380	10.4	1,800	13.3
Operators, fabricators, and laborers	16,349	13.5	17,902	12.1	1,553	9.5

Source: Bureau of Labor Statistics, *News*, 11/24/93, p. 7.

Employer Size

The vast majority of jobs and job growth occur in small business. Two telling examples highlight this.[2] First, in 1991, the Fortune 500 employers (the top 500 private firms in terms of total sales) accounted for less than 11% of total nonfarm employment in the United States. This was down from a peak of 21% in 1969, and there is every reason to expect this decline to continue. Second, in 1991, 16% of jobs were found in businesses with ten or fewer employees.

Labor Demand: Quality

Qualitative characteristics (KSAOs, motivation) of employers' demand for labor are difficult to describe, given the paucity of data available. Surveys of employers' preferences regarding labor quality, and an attempt to develop a national taxonomy of skills necessary for jobs, provide a glimpse at patterns in this area.

Employer Preferences

A recent survey of more than 400 senior HR executives revealed a major concern with issues reflecting labor quality. Of particular salience for staffing was the "poor quality of education among new job applicants" that these executives reported. This factor was viewed as the second most important factor affecting their competitiveness, behind only "increased cost of health benefits."[3]

A more focused national survey of employers sought their opinions on the kinds of skills they felt needed enhancement in current and prospective employees. Presumably, these skills are of direct relevance to organizational goals and competi-

---

EXHIBIT 2.4   Employer Opinions About Needed Skills Enhancement

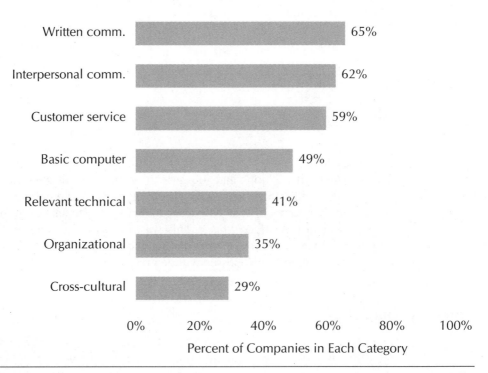

SKILLS NEEDING ENHANCEMENT
Among Current and Prospective Employees

Written comm. — 65%
Interpersonal comm. — 62%
Customer service — 59%
Basic computer — 49%
Relevant technical — 41%
Organizational — 35%
Cross-cultural — 29%

Percent of Companies in Each Category

Source: Olsten Corporation, Westbury, NY. *Olsten Forum ™ on Human Resource Issues and Trends, Skills for Success: Training and Developing the Work Force of the 1990s*, p. 5. Reprinted with permission.

EXHIBIT 2.5   SCANS Competencies and Skills: Foundation Skills

---

Basic Skills	Reading
	Writing
	Arithmetic
	Mathematics
	Listening
	Speaking
Thinking Skills	Creative thinking
	Decision making
	Problem solving
	Seeing things in the mind's eye
	Knowing how to learn
	Reasoning
Personal Qualities	Responsibility
	Self-esteem
	Social
	Self-management
	Integrity/honesty

Source: Secretary's Commission on Achieving Necessary Skills (SCANS), *Skills and Tasks for Jobs* (Washington, D.C.: U.S. Government Printing Office, 1992), pp. 1–5.

tiveness. The results are shown in Exhibit 2.4. As can be seen, the top two skills needing enhancement are written and interpersonal skills. These are followed by customer service skills, basic computer literacy, relevant technical skills, organizational knowledge, and cross-cultural knowledge.

SCANS Report

The Department of Labor established a special commission (Secretary's Commission on Achieving Necessary Skills) to study the possibility of identifying a taxonomy of skills that would be applicable to jobs on a national basis. Such a taxonomy would represent a common way of describing jobs in terms of skill requirements, and it would make possible the development of skill measures that could then be used to gauge skill levels of the workforce. Employers could also use the taxonomy as a way of focusing on and developing their own qualitative demands for labor.

The commission presented such a skill taxonomy in the SCANS report.[4] The taxonomy contains two levels of skills—foundation skills (Exhibit 2.5) and competencies (Exhibit 2.6). The foundation skills involve the traditional basic skills, plus thinking and cognitive skills, and personal qualities. These core skills are prerequisites for the competencies, which pertain to resource, information, interpersonal, systems, and technology skills.

EXHIBIT 2.6   SCANS Competencies and Skills: Competencies

Resources	Allocates time
	Allocates money
	Allocates material and facility resources
	Allocates human resources
Information	Acquires and evaluates information
	Organizes and maintains information
	Interprets and communicates information
	Uses computers to process information
Interpersonal	Participates as a member of a team
	Teaches others
	Serves clients/customers
	Exercises leadership
	Negotiates to arrive at a decision
	Works with cultural diversity
Systems	Understands systems
	Monitors and corrects performance
	Improves and designs systems
Technology	Selects technology
	Applies technology to task
	Maintains and troubleshoots technology

Source: Secretary's Commission on Achieving Necessary Skills (SCANS), *Skills and Tasks for Jobs* (Washington, D.C.: U.S. Government Printing Office, 1992), pp. 1–5.

The foundation skills and competencies will be discussed in more detail in Chapter 5 (Job Analysis) where their possible incorporation into job analysis for purposes of establishing KSAO requirements for particular jobs is explored.

Labor Supply: Quantity

Quantity of labor supplied is measured and reported periodically through a formal labor force survey process. The resulting data can then be combined with other data to study labor force trends.

Measuring the Labor Force

The Bureau of Labor Statistics, housed in the Department of Labor, collects data through use of a monthly survey. It also conducts special labor force surveys, usually focusing on a labor force segment (e.g., older workers) or issue (e.g., part-time employment).

The monthly survey is the most fundamental tool for collecting labor force statistics. It is conducted among approximately 60,000 households throughout the United States each month, with 25% of the households being new inclusions each time. Based on their responses to a detailed set of questions, individuals are placed into certain categories for purposes of statistical calculation and reporting, using standard definitions of terms. The major categories and definitions used in this process are shown in Exhibit 2.7.

This exhibit shows that each individual is placed into one of four categories— employed, unemployed, not in the labor force, or institutionalized and/or less than 16 years of age. Though the definitions for each category are seemingly straight-forward, there is a bit of fuzziness to them. For example, the line between being

---

EXHIBIT 2.7   Categories and Definitions for Labor Force Statistics

A. Categories

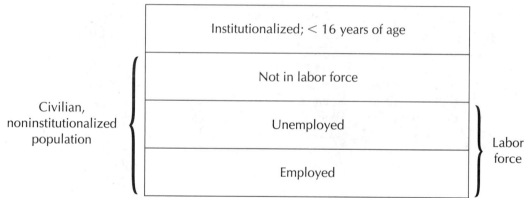

B. Definitions
1. Employed—worked for pay one or more hours during survey week; tempo-rarily absent from regular job; self-employed.
2. Unemployed—no work during survey week; available for work; looked for work in last four weeks.
3. Not in labor force—retired; homemaker; attending school; long-term illness; discouraged from seeking work because of personal or job-market factors; voluntarily idle.
4. Institutionalized—inmate of penal or mental institution, sanitarium, home for aged, infirm, or needy; member of armed forces in U.S.
5. Unemployment rate—percentage of labor force unemployed.
6. Labor force participation rate—percentage of civilian noninstitutionalized population in the labor force.

EXHIBIT 2.8   Labor Force Statistics for 1993 and 1994

	1993	1994
Civilian noninstitutionalized population	193.5	196.8
Civilian labor force	128.0	131.1
participation rate	66.2%	66.6%
Employed	119.3	123.1
Employment-population ratio	61.6%	62.5%
Unemployed	8.7	8.0
Unemployment rate	6.8%	6.1%
Not in labor force	65.5	65.8

Note: Numbers in millions

Source: U.S. Department of Labor, *Monthly Labor Review*, 1995, 118 (7), p. 92.

unemployed and not in the labor force (such as with unemployed workers who have become so discouraged in their job search that they quit looking for work) is a fine one.

Using the nomenclature shown in Exhibit 2.7, labor force statistics are reported on a monthly basis (the monthly unemployment rate has become a "hot" number for the media to report and mull over). These data are also aggregated and reported on an annual basis. Examples of the annual figures for 1993 and 1994 are shown in Exhibit 2.8. The civilian noninstitutionalized population was just under 200 million, and, of those, about 66% participated in the labor force in both years. The unemployment rate fell from 6.8% to 6.1% during that period.

Labor Force Trends

Two labor force trends have particular relevance for staffing organizations. These are the slow rate of labor force growth and increased demographic diversity.

Labor force growth is slowing, going from an annual growth rate of around 2% in the early 1990s to a projected rate of 1.3% by the year 2005. There are increasingly fewer new entrants to the labor force. This trend, coupled with the severe KSAO deficiencies that many of the new entrants will have, creates major adaptation problems for organizations.[5]

Demographically, the labor force has become more diverse, and this trend will continue. The data in Exhibit 2.9 clearly show this. If current demographic levels are extrapolated to the year 2005, it can be seen that the composition of the labor force will include (a) fewer men and more women; (b) fewer whites; (c) more Blacks, Asians, and Hispanics; (d) fewer younger (16–24) workers; and (e) more older (55+) workers.

EXHIBIT 2.9   Labor Force Demographics: Current and Projected

Civilian labor force by sex, age, race, and Hispanic origin, 1975, 1990, and 2005

	Level (Mill.)			Change		Percent Distribution			Annual Growth Rate	
	1975	1990	2005	1975–90	1990–2005	1975	1990	2005	1975–90	1990–2005
Total, 16 years and over	93.8	124.8	150.7	31.0	25.9	100.0	100.0	100.0	1.9	1.3
Men, 16 years and over	56.3	68.2	79.3	11.9	11.1	60.0	54.7	52.6	1.3	1.0
Women, 16 years and over	37.5	56.6	71.4	19.1	14.8	40.0	45.3	47.4	2.8	1.6
16 to 24	22.6	21.3	24.0	−1.4	2.8	24.1	17.0	16.0	−0.4	0.8
25 to 54	56.9	88.1	104.6	31.3	16.4	60.6	70.6	69.4	3.0	1.1
55 and over	14.3	15.4	22.1	1.1	6.7	15.3	12.3	14.7	0.5	2.4
White, 16 years and over	82.8	107.2	125.8	24.3	18.6	88.3	85.9	83.4	1.7	1.1
Black, 16 years and over	9.3	13.5	17.8	4.2	4.3	9.9	10.8	11.8	2.5	1.9
Asian and other, 16 years and over (1)	1.7	4.1	7.2	2.4	3.1	1.8	3.3	4.8	6.2	3.8
Hispanic, 16 and over (2)		9.6	16.8		7.2		7.7	11.1	(3) 5.9	3.8

(1) The "Asian and other" group includes (a) Asians and Pacific Islanders, and (b) American Indians and Alaskan Natives. The historic data are derived by subtracting "Black" from the "Black and other" group; projections are made directly.
(2) Persons of Hispanic origin may be of any race. Data for Hispanics are not available before 1980.
(3) This growth rate is from 1976 to 1990.

Source: Adapted from H. N. Fullerton, Jr., "Labor Force Projections: The Baby Boom Moves On," *Monthly Labor Review*, 1991, 114 (11), p. 36.

Labor Supply: Quality

Using the person/job matching model, the quality of labor may be thought of in KSAO and motivation terms. Each person possesses a bundle of KSAOs and motivation, and the labor force is nothing more than an aggregation of these individual bundles. The issue for study is what we know about these collective bundles that help us make characterizations about labor supply quality.

Ideally, we would have standard classifications or taxonomies of KSAOs and motivation, and measures to accompany them. We could then periodically survey KSAO and motivation characteristics of the labor force to learn about and track labor supply quality. Unfortunately, we do not have such taxonomies and measurements. Hence, we gather data in limited kinds of ways and use the results to try to derive some quality indications. We have some such data on KSAOs, and virtually none on motivation.

KSAOs

The most common, and broad, indicator of labor force quality is educational attainment level. Using data for 1992, about 27% of the population 25 and older had attained a college degree or higher, while 12% had less than a high school diploma; the remainder had education attainment levels within this band. The data also show differences in attainment level among whites, blacks, and hispanics, with whites generally having the highest level of formal education.[6]

A second, related indication of labor force quality pertains to literacy. Here, studies of new labor force entrants suggest problems for employers. In these studies, performance is measured in terms of prose, reading documents (tables, charts), and quantitative data. Scores for these skills were obtained for multiple samples and then divided into five categories measuring level of literacy. One-half to one-third of the new entrants fell into the bottom two categories.[7]

Another study also suggests KSAO problems. Among a large sample of employers it was found they considered 35% of their job applicants to be deficient in the ability to read instructions, do arithmetic, or write reports. Many of these organizations reported deficiency rates in excess of 50%.[8]

Results of education and literacy level studies are compared with what are felt to be the KSAO requirements of current or future jobs. These comparisons converge on a common conclusion, namely that there is a KSAO gap or skill shortage among workers, and that the gap will widen.[9] A recent example of such a conclusion is drawn from a massive study on workforce skill preparation by the Department of Labor.[10]

> The kinds of skills that people need to have—even if they hold the same job as before—have changed in the direction of higher skills, and more of them. The competitive work-place of today—regardless of the product or service—is a high skill environment designed around technology and people who are technically competent. Assembly line workers must now understand their

work as part of a much larger whole. Many workers must be comfortable with computer-numerically-controlled equipment. Front-line supervisors must confront tasks like budgeting and fiscal planning; clerical and other support personnel must handle complex word-processing and spreadsheet functions. Relatively few of these workers are likely to have graduated from college, while not long ago most of those skills would have been demanded only of the college-educated.

Motivation

Direct data on the motivational levels of workers in the labor force are virtually nonexistent. Development of such measures presents thorny questions pertaining to definitions of motivational goals (e.g., performance, attendance, retention of workers) and measures of motivation (e.g., self-reporting; behavioral indicators such as productivity, attendance record, length of service).

Compounding these problems is a general recognition that levels of motivation among workers are very much a function of the work environment they are part of. Motivation is thus not a hard-and-fast, stable characteristic or some general energy level that individuals maintain over extended periods of time. Measurements of motivation, if they could be made, would thus be very unreliable and depend upon the samples from which they are drawn.

Employment Arrangements

Though labor market forces bring organizations and job seekers together, the specific nature of the employment arrangement can assume many forms. One form is whether the person will be employed on a full-time or a part-time basis. Data show that about 82% of people work full time and 18% work part time.[11]

A second arrangement involves the issue of regular or shift work. About 82% of employees work a regular schedule, while 18% perform shift work. The latter, in turn, have a variety of different shift arrangements possible, such as evening, night, split, and rotating shifts.[12]

Two other types of arrangements, often considered in combination, are various "alternative" arrangements to the traditional employer-employee one, and the use of contingent employees. Alternative arrangements include the organization filling its staffing needs through use of independent contractors, on-call workers and day laborers, temporary help agency employees, and employees provided by a contract firm that provides a specific service (e.g., landscaping). Contingent employees do not have an explicit or implicit contract for long-term employment; they expect their employment to be temporary rather than long term. Contingent employees may occur in combination with any of the four alternatives given above.

National data on the use of alternative employment arrangements and contingent employees are shown in Exhibit 2.10. It can be seen that 90% of surveyed individuals worked in a traditional employer-employee arrangement, and the vast ma-

Exhibit 2.10   Usage of Alternative Employment Arrangements and Contingent Workers

Arrangement	Total (millions)	Percent	Percent Contingent	Percent Non-contingent
Alternative Arrangements				
Independent contractor	8.3	6.7%	3.8%	96.2%
On-call workers and day laborers	2.1	1.7%	38.1%	61.9%
Temporary help agency workers	1.2	1.0%	66.5%	33.5%
Workers provided by contract firm	.7	.6%	19.8%	80.2%
Traditional Arrangements	111.1	90.0%	3.6%	96.4%
	123.4	100 %		

Source: U.S. Department of Labor, Bureau of Labor Statistics, *Contingent and Alternative Employment Arrangements,* 1995, p.17.

jority of these (96.4%) considered themselves noncontingent. The most prevalent alternative was to work as an independent contractor (6.7%), followed by on-call employees and day laborers (1.7%), temporary help agency employees (1.0%), and employees provided by a contract firm (.6%). The percent of contingent employees in these alternative arrangements ranged from 3.8% (independent contractors) to 66.5% (temporary help employees).

Additional data are available on temporary help agency employees. Over a recent five-year period, employment growth has been substantially greater in temporary help agencies (43%) than in the labor force generally (5%). The average wage for a temporary employee is $7.74, compared to $11.13 for nonsupervisory employees in general. Also, many temporary agencies offer some benefits, particularly paid holidays and vacations, and health insurance. Relatively few temporary employees receive these benefits, however, because they fail to meet minimum eligibility requirements (e.g., minimum hours of service per year) or because they choose not to participate in the health insurance plan.[13]

Impacts on Staffing

Labor market forces strike at all staffing systems. Such forces cannot be ignored or denied; they create both staffing opportunities and threats for the organization.

On the opportunity side, for example, the gradually increasing age of the typical organization's workforce may contribute to greater workforce effectiveness. The reason for this is that organizations' managers rate older employees highly (compared to younger employees) on experience, judgment, commitment to quality, retention, and attendance/punctuality.[14] Another opportunity example involves labor surplus situations, where labor supply is plentiful relative to demand. Such "loose" labor markets allow the organization easy access to a ready labor supply, as well as one in which salary and benefit costs may be held in line. Surpluses occur in geographic areas, such as those experiencing unfavorable economic conditions (layoffs, plant closings); they also occur in occupations, such as among the large number of managers and professional employees experiencing layoffs due to downsizing and reengineering. Under conditions of labor surplus, recruitment elements of staffing often become relatively passive and benign activities for the organization.

The most ominous, general staffing threat is that of a recurring labor shortage, resulting from a relatively low growth in the labor force. With the labor force participation rate plateauing for women, and continuing to decline for men, persistent labor shortages will loom on the horizon for most organizations. This will require more aggressive, targeted, and expensive staffing activities by the organization.

One example of a shortage causing severe staffing problems involves poultry processing jobs.[15] These are low skill jobs growing rapidly in number due to surges in consumer demand for poultry products. The jobs are physically demanding, fast paced, hygienically distasteful, and low paid. These attributes yield employee turnover rates approaching 100%, so that poultry plants are continuously understaffed and seeking new employees.

Many organizations confront shortages at higher skill levels. For example, automobile companies face continued shortages of mechanical, manufacturing, and electrical engineers. This is due to heightened demand for them because of increasingly sophisticated technological production processes, and a dwindling supply of new employees coming out of engineering schools. In response, the companies recruit very aggressively, often poaching engineers from each other.[16]

Trucking companies are desperate for over-the-road drivers. A combination of lower wages (reflecting heightened competition among companies due to deregulation) and a lessening supply of 21- to 29-year-olds (the prime age category for driver recruits) has lead to several innovative staffing activities. There are attempts to expand recruitment pools beyond the traditional white male ranks to include women, minorities, and retirees; recruitment is being stepped up into labor markets where there are labor surpluses due to plant closings and layoffs; and jobs are being restructured (e.g., through shorter hauls) to make them more attractive.[17]

Manufacturing organizations are confronted with the anomaly of massive numbers of job applicants but a shortage of new hires due to low levels of qualifications among the applicants; they are lacking in required math, communication, and computer skills. Consequently, extraordinary recruitment and selection activities are under way. These include recruiting at local ROTC units, conducting nationwide searches for machinists, and holding open houses for high school teachers and career counselors in order to better communicate their needs. One organization spent $400,000 to staff its newly-opened plant; it screened 14,176 applicants to come up with the necessary 174 new hires; the selection and screening process involved 28 hours of applicant testing.[18]

As a final illustration of how shortages can affect staffing, consider small businesses. Many of them (e.g., research and development companies) are experiencing shortages of fully-qualified employees, and they cannot afford to hire people for whom they must invest heavily in training. A survey of small business owners found that 25% of them cited a shortage of qualified employees as a direct challenge to their growth.[19]

Both opportunities and threats are present in the growth of nontraditional employment arrangements and contingent workers. For an organization, such growth reflects an increasing opportunity for achieving staffing flexibility and avoiding long-term commitments to employees. The threat is that people may rebel against such arrangements and treatment, resulting in labor shortages as people shun employment through these alternative arrangements. Older employees may also present a combined opportunity/threat to the organizations. Despite the favorable attributes of older employees as rated by managers (see above), older employees are also rated by them as lower on flexibility, acceptance of new technology, ability to learn new skills, and physical ability to perform strenuous jobs.[20] Thus, even though their ranks are growing and they are rated as having some desirable KSAOs (opportunities), older employees also are perceived as having KSAO deficiencies (threats).

The undercurrents of labor supply and demand thus exert substantial influences on overall staffing strategy and practice for organizations. Organizational staffing systems must detect and fashion responses to these forces.

Recruitment activities help focus the organization on identifying and notifying potentially qualified segments of the labor force about employment needs and opportunities. Once identified, these applicants must be attracted to the organization through knowledge provided by the organization of specific job requirements and rewards, and then enter the applicant flow. Once a part of that flow, the organization must begin to assess the applicants' KSAOs and motivation, which is the major purpose of selection activities. Following that, hiring decisions must be made on the basis of the information gathered.

In all of these ways, the organization takes the initiative in attracting and assessing applicants from the labor force. It is through these staffing activities that individuals in the labor force become matched with jobs in the organization. Without specific staffing activities, person/job matches would likely be sporadic, chance-driven occurrences.

LABOR UNIONS

Labor union members are found across the spectrum in craft, production, professional, technical, clerical, transportation, maintenance, and sales jobs, as well as others. Managerial and supervisory employees, by law, are not permitted to be union members since they are involved in the establishment and administration of job requirements and rewards. If they were union members, they would have a conflict between allegiance to the union and their employer. Currently, about 15.5% of the labor force is unionized; the rates are 10.9% and 38.7% in the private and public sectors, respectively.[21]

Labor unions themselves are legally recognized and protected organizations whose purpose is to organize and to represent workers in matters affecting the employment relationship. It is the representation as opposed to organizing purpose of unions that is of most relevance to staffing organizations. Representation involves the establishment of the terms and conditions that will govern the employment relationship. It thus directly affects job requirements and rewards, as well as the person/job matching process.

Those effects are felt and expressed through provisions found in the labor contract. In terms of staffing, these provisions pertain to general characteristics of labor contracts and to specific contract clauses affecting staffing.

Labor Contracts

A labor contract is a legally enforceable, binding agreement between the organization and the union that represents the covered workers. It contains a set of terms and conditions that both parties have agreed to abide by during the duration of the contract.

For management, the impact of a labor contract is twofold. First, it standardizes terms and conditions of employment, making them uniform for all covered employees. The contract is thus a collective one, and cannot be replaced or supplemented by individual contracts between employees and the organization. Second, the contract explicitly restricts management authority and flexibility. Management cannot unilaterally establish or change terms and conditions of employment. The labor contract thus establishes, and "locks in," many job requirements and rewards.

Various federal and state laws govern collective bargaining and the labor–management relationship. Under those laws both parties generally have a mutual obligation to bargain in good faith over wages, hours, and other terms and conditions of employment.

As the law is interpreted, there are three types of issues that fall in the area of "terms and conditions"—those that are mandatory, those that are permissible, and those that are prohibited.[22] Mandatory issues include wages and hours as well as any issues regarding practices that have a direct and immediate effect on members' jobs and are strongly determined by labor cost factors. Prohibited issues are ones that labor and management are statutorily prohibited from bargaining over. Permissible issues are those that are neither mandatory nor prohibited. As regards staffing, most issues are mandatory subjects of bargaining because of their direct impact on jobs and labor costs.

Contract Clauses Affecting Staffing

Because of the mandatory nature of most staffing issues, contract clauses are negotiated for a wide array of staffing practices.[23] Several of the most prominent of these are discussed here.

Management Rights

A management rights clause specifies what rights management has to act unilaterally without prior consultation or negotiation with the union. Such a clause is found in almost every labor contract.

The clause may be a so-called savings clause, which says that management saves or retains all rights (including any regarding staffing) that are not explicitly covered by the contract. Or, the clause may contain explicit restrictions on management rights in certain areas. Examples of such areas are subcontracting, supervisory performance of union members' jobs, introduction of technological change, and plant shutdowns or relocations. All of these areas clearly pertain to matters having strong staffing overtones, particularly regarding labor demand.

Jobs and Job Structures

Individual job tasks and job titles are negotiable. An organization must decide what an electrician does, and whether it wants to use that title to describe a job. Also negotiable are job structures involving lines of task demarcation among jobs (e.g., does the electrician or carpenter rip out old wiring?), and internal mobility paths among jobs (into which jobs can someone be transferred or promoted?). Results of negotiations on jobs and job structures establish the structural features of the organization's internal labor market.

Recently, some organizations have tried to negotiate sweeping revisions in their contracts on matters relating to jobs and job structures. The reason for this is that jobs and structures had been too restrictive, giving management little flexibility in hiring, work assignments, and job transfers and promotions. For example, the GM Saturn automobile manufacturing plant, in order to create flexibility, has only one broad job classification—"operating technician"—instead of many narrow ones, for all nonskilled workers, and five job classifications for skilled trades workers. This is in comparison with the dozens of job classifications found in other GM plants. These job classifications for both Saturn and other GM plants are incorporated into the labor contracts between GM and the United Automobile Workers.[24]

External Staffing

Normally, external staffing is not an important topic of negotiation, and labor contracts are relatively void of contract clauses pertaining to it. The reason for this is that, by law, requiring union membership as a condition of employment ("closed shop" practices) is prohibited, except in certain narrow circumstances. With this restriction, unions are relatively indifferent as to whom management hires, and how it goes about doing that. Unions do not want to negotiate about the types of people that management must hire, nor would management want to do this.

Occasionally, there will be contract clauses pertaining to external staffing. There may be a clause requiring a preference for hiring people in the local geographic area or in the industry (e.g., by contract clause, the new Saturn automobile manufacturing plant was staffed primarily by GM employees from other plants or on layoff). In other instances, the union may have a direct hand in the administration of the staffing system, including the making of selection decisions. This occurs in referral or hiring hall arrangements (common in construction), as well as through joint labor–management apprenticeship committees.

Internal Staffing

Unions are extremely active in negotiating and administering contract clauses pertaining to internal staffing. The nature of jobs and job rewards, and access to them, are matters of great concern to their membership. Specific contract clauses pertaining to job postings, lines of movement, and seniority are of great relevance to internal staffing.

Job Posting   Many contracts contain provisions requiring the posting of job vacancies, as well as specifying procedures for applying for those vacancies. Job posting creates a very open internal mobility system, one that allows employees an active role in gathering information about vacancies and deciding whether to apply for them.

Lines of Movement   Lateral and upward lines of movement among jobs, and the rules and procedures for governing that movement, receive considerable attention from both labor and management. These transfer and promotion systems contain plenty of grist for the negotiating mill. Union leadership and management must decide upon the operational or procedural characteristics of the internal labor market. For example: To which other jobs are employees eligible to move? Will there be restrictions upon movement by department, function, shift, or location of facility? Who will be eligible for job moves, and what factors will be taken into account in making promotion and transfer decisions? This latter question raises important seniority concerns.

Seniority   Seniority clauses in contracts treat both definitional and decision-making issues. They lay out when seniority begins (e.g., date of hire or date reporting for work); what happens when seniority is interrupted (e.g., due to medical leave or layoff); in what way one builds up seniority and may exercise seniority rights (department, division, plant, organization); and whether seniority may be carried across the normal seniority unit (e.g., from one department to another). Answers to these types of questions are negotiated and incorporated into contract clauses.

The resultant clauses may create seniority calculation questions, and employees will want to know exactly how much seniority they have. In response, the contract may also contain a clause requiring posting of seniority lists or rosters.

In terms of seniority and decision making, the basic issue is what role seniority will play in transfer and promotion decisions and how much weight will be accorded seniority as opposed to other qualifications. Typically, a contract clause will specify seniority's weight.

Grievance Procedure

Terms of the contract need to be administered during its duration. This means addressing problems of interpretation and application of contract clauses. When interpretation and application problems arise, normally management and labor will attempt to handle and resolve them informally. Should they not be successful, there will, in all likelihood, be a grievance/arbitration process specified in the labor contract to which they can turn.[25] That process will be a formal one, specifying the steps that must be followed to resolve the grievance. Thus, aspects of the organization's staffing system are open not only to bargaining, but to grievance as well. Both of these facts restrict management's discretion and flexibility in staffing.

Guarantees Against Discrimination

Most contracts contain a nondiscrimination clause, guaranteeing no discrimination against persons because of race, color, religion, sex, national origin, or disability. Where such discrimination is alleged to occur, the claim may be pursued and resolved through the grievance procedure (as opposed to the legal system).

Impacts on Staffing

Labor unions have direct and powerful impacts on staffing systems. The labor contract, which must be negotiated with the union, specifies the terms and conditions of employment. Thus, job requirements and rewards are determined, as are characteristics of external and (especially) internal staffing systems. When terms of the contract are felt to have been violated, the violation claim may be pursued through the grievance procedure.

Even in nonunion situations the union influence can be felt through "spillover effects" in which management tries to emulate practices found in unionized settings. This may involve providing comparable wage and benefit packages, creating structured and well-defined internal labor markets, developing written staffing policies and procedures, and providing a grievance procedure.

SUMMARY

Economic conditions are composed of general economic forces that establish the overall economic environment in which the organization must function. That environment, in turn, affects the rate and direction of job growth. A positive rate of growth creates a positive impact on the movement of people into, within, and out of organizations. Staffing activities exist to anticipate and manage the "people flow" that comes about from job growth.

Labor markets are composed of labor demand and labor supply forces, as well as the interactions between them. Both supply and demand contain quantitative and qualitative elements. Various labor demand data provide indications about employment distributions and trends; relatively little is known about qualitative aspects of demand. Labor supply data provide descriptions of various characteristics of the labor force (e.g., numbers employed and unemployed, unemployment and labor force participation rates), as well as education, literacy, and skill levels. The organization's staffing systems serve as the interface between the labor market and the fulfillment of specific person/job matches. Labor market forces present many opportunities and threats for staffing systems, particularly when shortages of qualified applicants are confronted.

Labor unions affect staffing activities through their role as the employees' representative to negotiate and administer labor contracts. Contained in these contracts are the terms and conditions of employment that will govern the employment relationship for all represented employees over the life of the contract. Of particular importance to staffing are clauses pertaining to management rights, jobs and job structures, external staffing, and especially internal staffing. The contract also contains provisions for a grievance process to resolve problems of interpretation and application of these clauses, as well as a clause guaranteeing nondiscrimination. The labor contract clauses not only determine an organization's staffing policies and procedures, but may also have a spillover impact on staffing systems in nonunion organizations.

DISCUSSION QUESTIONS

1. Think of an organization you have worked for and describe how economic conditions have influenced its staffing activities. (Hint: Use Exhibit 2.1 to help you.)

2. What are some of the reasons there will be occupational "winners" (those who experience employment growth) and "losers" (those who experience employment decline) over the next decade?

3. Describe various ways you have experienced or seen a previous or current employer adjust staffing practices in order to best manage its labor demand.

4. How will a more demographically diverse workforce influence the person/job matching process in organizations?

5. Using the person/job matching model, why do unions seek to negotiate over job posting, lines of movement, and seniority?

APPLICATIONS

Staffing a Management Training Program

Doyton's is a medium-sized retailing organization (annual sales of $400 million) with corporate headquarters in Gary, Indiana and 25 stores located in both urban and suburban locations in a six-state region (Indiana, Illinois, Ohio, Wisconsin, Iowa, and Kansas). The company has major sales lines in ready-to-wear apparel, hardware, outdoor lawn furniture, lawn care products, and electronic sound systems.

Originally a one-store company, Doyton's has grown to its current size through use of a combined external/internal staffing strategy. It has used external staffing for filling entry-level jobs in sales, customer service, maintenance, marketing, and distribution jobs. Employees on these jobs have risen into entry-level management jobs through a very active and widely-used promotion-from-within system. Filling the entry-level nonmanagement jobs has been "a snap" because the company is able to couple above-market starting pay with strong advancement possibilities to create a very alluring job offer for external recruits.

Recently, however, the company had to abandon this strong promotion-from-within program for obtaining new management talent. The quality (KSAOs and motivation) of new hires into nonmanagerial jobs had fallen off, in the company's opinion. This meant that there were fewer well-qualified internal applicants for the entry-level management jobs, and those that were promoted usually required considerably more training than in the past. Consequently, the company has developed a management trainee program that will be used as the sole source of new entry-level managers. Both internal and external applicants will be sought for the program.

The program was designed by a team of top management and HR department staff members. The program will be conducted at corporate headquarters in Gary, and it will last for 18 months. It will combine classroom training, field trips, and rotating job assignments through various stores within 50 miles of Gary. At the end of training, each trainee will be assessed for final proficiency by a team of managers and HR staff members. Those who receive a passing assessment will be placed in an entry-level management job at one of the 25 existing stores, or new stores to be opened. While details of the program are still being worked out, the company wants to begin the staffing process necessary to obtain 30 trainees for the first class of the program.

The HR department has developed what it thinks will be a simple, cost-effective way to find and hire these new trainees. Its general strategy is to "beat the market," which means offering applicants a hiring package that exceeds what is being offered trainees in this and other industries. Based on market surveys, it has determined that starting pay for trainees is between $28,000 and $31,500 per year, with health insurance, retirement, and vacation pay (one week) eligibility after completion of the first year of the program. Doyton's will offer $32,000, health insurance (employee and employer split the cost of the premium) after six months, one week of vacation during the first year, and immediate participation in a 401(k) retirement plan. To recruit applicants, a general ad has been developed for placement in the internal company monthly newsletter, and for placement in the Sunday paper in every location in which it has a store. The ad will indicate the terms and conditions noted above, and readers will be asked to submit a resume to the corporate HR department. The HR department is very confident that this market-oriented staffing strategy will attract more than enough highly qualified applicants.

1. Do you share the company's optimism that the above staffing strategy will be sufficient by itself to yield an applicant pool from which 30 qualified new hires can be identified? Why or why not?
2. What specific recommendations (if any) would you make for improvements in, and additions to, the current staffing plan?

Staffing When There Are Labor Shortages

Identify and choose an organization to contact for a short (probably one-half hour) visit or telephone interview. You will want to interview either (a) a member of the HR department with responsibility for staffing, or (b) a line manager or owner who conducts staffing for the organization or one of its units. The purpose of the interview or visit is to learn about how the organization attempts to handle situations in which it is faced with shortages of applicants (numbers of applicants of any kind, and/or numbers of qualified applicants) for filling vacancies that it has currently, or has experienced in the past. If the organization has never faced shortages, you can ask how they would handle a shortage situation if it occurred.

Your questions should focus on learning about specific examples of what the organization does in terms of recruitment, selection, and employment activities as ways of meeting the shortage challenge. For example, for recruitment you might ask if the organization has used new methods of recruitment, or has sought to target new types of applicants it has traditionally not drawn from. For selection, you might determine if the organization has altered or dropped use of certain selection techniques, such as the interview, drug testing, or reference checks. For employment, consider asking questions about whether hiring standards have been lowered in order to be able to hire applicants that normally would not be hireable, or whether the organization has raised its wages or offered other inducements as ways of making a job more attractive.

ENDNOTES

1. G. T. Silvestri, "Occupational Employment: Wide Variations in Growth," *Monthly Labor Review*, 1993, 116(10), pp. 58–86.

2. D. Crispell, "People Patterns," *Wall Street Journal*, Aug. 6, 1993, p. B1; D. Hale, "For New Jobs, Help Small Business," *Wall Street Journal*, Aug. 10, 1992, p. B1.

3. A. A. Johnson and F. Linden, *Availability of a Quality Workforce* (New York: The Conference Board, 1992), p. 14.

4. Secretary's Commission on Achieving Necessary Skills (SCANS), *Skills and Tasks for Jobs* (Washington, D.C.: U.S. Government Printing Office, 1992).

5. W. B. Johnston, "The Coming Labor Shortage," *Journal of Labor Research*, 1992, 13, pp. 1–10.

6. U.S. Department of Labor, *News*, July 10, 1993.

7. A. Packer, "Skill Deficiencies: Problems, Policies, and Prospects," *Journal of Labor Research*, 1993, 14, pp. 227–247.

8. American Management Association, "1994 AMA Survey on Basic Skills Testing and Training," (New York: author, 1995).

9. A. Packer, "Skill Deficiencies: Problems, Policies, and Prospects."

10. U.S. Department of Labor, *Economic Change and the American Workforce* (Washington, D.C.: author, 1992), p. 3.

11. U.S. Department of Labor, *Monthly Labor Review*, 1995, 118(8), p. 93.

12. U.S. Department of Labor, *News*, Aug. 14, 1992, p. 5.

13. U.S. Department of Labor, *News*, Sept. 6, 1995, pp. 1–6.

14. American Association of Retired Persons, *Valuing Older Workers: A Case Study of Costs and Productivity,* (Washington, D.C.: author), pp. 22–23.

15. T. Horowitz, "These Six Growth Jobs Are Dull, Dead-End, Sometimes Dangerous," *Wall Street Journal*, Dec. 1, 1994, p. A1.

16. K. Miller, "Dwindling Supply of Engineers Brings a Sense of Desperation to Auto Makers," *Wall Street Journal*, June 7, 1994, p. B1.

17. D. Machalaba, "Trucking Firms Find It Is a Struggle to Hire and Retain Drivers," *Wall Street Journal*, Dec. 28, 1993, p. A1.

18. R. Narisetti, "Manufacturers Decry a Shortage of Workers While Rejecting Many," *Wall Street Journal*, Sept. 8, 1995, p. A1.

19. S. Mehta, "Companies Plan More Hires but Worry That Qualified Labor Pool Is Shrinking," *Wall Street Journal*, Aug. 2, 1995, p. B2.

20. American Association of Retired Persons, *Valuing Older Workers: A Case Study of Costs and Productivity.*

21. U.S. Department of Labor, "Union Members in 1994," *News*, Feb. 8, 1995.

22. J. A. Fossum, *Labor Relations: Development, Structure, Process*, sixth ed. (Homewood, IL: Irwin, 1995), pp. 191–192.

23. Bureau of National Affairs, *Basic Patterns in Union Contracts*, fourteenth ed. (Washington, D.C.: author, 1995).

24. B. Geber, "Saturn's Grand Experiment," *Training*, June 1992, pp. 27–33.

25. J. A. Fossum, *Labor Relations: Development, Structure, Process*, pp. 408–434.

CHAPTER THREE

Laws and Regulations

The Employment Relationship
Employer-Employee
Independent Contractors
Temporary Employees

Laws and Regulations
Need for Laws and Regulations
Sources of Laws and Regulations

EEO/AA: Preliminary Issues
EEO, AA, and Quotas
Disparate Treatment and Disparate Impact

EEO/AA Laws: General Provisions and Enforcement
General Provisions
Enforcement: EEOC
Enforcement: OFCCP

EEO/AA Laws: Specific Staffing Provisions
Civil Rights Act
Age Discrimination in Employment Act
Americans With Disabilities Act
Rehabilitation Act
Executive Order 11246

EEO/AA: Regulations and Information
Regulations and Guidelines
Information Sources

Other Staffing Laws
Federal Laws
State and Local Laws
Civil Service Laws and Regulations

Legal Issues in Remainder of Book

Summary

Discussion Questions

Applications

L aws and regulations have assumed an importance of major proportions in the process of staffing organizations. Virtually all aspects of staffing are subject to their influence. No organization can or should ignore provisions of the law; in this case, ignorance truly is not bliss.

This chapter begins by discussing the formation of the employment relationships from a legal perspective. It first defines what is an employer, along with the rights and obligations of being an employer. The employer may acquire people to work for it in the form of employees, independent contractors, and temporary employees. Legal meanings and implications for each of these terms is provided.

For many reasons, the employment relationship has become increasingly regulated. Reasons for the myriad laws and regulations affecting the employment relationship are suggested. Then, the major sources of the laws and regulations controlling the employment relationship are indicated.

Equal employment opportunity and affirmative action (EEO/AA) laws and regulations have become dominant in the eyes of most who are concerned with staffing organizations. This dominance is illustrated first by a general discussion of EEO, AA, and quotas, as well as the two approaches for bringing forth and resolving discrimination charges. Following that, the general provisions of five major EEO/AA laws are summarized, along with indications of how these laws are administered and enforced.

For these same five laws, their specific (and numerous) provisions regarding staffing are then presented in detail. It is within this presentation that the true scope, complexity, and impact of the laws as regards to staffing become known.

Numerous regulations and guidelines have been issued to assist in interpretation, implementation, and enforcement of these five laws. The most prominent are the Uniform Guidelines on Employee Selection Procedures, Revised Order No. 4, and the Employment Regulations of the Americans With Disabilities Act. Each of these is introduced (their full text is found in Appendixes A, B, and C). Also, numerous information sources about EEO/AA laws and regulations are presented.

Attention then turns to other staffing laws and regulations. These involve a myriad of federal laws, state and local laws, and civil service laws and regulations. These laws, like federal EEO/AA ones, have major impacts on staffing activities.

Finally, the chapter concludes with an indication that each of the chapters that follows this one has a separate section, "Legal Issues," at the end of it. In these sections, specific topics and applications of the law are presented. Their intent is to provide guidance and examples (not legal advise per se) regarding staffing practices that are permissible, impermissible, and required.

THE EMPLOYMENT RELATIONSHIP

The definition of staffing (Chapter 1) refers to formation of the employment relationship. That relationship involves several different types of arrangements between the organization and those who provide work for it. These arrangements have special and reasonably separate legal meaning. This section explores those arrangements: employer–employee, independent contractor, and temporary employee.

Employer–Employee

By far the most prevalent form of the employment relationship is that of employer–employee. This arrangement is the result of the organization's usual staffing activities—a culmination of the person/job matching process. As shown in Exhibit 3.1, the employer and employee negotiate and agree upon the terms and conditions that will define and govern their relationship. The formal agreement represents an employment contract, the terms and conditions of which represent the promises and expectations of the parties (job requirements and rewards, and KSAOs and motivation).[1] Over time, the initial contract may be modified due to changes in requirements or rewards of the current job, or employee transfer or promotion. The contract may also be terminated by either party, thus ending the employment relationship.

EXHIBIT 3.1   Matching Process, Employment Contract, and Employment Relationships

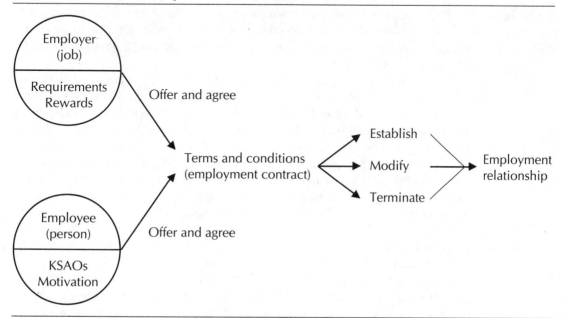

Employment contracts come in a variety of styles. They may be written or oral (both types are legally enforceable), and their specificity may vary from extensive to "bare bones." In some instances, where the contract is written, terms and conditions are described in great detail. Examples of such contracts are collective bargaining agreements and contracts for professional athletes, entertainers, and upper-level executives. At the other extreme, the contract may be little more than some simple oral promises about the job, such as promises about wages and hours, and agreed to on the basis of a handshake.

From a legal perspective, an employer is an entity that employs others (employees or independent contractors) to do its work or work on its behalf.[2] When these "others" are employees, the employer has the right to specify both the work output (results) expected and the work methods to be followed by its employees. In exchange for this right to control its employees, the employer incurs certain legal responsibilities and liabilities. Specifically, the employer becomes (a) required to withhold employee payroll taxes (income, social security), (b) required to pay taxes (unemployment compensation, employer's share of social security and medicare), (c) covered under the myriad laws and regulations governing the employment relationship, and (d) liable for the acts of its employees during employment.

When and how the employment relationship may end is a matter of great importance to the employer and the employee. For the employer, it bears on the degree of staffing flexibility possible to quickly terminate employees without constraint. For employees, the issue is the degree of continued employment and job security that will be expected. Under the common-law principle of employment-at-will, in the absence of any contract language to the contrary, the employment relationship is strictly an at-will one, meaning that either the employer or the employee may terminate the employment relationship at any time, for any reason, without prior notification.[3]

Restrictions on the employment-at-will right are usually established as part of the employment contract. For example, a set-term contract specifies a definite duration and ending date; normally it will (or should) have a clause stating that it may not be terminated during that time period without showing "just cause" or "failure to perform." As another example, labor union contracts usually contain a provision stating that an employee can be terminated only for "just cause." As another example, a letter of appointment to a new hire may contain a clause saying it is the policy of the organization to terminate its employees only "for cause." For an organization wishing to avoid such restrictions and to be governed by employment-at-will, it must take care to ensure that its employment contracts explicitly state that there will be an employment-at-will relationship, and that the contracts contain no language providing restrictions on such a relationship.

There are numerous exceptions to employment-at-will, outside of specific contract language restrictions, that limit the right of the employer to terminate the employment relationship at will.[4] These include prohibitions of discharge on the basis of legally protected characteristics (e.g., age, sex, race), for exercising rights guaranteed by law (e.g., filing a discrimination charge against the employer), or for refusing to engage in illegal acts for the employer.

Independent Contractors

The employer may also hire independent contractors to work for it. An independent contractor is not legally considered an employee, however, and because of this the rights and responsibilities the employer has toward the independent contractor are different than those for its employees.[5] Classifying and using a person as an independent contractor frees the employer of the tax withholding and tax payment obligations it has for employees. It may also reduce employer exposure under laws and regulations governing the employment relationship. For example, nondiscrimination laws (e.g., Civil Rights Act) apply to the employer and its employees but not to its independent contractors.

In exchange for these advantages of using independent contractors, the employer substantially loses the right to control the contractor. In particular, while the employer can still control expected results, the employer cannot dictate where, when, or how work is to be done. Thus, the employer loses control over the means (work processes, tools, equipment, work schedules, and so forth) by which the work is performed.

Beyond this crucial distinction, the line of demarcation between what constitutes an employee and what constitutes an independent contractor is often fuzzy. Numerous other factors come into play. For example, a person is more likely to be considered an independent contractor than an employee when

- working in a distinct occupation or business
- working without supervision or oversight from the employer
- paying one's own business and travel expenses
- setting one's own hours of work
- possessing a high degree of skill
- using one's own tools, materials, office
- working on a project with a definite completion date
- working on relatively short projects
- being paid by the project or commission, rather than by the time spent

The above examples are based on common-law interpretations, and on a list of 20 criteria used by the Internal Revenue Service to determine the appropriate classification of people as employees or independent contractors. Misclassification of people as independent contractors can result in substantial tax liabilities and fines for the employer.

Temporary Employees

Temporary employees do not have special legal stature. They are considered employees of the temporary help agency that obtained them through its own staffing process. Temporary employees are then given job assignments with other employers (clients) by the agency. During these assignments the temporary employee remains on the payroll of the agency, and the client employer simply reimburses the agency for its wage and other costs. The client employer must recognize that it has a severely limited right to control temporary employees that it utilizes since they are not its employees, but employees of the agency.

Use of temporary employees often raises issues of coemployment, in which the client employer and the temporary agency share the traditional role of employer.[6] Because both function to an extent as employers, there is a need to sort out their obligations and liabilities under various laws. Depending on the specific issue and law involved, both the client employer and agency may be legally considered the employer. Employment discrimination laws such as the Civil Rights Act, for example, apply to both the client employer and the agency. Thus, usage of temporary employees by a client employer should be proceeded by a thorough review of the coemployment legal ramifications.

LAWS AND REGULATIONS

Establishment and maintenance of the employment relationship involves exercising discretion on the part of both the employer and the employee. Broadly speaking, laws affecting the employment relationship spring from a need to define the scope of permissible discretion and place limits on it. Their purpose is to create a reasonable balance of power between employer and employee, as well as to provide protections for each.

Need for Laws and Regulations

Balance of Power

Entering into and maintaining the employment relationship involves negotiating issues of power.[7] The employer has something desirable to offer the employee (a job with certain requirements and rewards), and the employee has something to offer the employer (KSAOs and motivation). Both parties seek to use to their own advantage what they have to offer in establishing the terms and conditions of employment.

Usually, the employer has the upper hand in this power relationship because the employer has more to offer, and more control over what to offer, than does the employee. It is the employer who controls the creation of jobs; the definition of jobs in terms of requirements and rewards; access to those jobs via staffing systems; movement of employees among jobs over time; and ultimately, the retention or termination of employees. While employees participate in these processes and decisions to varying degrees, it is seldom as an equal or a partner of the employer. Employment laws and regulations exist, in part, to reduce or limit the employer's power in the employment relationship. Laws pertaining to wages, hours, equal employment opportunity, and so forth, all seek to limit employer discretion in the establishment of the terms and conditions of employment.

Protection of Employees

Laws and regulations seek to provide specific protections to employees that they could conceivably, though improbably, acquire individually in an employment contract.[8] These protections pertain to employment standards, individual workplace rights, and consistency of treatment.

Employment Standards   Employment standards usually represent minimum acceptable terms and conditions of employment. Examples of these standards include minimum wage laws, overtime pay requirements, and safety and health standards. Sometimes employment standards represent maximums, such as maximum permissible hours of work for minors and maximum permissible levels of exposure to work environment elements (e.g., noise and toxic substances).

Individual Rights   Laws and regulations provide employees with individual rights that they could not acquire alone in a contract with their employers. An example of these are the organizing and collective bargaining rights granted employees under the Railway Labor Act and the National Labor Relations Act. Another, more recent, example are civil rights protections afforded employees by the various civil rights laws discussed in following sections.

A final example are the protections given employees through constraints that have been developing on employment-at-will. These constraints place limits on the right of the employer to unilaterally terminate the employment relationship. Laws prohibit discharge on the basis of union preference, race, sex, disability, and so forth. Common law also increasingly recognizes limits or exceptions to employment-at-will as the norm in employment contracts. For example, statements about job security for employees in an employee handbook may be treated as an implied contract that restricts the right of the employer to terminate employees at will.

Consistency of Treatment   As the previous examples show, laws and regulations, in effect, provide guarantees of consistency of treatment among employees. They constitute a constraint on the employer to treat employees differently from one another in terms and conditions of employment and afford employees some measure of procedural justice, or fairness in the process whereby decisions are made about them. Hiring and promotion decisions, for example, cannot be made on the basis of protected employee characteristics (e.g., race, sex). Ensuring this in essence requires the employer to develop and implement standardized staffing systems (e.g., all job applicants receive the same interview and must provide the same biographical data about themselves).

Protection of Employers

While the preceding discussion suggests a general proemployee tenor or slant to employment laws and regulations, employers also gain protections in the process.

Permissible/Impermissible Practices   Given the inherent fuzziness of the employment relationship and the ground rules surrounding it, laws and regulations provide guidance to employers as to what are permissible practices as well as impermissible practices. The Civil Rights Act, for example, not only forbids certain types of discrimination on the basis of race, color, religion, sex, and national origin, but also specifically mentions employment practices that are permitted. One of those practices, for example, is the use of professionally developed ability tests, a practice that has major implications for external and internal selection.

Administrative Predictability and Stability   New laws and regulations initially create uncertainty and turbulence for an employer. What do the laws mean, and exactly what do they require? Over time, these questions are clarified through many avenues—court decisions, policy statements from government agencies, informal guidance from enforcement officials, and networking with other employers. The result is increasing convergence upon what is required in order to comply with the laws. This allows the employer to implement needed changes, which then become standard operating procedure in staffing systems. In this manner, for example, affirmative action programs have developed and been incorporated into the administrative mainstream for many employers.

Sources of Laws and Regulations

There are numerous sources of law and regulation that govern the employment relationship. Exhibit 3.2 provides examples of these as they pertain to staffing. Each of these is commented on next.

Common Law

Common law, which has its origins in England, is court-made law, as opposed to law from other sources such as the state. It consists of the case-by-case decisions of the court, which determine over time permissible and impermissible practices, as well as their remedies. There is a heavy reliance in common law on the precedence established in previous court decisions. Each state develops and administers its own common law. Employment-at-will and workplace tort cases, for ex-

---

EXHIBIT 3.2   Sources of Laws and Regulations

SOURCE	EXAMPLES
Common law	Employment-at-will Workplace torts
Constitutional	Fifth Amendment Fourteenth Amendment
Statutory	Civil Rights Act Age Discrimination in Employment Act Americans With Disabilities Act Rehabilitation Act Immigration Reform and Control Act Immigration Act Employee Polygraph Protection Act State and local laws Civil service laws
Executive order	11246 (nondiscrimination under federal contracts)
Agencies	Equal Employment Opportunity Commission (EEOC) Department of Labor (DOL) Office of Federal Contract Compliance Programs (OFCCP) State Fair Employment Practice (FEP) agencies

---

ample, are treated at the state level. As noted, employment-at-will involves the rights of employer and employee to terminate the employment relationship at will. A tort is a civil wrong that occurs when the employer violates a duty owed to its employees or customers that leads to harm or damages suffered by them. Staffing tort examples include negligent hiring of unsafe or dangerous employees, fraud and misrepresentation regarding employment terms and conditions, defamation of former employees, and invasion of privacy.[9]

Constitutional Law

Constitutional law is derived from the U.S. Constitution and its amendments. It supersedes any other source of law or regulation. Its major application is in the area of the rights of public employees, particularly their due process rights.

Statutory Law

Statutory law is derived from written statutes that are passed by legislative bodies. These bodies are federal (Congress), state (legislatures and assemblies), and local (municipal boards and councils). Legislative bodies may create, amend, and eliminate laws and regulations. They may also create agencies to administer and enforce the law.

Agencies

Agencies exist at the federal, state, and local level. Their basic charge is to interpret, administer, and enforce the law. At the federal level, the two major agencies of concern to staffing are the Department of Labor (DOL) and the Equal Employment Opportunity Commission (EEOC). Housed within DOL are several separate units for administration of employment law, notably the Office of Federal Contract Compliance Programs (OFCCP).

Agencies rely heavily on written documents to perform their functions. These documents are variously referred to as rules, regulations, guidelines, and policy statements. Rules, regulations, and guidelines are published in the *Federal Register*, as well as incorporated into the Code of Federal Regulations (CFR), and have the weight of law. Policy statements are somewhat more benign in that they do not have the force of law. They do, however, represent the agency's official position on a point or question.

EEO/AA: PRELIMINARY ISSUES

The numerous and complex equal employment opportunity and affirmative action (EEO/AA) laws and regulations are major sources of influence on staffing. Understanding them requires familiarity first with some preliminary issues that set the context for the specifics of the laws and regulations.

EEO, AA, and Quotas

The terms equal employment opportunity (EEO), affirmative action (AA), and quotas are encountered frequently, and often lead to confusion. There are conceptual, semantic, and practical differences among these three terms as they apply to staffing.[10] What follows is a brief overview of the distinctions to help clarify their meaning and usage.

EEO

As applied to staffing, EEO refers to practices that are designed and used in a "facially neutral" manner, meaning that all applicants and employees are treated similarly without regard to protected characteristics such as race and sex. Consistent application of and adherence to these practices is thought to create an equal opportunity for everyone to obtain a job or promotion.

To illustrate, consider a simple example where an organization is filling a vacant position and uses both a written job knowledge test and an interview in assessing job applicants. Anyone is free to apply for the position, and all that do so will be given both the test and the interview. How well each performs on the test and in the interview determines who is hired. Thus, all applicants have an equal chance or opportunity to be considered for the job, and which applicant receives the job offer depends upon an unbiased assessment of applicants' job qualifications.

AA

AA requirements in staffing must be placed in the context of past practices that were discriminatory against minorities and women, as well as other groups. Through changing existing staffing practices and adding new ones, AA seeks to rectify the discriminatory effects of these past practices. In this sense, AA is less than completely facially neutral. AA may be voluntarily undertaken by an employer, without anyone "pointing a finger" at specific actions. AA may also be court-ordered, or agreed to, as a remedy for past actions that indeed were discriminatory.

Consider again the preceding staffing example, and assume that the staffing system has operated in the same way for many years. Several features of the system may have created potentially unequal employment opportunities for women and minorities, resulting in their being numerically underrepresented relative to their availability and qualifications in the labor market. For example, there may have been an outright refusal to recruit women and minorities, or the recruitment methods used—referrals from current, mostly male, employees—may have greatly favored male applicants. As another example, women and minorities may have scored poorly on the job knowledge test because of lack of access to the types of training and/or job experience necessary to acquire that job knowledge. Special affirmative actions, voluntary or court-imposed, seek to enhance the employment of women and minorities and help deal with these sorts of historical problems.[11]

What might these actions entail? The organization might undertake special recruiting methods, other than just employees' referral, to identify and attract women and minority applicants. Management might establish specific hiring goals and timetables for achieving those goals for women and minorities. The organization would make good faith efforts to meet the hiring goals and timetables. Also, the organization could place less weight on the job knowledge test when making hiring decisions and create a training program for new job entrants to provide them the types of job knowledge they need in order to perform effectively on the job.

Quotas

Quotas represent more rigid hiring and promotion requirements that must be adhered to. Quotas do not leave staffing to the somewhat ill-defined concept of affirmative action; quotas focus on and demand staffing results. If a quota staffing system were applied in the previous example, a hiring formula would be established that specifies the number or percentage of women and minorities to be hired so that their numerical representation in the workplace reflects the percentage of potentially qualified women and minorities in the population. Quota staffing systems of this kind are legally permissible as a judicial remedy for past discrimination, though there are limitations on their usage and features.[12] AA quotas have raised substantial legal turmoil, as well as more practical questions as to whether they have in fact worked to effectively advance the hiring and promotion of minorities and women. Of utmost concern are issues of "reverse discrimination" or special racial or gender preferences that weigh too heavily into hiring and promotion decisions, relative to the qualifications of candidates for the job.[13] The permissibility and legal status of AA and quotas are explained in detail in Chapter 6, along with a description of AA plan requirements and the content of AA programs.

Disparate Treatment and Disparate Impact

Claims of discrimination in staffing ultimately require evidence and proof, particularly as these charges pertain to the staffing system itself and its specific characteristics as it has operated in practice. Toward this end, there are two different avenues or paths to follow—disparate treatment and disparate impact.[14]

Disparate Treatment

Claims of disparate treatment involve allegations of intentional discrimination where it is alleged that the employer knowingly and deliberately discriminated against people on the basis of specific characteristics such as race or sex. Evidence for such claims may be of several sorts.

First, the evidence may be direct. It might, for example, involve reference to an explicit, written policy of the organization such as one stating that "women are not to be hired for the following jobs. . . ."

The situation may not involve such blatant action, however, but may consist of what is referred to as a mixed motive. Here, both a prohibited characteristic (e.g., sex) and a legitimate reason (e.g., job qualifications) are mixed together to contribute to a negative decision about a person, such as a failure to hire or promote. If an unlawful motive, such as sex, plays any part in the decision, it is illegal, despite the presence of a lawful motive as well.

Finally, the discrimination may be such that evidence of a failure to hire or promote because of a protected characteristic must be inferred from several situational factors. Here, the evidence involves four factors:

1. The person belongs to a protected class.
2. The person applied for, and was qualified for, a job the employer was trying to fill.
3. The person was rejected despite being qualified.
4. The position remained open and the employer continued to seek applicants as qualified as the person rejected.

Most disparate treatment cases involve and require the use of these four factors to initially prove a charge of discrimination.

Disparate Impact

Disparate impact is also known as adverse impact and focuses on the effect of employment practices, rather than on the motive or intent underlying them. Accordingly, the emphasis here is on the need for direct evidence that, as a result of a protected characteristic, people are being adversely affected by a practice. Statistical evidence must be presented to support a claim of adverse impact.[15] Three types of statistical evidence may be used, and these are shown in Exhibit 3.3.

Shown first in the exhibit are applicant flow statistics, which look at differences in selection rates (proportion of applicants hired) among different groups for a particular job. If the differences are large enough, this suggests that the effect of the selection system is discriminatory. In the example, the selection rate for men is .50 (or 50%) and for women it is .11 (or 11%), suggesting the possibility of discrimination.

A second type of statistical evidence, shown next in the exhibit, involves the use of stock statistics. Here, the percentage of women or minorities actually employed in a job category is compared with their availability in the relevant popu-

---

EXHIBIT 3.3   Types of Disparate Impact Statistics

A. FLOW STATISTICS

Definition:

Significant differences in selection rates between groups

Example

Job Category: Customer Service Representative					
No. of Applicants		No. Hired		Selection Rate (%)	
Men	**Women**	**Men**	**Women**	**Men**	**Woman**
50	45	25	5	50%	11%

B. STOCK STATISTICS

Definition:

Underutilization of women or minorities relative to their availability in the relevant population

Example

Job Category: Management Trainee			
Current Trainees (%)		Availability (%)	
Nonminority	**Minority**	**Nonminority**	**Minority**
90%	10%	70%	30%

C. CONCENTRATION STATISTICS

Definition:

Concentration of women or minorities in certain job categories

Example				
	Job Category			
	Clerical	**Production**	**Sales**	**Managers**
% Men	3%	85%	45%	95%
% Women	97%	15%	55%	5%

lation. Relevant is defined in terms of such things as "qualified," "interested," or "geographic." In the example shown, there is a disparity in the percentage of minorities employed (10%) compared with their availability (30%), which suggests their underutilization.

The third type of evidence involves use of concentration statistics. Here, the percentages of women or minorities in various job categories are compared to see if women are concentrated in certain workforce categories. In the example shown, there is a concentration of women in clerical jobs (97%), a concentration of men in production (85%) and managerial (95%) jobs, and roughly equal concentrations of men and women in sales jobs (45% and 55%, respectively).

EEO/AA LAWS: GENERAL PROVISIONS AND ENFORCEMENT

In this section, the major federal EEO/AA laws are summarized in terms of their general provisions. Mechanisms for enforcement of the laws are also discussed.[16]

General Provisions

The federal EEO/AA laws that are major follow:

1. Civil Rights Acts (1964, 1991)
2. Age Discrimination in Employment Act (1967)
3. Americans With Disabilities Act (1990)
4. Rehabilitation Act (1973)
5. Executive Order 11246 (1965)

Exhibit 3.4 contains a summary of the basic provisions of these laws, pertaining to coverage, prohibited discrimination, enforcement agency, and important rules, regulations, and guidelines.

Inspection of Exhibit 3.4 suggests that these laws are appropriately labeled major for several reasons. First, the laws are very broad in their coverage of employers. Second, they specifically prohibit discrimination on the basis of several individual characteristics (race, color, religion, sex, national origin, age, disability, handicap). Third, separate agencies have been created for their administration and enforcement. Finally, these agencies have issued numerous rules, regulations, and guidelines to assist in interpreting, implementing, and enforcing the law.

Enforcement: EEOC

As shown in Exhibit 3.4, the EEOC has responsibility for enforcing the Civil Rights Act, Age Discrimination in Employment Act, and Americans With Dis-

EXHIBIT 3.4 Major Federal EEO/AA Laws: General Provisions

Law or Executive Order	Coverage	Prohibited Discrimination	Enforcement Agency	Important Rules, Regulations, and Guidelines
Civil Rights Act (1964, 1991)	Private employers with 15 or more employees Federal, state, and local governments Educational institutions Employment agencies Labor unions	Race, color, religion, national origin, sex	EEOC	Uniform Guidelines on Employee Selection Procedures Sex Discrimination Guidelines Religious Discrimination Guidelines National Origin Discrimination Guidelines
Age Discrimination in Employment Act (1967)	Private employers with 20 or more employees Federal, state, and local governments Employment agencies Labor unions	Age (40 or over)	EEOC	Interpretations of the Age Discrimination in Employment Act
Americans with Disabilities Act (1990)	Private employers with 15 or more employees State and local governments	Qualified individual with a disability	EEOC	ADA—Employment Regulations Definition of the term Disability Pre-Employment Disability-Related Questions and Medical Examinations
Rehabilitation Act (1973)	Federal contractors with contracts in excess of $2,500	Individual with a handicap	DOL (OFCCP)	Affirmative Action Regulations on Handicapped Workers
Executive Order 11246 (1965)	Federal contractors with contracts in excess of $10,000	Race, color, religion, national origin, sex	DOL (OFCCP)	Sex Discrimination Guidelines Affirmative Action Guidelines—Revised Order No. 4

NOTE: Full text of the laws and Executive Order, as well as the important rules, regulations, and guidelines, may be found in the Bureau of National Affairs publication, *Fair Employment Practices*, Volume 1 (Washington, D.C.: author, periodically updated).

abilities Act. While each law requires separate enforcement mechanisms, some generalizations about their collective enforcement are possible.[17]

Initial Charge and Conciliation

Enforcement proceedings begin when a charge is filed by an employee or job applicant (the EEOC itself may also file a charge). In states where there is an EEOC-approved fair enforcement practice (FEP) law, the charge is initially deferred to the state. An investigation of the charge occurs to determine if there is "reasonable cause" to assume discrimination has occurred. If such reasonable cause is not found, the charge is dropped. If reasonable cause is found, however, the EEOC attempts conciliation of the charge. Conciliation is a voluntary settlement process that seeks agreement by the employer to stop the practice(s) in question and abide by proposed remedies. This is the EEOC's preferred method of settlement.

Complementing conciliation is the use of alternative dispute resolution (ADR). With ADR, a neutral third-party mediator is used to mediate the dispute between the employer and the EEOC, and to obtain an agreement between them that resolves the dispute. Participation in ADR is voluntary, and either party may opt out of it for any reason. ADR proceedings are confidential. Any agreement reached between the parties is legally enforceable.[18]

Litigation

Should conciliation fail, suit is filed in federal court. The ensuing litigation process is shown in Exhibit 3.5. As can be seen, the charge of the plaintiff (charging party) will follow either a disparate treatment or disparate impact route. In either event, the plaintiff has the initial burden of proof. Such a burden requires the plaintiff to establish a prima facie case that demonstrates reasonable cause to assume discrimination has occurred. Assuming this case is successfully presented, the defendant must rebut the charge and accompanying evidence.

In disparate treatment cases, the defendant must provide nondiscriminatory reasons during rebuttal for the practice(s) in question. In disparate impact cases, the employer must demonstrate that the practices in question are job-related and consistent with business necessity.

Following rebuttal, the plaintiff may respond to the defense provided by the defendant. In disparate treatment cases, that response hinges on a demonstration that the defendant's reasons for a practice are a pretext, or smokescreen, for the practice. In disparate impact cases, the plaintiff's response will focus on showing that the defendant has not shown its practices to be job-related and/or that the employer refuses to adopt a practice that causes less adverse impact.

Who bears the final, or ultimate, burden of proof? In disparate treatment cases it is the plaintiff who must ultimately prove that the defendant's practices are discriminatory. For disparate impact cases, on the other hand, the burden is on the

EXHIBIT 3.5   Basic Litigation Process: EEOC

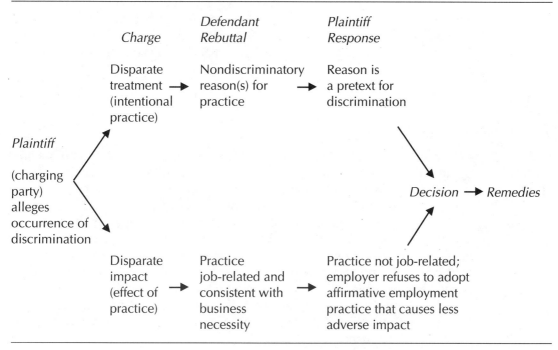

defendant. That is, it is the defendant who must prove that its practices are not discriminatory.

The plaintiff and defendant have an opportunity to end their dispute through a consent decree. This is a voluntary, court-approved agreement between the two parties. The consent decree may contain not only an agreement to halt certain practices, but also an agreement to implement certain remedies, such as various forms of monetary relief and AA programs. A rather dramatic example of a consent decree—atypical in terms of size—involves an agreement between black applicants and employees, and Shoney's (a restaurant chain) for $105 million in monetary relief (back pay) plus implementation of an affirmative action plan.[19]

In the absence of a consent decree, the court will fashion its own remedies from those permitted under the law. There are several remedies available. First, the court may enjoin certain practices, which means requiring the defendant to halt the practices. Second, the court may order the hiring or reinstatement of individuals. Third, the court may fashion various forms of monetary relief, such as back pay, front pay, attorney's fees, and compensatory and punitive damages. These compensatory and punitive damages may be applied only in cases involving disparate treatment, and there is a cap of $300,000 on them. Finally, under the Civil Rights

Act and Americans With Disabilities Act, the court may order "such affirmative action as may be appropriate," as well as "any other equitable relief" that the court deems appropriate. Through these provisions, the court has considerable latitude in the remedies it imposes. Note that this court's prerogative includes imposition of affirmative action plans, as well as hiring and promotion quota systems.

Enforcement: OFCCP

Enforcement mechanisms used by the OFCCP are very different from those used by the EEOC.[20] Most covered employers are required to develop and implement written AA plans for women and minorities. Specific AA plan requirements for employers under EO 11246 are spelled out in Revised Order No. 4.

To enforce these requirements, the OFCCP conducts employer site visits and compliance reviews of employers' AA plans. It also investigates complaints charging noncompliance. Employers found to be in noncompliance are urged to change their practices through a conciliation process. Summaries of conciliation agreements for three organizations are shown in Exhibit 3.6. Should conciliation not be successful, employers are subject to various penalties that affect their status as a federal contractor. These include cancellation of contracts and debarment from bidding on future contracts.

EEO/AA LAWS: SPECIFIC STAFFING PROVISIONS

Each of the major laws covered in the previous section contains specific provisions pertaining to staffing practices by organizations. This section summarizes those specific provisions.[21] Phrases in quotation marks are direct quotations from the laws themselves. Applications of these provisions to staffing policies, practices, and actions occur throughout the remainder of the book.

Civil Rights Acts (1964, 1991)

The provisions of the Civil Rights Acts of 1964 and 1991 are combined for discussion purposes here. The 1991 law is basically a series of amendments to the 1964 law, though it does contain some provisions unique to it.

Unlawful Employment Practices
This section of the law contains a comprehensive statement regarding unlawful employment practices. Specifically, it is unlawful for an employer

EXHIBIT 3.6   Summaries of Three Conciliation Agreements

Three employers—Goodyear Tire and Rubber Company in Houston, the University of California at San Diego, and American of Martinsville in Va.—will pay more than $1.25 million in back pay and salary adjustments to resolve alleged federal equal employment opportunity law violations, Secretary of Labor Robert B. Reich announced today.

"These settlements clearly demonstrate our strong commitment to ensure that our nation's workers are protected and have access to equal employment opportunity in the workplace," Reich said. "Employers must understand that we take our mandate to enforce the law in a fair and responsible manner very seriously and will take necessary action to ensure compliance."

The conciliation agreements resolve alleged discrimination based on race and gender and other faulty personnel practices identified in compliance reviews conducted by the department's Office of Federal Contract Compliance Programs (OFCCP). OFCCP monitors federal contractors and subcontractors to ensure they are in compliance with federal antidiscrimination laws.

Details of the conciliation agreements follow:

—The University of California at San Diego has agreed to pay $608,403 in back pay to 28 individuals. The university will pay $600,000 to 27 women and minorities who were denied jobs or promotions although they were fully qualified. An additional $8,403 will be paid a current employee who was given a retroactive promotion to July 1992.

—American of Martinsville, Martinsville, Va., a furniture manufacturer, has agreed to pay $417,000 to resolve alleged discriminatory employment practices. About $217,123 in back pay is to be paid to nearly 200 minorities and women. Back pay, based on length of service from one to 48 years, ranges from $100 to $2,700 per individual. The company also has agreed to pay about $200,000 in front pay. Front pay is the difference between the new and old pay systems, which will be paid retroactively from the period July 1 to January 1995 when the new system is fully operational. In addition, the company will spend approximately $200,000 to design and implement a completely revised blue-collar pay system to be in place no later than Jan. 1, 1995.

—Goodyear Tire and Rubber Company in Houston has agreed to pay $229,361 in back wages to 42 employees and applicants who were alleged victims of racial discrimination. The settlement resolves discriminatory hiring and personnel practices identified in a combined compliance review and a class action complaint investigation. OFCCP identified 33 victims of discrimination due to Goodyear's promotion policies and practices; seven minorities were paid unequal wages compared to non-minority workers, and two applicants were denied employment because of their ethnic identification.

Source: U.S. Department of Labor, OFCCP, *News,* (Washington, D.C. author, 10/28/95).

1. "to fail or refuse to hire or to discharge any individual, or otherwise discriminate against any individual with respect to his compensation, terms, conditions, or privileges of employment, because of such individual's race, color, religion, sex, or national origin"; or

2. "to limit, segregate, or classify his employees or applicants for employment in any way which would deprive or tend to deprive any individual of employment opportunities or otherwise adversely affect his status as an employee because of such individual's race, color, religion, sex, or national origin."

These two statements are the foundation of civil rights law. They are very broad and inclusive, applying to virtually all staffing practices by an organization. There are also separate such statements for employment agencies and for labor unions.

Establishment of Disparate Impact

As discussed previously, a claim of discrimination may be pursued via a disparate impact or disparate treatment approach. The law makes several points regarding the former approach.

First, staffing practices that do not cause adverse impact are not illegal (assuming, of course, that no intention to discriminate underlies them). Thus, while certain practices may somehow seem unfair, outrageous, or of dubious value to the employer, they are a matter of legal concern only if their usage causes disparate impact.

Second, staffing practices that the plaintiff initially alleges to have caused adverse impact are unlawful unless the employer can successfully rebut the charges. To do this, the employer must show that the practices are "job-related for the position in question and consistent with business necessity." Practices that fail to meet this standard are unlawful.

Third, the plaintiff must show adverse impact for each specific staffing practice or component. For example, if an employer has a simple selection system in which applicants first take a written test, and those who pass it are interviewed, the plaintiff must show adverse impact separately for the test and the interview, rather than for the two components combined.

Disparate Treatment

Intentional discrimination with staffing practices is prohibited, and the employer may not use a claim of business necessity to justify intentional use of a discriminatory practice.

Mixed Motives

An employer may not defend an action by claiming that while a prohibited factor, such as sex, entered into a staffing decision, other factors, such as job qualifications, did also. Such "mixed motive" defenses are not permitted.

Bona Fide Occupational Qualification (BFOQ)

An employer may attempt to justify use of a protected characteristic, such as national origin, as being a bona fide occupational qualification, or BFOQ. The law permits such claims, but only for sex, religion, and national origin—not race or color. The employer must be able to demonstrate that such discrimination is "a bona fide occupational qualification reasonably necessary to the normal operation of that particular business or enterprise." Thus, a maximum security prison with mostly male inmates might hire only male prison guards on the grounds that by doing so it ensures the safety, security, and privacy of inmates. However, it must be able to show that doing so is a business necessity.

Testing

The law explicitly permits the use of tests in staffing. The employer may "give and act upon the results of any professionally developed ability test, provided that such test, its administration, or action upon the basis of results is not designed, intended, or used to discriminate because of race, color, religion, sex, or national origin."

Interpretation of this provision has been difficult. What exactly is a "professionally developed ability test"? How does an employer use a test to discriminate? Not discriminate? The need for answers to such questions gave rise to the Uniform Guidelines on Employee Selection Procedures (UGESP), contained in Appendix A.

Test Score Adjustments

Test scores are not to be altered or changed in order to somehow make them more fair; test scores should speak for themselves. Specifically, it is an unlawful employment practice "to adjust the scores of, use different cutoff scores for, or otherwise alter the results of employment related tests on the basis of race, color, religion, sex, or national origin." This provision bans so-called race norming in which people's scores are compared only to members of their own racial group and separate cutoff or passing scores are set for each group.

Seniority or Merit Systems

The law explicitly permits the use of seniority and merit systems as a basis for applying different terms and conditions to employees. However, the seniority or merit system must be a "bona fide" one, and it may not be the result of an intention to discriminate.

This provision has particular relevance to internal staffing systems. It in essence allows the employer to take into account seniority (experience) and merit (e.g., KSAOs, promotion potential assessments) when making internal staffing decisions.

Employment Advertising

Discrimination in employment advertising is prohibited. Specifically, the employer may not indicate "any preference, limitation, specification, or discrimination based on race, color, religion, sex, or national origin." An exception to this is if sex, religion, or national origin is a BFOQ.

Preferential Treatment and Quotas

The law does not require preferential treatment or quotas. Thus, the employer is not required to have a balanced workforce, meaning one whose demographic composition matches or mirrors the demographic makeup of the surrounding population from which it draws its employees.

Note that the law does not prohibit preferential treatment, AA, and quotas. It merely says they are not required. Thus, they may be used in certain instances, such as a voluntary AA plan or a court-imposed remedy.

Age Discrimination in Employment Act (1967)

Prohibited Age Discrimination

The law explicitly and inclusively prohibits discrimination against those 40 and older. It is unlawful for an employer

> 1. "to fail or refuse to hire or to discharge any individual or otherwise discriminate against any individual with respect to his compensation, terms, conditions or privileges of employment, because of such individual's age"; and
> 2. "to limit, segregate, or classify his employees in any way which would deprive or tend to deprive any individual of employment opportunities or otherwise adversely affect his status as an employee, because of such individual's age."

Bona Fide Occupational Qualification (BFOQ)

Like the Civil Rights Act, the law contains a BFOQ provision. Thus, it is not unlawful for an employer to differentiate among applicants or employees on the basis of their age "where age is a bona fide occupational qualification reasonably necessary to the normal operation of the particular business."

Factors Other Than Age

The employer may use "reasonable factors other than age" in making employment decisions. Such factors must be applied equally to all applicants, cannot include age in any way, must be job-related, and cannot result in discrimination on the basis of age.

Seniority Systems

The law permits the use of seniority systems (merit systems are not mentioned). Thus, the employer is permitted "to observe the terms of a bona fide seniority system that is not intended to evade the purposes" of the act.

Employment Advertising

Age discrimination in employment advertising is prohibited. Ads may not indicate "any preference, limitation, specification, or discrimination based on age."

Americans With Disabilities Act (1990)

The ADA is a new and sweeping piece of legislation whose application to employment did not occur until mid-1992. Its basic purpose is to prohibit discrimination against qualified individuals with disabilities, and to require the employer to make reasonable accommodation for such individuals unless that would cause undue hardship for the employer.

Prohibited Discrimination

The law contains a broad prohibition against disability discrimination. It specifically says that an employer may not "discriminate against an individual with a disability because of the disability of such individual in regard to job application procedures, the hiring, advancement or discharge of employees, employee compensation, job training, and other terms, conditions, and privileges of employment."

The law does not apply to all disabled people, only those who are "otherwise qualified." It therefore does not require the hiring, promotion, or retention of unqualified people. There is thus an important emphasis on the determination of qualifications for decision-making purposes. This emphasis is very consistent with the person/job matching model.

Definition of Disability

Disability refers to both physical and mental impairments that substantially limit a major life activity of the person (e.g., breathing, walking, working). It also refers to persons who have a record of such impairment in the past or are regarded by others as having such an impairment.

Disability refers not only to obvious impairments, such as blindness, but to many others as well—for example, cancer, AIDS, and many mental illnesses. Current users of illegal drugs are excluded from coverage. Recovering former drug users, though, are covered, as are both practicing and recovering alcoholics.

The EEOC has provided written clarification of the meaning of the term "disability." First, the EEOC defines an impairment as "a physiological disorder affecting one or more of a number of body systems or a mental or psychological disorder." Excluded from this definition are (a) environmental, cultural, and economic disadvantages, (b) homosexuality and bisexuality, (c) pregnancy, (d) physical characteristics, (e) common personality traits, and (f) normal deviations in height, weight, or strength. Second, the EEOC expanded major life activities to include "sitting, standing, lifting, and mental and emotional processes such as thinking, concentrating, and interacting with others." Third, whether an impairment is substantially limiting depends on its nature and severity, duration or expected duration, and its permanency or long-term impact. For example, a broken arm or leg would generally not be considered a disability. Fourth, to be substantially limiting the impairment must prevent or significantly restrict the individual from performing a class of jobs or a broad range of jobs in various classes. For example, an impairment that prevented the individual from performing only a single job likely would not be considered a disability.[22]

Qualified Individual with a Disability

A qualified individual with a disability is "an individual with a disability who, with or without reasonable accommodation, can perform the essential functions of the employment position that such individual holds or desires."

Essential Job Functions

The law provides little guidance as to what are essential job functions. It would seem that they are the major, nontrivial tasks required of an employee. The employer has great discretion in such a determination. Specifically, "consideration shall be given to the employer's judgment as to what functions of a job are essential, and if an employer has prepared a written description before advertising or interviewing applicants for the job, this description shall be considered evidence of the essential functions of the job." Subsequent regulations (Appendix C) amplify on what are essential job functions; these are explored in Chapter 5.

Reasonable Accommodation and Undue Hardship

Unless it would pose an "undue hardship" on the employer, the employer must make "reasonable accommodation" to the "known physical or mental impairments of an otherwise qualified, disabled job applicant or employee." The law provides actual examples of such accommodation. They include changes in facilities (e.g., installing wheelchair ramps); job restructuring; changes in work schedules; employee reassignment to a vacant position; purchase of adaptive devices; provision of qualified readers and interpreters; and adjustments in testing and training material. In general, only accommodations that would require significant difficulty or expense are considered to create an undue hardship.

Selection of Employees

The law deals directly with discrimination in the selection of employees. Prohibited discrimination includes

1. "using qualification standards, employment tests or other selection criteria that screen out or tend to screen out an individual with a disability or a class of individuals with disabilities unless the standard, test, or other selection criteria, as used by the covered entity, is shown to be job related for the position in question and is consistent with business necessity"; and

2. "failing to select and administer tests concerning employment in the most effective manner to ensure that, when such a test is administered to a job applicant or employee who has a disability that impairs sensory, manual, or speaking skills, such results accurately reflect the skills, aptitude or whatever other factor of such applicant or employee that such test purports to measure, rather than reflecting the impaired sensory, manual, or speaking skills of such employee or applicant (except where such skills are the factors that the test purports to measure)."

These provisions seem to make two basic requirements of staffing systems. First, if selection procedures cause disparate impact against people with disabilities, the employer must show that the procedures are job-related and consistent with business necessity. The requirement is similar to that for selection procedures under the Civil Rights Act. Second, the employer must ensure that employment tests are accurate indicators of the KSAOs they attempt to measure.

Medical Exams for Job Applicants

Prior to making a job offer, the employer may not conduct medical exams of job applicants, or inquire whether or how severely a person is disabled. Specific inquiries about a person's ability to perform essential job functions, however, are permitted.

After a job offer has been made, the employer may require the applicant to take a medical exam. The job offer may be contingent upon the applicant successfully passing the exam. Care should be taken to ensure that all applicants are required to take and pass the same exam. Medical records should be confidential and maintained in a separate file.

Affirmative Action

There are no affirmative action requirements for employers.

Rehabilitation Act (1973)

This law has many similarities to the ADA. Indeed, the ADA draws heavily on it and complements it in providing similar coverage to employers who are not federal contractors. Hence, its provisions are mentioned only briefly.

Prohibited Discrimination

According to the law, "no otherwise qualified individual with handicaps . . . shall, solely by reason of his handicaps, be excluded from participation in, or denied the benefits of, or be subjected to discrimination under any program or activity receiving federal assistance. . . ." The term "handicaps" is used in a similar fashion and with similar meaning to the term "disability" under the ADA. There are other similarities between the two laws as well. Both, for example, use the terms "otherwise qualified," "essential job functions," and "reasonable accommodation."

Affirmative Action

The law explicitly requires employers to undertake affirmative action. It says that the federal contractor "shall take affirmative action to employ and advance in employment qualified individuals with handicaps."

Executive Order 11246 (1965)

Prohibited Discrimination

The federal contractor is prohibited from discrimination on the basis of race, color, religion, sex, and national origin. (A similar prohibition against age discrimination by federal contractors is contained in Executive Order 11141).

Affirmative Action

The order plainly requires affirmative action. It says specifically that "the contractor will take affirmative action to ensure that applicants are employed, and that employees are treated during employment, without regard to their race, color, religion, sex, or national origin. Such actions shall include, but not be limited to the following: employment, upgrading, demotion, or transfer; recruitment or recruitment advertising; layoff or termination; rates of pay or other forms of compensation; and selection for training, including apprenticeship." (Executive Order 11141 does not require affirmative action.) Regulations for these affirmative action requirements, known as Revised Order No. 4, are contained in Appendix B.

EEO/AA: REGULATIONS AND INFORMATION

As noted previously, and in Exhibit 3.4, numerous regulations and guidelines have been issued to further implement the enforcement of the EEO/AA law. Three major sets of these, with particular relevance to staffing, are briefly mentioned in the following sections. Also briefly mentioned are various information sources that are useful to consult regarding EEO/AA regulations and guidelines.

Regulations and Guidelines

Staffing policies and practices are most directly affected by the Uniform Guidelines on Employee Selection Procedures (UGESP), Revised Order No. 4, and

Employment Regulations for the Americans With Disabilities Act. The general content of each of these is indicated next. The full text of each is contained in Appendixes A (UGESP), B (Revised Order No. 4), and C (Employment Regulations for the ADA).

UGESP

The UGESP deals with adverse impact issues, requiring the organization to keep detailed records about the demographics of its applicants and new hires, and to use these data to generate applicant flow statistics (selection rates). If significant differences in selection rates between protected groups are found—that is, there is adverse impact—the UGESP requires the organization to take steps to eliminate it, or to justify it through the conduct of validation studies. Detailed technical standards for these studies are provided. The UGESP also indicates the relationship between its requirements and AA obligations of the organization.

Revised Order No. 4

This order applies to most federal contractors. It requires them to conduct utilization analysis. The analysis is to use stock statistics to identify if, and in what jobs, women and minorities are underutilized relative to their availability in the population. Eight availability factors or criteria are provided for use in the utilization analysis. The contractor is also required to develop and implement AA plans and programs (AAPs) that address identified underutilization. The AAP must include hiring and promotion goals and timetables for their achievement. A thorough review must be conducted of all HR activities to ensure that they will not hinder, but in fact further, the attainment of AA goals. The contractor is required to put forth a good faith effort to achieve AA goals and timetables, and compliance with the order will be judged—at least partially—on the extent to which such efforts are shown.

Employment Regulations for ADA

These regulations seek to clarify the meanings of terms used in the ADA, such as "disability," "qualified individual with a disability," and "reasonable accommodation." There are several sections explicitly dealing with selection of new employees. These pertain to the use and administration of tests and other selection procedures, as well as hiring standards. Medical examinations also receive detailed treatment. Employer defenses to discrimination charges, both disparate treatment and disparate impact, are specified. Finally, the regulations contain a lengthy appendix providing additional interpretive guidance.

Information Sources

The sheer volume and complexity of EEO/AA laws and regulations is staggering. Several key information sources are available that collect, categorize, and summarize the information in very understandable, user-friendly ways. Each of these sources is described next, and the reader is well-advised to become familiar with these sources and consult them for assistance.

Information Services

The Bureau of National Affairs publishes *Fair Employment Practices,* a three-volume loose-leaf reference manual that is continually updated.[23] The first volume is the most useful overall and contains the following:

1. text of federal laws and executive orders
2. text of federal rules, regulations, and guidelines
3. text of federal policy statements
4. federal law—who is covered
5. federal law—what discrimination is forbidden
6. federal law—administration and enforcement
7. federal law—reports, records

The other two volumes contain a section on affirmative action, plus the full text of states' fair employment practice (FEP) laws.

The Bureau of National Affairs also publishes *FEP Cases.* It provides the text of federal and state court rulings, as well as summaries of decisions. In a similar vein, the Commerce Clearing House publishes *Employment Practice Decisions.*[24]

Compliance Manuals

Various compliance manuals are published that provide very practical, hands-on suggestions and guidance for employers' compliance attempts. The Bureau of National Affairs publishes the *EEOC Compliance Manual,* covering the Civil Rights Acts, the Age Discrimination in Employment Act, and the Americans With Disabilities Act, and the *Affirmative Action Compliance Manual for Federal Contractors,* covering Executive Order 11246 and the Rehabilitation Act. The Equal Employment Opportunity Commission publishes the *Technical Assistance Manual,* covering the Americans With Disabilities Act.[25]

Reference Books

There are certain books that review and summarize permissible and impermissible practices, as well as court cases pertaining to them. Examples include *Federal Law of Employment Discrimination, Employment Discrimination Law, Employment Law Manual,* and *Fair Employment Practices.*[26] These books contain a wealth of summarized and condensed material.

Professional Associations

Most professional associations provide informational services to their members. For example, the Society for Human Resource Management publishes *HR Mag-*

azine, a monthly journal frequently containing staffing and EEO/AA articles. The society also puts out a monthly newsletter, which often contains EEO/AA material. The Employment Management Association publishes its own journal, the *EMA Journal,* and it, too, provides a newsletter to members pertaining to staffing issues. Likewise, the International Personnel Management Association publishes *Public Personnel Management* and a monthly newsletter.

OTHER STAFFING LAWS

In addition to the EEO/AA laws, there are a variety of other laws and regulations affecting staffing. At the federal level are the Immigration Reform and Control Act, and the Employee Polygraph Protection Act. At the state and local level are a wide array of laws pertaining to EEO, as well as a host of other areas. Finally, there are civil service laws and regulations that pertain to staffing practices for federal, state, and local government employers.

Federal Laws

Immigration Reform and Control Act (1986)
The purpose of this law is to prohibit the employment of unauthorized aliens, and to provide civil and criminal penalties for violations of this law. The law was amended by the Immigration Act of 1990, and those amendments are incorporated into the discussion that follows.

Prohibited Discrimination   The law prohibits the initial or continuing employment of unauthorized aliens. Specifically,

> 1. "it is unlawful for a person or other entity to have, or to recruit or refer for a fee, for employment in the United States an alien knowing the alien is an unauthorized alien with respect to such employment"; and
> 2. "it is unlawful for a person or other entity, after hiring an alien for employment . . . to continue to employ the alien in the United States knowing the alien is (or has become) an unauthorized alien with respect to such employment." (This does not apply to the continuing employment of aliens hired before November 6, 1986.)

The law also prohibits employment discrimination on the basis of national origin or citizenship status. The purpose of this provision is to discourage employers from attempting to comply with the prohibition against hiring unauthorized aliens by simply refusing to hire applicants who are foreign-looking in appearance or have foreign-sounding accents.

Employment Verification System The employer must verify that the individual is not an unauthorized alien and is legally eligible for employment. This is accomplished by the examination of one or more documents that serve to establish employment verification (e.g., U.S. passport, certificate of U.S. citizenship, certificate of naturalization, unexpired foreign passport, or resident alien card).

The individual seeking employment must attest to being an authorized alien. There is a particular form (commonly referred to as the I-9 form) that the individual and employer must then sign, indicating employment verification. This form must be retained by the employer and made available for enforcement inspection.

Temporary Foreign Workers Employers may apply for temporary (3-year) H-1B visas for skilled foreign workers in certain specialty occupations (e.g., computer programmers, engineers, physical therapists) to enter and work in the U.S. The employer must attest that the visa will not displace any U.S. workers, and must pay the alien worker at least the prevailing wage rate for the occupation in the geographic area.[27]

Enforcement The law is enforced by the Department of Justice. Noncompliance may result in fines of up to $10,000 for each unauthorized alien employed, as well as imprisonment for up to six months for a pattern or practice of violations. Federal contractors may be barred from federal contracts for one year.

Employee Polygraph Protection Act (1988)

The purpose of this law is to prevent most private employers from using the polygraph or lie detector on job applicants or employees. The law does not apply to other types of "honesty tests," such as paper-and-pencil ones.

Prohibited Practices The law prohibits most private employers (public employers are exempted) from (a) requiring applicants or employees to take a polygraph test, (b) using the results of a polygraph test for employment decisions, and (c) discharging or disciplining individuals for refusal to take a polygraph test.

There are three explicit instances in which the polygraph may be used. First, it may be used by employers who manufacture, distribute, or dispense controlled substances, such as drugs. Second, the polygraph may be used by private security firms that provide services to businesses affecting public safety or security, such as nuclear power plants or armored vehicles. Third, the polygraph may be used in an investigation of theft, embezzlement, or sabotage that caused economic loss to the employer.

Enforcement The law is enforced by the Department of Labor. Penalties for noncompliance are fines of up to $10,000 per individual violation. Also, individuals may sue the employer, seeking employment, reinstatement, promotion, and back pay.

State and Local Laws

The emphasis in this book is on federal laws and regulations. It should be remembered, however, that an organization is subject to law at the state and local level as well.[28] This greatly increases the array of applicable laws to which the organization must attend.

EEO/AA Laws

These laws are often patterned after federal law. Their basic provisions, however, vary substantially from state to state. Compliance with federal EEO/AA law does not ensure compliance with state and local EEO/AA law, and vice versa. Thus, it is the responsibility of the organization to be explicitly knowledgeable of the laws and regulations that apply to it. The text of relevant state (but not local) law is located in *Fair Employment Practices* (volumes 2 and 3).

Of special note is the fact that state and local EEO/AA laws and regulations often provide protections beyond those contained in the federal laws and regulations. State laws, for example, may apply to employers with fewer than 15 employees, which is the cutoff for coverage under the Civil Rights Act. State laws may also prohibit certain kinds of discrimination not prohibited under federal law, for example, sexual preference. The law for the District of Columbia prohibits 13 kinds of discrimination, including sexual orientation, physical appearance, matriculation, and political affiliation. Finally, state law may deviate from federal law with regard to enforcement mechanisms and penalties for noncompliance.

Other State Laws

Earlier reference was made to employment-at-will and workplace torts as matters of common law, which, in turn, are governed at the level of state law. The common law pertaining to staffing and employment has been characterized as fractured, and the following explanation has been provided for this characterization:

> Each state has adopted and adapted the common law to its own needs. The success of common law in the United States is attributable, in significant part, to its ability to draw upon the ingenuity of individuals and courts and on the experience of individual states in advancing the law of any particular jurisdiction. Each jurisdiction acts, in effect, as a laboratory in which new legal rights are tested. While generally not bound by the decisions of courts in other states, courts may review those decisions and are free to adopt the reasoning of those decisions that they find persuasive.[29]

Statutory state laws applicable to staffing, in addition to EEO/AA laws, are also plentiful. Examples of areas covered in addition to EEO/AA include criminal record inquiries by the employer, polygraph and "honesty testing," drug testing, AIDS testing, and employee access to personnel records.

Civil Service Laws and Regulations

Federal, state, and local government employers are governed by special statutory laws and regulations collectively referred to as civil service. Civil service is guided by so-called merit principles that serve as the guide to staffing practices. Following these merit principles results in notable differences between public and private employers in their staffing practices.

Merit Principles and Staffing Practices

The essence of merit principles relevant to staffing is fourfold:

1. to recruit, select, and promote employees on the basis of their KSAOs
2. to provide for fair treatment of applicants and employees without regard to political affiliation, race, color, national origin, sex, religion, age, or handicap
3. to protect the privacy and constitutional rights of applicants and employees as citizens
4. to protect employees against coercion for partisan political purposes[30]

Merit principles are codified in civil service laws and regulations. In the state of Wisconsin, for example, Chapter 230 of the Wisconsin Statutes governs state employment relations. The merit policy of the state at the beginning of that Chapter, as well as its topical contents, is shown in Exhibit 3.7. The Chapter 230 statutes, in turn, are implemented and interpreted through the Wisconsin Administrative Code.

Comparisons with Private Sector

The merit principles and civil service laws and regulations combine to shape the nature of staffing practices in the public sector. This leads to some notable differences between the public and private sectors. Examples of public sector staffing practices are:

1. open announcement of all vacancies, along with the content of the selection process that will be followed
2. very large numbers of applicants due to applications being open to all persons
3. legal mandate to test applicants only for KSAOs that are directly job-related
4. limits on discretion in the final hiring process, such as number of finalists, ordering of finalists, and affirmative action considerations
5. rights of applicants to appeal the hiring decision, testing process, or actual test content and method[31]

These examples are unlikely to be encountered in the private sector. Moreover, they are only illustrative of the many differences in staffing practices and context between the private and public sectors. A more thorough summary of the differences between the two sectors is shown in Exhibit 3.8.

LEGAL ISSUES IN REMAINDER OF BOOK

The laws and regulations applicable to staffing practices by organizations are multiple in number and complexity. The emphasis in this chapter has been on an understanding of the need for law, the sources of law, general provisions of the law, and a detailed presentation of specific provisions that pertain to staffing activities. Little has been said about practical implications and applications.

In the remaining chapters of the book, the focus shifts to the practical, with guidance and suggestions on how to align staffing practices with legal requirements. The last section of each remaining chapter is devoted to "Legal Issues" and discusses major issues from a compliance perspective. The issues so addressed, and the chapter in which they occur, are shown in Exhibit 3.9. Inspection of the exhibit should reinforce the importance accorded laws and regulations as an external influence on staffing activities.

It should be emphasized that there is a selective presentation of the issues in Exhibit 3.9. Only certain issues have been chosen for inclusion, and only a summary of their compliance implications is presented. It should also be emphasized that the discussion of these issues does not constitute professional legal advice.

EXHIBIT 3.7   Example of Civil Service Statutes—State of Wisconsin

---

Statement of Merit Policy

(1) It is the purpose of this chapter to provide state agencies and institutions of higher education with competent personnel who will furnish state services to citizens as fairly, efficiently, and effectively as possible.

(2) It is the policy of the state and the responsibility of the secretary and the administrator to maintain a system of personnel management which fills positions in the classified service through methods which apply the merit principle, with adequate civil service safeguards. It is the policy of this state to provide for equal employment opportunity by ensuring that all personnel actions including hire, tenure or term, and condition or privilege of employment be based on the ability to perform the duties and responsibilities assigned to the particular position without regard to age, race, creed or religion, color, handicap, sex, national origin, ancestry, sexual orientation or political affiliation. It is the policy of this state to take affirmative action which is not in conflict with other provisions of this chapter. It is the policy of the state to ensure its employees opportunities for satisfying careers and fair treatment based on the value of each employee's services. It is the policy of this state to encourage disclosure of information under subchapter III and to ensure that any employee employed by a governmental unit is protected from retaliatory action for disclosing information under subchapter III. It is the policy of this state to correct pay inequities based on gender or race in the state civil service system.

(continued)

EXHIBIT 3.7 Continued

Contents of Chapter 230

State Employment Relations

SUBCHAPTER I
ADMINISTRATIVE SERVICES

230.01	Statement of policy
230.02	Liberal construction of statutes
230.03	Definitions
230.04	Powers and duties of the secretary
230.046	Training programs
230.047	Temporary interchange of employees
230.048	Daycare for children of state employees

SUBCHAPTER II
CIVIL SERVICE

230.05	Powers and duties of the administrator
230.06	Powers and duties of appointing authorities
230.08	Classification of civil service
230.09	Classification
230.10	Compensation plan coverage
230.12	Compensation
230.13	Closed records
230.14	Recruitment
230.147	Employment of aid recipients
230.148	Unclassified service reappointments
230.15	Appointments, promotions, changes in classified service
230.16	Applications and examinations
230.17	Applicants and eligibles may be barred; bonds may be required
230.18	Discrimination prohibited
230.19	Promotion
230.20	Recommendations
230.21	Unskilled labor and critical recruitment selection
230.215	Part-time employment and flexible-time schedules
230.22	Entry profession selection
230.24	Career executive selection
230.25	Certification, appointments and registers
230.26	Limited term appointments
230.27	Project positions
230.28	Probationary period
230.29	Transfers
230.30	Employing units; establishment and revision
230.31	Restoration of employment and reinstatement privileges
230.32	Restoration after military leave
230.33	Leave of absence and pay while serving in unclassified position
230.335	Rights of unclassified division administrators
230.337	Rights of employees: corrections or parole
230.34	Demotion, suspension, discharge and layoff
230.35	State office hours; standard workweek; leaves of absence; holidays
230.36	Hazardous employment, injuries, pay continued
230.37	Standards of performance and ratings
230.40	Political activities; public office
230.41	Invalid appointments
230.43	Misdemeanors; how punished
230.44	Appeal procedures
230.45	Powers and duties of personnel commission
230.46	Duties of council on affirmative action
230.48	State employees' suggestion board

SUBCHAPTER III
EMPLOYEE PROTECTION

230.80	Definitions
230.81	Employee disclosure
230.82	Processing of information
230.83	Retaliatory action prohibited
230.85	Enforcement
230.86	Discipline based on surveillance
230.87	Judicial review
230.88	Payment of award, judgment or settlement; effect of order, arbitration award or commencement of court action
230.89	Rule making and reporting

Source: Wisconsin Statutes, Chapter 230 (State Employment Relations).

EXHIBIT 3.8   Staffing Differences Between Private and Public Sector

---

Area	Private Sector	Public Sector
Goal	Select good people	Allow all to apply and select the best among them
Laws	State/federal law on discrimination	State/federal law on discrimination State/federal/municipal law on merit and civil service (CS)
Ethics	Corporate principles and policies	State ethics laws on conflict of interest and patronage Executive orders banning discrimination
Fairness	Fairness is an ideal goal Patronage is inefficient	Fairness is legally mandated Patronage is illegal
Appeals and reviews	Internal review by personnel/AA office Review by federal agencies	Inter nal review by agency personnel/ AA office Review by federal agencies Appeals by individuals Routine audits by central CS
Speed	Speed in hiring possible	Speed difficult to achieve
Power	Centralized in CEO and board of directors Unions	Three equal branches of government News media Unions Special interest groups
Ease of change	Procedures and policies based on consensus or fiat Easy to innovate Change controlled by managers Exceptions to procedures possible Few legal ramifications or exceptions Flexible Change to corporate policy or union contracts most difficult	Procedures and policies based on law Difficult to innovate Change controlled by legislature and executive Exceptions to rules, policy and procedure are difficult and may be subject to appeal/review Exceptions may be grounds for appeal Appeal at each step by persons involved Little flexibility
Public interest	Public has little interest in personnel matters	Public has great interest in personnel matters
Central control	Degree of central control varies	Degree of central control varies
Recruitment	Area often local, may be countrywide Period may be arbitrarily short	Area usually jurisdiction-wide, may be countrywide Recruitment period act by law, rule or regulation
Paperwork	Documentation desirable	Documentation required

Source: J. P. Wiesen, N. Abrams, and S. A. McAttee, *Employment Testing: A Public Sector Viewpoint,* 1990. Reprinted with permission of the International Personnel Management Association Assessment Council, Monograph Vol. 2 #3.

EXHIBIT 3.9   Legal Issues Covered in Other Chapters

Chapter Title and Number	Topic
Strategy and Planning (4)	Affirmative action plans (AAPs) and Revised Order No. 4
	Legality of AAPs
	Diversity programs
Job Analysis (5)	Job-relatedness and court cases
	Job analysis and selection
	Essential job functions
Measurement (6)	Disparate impact statistics
	Standardization and validation
External Recruitment (7)	Definition of job applicant
	Targeted recruitment
	Recruitment sources
	Job advertisements
	Fraud and misrepresentation
Internal Recruitment (8)	Revised Order No. 4
	Bona fide seniority system
	Glass ceiling
External Selection I (9)	Disclaimers
	Reference checks
	Preemployment inquiries
	Bona fide occupational qualifications (BFOQs)
External Selection II (10)	Uniform Guidelines on Employee Selection Procedures (UGESP)
	Selection under the ADA
	Drug testing
Internal Selection (11)	UGESP
	Glass ceiling
Decision Making (12)	UGESP
	Choices among finalists
Final Match (13)	Authorization to work
	Negligent hiring
	Employment-at-will
Staffing System Management (14)	Recordkeeping and reports
	Audits
	Managing legal compliance

SUMMARY

Staffing involves the formation of the employment relationship. That relationship involves the employer acquiring individuals to perform work for it as employees, independent contractors, and temporary employees. The specific legal meanings and obligations associated with these various arrangements were provided.

Myriad laws and regulations have come forth from several sources to place constraints on the contractual relationship between employer and employee. These constraints seek to ensure a balance of power in the relationship, as well as provide protections to both the employee and employer.

Statutory federal laws pertaining to EEO/AA prohibit discrimination on the basis of race, color, religion, sex, national origin, age, and disability. This prohibition applies to staffing practices intentionally used to discriminate (disparate treatment), as well as to staffing practices that have a discriminatory effect (disparate or adverse impact). Equal employment opportunity, affirmative action, and quotas are each general attempts to bring staffing practices into compliance with these legal requirements.

Such attempts must occur within the specific provisions of the laws pertaining to staffing, which specify both prohibited and permissible practices. In both instances, the emphasis is on use of staffing practices that are job-related and focus on the person/job match.

Interpretation and implementation of the major EEO/AA laws occur through federal guidelines and regulations. The most prominent of these regarding staffing are the Uniform Guidelines on Employee Selection Procedures, Revised Order No. 4, and the Employment Regulations for the ADA.

Other laws and regulations also affect staffing practices. At the federal level, there is a prohibition on the employment of unauthorized aliens, and on the use of the polygraph (lie detector). State and local EEO/AA laws supplement those found at the federal level. Many other staffing practices are also addressed by state and local law. Finally, civil service laws and regulations govern staffing practices in the public sector. Their provisions create marked differences in certain staffing practices between public and private employers.

Legal issues will continue to be addressed throughout the remainder of this book. The emphasis will be on explanation and application of the laws' provisions to staffing practices.

DISCUSSION QUESTIONS

1. Do you agree that "the employer usually has the upper hand" when it comes to establishing the employment relationship? When might the employee have maximum power over the employer?

2. What is the nature of the distinction between AA and quotas?

3. What are the limitations of disparate impact statistics as indicators of potential staffing discrimination?

4. Why is each of the four situational factors necessary to establishing a claim of disparate treatment?

5. What factors would lead an organization to enter into a consent agreement rather than continue to pursue a suit in court?

6. What are the differences between staffing in the private and public sectors? Why would private employers probably resist adopting many of the characteristics of public staffing systems?

APPLICATIONS

Age Discrimination in a Promotion?

The Best Protection Insurance Company (BPIC) handled a massive volume of claims each year in the corporate claims function, as well as its four regional claims centers. Corporate claims was headed by the Senior Vice President of Corporate Claims (SVPCC); reporting to the SVPCC were two managers of corporate claims (MCC-Life and MCC-Residential) and a highly skilled corporate claims specialist (CCS). Each regional office was headed by a regional center manager (RCM); the RCM was responsible for both supervisors and claims specialists within the regional office. The RCMs reported to the Vice President of Regional Claims (VPRC). Here is the structure before reorganization:

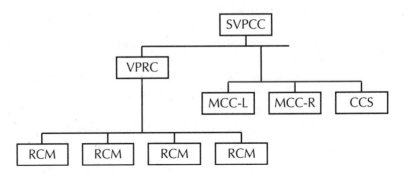

BPIC decided to reorganize its claims function by eliminating the four regional offices (and the RCM position) and establishing numerous small field offices throughout the country. The other part of the reorganization involved creating five new CCS positions. The CCS job itself was to be redesigned and upgraded in terms of knowledge and skill requirements. It was planned to staff these new CCS positions through internal promotions from within the claims function.

The plaintiff in the case was Gus Tavus, a 52-year-old RCM. Since his job was being eliminated, Gus was asked by the SVPCC to apply for one of the new CCS positions, as were the other RCMs, all of whom were over 40 years of age. Neither Gus nor the other RCMs were promoted to the CCS positions. Other candidates were also bypassed, and some of them were also over 40. The promotions went to five claims specialists and supervisors from within the former regional offices, all of whom were under 40 years of age. Two of these newly promoted employees had worked for, and reported to, Gus as RCM.

Upon learning of his failure to be promoted, Gus sought to determine why he was not promoted. What he learned (described below) lead him to feel he had been discriminated against because of his age. He then retained legal counsel, attorney Bruce Davis. Bruce met informally with the SVPCC to try to determine what had happened in the promotion process, and why his client Gus had not been promoted. He was told that there were a large number of candidates who were better qualified than Gus, and that Gus lacked adequate technical and communication skills for the new job of CCS. The SVPCC refused to reconsider Gus for the job and said that all his decisions were "etched in stone." Gus and Bruce then filed suit in federal district court, claiming a violation of the Age Discrimination in Employment Act. They also subpoenaed numerous BPIC documents, including the personnel files of all applicants for the CCS positions.

Based on these documents, and discussions with Gus, the following information emerged about the promotion process actually used by BPIC. The SVPCC and the two MCCs conducted the total process; they received no input from the VPRC or the HR department. There was no formal, written job description for the new CCS position, nor was there a formal internal job posting as required by company policy. The SVPCC and the MCCs developed a list of employees they thought might be interested in the job, including Gus, and then met to consider the list of candidates. At that meeting, the personnel files and previous performance appraisals of the candidates were not consulted. After deciding on the five candidates who would be offered the promotion (all five accepted), the VPCC and MCCs did scan the personnel files and appraisals of these five (only) to check for any disconfirming information about the employees. None was found. Inspection of all the files by Bruce Davis revealed no written comments suggesting age bias in past performance appraisals for any of the candidates, including Gus. Also, there was no indication that Gus lacked technical and communication skills. All of Gus' previous appraisal ratings were above average, and there was no evidence of decline in the favorability of the ratings recently. Finally, an interview with the VPRC (Gus' boss) revealed that he had not been consulted at all during the promotion process, that he was "shocked beyond belief" that Gus had not been promoted, and that there was "no question" but that Gus was qualified in all respects for the CCS job.

1. Based on the above facts, prepare a written report that presents a convincing disparate treatment claim that Gus had been intentionally discriminated against on the basis of his age.

2. Present a convincing rebuttal, from the viewpoint of BPIC, to this disparate treatment claim.

Disparate Impact: What Do the Statistics Mean?

Claims of discrimination can be pursued under an allegation of disparate impact. According to this approach, the effect or impact of staffing practices can be discriminatory and thus in violation of the Civil Rights Act. Such an impact could occur even though there may be no underlying intention to discriminate against members of a protected group or class (e.g. women or minorities). Pursuit of a disparate impact claim requires the use of various statistics to show that, in effect, women or minorities are being treated differently than men or nonminorities under the law.

Exhibit 3.3 shows three types of disparate impact statistics: flow statistics, stock statistics, and concentration statistics. Also shown is a statistical example of disparate impact for each type. For each of these three types of statistics, prepare a report in which you discuss the following:

1. How could an organization go about collecting and reporting these statistics in the form shown in Exhibit 3.3.

2. What "rule of thumb" or guidelines would you recommend for deciding whether statistical differences between men and women, or nonminorities and minorities, reflect discrimination occurring through its staffing system?

3. What types of staffing activities (recruitment, selection, employment) might be causing the statistical differences? For example, in Exhibit 3.3 the selection rate for men is 50% and for women is 11%. How would the organization collect the data necessary to compute these selection rates, how would you decide if the difference in selection rates (50% vs. 11%) is big enough to indicate possible discrimination, and what sorts of practices might be causing the difference in selection rates?

ENDNOTES

1. C. J. Bakaly, Jr. and J. M. Grossman, *The Modern Law of Employment Relationships* (Englewood Cliffs, NJ: Prentice Hall, 1995), pp. 1–23; A. G. Feliu, *Primer on Individual Employee Rights* (Washington, DC: Bureau of National Affairs, 1992), pp. 1–9.

2. D. L. Bennett-Alexander and L. B. Pincus, *Employment Law for Business* (Homewood, IL: Irwin, 1995), pp. 33–60; J. G. Frierson, *Preventing Employment Lawsuits* (Washington, DC: Bureau of National Affairs, 1994), pp. 58–61.

3. C. J. Bakaly, Jr. and J. M. Grossman, *The Modern Law of Employment Relationships*, pp. 1–23.

4. G. P. Panaro, *Employment Law Manual*, second ed. (Boston: Warren Gorham Lamont, 1993), pp. 7–1 to 7–89; M. J. Levine, "The Erosion of the Employment-At-Will Doctrine: Recent Developments," *Labor Law Journal*, 1994, 45, pp. 79–89.

5. D. P. O'Meara, "Question the Status of Independent Contractors," *HR Magazine*, August 1994, pp. 33–39; M. Selz and S. N. Mehta, "Small Business Gets Big Bills As IRS Targets Free-Lancers." *Wall Street Journal*, 8/24/95, p. B1; T. Stalnaker, *Employer's Guide to Using Independent Contractors* (Washington, DC: Bureau of National Affairs, 1993).

6. D. C. Feldman and B. S. Klaas, "Temporary Workers: Employee Rights and Employer Responsibilities," *Employee Rights and Responsibilities Journal*, 1996 (1), pp. 1–21; J. W. Tansky and P. A. Veglahn, "Legal Issues in Co-Employment," *Labor Law Journal*, 1995, 46, pp. 293–300.

7. A. G. Feliu, *Primer on Individual Employee Rights*, pp. 1–8.

8. A. G. Feliu, *Primer on Individual Employee Rights*, pp. 1–8.

9. R. M. Green and R. J. Reibstein, *Employer's Guide to Workplace Torts* (Washington, DC: Bureau of National Affairs, 1992).

10. Bureau of National Affairs, *Fair Employment Practices*, vols. 1 and 2 (Washington, DC: author, periodically updated); Commerce Clearing House, *1991 Guidebook to Fair Employment Practices* (Chicago: author, 1991), pp. 15–73, 153–162; B. S. Gamble (ed.), *Sex Discrimination Handbook* (Washington, DC: Bureau of National Affairs, 1992), pp. 149–174; M. A. Player, *Federal Law of Employment Discrimination* (St Paul, MN: West, 1992), pp. 47–49, 59–66, 217–225.

11. Bureau of National Affairs, *Fair Employment Practices*, vols. 1 and 2 (Washington, DC: author, periodically updated); Commerce Clearing House, *1991 Guidebook to Fair Employment Practices* (Chicago: author, 1991), pp. 15–73, 153–162; B. S. Gamble, ed., *Sex Discrimination Handbook* (Washington, DC: Bureau of National Affairs, 1992), pp. 149–174; M. A. Player, *Federal Law of Employment Discrimination* (St. Paul, MN: West, 1992), pp. 47–49, 59–66, 217–225.

12. Bureau of National Affairs, *Fair Employment Practices*, vol. 1, pp. 431:363–374; T. Johnson, "The Legal Use of Racial Quotas and Gender Preference by Private and Public Employers," *Labor Law Journal*, 1989, 40, pp. 419–425.

13. S. Meisinger, "Affirmative Action Comes Under Review by States, Nation—An Analysis of the Issue," *Society for Human Resource Management Mosaics*, April, 1995; R. K. Robinson, J. Seydel and H. J. Sloan, "Reverse Discrimination Employment Litigation: Defining the Limits of Preferential Promotion," *Labor Law Journal*, 1995, 46, pp. 131–141.

14. Bureau of National Affairs, *Fair Employment Practices*, vol. 1, pp. 431:225–250; M. A. Player, *Federal Law of Employment Discrimination*, pp. 67–114.

15. R. D. Arvey and R. H. Faley, *Fairness in Selecting Employees*, second ed. (Reading, MA: Addison-Wesley, 1988), pp. 73–80; J. C. Cook, "Preparing for Statistical Battles under the Civil Rights Act," *HR Focus*, May 1992, pp. 12–13; W. M. Howard, "The Decline and Fall of Statistical Evidence as Proof of Employment Discrimination," *Labor Law Journal*, 1994, 45, pp. 208–220.

16. Bureau of National Affairs, *Fair Employment Practices*, vol. 1, pp. 401:1–4241; R. C. West (ed.), *U.S. Labor and Employment Laws* (Washington, DC: author, 1991).

17. Bureau of National Affairs, *Fair Employment Practices*, vol. 1, pp. 431:1–55, 151–170, 301–375; P. E. Varca and P. Pattison, "Evidentiary Standards in Employment Discrimination: A View Toward the Future," *Personnel Psychology*, 1993, 40, pp. 239–258.

18. Equal Employment Opportunity Commission, *EEOC Policy Statement on Alternative Dispute Resolution* (Washington, DC: author, 1995).

19. Bureau of National Affairs, *Daily Labor Report*, 11/5/92, pp. A-3 to A-4.

20. Bureau of National Affairs, *Fair Employment Practices*, vol. 1, pp. 431:55–64, 481–490.

21. Bureau of National Affairs, *Fair Employment Practices*, vol. 1, pp. 401:1–4241; R. C. West, (ed.), *U.S. Labor and Employment Laws*.

22. Equal Employment Opportunity Commission, "Definition of the Term Disability," *Compliance Manual Section 902* (Washington, DC: author, 1995).

23. Bureau of National Affairs, *Fair Employment Practices*, vols. 1, 2, and 3.

24. Commerce Clearing House, *Employment Practice Decisions* (Chicago: author, periodically updated).

25. Bureau of National Affairs, *EEOC Compliance Manual* and *Affirmative Action Compliance Manual for Federal Contractors* (Washington, DC: author, periodically updated); Equal Employment Opportunity Commission, *Technical Assistance Manual of the Employment Provisions of the Americans with Disabilities Act* (Washington, DC: author, periodically updated).

26. Commerce Clearing House, *1994 Guidebook to Fair Employment Practices;* G. P. Panaro, *Employment Law Manual;* M. A. Player, *Federal Law of Employment Discrimination;* B. L. Schlei and P. Grossman, *Employment Discrimination Law* (Washington, DC: Bureau of National Affairs, 1987).

27. Bureau of National Affairs, "Labor Department Issues Final Rules for Program on Temporary Foreign Workers," *Daily Labor Report*, 12/20/94, p. AA-1.

28. R. M. Green and R. J. Reibstein, *Employer's Guide to Workplace Torts*.

29. A. G. Feliu, *Primer on Individual Employee Rights,* p. 284.

30. J. P. Wiesen, N. Abrams, and S. A. McAttee, *Employment Testing: A Public Sector Viewpoint* (Alexandria, VA: International Personnel Management Association Assessment Council, 1990), pp. 2–3.

31. J. P. Wiesen, N. Abrams, and S. A. McAttee, *Employment Testing: A Public Sector Viewpoint,* pp. 3–7.

STAFFING ORGANIZATIONS MODEL

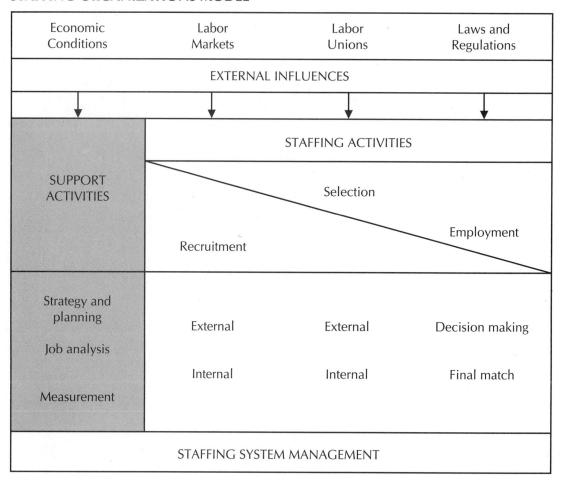

PART TWO

Support Activities

CHAPTER FOUR

Strategy and Planning

Strategic Issues
   HR Strategy
   Staffing Strategy

Human Resource Planning
   Process and Example
   Initial Decisions
   Forecasting HR Requirements
   Forecasting HR Availabilities
   External and Internal Environmental Scanning
   Reconciliation and Gaps
   Action Planning

Staffing Planning
   Staffing Planning Process
   Core Workforce
   Flexible Workforce

Legal Issues
   Affirmative Action Plans (AAPs)
   Legality of AAPs
   Diversity Programs

Summary

Discussion Questions

Applications

H R strategy represents key decisions that have been made to shape and guide HR programs, including staffing. HR planning is the process of forecasting the organization's future employment needs, and then developing action staffing plans and programs for fulfilling these needs in ways that are in alignment with strategy.

This chapter first presents HR strategy and how it relates to overall organization strategy. Staffing strategy is shown to be a crucial component of HR strategy; it is a reflection of decisions about how to acquire and deploy the workforces of the organization. Seven such decisions are identified and explained.

The HR planning process involves several components, simplified examples of which are presented for the sales and customer service unit of an organization. Then each of these components is described in detail. These components consist of making initial planning decisions, forecasting HR requirements, forecasting HR availabilities, scanning the external and internal environment, determining employee shortages and surpluses, and developing action plans. For each of these components specific examples are provided, drawing from the initial example of the sales and customer service unit.

Staffing planning is shown to be a logical outgrowth of HR planning. It generally involves setting staffing objectives, generating alternative staffing activities, and assessing and choosing from among these activities. Guided by staffing strategy, one of the key staffing planning areas involves planning for the core (permanent employees) and flexible (temporary employees and independent contractors) workforces. The unique nature and requirements for planning each type of workforce is indicated.

The major legal issue for HR strategy and planning is that of affirmative action plans (AAPs). The three basic components of an AAP are utilization analysis, staffing goals and timetables, and action plans. An illustration of these components is provided, along with the AAP requirements for federal contractors contained in Revised Order No. 4. A summary of the legality of AAPs is then presented. Finally, diversity programs represent a natural extension of AAPs. They seek to prepare organizational members for a diverse workforce, and to develop HR programs that will foster acceptance and success for all its members.

STRATEGIC ISSUES

HR strategies are both derived from and contribute to the formulation of the organization's strategy. Imbedded within, and flowing out of, HR strategy is staffing strategy. Staffing strategy reflects several key decisions about how to acquire and deploy the organizations' workforces. These decisions then guide more specific HR and staffing planning.

HR Strategy

Organizations formulate strategy to express an overall purpose or mission, and to establish broad goals and objectives that will guide the organization toward fulfillment of its mission. For example, a software development organization may have a mission to "help individuals and families manage all of their personal finances and records through electronic means." Based on this mission statement the organization might then develop goals and objectives pertaining to product development, sales growth, and competitive differentiation through superior product quality and customer service.

Underlying these objectives are certain assumptions about the size and types of workforces that will need to be acquired, trained, managed, rewarded, and retained. HR strategy represents the key decisions about how these workforce assumptions will be handled. Such HR strategy may not only flow from the organization strategy, but may actually contribute directly to the formulation of the organization's strategy.[1]

Consider again the software development organization and its objective pertaining to new product development. Being able to develop new products assumes sufficient, qualified product-development team members are available internally and externally, and assurances from the HR department about availability may have been critical in helping the organization to decide on its product development goals. From this general assumption, HR strategy may suggest (a) obtaining new, experienced employees from other software companies, rather than going after newly-minted college and graduate school graduates; (b) building a new facility for software development employees in a geographic area that will be an attractive place to work, raise families, and pursue leisure activities; (c) developing relocation assistance packages and family-friendly benefits; (d) offering wages and salaries above the market average, plus using sign-on (hiring) bonuses to help lure new employees away from their current employers; (e) creating special training budgets for each employee to use at his or her own discretion for skills enhancement; and (f) putting in place a promotion system that is fast-track and allows employees to rise upward in either their professional specialty or the managerial ranks. In all of these ways HR strategy seeks to align acquisition and management of the workforce with organization strategy.

Staffing Strategy

Staffing strategy is an outgrowth of the interplay between organization and HR strategy described above. It deals directly with key decisions regarding the acquisition and deployment of the organization's workforces.[2] Such decisions guide the development of recruitment, selection, and employment programs. In the software development illustration above, the strategic decision to acquire new employees from the ranks of experienced people at other organizations may lead the organization to develop very active, personalized, and secret recruiting activities for luring these people away. It may also lead to the development of special selection techniques for assessing job experiences and accomplishments. In such ways strategic staffing decisions shape the staffing process.

Exhibit 4.1 shows the interplays between organization, HR, and staffing strategy. It also contains seven strategic staffing decisions that must be confronted during the strategy formulation process. While each decision is shown as an "either-or" one, each is more appropriately thought of as lying on a continuum that

EXHIBIT 4.1   Organization, HR, and Staffing Strategy

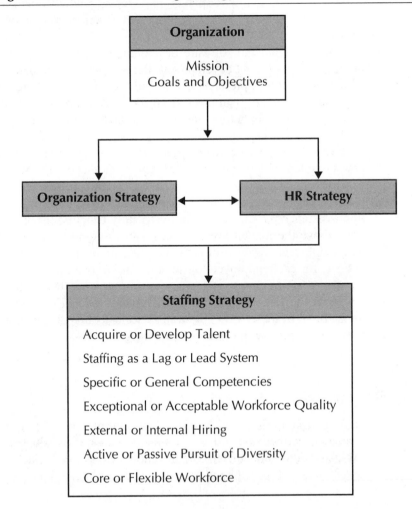

is anchored at each end by the either-or extremes. Each of these strategic staffing decisions is discussed separately below, though in reality they are interrelated.

Acquire or Develop Talent

To fulfill its staffing needs, a pure staffing strategy would have an organization concentrate on acquisition of new employees who can "hit the ground running" and be at peak performance the moment they arrive. These employees would bring their talents with them to the job, with little or no need for development. A pure development strategy would lead to acquisition of just about anyone, as long as they were willing and able to learn the KSAOs required by the job. Staffing strategy must position the organization appropriately along this "buy or make" your talent continuum. For critical positions and newly created ones, such as might occur in the software company example, the emphasis would likely be on acquiring talent because of the urgency of developing new products. There may be no time to train, nor may qualified internal candidates be available.

Staffing as a Lag or Lead System

The organization's staffing systems may develop in response to organization and HR strategy (lag system), or staffing considerations may serve as key inputs to organization and HR strategy (lead system). With staffing as a lag system, strategic organization objectives and plans are developed first, and staffing systems then are developed to deliver the numbers and types of employees needed. Using staffing as a lead system involves the acquisition of people and their accompanying skills without a formal blueprint for how many are needed or when. Such people are acquired to come into the organization and "make things happen," so that organization strategy becomes a reflection of newly-acquired employees' talents and ideas. In the software organization illustration, it may decide to "staff up" on good programmers whenever they can be found, thinking that their presence will help contribute to new product development.

Specific or General Competencies

Should the organization acquire people for a specific person/job match, or a more general person/organization match? The former means focusing on job-specific competencies, often of the job knowledge and technical skill variety. The latter requires a focus on KSAOs that will be applicable across a variety of jobs, both current and future. Examples of such KSAOs include flexibility and adaptability, ability to learn, written and oral communication skills, and algebra/statistics skills. An organization expecting rapid changes in job content, and new job creation, such as in the software development illustration, might position itself close to the general competencies end of the continuum.

Exceptional or Acceptable Workforce Quality

Strategically, the organization could seek to acquire a workforce that was pre-eminent KSAO-wise (exceptional quality), or one that was a more "ballpark" variety KSAO-wise (acceptable quality). Pursuit of the exceptional strategy would allow the organization to stock up on the "best and the brightest" with the hope that this exceptional talent pool would deliver truly superior performance. The acceptable strategy means pursuit of a less high-powered workforce, and probably a less expensive one as well. Owners of professional sports teams confront this choice and make their decisions accordingly. In football, for example, the Dallas Cowboys and San Francisco Forty-niners have opted for the exceptional quality choice, while other teams (name your own example) appear content and profitable with the acceptable quality choice.

External or Internal Hiring

When job vacancies occur, or new jobs are created, should the organization seek to fill them from the external or internal labor market? While some mixture of external and internal hiring will be necessary in most situations, the relative blend could vary substantially. To the extent that the organization wants to cultivate a stable, committed workforce, it will probably need to emphasize internal hiring. This will allow employees to use the internal labor market as a spring board for launching long-term careers within the organization. External hiring might then be restricted to specific entry-level jobs, as well as newly created ones for which there are no acceptable internal applicants. External hiring might also be necessary when there is rapid organization growth, such that the number of new jobs created outstrips internal supply available.

Active or Passive Pursuit of Diversity

As discussed in Chapter 2, the labor force is becoming increasingly diverse in terms of demographics, values, and languages. Does the organization want to actively pursue this diversity in the labor market so that its own workforce mirrors it, or does the organization want to more passively let diversity of its workforce happen to it? Advocates of an active diversity strategy argue it is not only legally and morally appropriate, but that a diverse workforce allows the organization to be more attuned to the diverse needs of the customers it serves. Those favoring a more passive strategy suggest that diversification of the workforce takes time because it requires substantial planning and assimilation activity. In the software development illustration, an active diversity strategy might be pursued as a way of acquiring workers who can help identify a diverse array of software products that might be received favorably by various segments of the marketplace.

Core or Flexible Workforce

The organization's core workforce is made up of individuals who are viewed (and view themselves) as permanent employees of the organization, either full-time or part-time. They are central to the core goods and services delivered by the organization. The flexible workforce is composed of more peripheral workers who are used on an as-needed, just-in-time basis. They are not viewed (nor do they view themselves) as "permanent," and legally most of them are not even employees of the organization. Rather, they are employees of an alternative organization, such as a temporary help agency or independent contractor, that provides these workers to the organization. Strategically, the organization must decide whether it wishes to use both core and flexible workforces, what the mixture of core vs. flexible workers will be, and in what jobs and units of the organization these mixtures will be deployed (this matter is explored below in a discussion of staffing planning). Within the software development organization, programmers might be considered as part of its core workforce, but ancillary workers (e.g., clericals) may be part of the flexible workforce, particularly since the need for them will depend on the speed and success of new product development.

HUMAN RESOURCE PLANNING

Human resource planning (HRP) is a process and set of activities undertaken to forecast an organization's labor demand (requirements) and internal labor supply (availabilities), to compare these projections to determine employment gaps, and to develop action plans for addressing these gaps. Action plans include staffing planning.

A general model depicting the process of HRP is presented first in this chapter. Following this, an operational example of HRP is presented; it casts the general model into an administrative mode that can be used by organizations to guide the conduct of actual HRP.[3]

Process and Example

The basic elements of virtually any organization's HRP are shown in Exhibit 4.2. As can be seen, the HRP process involves five sequential steps:[4]

1. determining future human resource requirements
2. determining future human resource availabilities
3. conducting external and internal environmental scanning
4. reconciling requirements and availabilities—that is, determining gaps (shortages and surpluses) between the two
5. developing action plans to close the projected gaps

Future HR Requirements
Future HR requirements represent the number and types (in terms of qualities or KSAOs) of employees that the organization will need in the future to produce its

EXHIBIT 4.2 Human Resource Planning (HRP) Process

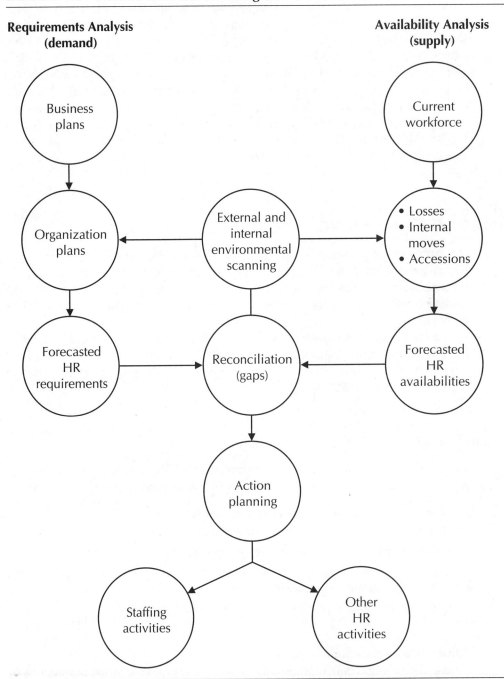

goods and services. The requirements represent the organization's desired workforce of the future.

These projections are derived from knowledge of the overall business plan of the organization, as well as accompanying organizational plans regarding structure and hierarchy. Business and organizational plans thus drive the future HR requirements of the organization. In many organizations, however, the process is reciprocal; tentative projections about HR requirements help shape the establishment of business and organizational plans.

Future HR Availabilities

Availability projections focus on the organization's current internal workforce. Their concern is with estimating the numbers and types of current employees that will be available in the future. More specifically, these estimates are concerned with the loss or exit of employees from the organization, the resulting distribution of employees who remain within the organization's internal labor market (promotions, transfers, and demotions), and the number of accessions (new hires) during the planning time frame.

External and Internal Environmental Scanning

The external portion of scanning involves tracking trends and developments in the external environment, discerning implications of these trends for HRM, and ensuring that these implications receive attention during the HRP process. Referring back to the general HR model, note that external scanning focuses on the external forces of economic conditions, labor markets, labor unions, and laws and regulations.

Internal scanning involves assessing the organization's internal environment as it relates to the workforce and the conduct of HR activities. It is important to be aware of the composition and diversity of the organization's workforce, and the types of HR policies and programs that have been developed, or need to be developed, in order to accommodate and encourage diversity. Also important is awareness of employees' changing preferences for certain job rewards (e.g., parental leave, day care) and their likely responses to such new rewards. In both of these examples, knowledge derived from internal scanning could be useful in the prediction of losses, internal moves, and accessions.

Reconciliation (Gaps)

Armed with estimates of future requirements and availabilities—estimates tempered with assessments based on external and internal environmental scanning—the organization must reconcile all of the data it has collected in order to arrive at predicted employment gaps. Gaps represent shortages and surpluses of employees, primarily in terms of numbers of employees. Gaps may also be thought of in more qualitative terms pertaining to shortages or surpluses of KSAOs. The discussion here, and in the remainder of the chapter, however, will focus on gaps in the numerical sense only.

Identification of, and agreement on, gap estimates are the "bottom line" objective of forecasting activities. With some sense of impending shortages and surpluses, the organization has the opportunity to begin planning how to best cope with them. In this way, the organization can be proactive in its HR policies and programs, and can avoid a reactive approach to HR problems involving shortages (e.g., "Mary just quit; find me a replacement immediately!") and surpluses (e.g., "Sales keep falling; we have no choice but to lay off some employees.").

Action Plans

Action plans spring forth and begin to take shape from identified employment gaps. They represent careful, intentional responses to likely future events. Many of these responses involve staffing activities. Shortages, for example, usually lead to the development and implementation of external staffing activities that yield sufficient numbers and types of new employees to meet the shortage challenge.

Other HR activities also flow from gap figures, usually in concert with staffing activities, or sometimes as substitutes for staffing. If the response to a predicted shortage is to increase hiring, for example, particular attention may need to be paid to starting pay and benefit issues in order to augment the staffing plan. As another example, shortages may be met by implementing a productivity improvement program involving current employees, rather than by hiring new employees.

An example of HRP, including results from forecasting requirements and availabilities, is shown in Exhibit 4.3. The exhibit shows a partial HRP being conducted by an organization for a specific unit (sales and customer service). It involves only two job categories (A or sales, and B or customer service) and two hierarchical levels for each category (1 or entry level, and 2 or manager level). All of the HRP steps are confined to this particular organizational unit and its job categories/levels, as shown.

The current workforce size (number of employees) is given for each job category/level. Requirements and availabilities are forecast for a one-year time frame, and the results are shown in the relevant columns. After the reconciliation process, final gap figures are agreed upon and entered into the gap column. It can be seen that in total there is an estimated shortage of $n = -145$ employees. This overall shortage is very unevenly distributed across the four job categories/levels. In three of these, there are shortages projected ($n = -39$, $n = -110$, and $n = -3$), and in the remaining one, there is a projected surplus ($n = +7$).

These gap data serve as the basic input to action planning. Because the gaps show both shortages and a surplus, and because the gaps vary in severity relative to the current workforce, a specific action plan will likely have to be developed and implemented for each job category/level. The resultant four staffing (and other) plans will hopefully bring staffing into an orderly balance of requirements and availabilities over the course of the planning period.

EXHIBIT 4.3   Operational Format and Example for Human Resource Planning (HRP)

Organizational Unit: Sales and Customer Service

Job Category and Level	Current Workforce	Forecast for Workforce— One Year		Reconciliation and Gaps	Action Planning
		Requirements	Availabilities		
A1 (Sales)	100	110	71	−39 (shortage)	Staffing activities
A2 (Sales manager)	20	15	22	+7 (surplus)	Recruitment Selection
B1 (Customer service representative)	200	250	140	−110 (shortage)	Employment Other HR activities
B2 (Customer service manager)	15	25	22	−3 (shortage)	Compensation Training & development
	335	400	255	−145 (shortage)	

The above process and example serve to identify and illustrate the rudiments of HRP. Within them are several distinct HRP components that require elaboration. We turn now to these components, emphasizing that each component represents a factor that must be considered in HRP, and that there are specific choices to be made regarding the operational details for each component.

Initial Decisions

Before HRP per se can be undertaken, there are several critical decisions that must be made.[5] These decisions will shape the nature of the resultant HRP process, and they will influence the output of the process, namely the gap estimates. The quality and potential effectiveness of the action plans developed from the gap estimates are thus at stake when these initial decisions are confronted and made.

Comprehensiveness of Planning

Often, HRP takes place as an integral part of an organization's business planning process; this is referred to as plan-based HRP. This is a logical approach since most organizations do business planning, and these plans almost always have HR implications. It is always a good idea to have a close, reciprocal linkage between business and HR plans.

Not all important business developments are captured in formal business plans, however, particularly if they occur rapidly or unexpectedly. Sudden changes in consumer preferences, or in legal requirements, for example, can wreak havoc on business plans. Organizational responses to these changes often occur in the form of special projects, rather than in changes in the total business plan. Part of each response requires consideration of HR implications, however, resulting in what is called project-based HRP. This type of planning helps ensure that the necessary creation of new jobs, changes in requirements and rewards for existing jobs, and employee job changes are undertaken systematically and without undue interruption.

In addition, many organizations do HRP outside the formal planning cycle for critical groups of employees on a regular basis. This often occurs for jobs in which there are perennial shortages of employees, both externally and internally. Examples here include nurses in health care organizations, faculty in certain specialized areas at colleges and universities, and until recently, teachers in elementary and secondary schools. Planning focused on a specific employee group is referred to as population-based HRP.

Planning Time Frame

Since planning involves looking into the future, the logical question for an organization to ask is, How far into the future should our planning extend? Typically, plans are divided into long-term (three plus years), intermediate (one to three years), and short-term (one year or less). Organizations vary in their planning time frame, often depending upon which of the three types of HRP is being undertaken.[6]

For plan-based HRP, the time frame will be the same as that of the business plan. In most organizations, this is between three and five years for so-called strategic planning and something less than three years for operational planning. Planning horizons for project-based HRP vary depending on the nature of the projects involved. Solving a temporary shortage of, say, salespeople for the introduction of a new product might involve planning for only a few months, while planning for the start-up of a new facility could involve a lead time of two or more years. Population-based HRP will have varying time frames, depending on the time necessary for labor supply (internal as well as external) to become available. As an example, for top-level executives in an organization, the planning time frame will be lengthy.

Job Categories and Levels

The unit of HRP and analysis is comprised of job categories and hierarchical levels among jobs. These job category/level combinations, and the types and paths of employee movement among them, form the structure of an internal labor market. Management must choose which job categories and which hierarchical levels to use for HRP. In Exhibit 4.3, for example, the choice involves two jobs (sales and customer service) and two levels (entry and manager) for a particular organizational unit.

Job categories are created and used on the basis of the unit of analysis for which projected shortages and surpluses are being investigated. These categories should be consistent with results of the job analysis. Major attention should also be paid to EEO/AA activities and commitments.

Hierarchical levels should be chosen so that they are consistent with or identical to the formal organizational hierarchy. The reason for this is that it is these formal levels which define employee promotions (up levels), transfers (across levels), and demotions (down levels). Having gap information by level facilitates planning of internal movement programs within the internal labor market. For example, it is difficult to have a systematic promotion-from-within program without knowing probable numbers of vacancies and gaps at various organizational levels.

Head Count (Current Workforce)

Exactly how does an organization count or tally the number of people in its current workforce for forecasting and planning purposes? Simply counting the number of employees on the payroll at the beginning of the planning period may be adequate for intended purposes. It ignores, however, two important distinctions.

First, it ignores the amount of scheduled time worked by each employee relative to a full workweek. For example, it treats full-time employees as synonymous with part-time employees. To rectify this, an employee head count may be made and stated in terms of full-time equivalents, or "FTEs." To do this, simply define what constitutes full-time work in terms of hours per week (or other time unit), and count each employee in terms of scheduled hours worked relative to a full work-week. If full-time is defined as 40 hours per week, a person who normally works 20 hours per week is counted as a .50 FTE, a person normally working 30 hours per week is a .75 FTE, and so on.

A second problem with current payroll head count is that it ignores vacancies that exist at the time of the count. Since most of such vacancies are probably so-called authorized ones, derived from previous HRP, they are better added into any head count tallies for the current workforce.

Roles and Responsibilities

Both line managers and staff specialists (usually from the HR department) become involved in HRP, so the roles and responsibilities of each must be determined as part of HRP. Most organizations take the position that line managers are ultimately responsible for the completion and quality of HRP. But the usual practice is to have HR staff assist with the process.

Initially, the HR staff take the lead in proposing which types of HRP will be undertaken and when, and in making suggestions with regard to comprehensive-ness, planning time frame, job categories and levels, and head counts. Final de-cisions on these matters are usually the prerogative of line management. Once an approach has been decided upon, task forces of both line managers and HR staff people are assembled to design an appropriate forecasting and action planning process and to do any other preliminary work.

Once these processes are in place, the HR staff typically assumes responsibility for collecting, manipulating, and presenting the necessary data to line manage-ment, and for laying out alternative actions plans (including staffing plans). Action planning usually becomes a joint venture between line managers and HR staff people, particularly as they gain experience with, and trust for, each other.

Forecasting HR Requirements

Forecasting HR requirements is a direct derivative of business and organizational planning. As such, it becomes a reflection of projections about a variety of factors, such as sales, production, technological change, productivity improvement, and the regulatory environment. Many specific techniques may be used to forecast HR requirements; these are either statistical or judgmental in nature, and are usually tailor-made by the organization.

Statistical Techniques

A wide array of statistical techniques is available for use in HR forecasting. Prom-inent among these are regression analysis, ratio analysis, time series analysis, and stochastic analysis. Brief descriptions of two of these techniques, regression analysis and ratio analysis, are given in Exhibit 4.4.

We will not elaborate on these techniques for several reasons. First, their very complexity would lead away from a staffing focus. Second, all of these techniques are designed simply to project the past into the future. These techniques thus have limited applicability in organizations whose immediate past and/or future forecast are characterized by significant alterations in products and services, technologies, or organizational structures. (Obviously, this includes a large percentage of organizations of varying size today.) Third, as they are dependent upon the discovery of historical relationships between certain so-called leading indicators (e.g., sales or production volume) and head count, often these relationships are difficult to find, and if found, they may not hold up in the future.

Judgmental Techniques

Judgmental techniques represent human decision-making models that are used for forecasting HR requirements. Unlike statistical techniques, it is the decision maker who collects and weighs the information subjectively and then turns it into fore-

---

EXHIBIT 4.4 Examples of Statistical Techniques to Forecast HR Requirements

(A) **Ratio Analysis**

1. Examine historical ratios involving workforce size

$$\text{Example:} \frac{\$ \text{ sales}}{1.0 \text{ FTE}} = ? \qquad \frac{\text{No. of new customers}}{1.0 \text{ FTE}} = ?$$

2. Assume ratio will be true in future
3. Use ratio to predict future HR requirements

$$\text{Example: (a)} \frac{\$4,000 \text{ sales}}{1.0 \text{ FTE}} \text{ is past ratio}$$

(b) Sales forecast is $4,000,000
(c) HR requirements = 100 FTEs

(B) **Regression Analysis**

1. Statistically identify historical predictors of workforce size

Example: FTEs $= a + b_1$ sales $+ b_2$ new customers

2. Only use equations with predictors found to be statistically significant
3. Predict future HR requirements, using equation

Example: (a) FTEs $= 7 + .0004$ sales $+ .02$ new customers

(b) Projected sales $= \$1,000,000$
   Projected new customers $= 300$

(c) HR requirements $= 7 + 400 + 6 = 413$

casts of HR requirements. The decision maker's forecasts may or may not agree very closely with those derived from statistical techniques.

Implementation of judgmental forecasting can proceed from either a "top-down" or "bottom-up" approach.[7] In the former case, top managers of the organization, organizational units, or functions rely on their knowledge of business and organizational plans to make predictions about what future head counts will be. At times, these projections may, in fact, be dictates rather than estimates, necessitated by strict adherence to the business plan. Such dictates are common in organizations undergoing significant change, such as restructuring, mergers, and cost-cutting actions.

In the bottom-up approach, lower-level managers make initial estimates for their unit (e.g., department, office, or plant) based on what they have been told, or presume, are the business and organizational plans. These estimates are then consolidated and aggregated upward through successively higher levels of management. It is then top management that establishes the HR requirements in terms of numbers.

Forecasting HR Availabilities

In Exhibit 4.3 head count data are given for the current workforce, and their availability as forecast, in each job category/level. These forecast figures take into account movement into each job category/level, movement out of each job category/level, and exit from the organizational unit or the organization. Exhibit 4.5 shows this.

Numerous techniques could have been used, alone or in combination, to generate the availabilities forecast from the current workforce figures shown in Exhibit 4.3. As with HR requirements, these techniques can be classified as statistical or judgmental.[8]

Statistical Techniques
Statistical techniques seek to predict availabilities on the basis of historical patterns of job stability and movement among employees. Referring again to Exhibit 4.5, note that between any two time periods, the following possibilities exist for each employee in the internal labor market:

1. job stability (remain in A1, A2, B1, B2)
2. promotion (move to a higher level: A1 to A2, A1 to B2, B1 to B2, B1 to A2)
3. transfer (move at the same level: A1 to B1, B1 to A1, A2 to B2, B2 to A2)
4. demotion (move to a lower level: A2 to A1, A2 to B1, B2 to B1, B2 to A1)
5. exit (move to another organizational unit or leave the organization)

EXHIBIT 4.5   A Forecast of Future Human Resource Availabilities

Job Category and Level	Current Work- force	Movement In			Movement Out			Exit		Availability
		Promotion	Transfer	Demotion	Promotion	Transfer	Demotion	Unit	Org.	
A1	100									71
A2	20			[specific cell entries not shown]						22
B1	200									140
B2	15									22
	335									255

These possibilities may be thought of in terms of flows, and rates of flow or movement rates. Past flows and rates may be measured, and then used to forecast the future availability of current employees, based on assumptions about the extent to which past rates will continue unchanged into the future. For example, if it is known that the historical promotion rate from A1 to A2 is .10 (10% of A1 employees are promoted to A2), we might predict that A1 will experience a 10% loss of employees due to promotion to A2 over the relevant time period.

To be beneficial, the study and use of flows and rates must capture all of them simultaneously within the internal labor market. That is, we must know all of the job stability, promotion, transfer, demotion, and exit rates for an internal labor market before we can forecast future availabilities. Markov Analysis is a statistical technique that accomplishes this, and it is discussed next. Other possible techniques, not discussed here, include renewal and goal programming models.

Markov Analysis The elements of Markov Analysis are shown in Exhibit 4.6 for the organizational unit originally presented in Exhibit 4.3. Refer first to part A of the exhibit. There are four job category/level combinations for which movement rates are calculated between two time periods (T and T + 1). This is accomplished as follows. For each job category/level, take the number of employees who were in it at T, and use that number as the denominator for calculating job stability and movement rates. Then, for each of those employees determine which job category/level they were employed in at T + 1. Then sum up the number of employees in each job category/level at T + 1, and use these as the numerators for calculating stability and movement rates. Finally, divide each numerator separately

---

EXHIBIT 4.6   Use of Markov Analysis to Forecast Availabilities

			T + 1			
A.	**Transition Probability Matrix** **Job Category and Level**	**A1**	**A2**	**B1**	**B2**	**Exit**
	A1	.60	.10	.20	.00	.10
	A2	.05	.60	.00	.00	.35
T	B1	.05	.00	.60	.05	.30
	B2	.00	.00	.00	.80	.20

		Current Workforce				
B.	**Forecast of Availabilities**					
	A1	100	60	10	20	0
	A2	20	1	12	0	0
	B1	200	10	0	120	10
	B2	15	0	0	0	12
			71	22	140	22

by the denominator. The result is the stability and movement rates expressed as proportions, also known as transition probabilities. The rates for any row (job category/level) must add up to 1.0.

For example, consider job category/level A1. Assume that at time T in the past there were a total of 400 people in it. Further assume that at $T + 1$, 240 of these employees were still in A1, 40 had been promoted to A2, 80 had been transferred to B1, 0 had been promoted to B2, and 40 had exited the organizational unit or the organization. The resultant transition probabilities, shown in the row for A1, are .60, .10, .20, .00, and .10. Note that these rates sum to 1.00.

By referring to these figures, and the remainder of the transition probabilities in the matrix, an organization can begin to understand the workings of the unit's internal labor market. For example, it becomes clear that 60–80% of employees experienced job stability and that exit rates varied considerably, ranging from 10% to 35%. Promotions occurred only within job categories (A1 to A2, B1 to B2), and not between job categories (A1 to B2, B1 to A2). Transfers were confined to the lower of the two levels (A1 to B1, B1 to A1). Only occasionally did demotions occur, and only within a job category (A2 to A1). Presumably, these stability and movement rates are a reflection of specific staffing policies and procedures that were in place between T and $T + 1$.

With these historical transitional probabilities, it becomes possible to forecast the future availability of the current workforce over the same time interval, T and $T + 1$, assuming that the historical rates will be repeated over the time interval and that staffing policies and procedures will not change. Refer now to part B of Exhibit 4.6. To forecast availabilities, simply take the current workforce column and multiply it by the transition probability matrix shown in part A. The resulting availability figures (note these are the same as those shown in Exhibits 4.3 and 4.4) appear at the bottom of the columns: A1 = 71, A2 = 22, B1 = 140, B2 = 22. The remainder of the current workforce (n = 80) are forecast to exit and will not be available at $T + 1$.

Limitations of Markov Analysis   Markov Analysis is an extremely useful way to capture the underlying workings of an internal labor market and then use the results to forecast future HR availabilities. Markov Analysis, however, is subject to some limitations that must be kept in mind.[9]

The first and most fundamental limitation is that of sample size, or the number of current workforce employees in each job category/level. As a rule, it is desirable to have n = 20 or more employees in each job category/level. Since this number serves as the denominator in the calculation of transition probabilities, with small sample sizes there can be substantial differences in the values of transition probabilities, even though the numerators used in their calculation are not that different (e.g., 2/10 = .20 and 4/10 = .40). Thus, transition probabilities based on small samples yield unstable estimates of future availabilities.

A second limitation of Markov Analysis is that it does not detect multiple moves by employees between T and T + 1; it only classifies employees and counts their movement according to their beginning (T) and ending (T + 1) job category/level, ignoring any intermittent moves. To minimize the number of undetected multiple moves, therefore, it is necessary to keep the time interval relatively short, probably no more than two years.

A third limitation pertains to the job category/level combinations created to serve as the unit of analysis. These must be meaningful to the organization for HRP purposes, both forecasting and action planning. Thus, extremely broad categories (e.g., managers, clericals) and categories without any level designations, should be avoided. It should be noted that this recommendation may conflict somewhat with HRP for affirmative action purposes, as discussed later.

Finally, the transition probabilities reflect only gross, average employee movement, and not the underlying causes of the movement. Stated differently, all employees in a job category/level are assumed to have an equal probability of movement. This is unrealistic, since organizations take many factors into account (e.g., seniority, performance appraisal results, and KSAOs) when making movement decisions about employees. Because of these factors, the probabilities of movement may vary among specific employees.

Judgmental Techniques

There are three judgmental techniques for forecasting availabilities that enjoy widespread acceptance: executive reviews, succession planning, and vacancy analysis. In this context, the main difference between statistical and judgmental techniques is that the former treat employees as numbers and forecast their movements based on probabilities. The latter treat them as individuals and forecast their movements person by person.

Executive Reviews   Executive reviews focus on small and unique groups of employees, most commonly top executives and other managers and professionals judged to have the potential to be top executives. Thus, executive reviews are a form of population-based HRP. The actual reviews are carried out through a series of meetings at which the top executives in a given unit consider anticipated human resource requirements and then thoroughly discuss each person under review to determine who is likely to be, or should be, promoted, reassigned, developed for future assignments, or drummed out of the organization. Determinations are made based on judgments about performance, promotability, and potential, taking into account the long-term career interests of the employee being considered. The process produces a clear indication of where the organization can expect to have managerial shortages or surpluses. It also provides career and development plans for individuals.

Succession Planning   This planning is often an adjunct to executive reviews.[10] It helps to identify backup candidates who are, or soon will be, qualified to replace current executives or upper-level managers. Succession planning results are typically summarized on charts such as the one shown in Exhibit 4.7. These greatly facilitate the planning of likely retirements, terminations, promotions, and transfers within and across organizational units. These charts also show which managers are in need of further development to become ready to fill job(s) for which they are (or might be) considered as replacements.

Vacancy Analysis   In vacancy analysis, judgments are made about likely employee movement on an individual basis, as in executive reviews and succession planning. Because large numbers of employees are usually involved, the results may be aggregated and summarized statistically. Vacancy analysis is akin to judgmental Markov Analysis; employee movement is "guesstimated" through managerial judgment rather than estimated statistically through calculation and use of transition probabilities.

Exhibit 4.8 shows a vacancy analysis, using the same four job categories/levels, current workforce numbers, and forecast of requirements, as in Exhibits 4.3, 4.5, and 4.6. Vacancy analysis begins with a forecast about numbers of exits from each job category/level. This yields an effective internal labor supply, which can then be compared to a forecast of demand to arrive at a gross shortage or surplus number for each job category/level. These numbers are then adjusted for likely movement into and out of the job category/levels, resulting in final gap figures. These gaps serve as the input to action planning. Since both shortages and surpluses were forecast in Exhibit 4.3, these plans are likely to involve both accessions (internal and external) and workforce reductions in head count and/or hours of work.

It should be noted that the data in Exhibit 4.8 were constructed to yield the same availability results and employment gaps as shown in Exhibits 4.3 and 4.5. Referring to Exhibit 4.8, note that A1 may be calculated as $(90+11-30 = 71)$, A2 as $(13+10-1 = 22)$, B1 as $(160+0-20 = 140)$, and B2 as $(12+10 - 0 = 22)$. In essence, the results of judgmental forecasting have been "rigged" to yield the same results as statistical forecasting. In actual practice, such a result is extremely unlikely. But our example does illustrate that if decision makers are knowledgeable about their internal labor markets, their judgments may yield results similar to those that would have been obtained from statistical forecasting, such as Markov Analysis.

External and Internal Environmental Scanning

External Scanning

This is the term applied to the process of tracking trends and developments in the outside world, documenting their implications for the management of human

EXHIBIT 4.7   Employee Replacement Chart for Succession Planning

Organizational Unit _____

Date _____

Position	
Incumbent _____	Current job: years: ___ Total service: years: ___
Promote to _____	Date ready: _____
Replacement (1) _____	Current job: years: ___ Total service: years: ___
Present position _____	Date promotable: _____
Replacement (2) _____	Current job: years: ___ Total service: years: ___
Present position _____	Date promotable: _____

Position	
Incumbent _____	Current job: years: ___ Total service: years: ___
Promote to _____	Date ready: _____
Replacement (1) _____	Current job: years: ___ Total service: years: ___
Present position _____	Date promotable: _____
Replacement (2) _____	Current job: years: ___ Total service: years: ___
Present position _____	Date promotable: _____

Position	
Incumbent _____	Current job: years: ___ Total service: years: ___
Promote to _____	Date ready: _____
Replacement (1) _____	Current job: years: ___ Total service: years: ___
Present position _____	Date promotable: _____
Replacement (2) _____	Current job: years: ___ Total service: years: ___
Present position _____	Date promotable: _____

Position	
Incumbent _____	Current job: years: ___ Total service: years: ___
Promote to _____	Date ready: _____
Replacement (1) _____	Current job: years: ___ Total service: years: ___
Present position _____	Date promotable: _____
Replacement (2) _____	Current job: years: ___ Total service: years: ___
Present position _____	Date promotable: _____

EXHIBIT 4.8   Vacancy Analysis for Sales and Customer Service Unit

Job Category and Level	Current Work-force	Exit Forecast Org.	Exit Forecast Unit	Effective Supply	Forecast of Demand	(Shortages) or Surpluses	Movements Within Unit Into	Movements Within Unit Out	Gap/Net Shortage or Surplus	Accessions From Other Units	Accessions External New Hires	Reductions
A1	100	8	2	90	110	(20)	11	30	(39)			
A2	20	4	3	13	15	(2)	10	1	7	Action planning		
B1	200	25	15	160	250	(90)	0	20	(110)			
B2	15	2	1	12	25	(13)	10	0	(3)			

resources, and ensuring that these implications receive attention in the HRP process. Many large corporations maintain fairly elaborate networks of line managers, technical specialists, and human resource specialists, who monitor large numbers of publications, broadcast media, futurist think tanks, and conferences for relevant data. Periodically, these data are assembled and trend reports are prepared and made available to those responsible for HRP. These reports usually include a summary of the major environmental trends and their implications for human resource management. Exhibit 4.9 shows an example of an environmental scan and its use at the First Chicago Corporation.

Of the various areas monitored through external scanning, the labor market is most directly relevant to staffing planning. For a start-up organization in genetic engineering, for example, the future availability of geneticists, biologists, and other types of scientists and engineers is an important strategic contingency. If tight labor markets for these skills are expected, the organization must plan to put considerable time and money into attracting and retaining the needed talent (for example, by raising salaries or offering day care programs) or into developing alternative means of accomplishing its key research and development work (for instance, by using technicians wherever possible, thus reducing the need for scientists and engineers).

Clearly, then, an organization's grasp of impending developments in the outside world is very helpful to human resource planners. It puts them in an excellent position to influence the nature of business plans (and thus the nature of future human resource requirements) and to ensure that planned HR activities are both realistic and supportive of these business plans.

Internal Scanning

Also important is a firm grasp of an organization's internal environment. Thus, planners must be out and about in their organizations, taking advantage of opportunities to learn what is going on. Informal discussions with key managers can help, as can employee attitude surveys, special surveys, and the monitoring of key indices such as employee performance, absenteeism, turnover, and accident rates. Of special interest is the identification of nagging personnel problems, as well as prevailing managerial attitudes concerning human resources.

Nagging personnel problems refer to recurring difficulties that threaten to interfere with the attainment of future business plans or other important organizational goals. High turnover in a sales organization, for example, is likely to threaten the viability of a business plan that calls for increased sales quotas or the rapid introduction of several new products.

The values and attitudes of managers, especially top managers, toward human resources are also important to HRP. Trouble brews when these are inconsistent with the organization's business plans. For example, a mid-sized accounting firm may have formulated a business plan calling for very rapid growth through aggressive marketing and selected acquisitions of smaller firms, but existing management talent

EXHIBIT 4.9   Example of an Environmental Scan and Its Use

First Chicago's HR Strategic Diagnostic

Pablo Picasso was known for painting in haptic style—that is, he painted the way people feel. If his portrait was one of a person with an injured finger, the finger would be painted disproportionately large to indicate pain.

According to Jim Alef, senior vice president and head of human resources at First Chicago Corporation, HR professionals often work in much the same fashion by giving their individual challenges a disproportionately large share of attention. The human resources strategic diagnostic is First Chicago's way of overcoming such tunnel vision and objectively prioritizing all issues related to HR management.

"As I looked at our HR activity, I saw a lot of well-intentioned people working on recommendations related to individual issues," he explains. "What I didn't see was an attempt to pull those recommendations together."

In 1989, under Alef's direction, the HR staff worked in concert to identify and prioritize all its HR issues. Extensive input was sought from other departments including corporate strategy, economics, government and legal affairs and the line areas. The resulting diagnostic was the company's first comprehensive, objective list of HR challenges.

Alef's staff uses the diagnostic to anticipate upcoming challenges and take early, decisive action on HR issues. What staff members may intuitively think are issues, the diagnostic confirms. By making decisions based on fact, not suspicion, the bank not only avoids potential problems, it experiences greater program success. Specifically, the document:

(1) Identifies and examines the major external and internal forces that have or will have implications for the management of First Chicago's human resources

(2) Establishes a sound data base that describes First Chicago's total work force as well as the work force composition of each major line of business

(3) Promotes possible courses of action for upcoming human resources challenges

(4) Crafts a time-phased agenda that reflects opportunities to put First Chicago ahead of those challenges

(5) Helps determine an appropriate organizational structure for the HR department, as well as corresponding staff and budget requirements.

The diagnostic, which is constantly being updated, measures the company's corporate business objectives against political, educational, demographic, economic, judicial and social issues. This "living document" is used as a strategic HR roadmap, allowing HR professionals to act on changing circumstances, rather than react to them.

Among the HR programs developed as a result of information revealed in the diagnostic are enhanced basic skills training efforts, a revised pensioner health care program, and stepped-up recruitment for entry-level, non-exempt positions.

"Upon compiling the diagnostic," says Alef, "we learned there are a vast number of things going on in this world that are HR-related, and, if we could do human resources right, what a tremendous competitive advantage we would have."

Source: S. Caudran, "Strategic HR at First Chicago," *Personnel Journal*, 1991, pp. 50–56.

may be inadequate to the task of operating a larger, more complex organization. Moreover, there may be a prevailing attitude among the top management against investing much money in management development and against bringing in talent from outside the firm. This attitude conflicts with the business plan, requiring a change in either the business plan or attitudes.

Reconciliation and Gaps

The reconciliation and gap determination process is best examined by means of an example. Exhibit 4.10 presents intact the example in Exhibit 4.3. Attention is now directed to the reconciliation and gaps column. It represents the results of bringing together requirements and availability forecasts with the results of external and internal environmental scanning. Gap figures must be decided upon and entered into the column, and the likely reasons for the gaps need to be identified.

Consider first job category/level A1. A relatively large shortage is projected, due to a mild expansion in requirements coupled with a substantial drop in availabilities. This drop is not due to an excessive exit rate, but to losses through promotions and job transfers (refer back to the availability forecasts in Exhibits 4.6 and 4.8).

For A2, decreased requirements coupled with increased availabilities lead to a projected surplus. Clearly, changes in current staffing policies and procedures will have to be made in order to stem the availability tide, such as a slowdown in the promotion rate into A2 from A1 or an acceleration in the exit rate, through an early retirement program.

Turning to B1, note that a huge shortage is forecast. This is due to a major surge in requirements and a substantial reduction in availabilities. To meet the shortage, the organization could increase the transfer of employees from A1. While this would worsen the already projected shortage in A1, it might be cost-effective to do this and would beef up the external staffing for A1 to cover the exacerbated shortage. Alternatively, a massive external staffing program could be developed and undertaken for B1 alone. Or, a combination of internal transfers and external staffing for both A1 and B1 could be attempted. To the extent that external staffing becomes a candidate for consideration, this will naturally spill over into other HR activities, such as establishing starting pay levels for A1 and B1.

Finally, for B2 there is a small projected shortage. This gap is so small, however, that for all practical purposes it can be ignored. The HRP process is too imprecise to warrant concern over such small gap figures.

In short, the reconciliation and gap phase of HRP involves coming to grips with projected gaps and likely reasons for them. Quite naturally, thoughts about future implications begin to creep into the process.[11] Even in the simple example shown, it can be seen that considerable action will have to be contemplated and undertaken in order to respond to the forecasting results for the organizational unit. That will

EXHIBIT 4.10   Operational Format and Example for Human Resource Planning (HRP)

Organizational Unit: Sales and Customer Service

Job Category and Level	Current Workforce	Forecast for Workforce— One Year		Reconciliation and Gaps	Action Planning
		Requirements	Availabilities		
A1 (Sales)	100	110	71	−39 (shortage)	Staffing activities Recruitment
A2 (Sales manager)	20	15	22	+7 (surplus)	Selection Employment
B1 (Customer service representative)	200	250	140	−110 (shortage)	Other HR activities Compensation
B2 (Customer service manager)	15	25	22	−3 (shortage)	Training & development
	335	400	255	−145 (shortage)	

involve mixtures of external and internal staffing, with compensation as another likely HR ingredient. It is through action planning that these possibilities become real.

Action Planning

Action planning involves four basic sequential steps:[12]

1. Set objectives.
2. Generate alternative activities.
3. Assess alternative activities.
4. Choose alternative activities.

Movement through these steps is a logical outgrowth of HRP and is greatly enhanced by its occurrence. Indeed, without HRP the organization rarely has the luxury of doing action planning. Instead, reaction becomes the mode of operation, leading to crash or crisis activities and programs.

These general statements apply to virtually all HR activities that are in any way dependent upon the existence of employment gaps and the need to close them. The focus in this chapter is on staffing planning as a specific form of action planning.

STAFFING PLANNING

The four stages of action planning translate directly into a general staffing planning process. After discussing this general process, staffing planning is divided into planning for the core and the flexible workforces.

Staffing Planning Process

Staffing Objectives

Staffing objectives are derived from identified gaps between requirements and availabilities. As such, they involve objectives responding to both shortages and surpluses. They may require the establishment of quantitative and qualitative targets.

Quantitative targets should be expressed in head count or FTE form for each job category/level and will be very close in magnitude to the identified gaps. Indeed, to the extent that the organization believes in the gaps as forecast, the objectives will be identical to the gap figures. A forecast shortage of $n = 39$ employees in A1, for example, should be transformed into a staffing objective of $n = 39$ accessions (or something close to it) to be achieved by the end of the forecasting time interval. Exhibit 4.11 provides an illustration of these points regarding quantitative staffing objectives.

Qualitative staffing objectives refer to the types or qualities of people, usually in KSAO-type terms. For external staffing objectives, these may be stated in terms of averages, such as average education level for new hires and average scores on ability tests. Internal staffing objectives of a qualitative nature may also be established. These may reflect desired KSAOs in terms of seniority, performance appraisal record over a period of years, types of on- and off-the-job training, and so forth.

Qualitative (KSAO) staffing concerns are usually not a part of the previously described forecast process. Gaps are thus not likely to be identified or expressed in qualitative terms. Hence, establishment of qualitative staffing objectives involves considerable judgment on the part of the organization. Ideally, the organization will have conducted job analysis and have available formal job specifications that it can use to guide it in establishing qualitative objectives.

Generating Alternative Staffing Activities

With quantitative and, possibly, qualitative objectives established, it is necessary to begin identifying possible ways of achieving them. This requires an identification of the fullest possible range of alternative activities, which, if pursued, might lead to achievement of the objectives. At the beginning stages of generating alternatives, it is wise not to prematurely close the door on any alternatives. Exhibit 4.12 provides an excellent list of the full range of options available for initial consideration.

Assessing and Choosing Alternatives

As should be apparent, there is a veritable smorgasbord of alternative staffing activities available to address staffing gaps. Each of these alternatives needs to be

---

EXHIBIT 4.11   Setting Numerical Staffing Objectives

Job Category and Level	Gap	Objectives					Total
		New Hires	Promotions	Transfers	Demotions	Exits	
A1	−39						+39
A2	+7	For each cell, enter a positive number for head count					−7
B1	−110	additions and a negative number for head count					+110
B2	−3	subtractions.					+3
Total							

Note: Assumes objective is to close each gap exactly.

EXHIBIT 4.12   Staffing Alternatives to Deal with Employee Shortages and Surpluses

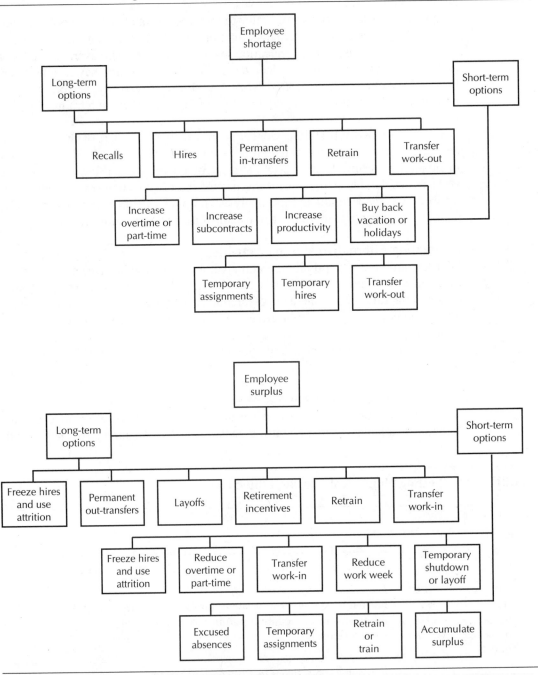

Source: Compliments of Dan Ward, GTE Corporation.

assessed systematically in order to help decision makers choose from among the alternatives.

The goal of such assessment is to identify one or more preferred activities. A preferred activity is one offering the highest likelihood of attaining the staffing objective, within the time limit established, at the least cost or tolerable cost, and with the fewest negative side effects. There are no standard or agreed upon programs or formats for conducting these assessments. Thus, the organization will need to develop its own internal mechanisms for assessment. Whatever overall mechanism is developed, it should ensure that two things occur. First, a common set of assessment criteria (e.g., time for completion, cost, probability of success) should be identified and agreed upon. Second, each alternative should be assessed according to each of these criteria. In this way, all alternatives will receive equal treatment, and tendencies to jump at an initial alternative will be minimized.

Responsibility for scrutinizing the proposed package of staffing alternatives and making final decisions rests with top management. Inconsistencies between positions and overlaps among them must be ferreted out, and the alternatives must be realistically placed within the context of the emerging business and organizational plans. The alternatives must be seen as viable by top management in terms of the budget and people likely to be available to implement them.

Top management's decisions form the basis of staffing planning. It is derived from a systematic process of identifying employment gaps, establishing staffing objectives to address the gaps, generating alternative programs for achieving the objectives, assessing each of these programs according to a set of common criteria, and then presenting the information (and usually recommendations) to top management for final decision making. Once final decisions have been made, the chosen staffing plans must be implemented.

A fundamental alternative that organizations are confronting increasingly is that of using core or flexible workforces. Each of these alternatives is discussed below regarding their advantages and disadvantages, as well as key factors involved in planning for their actual usage.

Core Workforce

Planning for the core workforce should begin by reviewing its specific advantages and disadvantages. This will serve as a final check on the wisdom of the strategic decision made about use of the core workforce.

The key advantage of the core workforce is that it provides stability, continuity, and predictability to the organization. The organization can "count on" the core workforce and build its strategic plans on top of it. Moreover, the permanence of the employer and employee commitment to each other fosters cohesion and a sense of shared purpose toward the organization's mission. Also, the use of legally-designated employees provides the organization the right to direct and control its core workforce, both in terms of results desired and methods used to obtain those results.

A key disadvantage of the core workforce is that the permanence of commitment to it "locks in" the organization to its core workforce, with a potential loss of staffing flexibility and adaptability. Additionally, the core workforce is usually more expensive (higher wages, salaries, and benefits) than the flexible workforce, and these costs are quite fixed relative to the labor cost variability possible with the flexible workforce. Finally, by having an employer-employee relationship for the core workforce, the organization assumes the numerous legal obligations associated with it (see Chapter 3).

If a review of the specific advantages and disadvantages confirms the strategic choice regarding core workforce usage, specific staffing planning for its use must begin. This will involve substantial planning of recruitment, selection, and employment activities; these topics are covered in subsequent chapters. However, two overarching issues need to be addressed very early on because of their impact on all of these specific staffing plans. The issues are staffing philosophy and staffing flows.

Staffing Philosophy

In conjunction with the staffing planning process, the organization's staffing philosophy should be reviewed. Results of this review help shape the direction and character of the specific staffing systems implemented. The review should focus on the following issues: internal versus external staffing, EEO/AA practices, and applicant reactions.

The relative importance to the organization of external or internal staffing is a critical matter because it so greatly shapes the nature of the staffing system, as well as sends signals to applicants and employees alike about the organization as an employer. For example, at the extreme, an exclusively external focus will require the organization to devote considerable resources to looking outward in order to identify applicant pools to activate and process. For potential applicants, this external focus will likely cause them to perceive any job as fair game, and will enhance the external reputation of the organization as a desirable place to seek employment at any level. Current employees, however, will perceive a lack of internal mobility possibilities, and this may cause such reactions as high turnover and negative feelings toward new external hires. Exhibit 4.13 highlights the advantages and disadvantages of external and internal staffing.

In terms of EEO/AA, the organization must be sure to consider, or develop, a sense of importance attached to being an EEO/AA-conscious employer, and the commitment it is willing to make in incorporating EEO/AA elements into all phases of the staffing system. Attitudes toward EEO/AA can range all the way from outright hostility and disregard, to benign neglect, to aggressive commitment and support. As should be obvious, the stance that the organization adopts will

EXHIBIT 4.13   Staffing Philosophy: Internal versus External Staffing

	Advantages	Disadvantages
Internal	• Positive employee reactions to promotion from within • Quick method to identify job applicants • Less expensive • Little orientation time required	• No new KSAOs into the organization • May perpetuate current underrepresentation of minorities and women • Small labor market to recruit from • Employees may require more training time
External	• Brings employees in with new KSAOs • Larger number of minorities and women to draw upon • Large labor market to draw from • Employees may require less training time	• Negative reaction by internal applicants • Time consuming to identify applicants • Expensive to search external labor market • New employees require more orientation time

have major effects on its operational staffing system, as well as on job applicants and employees.

As a final point about staffing philosophy, planners must continue to bear in mind that staffing is an interaction involving both the organization and job applicants as participants.[13] Just as organizations recruit and select applicants, so, too, do applicants recruit and select organizations (and job offers). Through their job search strategies and activities, applicants exert major influence on their own staffing destinies. Once the applicant has decided to opt into the organization's staffing process, the applicant is confronted with numerous decisions about whether to continue on in the staffing process or withdraw from further consideration. This process of self-selection is inherent to any staffing system. During staffing planning, those within the organization must constantly consider how the applicant will react to the staffing system and its components, and whether they want to encourage or discourage applicant self-selection.

Staffing Flows

Staffing an organization requires not only decisions about discrete staffing system characteristics (for example, which recruitment sources to use and what type of interviews to conduct), but also decisions about the overall flow of events that comprise a staffing system. This flow may be described in general terms or in specific terms. Organizations may use flowcharts to plan and designate the precise nature of the staffing system.

There are several discrete, but sequential, phases that comprise a general staffing flow—a flow that involves an applicant reduction process and consists of the following:

1. Eligible labor force—At the national level, this includes the employed, the unemployed, discouraged workers, new labor force entrants, and labor force reentrants. Eligible labor forces also exist at the level of state, region, county, SMSA (standard metropolitan statistical area), and so forth.

2. Potential applicant population—These are individuals from the eligible labor force with at least the minimum qualifications (KSAOs) for the job, as well as interest and availability for the job.

3. Applicants—These are the individuals who formally become identified as job applicants, by a process of organization and/or self identification.

4. Candidates—These are the applicants who survive the initial screening and remain interested in the organization.

5. Finalists—These are the candidates who survive all but the final selection activities.

6. Offer receiver—This is the finalist(s) who receives the offer of a job.

7. New hire(s)—The offer receiver who accepts the offer and formally begins the employment relationship.

This general staffing flow has external staffing activities as its apparent referent. However, it also may be used to describe the internal staffing process entailed in promotion and transfer systems. The eligible labor force is the organization's total workforce, comprised of those employed, otherwise hired (e.g., temporary workers), and on layoff. The potential applicant population consists of those eligible individuals who also have the required KSAOs, including seniority and experience minimums. Applicants are those individuals who formally apply for the vacancy (such as through a job posting system) or are identified as candidates for the position by the organization (such as through succession planning and replacement charts). Candidates are those who survive initial screening. Finalists are those who remain in contention for the post after organization and self-selection. The offer receiver is the person offered the promotion or the transfer. The new hire is the person who actually assumes the new position and becomes a job incumbent.

General staffing flow operations may be expanded to take into account all the specific methods, techniques, and decision points that operationally define a staffing system. Moreover, these flows can be (and should be) visualized and charted from both organizational and applicant viewpoints. Developing such flowcharts represents the final stage of staffing planning.

Organization Staffing Flowchart   An example of a staffing flowchart from an organization's perspective is shown in Exhibit 4.14. It is a flowchart that depicts the staffing system of a medium-sized (n = 580 employees) high-tech printing and lithography company. It shows the actual flow of staffing activities, and both organization and applicant decision points, from the time a vacancy occurs until the time it is filled with a new hire.

A detailed inspection of the chart reveals the following sorts of information about the company's staffing system:

1. It is a generic system used for both entry-level and higher-level jobs.
2. For higher-level jobs, vacancies are first posted internally (thus showing a recruitment philosophy emphasizing a commitment to promotion from within). Entry-level jobs are filled externally.
3. External recruitment sources (colleges, newspaper ads, employment agencies) are used only if the current applicant file yields no qualified applicants.
4. Initial assessments are made using biographical information (application blanks, resumes), and results of these assessments determine who will be interviewed.
5. Substantive assessments are made through the interview(s) conducted by the HR manager and the hiring supervisor, and results of these assessments determine who receives the job offer.
6. The applicant may counteroffer, and acceptance by the applicant of the final offer is conditional upon passing drug/alcohol and physical tests.
7. The new hire undergoes a six-month probationary employment period before becoming a so-called permanent employee.

Applicant Staffing Flowchart   It is useful for an organization also to chart the staffing flow from the viewpoint of the job applicant. This helps the organization better understand what experiences their staffing system creates for the applicant, as well as potential applicant reactions to those experiences.

EXHIBIT 4.14   Staffing Flowchart for Medium-Sized Printing Company: Company Perspective

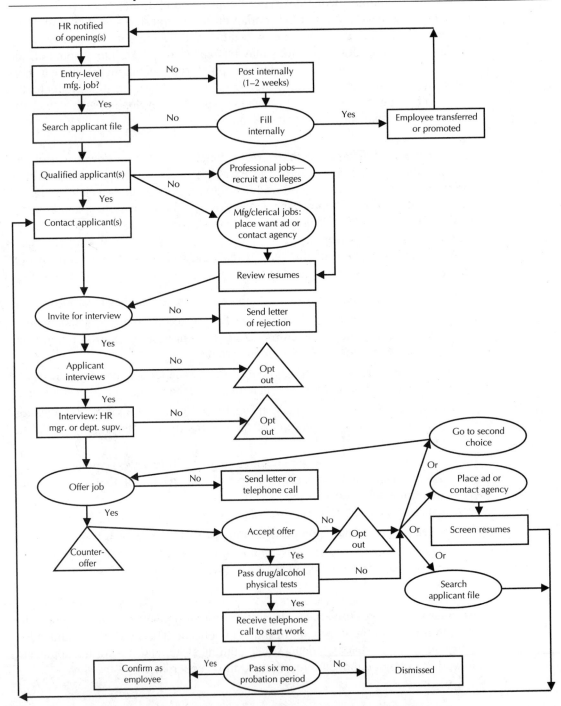

Using the preceding example of a printing and lithography company, and drawing upon its organizational staffing flowchart, the company's applicant staffing flowchart is developed as in Exhibit 4.15. Inspection of that flowchart reveals that the organization does not actively seek out external applicants for entry-level jobs; it waits for applicants to come to it. For higher-level jobs, resume submission in response to knowledge of vacancies gained through the internal posting or external recruitment sources is used by applicants. There are several identifiable decision points at which the applicant may self-select out of the staffing process. Occasionally, and outside the formal staffing process (as shown by the dotted line), the applicant may receive a plant tour. For the applicant, this tour may be very useful for learning more about both job requirements and rewards. If the applicant receives and accepts an offer, he or she may not be told a specific starting date, but must await a phone call to report to work as a new hire. Finally, the new hire knows that the first six months of employment are probationary, and that failure to pass the probationary period will result in dismissal.

Flexible Workforce

Planning for the flexible workforce, as for the core workforce, should begin with a review of its advantages and disadvantages.[14] The key advantage is the staffing flexibility and adaptability for adjusting staffing levels quickly in response to changing conditions, such as technological and consumer demand changes. Accompanying this flexibility is sometimes lower labor costs, and certainly more variable labor costs, relative to the core workforce. Also, since flexible workers are usually not legally considered employees of the organization, it is relieved of the legal obligations associated with an employer-employee relationship. Finally, the organization is usually relieved of the need to do its own recruitment and selection since these are done for it by the organization (e.g., temporary help agency, independent contractor) supplying the flexible workforce to it.

The flexibility and cost advantages must be weighed against several potential disadvantages. Most important is the legal loss of control over flexible workers because they are not employees of the organization. Thus, while the organization can assign flexible workers to jobs (the person/job match), it cannot supervise and direct the performance of these workers or their interactions with core workers except in a very limited sense. Frictions between flexible and core workers may also arise. Core workers, for example, may feel that flexible workers lack knowledge and experience, are just "putting in time," receive the easy job assignments, and do not act like committed "team players." Finally, flexible workers may lack familiarity with equipment, policies, procedures, and important customers; such deficiencies may be compounded by a lack of training in specific job requirements.

If the review of advantages and disadvantages of flexible workers confirms the strategic choice to use them in staffing, plans must be developed for the organi-

EXHIBIT 4.15 **Staffing Flowchart for Medium-Sized Printing Company: Applicant Perspective**

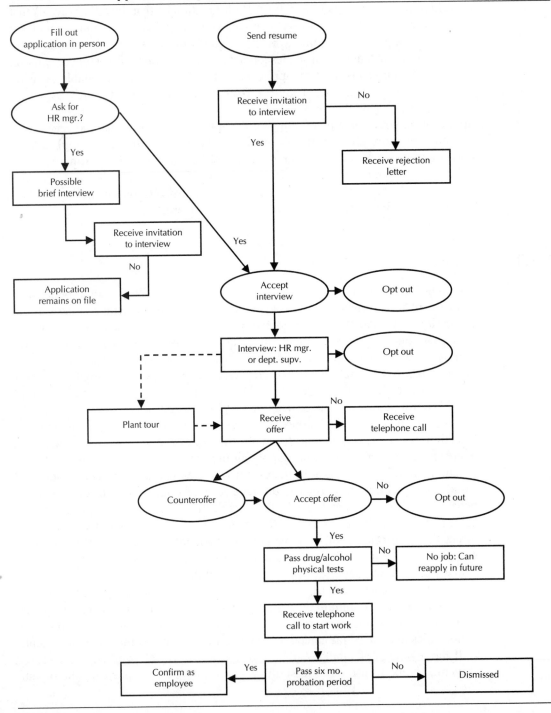

zation units and jobs in which they will be used, and for how they will be acquired. Acquisition plans normally involve the use of temporary help agencies and independent contractors, both of which perform the traditional staffing activities for the organization. Hence, in contrast to the substantial and sustained staff planning that must occur for the core workforce, planning for the flexible workforce is primarily a matter of becoming knowledgeable about these potential sources and "lining them up" in advance of when they are actually needed.

Temporary Help Agencies

Recall that temporary help agencies are the legal employers of the workers being supplied, though there may also be matters of coemployment that may arise. Hence, the agency conducts recruitment, selection, training, compensation, performance appraisal, and retention activities for the flexible workers. The agency also is responsible for their on-site supervision and management, as well as all payrolling and the payment of legally required insurance premiums. For such services the agency charges the organization a general fee for its labor costs (wages and benefits) plus a "markup" percentage of labor costs (usually 40–50%) to cover these services costs plus provide a profit. There may be additional charges for specially provided services such as extra testing or background checks, or skill training. Sometimes temporary workers are hired away from the agency (with its permission) by the organization to become permanent employees in the core workforce, a practice known as "temp-to-perm." For larger clients the agency may provide an on-site manager to help the organization plan out its specific staffing needs, supervise and appraise the performance of the temporary workers, handle discipline and complaints, and facilitate agency-organization relations. With such additional staffing services the agency functions increasingly like a staffing partner, rather than just a staffing supplier.[15]

Planning for use of temporary help agencies requires advance planning, rather than a panicky phone call to an agency at the moment of staffing need. In addition to becoming aware of agencies that might be accessed, it is wise to become very familiar with their characteristics and services. Shown in Exhibit 4.16 are descriptions of the various factors and issues to become knowledgeable about for any agency.

When an agency is actually chosen for use, a formal written agreement should be entered into by both parties. That agreement should cover such matters as specific services to be provided, costs, steps to ensure that the flexible workers are employees of the agency (such as having an on-site manager for them), and the process for terminating the agency-organization relationship. It is best to have the agreement prepared/reviewed by legal counsel.

Occasionally the organization may decide to establish its own in-house temporary agency. When this is done, the employees of the agency may even be employees of the organization. Managers thus have readily available flexible work-

---

EXHIBIT 4.16 Factors to Consider When Choosing a Temporary Help Agency

Factor	Issues
Agency and Its Reputation	How long in business; location; references from clients available.
Types of Workers Provided	What occupation and KASO levels; how many available.
Planning and Leadtime	Does agency help client plan staffing levels and needs; how quickly can workers to provided.
Services Provided	
Recruitment	What methods are used; how targeted and truthful is recruitment process.
Selection	What selection techniques are used to assess KSAOs.
Training	What types of training, if any, provided before workers placed with client.
Wages and Benefits	How are wages determined; what benefits are provided.
Orientation	How does the agency prepare workers for assignment with client; does agency have an employee handbook for its workers.
Supervision	How does agency supervise its workers on site of client; does agency provide on-site manager.
Temp-to-Perm	Does agency allow client to hire its temporary workers as permanent employees.
Client Satisfaction	How does agency attempt to gauge client satisfaction with services, workers, costs.
Worker Effectiveness	
Punctuality and Attendance	Does the agency monitor these; what is their record with previous clients.
Job Performance	Is it evaluated; how are the results used.
Retention	How long do workers remain on an assignment voluntarily; how are workers discharged by the agency.
Cost	
Markup	What is the % over base wage charged to client (often it is 50% to cover benefits, overhead, profit margin).
For Special Services	What services cost extra beyond the markup (e.g., temp-to-perm), and what are those costs.

ers to whom they can turn, without having to go through all the planning steps mentioned above.

At AT&T, for example, both white collar and blue collar temporary agencies (pools) have been established. Employees in both agencies are full-time employees of AT&T, receiving full pay and benefits. The white collar agency, named Resource Link, has more than five hunderd managerial, professional, and technical employees available for assignment throughout AT&Ts twenty-eight business units. These employees are carefully recruited internally, often from the ranks of employees who have been displaced during a reorganization. The employees are also carefully screened in terms of specific skills, adaptability, flexibility, and customer focus. Their assignments usually last between three and eighteen months. The blue collar agency, named the Skills Match Center Administrative Intern Program, is run for general secretaries, advanced software specialists, administrative assistants, and word processors. Employees in these jobs are also carefully recruited and screened.[16]

Independent Contractors

An independent contractor (IC) provides specific task and project assistance to the organization, such as maintenance, bookkeeping, and advertising. The IC can be a single individual (self-employed, freelancer) or an employer with its own employees. Neither the IC nor its employees are intended to be employees of the organization utilizing their services, and care should be taken to ensure that the IC is not treated as an employee (see Chapter 3).[17]

As with temporary help agencies, the organization must take the initiative to identify and "check out" ICs for possible use in advance of when they are actually needed. It is desirable to solicit and examine references from past or current clients of the IC. Also, as much as possible the organization should seek to determine how the IC staffs, trains, and compensates its employees. This could occur during a preliminary, get-together meeting with the IC. In these ways, the organization will have cultivated and screened ICs prior to when they are actually needed.

It is recommended that the IC and the organization prepare and enter into a written agreement between them. In general, the agreement should clarify the nature and scope of the project and contain language that reinforces the intent to have the IC function as such, rather than as an employee. For example, the agreement should refer to the parties as "firm" and "contractor," describe the specific work to be completed, specify that payment will be for completion of the project (rather than time worked), make the IC responsible for providing all equipment and supplies, exclude the IC from any of the organization's benefits, and ensure that the IC is responsible for paying all legally required taxes. Preparation of such an agreement might well require the assistance of legal counsel.

LEGAL ISSUES

The major legal issue in HR and staffing planning is that of affirmative action plans and programs (AAPs). AAPs originate from many different sources—voluntary employer efforts, court-imposed remedies for discriminatory practices, conciliation or consent agreement, and requirements as a federal contractor. Regardless of source, all AAPs seek to rectify the effects of past employment discrimination by increasing the representation of certain groups (minorities, women, disabled) in the organization's workforce. This is to be achieved through establishing, and actively pursuing, hiring and promotion goals, and adhering to timetables for achieving those goals.

This section describes the general content of AAPs, discusses the affirmative action requirements for federal contractors under Revised Order No. 4, and provides some general indications as to the legality of AAPs. Also, a brief presentation is made of so-called diversity programs, which can augment, and potentially increase, the effectiveness of AAPs.

Affirmative Action Plans (AAPs)

AAPs are organization-specific plans and thus their content varies across organizations. Nonetheless, all AAPs share three general components, namely utilization analysis, staffing goals and timetables, and action plans.[18]

An example of a partial AAP with these three general components is shown in Exhibit 4.17. The example draws from the general HR planning example in Exhibits 4.2 and 4.3. The AAP shown is for only one job category (sales) and for only one group (women).

Inspection of the exhibit reveals that the organization has a current sales force of $n = 100$, of whom $n = 10$ (10%) are women. A utilization analysis with accompanying stock statistics (see Chapter 3) shows that the current percentage of female salespeople (10%) is less than their estimated availability (20%), based on consideration of eight availability factors. A comparison of these two percentages suggests that there is underutilization of women in the sales job category.

Based on the identified underutilization, the organization sets an affirmative action goal of 20% utilization and sets an ambitious timetable of one year to achieve that goal. Action plans are now developed for achieving this goal. These involve staffing plans and other HR plans.

In terms of staffing plans, the organization first considers the results of its general HR forecast for the next year, which had predicted a shortage of 39 salespeople. New hires may be obtained from both external and internal (job transfer) sources, consistent with past staffing practices. Based on its affirmative action goal and timetable, the organization sets a staffing target of $n = 24$ men and $n = 15$ women, for a total of $n = 39$ new salespeople. If, in fact, these targets are met,

EXHIBIT 4.17   Example of Affirmative Action Plan (AAP): Essential Components

Job Category: Sales
Affirmative Action Plan: Women

Current Workforce			Availability* (8 factors)		Utilization Analysis — Underutilization (?)	Goals and Timetables		Forecast of Gap	External Staffing		Action Plan (one year) — Other Plans
Total	%M	%F	%M	%F		Goal	Timetable		M	F	
100	90	10	80	20	Yes	%F 20	%F 1 year	−39 (shortage)	24	15	accelerated training program, day care program

* Availability determined on the basis of the eight factors contained in Revised Order No. 4. It includes both internal (current employees) and external (labor force) factors.

the organization will come close to its affirmative action goal of 20% women in the sales job category (the $n = 15$ new saleswomen plus whatever number of the $n = 10$ current saleswomen who remain in the job category, out of the total of $n = 112$ that were forecast in Exhibit 4.3).

Armed with this numerical staffing target, the organization can now develop specific plans for pursuing it. This involves development of detailed staffing plans, as discussed earlier in this chapter. It also involves consideration of other action plans to support the staffing plan. As shown in Exhibit 4.17, the development of an accelerated training program and the development of a child care program have been identified as two possible support plans.

This example illustrates the basics of an affirmative action plan (utilization analysis, staffing goals and timetables, and action plans). It is, however, a very simplified version of an AAP. It involves only one job category, one group (women), and a one-year time frame. Specifics of the utilization analysis, and action plans, are ignored. AAPs are, in reality, much more complex than this example suggests. They involve all job categories, multiple underrepresented groups (women, minorities, disabled), multiple-year time frames, internal administration and enforcement mechanisms, and very detailed staffing plans. A consideration of the actual AAP requirements for federal contractors under Revised Order No. 4 shows the complexities involved in AAPs.

Revised Order No. 4

Revised Order No. 4 (Appendix B) spells out in detail the requirements a federal contractor must adhere to as it develops, implements, and administers an AAP. Three basic features of the order should be emphasized—its broad scope, utilization analysis requirements, and judgment of contractor compliance status.

Scope   AAPs are very broad in scope under the order, touching on virtually all HR policies and practices of the organization. This breadth comes from the order's statement regarding "required ingredients of affirmative action programs." The order specifically requires

1. "development or reaffirmation of the contractor's equal employment policy in all personnel actions
2. formal internal and external dissemination of the contractor's policy
3. establishment of responsibilities for implementation of the contractor's affirmative action program
4. identification of problem areas (deficiencies) by organizational units and job classifications
5. establishment of goals and objectives by organizational units and job classifications, including timetables for completion

6. development and execution of action-oriented programs designed to eliminate problems and further designed to attain established goals and timetables

7. design and implementation of internal audit and reporting systems to measure effectiveness of the total program

8. compliance of personnel policies and practices with the Sex Discrimination Guidelines (41 CFR Part 60–20)

9. active support of local and national community action programs and community service programs designed to improve the employment opportunities of minorities and women

10. consideration of minorities and women not currently in the work force having requisite skills who can be recruited through affirmative action measures".

The content of Revised Order No. 4 is organized around these "required ingredients," all of which are amplified in detail in the order. A careful reading of these requirements in their entirety will show the breadth of their scope. To help cope with the sheer magnitude of the requirements, the organization should consult the EEO/AA information sources discussed in Chapter 3. Of particular usefulness are examples and samples of full-blown AAPs.[19]

Utilization Analysis Utilization analysis is critical in an AAP because through it are derived the numerical standards (availability percentages for women and minorities) against which the representativeness of the organization's workforce is to be judged. In Exhibit 4.17, for example, an availability percentage of 20% for women in the sales job category is shown. It is against this figure that the current percentage of women in the job category (10%) is compared in order to help determine if there is underutilization of women.

Where do availability statistics come from? The example in Exhibit 4.17 indicates that the number is determined on the basis of the eight factors contained in Revised Order No. 4. Those factors for women (there are also very similar ones for minorities) are as follows:

1. "the size of the female unemployment force in the labor area surrounding the facility

2. the percentage of the female work force as compared with the total work force in the immediate labor area

3. the general availability of women having the requisite skills in the immediate labor area

4. the availability of women having requisite skills in an area in which the contractor can reasonably recruit

5. the availability of women seeking employment in the labor or recruitment area of the contractor

6. the availability of promotable and transferable female employees within the contractor's organization

7. the existence of training institutions capable of training persons in the requisite skills

8. the degree of training which the contractor is reasonably able to undertake as a means of making all job classes available to women''.

These eight factors require the contractor to take many different considerations into account in determining availability statistics. These include requisite skills, general applicant availability, geographic recruitment area, training possibilities, and internal employees. Unfortunately, hard data for these factors are often difficult to come by; federal and state labor force statistics are of only limited usefulness. Hence, availability figures such as shown in Exhibit 4.17 should be treated as estimates, rather than precise indicators. Also, the organization should consult sources of assistance on the gathering and interpretation of availability statistics.[20]

Compliance Status   How is an organization's compliance with the order to be judged? Is failure to achieve affirmative action goals grounds for concluding there is noncompliance? The order makes clear that lack of goal attainment, by itself, does not constitute noncompliance. As long as the contractor sets reasonable, attainable goals and timetables, and then makes a good faith effort to achieve them, the contractor is meeting the requirements of the order. Specifically:

> The goals and timetables developed by the contractor should be attainable in terms of the contractor's analysis of his deficiencies and his entire affirmative action program. No contractor's compliance status shall be judged alone by whether or not he reaches his goals and meets his timetables. Rather, each contractor's compliance posture shall be reviewed and determined by reviewing the contents of his program, the extent of his adherence to the program, and his good faith efforts to make his program work toward the realization of the program's goals within the timetables set for completion.

The above statements make clear that AAPs under the order are not hiring quota ones.

Legality of AAPs

AAPs have been controversial since their inception, and there have been many challenges to their legality. Questions of legality are difficult to answer or provide guidance on because of complexities in the interpretations of the relevant laws, as well as complexities in the nature of AAPs themselves as adopted by organizations. Despite these problems, it is possible to provide several conclusions and recommendations regarding AAPs.

AAPs in general are legal in the eyes of the Supreme Court. However, to be acceptable, an AAP should be based on the following guidelines:[21]

1. The plan should have as its purpose the remedying of specific and identifiable effects of past discrimination.

2. There should be definite underutilization of women and/or minorities currently in the organization.

3. As regards nonminority and male employees, the plan should not unnecessarily interfere with their job interests and rights, not result in their discharge and replacement with minority or women employees, and not create an absolute bar to their promotion.

4. The plan should be temporary, and eliminated once affirmative action goals have been achieved (this occurred, for example, to the AAP for police officers in the city of Detroit).[22]

5. All candidates for positions should be qualified for those positions.

6. The plan should include organizational enforcement mechanisms, as well as a grievance procedure.

A recent Supreme Court ruling on the constitutionality (Fifth Amendment) of affirmative action programs by the federal government suggests that even more strict guidelines than those above may be necessary. Insofar as federal programs are concerned, racial preferences are subject to strict constitutional scrutiny. They may be used only when there has been specific evidence of identified discrimination, the remedy has been narrowly tailored to only the identified discrimination, only those who have suffered discrimination may benefit from the remedy, and other individuals will not carry an undue burden, such as job displacement, from the remedy.

This decision has touched off substantial debate over affirmative action and its role as a legitimate tool for addressing discrimination. Much of the debate centers around questions of whether affirmative action involves quota hiring and promotion, giving rise to reverse discrimination. Possible outcomes of the debate range from no change in present laws and practices all the way to amending the Civil Rights Act to prohibit affirmative action and preferential treatment and to scrapping EO 11246 and Revised Order No. 4 for federal contractors.[23]

AAPs are not separate staffing systems, but rather integral parts of general staffing systems. As such, AAPs should be incorporated into more general HR and staffing planning. In this way, there is a single, unified staffing system to serve both broad organizational goals and more specific affirmative action ones.

Diversity Programs

Staffing focuses on the initial acquisition of people and creation of the initial person/job match. AAPs likewise have this focus. Once the initial match has occurred, however, the organization must be concerned about employee adaptation to the job and maintenance of the employment relationship over time. Without such a concern, the effectiveness of AAPs can be severely undercut. In particular, satisfaction and retention problems for those acquired through the AAP can arise, and these problems in turn will thwart any meaningful, permanent change in the race/sex composition of the organization's workforce.

Recently, organizations have begun experimenting with diversity programs. These programs arise out of a recognition that the labor force, and thus the organization's workforce, is becoming more demographically diverse. The focus of diversity programs is on the assimilation and adaptation of a diverse workforce once it has been acquired. Diversity programs thus pick up where affirmative action programs leave off, and indeed may be viewed as a logical continuation of them.

A diverse workforce is a heterogeneous one in terms of individuals' KSAOs and motivation. Such individual diversity requires a diversity in programs designed to facilitate an effective, long-term person/job match.[24] Examples of the types of content found in diversity programs include flexible work schedules, telecommuting, training programs to heighten employee awareness and acceptance of diversity, mentoring relationships, special career and credential-building assignments, child care, and team building. Other, more traditional HR programs, especially performance management and career development ones, may also be included in an organization's diversity initiative.

Though in their infancy, and without any specific legal basis or requirement, diversity programs can be of assistance to organization AAPs in two major ways. First, having a diversity program may aid in the recruitment and attraction of a diverse workforce, thus contributing directly to the achievement of affirmative action goals and timetables. Second, with a diversity program, the organization may increase the retention rates of those acquired through the AAP. As a consequence, underutilization of underrepresented groups will lessen over time and, ideally, lead to the elimination of the need for an AAP in the first place.

SUMMARY

Organization and HR strategy work together to fulfill a mission and accompanying goals and objectives for the organization. HR strategy focuses on decisions about how the organization's workforces will be acquired, trained, managed, rewarded, and retained. Staffing strategy is an outgrowth of organization and HR strategy. It focuses on key decisions (seven are discussed) regarding the acquisition and deployment of the workforces.

Human resource planning (HRP) is described as a process and set of activities undertaken to forecast future HR requirements and availabilities, resulting in the identification of likely employment gaps (shortages and surpluses). Action plans are then developed for addressing the gaps. Before HRP begins, initial decisions must be made about its comprehensiveness, planning time frame, job categories and levels to be included, how to "count heads," and the roles and responsibilities of line and staff (including HR) managers.

A variety of statistical and judgmental techniques may be used in forecasting. Those used in forecasting requirements are typically used in conjunction with business and organization planning. For forecasting availabilities, techniques must be used that take into account the movements of people into, within, and out of the organization, on a job-by-job basis. Here, Markov Analysis is suggested as particularly useful in jobs with relatively large numbers of employees. For other situations, executive reviews, succession planning, and vacancy analysis may be more useful.

External and internal environmental scanning occur after forecasting. Their results temper, and aid in interpretation of, identified employment gaps. Analysis of gaps requires determining likely reasons for them. Such reasons can serve as stimuli for, and inputs into, action planning.

Staffing planning is a form of action planning. It is shown to generally require setting staffing objectives, generating alternative staffing activities, and assessing and choosing from among those alternatives. A fundamental alternative involves use of core or flexible workforces, as identified in staffing strategy. Plans must be developed for acquiring both types of workforces. Advantages and disadvantages of each type are provided; those should first be reviewed to reaffirm strategic choices about their use. Following that, planning can begin. For the core workforce, this first involves matters of staffing philosophy and staffing flowcharts; these will guide the planning of recruitment, selection, and employment activities (discussed in remainder of book). For the flexible workforce, the organization should establish early contact with the providers of the flexible workers (i.e., temporary help agencies and independent contractors). In general, it is recommended that the organization also enter into written agreements with these providers. Numerous issues need to be addressed in such agreements.

Affirmative Action Plans (AAPs) are an extension and application of general HR and staffing planning. AAPs have three basic components, namely utilization analysis, staffing goals and timetables, and action plans. Revised Order No. 4, which applies to federal contractors, specifies requirements for each of these three components. The legality of AAPs has been clearly established, but the courts have fashioned limits to their content and scope. Diversity programs are organizational initiatives to help effectively manage a diverse workforce. Such programs have the potential for successfully working in tandem with AAPs by contributing to the attraction and retention of AAP-targeted people.

DISCUSSION QUESTIONS

1. What are the types of experiences, especially staffing-related ones, that an organization will be likely to have if it does not engage in HR and staffing planning?
2. Why are decisions about job categories and levels so critical to the conduct and results of HRP?
3. What are the differences between statistical and judgmental techniques for forecasting future availabilities?
4. What is meant by reconciliation, and why can it be so useful as an input to staffing planning?
5. What criteria would you suggest using for assessing the staffing alternatives shown in Exhibit 4.12?
6. Some people object to staffing flowcharts as making the staffing process too mechanical, impersonal, and cold. Do you agree? Why?
7. What problems might an organization encounter in doing an AAP that it might not encounter in regular staffing planning?

APPLICATIONS

Markov Analysis and Forecasting

The Doortodoor Sports Equipment Company sells sports clothing and equipment for amateur, light sport (running, tennis, walking, swimming, badminton, golf) enthusiasts. It is the only company in the nation that does this on a door-to-door basis, seeking to bypass the retail sporting goods store and sell directly to the customer. Its sales people have sales kits that include both sample products, as well as a full-line catalogue it can use to show and discuss with customers. The sales function is composed of full-time and part-time sales people (level 1), assistant sales managers (level 2), and regional sales managers (level 3).

The company has decided to study the internal movement patterns of people in the sales function, as well as to forecast their likely availabilities in future time periods. Results will be used to help identify staffing gaps (surpluses and shortages) and to develop staffing strategy and plans for future growth.

To do this, the HR department first collected data for 1994 and 1995 to construct a transition probability matrix, as well as the number of employees for 1996 in each job category. It then wanted to use the matrix to forecast availabilities for 1997. The following data were gathered:

		Transition Probabilities (1994–95)					Current (1996)
Job Category	Level	SF	SP	ASM	RSM	Exit	No. Employees
Sales, Full-time (SF)	1	.50	.10	.05	.00	.35	500
Sales, Part-time (SP)	1	.05	.60	.10	.00	.25	150
Ass't. Sales Mgr. (ASM)	2	.05	.00	.80	.10	.05	50
Region. Sales Mgr. (RSM)	3	.00	.00	.00	.70	.30	30

Based on the above data:

1. Describe the internal labor market of the company in terms of job stability (staying on same job), promotion paths and rates, transfer paths and rates, demotion paths and rates, and turnover (exit) rates.

2. Forecast the numbers available in each job category in 1997.

3. Indicate potential limitations to your forecasts.

Deciding Whether to Use Flexible Staffing

The Kaiser Manufacturing Company (KMC) has been in existence for over fifty years. Its main products are specialty implements for use in both the crop and dairy herd sides of the agricultural business. Products include special attachments to tractors, combines, discers, etc., and add-on devices for milking and feeding equipment that enhance the performance and safety of the equipment.

KMC has a small corporate office plus four manufacturing plants (two in the midwest and two in the south). It has a core workforce of 725 production workers, 30 clericals, 32 professional and engineering workers, and 41 managers. All employees are full-time, and KMC has never used either part-time or temporary workers. It feels very strongly that its staffing strategy of using only a core workforce has paid big dividends over the years in attracting and retaining a committed and highly productive workforce.

Sales have been virtually flat at $175 million annually since 1990. At the same time KMC has begun to experience more erratic placement of orders for its products, making sales less predictable. This appears to be a reflection of more turbulent weather patterns, large swings in interest rates, new entrants into the specialty markets, and general uncertainty about the future direction and growth in the agricultural industry. Increased unpredictability in sales has been accompanied by steadily rising labor costs. This has been due to KMC's increasingly older workforce, as well as shortages of all types of workers (particularly production workers) in the immediate labor markets surrounding the four plants.

Assume you are the HR manager responsible for staffing and training at KMC. You have just been contacted by a representative of the Flexible Staffing Services

(FSS) Company, Mr. Tom Jacoby. Mr. Jacoby has proposed meeting with you and the president of KMC, Mr. Herman Kaiser, to talk about FSS and how it might be of service to KMC. You and Mr. Kaiser agree to meet with Mr. Jacoby. At that meeting, Mr. Jacoby makes a formal presentation to you in which he describes the services, operation, and fees of FSS, as well as highlights the advantages of using a more flexible workforce. During that meeting, you learn the following from Mr. Jacoby.

FSS is a recent entrant into what is called the staffing industry. Its general purpose is to furnish qualified employees to companies (customers) on an as-needed basis, thus helping the customer implement a flexible staffing strategy. It furnishes employees in four major groups: production, clerical, technical, and professional/managerial. Both full-time and part-time employees are available in each of these groups. Employees may be furnished to the customer on a strictly temporary basis ("temps"), or on a "temp-to-perm" basis in which the employees convert from being a temporary employee of FSS to being a permanent employee of the customer after a 90-day probationary period.

For both the temp and temp-to-perm arrangements, FSS offers the following services. In each of the four employee groups it will recruit, select, and hire people to work for FSS, which will in turn lease them to the customer. FSS performs all recruitment, selection, and employment activities. It has a standard selection system used for all applicants, composed of an application blank, reference checks, drug testing, and a medical exam (given after making a job offer). It also offers customized selection plans in which the customer chooses from among a set of special skill tests, a personality test, an honesty test, and background investigations. Based on the standard and/or custom assessments, FSS refers to the customer what it views as the top candidates. FSS tries to furnish two people for every vacancy, and the customer chooses from between the two.

New hires at FSS receive a base wage that is similar to the market wage, as well as close to the wage of the customer's employees with whom they will be directly working. In addition, new hires receive a paid vacation (one week for every six months of employment, up to four weeks), health insurance (with a 25% employee co-pay), and optional participation in a 401(k) plan. FSS performs and pays for all payroll functions and deductions. It also pays the premiums for workers' compensation and unemployment compensation.

The fees charged by FSS to the customer are as follows. There is a standard fee per employee furnished of $1.55 \times$ base wage $\times$ hours worked per week. The 1.55 is labeled "mark-up"; it covers all of FSS's costs (staffing, insurance, benefits, administration) plus a profit margin. On top of the standard fee is an additional fee for customized selection services. This fee ranges from .50 to .90 $\times$ base wage $\times$ hours worked per week. Finally, there is a special one-time fee for temp-to-perm employees (a one-month pay finders fee) payable after the employee has successfully completed the 90-day probationary period and transferred to being an employee of the customer.

Mr. Jacoby concludes his presentation by stressing three advantages of flexible staffing as provided by FSS. First, use of FSS employees on an as-needed basis will give KMC greater flexibility in its staffing to match fluctuating product demand, as well as movement from completely fixed labor costs to more variable labor costs. Second, FSS provides considerable administrative convenience, relieving KMC of most of the burden of recruitment, selection, and payrolling. Finally, KMC will experience considerable freedom from litigation (workers' comp, EEO, torts) since FSS and not KMC will be the employer.

After Mr. Jacoby's presentation, Mr. Kaiser tells you he is favorably impressed but that they clearly need to do some more thinking before they embark on the path of flexible staffing and use of FSS as its provider. He asks you to prepare a brief, preliminary report including:

1. a summary of the possible advantages and disadvantages of flexible staffing
2. a summary of the advantages and disadvantages of using FSS as a service provider
3. a summary of the type of additional information you recommend gathering and using as part of the decision-making process.

ENDNOTES

1. J. E. Butler, G. R. Ferris, and N. K. Napier, *Stretegy and Human Resources Management* (Cincinnati: Southwestern, 1991); C. R. Greer, *Strategy and Human Resources* (Englewood Cliffs, NJ: Prentice-Hall, 1995); C .D. Keen, "Tips for Effective Strategic Planning," *HR Magazine*, 1994, 39(8), pp. 84–87; E. Raimy, "Strategic Planning in the Trenches," *Human Resource Executive*, June, 1995, pp. 21–29.

2. C. C. Snow and S. A. Snell, "Staffing as Strategy," in N. Schmitt, W. C. Borman, and Associates (eds.), *Personnel Selection in Organizations* (San Francisco: Jassey-Bass, 1993), pp. 448–478; J. A. Sannenfeld and M. A. Peiperl, "Staffing Policy as a Strategic Response: A Typology of Career Systems," *Academy of Management Review*, 1988, 13, 588–600.

3. Major treatments of HRP are in: J. P. Begin, *Strategic Employment Policy* (Englewood Cliffs, NJ: Prentice-Hall, 1991); J. E. Butler, G. R. Ferris, and N. K. Napier, *Strategy and Human Resource Management* (Cincinnati: South-Western, 1991); L. Dyer (ed.), *Human Resource Planning: A Case Study Reference Guide to the Tested Practices of Five Major U.S. and Canadian Companies* (New York: Random House, 1986); H. G. Heneman III, D. P. Schwab, J. A. Fossum, and L. Dyer, *Personnel/Human Resource Management,* fourth ed. (Homewood, IL: Irwin, 1988); D. W. Jarrell, *Human Resource Planning* (Englewood Cliffs, NJ: Prentice-Hall, 1993); P. Osterman, "Internal Labor Markets in a Changing Environment," in D. Lewin, O. S. Mitchell, and P. D. Sherer (eds.), *Research Frontiers in Industrial Relations and Human Resources* (Madison, WI: Industrial Relations Research Association, 1992), pp. 273–308; G. T. Milkovich and T. M. Mahoney, "Human Resource Planning and PAIR Policy," in D. Yoder and H. G. Heneman, Jr. (eds.), *ASPA Handbook of Personnel and Industrial Relations* (Washington, D.C.: Bureau of National Affairs, 1979), pp. 2–1 to 2–28; S. E. Jackson and R. S. Schuler, "Human Resource Planning: Challenges for Industrial/Organizational Psychologists," *American Psychologist,*

1990, 45, pp. 223–239; J. W. Walker, *Human Resource Strategy* (New York: McGraw-Hill, 1992); R. Page and D. V. D. Voort, "Job Analysis and HR Planning," in W. F. Cascio (ed.), *Human Resource Planning* (Washington, D.C.: Bureau of National Affairs, 1989).

4. Heneman III, Schwab, Fossum, and Dyer, *Personnel/Human Resource Management,* pp. 201–243.

5. Heneman III, Schwab, Fossum, and Dyer, *Personnel/Human Resource Management,* pp. 205–209.

6. Jackson and Schuler, "Human Resource Planning: Challenges to Industrial/Organizational Psychologists," p. 225.

7. Heneman III, Schwab, Fossum, and Dyer, *Personnel/Human Resource Management,* p. 213; Walker, *Human Resource Strategy,* pp. 156–177.

8. Heneman III, Schwab, Fossum, and Dyer, *Personnel/Human Resource Management,* pp. 214–281; Jarrell, *Human Resource Planning,* pp. 256–281; L. T. Pinfield and M. Morishima, "Taking the Measure of Human Resource Management Flows," *Public Personnel Management,* 1991, 20, pp. 299–318.

9. H. G. Heneman III and M. H. Sandver, "Markov Analysis in Human Resource Administration: Applications and Limitations," *Academy of Management Review,* 1977, 2, pp. 535–542.

10. A. K. Deegan, *Succession Planning: Key to Corporate Excellence* (New York: Wiley, 1986).

11. C. R. Greer and T. C. Ireland, "Organizational and Financial Correlates of a Contrarian Human Resource Investment Strategy," *Academy of Management Review,* 1992, 35, pp. 956–984.

12. Heneman III, Schwab, Fossum, and Dyer, *Personnel/Human Resource Management,* pp. 227–233; Milkovich and Mahoney, "Human Resource Planning and PAIR Policy."

13. J. Breaugh, *Recruitment: Science and Practice* (Boston: PWS-Kent, 1992); J. Wanous, *Organizational Entry,* second ed. (Reading, MA: Addison-Wesley, 1992).

14. S. Caudron, "Contingent Workforce Spurs HR Planning," *Personnel Journal,* 1994, 73(7), pp. 52–60; D. C. Feldman, H. I. Doerphinghaus, and W. H. Turnley, "Managing Temporary Workers: A Permanent HRM Challenge," *Organizational Dynamics,* 1994, 23(2), pp. 49–63; D. Greenberger, C. Hippel, S. L. Mangum, and R.L. Heneman, "The Motivation of the Temporary Employee: The Importance of Skill-Enhancing Characteristics," paper presented at the Academy of Management meeting, Vancouver, B.C. 1995; G. Porter, R. L. Heneman, and S. Strasser, "Regular Employees' Attitudes May Be Influenced by the Presence of Contract Co-Workers," paper presented at the Academy of Management Meeting, Vancouver, 1995; S. Kahn and F. Foulkes, "Human Resource Challenges of the Burgeoning Temporary Work Force: Findings from a Survey of HR Managers," paper presented at the Academy of Management meeting, Vancouver, B.C.1995; L. M. Segal and D. G. Sullivan, "The Temporary Labor Force," *Economic Perspectives,* 1995, 19(2), pp. 2–19; A Davis-Blake, M. J. Waller, and T. P. Ammeter, "The Effects of Temporary Workers on the Commitment and Satisfaction of Permanent Employees in Small Firms," paper presented at the Academy of Management meeting, Vancouver, B.C.1995.

15. V. Zinno, "New Terms for Temps," *Human Resource Executive,* Sept. 1994. pp. 43–45.

16. V. C. Smith, "Temping the AT & T Way," *Human Resource Executive,* Sept. 1994, pp. 52–53.

17. D. P. O'Meara, "Question the Legal Status of Independent Contractors," *HR Magazine,* 1994, 39(8), pp. 33–39; T. Stalnaker, *Using Independent Contractors* (Washington, D.C.: Bureau of National Affairs, 1993).

18. Bureau of National Affairs, *Fair Employment Practice Manual* (Washington, D.C.: author, periodically updated), pp. 403:499–507; 431:11–16.

19. Bureau of National Affairs, *Fair Employment Practice Manual,* pp. 443:465–632.

20. Bureau of National Affairs, *Fair Employment Practice Manual,* pp. 443:201–208, 209–211, 9005–9010.

21. T. Johnson, "Affirmative Action as a Title VII Remedy: Recent U.S. Supreme Court Decisions, Racial Quotas and Preferences," *Labor Law Journal,* 1987, 38, pp. 574–581; T. Johnson, "The Legal Use of Racial Quotas and Gender Preferences by Public and Private Employers," *Labor Law Journal,* 1989, 40, pp. 419–425; G. P. Panaro, *Employment Law Manual* (Boston: Warren, Gorham, and Lamont, 1990), pp. 5–1 to 5–40; N. J. Sedmak and M. D. Levin-Epstein, *Primer on Equal Employment Opportunity* (Washington, D.C.: Bureau of National Affairs, 1991), pp. 135–140.

22. International Personnel Management Association, "Court Ends Affirmative Action Plan," *IPMA News,* June 1993, pp. 19–20.

23. F. Bloch, "Affirmative Action Hasn't Helped Blacks," *Wall Street Journal,* 3/1/95, p. A16; Bureau of National Affairs, "Affirmative Action after Adarand: A Legal, Regulatory, Legislative Outlook," *Daily Labor Report,* 3/23/95, pp. S-1 to S-98; Bureau of National Affairs, "Draft Report on Reverse Discrimination Commissioned by Labor Department," *Daily Labor Report,* 3/23/95, pp. E-1 to E-6; Bureau of National Affairs, "OFCCP Notice Reaffirming Affirmative Action Goals in Light of Adarand Decision, Administration Review," *Daily Labor Report,* 8/11/95, pp. E-1 to E-2.

24. S. E. Jackson and Associates, *Diversity in the Workplace* (New York: The Guilford Press, 1992); S. Caudron, "U.S. West Finds Strength in Diversity," *Personnel Journal,* 1992, March, pp. 40–44; B. Rosen and K. Lovelace, "Piecing Together the Diversity Puzzle," *HR Magazine,* 1991, June, pp. 78–84.

CHAPTER FIVE

Job Analysis

This chapter begins with a description of several types of jobs: traditional, evolving, flexible, idiosyncratic, and team-based. All such jobs have certain requirements (tasks, KSAOs, job context) and rewards (extrinsic and intrinsic) that must be identified and described. Job analysis is presented as the process for accomplishing this identification and description. Separate job analysis approaches are needed for job requirements and for job rewards.

The job requirements approach to job analysis is guided by the job requirements matrix, which contains three basic components (tasks, KSAOs, job context) that must be considered during a job analysis. Each of these components is described in some detail. Once the job requirements matrix has been completed, the results can be expressed in job descriptions and job specifications.

Collecting the necessary information for the job requirements matrix requires considering multiple job analysis methods, sources, and processes. All are described, along with indications of each one's advantages and disadvantages. Through this presentation, it is shown that there is no best or right way to conduct a job requirements job analysis.

Attention then shifts to the job rewards approach, which is guided by the job rewards matrix. It contains information about the extrinsic and intrinsic rewards of a job, along with indications about their amount, differentials among employees, and stability. Methods, sources, and processes for collecting this information are described.

Finally, three legal issues pertaining to job analysis are treated. All three issues involve the job requirements approach to job analysis as it applies to EEO/AA under the Civil Rights Act and the Americans With Disabilities Act.

TYPES OF JOBS

Jobs are the building blocks of an organization, in terms of both job content and the hierarchical relationships that emerge among them.[1] They are explicitly designed and aligned in ways that enhance the production of the organization's goods and services. Job analysis thus must be considered within the broader framework of the design of jobs, for it is through their design that jobs acquire their requirements and rewards in the first place. Several different types of jobs may be designed by the organization. These include traditional, evolving, flexible, idiosyncratic, and team-based jobs.

Traditional

The traditional way of designing a job is to identify and define its elements and tasks precisely, and then incorporate them into a job description. This task core includes virtually all tasks associated with the job, and from it a fairly inclusive list of KSAOs will flow. Thus defined, there are clear lines of demarcation between jobs in terms of both tasks and KSAOs, and there is little overlap between jobs on either basis. Each job also has its own set of extrinsic and intrinsic rewards. Such job design is marked by formal organization charts, clear and precise job descriptions and specifications, and well-defined relationships between jobs in terms of mobility (promotion and transfer) paths. Also, traditional jobs are very static ones, with little or no change occurring in tasks or KSAOs.

Certain terms are used frequently in discussions of traditional jobs. Definitions of some of the key terms, and examples of them, are provided in Exhibit 5.1. Note that the terms are presented in a logically descending hierarchy, starting with job category, or family, and proceeding downward through job, position, task dimension, task, and element.

Evolving

Traditionally designed and administered jobs may gradually change or evolve over time, yielding an evolving job. These changes are not radical, are usually intentional, and are often due to technological and workload changes. An excellent example of such an evolving job is that of "secretary."[2] Traditional or core tasks associated with the job include typing, filing, taking dictation, and answering

---

EXHIBIT 5.1   Terminology Commonly Used in Describing Jobs

TERM	DEFINITION
Job family	A grouping of jobs, usually according to function (e.g., production, finance, human resources, marketing)
Job category	A grouping of jobs according to generic job title or occupation (e.g., managerial, sales, clerical, maintenance), within or across job families
Job	A grouping of positions that are similar in their tasks and task dimensions
Position	A grouping of tasks/dimensions that constitute the total work assignment of a single employee; there are as many positions as there are employees
Task dimension	A grouping of similar types of tasks: sometimes called "duty," "area of responsibility," or "key results area"
Task	A grouping of elements to form an identifiable work activity that is a logical and necessary step in the performance of a job
Element	The smallest unit into which work can be divided without analyzing separate motions, movements, and mental processes

phones. However, in many organizations the job has evolved to include new tasks such as word processing, managing multiple projects, creating spreadsheets, purchasing supplies and office technology, and gathering information on the Internet. These task changes lead to new KSAO requirements, such as planning and coordination skills, and knowledge of spreadsheet software. Accompanying these changes is a change in job title to that of "administrative assistant."

Flexible

Flexible jobs have frequently changing task and KSAO requirements. Sometimes these changes are initiated by the job incumbent who constantly adds and drops (or passes off) new assignments or projects in order to work toward moving targets of opportunity. Other times the task changes may be dictated by changes in production schedules or client demands. Many small business owners, general managers of start-up strategic business units, and top management members perform such flexible jobs. These jobs are "loose cannon" ones, characterized by broad job titles (e.g., administrator, general manager, director, scientist) and job descriptions with only cursory statements about tasks and duties (e.g., "manages budget planning, human resources, and marketing processes"). Within this elastic job title-tasks combination the employee is free to rattle and roll around.

Another example of flexible jobs is project jobs. Here, specific projects are undertaken (e.g., designing an advertising campaign) and when they are completed, new projects emerge. Both managing and working on project-based jobs requires task and KSAO flexibility across projects.

Idiosyncratic

Idiosyncratic jobs are unique and created in response to the known (or anticipated) availability of a specific person with highly valued skills.[3] The person may be a current employee or an outsider to the organization. The person for whom the position is created may in fact even be the instigator of its creation. He or she may approach the organization and explicitly communicate availability and the type of position (both requirements and rewards) desired. Former politicians and high-level government employees are often hired into such idiosyncratically designed jobs.

Team-Based

Team-based jobs occur within work teams.[4] A work team is an interdependent collection of employees who share responsibility for achieving a specific goal. Examples of such goals include developing a product, delivering a service, winning a game, conducting a process, developing a plan, or making a joint decision.

Teams, and thus team-based jobs, occur in multiple forms. One classification of such forms is as follows:[5]

1. Advice/involvement teams—such as quality control circles, special committees, and advisory boards
2. Production/service teams—such as assembly, data processing, and client service teams
3. Project/development teams—such as research and development, project management, brand management, engineering, and task force teams
4. Action/negotiation teams—such as sports, collective bargaining, surgery, and flight crew teams.

Each of these teams is composed of two or more employees, and there is an identifiable collection of tasks that the team is to perform. Usually, these tasks will be grouped into specific clusters and each cluster constitutes a position or job. A project management team, for example, may have separate jobs and job titles for budget specialists, technical specialists, coordinators, and field staff. Each of these jobs may be a traditional, evolving, flexible, or idiosyncratic one.

While teams differ in many respects, two differences are very important in terms of their staffing implications. The first difference is in the extent to which each team member performs only one job, as opposed to multiple jobs. When members each perform only a single job, staffing each job requires a focus on recruitment and selection for only job-specific KSAOs. To the extent that members must perform multiple jobs, however, staffing must emphasize recruitment and selection for both job-specific KSAOs and job-spanning KSAOs. Other terms used to connote job-spanning KSAOs include general competencies and umbrella competencies. Many of these job-spanning KSAOs will involve flexibility, adaptability, and rapid learning skills that will facilitate performing, and switching between, multiple jobs. Exhibit 5.2 shows the relationships between jobs, and job-specific and job-spanning KSAOs, in team-based jobs.

As examples of the above points, a product development team may include mechanical engineers, computer-assisted design specialists, product safety experts, and marketing specialists. Each team member will likely perform only one of these jobs, and thus staffing these jobs will be targeted toward job-specific KSAOs. As a different example, a team responsible for assembly of lawnmower engines may require different members to perform different jobs at any particular moment, but it may also require each member to be (or become) proficient in all phases of engine assembly. Staffing this team will require acquisition of team members that have both job-specific and job-spanning KSAOs.

The second important difference between teams as regards staffing is the degree of task interdependence among team members. The greater the task interdependence, the greater the importance of KSAOs pertaining to interpersonal qualities (e.g., communicating, collaborating, and resolving conflicts) and team self-

---

EXHIBIT 5.2   Team-Based Jobs and KSAOs

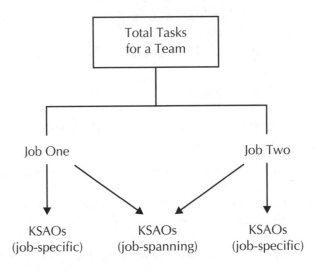

---

management qualities (e.g., setting group goals, inspecting each other's work). Thus, task interdependence brings behaviorally-oriented KSAOs to the forefront of job requirements for team-based jobs.

NATURE OF JOB ANALYSIS

Job analysis may be defined as the process of studying jobs in order to gather, analyze, synthesize, and report information about job requirements and rewards. Note in this definition that job analysis is an overall process, as opposed to a specific method or technique. Also note that in job analysis information is sought about both job requirements and job rewards. Traditionally, job analysis has been a process for seeking information only about tasks and KSAOs, and that remains its primary practical purpose as it is used by organizations today. Recently, however, the job analysis process has been extended to encompass gathering information on job rewards as well.

In job analysis, information is uncovered and then reported about jobs in ways that will be useful to the organization. In staffing, useful information is that which assists the organization in matching persons to jobs. More specifically, the information must focus on job requirements and job rewards, which combine to form overall job content. Armed with such information, the organization is able to conduct staffing activities, such as communicating with job applicants about job vacancies (recruitment); determining appropriate assessment devices for measuring applicant qualifications (selection); and deciding which applicants will receive job offers, as well as determining the content of the offers (employment).

Effective staffing requires job requirements and job rewards information for each of the types of jobs described above. Traditional and evolving jobs readily lend themselves to this. Their requirements and rewards are generally well-known and unlikely to change except in a gradual manner. For idiosyncratic, flexible, and team-based jobs, job analysis is more difficult and problematic. The requirements and rewards for these jobs may frequently be changing, difficult to pinpoint, and even unknown because they depend so heavily on how the job incumbent defines them. Despite the often ambiguous and fluid nature of these jobs, attempts must be made to identify their requirements and rewards through job analysis. Failure to do so is inviting the occurrence of person/job mismatches.

Job analysis and the information it provides thus serves as basic input to the totality of staffing activities for an organization. In this sense, job analysis is a support activity to the various functional staffing activities. Indeed, without thorough and accurate information about job requirements and rewards, the organization is greatly hampered in its attempts to acquire a workforce that will be effective in terms of HR outcomes such as performance, satisfaction, and retention. Job analysis thus is the foundation upon which successful staffing systems are constructed.

Some job analysis processes focus on the job requirements portion of job content; other job analyses concentrate on the job rewards part. The fundamentals of the job requirements approach are presented next, followed by a similar presentation of the job rewards approach.

JOB REQUIREMENTS JOB ANALYSIS

Overview

Any job has two related requirements that must be met by individuals in order for the job to be performed. These are (a) the job tasks, and (b) the underlying knowledge, skill, ability, and other characteristics (KSAOs) necessary for the performance of the tasks. Some processes of job analysis focus on the task component of job requirements, and these are referred to as task-oriented approaches. Other forms of job analysis, while not ignoring tasks, place emphasis on KSAOs, and these are referred to KSAO-oriented in nature.[6] Each of these approaches, and the logical relationships between them, is shown in Exhibit 5.3.

As demonstrated in Exhibit 5.3, task-oriented job analysis is used to identify job tasks and the context in which these tasks are performed, such as the physical

---

EXHIBIT 5.3   Job Requirements Approach to Job Analysis

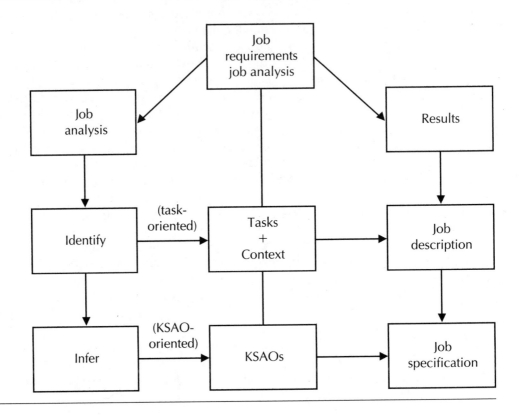

working environment. The results of this job analysis are typically reported in a job description. This document then becomes the written source of information that is incorporated into the HR activities of the organization, particularly staffing activities.

As Exhibit 5.3 displays, job analysis may proceed beyond identification of tasks and job context. In particular, the purpose of KSAO-oriented job analysis is to infer the KSAOs that are likely to be required for successful performance of job tasks, taking into account characteristics of the job context. For example, assume a task-oriented job analysis for the job of management trainee in a retail store, such as Kmart or Sears, reveals that the job entails a number of tasks that may be grouped together into a broader task dimension labeled "customer service." Using this specific task information, a KSAO-oriented job analysis should infer the specific types of KSAOs necessary for a management trainee in order to provide effective customer service. The resultant KSAOs might involve such things as product knowledge, interpersonal skills, verbal ability, and other characteristics pertaining to educational background (e.g., a major or specific courses).

The results of a KSAO-oriented job analysis, just like a task-oriented one, yield information that is reported in written documents, notably a job specification. In turn, these documents serve as basic sources of information that are stored, communicated throughout the organization, and used as input to the myriad staffing activities.[7]

The conceptual framework in Exhibit 5.3 can be transformed into a general operational framework, or job requirements matrix, that identifies the key components and results of job requirements job analysis. A job requirements matrix serves as a general guide to the design and conduct of job analysis, and it functions as an overlay to various methods, techniques, analysts, and so forth.

The job requirements matrix is presented below, followed by a discussion of key components and issues embedded within the matrix. Following that, potential methods of collecting job information and individuals who function as possible sources of job information are dealt with. This is followed by some general suggestions regarding the conduct of job analysis as a process, as well as a concrete, step-by-step example.

Job Requirements Matrix

Job requirements job analysis is best conceptualized by referring to the job requirements matrix shown in Exhibit 5.4. The matrix shows the key components of job requirements job analysis, each of which must be explicitly considered for inclusion in any job requirements job analysis. Completion of the cell entries in the matrix represents the information that must be gathered, analyzed, synthesized, and expressed in usable written form.

At the top of Exhibit 5.4 are entered a "job title" and a "job summary." A job summary is an overall, general statement of major tasks or duties associated with the job. The section dealing with "tasks" contains three columns. The first column is for a listing (from 1 to N) of tasks expressed in the form of task statements (e.g., takes and records orders from customers). The second column is for "dimensions," which are groupings (A,B, . . . Z) of similar tasks into more abstract, but meaningful categories (e.g., planning and customer service). Column three indicates the "importance" of tasks and/or dimensions. "Importance" is a generic term used to indicate the significance attached to tasks/dimensions in terms of such attributes as frequency, time spent, and criticalness. This section of the matrix, when completed, will provide a representation of job task requirements in terms of their nature, groupings into dimensions, and indications about their relative importance.

The KSAO section of the matrix contains columns for "nature" and for "importance" of KSAOs. The nature of each KSAO is derived by inference from the

---

EXHIBIT 5.4 Job Requirements Matrix

Job Title:

Job Summary:

Tasks			KSAOs							
			Nature				Importance			
Tasks	Dimensions	Importance	K	S	A	O	K	S	A	O
1	A									
2										
3										
4	B									
.	.									
.	.									
.	.									
N	Z									

Job Context: Physical and environmental

---

task section of the matrix. That is, for each task and associated task dimension, the underlying KSAOs necessary for performance of the tasks are inferred by various participants (sources) in the job analysis process. The importance of KSAOs represents judgments about their weight in terms of impact on, or contribution to, task performance.

Turning to the bottom of the job requirements matrix, the "job context" is represented as encompassing both tasks and KSAOs, for both of these occur within a particular job context. That context is usually analyzed and described in terms of physical demands and environmental characteristics (e.g., noise) surrounding the job.

When a job requirements job analysis process is finished, the final result or output is a completed job requirements matrix, a portion of which is shown in Exhibit 5.5 for the job of administrative assistant. This matrix serves as the basic informational source or document for any job in terms of its job requirements. Often, the task and job context parts of the matrix are converted to a job description, and the KSAO portion is converted to a job specification. However it is expressed exactly, the resultant information serves as a basic input and guide to all subsequent staffing activities.

As just noted, the job requirements matrix contains major sections, each of which represents a basic component of job requirements job analysis. We turn now to a fuller discussion of each of those components.

EXHIBIT 5.5   Portion of Job Requirements Matrix for Job of Administrative Assistant

Tasks			KSAOs	
Specific Tasks	**Task Dimensions**	**Importance (% time spent)**	**Nature**	**Importance to Tasks (1–5 rating)**
1. Arrange schedules with office assistant/volunteers to assure that office will be staffed during prescribed hours	A. Supervision	30%	1. Knowledge of office operations and policies	4.9
			2. Ability to match people to tasks according to their skills and hours of availability	4.6
2. Assign office tasks to office assistant/volunteers to assure coordination of activities	A. Supervision		3. Skill in interaction with diverse people	2.9
			4. Skill in determining types and priorities of tasks	4.0
3. Type/transcribe letters, memos, and reports from handwritten material or dictated copy to produce final copy, using word processor	B. Word processing	20%	1. Knowledge of typing formats	3.1
			2. Knowledge of spelling and punctuation	5.0
			3. Knowledge of graphics display software	5.0
4. Prepare graphs and other visual material to supplement reports, using word processor	B. Word processing		4. Ability to proofread and correct work	2.0
			5. Skill in use of WordPerfect (most current version)	5.0
5. Proofread typed copy and correct spelling, punctuation, and typographical errors in order to produce high quality materials	B. Word processing		6. Skill in creating visually appealing and understandable graphs	4.3
				3.4

Job Context: No excessive physical demands; safe, occasionally noisy, work environment.

Task Statements

The task-oriented approach to job analysis begins with the development of task statements, whose objective is to identify and record a set of tasks that both includes all of the job's major tasks and excludes nonrelevant or trivial tasks.[8] The resultant task statements serve as the building blocks for the remainder of the job requirements job analysis.

Identification and recording of tasks begins with the construction of task statements. These statements are objectively written descriptions of the behaviors or work activities engaged in by employees in order to perform the job. The statements are made in simple declarative sentences.

Ideally, each task statement will show several things. These are

1. what the employee does, using a specific action verb at the start of the task statement
2. to whom or what the employee does what he or she does, stating the object of the verb
3. what is produced, indicating the expected output of the verb
4. what materials, tools, procedures, or equipment are used

Use of the sentence analysis technique is very helpful for writing task statements that conform to these four requirements. An example of the technique is shown in Exhibit 5.6 for several tasks from very different jobs.

In addition to meeting the preceding four requirements, there are several other suggestions for effectively writing task statements. First, use specific action verbs that have only one meaning. Examples of verbs that do not conform to this suggestion include "supports," "assists," and "handles."

Second, focus on recording tasks, as opposed to specific elements that comprise a task. This requires use of considerable judgment, since the distinction between a task and an element is relative and often fuzzy. A useful rule to keep in mind here is that most jobs can be adequately described within a range of 15–25 task statements. Should a task statement list exceed this range, it is a warning that it may be too narrow in terms of activities defined.

Third, do not include minor or trivial activities in task statements; focus only on major tasks and activities. An exception to this recommendation occurs when a so-called minor task is judged to have great importance to the job (see the following discussion).

Fourth, take steps to ensure that the list of task statements is content valid and reliable.[9] The basic way to conform to this suggestion is to have two or more people ("analysts") independently evaluate the task statement list in terms of (a) inclusiveness, and (b) clarity. High agreement between people signifies high reliability and content validity, meaning that job content is consistently described in ways not deficient or contaminated. Should disagreements between people be discovered, the nature of the disagreements can be discussed and appropriate modifications to the task statements made.

EXHIBIT 5.6   Use of the Sentence Analysis Technique for Task Statements

Sentence Analysis Technique

What does the worker do?		Why does the worker do it? What gets done?	What is the final result or technological objective?
Worker action		Purpose of the worker actions	Materials, products, subject matter, and/or services
(Worker function)	(Work devices, people or information)	(Work field)	(MPSMS)
Verb	Direct object	Infinitive phrase	
		Infinitive	Object of the infinitive
Sets up *(setting up)*	various types of metal-working machines *(work device)*	to machine *(machining)*	metal aircraft parts. *(material)*
Persuades *(persuading)*	customers *(people)*	to buy *(merchandising)*	automobiles. *(product)*
Interviews *(analyzing)*	clients *(people)*	to assess *(advising– counseling)*	skills and abilities. *(subject matter)*
Drives *(driving– operating)*	bus *(work device)*	to transport *(transporting)*	passengers. *(service)*

Source: Vocational Rehabilitation Institute, *A Guide to Job Analysis* (Menominee, WI: University of Wisconsin-Stout, 1982), p. 8.

Fifth, have at least the manager and a job incumbent serve as the analysts, providing the content validity and reliability checks. It is important to have the manager participate in this process in order to verify that the task statements are inclusive and accurate. For the job incumbent, the concern is not only that of verification, but also acceptance of the task statements as adequate representations that will guide incumbents' performance of the job. Ideally, there should be multiple managers and job incumbents, along with a representative of the HR department, serving as analysts. This would expand the scope of input and allow for more precise content validity and reliability checks.

Finally, recognize that the accuracy or validity of task statements cannot be evaluated against any external criterion. The reason for this is that there is no external criterion available for use. Task descriptions are accurate and meaningful only to the extent that people agree on them. Because of this, the preceding recommendation regarding checks on content validity and reliability takes on added importance.

Task Dimensions

Task statement lists may be maintained in list form and subsequently incorporated into the job description. Often, however, it is useful to group sets of task statements into task dimensions, and then attach a name to each such dimension. Other terms for task dimensions are "duties," "accountability areas," "responsibilities," and "performance dimensions."

A useful way to facilitate the grouping process is to create a task dimension matrix. Each column in the matrix represents a potential task dimension, and a label is tentatively attached to it. Each row in the matrix represents a particular task statement. Cell entries in the matrix represent the assignment of task statements to task dimensions (the grouping of tasks). The goal is to have each task statement assigned to only one task dimension. The process is complicated by the fact that the dimensions and labels must be created prior to grouping; the dimensions and labels may have to be changed or rearranged in order to make task statements fit as one progresses through the assignment of task statements to dimensions.

Several things should be borne in mind about task dimensions. First, their creation is optional and should occur only if they will be useful. Second, there are many different grouping procedures, ranging from straightforward judgmental ones to highly sophisticated statistical ones.[10] For most purposes, a simple judgmental process is sufficient, such as having the people who participated in the creation of the task statements also create the groupings as part of the same exercise. As a rule, there should be 4–8 dimensions, depending on the number of task statements, regardless of the specific grouping procedure used. Third, it is important that the grouping procedure yield a reliable set of task dimensions acceptable to managers, job incumbents, and other organizational members. Finally, as with task statements, it is not possible to empirically validate task dimensions against some external criterion; for both task statements and dimensions, their validity is in the eyes of their definers and beholders.

Importance of Tasks/Dimensions

Rarely are all tasks/dimensions of a job thought to be of equal "weight" or importance. In some general sense, it is thus felt that these differences must be captured, expressed, and incorporated into job information, especially the job description. Normally, assessments of importance are made just for task dimensions, though it is certainly possible to make them for individual tasks as well.

Before actual weighting can occur, two decisions must be made. First, the specific attribute to be assessed in terms of importance must be decided (e.g., time spent on the task/dimension). Second, a decision is required regarding whether the attribute will be measured in categorical (e.g., essential-nonessential) or continuous (e.g., % of time spent, 1–5 rating of importance) terms. Exhibit 5.7 shows examples of the results of these two decisions in terms of commonly used importance attributes and their measurement.

Once these decisions are made, it is possible to proceed with the actual process of assessing or weighting the tasks/dimensions in terms of importance. It should be noted here that if the tasks/dimensions are not explicitly assessed in such a manner, all tasks/dimensions end up being weighted equally by default.

If possible, it is desirable for the assessments to be done initially by independent analysts (e.g., incumbents and managers). In this way, it will be possible to then check for the degree of reliability among raters. Where differences are found, they can be discussed and resolved. Just as it is desirable to have high reliability in the identification of tasks and dimensions, it is desirable to have high reliability in judgments of their importance.[11]

KSAOs

KSAOs are inferred or derived from knowledge of the tasks and task dimensions themselves. The inference process requires that the analysts explicitly think in specific cause-and-effect terms. For each task or dimension, the analyst must in essence ask, "Exactly what KSAOs do I think will be necessary for (will cause) performance on this task or dimension?" Then the analyst should ask "Why do I think this?" in order to think through the soundness of the inferential logic. Discussions among analysts about these questions are to be encouraged.

When asking and answering these questions, it is useful to keep in mind what is meant by the terms "knowledge," "skill," "ability," and "other characteristics." It is also very helpful to refer to research results that help us better understand the nature and complexity of these concepts.

Knowledge   Knowledge is a body of information (conceptual, factual, procedural) that can be applied directly to the performance of tasks. It tends to be quite focused or specific in terms of job, organization, or occupation. Generally, research has not been concerned with identifying and defining bodies of knowledge required for specific tasks, dimensions, or jobs. Because of this, a heavy responsi-

---

EXHIBIT 5.7   Examples of Ways to Assess Task/Dimension Importance

---

A. **Relative Time Spent**

For each task/dimension, rate the amount of time you spend on it, relative to all other tasks/dimensions of your job.

1	2	3	4	5
Very small amount		Average amount		Very large amount

B. **Percentage (%) Time Spent**

For each task/dimension, indicate the percentage (%) of time you spend on it (percentages must total to 100%).

Dimension _____   % Time spent _____

C. **Importance to Overall Performance**

For each task/dimension, rate its importance to your overall job performance.

1	2	3	4	5
Minor importance		Average importance		Major importance

D. **Need for New Employee Training**

Do new employees receive a standard, planned course of training for performance of this task, other than a customary job orientation?

_____ Yes

_____ No

---

bility is placed on the analysts to infer the specific knowledges actually required for task performance. Analysts should be particularly wary of using global or shorthand terms such as "knowledge of accounting principles." Here, it would be better to indicate which accounting principles are being utilized, and why each is necessary for task performance.

Skill   Skill refers to an observable competence to perform a particular task or closely related set of tasks. Skill requirements are directly inferred from observation or knowledge of tasks performed.

Considerable research has been devoted to identifying particular job-related skills and to organizing them into taxonomies. Job analysts should begin the skills inference process by referring to the results of this research.

An excellent example of such useful research is found in the SCANS project.[12]

It identifies two types of skills: competency and foundation. The competency skills are generic skills required for successful job performance in most if not all jobs, and the foundation skills are more basic skills or qualities underlying the competencies. Detailed definitions of each competency and foundation skill are contained in the report itself.

The SCANS report also identifies 35 jobs representative of the entire job spectrum in this country. They fall into five categories: health and human services; office, financial services, and government; accommodations and personal services; manufacturing, agribusiness, mining, and construction; and trade, transportation, and communication. For each of these jobs there is provided a detailed statement of the specific competency and foundation skills as they apply to that job, as well as a listing of all of the skills and their rated (1–5 rating scale) importance to the job. An example of the listing and importance ratings for the job of dietary manager is shown in Exhibit 5.8.

EXHIBIT 5.8   Dietary Manager: Job Summary, Competencies, Foundation Skills

---

Job Summary: Duties performed by the dietary manager combine clinical and administrative services. The managers are responsible for meal planning and preparation on a large scale. Some of the services include supervising and training staff, preparing budgets, purchasing food and equipment, and establishing policy.

Competencies	Mean	Standard Deviation
Interprets and communicates information	4.75	.50
Exercises leadership	4.75	.50
Acquires and evaluates information	4.50	.58
Understands systems	4.50	.58
Serves clients/customers	4.50	.58
Teaches others	4.50	.58
Participates as a member of a team	4.25	.96
Allocates human resources	4.25	.50
Improves and designs systems	4.25	.50
Negotiates to arrive at a decision	4.25	.50
Selects technology	4.00	.82
Works with cultural diversity	4.00	.82
Allocates time	4.00	.82
Allocates money	3.75	1.50
Monitors and corrects performance	3.75	.96
Organizes and maintains information	3.50	1.00
Allocates material and facility resources	3.50	.58
Uses computers to process information	3.25	1.50
Applies technology to tasks	2.50	1.29
Maintains and troubleshoots technology	2.25	.96

(continued)

EXHIBIT 5.8   Continued

Foundation Skills	Mean	Standard Deviation
Listening	4.75	.50
Integrity/honesty	4.75	.50
Responsibility	4.75	.50
Reading	4.75	.50
Problem solving	4.50	1.00
Speaking	4.50	1.00
Writing	4.50	.58
Reasoning	4.50	.58
Decision making	4.25	.96
Self-management	4.25	.96
Arithmetic	4.00	.82
Social	4.00	.82
Self-esteem	3.75	.96
Knowing how to learn	3.75	1.26
Creative thinking	3.50	.58
Mathematics	3.25	.50
Seeing things in the mind's eye	3.25	.50

NOTE: Mean and standard deviation calculated on 1–5 importance rating scale.

Source: U.S. Department of Labor, *Skills and Tasks for Jobs: A SCANS Report for America 2000* (Washington, D.C.: author, 1992), pp. 3–27 to 3–37.

Ability   An ability is an underlying capacity to perform a task. This capacity is possessed by the person at the time the task is first performed.

Substantial research has been conducted on the nature and classification of human abilities. Analysts should consult the results of that research when doing ability inference. Recent research suggests a taxonomy of 52 specific abilities, grouped into four major ability categories (cognitive, psychomotor, physical, and sensory/perceptual).[13] These are shown in Exhibit 5.9.

Each of these 52 specific abilities is accompanied by a definition, examples of specific tasks requiring the ability, titles of jobs commonly requiring these tasks, and examples of selection tests that assess the ability. An example for the cognitive ability "written comprehension" is shown in Exhibit 5.10.

There may be instances in which standard taxonomies may not be sufficient to cover all the specific abilities required for a particular job. Such gaps in coverage will need to be closed by the analysts conducting the ability inferences. When doing so, they should seek to follow the format shown in Exhibit 5.10, particularly those sections pertaining to definition, tasks, and jobs (test examples are not necessary at this point; they become relevant during the selection process).

EXHIBIT 5.9   Taxonomy of Human Abilities

Cognitive Abilities
1. Oral comprehension
2. Written comprehension
3. Oral expression
4. Written expression
5. Fluency of ideas
6. Originality
7. Memorization
8. Problem sensitivity
9. Mathematical reasoning
10. Number facility
11. Deductive reasoning
12. Inductive reasoning
13. Information ordering
14. Category flexibility
15. Speed of closure
16. Flexibility of closure
17. Spatial orientation
18. Visualization
19. Perceptual speed
20. Selective attention
21. Time sharing

Psychomotor Abilities
22. Control precision
23. Multi-limb coordination
24. Response orientation
25. Rate control
26. Reaction time
27. Arm-hand steadiness
28. Manual dexterity
29. Finger dexterity
30. Wrist-finger speed
31. Speed-of-limb movement

Physical Abilities
32. Static strength
33. Explosive strength
34. Dynamic strength
35. Trunk strength
36. Extent flexibility
37. Dynamic flexibility
38. Gross body coordination
39. Gross body equilibrium
40. Stamina

Sensory/Perceptual Abilities
41. Near vision
42. Far vision
43. Visual color discrimination
44. Night vision
45. Peripheral vision
46. Depth perception
47. Glare sensitivity
48. Hearing sensitivity
49. Auditory attention
50. Sound localization
51. Speech recognition
52. Speech clarity

EXHIBIT 5.10 Written Comprehension Ability:
Definition, Tasks, Jobs, and Test Examples

Definition: Written comprehension is the ability to understand written sentences and paragraphs. This ability involves reading and understanding the meaning of words, phrases, sentences, and paragraphs. It involves reading; it does not involve writing, listening to, or understanding spoken information.

Tasks: Written comprehension may be used in reading books, articles, technical manuals, written instructions, work orders, and apartment leases.

Jobs: Jobs that require high levels of written comprehension include those of an administrator, lawyer, reporter, scientist, translator, and journal editor.

Test Examples: Tests of written comprehension usually present subjects with one or more passages of information. They then answer multiple-choice questions about the information. The emphasis of the test may be on following directions, understanding the general meaning of paragraphs, or understanding the meaning of specific words. Other tests of written comprehension are strictly vocabulary-oriented, focusing on identifying definitions, synonyms, or antonyms.

Source: Modified and reproduced by special permission of the Publisher, Management Research Institute, Inc., Bethesda, MD 20817 from *Handbook of Human Abilities: Definitions, Measurements, and Job Task Requirements* by Edwin A. Fleishman and Maureen E. Reilly. Copyright 1992 by Management Research Institute, Inc. All rights reserved. Further reproduction is prohibited without the Publisher's written consent.

Other Characteristics This is a catchall category for factors that do not fit neatly into the K, S, and A categories. Despite the catchall nature of these requirements, they are very important for even being able to enter the employment relationship (legal requirements), being present to perform the job (availability requirements), and having values consistent with organizational culture and values (character requirements). Numerous examples of these factors are shown in Exhibit 5.11. Care should be taken to ensure that these factors truly are job requirements, as opposed to whimsical and ill-defined preferences of the organization.

KSAO Importance

As suggested in the job requirements matrix (Exhibit 5.4), the KSAOs of a job may differ in their weight or contribution to task performance. Hence, their relative importance must be explicitly considered, defined, and indicated. Failure to do so means that all KSAOs will be assumed to be of equal importance by default.

As with task importance, deriving KSAO importance requires two decisions. First, what will be the specific attribute(s) on which importance is judged? Second, will the measurement of each attribute be categorical (e.g., required-preferred) or continuous (e.g., 1–5 rating scale)? Examples of formats for indicating KSAO importance are shown in Exhibit 5.12.

EXHIBIT 5.11   Examples of Other Job Requirements

Legal Requirements
    Possession of license (occupational, drivers, etc.)
    Citizen or legal alien?
    Geographic residency (e.g., within city limits for public employees)
    Security clearance

Availabiity Requirements
    Starting date
    Worksite locations
    Hours and days of week
    Travel
    Attendance and tardiness

Character Requirements
    Moral
    Work ethic
    Background
    Conscientiousness
    Honesty and integrity

Job Context

As shown in the job requirements matrix, tasks and KSAOs occur within a broader job context. A job requirements job analysis should include consideration of the job context and the factors that are important in defining it. Such consideration is necessary because these factors may have an influence on tasks and KSAOs, and further, information about the factors may be used in the recruitment and selection of job applicants.

Consider, for example, a job context factor such as physical demands, which includes lifting and kneeling. These types of demands may influence how jobs and tasks are designed and subsequently performed. As such, consideration of these factors will have to be incorporated into the KSAO assessment procedures to be used in the selection of job applicants. In addition, information about the physical demands of a job may be communicated to job applicants in order to provide a realistic description of what the total job is like.

Two frequently considered job context factors are physical demands and environmental conditions. Physical demands refer to demands of the job per se, and not to the physical capacities or requirements of employees (these could obviously be derived as a part of the KSAO inference process). Environmental conditions refer to the surroundings in which a job is performed. They must be specific and have identifiable effects on tasks and/or employees performing them. Organization "climate" factors, such as trust and team spirit, are not included as environmental

---

EXHIBIT 5.12 Examples of Ways to Assess KSAO Importance

A. **Importance to (acceptable) (superior) task performance**
   1 = minimal importance
   2 = some importance
   3 = average importance
   4 = considerable importance
   5 = extensive importance

B. **Should the KSAO be assessed during recruitment/selection?**
   ☐ Yes
   ☐ No

C. **Is the KSAO required, preferred, or not required for recruitment/selection?**
   ☐ Required
   ☐ Preferred
   ☐ Not required (obtain on job and/or in training)

---

conditions and are more appropriately candidates for consideration under job rewards.

   The physical demands of jobs may be defined in terms of 20 specific factors, and environmental conditions defined in terms of 14 factors.[14] Both sets of factors are shown in Exhibit 5.13 along with the information provided as an example for one physical demand factor ("climbing") and one environmental condition ("atmospheric conditions"). When these factors are used in job analysis, the importance of the factor is assessed in terms of a categorical judgment about frequency (does not exist, exists up to 1/3 of the time, exists from 1/3 to 2/3 of the time, exists 2/3 or more of the time).

Job Descriptions and Job Specifications

   For administrative purposes, it is common practice to express the output or results of job requirements job analysis in written job descriptions and job specifications.[15] Referring back to the job requirements matrix, note that its sections pertaining to tasks and job context are similar to a job description, and the section dealing with KSAOs is similar to a job specification. The job requirements matrix thus not only provides an operational framework for job analysis, but also indicates the opera-

---

EXHIBIT 5.13   Job Context Factors: Physical Demands and Environmental Conditions

Physical Demands	Environmental Conditions
Strength	Exposure to weather
Balancing	Extreme cold
Stooping	Extreme heat
Kneeling	Wet and/or humid
Crouching	Noise intensity level
Crawling	Vibration
Climbing	Atmospheric conditions
Reaching	Moving mechanical parts
Handling	Electric shock
Fingering	High, exposed places
Feeling	Radiation
Talking	Explosives
Hearing	Toxic/caustic chemicals
Tasting/smelling	Other
Near acuity	
Far acuity	
Depth perception	
Accommodation	
Color vision	
Field of vision	

Example: Climbing	**Example: Atmospheric Conditions**
Ascending or descending ladders, stairs, scaffolding, ramps, poles and the like, using feet and legs or hands and arms. Bodily agility is emphasized.	Exposure to conditions such as fumes, noxious odors, dusts, mists, gases, and poor ventilation that affect the respiratory system, eyes, or skin.

Source: U.S. Department of Labor, *The Revised Handbook for Analyzing Jobs* (Washington, D.C.: author, 1991), pp. 12–1 to 12–18.

tional output for job analysis in the form of the information to be included in job descriptions and job specifications.

There are no standard formats or other requirements for either job descriptions or job specifications. In terms of content, however, a job description should usually include the following: job family, job title, job summary, task statements and dimensions, importance indicator(s), job context indicators, and date job analysis conducted. A job specification should usually include job family, job title, job summary, KSAOs (separate section for each), importance indicators, and date conducted. An example of a combined job description/specification is shown in Exhibit 5.14.

EXHIBIT 5.14 **Example of Combined Job Description/Specification**

FUNCTIONAL UNIT: CHILDREN'S REHABILITATION
JOB TITLE: REHABILITATION SPECIALIST
DATE: 12/5/96

JOB SUMMARY

Works with disabled small children and their families to identify developmental strengths and weaknesses, develop rehabilitation plans, deliver and coordinate rehabilitation activities, and evaluate effectiveness of those plans and activities.

PERFORMANCE DIMENSIONS AND TASKS   Time Spent (%)

1. Assessment   **10%**

Administer formal and informal motor screening and evaluation instruments to conduct assessments. Perform assessments to identify areas of strengths and need.

2. Planning   **25%**

Collaborate with parents and other providers to directly develop the individualized family service plan. Use direct and consultative models of service in developing plans.

3. Delivery   **50%**

Carry out individual and small group motor development activities with children and families. Provide service coordination to designated families. Work with family care and child care providers to provide total services. Collaborate with other staff members and professionals from community agencies to obtain resources and specialized assistance.

4. Evaluation   **15%**

Observe, interpret, and report on client in order to monitor individual progress. Assist in collecting and reporting intervention data in order to prepare formal program evaluation reports. Write evaluation reports to assist in developing new treatment strategies and programs.

JOB SPECIFICATIONS

1. License: License to practice physical therapy in the state
2. Education: B.S. in physical or occupational therapy required; M.S. preferred
3. Experience: Prefer (not required) one year experience working with children with disabilities and their families
4. Skills: Listening to and interacting with others (children, family members, coworkers)
Developing treatment plans
Organizing and writing reports

Collecting Job Information

Job analysis involves not only consideration of the types of information (tasks, KSAOs, and job context) to be collected, but also the methods, sources, and processes to be used for such collection. These issues are discussed next, and as will be seen, there are many alternatives to choose from for purposes of developing an overall job analysis system for any particular situation.[16]

Methods

Job analysis methods represent procedures or techniques for collecting job information. There have been many specific techniques and systems developed and named (e.g., Functional Job Analysis, Position Analysis Questionnaire). Rather than discuss each of the many techniques separately, we will concentrate on the major generic methods that underlie all specific techniques and applications. There are many excellent descriptions and discussions of the specific techniques available.[17]

Prior Information   For any job, there is usually some prior information available about it that could and should be consulted. Indeed, this information should routinely be searched for and used as a starting point for a job analysis.

There are many possible organizational sources of job information available, including current job descriptions and specifications, job-specific policies and procedures, training manuals, and performance appraisals. Externally, job information may be available from other employers, as well as trade and professional associations. The most important and public external source of information is the *Dictionary of Occupational Titles,* published by the Department of Labor.[18] It contains generic job summaries in the form of task statements for over 20,000 separate job titles, with accompanying occupational and industry (if relevant) designations. The DOT should be available and consulted for any job analysis. An example of the type of information provided in the DOT for the job title "job analyst" is shown in Exhibit 5.15.

The ready availability of prior job information needs to be balanced with some possible limitations. First, there is the general issue of completeness. Usually, prior information will be deficient in some important areas of job requirements, as in evolving or nontraditional types of jobs. Sole reliance upon prior information thus should be avoided. A second limitation is that there will be little indication of exactly how the information was collected, and relatedly, how accurate it is. These limitations suggest that while prior information should be the starting point for job analysis, it should not be the stopping point.

Observation   Simply observing job incumbents performing the job is an obviously excellent way to learn about tasks, KSAOs, and context. It provides a thoroughness and richness of information unmatched by any other method. It is also

---

EXHIBIT 5.15   Job of "Job Analyst": As Defined in *Dictionary of Occupational Titles*

Collects, analyzes, and prepares occupational information to facilitate personnel, administration, and management functions of organization. Consults with management to determine type, scope, and purpose of study. Studies current organizational occupational data and compiles distribution reports, organization and flow charts, and other background information required for study. Observes jobs and interviews workers and supervisory personnel to determine job and worker requirements. Analyzes occupational data, such as physical, mental, and training requirements of jobs and workers and develops written summaries, such as job descriptions, job specifications, and lines of career movement. Utilizes developed occupational data to evaluate or improve methods and techniques for recruiting, selecting, promoting, evaluating, and training workers, and administration of related personnel programs. May specialize in classifying positions according to regulated guidelines to meet job classification requirements of civil service system and be known as Position Classifier.

Source: U. S. Department of Labor, *Dictionary of Occupational Titles,* fourth ed. (Washington, D.C.: Author, 1991), p. 11.

the most direct form of gathering information since it does not rely on intermediary information sources, such as would be the case with other methods (e.g., interviewing job incumbents and supervisors).

The following potential limitations to observation should be borne in mind. First, it is most appropriate for jobs with physical (as opposed to mental) components, and ones with relatively short job cycles (i.e., amount of time required to complete job tasks before repeating them). Second, the method may involve substantial time and cost. Third, the ability of the observer to do a thorough and accurate analysis is open to question; it may be necessary to train observers prior to the job analysis. Fourth, the method will require coordination with, and approval from, many people (e.g., supervisors and incumbents). Finally, the incumbents being observed may distort their behavior during observation in self-serving ways, such as making tasks appear more difficult or time-consuming than they really are.

Interviews   Interviewing job incumbents and others, such as their managers, has many potential advantages. It respects the interviewee's vast source of information about the job. And, the interview format allows the interviewer to explain the purpose of the job analysis, how the results will be used, and so forth, thus enhancing likely acceptance of the process by the interviewees. It can be structured in format to ensure standardization of collected information.

As with any job analysis method, the interview is not without potential limitations. It is time-consuming and costly, and this may cause the organization to skimp on it in ways that jeopardize the reliability and content validity of the information gathered. The interview, not providing anonymity, may lead to suspicion and distrust on the part of interviewees. The quality of the information obtained, as well as interviewee acceptance, depends upon the skill of the interviewer. Careful selection, and possible training, of interviewers should definitely be considered when the interview is the method chosen for collecting job information. Finally, the success of the interview also depends on the skill and abilities of the interviewee, such as verbal communication skills and ability to recall tasks performed.

Task Questionnaire   A typical task questionnaire contains a lengthy list of task statements that cut across many different job titles, and is administered to incumbents (all or samples of them) in these job titles. For each task statement, the respondent is asked to indicate (a) whether or not the task applies to the respondent's job (respondents should always be given a DNA—does not apply—option), and (b) task importance (e.g., a 1–5 scale rating difficulty or time spent).

The advantages of task questionnaires are numerous. They are standardized in content and format, thus yielding a standardized method of information gathering. They can obtain considerable task information from large numbers of people. They are economical to administer and score, and the availability of scores creates the opportunity for subsequent statistical analysis. Finally, task questionnaires are (and should be) completed anonymously, thus enhancing respondent participation, honesty, and acceptance.

A task questionnaire is potentially limited in certain ways. The most important limitation pertains to task statement content. Care must be taken to ensure that the questionnaire contains task statements of sufficient content relevance, representativeness, and specificity. This suggests that if a tailor-made questionnaire is to be used, considerable time and resources must be devoted to its construction to ensure accurate inclusion of task statements. If a preexisting questionnaire (e.g., the Position Analysis Questionnaire) is considered, its task statement content should be assessed relative to the task content of the jobs to be analyzed prior to any decision to use the questionnaire.

A second limitation of task questionnaires pertains to potential respondent reactions. Respondents may react negatively if they feel the questionnaire does not contain task statements covering important aspects of their jobs. Respondents may also find completion of the questionnaire to be both tedious and boring, and this may cause them to commit rating errors. Interpretation and understanding of the task statements may be problematic for some respondents who have reading and comprehension skill deficiencies.

Finally, it should be remembered that a typical task questionnaire focuses on tasks. Other job requirement components, particularly KSAOs and those related to job context, may be ignored or downplayed if the task questionnaire is relied upon as the method of job information collection.

Combined Methods Only in rare instances does a job analysis involve use of only a single method. Much more likely is a "mix-and-match" eclectic approach using multiple methods. This makes job analysis a more complicated process to design and administer than implied by a description of each of the methods alone.

Criteria for Choice of Methods Some explicit choices regarding methods of job analysis need to be made. One set of choices involves decisions to use or not use a particular method of information collection. An organization must decide, for example, whether to use an "off-the-shelf" method or its own particular method that is suited to its own needs and circumstances. A second set of choices involves how to blend together a set of methods that will all be used, in varying ways and degrees, in the actual job analysis. Some criteria for guidance in such decisions are shown in Exhibit 5.16.

Sources to Be Used

Choosing sources of information involves considering who will be used to provide the information sought. While this matter is not entirely independent of job analysis methods (e.g., use of a task questionnaire normally requires use of job incumbents as the source), it is treated as such in the sections that follow.

Job Analyst A job analyst is someone who, by virtue of job title and training, is available and suited to conduct job analyses and to guide the job analysis process. The job analyst is also "out of the loop," being neither manager nor incumbent of the jobs analyzed. As such, the job analyst brings a combination of expertise and neutrality to the work.

EXHIBIT 5.16   Criteria for Guiding Choice of Job Analysis Methods

1. Degree of suitability/versatility for use across different types of jobs
2. Degree of standardization in the process and in the reporting of results
3. Acceptability of process and results to those who will serve as sources and/or users
4. Degree to which method is operational and may be used off-the-shelf without modification, as opposed to method requiring tailor-made development and application
5. Amount of training required for sources and users of job information
6. Costs of the job analysis, both in terms of direct administrative costs and opportunity costs of time involvement by people
7. Quality of resultant information in terms of reliability and content validity
8. Usability of results in recruitment, selection, and employment activities.

Source: Adapted from E. L. Levine, R. A. Ash, H. Hall, and F. Sistrunk, "Evaluation of Job Analysis Methods by Experienced Job Analysts," *Academy of Management Journal*, 1983, 26, 339–348.

Despite such advantages and appeals, reliance upon a job analyst as the job information source is not without potential limitations. First, the analyst may be perceived as an outsider by incumbents and supervisors, a perception that may eventuate in questioning the analyst's job knowledge and expertise, as well as trustworthiness. Second, the job analyst may, in fact, lack detailed knowledge of the jobs to be analyzed, especially in an organization with many different job titles. Lack of knowledge may cause the analyst to bring inaccurate job stereotypes to the analysis process. Finally, having specially designated job analysts (either as employees or outside consultants) tends to be expensive.

Job Incumbents   Job incumbents seem like a natural source of information to be used in job analysis, and indeed they are relied upon in most job analysis systems. The major advantage to working with job incumbents is their familiarity with tasks, KSAOs, and job context. In addition, job incumbents may become more accepting of the job analysis process and its results through their participation in it.

Some skepticism should be maintained about job incumbents as a source of workplace data, as is true for any source. They may lack the knowledge or insights necessary to provide inclusive information, especially if they are probationary or part-time employees. Some employees also may have difficulty in describing the tasks involved in their job, or in being able to infer and articulate the underlying KSAOs necessary for the job. Another potential limitation of job incumbents as an information source pertains to their motivation to be a willing and accurate source. Feelings of distrust and suspicion may greatly hamper employees' willingness to function capably as sources. For example, incumbents may intentionally fail to report certain tasks as part of their job so that those tasks are not incorporated into the formal job description. Or, incumbents may purposely inflate the importance ratings of tasks in order to make the job appear more difficult than it actually is.

Supervisors   Supervisors could and should be considered excellent sources for use in job analysis. They not only supervise employees performing the job to be analyzed, they may also have played a major role in defining it and later in adding/ deleting job tasks (as in evolving and flexible jobs). Moreover, supervisors ultimately have to accept the resultant descriptions and specifications for jobs they supervise, and inclusion of them as a source seems a way to ensure such acceptance.

Subject Matter Experts   Often times, the sources previously mentioned are called subject matter experts or SMEs.[19] Individuals other than those mentioned may also be used as SMEs. These people bring particular expertise to the job analysis process, an expertise thought not to be available through standard sources.

While the exact qualifications for being designated an SME are far from clear, examples of sources so designated are available. These include previous jobholders (e.g., recently promoted employees), private consultants, customer/clients, and citizens-at-large for some public sector jobs, such as superintendent of schools for a school district. Whatever the sources of SMEs, a common requirement for them is that they have recent, firsthand knowledge of the job being analyzed.

Combined Sources Combinations of sources, like combinations of methods, are most likely to be used in a typical job analysis. This is not only likely, but desirable. As noted previously, each source has some potentially unique insight to contribute to job analysis, as well as some limitations. It is through a pooling of such sources, and the information they provide, that an accurate and acceptable job analysis is most likely to result.

Job Analysis Process

Collecting job information through job analysis requires development and use of an overall process for doing so. Unfortunately, there is no set or best process to be followed; the process has to be tailor-made to suit the specifics of the situation in which it occurs. There are, however, many key issues to be dealt with in the construction and operation of the process.[20] Each of these is briefly commented on next.

Purpose The purpose(s) of job analysis should be clearly identified and agreed upon. Since job analysis is a process designed to yield job information, the organization should ask exactly what job information is desired and why. Here, it is useful to refer back to the job requirements matrix to review the types of information that can be sought and obtained in a job requirements job analysis. Management must decide exactly what types of information are desired (task statements, task dimensions, and so forth), and in what format. Once the desired output and results of job analysis have been determined, the organization can then plan a process that will yield the desired results.

Scope The issue of scope involves which job(s) to include in the job analysis. Decisions about actual scope should be based on consideration of (a) the importance of the job to the functioning of the organization, (b) the number of job applicants and incumbents, (c) whether the job is entry level and thus subject to constant staffing activity, (d) the frequency with which job requirements (both tasks and KSAOs) change, and (e) the amount of time lapsed since the previous job analysis.

Internal Staff or Consultant The organization may conduct the job analysis using its own staff, or it may procure external consultants. This is a difficult de-

---

EXHIBIT 5.17   Factors to Consider in Choosing Between Internal Staff or Consultants for Job Analysis

---

Internal Staff	Consultant
Cost of technical or procedural failure is low	Cost of technical or procedural failure is high
Project scope is limited	Project scope is comprehensive and/or large
Need for job data ongoing	Need for job data is a one-time, isolated event
There is a desire to develop internal staff skills in job analysis	There is a need for assured availability of each type and level of job analysis skill
Strong management controls are in place to control project costs	Predictability of project cost can depend on adhering to work plan
Knowledge of organization's norms, "culture," and jargon are critical	Technical innovativeness and quality are critical
Technical credibility of internal staff is high	Leverage of external "expert" status is needed to execute project
Process and products of the project are unlikely to be challenged	Process and products of the project are likely to be legally, technically, or politically scrutinized
Rational or narrative job analysis methods are desired	Commercial or proprietary job analysis methods are desired
Data collected are qualitative	Data collection methods are structured, standardized, and/or quantitative

---

Source: D. M. Van De Vort and B. V. Stalder, "Organizing for Job Analysis," in S. Gael (ed.), *The Job Analysis Handbook for Business, Industry, and Government.* Copyright © 1988 by John Wiley & Sons, Inc. Reprinted by permission of John Wiley & Sons, Inc.

cision to make since it involves not only the obvious consideration of cost, but many other considerations as well. Exhibit 5.17 highlights some of these concerns and the trade-offs involved.

Organization and Coordination   Any job analysis project, whether conducted by internal staff or external consultants, requires careful organization and coordination. There are two key steps to take to help ensure that this is achieved. First, an organizational member should be appointed to function as a project manager for the total process (if consultants are used, they should report to this project manager). The project manager should be assigned overall responsibility for the total project, including its organization and control. Second, the roles and relationships for the various people involved in the project—HR staff, project staff, line managers, and job incumbents—must be clearly established.

Communication   Clear and open communication with all concerned facilitates the job analysis process. Job analysis will be thought of by some employees as analogous to an invasive, exploratory surgical procedure, which, in turn, naturally raises questions in their minds about its purpose, process, and results. These questions and concerns need to be anticipated and addressed forthrightly.

Work Flow and Time Frame   Job analysis involves a mixture of people and paper in a process in which they can become entangled very quickly. The project manager should develop and adhere to a work-flow chart that shows the sequential ordering of steps to be followed in the conduct of the job analysis. This should be accompanied by a time frame showing critical completion dates for project phases, as well as a final deadline.

Analysis, Synthesis, and Documentation   Once collected, job information must be analyzed and synthesized through use of various procedural and statistical means. These should be planned in advance and incorporated into the work-flow and time-frame requirements. Likewise, provisions need to be made for preparation of written documents, especially job descriptions and job specifications, and their incorporation into relevant policy and procedure manuals.

Maintenance of the System   Job analysis does not end with completion of the project. Rather, mechanisms must be developed and put into place to maintain the job analysis and information system over time. This is critical because the system will be exposed to numerous influences requiring response and adaptation. Examples of these influences include (a) changes in job tasks and KSAOs—additions, deletions, and modifications; (b) job redesign, restructuring, and realignment; and (c) creation of new jobs. In short, job analysis must be thought of and administered as an ongoing organizational process.

Example of Job Analysis Process   Because of the many factors involved, there is no best or required job analysis process. Rather, the process must be designed to fit each particular situation. Exhibit 5.18 shows an example of the job analysis process with a narrow scope, namely for a single job—that of administrative assistant (secretary). This is a specially-conducted job analysis that uses multiple methods (prior information, observation, interviews), and multiple sources (job analyst, job incumbents, supervisors). It was conducted by a previous holder of the job (subject matter expert), and it took the person about 20 hours over a 30-day period to conduct and prepare a written job description as the output of the process.

EXHIBIT 5.18   Example of Job Requirements Job Analysis

1. Meet with manager of the job, discuss project

→

2. Gather existing job information from *Dictionary of Occupational Titles*, current job description, observation of incumbents

→

3. Prepare tentative set of task statements

→

4. Review task statements with incumbents and managers; add, delete, rewrite statements

→

5. Finalize task statements, get approval from incumbents and managers

→

6. Formulate task dimensions, assign tasks to dimension, determine % time spent (importance) for each dimension

→

7. Infer necessary KSAOs, develop tentative list

→

8. Review KSAOs with incumbents and managers; add, delete, and rewrite KSAOs

→

9. Finalize KSAOs, get approval from incumbents and manager

→

10. Develop job requirements matrix and/or job description in useable format

→

11. Provide matrix or job description to parties (e.g., incumbents, manager, HR department)

→

12. Use matrix or job description in staffing activities, such as communicating with recruits and recruiters, developing the selection plan

→

JOB REWARDS JOB ANALYSIS

Overview

Broadly speaking, every job has an array of rewards associated with it. Some of these rewards are external to the job itself and the tasks that comprise the job. Examples of such rewards include pay, benefits, promotion opportunities, and type of supervision. Collectively, these are referred to as extrinsic rewards. Other rewards, however, are internal to the job itself. They are usually a direct outgrowth of the tasks themselves and the feelings that an employee experiences while performing and completing the tasks. Feelings of autonomy, utilization of skills, and achievement of tasks and related goals are examples of these types of rewards. The label generally attached to these is intrinsic rewards.

The job rewards approach to job analysis focuses on both extrinsic and intrinsic rewards, as shown in Exhibit 5.19. As can be seen, the first purpose of job analysis is to identify the extrinsic rewards associated with the job. Usually this is a straightforward process since the extrinsic rewards have already been established by the organization as part of regular HR functional activities. As an example, the pay is specified as part of the organization's compensation activities, which detail starting pay and pay range. These terms are recorded and reported in a variety of ways, such as HR policy manuals, employee handbooks, labor contracts, and recruitment literature. The result of this job analysis is specification of extrinsic terms and conditions of employment.

A second form of analysis is concerned with inferring the intrinsic rewards associated with the job, as seen in Exhibit 5.19. These inferences are made by studying the tasks identified during the job analysis; for example, the extent of repetitive tasks in a job says something about how challenging it is. Inferences also are (and probably should be) made on the basis of responses from job incumbents to questionnaires designed to reveal their sense of on-the-job achievement, utilization of skills, and so forth. Results of analysis of intrinsic rewards is communicated as intrinsic terms and conditions of employment. They may be used as a basis for redesigning jobs (and thus task and KSAO requirements), developing recruitment information, and designing promotion systems that provide increases in both extrinsic and intrinsic rewards as employees advance upward in the organization's hierarchy.

Before proceeding, it should be noted that the treatment of job rewards job analysis will be relatively brief. This brevity is the result of two related factors. First, organizations typically pay little or no formal attention to this type of job analysis; whatever energy and resources are devoted to job analysis are usually given to the job requirements variety. Second, the research and knowledge base from which to draw our discussion of job rewards job analysis is quite recent and limited. Hopefully, these circumstances will change in the future. In the meantime,

---

EXHIBIT 5.19   Job Rewards Approach to Job Analysis

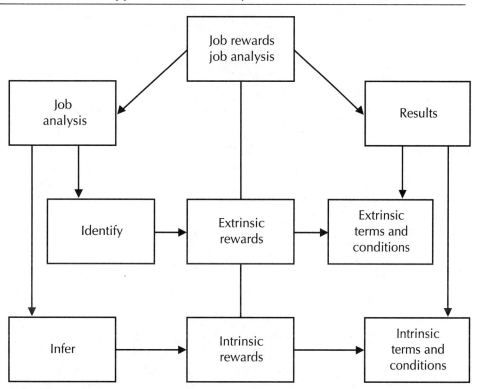

---

the discussion that follows should be viewed as tentative, but promising, in terms of job analysis practice and research.

Job Rewards Matrix

The operational framework for job rewards job analysis is specified in the job rewards matrix, shown in Exhibit 5.20. The matrix shows the key components to be addressed by the job analysis and the type of information that must be collected and reported.

At the top of the matrix is space for a job title and a job summary, just as in the job requirements approach. The far left column is labeled "rewards," and calls for a listing (from 1 to N) of the rewards associated with the job. The next column

---

EXHIBIT 5.20   Job Rewards Matrix

Job Title:

Job Summary:

Reward	Dimensions	Reward Characteristics		
		Amount	Differential	Stability
1	A			
2				
3				
4	B			
.	.			
.	.			
.	.			
N	Z			

is labeled "dimensions," and in it are placed the names of groupings (A,B, . . . Z) of broader reward dimensions. The remaining columns are used to indicate "reward characteristics," which are ways of describing the nature of rewards. There are three such characteristics in the matrix: "amount," "differential," and "stability." When completed, the job requirements matrix shows a virtual catalogue of information about a job's rewards. An example of a completed job rewards matrix for the job of administrative assistant is shown in Exhibit 5.21.

Bearing the job rewards matrix in mind, we now turn to a brief discussion of its components. Blended into this discussion are ideas regarding methods (e.g., interviews, questionnaires) and sources (e.g., incumbents, managers) for collecting the rewards information.

Rewards

This portion of the job analysis requires development of an inclusive set or list of rewards that are a part of the job and are experienced by job incumbents. Research has been quite successful in identifying sets or taxonomies of relatively independent rewards through the development of job reward measures. The two most prominent of these measures are the Minnesota Job Description Questionnaire (MJDQ) and the Job Diagnostic Survey (JDS).[21] The MJDQ provides information about 20 different rewards, and covers the spectrum of both extrinsic and intrinsic rewards. The JDS, alternatively, measures a total of seven rewards (five "core"

EXHIBIT 5.21   Portion of Job Rewards Matrix for Job of Administrative Assistant

Reward	Dimension	Amount	Reward Characteristics		
			Differential	Stability	
1. Starting pay	A. Individual pay (extrinsic)	$2,000/month minimum	May exceed minimum, depending on KSAOs	Changes according to market conditions	
2. Pay raises	A. Individual pay (extrinsic)	Typically 2–3%	Across the board (same % for all)	Range from 0% to 10%, annually	
3. Bonuses	A. Individual pay (extrinsic)	2.5% average	Range from 0% to 10%, depending on performance	Will vary each year, depending on size of bonus pool	
4. Doing different tasks	B. Skill variety (intrinsic)	x̄ = 4.8*	SD = .73*	Frequent change	
5. Using complex skills	B. Skill variety (intrinsic)	x̄ = 3.9*	SD = 1.54*	No recent changes; none anticipated	
6. Doing simple and repetitive tasks	B. Skill variety (intrinsic)	x̄ = 5.4*	SD = .37*	Will continue to be part of job	

*Rating scale (1–7) values, based on the three skill variety items from the Job Diagnostic Survey (JDS).

job characteristics plus two others), all of which are intrinsic in nature. Exhibit 5.22 shows listings of the rewards measured by the MJDQ and the JDS.

Reward sets such as those included on the MJDQ and JDS are a useful starting point for any job rewards job analysis. The sets could be amended by inclusion of additional rewards not covered by either of these measures, but clearly associated with the job. Such modifications could come about through consultation with various SMEs (e.g., incumbents, supervisors, HR staff representatives), using a variety of methods (e.g., interviews, questionnaires, observation). The desired end product of this part of the job analysis is a set of rewards that are agreed upon by all sources and methods as inclusive in scope and acceptable for purposes of capturing the reward domain of jobs.

Reward Dimensions

Once a reward set has been identified, the resulting list of rewards either must stand alone or must somehow be collapsed into a set of more general reward dimensions. Either choice is acceptable, and the decision made should be based on the ease with which the rewards are likely to be classified, as well as the usefulness of having rewards so cast.

EXHIBIT 5.22   Rewards Assessed by the Minnesota Job Description Questionnaire (MJDQ) and the Job Diagnostic Survey (JDS)

MJDQ	JDS
1. Ability utilization	1. Skill variety*
2. Achievement	2. Task identity*
3. Activity	3. Task significance*
4. Advancement	4. Autonomy*
5. Authority	5. Feedback from job*
6. Company policies and procedures	6. Feedback from agents
7. Compensation	7. Dealing with others
8. Co-workers	
9. Creativity	*Core job characteristics
10. Independence	
11. Moral values	
12. Recognition	
13. Responsibility	
14. Security	
15. Social service	
16. Social status	
17. Supervision—human relations	
18. Supervision—technical	
19. Variety	
20. Working conditions	

It is probably useful, and relatively easy, to distinguish rewards as either "extrinsic" or "intrinsic." Extrinsic rewards are those that are established and changed (usually by management) without any direct, intended effect on job requirements (tasks or KSAOs). Intrinsic rewards, alternatively, are inherent to the nature of the job itself and thus flow from job tasks and the KSAOs required to perform the tasks. As noted, all of the rewards on the JDS are considered intrinsic. The MJDQ, however, contains a mixture of extrinsic and intrinsic rewards.

It is possible to go beyond the straightforward extrinsic/intrinsic dichotomy. Extrinsic rewards may be classified into a series of dimensions such as direct compensation, benefits, work hours, and internal job mobility. Intrinsic rewards may be classified into dimensions having to do with breadth of tasks, utilization of KSAOs, and task goals/challenges. Any such classification is possible; the key consideration is whether it meets the tests of ease and usefulness mentioned earlier. It should also be noted that these considerations are compounded by the fact that little is known about how various methods and sources can be used most effectively to form reward dimensions.

Reward Characteristics

In the job rewards matrix it is suggested that the organization analyze and record three particular characteristics of rewards: amount, differential, and stability. Each of these characteristics is considered next.

Amount of Reward   Clearly, any analysis of job rewards would seek to provide some indication about their amount or level. For external rewards, this is a relatively straightforward process because the reward amounts are externally defined and specified (e.g., starting pay, hours of work, number of vacation days). Intrinsic reward amounts, by their very nature, are not so easily analyzed and specified. They are not externally established, and there are no objective measures of their amount (e.g., how does one objectively measure amount of task challenge?). The amount of an intrinsic reward thus must be inferred from what various sources (e.g., incumbents, supervisors) tell about it.

Subjective methods or measures thus are used to gather the desired information about intrinsic reward amounts. Here is where the MJDQ and JDS again are very useful, for both have a solid history of research supporting their reliability and validity as measures.[22] Both use a questionnaire method of measurement. For the MJDQ, respondents are asked to indicate how well 20 job rewards describe their job, using a unique ranking procedure. For the JDS, respondents rate the amount of each reward on a 1–7 rating scale. Respondents for the MJDQ are usually supervisors, and for the JDS, they are incumbents. Exhibit 5.23 shows one set of the rating scales for the seven rewards measured by the JDS (the full instrument contains two more sets of items for these same seven rewards as well). After respondents have completed the JDS, the average rating score for each reward is computed, and those averages then represent the amounts of the rewards present in the job.

EXHIBIT 5.23   Set of Items from the Job Diagnostic Survey

1. To what extent does your job require you to *work closely with other people* (either "clients," or people in related jobs in your own organization)?

1	2	3	4	5	6	7

    Very little; dealing with other people is not at all necessary in doing the job.

    Moderately; some dealing with others is necessary.

    Very much; dealing with other people is an absolutely essential and crucial part of doing the job.

2. How much *autonomy* is there in your job? That is, to what extent does your job permit you to decide *on your own* how to go about doing the work?

1	2	3	4	5	6	7

    Very little; the job gives me almost no personal say about how and when the work is done.

    Moderate autonomy; many things are standardized and not under my control, but I can make some decisions about the work.

    Very much; the job gives me almost complete responsibility for deciding how and when the work is done.

3. To what extent does your job involve doing a *whole and identifiable piece of work?* That is, is the job a complete piece of work that has an obvious beginning and end? Or is it only a small *part* of the overall piece of work, which is finished by other people or by automatic machines?

1	2	3	4	5	6	7

    My job is only a tiny part of the overall piece of work; the results of my activities cannot be seen in the final product or service.

    My job is a moderate-sized chunk of the overall piece of work; my own contribution can be seen in the final outcome.

    My job involves doing the whole piece of work, from start to finish; the results of my activities are easily seen in the final product or service.

4. How much *variety* is there in your job? That is, to what extent does the job require you to do many different things at work, using a variety of your skills and talents?

1	2	3	4	5	6	7

    Very little; the job requires me to do the same routine things over and over again.

    Moderate variety.

    Very much; the job requires me to do many different things, using a number of different skills and talents.

continued

EXHIBIT 5.23   Continued

5. In general, how *significant or important* is your job? That is, are the results of your work likely to significantly affect the lives or well-being of other people?

1	2	3	4	5	6	7

Not very significant; the outcomes of my work are *not* likely to have important effects on other people.

Moderately significant.

Highly significant; the outcomes of my work can affect other people in very important ways.

6. To what extent do *managers or co-workers* let you know how well you are doing on your job?

1	2	3	4	5	6	7

Very little; people almost never let me know how well I am doing.

Moderately; sometimes people may give me feedback; other times they may not.

Very much; managers or co-workers provide me with almost constant feedback about how well I am doing.

7. To what extent does *doing the job itself* provide you with information about your work performance? That is, does the actual *work itself* provide clues about how well you are doing aside from any feedback co-workers or supervisors may provide?

1	2	3	4	5	6	7

Very little; the job itself is set up so I could work forever without finding out how well I am doing.

Moderately; sometimes doing the job provides feedback to me; sometimes it does not.

Very much; the job is set up so that I get almost constant feedback as I work about how well I am doing.

If it is difficult or not possible to obtain actual ratings of amount of reward, simpler methods can be used. For example, job incumbents could be interviewed and asked to indicate whether each reward had a "high," "medium," or "low" amount. Their collective, modal response could then be placed into one of these three categories for each reward.

Unless the organization uses the MJDQ or JDS to measure intrinsic reward amounts, it must develop its own measure. If this is done, considerable care and caution should be exercised regarding the measure's development, reliability, and validity.

Reward Differential   This characteristic refers to the relative differences in reward amount that may be received or experienced by job incumbents. Do all have the same salary? Do all experience the same amount of skill variety? Such questions are at the heart of the reward differential issue.

Analyzing extrinsic job rewards in terms of their differential is quite straightforward. The analyst simply consults the relevant HR policies and activities to determine whether there are reward differentials or not, and if so, how many and how much. Consider the case of wage or salary. The analyst can look at the compensation policies for a job and determine whether all employees receive the same rate of pay, and if they do not, the range of pay rates (minimum and maximum) that are possible.

Analyzing intrinsic reward differentials is more difficult. Even though all employees on a given job may perform roughly the same tasks, they differ in how they perceive or experience the intrinsic rewards that flow from these tasks. The job analysis must be prepared to capture these differentials among employees for each intrinsic reward.

Measurement of reward differentials with questionnaire instruments such as the MJDQ and the JDS is easily accomplished. The analyst simply computes the standard deviation of ratings assigned to each reward by the respondents. The greater the standard deviation, the greater the variability in reward, as experienced and reported by the respondents. In the absence of a measure such as the MJDQ or JDS, the organization will have to build its own method of assessing reward differentials. For example, it may interview job incumbents about various intrinsic rewards, and based on their responses, classify each intrinsic reward as "high," "medium," or "low." Naturally, the reliability of this classification process is important to determine.

Reward Stability   Does the amount of a reward remain stable over time, or does it change? This is the matter of reward stability. For extrinsic rewards, assessment of stability is made by inspection of HR policies and activities that are explicitly designed to create stability or instability. Consider the extrinsic reward "pay raise." Analysis of the organization's pay raise policies will show whether or not pay raises are given, and if so, how frequently.

Assessing intrinsic reward stability will require gauging employees' perceptions of, or experiences with, these types of rewards over time. Perceptions of skill variety, for example, may change due to changes in actual task content, as occurs in evolving and flexible jobs.[23] Or, changes in employees themselves (e.g., KSAO changes due to new training and/or educational experiences) may lead them to perceive their intrinsic rewards differently over time.

Capturing the effects of these types of changes on employees and their perceptions of rewards may require a substantial commitment from the organization. For example, it may mean establishing and maintaining an intrinsic reward tracking system for employees in each particular job. This might require, for example, periodic (annual) administrations of the JDS to employees, followed by the necessary statistical analysis and interpretation of results as they pertain to trends in perceptions of rewards. Alternatively, in a more casual mode, summary written statements about stability may be made (and changed when necessary), as was done in Exhibit 5.21.

Results of Job Rewards Job Analysis

The job analysis produces a thorough description of the structure and pattern of rewards for a particular job. It is a description of the extrinsic and intrinsic terms and conditions of the job. The organization will thus have identified and defined such features as (a) the domain of relevant rewards; (b) broader groupings or dimensions of rewards, both extrinsic and intrinsic; (c) indications about the amount of each reward present; (d) how much difference there is among employees in the amounts of rewards they receive and experience; and (e) how stable or fluctuating are the rewards that employees receive.

Unfortunately, this wealth of job reward information may be difficult to translate into directly usable form. There are no standard procedures or formats for expressing the information. The job rewards matrix, however, is a good starting point for recording and communicating the job reward information that has been collected.

In addition, the organization can use its own creativity to develop its own unique and useful ways of putting the information into usable formats and then incorporating it into policy manuals, employee handbooks, recruitment literature, college relations programs, and the like. As will be discussed, having and using job rewards information in these ways may play a key role in the multitude of recruitment, selection, and employment activities.

LEGAL ISSUES

This chapter has emphasized the crucial role that job analysis plays in establishing the foundations for staffing activities. That crucial role continues from a legal perspective. Job analysis becomes intimately involved in court cases involving the job relatedness of staffing activities. It also occupies a prominent position in the Uniform Guidelines on Employee Selection Procedures (UGESP). Finally, the Americans With Disabilities Act requires that the organization determine the essential functions of each job, and job analysis can play a pivotal role in that process. As these issues are discussed in the following sections, note the direct relevance of the job requirements matrix and its development to them.

Job Relatedness and Court Cases

In EEO/AA court cases, the organization is confronted with the need to justify its challenged staffing practices as being job-related. Common sense suggests that this requires first and foremost that the organization conduct some type of job analysis as a way of identifying job requirements and rewards. In addition, it also is the case that specific features or characteristics of the job analysis make a difference in the organization's defense. Specifically, an examination of court cases indicates that for purposes of legal defensibility the organization should conform to the following recommendations:

1. "Job analysis must be performed and must be for the job for which the selection instrument is to be utilized.
2. Analysis of the job should be in writing.
3. Job analysts should describe in detail the procedure used.
4. Job data should be collected from a variety of current sources by knowledgeable job analysts.
5. Sample size should be large and representative of the jobs for which the selection instrument is used.
6. Tasks, duties, and activities should be included in the analysis.
7. The most important tasks should be represented in the selection device.
8. Competency levels of job performance for entry-level jobs should be specified.
9. Knowledge, skills, and abilities should be specified, particularly if a content validation model is followed."[24]

These recommendations are very consistent with our more general discussion of job analysis as an important tool and basic foundation for staffing activities. Moreover, even though these recommendations were made several years ago, there is little reason to doubt or modify any of them on the basis of more recent court cases.

Job Analysis and Selection

The UGESP (see Appendix A) places great emphasis on job analysis in the conduct of validation studies. In general, these guidelines indicate that any validation study should begin with a job analysis. More specifically, here is their exact language regarding job analysis for criterion-related and content validation studies:

1. Criterion-related validation: "Validity studies should be based on review of information about the job for which the selection procedure is to be used. The review should include a job analysis except as provided in section 14B(3) below with respect to criterion-related validity. Any method of job analysis may be used if it provides the information required for the specific validation strategy used.

There should be a review of job information to determine measures of work behavior(s) or performance that are relevant to the job or group of jobs in question. These measures or criteria are relevant to the extent that they represent critical or important job duties, work behaviors, or work outcomes as developed from the review of job information."

2. Content validation: "There should be a job analysis which includes an analysis of the important work behavior(s) required for successful performance and their relative importance and, if the behavior results in work product(s), an analysis of the work product(s). Any job analysis should focus on the work behavior(s) and the tasks associated with them. If work behaviors are not observable, the job analysis should identify and analyze those aspects of the behavior(s) that can be observed and the observed work products. The work behavior(s) selected for measurement should be critical work behavior(s) and/or important work behavior(s) constituting most of the job.

For any selection procedure measuring a knowledge, skill or ability the user should show that (a) the selection procedure measures and is a representative sample of that knowledge, skill or ability and (b) that knowledge, skill or ability is used in and is a necessary prerequisite to critical or important work behavior(s)."

Reflection on these statements reveals the crucial role accorded job analysis in the conduct of validation studies. It is essential for derivation of the content of both criterion and predictor measures and for establishment of links between tasks and KSAOs.

Essential Job Functions

Recall that under the ADA, the organization must not discriminate against a qualified individual with a disability who can perform the "essential functions" of the job, with or without reasonable accommodation. This requirement raises three questions: What are essential functions? What is evidence of essential functions? What is the role of job analysis?

What Are Essential Functions?

The ADA employment regulations (see Appendix C) provide the following statements about essential functions:

1. "The term essential functions refers to the fundamental job duties of the employment position the individual with a disability holds or desires. The

term essential function does not include the marginal functions of the position; and

2. A job function may be considered essential for any of several reasons, including but not limited to the following:

   - The function may be essential because the reason the position exists is to perform the function;
   - The function may be essential because of the limited number of employees available among whom the performance of that job function can be distributed; and/or
   - The function may be highly specialized so that the incumbent in the position is hired for his or her expertise or ability to perform the particular function."

Evidence of Essential Functions

The employment regulations go on to indicate what constitutes evidence that any particular function is in fact an essential one. That evidence includes, but is not limited to,

1. the employer's judgement as to which functions are essential
2. written job descriptions, prepared before advertising or interviewing applicants for the job
3. the amount of time spent on the job performing the function
4. the consequences of not requiring the incumbent to perform the function
5. the terms of a collective bargaining agreement
6. the work experience of past incumbents in the job
7. the current work experience of incumbents in similar jobs

Role of Job Analysis

What role(s) might job analysis play in identifying essential functions and establishing evidence of their being essential? The employment regulations are silent on this question. However, the EEOC has provided substantial and detailed assistance to organizations to deal with this, and many other issues, under the ADA.[25] The specific statements regarding job analysis and essential functions of the job are shown in Exhibit 5.24.

Examination of the statements in Exhibit 5.24 suggests the following. First, while job analysis is not required by law as a means of establishing essential functions of a job, it is strongly recommended. Second, the job analysis should focus on tasks associated with the job. Where KSAOs are also studied or specified, they should be derived from an explicit consideration of their probable links to the essential tasks. Finally, with regard to tasks, the focus should be on the tasks themselves and the outcome or results of the tasks, rather than the methods by which they are performed.

EXHIBIT 5.24   Job Analysis and Essential Functions of the Job

Job Analysis and the Essential Functions of a Job

The ADA does not require that an employer conduct a job analysis or any particular form of job analysis to identify the essential functions of a job. The information provided by a job analysis may or may not be helpful in properly identifying essential job functions, depending on how it is conducted.

The term "job analysis" generally is used to describe a formal process in which information about a specific job or occupation is collected and analyzed. Formal job analysis may be conducted by a number of different methods. These methods obtain different kinds of information that is used for different purposes. Some of these methods will not provide information sufficient to determine if an individual with a disability is qualified to perform "essential" job functions.

For example: One kind of formal job analysis looks at specific job tasks and classifies jobs according to how these tasks deal with data, people, and objects. This type of job analysis is used to set wage rates for various jobs; however, it may not be adequate to identify the essential functions of a *particular* job, as required by the ADA. Another kind of job analysis looks at the kinds of knowledge, skills, and abilities that are necessary to perform a job. This type of job analysis is used to develop selection criteria for various jobs. The information from this type of analysis sometimes helps to measure the importance of certain skills, knowledge and abilities, but it does not take into account the fact that people with disabilities often can perform essential functions using other skills and abilities.

Some job analysis methods ask current employees and their supervisors to rate the importance of general characteristics necessary to perform a job, such as "strength," "endurance," or "intelligence," without linking these characteristics to *specific* job functions or specific tasks that are part of a function. Such general information may not identify, for example, whether upper body or lower body strength is required, or whether muscular endurance or cardiovascular endurance is needed to perform a particular job function. Such information, by itself, would not be sufficient to determine whether an individual who has particular limitations can perform an essential function with or without an accommodation.

As already stated, the ADA does not require a formal job analysis or any particular method of analysis to identify the essential functions of a job. A small employer may wish to conduct an informal analysis by observing and consulting with people who perform the job, or have previously performed it, and their supervisors. If possible, it is advisable to observe and consult with several workers under a range of conditions, to get a better idea of all job functions and the different ways they may be performed. Production records and workloads also may be relevant factors to consider.

(continued)

EXHIBIT 5.24   Continued

To identify essential job functions under the ADA, a job analysis should focus on the purpose of the job and the importance of actual job functions in achieving this purpose. Evaluating importance may include consideration of the frequency with which a function is performed, the amount of time spent on the function, and the consequences if the function is not performed. The analysis may include information on the work environment (such as unusual heat, cold, humidity, dust, toxic substances or stress factors). The job analysis may contain information on the manner in which a job currently is performed, but should not conclude that ability to perform the job in that manner is an essential function, unless there is no other way to perform the function without causing undue hardship. A job analysis will be most helpful for purposes of the ADA if it focuses on the results or outcome of a function, not solely on the way it customarily is performed.

For example:

- An essential function of a computer programmer job might be described as "ability to develop programs that accomplish necessary objectives," rather than "ability to manually write programs." Although a person currently performing the job may write these programs by hand, that is not the essential function, because programs can be developed directly on the computer.

- If a job requires mastery of information contained in technical manuals, this essential function would be "ability to learn technical material," rather than "ability to read technical manuals." People with visual and other reading impairments could perform this function using other means, such as audiotapes.

- A job that requires objects to be moved from one place to another should state this essential function. The analysis may note that the person in the job "lifts 50-pound cartons to a height of 3 or 4 feet and loads them into truck-trailers 5 hours daily," but should not identify the "ability to *manually* lift and load 50-pound cartons" as an essential function unless this is the only method by which the function can be performed without causing an undue hardship.

A job analysis that is focused on outcomes or results also will be helpful in establishing appropriate qualification standards, developing job descriptions, conducting interviews, and selecting people in accordance with ADA requirements. It will be particularly helpful in identifying accommodations that will enable an individual with specific functional abilities and limitations to perform the job.

Source: Equal Employment Opportunity Commission, *Technical Assistance Manual for the Employment Provisions (Title I) of the Americans With Disabilities Act* (Washington, D.C.: author, 1992), pp. II-18 to II-20.

SUMMARY

Organizations design and use various types of jobs—traditional, evolving, flexible, idiosyncratic, and team-based. These design approaches all result in job content in the form of job requirements and rewards. Job analysis is described as the process used to gather, analyze, synthesize, and report information about job content. The job requirements approach to job analysis focuses on tasks, KSAOs, and job context. The job rewards approach is concerned with extrinsic and intrinsic job rewards and various characteristics of them.

The job requirements approach is guided by the job requirements matrix. The matrix calls for information about tasks and task dimensions, as well as their importance. In a parallel fashion, it requires information about KSAOs required for the tasks, plus indications about the importance of those KSAOs. The final component of the matrix deals with the job context, both physical demands and environmental conditions.

When gathering the information called for by the job requirements matrix, the organization is confronted with a multitude of choices. Those choices are shown to revolve around various job analysis methods, sources, and processes. The organization must pick and choose from among these; all have advantages and disadvantages associated with them. The choices should be guided by a concern for the accuracy and acceptability of the information that is being gathered.

The job rewards matrix is suggested for use in a job rewards job analysis. The matrix indicates a need to identify the extrinsic and intrinsic rewards offered by the job. It also requires indication of the rewards' amounts, differences among employees, and stability. Instruments and processes for collecting the necessary information are in their infancy, as is the formal incorporation and use of the information in staffing activities.

From a legal perspective, job analysis is shown to assume major importance in creating staffing systems and practices that are in compliance with EEO/AA laws and regulations. The employer must ensure (or be able to show) that its practices are job-related. This requires not only having conducted a job requirements job analysis, but also using a process that itself has defensible characteristics. The UGESP clearly accords job analysis a prominent place in the conduct of validation studies. Indeed, it is required as an initial step in both criterion-related and content validation. Under the ADA, the organization must identify the essential functions of the job. While this does not require a job analysis, the organization should strongly consider it as one of the tools to be used. Over time, we will learn more about how job analysis is treated under the ADA.

DISCUSSION QUESTIONS

1. Identify a team-based job situation. What are examples of job-spanning KSAOs required in that situation?

2. How should task statements be written, and what sorts of problems might you encounter in asking a job incumbent to write these statements?

3. Would it be better to first identify task dimensions and then create specific task statements for each dimension, or should task statements be identified first and then used to create task dimensions?

4. What would you consider when trying to decide what criteria (e.g., % time spent) to use for gathering indications about task importance?

5. How might existing skill (e.g., SCANS) and ability (e.g., Fleishman and Reilly) taxonomies be used to help identify KSAOs in a job analysis?

6. What are the advantages and disadvantages to using multiple methods of job analysis for a particular job? Multiple sources?

7. Why might an organization resist doing a job rewards job analysis and using the results in staffing activities?

APPLICATIONS

Conducting a Job Requirements or Job Rewards Job Analysis

Job analysis is defined as "the process of studying jobs in order to gather, synthesize, and report information about job content." Based on the person/job match model, job content consists of job requirements (tasks and KSAOs) and job rewards (extrinsic and intrinsic). There are thus two forms of job analysis: job requirements, and job rewards. The goal of the job requirements job analysis is to produce the job requirements matrix. The goal of the job rewards job analysis is to produce the job rewards matrix.

Your assignment is to conduct either a job requirements or job rewards job analysis. In this assignment you will choose a job you wish to study, conduct either a job requirements or job rewards job analysis of that job, and prepare a written report of your project.

Your report should include the following sections:

1. The Job—What job (job title) did you choose to study and why?

2. The Form of Job Analysis—Did you choose the job requirements or job rewards form, and why?

3. The Methods Used—What methods did you use (prior information, observation, interviews, task questionnaires, combinations of these) and exactly how did you use them?

4. The Sources Used—What sources did you use (job analyst, job incumbent, supervisor, subject matter experts, combinations of these) and exactly how did you use them?

5. The Process Used—How did you go about gathering, synthesizing, and reporting the information? Refer back to Exhibit 5.18 for an example.

6. The Matrix—Present the actual job requirements or job rewards matrix.

Maintaining Job Descriptions

The InAndOut, Inc. company provides warehousing and fulfillment (order receiving and filling) services to small publishers of books with small print runs (number of copies of a book printed). After the books are printed and bound at a printing facility, they are shipped to InAndOut for handling. Books are received initially by Handlers who unload the books off of trucks, place them on pallets, and move them via forklifts and conveyors to their assigned storage space in the warehouse. The Handlers also retrieve books and bring them to the shipping area when orders are received. The books are then packaged, placed in cartons, and loaded on delivery trucks (to take to air or ground transportation providers) by Shippers. Book orders are taken by Customer Service Representatives via written, phone, or electronic (E-mail, fax) forms. New accounts are generated by Marketing Representatives, who also service existing accounts. Order Clerks handle all the internal paperwork. All of these employees report to either the Supervisor–Operations or Supervisor–Customer Service, who in turn reports to the General Manager.

The owner and President of InAndOut, Inc., Alta Fossom, is independently wealthy and delegates all day-to-day management matters to the General Manager, Marvin Olson. Alta requires, however, that Marvin clear any new ideas or initiatives with her prior to taking action. The company is growing and changing rapidly. Many new accounts, often larger than the past norm, are opening. Publishers are demanding more services and quicker order fulfillment. Information technology is constantly being upgraded, and new machinery (forklifts, computer-assisted conveyor system) is being utilized. And the workforce is growing in size to meet the business growth. There are now 37 employees, and Marvin expects to hire another 15–20 new employees within the next year.

Job descriptions for the company were originally written by a consultant about eight years ago. They have never been revised and are hopelessly outdated. And for the job of Marketing Representative there is no job description at all since the job was created only five years ago. As General Manager, Marvin is responsible for all human resource (HR) management matters, but he has little time to devote to them. To help him get a better grip on his HR responsibilities, Marvin has hired you as a part-time HR intern. He has a "gut feel" that the job descriptions need to be updated or written for the first time, and has assigned you that project. Since Marvin has to clear new projects with Alta, he wants you to prepare a brief proposal that he can use to approach Alta for seeking approval. In that proposal he wants to be able to suggest to Alta

1. reasons why it is important to update, and write new, job descriptions
2. an outline of a process that might be followed for doing this that will yield a set of thorough, current job descriptions
3. a process to be used in the future for periodically reviewing and updating these new job descriptions

(*continued*)

(continued)
Marvin wants to meet with you and discuss each of these points. He wants very specific suggestions and ideas from you that he can use to prepare his proposal. What exactly would you suggest to Marvin?

ENDNOTES

1. D. R. Ilgen and J. R. Hollenbeck, "The Structure of Work: Job Design and Roles," in M. D. Dunnette and L. M. Hough (eds.), *Handbook of Industrial and Organizational Psychology,* Vol. 2 (Palo Alto, CA: Consulting Psychologists Press, 1991), pp. 165–207.

2. L. S. Vines, "The New Clerical," *Human Resource Executive,* 1992, 6(10), pp. 57–79.

3. A. S. Miner, "Idiosyncratic Jobs in Formalized Organizations," *Administrative Science Quarterly,* 1987, 32, pp. 327–351.

4. W. Bridges, "The End of the Job," *Fortune,* Sept. 19, 1994, pp. 62–74; B. Dumaine, "The Trouble with Teams," *Fortune,* Sept. 5, 1994, pp. 86–92; R. J. Klimoski and R. G. Jones, "Staffing for Effective Group Decision Making: Key Issues in Matching People and Teams," in R. A. Guzzo, E. Salas, and Associates, *Team Effectiveness and Decision Making in Organizations* (San Francisco: Jossey-Bass, 1995), pp. 291–332; M. J. Stevens and M. A. Campion, "The Knowledge, Skill, and Ability Requirements for Teamwork: Implications for Human Resource Management," *Journal of Management,* 1994, 20, pp. 503–530; R. S. Wellins, W. C. Byham, and G. R. Dixon, *Inside Teams* (San Francisco: Jossey-Bass, 1994).

5. E. Sundstrom, K. P. DeMeuse, and D. Futrell, "Work Teams: Applications and Effectiveness," *American Psychologist,* 1990, 45, pp. 120–133.

6. For excellent overviews and reviews, see S. Gael (ed.), *The Job Analysis Handbook for Business, Industry and Government,* Vols. 1 and 2 (New York: Wiley, 1988); J. V. Ghorpade, *Job Analysis* (Englewood Cliffs, NJ: 1988); R. J. Harvey, "Job Analysis," in Dunnette and Hough, *Handbook of Industrial and Organizational Psychology,* pp. 71–163.

7. M. A. Campion, "Ability Requirement Implications of Job Design: An Interdisciplinary Perspective," *Personnel Psychology,* 1989, 42, pp. 1–24; R. D. Gatewood and H. S. Feild, *Human Resource Selection,* second ed. (Chicago: Dryden, 1990), pp. 251–282; Harvey, "Job Analysis."

8. U.S. Department of Labor, *Revised Handbook for Analyzing Jobs* (Washington, D.C.: author, 1991), pp. 13–1 to 13–13.

9. For a summary of research on these points and on job analysis in general, see E. T. Cornelius III, "Practical Findings from Job Analysis Research," in S. Gael, *Handbook of Job Analysis for Business, Industry and Government,* Vol. 1, pp. 48–70.

10. C. J. Cranny and M. E. Doherty, "Importance Ratings in Job Analysis: Note on the Misinterpretation of Factor Analysis," *Journal of Applied Psychology,* 1988, 73, 320–322.

11. Gatewood and Feild, *Human Resource Selection,* pp. 252–254; Harvey, "Job Analysis," in Dunnette and Hough, pp. 75–79.

12. U.S. Department of Labor, Secretary's Commission on Achieving Necessary Skills, *Skills and Tasks for Jobs* (Washington, D.C.: author, 1992).

13. E. A. Fleishman and M. E. Reilly, *Handbook of Human Abilities* (Palo Alto, CA: Consulting Psychologists Press, 1992); E. A. Fleishman and M. A. Quaintance, *Taxonomies of Human Performance: The Description of Human Tasks* (Bethesda, MD: Management Research Institute, 1984).

14. U.S. Department of Labor, *Revised Handbook for Analyzing Jobs,* pp. 12–1 to 12–18.

15. S. Gael, "Job Descriptions," in S. Gael, *Handbook of Job Analysis for Business, Industry and Government,* pp. 71–89.

16. For detailed treatments, see Gael, *The Job Analysis Handbook for Business, Industry and Government,* pp. 315–468; Harvey, "Job Analysis," in Dunnette and Hough; E. Levine, *Everything You Always Wanted to Know About Job Analysis But Were Afraid to Ask* (Tampa, FL: Mariner, 1983).

17. These are described in the sources cited in endnote 16.

18. U.S. Department of Labor, *Dictionary of Occupational Titles,* fourth ed. (Washington, D.C.: author, 1991).

19. F. J. Landy and J. Vasey, "Job Analysis: The Composition of SME Samples," *Personnel Psychology,* 1991, 44, pp. 27–50.

20. See Gael, *Job Analysis Handbook for Business, Industry and Government,* pp. 315–390.

21. F. H. Borgen, "Occupational Reinforcer Patterns," in S. Gael, *The Job Analysis Handbook for Business, Industry and Government,* Vol. 2, pp. 902–916; R. V. Dawis, "Person-Environment Fit and Job Satisfaction," in C. J. Cranny, P. C. Smith, and E. F. Stone (eds.), *Job Satisfaction* (New York: Lexington, 1992); C. T. Kulik and G. R. Oldham, "Job Diagnostic Survey," in S. Gael, *Handbook for Analyzing Jobs in Business, Industry and Government,* Vol. 2, pp. 936–959.

22. See the citations in endnote 7, plus T. D. Taber and E. Taylor, "A Review and Evaluation of the Psychometric Properties of the Job Diagnostic Survey," *Personnel Psychology,* 1990, 43, pp. 467–500.

23. Campion, "Ability Requirement Implications of Job Design: An Interdisciplinary Perspective."

24. D. E. Thompson and T. A. Thompson, "Court Standards for Job Analysis in Test Validation," *Personnel Psychology,* 1982, 35, pp. 865–874.

25. Equal Employment Opportunity Commission, *Technical Assistance Manual on the Employment Provisions (Title 1) of the Americans With Disabilities Act* (Washington, D.C.: author, 1992), pp. II–19 to II–21.

CHAPTER
SIX

Measurement

In staffing, measurement is a process used to gather and express information about persons and jobs in numerical form. A common example where management employs measurement is to administer a test to job applicants and evaluate their responses to determine a test score for each of them. The first part of this chapter presents a view of the process of measurement, then provides several specific examples of how measures are used in staffing.

After showing the vital importance and uses of measurement in staffing activities, three key concepts are then discussed. The first concept is that of measurement itself, along with the issues raised by it—standardization of measurement, levels of measurement, and the difference between objective and subjective measures. The second concept is that of scoring and how to express scores in ways that aid in their interpretation. The final concept is that of correlations between scores, particularly as expressed by the correlation coefficient and its significance. Calculating correlations between scores is a very useful way to learn even more about the meaning of scores.

What is the quality of the measures used in staffing? How sound an indicator of the attributes measured are they? Answers to these questions lie in the reliability and validity of the measures and the scores they yield. There are multiple ways of doing reliability and validity analysis; these are discussed in conjunction with numerous examples drawn from staffing situations. As these examples show, the quality of staffing decisions (e.g., who to hire or reject) depends heavily on the quality of measures and scores used as inputs to these decisions.

Measurement concepts and procedures are directly involved in legal issues, particularly EEO/AA ones. Organizations must perform various statistical analyses to help determine if disparate or adverse impact in staffing is occurring. This requires collection and analysis of applicant flow and stock statistics. Requirements for doing these analyses, as expressed in the Uniform Guidelines on Employee Selection Procedures (UGESP) and Revised Order No. 4, are reviewed. Also reviewed are implications of the results of disparate impact analysis for standardization and validation of measures, particularly as required by the UGESP.

IMPORTANCE AND USE OF MEASURES

Measurement is one of the key ingredients for, and tools of, staffing organizations. A general illustration of this is shown next, followed by a discussion of the major specific uses of measurement: measuring jobs, measuring individuals, measuring HR outcomes, monitoring and recordkeeping, and research and evaluation.

Measurement and Staffing

Staffing organizations is highly dependent upon the availability and use of measures. Indeed, it is virtually impossible to have any type of systematic staffing process that does not use measures and an accompanying measurement process.

Measures are methods or techniques for describing and assessing attributes of objects that are of concern to us. Examples include tests of applicant KSAOs, evaluations of employees' job performance, and applicants' ratings of their preferences for various types of job rewards. These assessments of attributes are gathered through the measurement process. That process consists of (a) choosing an attribute of concern, (b) developing an operational definition of the attribute, (c) constructing a measure of the attribute (if no suitable measure is available) as it is operationally defined, and (d) using the measure to actually gauge the attribute.

Results of the measurement process are expressed as numbers or scores—for example, applicants' scores on an ability test, employees' performance evaluation rating scores, or applicants' ratings of rewards in terms of their importance. These scores become the indicators of the attribute. Through the measurement process, the initial attribute and its operational definition have been transformed into a numerical expression of the attribute.

An example of these points, in a staffing context, is shown in Exhibit 6.1. The process starts with identification of an attribute of concern, in this case knowledge of mechanical principles. Once the attribute has been chosen, the measurement process unfolds, culminating in the use of actual scores generated by the measure to make hiring decisions about job applicants.

Specific Uses of Measures in Staffing

The example in Exhibit 6.1 has embedded within it several specific uses of measurement in staffing. Each of these uses is described.

Measuring Jobs

In the person/job matching model, jobs are said to have both requirements and rewards associated with them. These requirements and rewards need to be identified, defined, and measured in order to make the matching concept come to life for staffing purposes. This occurs through the process of job analysis, which is discussed in Chapter 5.

Through job analysis, job requirements become specified in terms of tasks and the KSAOs thought to be necessary for the performance of those tasks. Throughout the job analysis process, measurement processes are used.[1] For example, a task questionnaire might be administered to job incumbents where they are asked to rate the importance of each of a set of tasks for the performance of their job. The resultant scores would then be analyzed to develop a numerical profile of task requirements. This profile, in turn, could be used to identify the types of KSAOs likely to be necessary for the job.

To understand, refer again to the example in Exhibit 6.1. Assume that the job involved is that of maintenance mechanic in a food processing plant. A job analysis

EXHIBIT 6.1 Use of Measures in Staffing

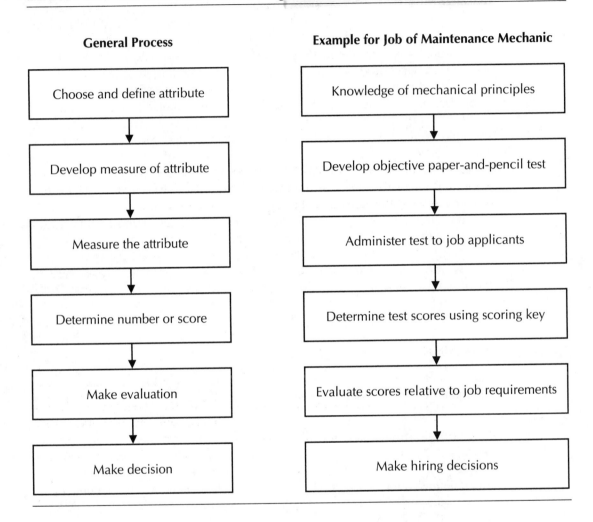

General Process

Choose and define attribute

↓

Develop measure of attribute

↓

Measure the attribute

↓

Determine number or score

↓

Make evaluation

↓

Make decision

Example for Job of Maintenance Mechanic

Knowledge of mechanical principles

↓

Develop objective paper-and-pencil test

↓

Administer test to job applicants

↓

Determine test scores using scoring key

↓

Evaluate scores relative to job requirements

↓

Make hiring decisions

may have revealed that the job involves troubleshooting and diagnosis of equipment failure, and that 30% of the job involves these tasks. With this task knowledge, it was inferred that knowledge of mechanical principles is an essential KSAO for the job. Furthermore, the specific sets of principles necessary for this particular job may have been specified, and their relative importance to job performance may have been rated by a group of job incumbents and their supervisors. In these ways, an attribute to measure has been chosen, and an operational definition of it has been developed.

Measuring Individuals

People possess a vast number of KSAOs. Some of these KSAOs will be of particular importance to the organization because they match identified KSAO requirements of jobs. Selecting individuals who possess these KSAO requirements as employees is greatly facilitated by having and using measures of individual applicants' job-relevant KSAOs.

There are a multitude of KSAOs to measure, and a corresponding multitude of measures of them that have been developed. Refinements of existing measures, as well as construction of new ones, occur on a continual basis. For example, tests of word processing skills were nonexistent 20 years ago, and the newly developed tests are revised constantly as changes in word processing technology occur.

The study of people's KSAOs has revealed two facts about people that have major staffing implications.[2] First, there are typically substantial interindividual differences, or differences among people, for any particular KSAO. Thus, if a particular ability test is administered to a group of people, inspection of their scores reveals substantial differences among them in performance on the test and, by inference, how much or little of the measured ability they possess.

The second fact revealed by studying KSAOs is that there are substantial intraindividual differences, or differences within an individual, as well. If a battery of ability tests, measuring several different abilities, were administered to a particular individual, inspection of the person's scores would show that the person scored better on some of the tests than on others.

The concept of inter- and intraindividual differences is illustrated in Exhibit 6.2. Notice that for any given ability there are differences in scores among people, and that for any given person there are differences in scores among abilities.

The importance of these pervasive differences to staffing should be apparent in the context of the person/job matching model. For KSAOs that are job-relevant, the existence of interindividual differences means that, for any particular KSAO,

---

EXHIBIT 6.2   Illustration of Inter- and Intraindividual Differences in Ability

| Person | Ability Test Scores | | | |
	Verbal Comprehension	Word Fluency	Number Aptitude	Inductive Reasoning
A	85	112	95	93
B	125	102	103	98
C	93	85	95	91
D	101	98	120	112
E	117	125	78	96
F	99	102	87	100

some individuals will be more qualified (better matched to job requirements) than will others. In terms of intraindividual differences, not all jobs have the same KSAO requirements, and thus, any given person will be more suited to perform some jobs than others. As a result of inter- and intraindividual differences, it is crucial that the organization be able to measure KSAOs so that applicants can be hired for jobs for which they are best suited.

In staffing, measures of KSAO characteristics of individuals are referred to as predictors, or tests. These predictors, and scores derived from them for individuals, serve as fundamental guides for staffing activities. In recruitment, for example, applicants may be informed that the selection process will require taking and passing a particular test; they may use this knowledge to help decide whether they truly want to apply for the position or want to self-select out of the staffing process. In the selection process, the predictor is administered to applicants, and then scored. These test score results are then fed into the employment activities, which require setting a passing (cutoff) score on the test, determining which applicants actually passed the test, and making job offers.

These types of staffing activities, driven by measurement concerns, are clearly illustrated in Exhibit 6.1. In this example, a test of knowledge of mechanical principles is developed, and applicants are informed that this predictor will be administered to them. For those who choose to take the test, it is administered and scored. Their scores are evaluated relative to job requirements (the passing or cutoff score), and this information serves as input to the hiring decisions made about the applicants.

Measuring Outcomes

Outcomes of the person/job matching process include factors such as job performance and retention. In order to determine and track the levels being attained on these outcomes, measures of them must be developed and used. In staffing, these outcome measures are referred to as criterion measures.[3] Scores on criterion measures include performance ratings and turnover rates, and may be used to help the organization decide if outcomes are occurring at acceptable levels, and if not, what corrective actions are necessary. These actions may include staffing activities.

Return again to the example in Exhibit 6.1. Perhaps the organization had a performance appraisal system that measured and tracked the performance of its maintenance mechanics. Appraisal results (criterion scores) may have indicated unacceptably low levels of performance. Diagnosis of the situation may have indicated that employees were deficient in their knowledge of mechanical principles. Based on this diagnosis, the organization could develop strategies for remedying the knowledge deficiency. One alternative would be to develop a training program for current employees and new hires for the job. A different strategy would be to impose a stringent knowledge requirement for new hires. If this alternative were chosen, it might necessitate the flow of events shown in the exhibit.

Monitoring and Record Keeping

Monitoring and record keeping are (or should be) an integral part of any staffing system. Through these activities, the organization gathers and records numerical information that may be used for numerous staffing-related purposes. These purposes include determining how well staffing activities conform to staffing policies and procedures, tracking numerically how applicant pools are reduced as applicants proceed through the staffing process (so-called applicant flow statistics), and determining compliance with legal requirements.

In the example in Exhibit 6.1, the organization could have developed a monitoring and record keeping program as part of the overall staffing system for the job of maintenance mechanic. The program might record information such as (a) date of initial application; (b) gender, age, and ethnicity of applicants; (c) scores on the test of knowledge of mechanical principles; (d) whether an offer was extended, and if so, if and when it was accepted; and (e) total elapsed time from date of application to date of acceptance or rejection. These data could then be analyzed periodically to provide indications of such things as (a) demographic composition of the applicant pool; (b) average and range of applicant test scores; (c) overall pass rate on the test, as well as specific pass rates for gender and ethnicity categories (in order to collect adverse impact statistics); and (d) speed in processing applicants.

Research and Evaluation

The maintenance and availability of staffing data leads naturally into more formal staffing research and evaluation activities. Such activities are primarily concerned with rigorously determining the effectiveness of specific staffing activities, as well as the overall effectiveness of the staffing system.

Consider once again the example in Exhibit 6.1. There are several types of research and evaluation projects the organization might wish to undertake. First, it might decide to investigate the reliability and validity of the results of its test of knowledge of mechanical principles. Conducting this evaluation project would require several types of research and data analysis, the nature of which is discussed in sections that follow. A second project might involve an analysis of pass rates on the test for the various gender and ethnic categories of job applicants. This is called adverse impact analysis, and it, too, is discussed. A third project might involve an assessment of the more routine processing aspects of the staffing system, with an eye toward efficiency, as well as reasonable treatment from the applicants' point of view (e.g., no excessive time delays in scheduling appointments or providing feedback).

KEY CONCEPTS

This section covers a series of key concepts in three major areas: measurement, scores, and correlation between scores.

Measurement

In the preceding discussion, the essence of measurement and its importance and use in staffing were described. It is now important to define the term "measurement" more formally and explore implications of that definition.

Definition

Measurement may be defined as the process of assigning numbers to objects to represent quantities of an attribute of the objects.[4] In the example in Exhibit 6.1, the attribute being measured is knowledge of mechanical principles, and the objects being measured are job applicants. Each job applicant received a number or score based on rules that had been determined in advance to measure correct and incorrect responses to each question on the test.

Several implications follow from this definition and example of measurement. First, the attribute, which is also called a construct, represents the concept to be measured. Second, the attribute is a particular characteristic of the object chosen for measurement, and it is the attribute, not the object, that is measured. Third, a particular method is selected to measure an attribute, such as a paper-and-pencil test. The numbers or scores that result are thus a direct function of the particular method of measurement used. Fourth, the amount of an attribute possessed by an object is expressed numerically, and that number is determined through the use of rules that have been developed. Ideally, those rules are determined in advance and are agreed upon as reasonable. If these conditions do not hold, then there will be disagreements about the scores that should be assigned. There may also be disagreement over the meaning of the scores that are assigned.

Standardization

The hallmark of sound measurement practice is standardization.[5] Standardization is a means of controlling the influence of outside or extraneous factors on the scores generated by the measure, and ensuring that, as much as possible, the scores obtained are a reflection of the attribute measured.

A standardized measure has three basic properties:

1. The content is identical for all objects measured (e.g., all job applicants take the same test).
2. The administration of the measure is identical for all objects (e.g., all job applicants have the same time limit on a test).
3. The rules for assigning numbers are clearly specified and agreed upon in advance (e.g., a scoring key for the test is developed before it is administered).

These seemingly simple and straightforward characteristics of standardization of measures have substantial implications for the conduct of many staffing activities. These implications will become apparent throughout the remainder of this text. For example, assessment devices, such as the employment interview and letters of reference, often fail to meet the requirements for standardization, and organizations must undertake steps to make them more standardized.

Levels of Measurement

There are varying degrees of precision in measuring attributes and in representing differences among objects in terms of attributes. Accordingly, there are different levels or scales of measurement.[6] It is common to classify any particular measure as falling into one of four levels of measurement: nominal, ordinal, interval, or ratio.

Nominal   With nominal scales, a given attribute is categorized and numbers are assigned to the categories. With or without numbers, however, there is no order or level implied among the categories. The categories are merely different, and none is higher or lower than the other. For example, each job title could represent a different category, with a different number assigned to it: managers = 1, clericals = 2, sales = 3, and so forth. Clearly, the numbers do not imply any ordering among the categories.

Ordinal   With ordinal scales, objects are rank-ordered according to how much of the attribute they possess. Thus, objects may be ranked from "best" to "worst," or from "highest" to "lowest." For example, five job candidates, each of whom has been evaluated in terms of overall qualification for the job, might be rank-ordered from 1 to 5, or highest to lowest, according to their job qualifications.

Rank orderings only represent relative differences among objects, and they do not indicate the absolute levels of the attribute. Thus, the rank ordering of the five job candidates does not indicate exactly how qualified each of them is for the job, nor are the differences in their ranks necessarily equal to the differences in their qualifications. The difference in qualifications between applicants ranked 1 and 2 may not be the same as the difference between those ranked 4 and 5.

Interval   Like ordinal scales, interval scales allow us to rank order objects. However, the differences between adjacent points on the measurement scale are now equal in terms of the attribute. If an interval scale is used to rank order of the five job candidates, the differences in qualifications between those ranked 1 and 2 are equal to the differences between those ranked 4 and 5.

It should be pointed out that there are many instances in which the level of measurement falls somewhere between an ordinal and interval scale. That is, objects can be clearly rank-ordered, but the differences between the ranks are not necessarily equal throughout the measurement scale. In the example of the five job candidates, the difference in qualifications between those ranked 1 and 2 might be slight compared with the distance between those ranked 4 and 5.

Unfortunately, this in-between level of measurement is characteristic of many of the measures used in staffing. While it is not a major problem, it does signal caution in interpreting the meaning of differences in scores among people.

Ratio   Ratio scales are like interval scales in that there are equal differences between scale points for the attribute being measured. In addition, however, ratio scales have a logical or absolute true zero point. Because of this, how much of the attribute each object possesses can be stated in absolute terms.

Normally, ratio scales are involved in counting or weighing things. There are many such examples of ratio scales in staffing. Assessing how much weight a candidate can carry over some distance for physically demanding jobs such as fire fighting or general construction is an example of this. Perhaps the most common example is counting how much previous job experience, general or specific, job candidates have had.

Objective and Subjective Measures

Frequently, staffing measures are described as being either "objective" or "subjective." Often, the term subjective is used in disparaging ways ("I can't believe how subjective that interview was; there's no way they can rate me fairly on the basis of it"). Exactly what is the difference between so-called objective and subjective measures?

The difference, in large part, pertains to the rules used to assign numbers to the attribute being assessed. With objective measures, the rules are predetermined and usually communicated and applied via some sort of scoring key or system. Most paper-and-pencil tests are considered objective. The scoring systems in subjective measures are more elusive, and often involve a rater or judge who assigns the numbers. Many employment interviewers fall in this category, especially those with an idiosyncratic way of evaluating people's responses, one that is not known or shared by other interviewers.

In principle, any attribute can be measured objectively, subjectively, or both. Research shows that when an attribute is measured by both objective and subjective means, there is often relatively low agreement between scores from the two types of measures. A case in point pertains to the attribute of "job performance." It may be measured objectively through quantity of output, and it may be measured subjectively through performance appraisal ratings. A review of the research shows that there is very low correlation between scores from the objective and subjective performance measures.[7] Undoubtedly, the raters' lack of sound scoring systems for rating job performance was a major contributor to the lack of obtained agreement.

It thus appears that whatever type of measure is being used to assess attributes in staffing, serious attention should be paid to the scoring system or key that is used. This requires nothing more, in a sense, than having a firm knowledge of exactly what the organization is trying to measure in the first place. This is true for both paper-and-pencil (objective) measures and judgmental (subjective) measures such as the employment interview. It is simply another way of emphasizing the importance of standardization in measurement.

Scores

Measures yield numbers or scores to represent the amount of the attribute being assessed. Scores thus are the numerical indicator of the attribute. Once scores have been derived, they can be manipulated in various ways to give them even greater meaning, and to help better describe characteristics of the objects being scored.[8]

Central Tendency and Variability
Assume that a group of job applicants was administered the test of knowledge of mechanical principles shown in Exhibit 6.1. The test is scored, using a scoring key, and each applicant receives a score on the test, known as a raw score. Their scores are shown in Exhibit 6.3.

Some features of this set of scores may be summarized through the calculation of summary statistics. These pertain to central tendency and variability in the scores and are also shown in Exhibit 6.3.

The indicators of central tendency are the mean, median, and mode. Since it was assumed that the data were interval-level data, it is permissible to compute all three indicators of central tendency. Had the data been ordinal, the mean should not be computed. For nominal data, only the mode would be appropriate.

The variability indicators are the range and the standard deviation. The range shows lowest to highest actual score for the job applicants. The standard deviation shows, in essence, the average amount of deviation of individual scores from the average score. It summarizes the amount of "spread" in the scores. The larger the standard deviation, the greater the variability, or spread, in the data.

Percentiles
A percentile score for an individual is the percentage of people scoring below the individual in a distribution of scores. Refer again to Exhibit 6.3, and consider applicant C. That applicant's percentile score is the 10th percentile (2/20 $\times$ 100). Applicant S is in the 90th percentile (18/20 $\times$ 100).

Standard Scores
When interpreting scores, it is natural to compare individuals' raw scores to the mean, that is, to ask whether scores are above, at, or below the mean. But a true understanding of how well an individual did relative to the mean takes into account the amount of variability in scores around the mean (the standard deviation). That is, the calculation must be "corrected" or controlled for the amount of variability in a score distribution to accurately present how well a person scored relative to the mean.

EXHIBIT 6.3   Central Tendency and Variability: Summary Statistics

Data		Summary Statistics
Applicant	**Test Score (x)**	
A	10	**A. Central tendency**
B	12	Mean ($\bar{x}$) = 338/20 = 16.9
C	14	Median = middle score = 17
D	14	Mode = most frequent score = 15
E	15	
F	15	**B. Variability**
G	15	Range = 10 to 24
H	15	Standard deviation (SD) =
I	15	
J	17	$\sqrt{\dfrac{\Sigma\,(x-\bar{x})^2}{N}} = 3.52$
K	17	
L	17	
M	18	
N	18	
O	19	
P	19	
Q	19	
R	22	
S	23	
T	24	
Total (Σ) = 338		
N = 20		

Calculation of the standard score for an individual is the way to accomplish this correction. The formula for calculation of the standard score, or Z, is as follows:

$$Z = \frac{X - \bar{X}}{SD}$$

Applicant S in Exhibit 6.3 had a raw score of 23 on the test; the mean was 16.9 and the standard deviation was 3.52. Substituting into the above formula, applicant S has a Z score of 1.7. Thus, applicant S scored about 1.7 standard deviations above the mean.

Standard scores are also useful for determining how a person performed, in a relative sense, on two or more tests. For example, assume the following data for a particular applicant:

	Test 1	**Test 2**
Raw score	50	48
Mean	48	46
SD	2.5	.80

On which test did the applicant do better? To answer that, simply calculate the applicant's standard scores on the two tests. The Z score on test 1 is .80, and the Z score on test 2 is 2.5. Thus, while the applicant got a higher raw score on test 1 than on test 2, the applicant got a higher Z score on test 2 than on test 1. Viewed in this way, it is apparent that the applicant did better on the second of the two tests.

Correlation Between Scores

Frequently, in staffing there are scores on two or more measures for a group of individuals. One common occurrence is to have scores on two (or often even more than two) KSAO measures. For example, there could be a score on the test of knowledge of mechanical principles and also an overall rating of the applicant's probable job success based on the employment interview. In such instances, it is logical to ask whether there is some relation between the two sets of scores. Is there a tendency for an increase in knowledge test scores to be accompanied by an increase in interview ratings?

As another example, an organization may have scores on a particular KSAO measure (e.g., the knowledge test) and a measure of job performance (e.g., performance appraisal ratings) for a group of individuals. Is there a correlation between these two sets of scores? If there is, then this would provide some evidence about the probable validity of the knowledge test as a predictor of job performance. This evidence would help the organization decide whether to incorporate the use of the test into the selection process for job applicants.

Investigation of the relationship between two sets of scores proceeds through the plotting of scatter diagrams, and through calculation of the correlation coefficient.

Scatter Diagrams

Assume two sets of scores for a group of people, scores on a test and scores on a measure of job performance. A scatter diagram is simply the plot of the joint distribution of the two sets of scores. Inspection of the plot provides a visual representation of the type of relationship that exists between the two sets of scores. Exhibit 6.4 provides three different scatter diagrams for the two sets of scores. Each X represents a test score and job performance score combination for an individual.

Example A in Exhibit 6.4 suggests very little relationship between the two sets of scores. Example B shows a modest relationship between the scores, and example C shows a somewhat strong relationship between the two sets of scores.

Correlation Coefficient

The relationship between two sets of scores may also be investigated through calculation of the correlation coefficient. The symbol for the correlation coefficient is r. Numerically, r values can range from $r = -1.0$ to $r = 1.0$. The larger the absolute value of r, the stronger the relationship. When an r value is shown without the plus or minus sign, the value is assumed to be positive.

Naturally, the value of r bears a close resemblance to the scatter diagram. As a demonstration of this, Exhibit 6.4 also shows the approximate r value for each of the three scatter diagrams. In example A, a low r is indicated ($r = .10$). The r in example B is moderate ($r = .25$), and the r in example C is high ($r = .60$).

Actual calculation of the correlation coefficient is straightforward. An example of this calculation, and the formula for r, are shown in Exhibit 6.5. In the exhibit, there are two sets of scores for $n = 20$ people. The first set of scores is the set of test scores for the 20 individuals in Exhibit 6.3. The second set of scores is an overall job performance rating (on a 1–5 rating scale) for these people. As can be seen from the calculation, there is a correlation of $r = .58$ between the two sets of scores.

The calculation of the correlation coefficient is straightforward. The resultant value of r is a value that succinctly summarizes both the strength of the relationship between two sets of scores and the direction of the relationship. Despite the simplicity of its calculation, there are several notes of caution to sound regarding the correlation.

First, the correlation does not connote a proportion or percentage. An $r = .50$ between variables X and Y does not mean that X is 50% of Y, or that Y can be predicted from X with 50% accuracy. The appropriate interpretation is to square the value of r, for r^2, and then say that the two variables share that percentage of common variation in their scores. Thus, the proper interpretation of $r = .50$ is that the two variables share 25% ($.5^2 \times 100$) common variation in their scores.

Second, the value of r is affected by how much variation there actually is in each set of scores. Other things being equal, the less variation there is in either or both sets of scores, the smaller will be the calculated value of r. At the extreme, if there is no variation in one of the sets of scores, the correlation will be $r = .00$. That is, for there to be a correlation there must be variation in both sets of scores. The lack of variation in scores is called the problem of restriction of range.

Third, the formula used to calculate the correlation in Exhibit 6.5 is based on the assumption that there is a linear relationship between the two sets of scores. This may not always be a good assumption; something other than a straight line may best capture the true nature of the relationship between scores. To the extent that two sets of scores are not related in a linear fashion, use of the formula for

EXHIBIT 6.4   Scatter Diagrams and Corresponding Correlations

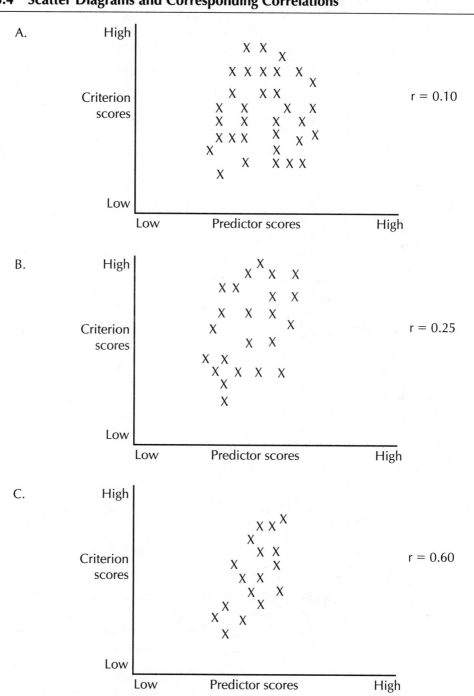

EXHIBIT 6.5   Calculation of Product-Moment Correlation Coefficient

---

Person	Test Score (X)	Performance Rating (Y)	(X²)	(Y²)	(XY)
A	10	2	100	4	20
B	12	1	144	1	12
C	14	2	196	4	28
D	14	1	196	1	14
E	15	3	225	9	45
F	15	4	225	16	60
G	15	3	225	9	45
H	15	4	225	16	60
I	15	4	225	16	60
J	17	3	289	9	51
K	17	4	289	16	68
L	17	3	289	9	51
M	18	2	324	4	36
N	18	4	324	16	72
O	19	3	361	9	57
P	19	3	361	9	57
Q	19	5	361	25	95
R	22	3	484	9	66
S	23	4	529	16	92
T	24	5	576	25	120
	$\Sigma X = 338$	$\Sigma Y = 63$	$\Sigma X^2 = 5948$	$\Sigma Y^2 = 223$	$\Sigma XY = 1109$

$$r = \frac{N\Sigma XY - (\Sigma X)(\Sigma Y)}{\sqrt{[N\Sigma X^2 - (\Sigma X)^2][N\Sigma Y^2 - (\Sigma Y)^2]}} = \frac{20(1109) - (338)(63)}{\sqrt{[20(5948) - (338)^2][20(223) - (63)^2]}} = .58$$

---

calculation of the correlation will yield a value of r that understates the actual strength of the relationship.

Finally, the correlation between two variables does not imply causation between them. A correlation simply says how two variables co-vary or co-relate; it says nothing about one variable necessarily causing the other one.

Significance of the Correlation Coefficient
Once the correlation coefficient is calculated, questions frequently arise as to the significance of the correlation. These questions may be addressed through consideration of a correlation's practical and statistical significance.

Practical Significance   The practical significance of the correlation refers to its size, regardless of its sign. The larger the r, the greater its practical significance.

This interpretation is a very appealing one. Recall that the correlation is really the amount of common or shared variation between two variables. The greater the degree of that covariation, the more we can use one variable to help us understand or predict another variable.

Consider again the correlation between the knowledge of mechanical principles test and the job performance ratings. The greater the r between those two variables, the greater the certainty that knowledge of mechanical principles is a key underlying KSAO of job performance, and that scores on this test are useful in predicting the likely performance of individuals at the time they are job applicants. Indeed, prediction such as this is a major purpose of staffing systems. Calculation and use of correlations is thus an extremely important tool for staffing activities.

Statistical Significance   When a correlation is computed for a particular group of individuals, it describes the relationship between two variables for that group only. However, to the extent that the group is drawn from, or representative of, some larger population, there may also exist a correlation in that population. For example, if there were a correlation between test scores and subsequent job performance ratings for a sample of current job applicants, it is possible to infer that there is a correlation in the population of future job applicants as well. Having made this inference, the organization could use the test to help select future applicants from that population.

The statistical significance of a correlation refers to the likelihood that a correlation exists in a population, based on knowledge of the actual value of r in a sample from that population. Concluding that a correlation is indeed statistically significant means that there is most likely a correlation in the population.

More formally, r is calculated in an initial group, called a sample. From this piece of information, the question arises whether to infer that there is also a correlation in the *population*. To do this, compute the t value of our correlation using the following formula,

$$t = \frac{r}{\sqrt{(1-r^2)/n-2}}$$

where r is the value of the correlation and n is the size of the sample.

A t distribution table in any elementary statistics book shows the significance level of r.[9] The significance level is expressed as p < some value, for example, p < .05. This p level tells the probability of concluding that there is a correlation in the population when, in fact, there is not a relationship. Thus, a correlation with p < .05 means there are fewer than 5 chances in 100 of concluding that there is a relationship in the population when, in fact, there is not. This is a relatively small probability, and usually leads to the conclusion that a correlation is indeed statistically significant.

It is important to avoid concluding that there is a relationship in the population when in fact there is not. Because of this, one usually chooses a fairly conservative or stringent level of significance that the correlation must attain before concluding that it is "significant." Typically, a standard of $p < .05$ or less (another common standard is $p < .01$) is chosen. The actual significance level (based on the t value for the correlation) is then compared to the desired significance level, and a decision reached whether the correlation is statistically significant or not. Here are some examples:

Desired Level	Actual Level	Conclusion about Correlation
$p < .05$	$p < .23$	Not significant
$p < .05$	$p < .02$	Significant
$p < .01$	$p < .07$	Not significant
$p < .01$	$p < .009$	Significant

Both the practical and statistical significance of the correlation are of concern in interpreting its significance. For example, if $r = .25$ and $p < .05$, the following kind of interpretation is made about significance. The correlation has moderate practical significance ($r^2 = .06$), and it meets a normal threshold for statistical significance. There is thus likely a relationship between the two variables in the population, based on what was found to be the relationship in this particular sample.

QUALITY OF MEASURES

Measures are developed and used to gauge attributes of objects. Results of measures are expressed in the form of scores, and various manipulation may be done to them. Such manipulations lead to better understanding and interpretation of the scores, and thus the attribute represented by the scores.

For practical reasons, in staffing the scores of individuals are treated as if they were, in fact, the attribute itself, rather than merely indicators of the attribute. For example, scores on a mental ability test are interpreted as being synonymous with how intelligent individuals are. Or, individuals' job performance ratings from their supervisors are viewed as indicators of their true performance.

Treated in this way, scores become a major input to decision making about individuals. For example, scores on the mental ability test are used and weighted heavily to decide which job applicants will receive a job offer. Or performance ratings may serve as a key factor in deciding which individuals will be eligible for an internal staffing move, such as a promotion. In these, and numerous other ways, management acts on the basis of scores to guide the conduct of staffing activities in the organization. This is illustrated through such phrases as "let the numbers do the talking," "we manage by the numbers," and "never measured, never managed."

The quality of the decisions and actions taken are unlikely to be any better than the quality of the measures on which they are based. Thus, there is a lot at stake in the quality of the measures used in staffing. Such concerns with the quality of measures are best viewed in terms of reliability and validity of measures.[10]

Reliability of Measures

Reliability of measurement refers to the consistency of measurement of an attribute.[11] A measure is reliable to the extent that it provides a consistent set of scores to represent an attribute. Rarely is perfect reliability achieved, because of the occurrence of measurement error. Reliability is thus a matter of degree.

Reliability of measurement is of concern both within a single time period in which the attribute is being measured, and between time periods. Moreover, reliability is of concern for both objective and subjective measures. These two concerns help create a general framework for better understanding reliability.

The key concepts for the framework are shown in Exhibit 6.6. In the exhibit, a single attribute, "A" (e.g., knowledge of mechanical principles), is being measured. Scores are available for $n = 15$ individuals, and scores range from 1 to 5. A is being measured in time period 1 (T_1) and time period 2 (T_2). In each time period, A may be measured objectively, with two test items, or subjectively, with two raters. The same two items or raters are used in each time period. (In reality, more than two items or raters would probably be used to measure A, but for simplicity's sake, only two are used here.) Each test item or rater in each time period is a submeasure of A. There are thus four submeasures of A—designated X_1, X_2, Y_1, and Y_2—and four sets of scores. In terms of reliability of measurement, the concern is with the consistency or similarity in the sets of scores. This requires various comparisons of the scores.

Comparisons Within T_1 or T_2

Consider the four sets of scores as coming from the objective measure, which used test items. Comparing sets of scores from these items in either T_1 or T_2 is called internal consistency reliability. The relevant comparisons are X_1 and Y_1, and X_2 and Y_2. It is hoped that the comparisons will show high similarity, because both the items are intended to measure A within the same time period.

Now treat the four sets of scores as coming from the subjective measure, which relied upon raters. Comparisons of these scores involve what is called interrater reliability. The relevant comparisons are the same as with the objective measure scores, namely X_1 and Y_1, and X_2 and Y_2. Again, it is hoped that there will be high agreement between the raters, because they are focusing on a single attribute at a single moment in time.

[handwritten margin note: different raters same time period]

Comparisons Between T_1 and T_2

Comparisons of scores between time periods involve assessment of measurement stability. When scores from an objective measure are used, this is referred to as test-retest reliability. The relevant comparisons are X_1 and X_2, and Y_1 and Y_2. To

---

EXHIBIT 6.6   Framework for Reliability of Measures

Scores on Attribute A

Person	Objective (Test Items)				Subjective (Raters)			
	Time 1		Time 2		Time 1		Time 2	
	X_1	Y_1	X_2	Y_2	X_1	Y_1	X_2	Y_2
A	5	5	4	5	5	5	4	5
B	5	4	4	3	5	4	4	3
C	5	5	5	4	5	5	5	4
D	5	4	5	5	5	4	5	5
E	4	5	3	4	4	5	3	4
F	4	4	4	3	4	4	4	3
G	4	4	3	4	4	4	3	4
H	4	3	4	3	4	3	4	3
I	3	4	3	4	3	4	3	4
J	3	3	5	3	3	3	5	3
K	3	3	2	3	3	3	2	3
L	3	2	4	2	3	2	4	2
M	2	3	4	3	2	3	4	3
N	2	2	1	2	2	2	1	2
O	1	2	3	2	1	2	3	2

NOTE: X_1 and X_2 are the **same** test item or rater; Y_1 and Y_2 are the same test item or rater. The subscript "1" refers to T_1, and the subscript "2" refers to T_2.

---

the extent that A is not expected to change between T_1 and T_2, there should be high test-retest reliability.

When subjective scores are compared between T_1 and T_2, the concern is with intrarater reliability. Here the same rater evaluates individuals in terms of A in two different time periods. To the extent that A is not expected to change, there should be high intrarater reliability.

In summary, reliability is concerned with consistency of measurement. There are multiple ways of treating reliability, depending on whether scores from a measure are being compared for consistency within or between time periods, and depending on whether the scores are from objective or subjective measures. These points are summarized in Exhibit 6.7. Ways of actually computing agreement between scores will be dealt with shortly, after the concept of measurement error is explored.

Measurement Error

Rarely will any of the comparisons among scores discussed previously yield perfect similarity or reliability. Indeed, none of the comparisons in Exhibit 6.7 visually

---

EXHIBIT 6.7   Summary of Types of Reliability

	Compare scores within T_1 or T_2	Compare scores between T_1 and T_2
Objective measure (test items)	Internal consistency	Test–retest
Subjective measure (raters)	Interrater	Intrarater

---

shows complete agreement among the scores. The lack of agreement among the scores may be due to the occurrence of measurement error. This type of error represents "noise" in the measure and measurement process. Its occurrence means that the measure did not yield perfectly consistent scores, or so-called true scores, for the attribute.

The scores actually obtained from the measure thus have two components to them, a true score and measurement error. That is,

$$\text{actual score} = \text{true score} + \text{error}$$

The error component of any actual score, or set of scores, represents unreliability of measurement. Unfortunately, unreliability is a fact of life for the types of measures used in staffing. To help understand why this is the case, the various types or sources of error that can occur in a staffing context must be explored. These errors may be grouped under the categories of deficiency and contamination error.[12]

Deficiency Error   Deficiency error occurs when there is failure to measure some portion or aspect of the attribute assessed. For example, if knowledge of mechanical principles involves gear ratios, among other things, and our test does not have any items (or an insufficient number of items) getting at this aspect, then the test is deficient. As another example, if an attribute of job performance is "planning and setting work priorities," and the raters fail to rate people on that dimension during their performance appraisal, then the performance measure is deficient.

Deficiency error can occur in several related ways. First, there can be an inadequate definition of the attribute in the first place. Thus, the test of knowledge of mechanical principles may fail to get at familiarity with gear ratios because it was never included in the initial definition of mechanical principles. Or, the performance measure may fail to require raters to rate their employees on "planning and setting work priorities" because this attribute was never considered to be an important dimension of their work.

A second way that deficiency error occurs is in the construction of measures used to assess the attribute. Here, the attribute may be well defined and understood, but there is a failure to construct a measure that adequately gets at the totality of the attribute. This is akin to poor measurement by oversight, which happens when measures are constructed in a hurried, ad hoc fashion.

Deficiency error also occurs when the organization opts to use whatever measures are available because of ease, cost considerations, sales pitches and promotional claims, and so forth. The measures so chosen may turn out to be deficient.

Contamination Error Contamination error represents the occurrence of unwanted or undesirable influence on the measure and on individuals for whom the measure is being used. These influences muddy the scores and make them difficult to interpret.

Sources of contamination abound, as do examples of them. Several of these sources and examples are shown in Exhibit 6.8, along with some suggestions for how they might be controlled. These examples show that contamination error is multifaceted, making it difficult to minimize and control.

Calculation of Reliability Estimates

There are numerous procedures available for calculating actual estimates of the degree of reliability of measurement.[13] The first two of these (coefficient alpha, interrater agreement) assess reliability within a single time period. The other two procedures (test-retest, intrarater agreement) assess reliability between time periods.

Coefficient Alpha Coefficient alpha may be calculated in instances where there are two or more items (or raters) for a particular attribute. Its formula is

$$\alpha = \frac{n\,(\bar{r})}{1 + \bar{r}\,(n-1)}$$

where $\bar{r}$ is the average intercorrelation among the items (raters) and n is the number of items (raters). For example, if there are five items ($n = 5$), and the average correlation among those five items is $\bar{r} = .80$, then coefficient alpha is .94.

It can be seen from the formula and example that coefficient alpha depends on just two things—the number of items and the amount of correlation between them. This suggests two basic strategies for increasing the internal consistency reliability of a measure—increase the number of items and increase the amount of agreement

EXHIBIT 6.8 Sources of Contamination Error and Suggestions for Control

Source of Contamination	Example	Suggestion for Control
Content domain	Irrelevant material on test	Define domain of test material to be covered
Standardization	Different time limits for same test	Have same time limits for everyone
Chance response tendencies	Guessing by test taker	Impossible to control in advance
Rater	Rater gives inflated ratings to people	Train rater in rating accuracy
Rating situation	Interviewees are asked different questions	Ask all interviewees same questions

between the items (raters). It is generally recommended that coefficient alpha be at least .80 for a measure to have an acceptable degree of reliability.

Interrater Agreement   When raters serve as the measure, it is often convenient to talk about interrater agreement, or the amount of agreement among them. For example, if members of a group or panel interview and independently rate a set of job applicants on a 1–5 scale, it is logical to ask how much they agreed with each other.

A simple way to determine this is to calculate the percentage of agreement among the raters. An example of this is shown in Exhibit 6.9.

There is no commonly accepted minimum level of interrater agreement that must be met in order to consider the raters sufficiently reliable. Normally, a fairly high level should be set, 75% or higher. The more important the end use of the ratings, the greater should be the agreement required. Critical uses, such as hiring decisions, demand very high levels of reliability, well in excess of 75% agreement.

Test-Retest Reliability   To assess test-retest reliability, the test scores from two different time periods are correlated through calculation of the correlation coefficient. The r may be calculated on total test scores, or a separate r may be calculated for scores on each item. The resultant r provides an indication of the stability of measurement; the higher the r, the more stable the measure.

Interpretation of the r is made difficult by the fact that the scores are gathered at two different points in time. Between those two time points, the attribute being measured has an opportunity to change. Interpretation of test-retest reliability thus requires some feeling for how much the attribute may be expected to change, and what the appropriate time interval between tests is. Usually, for very short time

---

EXHIBIT 6.9   Calculation of Percentage Agreement Among Raters

---

Person (ratee)	Rater 1	Rater 2	Rater 3
A	5	5	2
B	3	3	5
C	5	4	·4
D	1	1	5
E	2	2	4

$$\% \text{ Agreement} = \frac{\# \text{ agreements}}{\# \text{ agreements} + \# \text{ disagreements}} \times 100$$

% Agreement
   Rater 1 and Rater 2 = 4/5 = 80%
   Rater 1 and Rater 3 = 0/5 = 0%
   Rater 2 and Rater 3 = 1/5 = 20%

---

intervals (hours or days), most attributes are quite stable, and a large test-retest r ($r = .90$ or higher) should be expected. Over longer time intervals, it is usual to expect much lower r's, depending upon the attribute being measured. For example, over six months or a year, individuals' knowledge of mechanical principles might change. If so, there will be lower test-retest reliabilities (e.g., $r = .50$).

Intrarater Agreement   To calculate intrarater agreement, scores assigned the same people by a rater in two different time periods are compared. The calculation could involve computing the correlation between the two sets of scores, or it could involve use of the same formula as for interrater agreement (see Exhibit 6.9).

Interpretation of intrarater agreement is made difficult by the time factor. For short time intervals between measures, a fairly high relationship is expected (e.g., $r = .80$, or percentage agreement = 90%). For longer time intervals, the level of reliability may reasonably be expected to be lower.

Implications of Reliability

The degree of reliability of a measure has two implications. The first of these pertains to interpreting individuals' scores on the measure and the standard error of measurement. The second implication pertains to the effect that reliability has on the measure's validity.

Standard Error of Measurement   Measures yield scores, which, in turn, are used as critical inputs for decision making in staffing activities. For example, in Exhibit 6.1 a test of knowledge of mechanical principles was developed and administered to job applicants. The applicants' scores then were used as a basis for making hiring decisions.

The discussion of reliability suggests that measures and scores will usually have some amount of error in them. Hence, scores on the test of knowledge of mechanical principles most likely reflect both true knowledge and error. Since only a single score is obtained from each applicant, the critical issue is how accurate that particular score is as an indication of each applicant's true level of knowledge of mechanical principles alone.

The standard error of measurement addresses this issue. It provides a way to state, within limits, a person's likely score on a measure. The formula for the standard error of measurement (SEM) is

$$SEM = SD_x \sqrt{1 - r_{xx}}$$

where SD_x is the standard deviation of scores on the measure and r_{xx} is an estimate of the measure's reliability. For example, if $SD_x = 10$, and $r_{xx} = .75$ (based on coefficient alpha), then $SEM = 5$.

With the SEM known, the range within which any individual's true score is likely to fall can be estimated. That range is known as a confidence interval or limit. There is a 95% chance that a person's true score lies within ± 2 SEM of his or her actual score. Thus, if an applicant received a score of 22 on the test of knowledge of mechanical principles, the applicant's true score is most likely to be within the range of 22 $\pm$ 2(5), or 12–32.

Recognition and use of the SEM allows for care in interpreting people's scores, as well as differences between them in terms of their scores. For example, using the preceding data, if the test score for applicant 1 = 22, and the score for applicant 2 = 19, what should be made of the difference between the two applicants? Is applicant 1 truly more knowledgeable of mechanical principles than applicant 2? The answer is probably not. This is because of the standard error of measurement and the large amount of overlap between the two applicants' intervals (12–32 for applicant 1, and 9–29 for applicant 2).

In short, there is not a one-to-one correspondence between actual scores and true scores. Most measures used in staffing are sufficiently unreliable that small differences in scores are likely to be due to error of measurement and should be ignored.

Relationship to Validity   The validity of a measure is defined as the degree to which it measures the attribute it is supposed to be measuring. For example, the validity of the test of knowledge of mechanical principles is the degree to which it measures that knowledge. There are specific ways to investigate validity, and these are discussed in the next section. Here, it simply needs to be recognized that the reliability with which an attribute is measured has direct implications for the validity of the measure.

The relationship between the reliability and validity of a measure is

$$r_{xy} \leq \sqrt{r_{xx}}$$

where r_{xy} is the validity of a measure and r_{xx} is the reliability of the measure. For example, it had been assumed previously that the reliability of the test of knowledge of mechanical principles was $r = .75$. The validity of that test thus cannot exceed $\sqrt{.75} = .86$.

Thus, the reliability of a measure places an upper limit on the possible validity of a measure. It should be emphasized that this is only an upper limit. A highly reliable measure is not necessarily a valid one. Reliability does not guarantee validity; it only makes validity possible.

Validity of Measures

The validity of a measure is defined as the degree to which it is measuring the attribute it is intended to measure.[14] Refer back to Exhibit 6.1, which involved the development of a test of knowledge of mechanical principles that was then to be used for purposes of selecting job applicants. The validity of that test is the degree to which it truly measures the attribute or construct "knowledge of mechanical principles."

Judgments about the validity of a measure occur through the process of gathering data and evidence about the measure to assess how it was developed, and whether accurate inferences can be made from scores on the measure. This process can be illustrated in terms of concepts pertaining to accuracy of measurement and accuracy of prediction. These concepts may then be used to demonstrate how validation of measures occurs in staffing.

Accuracy of Measurement

How accurate is the test of knowledge of mechanical principles? This question asks for evidence about the accuracy with which the test portrays individuals' true levels of that knowledge. This is akin to asking about the degree of overlap between the attribute being measured and the actual measure of the attribute.

Refer to Exhibit 6.10. It shows the concept of accuracy of measurement in Venn diagram form. The circle on the left represents the construct "knowledge of mechanical principles," and the circle on the right represents the actual test of knowledge of mechanical principles. The overlap between the two circles represents the degree of accuracy of measurement for the test. The greater the overlap, the greater the accuracy of measurement.

Notice that perfect overlap is not shown in Exhibit 6.10. This signifies the occurrence of measurement error with the use of the test. These errors, as indicated in the exhibit, are the errors of deficiency and contamination previously discussed.

So how does accuracy of measurement differ from reliability of measurement, since both are concerned with deficiency and contamination? There is disagreement among people on this question. Generally, the difference may be thought of

EXHIBIT 6.10   Accuracy of Measurement

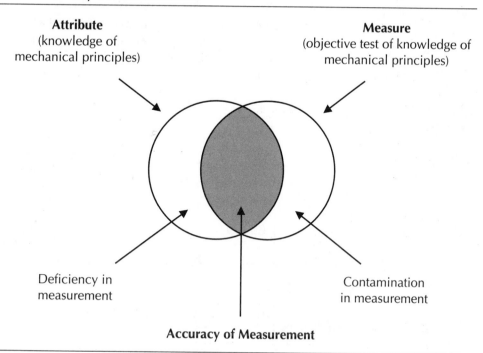

Attribute
(knowledge of
mechanical principles)

Measure
(objective test of knowledge of
mechanical principles)

Deficiency in
measurement

Contamination
in measurement

Accuracy of Measurement

as follows. Reliability refers to consistency among the scores on the test, as de-termined by comparing scores as previously described. Accuracy of measurement goes beyond this to assess the extent to which the scores truly reflect the attribute being measured—the overlap shown in Exhibit 6.10. Accuracy requires reliability, but it also requires more by way of evidence. For example, accuracy requires knowing something about how the test was developed. Accuracy also requires some evidence concerning how test scores are influenced by other factors—for example, how do test scores change as a result of employees attending a training program devoted to providing instruction in mechanical principles? Accuracy thus demands greater evidence than reliability.

Accuracy of Prediction

Measures are often developed because they provide information about people that can be used to make predictions about those people. In Exhibit 6.1, the knowledge test was to be used to help make hiring decisions, which are actually predictions about which people will be successful at a job. Knowing something about the accuracy with which a test predicts future job success requires examining the relationship between scores on the test and scores on some measure of job success for a group of people.

Accuracy of prediction is illustrated in the upper half of Exhibit 6.11. Where there is an actual job success outcome (criterion) to predict, the test (predictor) will be used to predict the criterion. Each person is classified as high or low on the predictor and high or low on the criterion, based on predictor and criterion

---

EXHIBIT 6.11   Accuracy of Prediction

A. General Illustration

		D	A
Actual criterion	High	Errors in predictions	Correct predictions
		C	B
	Low	Correct predictions	Errors in predictions
		Low	High

Predicted criterion

$$\text{Accuracy} = \frac{A+C}{A+B+C+D} \times 100$$

B. Selection Example (n=100 job applicants)

Actual performance	High	20	45
	Low	25	10
		Low	High

Predicted performance
(based on test scores)

$$\text{Accuracy} = \frac{45+25}{45+10+25+20} \times 100 = 70\%$$

scores. Individuals falling into cells A and C represent correct predictions, and individuals falling into cells B and D represent errors in prediction. Accuracy of prediction is the percentage of total correct predictions. Accuracy can thus range from 0% to 100%.

The bottom half of Exhibit 6.11 shows an example of the determination of accuracy of prediction using a selection example. The predictor is the test of knowledge of mechanical principles, and the criterion is an overall measure of job performance. Scores on the predictor and criterion measures are gathered for $n = 100$ job applicants, and dichotomized into high or low scores on each. Each individual is placed into one of the four cells. The accuracy of prediction for the test is 70%.

Validation of Measures in Staffing

In staffing, there is concern with the validity of predictors in terms of both accuracy of measurement and accuracy of prediction. It is important to have and use predictors that are accurate representations of the KSAOs to be measured, and those predictors need to be accurate in their predictions of job success. The validity of predictors is explored through the conduct of validation studies.

There are two types of validation studies typically conducted. The first of these is criterion-related validation, and the second is content validation. A third type of validation study, known as construct validation, involves components of reliability, criterion-related validation, and content validation. Each component is discussed separately in this book, and thus no further reference is made to construct validation.

Criterion-Related Validation

Exhibit 6.12 shows the components of criterion-related validation and their usual sequencing.[15] The process begins with job analysis. Results of job analysis are then fed into criterion and predictor measures. Scores on the predictor and criterion are obtained for a sample of individuals; the relationship between the scores is then examined to make a judgment about the predictor's validity.

Job Analysis   Job analysis is undertaken to identify and define important tasks (and broader task dimensions) of the job. The KSAOs and motivation thought to be necessary for performance of these tasks are then inferred. Results of the process of identifying tasks and underlying KSAOs are expressed in the form of the job requirements matrix. The matrix is a task $\times$ KSAO matrix; it shows the tasks required, combined with the relevant KSAOs for each task.

EXHIBIT 6.12 Criterion-Related Validation

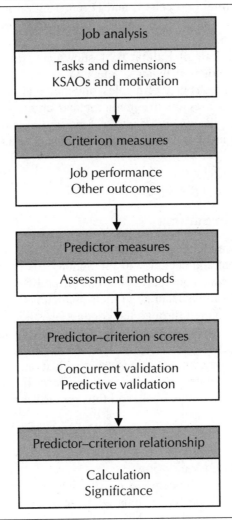

Criterion Measures Measures of performance on tasks and task dimensions are needed. These may already be available as part of an ongoing performance appraisal system, or they may have to be developed. However gathered, the critical requirement is that the measures be as free from measurement error as possible.

Criterion measures need not be restricted to performance measures. Others may be used, such as measures of attendance, retention, safety, and customer service. As with performance-based criterion measures, these alternative criterion measures should also be as error free as possible.

Predictor Measure   The predictor measure is the measure whose criterion-related validity is being investigated. Ideally, it taps one or more of the KSAOs identified in job analysis. Also, it should be the type of measure most suitable to assess the KSAOs. Knowledge of mechanical principles, for example, is probably best assessed with some form of written, objective test.

Predictor-Criterion Scores   Predictor and criterion scores must be gathered from a sample of current employees or job applicants. If current employees are used, this involves use of a concurrent validation design. Alternatively, if job applicants are used, a predictive validation design is used. The nature of these two designs is shown in Exhibit 6.13.

EXHIBIT 6.13   Concurrent and Predictive Validation Designs

Concurrent Validation Design

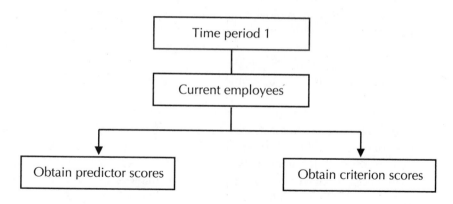

Predictive Validation Design

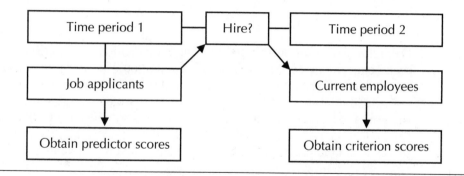

Concurrent validation has some definite appeal. Administratively, it is convenient and can often be done quickly. Moreover, results of the validation study will be available soon after the predictor and criterion scores have been gathered.

Unfortunately, some serious problems can arise with use of a concurrent validation design. One problem is that if the predictor is a test, current employees may not be motivated in the same way that job applicants would be in terms of desire to perform well on the test. Yet, it is future applicants for whom the test is intended to be used.

In a related vein, current employees may not be similar to, or representative of, future job applicants. Current employees may differ in terms of demographics such as age, race, sex, disability status, education level, and previous job experience. Hence, it is not certain that the results of the study will generalize to future job applicants. Also, some unsatisfactory employees will have been terminated, and some high performers may have been promoted. This leads to restriction of range on the criterion scores, which in turn will lower the correlation between the predictor and criterion scores.

Finally, current employees' predictor scores may be influenced by the amount of experience and/or success they have had on their current job. For example, scores on the test of knowledge of mechanical principles may reflect not only that knowledge, but how long people have been on the job and how well they have performed it. This is undesirable because we want predictor scores to be predictive of the criterion, rather than a result of it.

Predictive validation overcomes the potential limitations of concurrent validation, since the predictor scores are obtained from job applicants. Applicants will be motivated to do well on the predictor, and they are more likely to be representative of future job applicants. And applicants' scores on the predictor cannot be influenced by success and/or experience on the job, since the scores were gathered prior to their being on the job.

Predictive validation is not without potential limitations, however. It is neither administratively easy nor quick. Moreover, results will not be available immediately, since some time must lapse before criterion scores can be obtained. Despite these limitations, predictive validation is considered the more sound of the two designs.

Predictor-Criterion Relationship Once predictor and criterion scores have been obtained, the correlation r, or some variation of it, must be calculated. The value of the r is then referred to as the validity of the scores on the predictor. For example, if an r = .35 was found, the predictor would be referred to as having a validity of .31. Then, the practical and statistical significance of the r should be determined. Only if the r meets desired levels of practical and statistical significance should the predictor be consider "valid," and thus potentially usable in the selection system.

Illustrative Study   A study involving n = 52 law enforcement agency managers, holding ranks of sergeant through major, used a predictive validation design.[16] Predictor data were gathered in 1977, and criterion data in 1979, 1981, and 1984.

There were two predictors: assessment center ratings and subordinate ratings. Assessment center ratings were gathered during a two-day assessment. Managers participated in four exercises (leaderless group discussion, in-basket, subordinate counseling, and oral presentation). Upper-level managers rated participants' performance in the exercises on several dimensions (e.g., quality of ideas, interpersonal relations, and organization and planning). Ratings were summed up to form an overall assessment rating (OAR) for each participant. Subordinates also anonymously rated their managers annually on several performance dimensions. Ratings were summed up to form an overall subordinate rating.

There were three criterion measures, as follows:

1. Subordinate performance ratings, as already described, were gathered in 1979, 1981, and 1984.

2. Supervisory performance ratings were the sum of ratings on several performance dimensions.

3. Promotions were whether or not the manager was promoted in the time period. Decision makers had access to the OAR when making promotion decisions, so there was criterion contamination by knowledge of the OAR. This was not a problem with the other two criteria.

Results of the study are shown in Exhibit 6.14. The OAR significantly predicted near (1977) and long-term (1984) supervisory and subordinate performance ratings, as well as promotions (not unexpected, due to criterion contamination). Subordinate ratings significantly predicted all four sets of supervisory performance ratings, as well as all three sets of future subordinate ratings. These validities for the ratings were much more significant (both statistical and practical) than were those for the promotion criterion.

Content Validation

Content validation differs from criterion-related validity in one important respect: there is no criterion measure used in content validation. Thus, predictor scores cannot be correlated with criterion scores as a way of gathering evidence about a predictor's validity. Rather, a judgment is made about the probable correlation, had there been a criterion measure. For this reason, content validation is frequently referred to as judgmental validation.[17]

Content validation is most appropriate, and most likely to be found, in two circumstances: when there are too few people to form a sample for purposes of criterion-related validation, and when criterion measures are not available, or they are available but are of highly questionable quality. At an absolute minimum, an n = 30 is necessary for criterion-related validation.

EXHIBIT 6.14   Results of Validation Study for Law Enforcement Managers

Concurrent and Predictive Validity Coefficients for Two Predictors and Three Criteria over Seven Years

1977 Predictors	Criteria[a]										
	Supervisory Performance Ratings				Ratings by Subordinates				Promotions		
	1977	1979	1981	1984	1977	1979	1981	1984	1979	1981	1984
Assessment center OAR	.38**	.19***	.21	.41**	.29*	.19	−.14	.43**	.69***b	.69***b	.68***b
	(41)	(47)	(48)	(32)	(45)	(44)	(43)	(35)	(49)	(48)	(49)
Ratings by subordinates	.26*	.46***	.39**	.27*	NA[c]	.64***	.33**	.37*	.17	.20	.22*
	(49)	(56)	(54)	(38)		(51)	(48)	(37)	(.59)	(54)	(58)

[a]Numbers in parentheses are sample sizes.
[b]As noted in the text of the article, these very high correlations should not be interpreted as predictive validity coefficients because of the direct use of OARs in promotion decisions.
[c]NA = Not Applicable
*p < .05; **p < .01; ***p < .001

Source: G. M. McEvoy and R. W. Beatty, " Assessment Centers and Subordinate Appraisals of Managers: A Seven-Year Examination of Predictive Validity," *Personnel Psychology,* 1989, 42, p. 46.

Exhibit 6.15 shows the three basic steps in content validation—conducting a job analysis, constructing a job requirements matrix, and choosing or developing a predictor. These steps are commented on next. Comparing the steps in content validation with those in criterion-related validation (see Exhibit 6.12) shows that the steps in content validation are a part of criterion-related validation. Because of this, the two types of validation should be thought of as complementary, with content validation being a subset of criterion-related validation.

Job Analysis As with criterion-related validation, content validation begins with job analysis, which, in both cases, is undertaken to identify and define tasks and task dimensions, and to infer the necessary KSAOs and motivation for those tasks. Results are expressed in the job requirements matrix.

Predictor Measures Sometimes the predictor will be one that has already been developed and is in use. An example here is a commercially available test, interviewing process, or biographical information questionnaire. Other times, there will not be such a measure available. This occurs frequently in the case of job knowledge, which is usually highly specific to the particular job involved in the validation.

Lacking a readily available or modifiable predictor means that the organization will have to construct its own predictors. At this point, the organization has built predictor construction into the predictor validation process. Now, content validation and the predictor development processes occur simultaneously. The organization becomes engaged in test construction, a topic beyond the scope of this book.[18]

It should be emphasized that content validation procedures can be applied to any type of predictor, or combination of predictors, as illustrated in a content

---

EXHIBIT 6.15   Content Validation

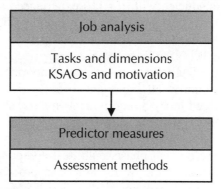

validation study involving police emergency telephone operators.[19] A job analysis identified six critical KSAO requirements for the job (communication skills, emotional control, judgment, cooperativeness, memory, and clerical/technical skills). The predictors included

1. a spelling test in which applicants received ten tape-recorded telephone calls and had to accurately record the pertinent information from each call on a form
2. a test in which applicants had to accurately record information received from monitoring police units
3. a typing test measuring both speed and accuracy
4. a situational interview in which applicants were asked how they would behave in a series of job-related situations
5. a role-playing exercise in which applicants assumed the role of police and telephone operators taking calls from complainants

This example makes clear that content validation is a flexible process for establishing task–KSAO–predictor linkages. At the same time that these linkages are being established administratively, validation evidence is emerging from a built-in process of content validation.

A final note about content validation emphasizes the importance of continually paying attention to the need for reliability of measurement and standardization of the measurement process. While these are always matters of concern in any type of validation effort, they are of paramount importance in content validation. The reason for this is that without an empirical correlation between the predictor and criterion, only the likely r can be judged. It is important, in forming that judgment, to pay considerable attention to reliability and standardization.

Illustrative Study This study is concerned with the development of a computerized testing procedure for the selection of secretarial applicants to a large manufacturing organization.[20] The first phase of the study involved job analysis. Interviews were conducted with n = 110 experienced secretaries (so-called subject matter experts or SMEs) and focused on the identification of tasks, KSAOs, and linkages between the two. Tasks were grouped into task dimensions; interrater reliability of the SMEs in this process was very acceptable, with an r = .90. KSAOs were rated by the SMEs in terms of their importance to successful task performance (from 1 = not at all important to 5 = critical). The task dimensions and KSAOs were placed in a job requirements matrix, shown in Exhibit 6.16. Each X represents a KSAO receiving an average importance rating of 3 or higher for a given task dimension. The matrix then served as the blueprint for test development.

In the test development phase, eight test components were identified to form the total test portion of the overall selection procedure. These test components were derived from the previously identified KSAOs and matched to them. The components deal with word processing, corrections, data bases, letters, travel expense forms, mail logs, electronic mail messages, and telephone messages.

Tests were tailor-made for the eight selection components. Care was taken to ensure a strong fidelity between test content and actual job content (e.g., type of computer, software commands). Also, 30 secretaries from a secretarial help agency were hired to go through a dry run of the selection procedure and provide reactions to it. This was used to fine-tune the tests. All tests were highly standardized in their construction and administration, as were their scoring keys.

The procedure was then tested on a sample of 43 individuals. Results of this test showed that (a) there were relatively high standard deviations in test scores, indicating good interindividual differences; (b) the intercorrelations among the test components were low, indicating they were measuring different KSAOs, as intended; and (c) there was high interrater reliability in the scoring of people's responses to the tests, indicating that the scoring keys could be used in a consistent fashion by multiple raters.

Validity Generalization

In the preceding discussions of validity and validation, an implicit premise is being made that validity is situation-specific and therefore validation of predictors must occur in each specific situation. All of the examples involve specific types of measures, jobs, individuals, and so forth. Nothing is said about generalizing validity across those jobs and individuals. For example, if a predictor is valid for a particular job in organization X, would it be valid for the same type of job in organization Y? Or, is validity specific to the particular job and organization?

The situation-specific premise is based on the following scenario, which, in turn, has its origins in findings from decades of previous research. Assume a large number of criterion-related validation studies have been conducted. Each study involves various predictor measures of a common KSAO attribute (e.g., general mental ability) and various criterion measures of a common outcome attribute (e.g., job performance). The predictor will be designated "X," and the criterion will be designated "Y." The studies are conducted in many different situations (types of jobs, types of organizations), and they involve many different samples (sample sizes, types of employees). In each study, r_{xy} is calculated. The results from all the studies reveal a wide range of different size r_{xy} values, though the average is $\bar{r}_{xy} = .25$. These results suggest that while on average there seems to be some validity to X, the validity varies substantially from situation to situation. Based on these findings, the best conclusion is that validity most likely is situation-specific, and thus cannot be generalized across the situations.

The concept of validity generalization questions this premise.[21] It says that much of the variation in the r_{xy} values is due to the occurrence of a number of methodological and statistical differences across the studies. If these differences were

EXHIBIT 6.16   Content Validation Study: Secretarial Job

JOB REQUIREMENTS MATRIX

Task Dimension	KSA															
	1	2	3	4	5	6	7	8	9	10	11	12	13	14	15	16
1. Maintaining and developing databases and spreadsheets, including collecting and entering information. Using databases and spreadsheets to obtain summaries and answer questions.		X[a]	X	X					X	X		X				X
2. General computer activities. Working with data files and preparing printed documents. Answering questions about computer use and printing options.		X		X				X	X	X		X			X	X
3. Creating and completing various company forms and insuring that they are filed and/or distributed to appropriate personnel.	X	X		X	X		X		X	X	X					X
4. General clerical activities including answering phone, filing, handling mail, and duplicating.	X	X		X	X	X	X	X	X		X		X	X		X
5. Note-taking, typing, and letter preparation, including editing and revising.	X	X		X	X	X	X	X	X		X		X	X	X	X
6. Handling travel arrangements, securing reimbursements, and completing travel expense reports.	X	X	X	X	X	X	X	X	X		X			X		

(continued)

EXHIBIT 6.16 Continued

JOB REQUIREMENTS MATRIX

Task Dimension	KSA															
	1	2	3	4	5	6	7	8	9	10	11	12	13	14	15	16
7. Personnel-related record keeping and handling payroll duties, including auditing and resolving discrepancies. Maintaining unit personnel files.	X		X	X	X	X	X		X		X					X
8. Coordinating office and building functions and maintaining equipment/supplies. Scheduling meetings and conferences, insuring that necessary people and equipment arrive.	X	X		X	X	X	X	X	X					X		X
9. Generating reports, charts, and graphs from notes/data and insuring their accuracy.		X	X	X	X		X		X	X		X				X
10. Coordinating and administering training and substituting activities.				X		X		X						X		X
11. Using electronic communication systems to send and receive information (file, messages, data, etc.).		X					X		X	X		X	X		X	X

[a]X = Those KSAs for which performance of a task was considered important by expert judges, that is, mean ratings were 3.00 or above.
NOTE: The KSAs are (1) ability to follow oral directions, (2) ability to read and follow manuals, (3) ability to perform basic arithmetic operations, (4) ability to organize, (5) judgment/decision making, (6) oral communication, (7) written communication, (8) interpersonal skills, (9) typing skills, (10) knowledge of computer software, (11) knowledge of company policies, (12) knowledge of basic computer operations, (13) knowledge of how to use office machines, (14) flexibility in dealing with job demands, (15) knowledge of communication software, (16) ability to attend to detail.

Source: N. Schmitt, S. W. Gilliland, R. S. Landis, and D. Devine, "Computer-Based Testing Applied to Selection of Secretarial Applicants," *Personnel Psychology*, 1993, 46, p. 152.

controlled for statistically, the variation in values would shrink and converge toward an estimate of the true validity of X. If that true r is significant (practically and statistically), one can indeed generalize validity of X across situations. Validity thus is not viewed as situation-specific. The logic of this validity generalization premise is shown in Exhibit 6.17.

The distinction between situation-specific validity and validity generalization is important for two related reasons. First, from a scientific viewpoint, it is important to identify and make statements about X and Y relationships in general, without always having to say that everything depends on the sample, criterion measure, and so forth. In this regard, validity generalization clearly allows greater latitude than does situation specificity. Second, from a practical standpoint, it would be convenient and less costly not to have to conduct a separate validation study for predictor X in every situation in which its use was a possibility. Validity generalization allows that to happen, while situation specificity does not.

Evidence is beginning to surface that is supportive of the validity generalization premise. For example, evidence suggests that tests of general mental ability have meaningful, practical validity for predicting job performance across a wide variety of types of employees and jobs. Until more is known about validity generalization, however, caution is called for in its use in either scientific or practical terms. In this light, the following recommendations are offered as guides to staffing practice:

1. At a minimum, all predictors should routinely be subject to content validation.

2. When feasible, criterion-related validation studies should be conducted unless there is sufficient validity generalization evidence available to support use of a predictor without prior validation.

3. Any claims of validity or validity generalization that are based on no criterion-related validity studies, or only a small number of them, should be suspect.

4. Organizations should become involved in various cooperative arrangements devoted to validation research in order to explore the extent to which validity may be generalized.

EXHIBIT 6.17   The Logic of Validity Generalization

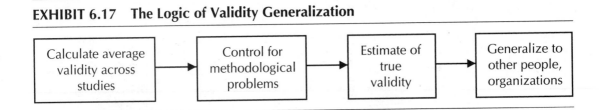

| Calculate average validity across studies | → | Control for methodological problems | → | Estimate of true validity | → | Generalize to other people, organizations |

A particular form of validity generalization that has proved useful is called meta-analysis. In meta-analysis the focus is on determining the average correlation between X and Y (i.e., $\bar{r}_{xy}$) noted above, such as between a particular selection technique (X) and job performance (Y), after controlling for methodological problems in the validation studies. For example, the average validity of general cognitive ability tests for predicting job performance is $\bar{r}_{xy} = .50$ (see Chapter 10). This represents our best statement of the average degree of validity found for mental ability tests to date, as well as an expectation of the validity we would likely find for general mental ability tests in future validation studies. We can also compare this $\bar{r}_{xy}$ to the $\bar{r}_{xy}$ of another selection technique, such as the unstructured interview, as a way of indicating the relative validity of the two techniques. Meta-analysis results and comparisons for numerous selection techniques are presented in Chapters 9 and 10.

LEGAL ISSUES

Staffing laws and regulations, particularly EEO/AA laws and regulations, place great reliance on the use of measurement concepts and processes. Here, measurement is an integral part of (a) judging an organization's compliance through the conduct of disparate impact analysis, and (b) requiring standardization and validation of measures.

Disparate Impact Statistics

In Chapter 3, disparate (adverse) impact was introduced as a way of determining whether staffing practices were having potentially illegal impacts on individuals because of race, sex, and so forth. Such a determination requires the compilation and analysis of statistical evidence, primarily applicant flow and applicant stock statistics.

Applicant Flow Statistics

Applicant flow statistical analysis requires the calculation of selection rates (proportions or percentages of applicants hired) for groups, and the subsequent comparison of those rates to determine if they are significantly different from one another.[22] This may be illustrated by taking the example from Exhibit 3.3:

	Applicants	**Hires**	**Selection Rate**
Men	50	25	.50 or 50%
Women	45	5	.11 or 11%

It may be seen in this example that there is a sizeable difference in selection rates between men and women (.50 as opposed to .11). Does this difference indicate adverse impact?

The Uniform Guidelines on Employee Selection Procedures (UGESP) speak directly to this question (see Appendix A). Several points need to be made regarding the determination of disparate impact analysis.

First, the UGESP requires the organization to keep records that will permit calculation of such selection rates, also referred to as applicant flow statistics. These statistics are a primary vehicle by which compliance with the law (Civil Rights Act) is judged.

Second, the UGESP requires calculation of selection rates (a) for each job category, (b) for both external and internal selection decisions, (c) for each step in the selection process, and (d) by race and sex of applicants. In order to meet this requirement, the organization must keep detailed records of its staffing activities and decisions. Such record keeping should be built directly into the organization's staffing system routines.[23]

Third, comparisons of selection rates among groups in a job category for purposes of compliance determination should be based on the 80% rule in the UGESP, which states that "a selection rate for any race, sex or ethnic group which is less than four-fifths (4/5) (or eighty percent) of the rate for the group with the highest rate will generally be regarded by federal enforcement agencies as evidence of adverse impact, while a greater than four-fifths rate will generally not be regarded by federal enforcement agencies as evidence of adverse impact."

If this rule is applied to the previous example, the group with the highest selection rate is men (.50). The rate for women should be within 80% of this rate, or .40 (.50 × .80 = .40). Since the actual rate for women is .11, this suggests the occurrence of adverse impact.

Fourth, the 80% rule is truly only a guideline. Note the use of the word "generally" in the rule with regard to differences in selection rates. Also, the 80% rule goes on to provide for other exceptions, based on sample size considerations and issues surrounding statistical and practical significance of difference in selection rates. Despite these exceptions, organizations are encouraged to use the 80% rule with stringency for purposes of self-analysis. Deviations from the rule should be treated as red flags that trigger an examination into possible reasons for their occurrence.

Applicant Stock Statistics

Applicant stock statistics require the calculation of the percentages of women and minorities (a) employed, and (b) available for employment in the population.[24] These percentages are compared to search for disparities in the percentages. This is referred to as utilization analysis.

To illustrate, the example from Exhibit 3.3 is shown here:

	Employed	**Availability**
Nonminority	90%	70%
Minority	10%	30%

It can be seen that 10% of employees are minorities, while their availability in the population is 30%. A comparison of these two percentages suggests an underutilization of minorities.

Utilization analysis of this sort is an integral part of not only compliance assessment, but affirmative action plans (AAPs). Indeed, utilization analysis is the starting point for the development of AAPs. This may be illustrated by reference to Revised Order No. 4 (see Appendix B), which specifies the affirmative action requirements for federal contractors.

The order requires the organization to conduct a formal utilization analysis of its workforce. That analysis must be (a) conducted by job category, and (b) done separately for women and minorities. While calculation of the numbers and percentages of persons employed is relatively straightforward, determination of their availability in the population is not. The order requires that the availabilities take into account eight factors, such as proximity to the organization and KSAO qualifications (these eight factors and utilization analysis are also covered in Chapter 4). Accurate measurement and/or estimation of availabilities that take into account these eight factors is extremely difficult. In large part, this is a reflection of difficulties in measuring characteristics of the labor force more generally.

Despite these measurement problems, the order requires comparison of the percentage of women and minorities employed with their availability. Based on this comparison, the organization must then determine if, and where, it is underutilizing these two groups. Unfortunately, the order does not provide any specific guidance to help determine how big a difference in percentages is tolerable before concluding that underutilization is occurring. Thus, the organization must exercise considerable discretion in the determination of adverse impact through the use of applicant stock statistics.

Standardization and Validation

When it has been determined that an organization is in noncompliance with the law, such as through adverse impact statistics, it must take certain steps to move toward compliance. While the specific steps will obviously depend on the situation, measurement activities invariably will be actively involved in them. These activities will revolve around standardization and validation of measures.

Standardization

A lack of consistency in treatment of applicants is one of the major factors contributing to the occurrence of discrimination in staffing. This is partly due to a lack of standardization in measurement, in terms of both what is measured and how it is evaluated or scored.

An example of inconsistency in what is measured is that the types of background information required of minority applicants may differ from that required of nonminority applicants. Minority applicants may be asked about credit ratings and criminal conviction records, while nonminority applicants are not. Or, the type of interview questions asked male applicants may be different from those asked female applicants.

Even if information is consistently gathered from all applicants, it may not be evaluated the same for all applicants. A male applicant who has a history of holding several different jobs may be viewed as a "career builder," while a female with the same history may be evaluated as an unstable "job hopper." In essence, different scoring keys are being used for men and women applicants.

Reducing, and hopefully eliminating, such inconsistency requires a straightforward application of the three properties of standardized measures discussed previously. Through standardization of measurement comes consistent treatment of applicants, and with it, the possibility of lessened adverse impact.

Validation

Even with standardized measurement, adverse impact may occur. Under these circumstances, the question is whether adverse impact is still justified. The UGESP addresses this issue directly. When there is adverse impact, the organization must either eliminate it or justify it through presentation of validity evidence regarding the measure(s) causing the adverse impact.

The types of validity evidence required under the UGESP are precisely those presented in this chapter. There are also detailed technical standards governing the conduct of these validation studies in the UGESP. The purpose of these requirements is to ensure that, if an organization's staffing system is causing adverse impact, it is for job-related reasons. Evidence of job relatedness thus becomes the employer's rebuttal to the plaintiff's charges of discrimination. In the absence of such validation evidence, the employer must take steps to eliminate the adverse impact. These steps will involve various recruitment, selection, and employment activities that will be discussed throughout the remainder of the book.

SUMMARY

Measurement is an integral part of the foundation of staffing activities. Measures are used in staffing to assess job requirements and rewards, individuals' KSAOs, and HR outcomes; they are also used in monitoring and record keeping, as well as research and evaluation.

Measurement is defined as the process of using rules to assign numbers to objects to represent quantities of an attribute of the objects. Standardization of the measurement process is sought. This applies to each of the four levels of measurement: nominal, ordinal, interval, and ratio. Standardization is also sought for both objective and subjective measures.

Measures yield scores that represent the amount of the attribute being measured. Scores are manipulated in various ways to aid in their interpretation. Typical manipulations involve central tendency and variability, percentiles, and standard scores. Scores are also correlated to learn about the strength and direction of the relationship between two attributes. The significance of the resultant correlation coefficient is then judged in statistical and practical terms.

The quality of measures involves issues of reliability and validity. Reliability refers to consistency of measurement, both at a moment in time and between time periods. Various procedures are used to estimate reliability, including coefficient alpha, interrater and intrarater agreement, and test-retest. Reliability places an upper limit on the validity of a measure.

Validity refers to accuracy of measurement and accuracy of prediction, as reflected by the scores obtained from a measure. Criterion-related and content validation studies are conducted to help learn about the validity of a measure. In criterion-related validation, scores on a predictor (KSAO) measure are correlated with scores on a criterion (HR outcome) measure. In content validation, there is no criterion measure, so judgments are made about the content of a predictor relative to the HR outcome it is seeking to predict. Traditionally, results of validation studies were treated as situation-specific, meaning that the organization ideally should conduct a new and separate validation study for any predictor in any situation in which the predictor is to be used. Recently, however, results from validity generalization studies have suggested that the validity of predictors may generalize across situations, meaning that the requirement of conducting costly and time-consuming validation studies in each specific situation could be relaxed.

Measurement is also said to be an integral part of an organization's EEO/AA compliance activities, as the Uniform Guidelines on Employee Selection Procedures (UGESP) and Revised Order No. 4 make clear. The organization must calculate disparate impact statistics of both applicant flows and applicant stocks. These statistics are then used to help determine if and where the organization's staffing activities are causing disparate (adverse) impact. When adverse impact is found, changes in measurement practices may be legally necessary. As specified in the UGESP and Revised Order No. 4, these changes will involve movement toward standardization of measurement and the conduct of validation studies.

DISCUSSION QUESTIONS

1. Imagine and describe a staffing system for a job in which there are no measures used.

2. Describe how you might go about determining scores for applicants' responses to (a) interview questions, (b) letters of recommendation, and (c) questions about previous work experience.

3. Describe examples of when you would want the following for a written job knowledge test: (a) a low coefficient alpha (e.g., $\alpha = .35$), and (b) a low test-retest reliability.

4. Assume you gave a general ability test, measuring both verbal and computational skills, to a group of applicants for a specific job. Also assume that because of severe hiring pressures, you hired all of the applicants, regardless of their test scores. How would you investigate the criterion-related validity of the test?

5. Using the same example as in question four, how would you go about investigating the content validity of the test?

APPLICATIONS

Evaluation of Two New Assessment Methods for Selecting Telephone Customer Service Representatives

The Phonemin Company is a distributor of men's and women's casual clothing. It sells exclusively through its merchandise catalog, which is published four times per year to coincide with seasonal changes in customers' apparel tastes. Customers may order merchandise from the catalog via mail or over the phone. Currently, 70% of orders are phone orders, and the company expects this to increase to 85% within the next few years.

The success of the company is obviously very dependent upon the success of the telephone ordering system and the Customer Service Representatives (CSRs) who staff the system. There are currently 185 CSR employees, and that should increase to about 225 CSRs to handle the anticipated growth in phone order sales. Though the CSRs are trained to use very standardized methods and procedures for handling phone orders, there are still seemingly large differences among them in their job performance. The CSRs performance is routinely measured in terms of error rate, speed of order taking, and customer complaints. The top 25% and lowest 25% of performers on each of these measures differ by a factor of at least 3 (e.g., the error rate of the lowest group is three times as high as that of the top group). Strategically, the company knows that it could enhance CSR performance (and ultimately sales) substantially if it could improve its staffing "batting average" by more accurately hiring new CSRs who are likely to be top performers.

The current staffing system for CSRs is straightforward. Applicants are recruited through a combination of employee referrals and newspaper ads. Because turnover among CSRs is so high (50% annually), recruitment is a continuous process at the company. Applicants complete a standard application blank which asks for information about education and previous work experience. The information is reviewed by the staffing specialist in the HR department. Only obvious misfits are rejected at this point; the others (95%) are asked to have an interview with the specialist. The interview lasts 20–30 minutes, and at the conclusion the applicant is either rejected or offered a job. Due to the tightness of the labor market and the constant presence of vacancies to be filled, 90% of the interviewees receive job offers. Most of those offers are accepted (95%), and the new hires then attend a one-week training program before being placed on the job.

The company has decided to investigate fully the possibilities of increasing CSR effectiveness through sounder staffing practices. In particular, it is not pleased with its current methods of assessing job applicants; it feels that neither the interview nor the application blank provides the accurate and in-depth assessments of the KSAOs truly needed to be an effective CSR. Consequently, it has engaged the services of a consulting firm whose product line includes various methods of KSAO assessment, along with validation and installation services. In cooperation with the HR staffing specialist, the consulting firm conducted the following study for the company.

A special job analysis lead to the identification of several specific KSAOs likely to be necessary for successful performance as a CSR. Three of these (clerical speed, clerical accuracy, interpersonal skills) were singled out for further consideration because of their seemingly high impact on job performance. Two new methods of assessment, provided by the consulting firm, were chosen for experimentation. The first was a paper-and-pencil clerical test that assesses clerical speed and accuracy. It is a 50 item test with a 30-minute time limit. The second was a brief work sample that could be administered as part of the interview process. In the work sample the applicant must respond to four different phone calls: from a customer irate about an out-of-stock item, from a customer wanting more product information about an item than was provided in the catalog, from a customer who wants to change an order placed yesterday, and from a customer with a routine order to place. The applicant is rated by the interviewer (using a 1–5 rating scale) in terms of tactfulness (T) and in terms of concern for customers (C). The interviewer is provided with a rating manual containing examples of exceptional (5), average (3), and unacceptable (1) responses by the applicant.

A random sample of n = 50 current CSRs were chosen to participate in the study. At Time 1 they were administered the clerical test and the work sample; performance data were also gathered from company records for error rate (number of errors per 100 orders), speed (number of orders filled per hour), and customer complaints (number of complaints per week). At Time 2, one week later, the clerical test and the work sample were re-administered to the CSRs. A member of the consulting firm sat in on all the interviews and served as a second rater of applicants' performance on the work sample.

Results for Clerical Test

	Time 1	Time 2
Mean score	31.61	31.22
Standard deviation	4.70	5.11
Coefficient alpha	.85	.86
Test-retest r		.92**
r with error rate	.31**	.37**
r with speed	.41**	.39**
r with complaints	.11	.08
r with work sample (T)	.21	.17
r with work sample (C)	.07	.15

Results for Work Sample (T)

	Time 1	Time 2
Mean score	3.15	3.11
Standard deviation	.93	1.01
% agreement (raters)	88%	79%
r with work sample (C)	.81**	.77**
r with error rate	.13	.12
r with speed	.11	.15
r with complaints	.37**	.35**

Results for Work Sample (C)

	Time 1	Time 2
Mean score	2.91	3.07
Standard deviation	.99	1.10
% agreement (raters)	80%	82%
r with work sample (T)	.81**	.77**
r with error rate	.04	.11
r with speed	.15	.14
r with complaints	.40**	.31**

(Note: ** means that r was significant at $p < .05$)

Based on the description of the study and results above:

1. How do you interpret the reliability results for the clerical test and work sample? Are they favorable enough for the company to consider using them "for keeps" in selecting new job applicants?

2. How do you interpret the validity results for the clerical test and work sample? Are they favorable enough for the company to consider using them "for keeps" in selecting new job applicants?

(*continued*)

3. What limitations in the above study should be kept in mind when interpreting the results and deciding whether or not to use the clerical test and work sample?

Conducting Empirical Validation and Adverse Impact Analysis

Yellow Blaze Candle Shops provide a full line of various types of candles and accessories such as candle holders. There are 150 shops located in shopping malls and strip malls throughout the country. There are over 600 sales people staffing these stores, each of which has a full-time manager. Staffing the manager's position, by policy, must occur by promotion from within the sales ranks. The company is interested in trying to improve its identification of sales people most likely to be successful store managers. It has developed a special technique for assessing and rating the suitability of sales people for the manager's job.

To experiment with this technique, the regional HR department representative met with the store managers in the region to review and rate the promotion suitability of each manager's sales people. They reviewed sales results, customer service orientation, and knowledge of store operations for each sales person, and then assigned a 1–3 promotion suitability rating (1 = not suitable, 2 = maybe suitable, 3 = definitely suitable) on each of these three factors. A total promotion suitability (PS) score, ranging from 3 to 9, was then computed for each sales person.

The PS scores were gathered, but not formally used in promotion decisions, for all sales people. Over the past year n=30 sales people have been promoted to store manager. Now it is time for the company to preliminarily investigate the validity of the PS scores, and to see if their use might lead to the occurrence of adverse impact against women or minorities. Each store manager's annual overall performance appraisal rating, ranging from 1 (low performance) to 5 (high performance), was used as the criterion measure in the validation study. The following data were available for analysis:

Employee ID	PS Score	Performance	Sex M/F	Minority Status (M = Minority NM = Nonminority)
11	9	5	M	NM
12	9	5	F	NM
13	9	1	F	NM
14	9	5	M	M
15	8	4	F	M
16	8	5	F	M
17	8	4	M	NM
18	8	5	M	NM
19	8	3	F	NM
20	8	4	M	NM

(continued)

Employee ID	PS Score	Performance	Sex M/F	Minority Status (M = Minority NM = Nonminority)
21	7	5	F	M
22	7	3	M	M
23	7	4	M	NM
24	7	3	F	NM
25	7	3	F	NM
26	7	4	M	NM
27	7	5	M	M
28	6	4	F	NM
29	6	4	M	NM
30	6	2	F	M
31	6	3	F	NM
32	6	3	M	NM
33	6	5	M	NM
34	6	5	F	NM
35	5	3	M	NM
36	5	3	F	M
37	5	2	M	M
38	4	2	F	NM
39	4	1	M	NM
40	3	4	F	NM

Based on the above data calculate:

1. Average PS scores for the whole sample, males, females, nonminority, minority.
2. The correlation between PS scores and Performance ratings, and its statistical significance (an r = .37 or higher is needed for significance at $p<.05$).
3. Adverse impact (selection rate) statistics for males and females, and nonminorities and minorities. Use a PS score of 7 or higher as a hypothetical passing score (the score that might be used to determine who will or will not be promoted).

Using the data, results, and description of the study, answer the following questions:

1. Is the PS assessment a valid predictor of performance as a store manager? Would you recommend the PS be used in the future to select sales people for promotion to store manager?
2. With a cut score of 7 on the PS, would its use lead to adverse impact against women? minorities? If there is adverse impact, does the validity evidence justify use of the PS anyway?

(*continued*)

(*continued*)
3. What are limitations of this study?
4. Would you recommend YellowBlaze now actually use the PS for making promotion decisions? Why or why not?

ENDNOTES

1. E. T. Cornelius III, "Analyzing Job Analysis Data"; E. L. Levine, J. N. Thomas, and F. Sistrunk, "Selecting a Job Analysis Approach," both in S. Gael (ed.), *The Job Analysis Handbook for Business, Industry and Government,* Vol. 1 (New York: Wiley, 1988), pp. 353–368 and pp. 339–352.

2. P. L. Ackerman and L. G. Humphreys, "Individual Difference Theory in Industrial and Organizational Psychology," in M. D. Dunnette and L. M. Hough (eds.), *Handbook of Industrial and Organizational Psychology,* Vol. 1 (Palo Alto, CA: Consulting Psychologists Press, 1990), pp. 223–282.

3. W. C. Borman, "Job Behavior, Performance, and Effectiveness," in M. D. Dunnette and L. M. Hough (eds.), *Handbook of Industrial and Organizational Psychology,* Vol. 2 (Palo Alto, CA: Consulting Psychologists Press, 1991), pp. 271–326. See also M. A. Campion, "Meaning and Measurement of Turnover: Comparison of Alternative Measures and Recommendations for Research," *Journal of Applied Psychology,* 1991, 76, pp. 19–212; D. L. Deadrick and R. M. Madigan, "Dynamic Criteria Revisited: A Longitudinal Study of Performance Stability and Predictive Validity," *Personnel Psychology,* 1990, 43, pp. 717–744; C. H. Campbell, P. Ford, M. G. Rumsey, E. D. Pulakos, W. C. Borman, D. B. Felker, M. V. D. Vera, and B. J. Riegelhaupt, "Development of Multiple Job Performance Measures in a Representative Sample of Jobs," *Personnel Psychology,* 1990, 43, pp. 277–300; K. R. Murphy and J. L. Cleveland, *Performance Appraisal* (Boston: Allyn and Bacon, 1991); A. K. Wigdor and B. F. Green, Jr., *Performance Assessment in the Workplace,* Vols. 1 and 2 (Washington, D.C.: National Academy Press, 1991).

4. E. F. Stone, *Research Methods in Organizational Behavior* (Santa Monica, CA: Goodyear, 1978), pp. 35–36.

5. F. G. Brown, *Principles of Educational and Psychological Testing* (Hinsdale, IL: Dryden, 1970), pp. 38–45.

6. E. F. Stone, *Research Methods in Organizational Behavior,* pp. 36–40.

7. R. L. Heneman, "The Relationship Between Supervisory Ratings and Results-Oriented Measures of Performance: A Meta-Analysis," *Personnel Psychology,* 1986, 39, pp. 811–826; W. H Bommer, J. L. Johnson, G. A. Rich, P. M. Podsakoff, and S. B. McKenzie, "On the Interchangeability of Objective and Subjective Measures of Employee Performance: A Meta-analysis," *Personnel Psychology,* 1995, 48, pp. 587–606.

8. This section draws on F. G. Brown, *Principles of Educational and Psychological Testing,* pp. 158–197; L. J. Cronbach, *Essentials of Psychological Testing,* fourth ed. (New York: Harper and Row, 1984), pp. 81–120; N. W. Schmitt and R. J. Klimoski, *Research Methods in Human Resources Management* (Cincinnati: Southwestern, 1991), pp. 41–87.

9. J. T. McClave and P. G. Benson, *Statistics for Business and Economics,* third ed. (San Francisco: Dellan, 1985).

10. For an excellent review, see N. W. Schmitt and R. J. Klimoski, *Research Methods in Human Resources Management,* pp. 88–114.

11. This section draws on E. G. Carmines and R. A. Zeller, *Reliability and Validity Assessment* (Beverly Hills, CA: Sage, 1979).

12. D. P. Schwab, "Construct Validity in Organization Behavior," in B. Staw and L. L. Cummings (eds.), *Research in Organizational Behavior* (Greenwich, CT: JAI Press, 1980), pp. 3–43.

13. E. G. Carmines and R. A. Zeller, *Reliability and Validity Assessment;* J. M. Cortina, "What is Coefficient Alpha? An Examination of Theory and Application," *Journal of Applied Psychology,* 1993, 78, pp. 98–104; N. W. Schmitt and R. J. Klimoski, *Research Methods in Human Resources Management,* pp. 89–100.

14. This section draws on R. D. Arvey, "Constructs and Construct Validation," *Human Performance,* 1992, 5, pp. 59–69; W. F. Cascio, *Applied Psychology in Personnel Management,* fourth ed. (Englewood Cliffs, NJ: Prentice-Hall, 1991), pp. 149–170; H. G. Heneman III, D. P. Schwab, J. A. Fossum, and L. Dyer, *Personnel/Human Resource Management,* fourth ed. (Homewood, IL: Irwin, 1989), pp. 300–329; N. Schmitt and F. J. Landy, "The Concept of Validity," in N. Schmitt, W. C. Borman and Associates, *Personnel Selection in Organizations* (San Francisco: Jossey-Bass, 1993), pp. 275–309; D. P. Schwab, "Construct Validity in Organization Behavior"; S. Messick, "Validity of Psychological Assessment," *American Psychologist,* September, 1995, pp. 741–749.

15. H. G. Heneman III, D. P. Schwab, J. A. Fossum, and L. Dyer, *Personnel/Human Resource Management,* pp. 300–310.

16. G. M. McEvoy and R. W. Beatty, "Assessment Centers and Subordinate Appraisals of Managers: A Seven-Year Examination of Predictive Validity," *Personnel Psychology,* 1989, 42, pp. 37–52.

17. I. L. Goldstein, S. Zedeck, and B. Schneider, "An Exploration of the Job Analysis-Content Validity Process," in N. Schmitt, W. C. Borman, and Associates, *Personnel Selection in Organizations* (San Francisco: Jossey-Bass, 1993), pp. 3–34; H. G. Heneman III, D. P. Schwab, J. A. Fossum, and L. Dyer, *Personnel/Human Resource Management,* pp. 311–315; P. R. Sackett and R. D. Arvey, "Selection in Small N Settings," in N. Schmitt, W. C. Borman and Associates, *Personnel Selection in Organizations,* pp. 418–447; D. A. Joiner, *Content Valid Testing for Supervisory and Management Jobs: A Practical/Common Sense Approach* (Alexandria, VA: International Personnel Management Association, 1987).

18. R. S. Barrett, "Content Validation Form," *Public Personnel Management,* 1992, 21, pp. 41–52; E. E. Ghiselli, J. P. Campbell, and S. Zedeck, *Measurement Theory for the Behavioral Sciences* (San Francisco: W. H. Freeman, 1981).

19. N. Schmitt and C. Ostroff, "Operationalizing the Behavioral Consistency Approach: Selection Test Development Based on a Content-Oriented Strategy," *Personnel Psychology,* 1986, 39, pp. 91–108.

20. N. Schmitt, S. W. Gilliland, R. S. Landis, and D. Devine, "Computer-Based Testing Applied to Selection of Secretarial Applicants," *Personnel Psychology,* 1993, 46, pp. 149–165.

21. R. M. Guion, "Personnel Assessment, Selection and Placement," in M. D. Dunnette and L. M. Hough (eds.), *Handbook of Industrial and Organizational Psychology,* Vol. 2, pp. 360–365; F. L. Schmidt and J. E. Hunter, "Development of a General Solution to the Problem of Validity Generalization," *Journal of Applied Psychology,* 1977, 62, 529–540; N. Schmitt, W. C. Borman, and Associates, *Personnel Selection in Organizations,* pp. 295–296.

22. R. D. Arvey and R. H. Faley, *Fairness in Selecting Employees,* (Reading, MA: Addison-Wesley, 1988), pp. 73–78; J. Ledvinka and V. G. Scarpello, *Federal Regulation of Personnel and Human Resource Management,* second ed. (Boston: PWS-Kent, 1991), pp. 142–151.

23. J. C. Cook, "Preparing For Statistical Battles Under the Civil Rights Act," *HR Focus,* 1992 (May), pp. 12–13.

24. Bureau of National Affairs, *Fair Employment Practices* (Washington, D.C.: author, periodically updated), pp. 443: 201, 209; J. Ledvinka and V. Scarpello, *Federal Regulation of Personnel and Human Resource Management,* pp. 124–142.

STAFFING ORGANIZATIONS MODEL

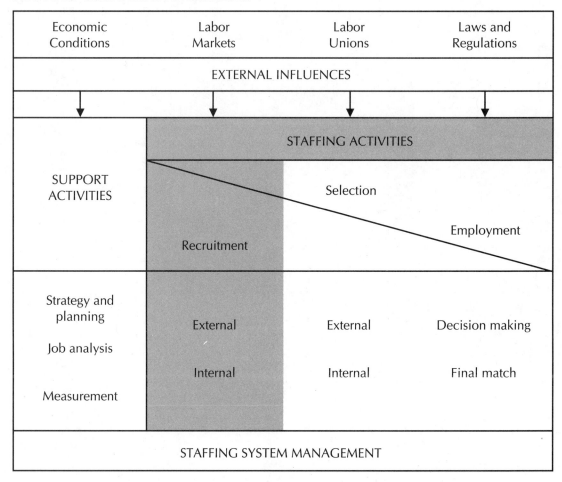

PART THREE

Staffing Activities: Recruitment

CHAPTER SEVEN

External Recruitment

Recruitment Planning
    Organizational Issues
    Administrative Issues

Strategy Development
    Where to Look
    How to Look
    When to Look

Searching
    Communication Message
    Communication Medium

Applicant Reactions

Transition to Selection

Legal Issues
    Definition of Job Applicant
    Targeted Recruitment
    Recruitment Sources
    Job Advertisements
    Fraud and Misrepresentation

Summary

Discussion Questions

Applications

The objective of the external recruitment process is to identify and attract job applicants from outside the organization. It is from among these applicants that hiring decisions are to be made.

The recruitment process begins with a planning phase where both organizational and administrative issues regarding the identification and attraction of applicants are addressed. Organizational issues include in-house versus external recruitment locations, individual versus cooperative recruitment alliances, and centralized versus decentralized recruitment functions. Administrative issues include requisitions; number and types of contracts; the recruitment budget; development of a recruitment guide; and the selection, training, and rewarding of recruiters.

Next, a recruitment strategy is formed in order to know where, how, and when to look for qualified applicants. Knowing where to look requires an understanding of open and targeted recruitment strategies. Knowing how to look requires an understanding of recruitment sources. Knowing when to look requires an understanding of lead time concerns and time sequence concerns.

Following the formation of strategy, the message to be communicated to job applicants is established and it is decided which communication medium should be used to communicate the message. The message may be traditional, realistic, attractive, or targeted. It may be communicated with recruitment brochures or videos, advertisements, voice messages, and video conferencing, and on-line.

Special consideration must be given to applicant reactions to recruiters and the recruitment process in undertaking each of these phases of the external recruitment process. Close attention must also be given to legal issues. This includes consideration of the definition of job applicant, disclaimers, targeted recruitment, recruitment sources, job advertisements, and fraud and misrepresentation.

RECRUITMENT PLANNING

Before actually identifying and attracting applicants to the organization, two issues must be resolved. First, organizational plans must be made to coordinate the identification and attraction of applicants. Second, administrative issues, such as the number of contacts to be made, recruiters to be used, and the budget to be spent, need to be considered to ensure that there are adequate resources to conduct a successful recruitment campaign.

Organizational Issues

The recruitment process in an organization can be organized in a variety of ways. It can be coordinated in-house or by an external recruitment agency. An organization can do its own recruiting or cooperate with other organizations in a recruitment alliance. Authority to recruit may be centralized or decentralized in the organization.

In-House versus External Recruitment Agency

Most organizational recruiting is done in-house. Smaller organizations may rely on external recruitment agencies rather than an in-house function to coordinate their recruitment efforts since smaller organizations may not have the staff or budget to run their own recruitment functions. Organizations with low turnover rates may also prefer to use external recruitment agencies because they recruit so infrequently it would not make sense to have a recruitment function of their own.

External recruitment agencies are growing in number. Some agencies, such as Elaine R. Shepherd Company, provide full-scale recruitment services ranging from identifying recruitment needs to advertising for applicants and checking references. Others, such as National Advertising Services, Inc., simply perform one recruitment activity. Although these services are expensive, the costs may be justified for organizations without a recruitment function or for employers with infrequent vacancies.

Large organizations and ones with frequent recruitment needs should have their own in-house recruitment function. An in-house function is needed to ensure that recruitment costs are minimized, recruitment searches are consistent from opening to opening, and the specific needs of the organization are being met.

Individual versus Cooperative Recruitment Alliances

Most organizations, especially ones that compete with one another in the same product and labor markets, do not cooperate with one another when recruiting. They do not cooperate because one organization's gain (a well-qualified hire) is another organization's loss (loss of a well-qualified candidate). Instead, they conduct their own recruitment programs to maintain a competitive advantage.

There are times, however, when even competitors may enter into cooperative recruitment alliances where arrangements are made to share recruitment resources.[1] Smaller organizations may gain from cooperating with one another in order to minimize recruitment costs. If there is an abundance of applicants in the labor market, with enough good applicants to go around, it may also make sense to cooperate. For example, a group called Hospital Personnel Exchange, in Melbourne, Florida, temporarily transfers personnel among hospitals to eliminate the problems of seasonal over- and understaffing for hospitals.

Even in a tight market it may make sense to cooperate when it comes to the spouses of job applicants. For example, the Personnel Association of Central Ohio (PACO) has a "trailing spouse network," where employers have a common pool of resumes from spouses following their partners' career move to central Ohio. All PACO members take from and contribute to the resume pool. By doing so, they are able to hire those job applicants who are unable to relocate unless their spouses find a job in the same area.

Centralized versus Decentralized Recruitment

The recruitment of external job applicants can be centralized or decentralized by an organization. A centralized recruitment function is one where recruitment activities are coordinated by a central group, usually human resource professionals in the corporate offices. A decentralized recruitment system is one where recruitment activities are coordinated by individual business units or individual managers. In most larger organizations, the recruitment function is centralized.[2] Although the ultimate hiring decision resides in the business unit, most organizations centralize the administrative activities associated with recruiting and screening applicants.

One advantage to a centralized recruitment function is that duplications of effort are eliminated. For example, when recruiting at a school, only one advertisement is placed rather than multiple ads for multiple business units. Another advantage to a centralized approach is that it ensures that policy is being interpreted consistently across business units. Along the same lines, a centralized function helps to ensure compliance with relevant laws and regulations.

Some organizations do have decentralized recruitment functions. One advantage to decentralized recruitment is that recruitment efforts may be undertaken in a more timely manner when there are fewer people to recruit than when a centralized approach is used. Also, the recruitment search may be more responsive to the business unit's specific needs because those involved with recruitment may be closer to the day-to-day operations of the business unit than their corporate counterparts.

Administrative Issues

In the planning stage of recruitment, attention must be given to administrative as well as organizational issues.

Requisitions

A requisition is a formal document that authorizes the filling of a job opening indicated by the signatures of top management.[3] Supervisors are not given discretion to authorize the filling of job openings. Top managers rather than supervisors are more likely to be familiar with staffing planning information for the entire organization, and their approval is needed instead to ensure that recruitment activities are coordinated with staffing planning activities.

An example of a requisition is shown in Exhibit 7.1. A well-developed requisition will specify clearly both the quantity and the quality (KSAOs) of labor to be hired. Hence, each requisition will list the number of openings per job and the minimum qualifications an applicant must have.[4] Qualifications should be based on the job requirements matrix.

Many smaller organizations do not have requisitions. They should, however, for two reasons. First, the procedure ensures that staffing activities are consistent

EXHIBIT 7.1 Personnel Requisition

Position Title	Division	Department	Department #
Salary/Grade Level	Work Hours	Location	Reports to

Position eligible for the following incentive programs	Budgeted
☐ Sales Commission ☐ Key Contributor ☐ Production Incentive ☐ Other (specify) ☐ Management Incentive ☐ _____	☐ Replacement for:_____ ☐ Yes Transfer/Term Date_____ ☐ No ☐ Addition to staff

POSITION OVERVIEW

Instructions: (1) Complete Parts I, II, and III. (2) Attach Position Description Questionnaire (if available) or complete reverse side.

I. POSITION PURPOSE: Briefly state in one or two sentences the primary purpose of this position.

II. POSITION QUALIFICATIONS: List the *minimum* education, formal training, and experience required to perform this position.

III. SPECIAL SKILLS: List the specialized clerical, administrative, technical, or managerial skills needed to perform this position.

Do current or previous incumbents possess these qualifications and skills? If no, please describe the reason for these requirements when hiring for this position.

APPROVALS	FOR HUMAN RESOURCES USE ONLY
Party Responsible for Conducting Second Interview	Posting Date_____Advertising Date_____
_____ Hiring Supervisor/Manager Date	Req Number _____ Job Number _____
_____ Next Approval Level Date	Acceptance Date _____ Start Date _____
_____ Human Resources Approval Date	New Employee _____ Source _____

Source: Reprinted with permission from United Health Care Corporation.

with the business plan of the organization. Second, it ensures that the qualifications of the job are clearly detailed so that a good person/job match is made.

Number of Contacts

The pool of applicants to be selected almost always needs to be larger than the number of applicants that will be hired eventually. Some applicants who are contacted may not be interested in the position, and others may not be qualified.

It is very difficult to identify the exact number of contacts needed to fill a particular vacant position. However, historical data is very useful in establishing the targeted number of contacts. If careful records are kept, then yield ratios can be calculated to summarize the historical data and to guide decisions about the number of contacts to make. A yield ratio expresses the relationship of applicant inputs to outputs at various decision points. For example, if 90 people were contacted (as identified by the number of resumes submitted) to fill one position, then the yield ratio would be 90:1. To fill two identical positions, it would be necessary to contact 180 applicants, based on the historical yield ratio of 90:1.

Types of Contacts

The types of contacts to be made depend upon two factors. First, it is essential that the qualifications needed to perform the job be clearly established. This is done through the process of job analysis, which results in the job requirements matrix. The more clearly these requirements are specified, the fewer the number of applicants who must be contacted to yield a successful candidate, and the narrower the recruitment search can be.

Second, consideration must be given to the job search and choice process used by applicants.[5] That is, the organization must be aware of where likely applicants search for employment opportunities and what it will take to attract them to the organization. One consistent finding in the research is that job seekers are more likely to find out about jobs through friends and family than they are through employment agencies. Another consistent finding in the research is that job seekers rely heavily upon advertisements.[6]

How proactive the organization should be in soliciting applicants is a policy issue that arises when deciding on the types of contacts the organization will make.[7] Some organizations spend very few resources identifying contacts and actively soliciting applicants from these sources. For example, many times grocery stores simply post a job opening in their store window to fill a vacancy. Other organizations, however, are very proactive in making their presence known in the community. For example, Spartan Stores in Michigan has formed a partnership with a local high school so that they will have higher quality applicants for entry-level positions in their grocery stores.[8] Many organizations are becoming involved with educational institutions through scholarships, adopt-a-school programs, mentorships, equipment grants, internships, and career planning services.[9] NASA has programs to help educate teachers, students, and administrators on the application of science and math.[10] These approaches are likely to build goodwill toward an organization in the community and, as a result, foster greater informal contacts with job applicants.

Research has shown that greater employer involvement with prospective applicants is likely to improve the image of the organization. In turn, a better image of the organization is likely to result in prospective applicants pursuing contact with the organization.[11]

Recruitment Budget

The recruitment process is a very expensive component of organizational staffing. The average cost per hire for exempt positions is $4,000, and the average cost per hire for nonexempt positions is $1,000.[12] As a result of these high costs, many organizations are currently using cost containment programs in their recruitment efforts. Examples here include the elimination of display advertising, greater reliance on state employment agencies, and the reduction of on-campus visits for college recruitment.[13] An example of a recruitment budget is shown in Exhibit 7.2.

EXHIBIT 7.2   Example of a Recruitment Budget for 500 New Hires

---

Administrative Expenses

Staff	32,000
Supplies	45,000
Equipment	10,000
	$87,000

Recruiter Expenses

Salaries	240,000
Benefits	96,000
Expenses	150,000
	$486,000

Candidate Expenses

Travel	320,000
Lodging	295,000
Fees	50,000
Relocation	150,000
	$815,000

Total Recruitment Expenses

87,000 + 486,000 + 815,000 = $1,388,000

Total Cost Per Hire

$1,388,000/500 new hires = $2,776

Due to pressures to contain costs, recruitment budgets have been reduced. In one survey, budgets were reduced in 61% of the surveyed organizations from 1991 to 1992.[14]

The high costs of recruitment also point to the importance of establishing a well-developed recruitment budget. Two issues need to be addressed in establishing a recruitment budget.[15] First, a top-down or bottom-up procedure can be used to gather the information needed to formulate the budget. With a top-down approach, the budget for recruitment activities is set by top management on the basis of the business plan for the organization and on the basis of projected revenues. With a bottom-up approach, the budget for recruitment activities is set up on the basis of the specific needs of each business unit. The former approach works well when the emphasis is on controlling costs. The latter approach works better when commitment to the budget by business unit heads is the goal. A cumbersome, yet useful, method is to combine these two approaches into program-oriented budgeting where there is heavy involvement in the budgeting process by both top management and business unit leaders.

A second issue that needs to be addressed in establishing a well-developed recruitment budget is to decide whether to charge recruitment costs to business unit users. That is, should recruitment expenses be charged to human resources or to the business unit using human resources' services? Most organizations charge the human resources department for the costs of recruitment rather than the business unit users of recruitment activities.[16] Perhaps this is done in order to encourage each business unit to use the recruitment services of the human resources group. However, it should be recognized that this practice of not charging the business unit may result in the business unit users not being concerned about minimizing recruitment costs.

Development of a Recruitment Guide

A recruitment guide is a formal document that details the process to be followed to attract applicants to a job.[17] It should be based on the organization's staffing flowcharts, if available. Included in the guide are details such as the time, money, and staff required to fill the job as well as the steps to be taken to do so. An example of a recruitment guide is shown in Exhibit 7.3.

Although a recruitment guide takes time to produce—time that may be difficult to find in the face of an urgent requisition to be filled—it is an essential document. It clarifies expectations for both the recruiter and the requesting department as to what will be accomplished, what the costs are, and who will be held accountable for the results. It also clarifies the steps that need to be taken to ensure that they are all followed in a consistent fashion and in accordance with organization policy as well as relevant laws and regulations. In short, a recruitment guide safeguards the interests of the employer, applicant, and recruiter.

EXHIBIT 7.3 Recruitment Guide for Director of Claims

Position: Director, Claims Processing

Reports to: Senior Director, Claims Processing

Qualifications: 4-year degree in business;
8 years experience in health care, including 5 in claims, 3 of which should be in management

Relevant labor market: Regional midwest

Time line: week of 1/17: Conduct interviews with qualified applicants
2/1/93: Targeted hire date

Activities to undertake to source well-qualified candidates:

Regional newspaper advertising

Request employee referrals

Contact regional health and life insurance associations

Call HR departments of regional health and life insurance companies to see if any are outplacing any middle managers.

Contact, if necessary, executive recruiter to further source candidates.

Staff members involved:

HR Recruiting Manager
Sr. Director, Claims Processing
V.P. Human Resources
Potential peers and direct reports

Budget:

$3,000–$5,000

Selecting Recruiters

Many studies have been conducted to assess desirable characteristics of recruiters. Reviews of these studies indicate that an ideal recruiter would possess the following characteristics:[18] strong interpersonal skills; knowledge about the organization, jobs, and career-related issues; and enthusiasm about the organization and job candidates. These characteristics represent a start on developing a set of KSAOs to select recruiters.

These characteristics are only a start at developing a job requirements matrix due to limitations in the research to date.[19] For example, the results are based on the special case of college recruitment, and college recruitment is only one of many forms of recruitment. It remains to be seen if characteristics of ideal college recruiters are the same as the characteristics of recruiters in noncollege settings. Hence, care should be taken to develop a job requirements matrix for the position of recruiter just as should be done for the recruitment of people to any position in an organization.

Not only do characteristics of the ideal recruiter need to be considered in selecting recruiters, but the characteristics of the job of recruiter also need to be considered. The research to date has focused primarily on the recruiter's job in the initial campus interview, but the job itself entails much more.[20] The job may consist of any or all of the steps shown in this book, ranging from the identification of appropriate sources to recruiting candidates to extending job offers.

Actual recruiters used by organizations come from a variety of sources including human resource professionals, line managers, and employees. Each of these sources generally has some distinct advantages and disadvantages relative to the list of desirable characteristics for recruiters. Human resource professionals may be very knowledgeable about career development issues and be enthusiastic about the organization, but lack detailed knowledge regarding specific job responsibilities. Line managers may have detailed knowledge about the company and jobs that they supervise, but not be particularly knowledgeable about career development opportunities. Similarly, employees may have an in-depth understanding of their own jobs, but not have much knowledge of the larger organization. As a result of these tradeoffs, there is no one ideal source to draw recruiters from and all recruiters need training to compensate for their shortcomings.

Training Recruiters

Many recruiters who come from areas outside human resources do not have any specialized training in human resources. Hence, the training of recruiters is essential. Unfortunately, very few recruiters ever receive any training. Based on current organizational practices, recruiters should receive training in the following areas:[21] interviewing skills, job analysis, interpersonal aspects of recruiting, laws and regulations, forms and reports, company and job characteristics, and recruitment targets. Important training aids for recruiter training are the job requirements matrix and the job rewards matrix.

Rewarding Recruiters

In order to reinforce effective recruitment practices, it is essential that recruiter performance—both effective recruitment behaviors and end results—be monitored and rewarded. Measures of performance commonly used include being on time for appointments, favorable comments from students, meeting affirmative action goals, and feedback from line managers.[22] Unfortunately, very few organizations collect the data needed to make an objective assessment of these factors.

Rewards can be coupled with performance standards. For example, in one interesting study, it was shown that the efforts of Navy recruiters were substantially heightened when there was the promise of a monetary reward for meeting their recruitment quotas.[23] In addition to rewarding recruiters for the successful completion of results, rewards should also be provided for the demonstration of critical behaviors.[24] For example, although good public relations activities may not result in more hires, they may result in more customer satisfaction, which is a major goal of most business organizations today. Accordingly, both the successful attraction of candidates and successful publicity concerning the organization should be rewarded.

Process Flow and Record Keeping

Prior to deciding where and how to look for applicants, it is essential that the organization prepare for the high volume of data entry and correspondence that accompanies the filling of vacancies. This high volume of correspondence and data entry results from the use of multiple sources to identify candidates (e.g., advertisements, walk-ins, employment agencies), the need to circulate the applicant's credentials to multiple parties (e.g., hiring managers, human resources), and the need to communicate with candidates regarding the status of their application. If process flow and record keeping issues are not addressed before the recruitment search, then the organization may become overwhelmed with correspondence that is not dealt with in a timely and professional manner; in turn, the organization may lose well-qualified applicants.

To manage the process flow and record keeping requirements, an information system must be created for recruitment efforts.[25] An effective information system for recruitment purposes allows the candidate, hiring manager, and human resource representatives to know the status of an applicant's application file at any point in time. The information system "tracks" the status of the candidate's file as it flows through the recruitment process in the organization. The information system can also periodically issue reports on the timeliness and accuracy with which applicant information is being processed.

The point of entry for most applicants is the presentation of a resume and/or application to the organization. Upon receipt of these materials, a "file" is created by the organization for each applicant. Once a file has been created, many steps must be taken to process this file. These steps include the coding (manually or with an optical scanner) of applicant's credentials, the recording of equal employment opportunity data to be reported to the federal government, the coding of the source from which the applicant came (e.g., advertisement, school, employment agency) in order to evaluate the effectiveness of each source, the routing (manually or by computer) of the file to hiring managers, and the sending of a letter to the applicant acknowledging receipt of their materials.

As the applicant progresses through the hiring process, additional record keeping is required. Information needs to be kept as to who has reviewed the file, how long each has had the file to be reviewed, what decision has been reached (e.g., reject, invite in for a visit, conduct a second interview), and what step needs to be taken next (e.g., arrange for a flight and accommodations, schedule an interview).

Throughout the process, communications with the applicant must also be tracked to ensure that applicants know when and if their credentials will receive further review and also to know what other steps, if any, they need to take to secure employment.

Even when an applicant is rejected for a position, there are record keeping responsibilities. The applicant's file should be stored in the event that another search arises that requires someone with the applicant's qualifications. Such storage should be for a maximum of one year (see Legal Issues below).

STRATEGY DEVELOPMENT

Once the recruitment planning phase is complete, the next phase is the development of a strategy. In essence, strategy development helps to assess those issues fundamental to the organization: where to look, how to look, and when to look. Each of these issues will be addressed in turn.

Where to Look

Once a requisition has been received, one of the most difficult aspects of recruitment is knowing where to look for applicants. In theory, the pool of potential job applicants is the eligible labor force (employed, unemployed, discouraged workers, new labor force entrants, and labor force reentrants). In practice, the organization must narrow down this vast pool into segments or strata of workers believed to be the most desirable applicants for the organization. To do so, organizations can use open or targeted recruitment methods.

Open Recruitment

With an open recruitment approach, organizations cast a wide net to identify potential applicants for specific job openings. Very little effort is made in segmenting the market into applicants with the most desirable KSAOs. This approach is very passive in that anyone can apply for an opening. All who apply for a position are considered regardless of their qualifications. This approach is sometimes taken by public sector organizations which typically have a high volume of applicants for positions. The advantage to an open recruitment method is that it is often seen as being 'fair' by applicants in that everyone has the opportunity to apply. The disadvantage to this approach is that qualified applicants may be overlooked as a concerted effort is not made to identify those markets with the most qualified applicants.

Targeted Recruitment

A targeted recruitment approach is one whereby the organization identifies those segments of the labor market where qualified candidates are likely to be. In doing so, qualified candidates are less likely to be overlooked. Also, this system may be seen as less "fair," because not all applicants are targeted. Yet, the system may be actually more fair in that people with special availabilities (e.g., teenagers, older workers, people with disabilities), who are sometimes unaware of positions with open recruitment systems, can be targeted for recruitment efforts. To target the labor market for applicants, consideration should be given to the job requirements matrix, demographics, geographic areas, recruitment sources, applicant interests, and special availabilities.

Job Requirements Matrix   As with all aspects of staffing, the starting point for targeted recruitment is the job requirements matrix. By knowing the KSAOs needed to perform the job, the applicant pool is narrowed. For example, the fact that a college degree is required to perform the job eliminates from the population those candidates with a high school degree only. The fact that a major in statistics is required eliminates from the sample the nonstatistics majors with a college degree. This iterative process is followed for all the KSAOs specified in the job requirements matrix.

Demographics   Demographics can also be used to target the applicant pools. Care must be taken not to use demographics to systematically exclude women and minorities from the applicant pool. Job-related demographics, as shown in the job requirements matrix, can and should be used. For example, some positions may require a certain number of years of experience.

Geographic Area   In targeting the applicant pool, one can look on a local, county, regional, state, national, or international basis. In general, the lower the skill levels required to perform the job, the more employers narrow the pool down to close geographic proximity to the organization. This is done to minimize recruitment and selection costs. Chances are that with low-skill jobs, the availability of those people will be high in the local labor market. Hence, an employer will not have to pay for ads in national magazines, relocation costs, and so forth.

On the other hand, for high-skill jobs, the employer is more likely to broaden the search. Although more costly, this is done in order to locate people who have the requisite high level of KSAOs needed to perform the job.

Recruitment Sources   A critical factor in narrowing down the applicant pool is an organization's previous successes and failures with alternative recruitment sources. Through previous searches, for example, an organization may find that the yield of high-quality candidates is best when applicants from professional societies, rather than applicants from placement agencies, are attracted.

Tradition   Some organizations have a rich history of successful recruitment with various segments of the population. Through their affirmative action efforts, for example, some organizations have hired many successful minority individuals from schools with large minority enrollments. In turn, these schools provide excellent services to these companies for the placement of their students. As a result, there is a tradition of certain schools placing students with certain employers.

Applicant Interest and Availability   Applicants self-select out of the potential applicant pool for a variety of reasons. Some are so-called discouraged workers who are no longer a part of the labor force. Others are gainfully employed and very happy to remain with a current employer. Another segment may be unwilling to relocate to a different geographic area. Many people, for example, have family constraints that prevent them from moving.

Special Availabilities   Employers traditionally have limited themselves to applicants who are members of the labor force and are between the ages 18 and 65. This traditional approach has excluded many potential applicants who are fully capable of performing the job even though they do not fit this traditional description. Many organizations have been forced to break away from this traditional view in order to adequately fill jobs when there is a shortage of entry-level employees.[26] Examples of such potential applicants include teenagers, older workers, welfare recipients, people with disabilities, the homeless, veterans, and homemakers.

Teenagers are an excellent source of potential applicants for entry-level positions in service jobs, such as cashier. Although they may not be able to work as many hours as more senior employees, teenagers may be less costly to hire. And their initial employment experiences, if favorable, may lead them to pursue other jobs in the organization as they acquire additional skills and education.

Older people who have withdrawn from the labor force represent another group with special availabilities. The older worker may be inclined to return to the workforce in order to enhance retirement funds or to meet social needs by working with others. A recent study showed that turnover rates are lower for older workers than for younger workers.[27] This is a distinct advantage in jobs, such as cashier, where turnover rates can be over 100%. Another study of older workers indicates that older workers bring some important competencies to the job, such as well-developed skills, flexibility in scheduling, low absenteeism, high motivation, and mentoring abilities for younger employees.[28]

Older workers represent many diverse categories of potential applicants.[29] Each category has special needs, interests, and skills which organizations can target. Midlife career changers are "younger" older workers who may be burned out in their current career or are at the end of the line in terms of job advancement. They may have well-developed skills, and are seeking the opportunity for advancement, and interested in full-time work with benefits. Displaced workers under age 62 usually have recent work experience, are not yet receiving social security benefits, and need full-time employment with benefits. Retirees under age 62 most likely have a pension, but do not receive social security, may be bored with retirement, looking for challenging assignments on a full- or part-time basis. Retirees with social security benefits are more likely to be seeking part-time employment opportunities because of the hourly limitations imposed by social security.

America Works is a temporary employment agency on the East Coast. Its mission is to take people off welfare and find them gainful employment. So far the agency has been successful at placing over 2,000 people. Part of the success has been attributed to the training and follow-up the company provides along with its insistence on no tardiness as a requirement to remain in the program.[30]

It is estimated that in this country the number of people with disabilities is about 36 million. People with disabilities include not only those needing wheelchairs, but those with AIDS, lower-back pain, mental illness, and a whole host of other physically challenging conditions. Many organizations have taken advantage of this large population to fill vacant jobs on an ongoing basis. For example, the Friendly Restaurant Corporation has developed a systematic recruitment procedure to attract and hire people with disabilities.[31] As shown in Exhibit 7.4, there are many unwarranted stereotypes about individuals with disabilities that need to be overcome in order for people with disabilities to be included in an organization's applicant pool.

The homeless do not have normal access to the labor market. Through rehabilitation centers, churches, and shelters they may receive the training and assistance needed to hold a job. Days Inn, for example, has hired the homeless since

---

EXHIBIT 7.4   Overcoming Objections about Applicants with Disabilities

Leonard describes a good case study of the process. "Our sales department needed to fill an opening. I was contacted by Lighthouse. I tried to get the manager to stop focusing on the problem and look at what the person has achieved. We had a meeting with a representative from the Lighthouse, the EEO manager and the sales manager, and walked the manager through each of his objections. When he saw the facts, he was still skeptical but open. We moved the manager from a rejection mode to a listening mode.

Next, we presented the candidate to the manager and discussed the line manager's concerns. The job candidate was well dressed, intelligent, articulate and confident. He uses a scanner attached to a voice box to read memos and other materials. He uses a cane to navigate around the room. He is pleasant and establishes relationships easily. He is good on the phone.

The manager went from a listening mode to a being-open mode. The candidate was hired, performed well and was eventually promoted."

Source: J. E. Peters, "How to Bridge the Hiring Gap," *HR Magazine,* October 1989, pp. 83–84. Reprinted with the permission of HR Magazine (formerly Personnel Administrator) published by the Society for Human Resource Management, Alexandria, VA.

1988, and about half of those employed have turned out to be successful by company standards.[32] One stumbling block to hiring the homeless has been the inability of organizations to contact them. Organizations may not be able to contact the homeless because they may not have access to a phone. Fortunately, in several communities, such as Columbus, Cincinnati, and Seattle, this obstacle has been removed. Businesses and social service agencies in these communities are setting up voice mail boxes for the homeless so that they can be contacted regularly. It is estimated that 30–40 cities have these programs.[33]

The U.S. Department of Defense is downsizing and, in the process, is creating a rich source of potential job applicants. The source is rich because it consists of trained and experienced personnel. It is estimated that about 600,000 people will be released from the military over the next five years.[34] Many, but not all, of the skills learned in the military are transferable to the civilian sector of the economy.[35]

Many women are forced to enter the labor force because of the death of a spouse, a divorce, or an abusive home situation. Many of their skills as homemakers are transferable to jobs in the labor force.[36] A group that helps them meet their needs, including employment, is the Displaced Homemakers Network in Washington, DC.

How to Look

Fortunately for employers, when conducting a search for applicants, they do not have to identify each possible job applicant. Instead, there are institutions in our economy where job seekers congregate. Moreover, these institutions often act as intermediaries between the applicant and employer to ensure that a match takes place. These institutions are called recruitment sources or methods in staffing. Some are very conventional and have been around for a long time. Others are more innovative and have less of a track record. Choices from among these sources should be guided by several criteria.

Sources

Unsolicited   It is a common practice for employers to accept applications from job applicants who physically walk into the organization to apply for a job or who send in resumes. The usual point of contact for unsolicited walk-ins or resume senders is the receptionist in smaller organizations and the employment office in larger organizations.

Organizations that rely upon unsolicited walk-ins and resume senders must be prepared to deal with the physical demands created by this process. In order for walk-ins not to disrupt the normal work flow in an organization, a contact person who is responsible for processing walk-ins needs to be assigned. Space needs to be created for walk-ins to complete application blanks and preemployment tests. Hours need to be established when applicants can apply for jobs. Procedures must be in place to ensure that data from walk-ins and resume senders are entered into the applicant flow process. If these steps are not taken, not only may the organizational work flow be disrupted, but the image of the organization may be tarnished as well. If walk-ins or resume senders are treated as being unexpected intruders, they may communicate a very negative image about the organization in the community. In turn, this negative image may have a chilling effect on other recruitment efforts by the organization (e.g., advertising). Similarly, unsolicited resumes should immediately be acknowledged by sending the applicants a card or letter to let them know that their resume has been received and how it will be processed.

Employee Referrals Employees currently working for an employer are a valuable source for finding job applicants. The employees can refer people they know to their employer for consideration. In some organizations, a cash bonus is given to employees who refer job candidates who prove to be successful on the job for a given period of time. In order to ensure that there are adequate returns on bonuses for employee referrals, it is essential that there be a good performance appraisal system in place to measure the performance of the referred new hire. There also needs to be a good applicant tracking system to ensure that new hire performance is maintained over time before a bonus is offered.

Employee referral programs sometimes fail to work because current employees lack the motivation or ability to make referrals.[37] Employees sometimes don't realize the importance of recruitment to the organization. As a result, the organization may need to encourage employee participation by providing special awards and public recognition along with bonuses for successful referrals. Employees may not be able to match people with jobs because they do not know about open vacancies and the requirements needed to fill them. Hence, communications regarding job vacancies and the requirements needed to fill these vacancies need to be constantly provided to employees.

An excellent example of both steps comes from the "Seek Talent and Find Fortune" (STAFF) program at Goodyear Aerospace. To participate in the program, employees must read a description of the jobs that are available and submit resumes of interested applicants. Employees that make a referral receive a coffee mug and become eligible for a sweepstakes drawing which includes many prizes up to a week-long cruise. If a referral is hired, the employee who made the referral receives a $1,000 bonus.

Advertisements A convenient way to attract job applicants is to write an ad that can be placed in newspapers, trade journals, and the like. Advertisements can also be recorded and placed on radio or television. Cable television channels, for example, sometimes have "job shows." Advertisements can be very costly and need to be monitored closely for yield. Advertisements in some periodicals may yield more and better qualified candidates than others. By carefully monitoring the results of each ad, the organization can then make a more informed decision as to which ads should be run next time a position is vacant. To track ads, each ad should be coded to assess the yield. Then, as resumes come into the organization in response to the ad, they can be recorded, and the yield for that ad can be calculated.

Coding an ad is a very straightforward process. For example, in advertising for a vice president of human resources, ads may be placed in a variety of human resources periodicals, such as *HR Magazine,* and business publications, such as the *Wall Street Journal.* To track responses sent, applicants for the vacant position are asked to respond to Employment Department A for *HR Magazine* and Employment Department B for the *Wall Street Journal.* (The other part of the return address is, of course, the same for each periodical.) As resumes arrive, those that are addressed to Department A are coded as responses from the *HR Magazine,* and those addressed to Department B are coded as responses from the *Wall Street Journal.*

Colleges and Placement Offices   Colleges are a source of people with specialized skills for professional positions. Most colleges have a placement office or officer who is in charge of ensuring that a match is made between the employer's interests and the graduating student's interests. Recruitment at colleges is usually performed at no cost to the employer.

In most cases, the placement office is the point of contact with colleges. It should be noted, however, that not all students use the services of the placement office.[38] Students sometimes avoid placement offices because they believe they will be competing against the very best students and be unlikely to receive a job offer. Additional points of contact for students at colleges include individual professors, department heads, professional fraternities, honor societies, recognition societies, and national professional societies. Sometimes small colleges are overlooked as a recruitment source by organizations because the small number of students does not make it seem worth the effort to visit. In order to present a larger number of students to choose from, some small colleges band together in consortia. For example, the Oregon Liberal Arts Placement Consortia provide a centralized recruitment source for eight public and private small colleges and universities. It is essential that appropriate colleges and universities be selected for a visit. Fortunately, many sound guidelines have been written on how to select campuses to visit.[39] A summary of the recommended factors to consider in selecting campuses follows:

- It is essential that schools have degree programs in the areas where job openings exist in the organization. To make the match between the curriculum and organizational needs, there must be careful assessment of the job requirements matrix as it relates to the specific classes offered on campus. Conversation with faculty members is often required to make this match as the description of courses in a course bulletin may be out of date.

- Many surveys have been conducted on the quality of the educational setting. Each year, *Business Week* reports the results of a survey on top MBA programs in the country, and *Peterson's Guide* reports on the quality of undergraduate programs. Care must be exercised in reviewing these reports. Though helpful in establishing school reputation, they may fail to consider important criteria to judge reputation. For example, to ensure that students are being provided with state-of-the-art information, attention should be paid to the research quality of the faculty. Unfortunately, few surveys use faculty research quality as a criterion in the assessments.

- The closer the school is to the organization, the less the transportation cost involved in recruitment may be. Many organizations have found that turnover rates are decreased by recruiting locally. Job applicants already have a realistic idea of what it is like to live in the area.

- The quality of applicants, as measured by both the performance of students while on campus and their subsequent performance on the job, must also be assessed. Hence, one should monitor student GPAs, work experience levels, and other KSAOs while on campus. Also, one should monitor the performance and turnover levels of new hires from various campuses.

- Previous success at attracting applicants on various campuses should be considered. Indicators to pay attention to here include overall yield ratios, as well as specific ones for women and minorities.

After selecting schools to visit, attention must be devoted to developing a college recruitment program for each school. A uniform college recruitment program is destined to fail. Schools vary considerably on the criteria just reviewed as well as on other characteristics. Consequently, the organization must target its efforts to the specific characteristics of each school. With large schools, the organization may need to target its efforts at the program level as well. Issues to consider in targeting a college recruitment program are life cycle, quality, and structure.

The relationship between college or university placement offices and organizations follows a life cycle. Just as individuals are born, grow, mature, and decline over time, so do relationships between placement offices and hiring organizations. Steps taken by hiring organizations need to be different depending upon the stage of the relationship.[40] For example, as an organization enters into a recruitment arrangement with a school or program for the first time, it is unlikely to recruit very many students because the new recruits are a somewhat unknown commodity. As a result, the organization is unlikely to offer scholarships to students at that school or program.

As its relationship to the school grows and matures, however, the organization is likely to recruit many more candidates and offer scholarships. More candidates are recruited because they are now a proven commodity, and scholarships are offered to maintain a steady flow of well-qualified candidates into the organization.

Other recruitment activities, such as internships and advertising, also need to be considered in relation to the life cycle.

In order to establish high-quality relationships on campus, AT&T has developed a customer–supplier model to guide the relationship between career service offices on campus and the recruitment function in organizations.[41] The model is shown in Exhibit 7.5.

This model shows that both the organization (AT&T) and university serve as customers and suppliers to one another. In terms of being a customer, AT&T employs the services of students graduated by the university. The university is also a customer as it receives special services provided by AT&T. These special services include the training of university placement counselors on effective counseling techniques. In terms of being a supplier, AT&T supplies training services to university placement counselors. The university is also a supplier as it supplies AT&T with students for employment.

The key to arranging college recruitment activities according to this model is for both parties to clearly define their requirements of one another as customers and suppliers. Then, periodic feedback needs to be exchanged between the parties to ensure compliance with these requirements.

In terms of structure, a college recruitment program can but does not have to be housed in a single location.[42] A college recruitment program may have multiple structures depending upon the stage of its relationship with colleges and depending upon the requirements of the organization and program. For example, recruiters may work out of a central office on a full-time basis. They travel to schools to recruit and may recruit by region, size of school, program, or special characteristics of school. Alternatively, managers can be assigned schools within their geographic area, where they recruit on a part-time basis.

Employment Agencies   A source of nonexempt employees and lower-level exempt employees is employment agencies or body shops, as they are sometimes

---

EXHIBIT 7.5   The Customer–Supplier Model of College Recruitment at AT&T

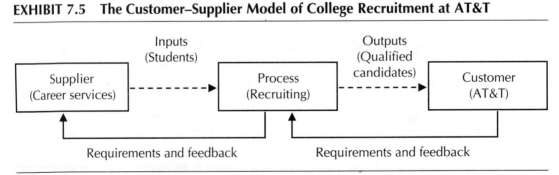

Source: Reprinted with permission from Gale Hiering Varma.

called. These agencies collect, screen, and present applicants to employers for a fee. The fee is contingent upon successful placement of a candidate with an employer and is a percentage, around 25%, of the candidate's starting salary. During difficult economic periods, employers cut back on the use of these agencies and/or attempt to negotiate lower fees in order to contain costs.[43]

Care must be exercised in selecting an employment agency. It is a good idea to check the references of employment agencies with other organizations that have used their services. Allegations abound regarding the shoddy practices of these agencies. They may, for example, flood the organization with resumes. Unfortunately, this flood may include both qualified and unqualified applicants. A good agency will screen out unqualified applicants and not attempt to dazzle the organization with a large volume of resumes. Poor agencies may misrepresent the organization to the candidate and the candidate to the organization. Misrepresentation may take place when the agency is only concerned about a quick placement (and fee) without regard to the costs of poor future relationships with clients. A good agency will be in business for the long run and not misrepresent information and invite turnover. Poor agencies may pressure managers to make decisions when they are uncertain or do not want to do so. Also, they may "go around" the human resources staff in the organization to negotiate "special deals" with individual managers. Special deals may result in paying higher fees than agreed upon with human resources and overlooking qualified minorities and women. A good agency will not pressure managers, make special deals, or avoid the human resources staff.

Executive Search Firms For higher-level professional positions, or jobs with salaries of $100,000 and higher, executive search firms, or "headhunters," may be used. Like employment agencies, these firms collect, screen, and present resumes to employers. Unlike employment agencies, they operate on the basis of a retainer fee rather than a contingency fee. This means that they collect a fee from the employer regardless of whether a successful placement is made. Thus, their services are retained by a fee in advance of a placement. The fee is paid up front so that the search firm has the resources to conduct exhaustive searches and has a travel budget to help screen candidates.

Professional Associations and Meetings Many technical and professional organizations have annual meetings around the country at least once a year. Many of these groups run a placement service for their members. There may be a fee to recruit at these meetings. This source represents a way to attract applicants with specialized skills or professional credentials. Also, some meetings represent a way to attract women and minorities. For example, the National Council of Black Engineers and Scientists holds an annual meeting.[44] In addition to having placement activities at annual conventions, professional associations also may have a placement function throughout the year. For example, it is a common practice in professional association newsletters to advertise both positions available and interested applicants. Others may also have a computerized job and applicant bank.

State Employment Services   All states have an employment or job service. These services are funded by employer-paid payroll taxes.[45] This service is provided by the states to help secure employment for those seeking employment, particularly those currently unemployed. Typically, these services refer low- to middle-level employees to employers. In order for jobs to be filled properly, the hiring organization must maintain a close relationship with the employment service. Job qualifications need to be communicated clearly to ensure that proper screening takes place by the agency. Positions that have been filled must be reported promptly to the agency so that resumes are not sent for closed positions. The state employment services are now all networked together through the Interstate Job Bank Center which has an on-line job search service to match organizations and job seekers. Organizations no longer need to separately contact each state employment service.[46]

The U.S. Department of Labor has provided the funding for states to develop one-step career centers which will provide workers with various programs, benefits, and opportunities related to finding jobs. The centers' emphasis is on providing customer friendly services which reach large segments of the population and are fully integrated with state employment services.[47]

Outplacement Services   Some organizations retain an outplacement firm to provide assistance to employees who are losing their jobs. Outplacement firms usually offer job seekers assistance in the form of counseling and training to help facilitate a good person/job match. Most large outplacement firms have job banks, which are computerized listings of applicants and their qualifications. Registration by employers to use these job banks is usually free.

Larger organizations experiencing a downsizing may have their own internal outplacement function and perform the activities traditionally found in external outplacement agencies. They may also hold in-house job fairs. The reason for this in-house function is to save on the costs of using an external outplacement firm and to build the morale of those employees who remain with the organization and are likely to be affected by their friends' loss of jobs.

Community Agencies   Some agencies in local communities may also provide outplacement assistance for the unemployed who cannot afford outplacement services. The applicants who use these services may also be listed with a state employment service as well. Community agencies may also offer counseling and training.

Job Fairs   Professional associations, schools, employers, the military, and other interested organizations hold career or job fairs to attract job applicants.[48] Typically, the sponsors of a job fair will meet in a central location with a large facility in order to provide information, collect resumes, and screen applicants. Often, there is a fee for the employer to participate. Job fairs may provide both short- and long-term gains. In the short run, the organization may identify qualified applicants. In the long run, it may be able to enhance its visibility in the community, which, in turn, may improve its image and ability to attract applicants for jobs.

In order for a job fair to yield a large number of applicants, it must be advertised well in advance. Moreover, advertisements may need to be placed in specialized publications likely to attract minorities and women. In order for an organization to attract quality candidates from all of those in attendance, the organization must be able to differentiate itself from all the other organizations competing for applicants at the job fair. To do so, giveaways such as mugs and key chains, with company logos, can be distributed to remind the applicants of employment opportunities at a particular organization. An even better promotion may be to provide attendees at the fair with assistance in developing their resumes and cover letters.

Co-ops and Internships   Students currently attending school are sometimes available for part-time work. Two part-time working arrangements are known as co-ops and internships. Under a co-op arrangement, the student works with one employer on an alternating quarter basis. In one quarter the student works full-time, and the next quarter, attends school full-time. Under an internship arrangement, the student has a continuous period of employment with an employer for a specified period of time. These approaches allow an organization to obtain services from a part-time employee for a short period of time, but they also allow the organization the opportunity to assess the person for a full-time position upon graduation. In turn, interns have better employment opportunities as a result of their experiences.[49]

Not only can the co-ops and interns themselves be a good source of candidates for full-time jobs, but they can also be a good referral source. Those with a favorable experience with an employer are more likely to refer others from their schools for jobs. In order for this to occur, the students' experiences must be favorable. To ensure this happens, students should not be treated as cheap commodities. Care must be taken to provide them with meaningful job experiences and with the training necessary to do a good job.

Internships and co-op assignments can take a variety of different forms.[50] One type of assignment is to have the student perform a part of the business that occurs on a periodic basis. For example, some amusement parks that operate only in the summer in northern climates may have a large number of employees who need to be hired and trained in the spring. A student with a background in human resources could perform these hiring and training duties. Another type of assignment is to have students apply their knowledge of current advancements in their field by critiquing existing programs and developing new programs based on the latest advancements. Students can also conduct research for the organization by conducting literature reviews or benchmarking current employer practices. Occasionally, experience shows that some internships and co-op assignments do not provide these meaningful experiences that build on the qualifications of the student.

Meaningful experiences are of benefit to both the organization and the student. The organization gains from the influence of new ideas the student has been exposed to in their curriculum, and the student gains from having the experience of having to apply concepts when facing the realities of organizational constraints. For both parties to gain, it is important that a learning contract be developed and signed by the student, the student's adviser, and the corporate sponsor. The learning contract becomes, in essence, a job description to guide the student's activities. Also, it establishes the criteria by which the student's performance is assessed for purposes of a grade by the academic adviser and for purposes of successful completion of the project for the organization. In the absence of a learning contract, internships can result in unrealistic expectations by the corporate sponsor which, in turn, can result in disappointment when these unspoken expectations are not met.

To secure the services of students, organizations can contact the placement offices of high schools, colleges, universities, and vocational technology schools. Also, teachers, professors, and student chapters of professional associations can be contacted to obtain student assistance. Placement officials can provide the hiring organization with the policies that need to be followed for placements, while teachers and professors can give guidance on the types of skills students could bring to the organization and the organizational experiences the students would benefit from the most.

Contingent Workers A very large and growing segment of our labor market is composed of contingent workers. They include the self-employed, temporary or leased employees (those who work for an agency who provides temporary workers to employers), and independent contractors (those who work for themselves or for a firm specializing in providing a product or service to employers).[51] Contingent workers can be used when work is of limited duration, but may not always produce satisfactory results if they are not committed to the goals and objectives of the organization. In response to this possible problem, some organizations have created in-house temporary pools to fill limited-term positions. Monsanto Company is one such organization to create an in-house temporary pool known as Retiree Resource Corps (RRC).[52] The RRC is composed of and run by retirees from Monsanto. When Monsanto needs someone for a temporary position, it turns first to the RRC because, unlike external temporary agencies, the RRC temporaries are very knowledgeable about the Monsanto culture and methods of operations. By using the RRC, Monsanto saves the cost of training and orienting temporaries unfamiliar with the company.

Computerized Resume Services Many organizations now offer employers computerized resume services. A large bank of resumes is stored in a computer, and for a fee, the data base is searched for applicants who meet the employer's specifications. Organizations that provide this service include Job Bank USA, which has resumes for a large number of professions, and Connexion, which has an international data bank.[53]

Alumni Associations Another source for experienced personnel is alumni associations at schools. Some schools, such as the Georgia Institute of Technology, offer placement services for past as well as current students.[54] A small fee is assessed for the service. Placement opportunities are made known, and training and career counseling are offered.

Unemployed Youth Services Youth unemployment is very high relative to that of other demographic groups in the United States. In order to reach this group for entry-level positions, employers can use unemployed youth services, which provide placement opportunities for youths as well as counseling and training in some local communities.

Religious Organizations These organizations (e.g., churches) provide another source of labor often overlooked. Such institutions typically have many senior and teenage human resources. Organizations can attract members by sponsoring events such as socials and by making donations to charitable causes endorsed by them.

Interest Groups There are many associations that help facilitate the interests of their members. Two such groups are the American Association for Retired Persons (AARP) and the National Association for the Advancement of Colored People (NAACP). An example of how these groups provide for the employment interests of their members is the NAACP job fair conducted by BPI Tech Fair in Minneapolis.[55]

Realtors Some realtors now offer employment services for trailing partners. When one person in a relationship must relocate to further a career, the realtor may also help the trailing partner to find a new job.

Senior Networks Many networks have been formed to advance the employment interests of older workers. These networks include Senior Community Service Employment Programs, the Job Training Partnership Act, Forty Plus, Operation ABLE, the National Clearinghouse on State and Local Older Workers Programs, the National Caucus for Black Aged, the National Association of Spanish-Speaking Elderly, and the Older Women's League. These organizations provide many employment services such as the training, counseling, and placement of older workers along with programs for employers on how to best utilize the talents of older workers.[56]

Direct Mail Solicitations   Drawing upon marketing tactics in business, some organizations now recruit by direct mail solicitations. Likely segments of the labor market are targeted and sent direct mail to inform them of employment opportunities. In addition to mailing letters, employers also communicate with potential applicants via door hangers, bargain shoppers, welcome wagons, point-of-sale messages, and talent scout cards.[57]

Choice of Source

There is no one best source for recruitment; each source has its strengths and weaknesses. The following criteria can be used to select which sources are most appropriate for each search.

Quantity of Labor   Some sources, such as advertisements, produce a large number of applicants. Such a source is appropriate when a large head count is needed by the organization. When number of hours of work is the quantity indicator, temporary employee sources may be most beneficial.

Quality of Labor   If a premium is to be paid for high-quality candidates in the recruitment process, then some sources are better than others. If a very high level of KSAOs is required, an executive search firm is helpful. If certain skills are needed, then some schools that emphasize these skills may be better sources of employees than others.

Availability of Sources   Not all of the possible sources are available to a given organization. For example, one is unlikely to find temporary agencies in rural areas. Similarly, some jobs do not have members who belong to professional associations.

Past or Promised Experiences   Many organizations have a past track record with various sources. Organizations who have not used a certain source in the past can look to the past experiences of other organizations, or the promises made by the source, for validation of its effectiveness. Issues to be considered in evaluating experiences with the source include its process and outcomes. Process issues to be considered include the types of services provided, the quality of services, and the timing and dependability of services offered. Outcomes of concern include not only the number of candidates, but the quality of candidates as well.

Budget Constraints   Some organizations have large enough budgets that they can perform many of the services offered by institutions who act as intermediaries in the labor market, such as employment agencies. Other organizations, due to a lack of resources, small size, or infrequency of search, cannot replicate these services in-house.

Contractual Obligations   In organizations where all or part of the workforce is organized by a union, the labor agreement may spell out the conditions under which external and internal sources can be used. Even in nonunion organizations, there may be an agreement between the employment function, where external recruitment is housed, and placement, where internal recruitment is housed, concerning when and which sources can be used to recruit externally.

Effectiveness

A considerable amount of research has been conducted on the effectiveness of various recruitment sources and can be used as a starting point as to which sources are likely to be effective.[58] Research has defined effectiveness as the impact of recruitment sources on increased employee satisfaction, performance, and retention. Unfortunately, this research has focused on the effectiveness of only a few different sources (walk-ins, employee referrals, advertisements). Hence, organizations need to systematically collect their own data to gauge effectiveness and to guide their choice of recruitment sources. For example, organizations may need to code sources to ascertain which sources produce the greatest yield of qualified applicants.

When to Look

Two factors that drive the decision of when to look for job applicants are lead time concerns and time sequence concerns.

Lead Time Concerns

Although managers would like to have each position filled immediately upon approval of requisitions, this goal is not possible, as recruiters handle an average of seventeen vacancies at any one time.[59] It is possible, however, to minimize the delay in filling vacancies by planning for openings well in advance of their actual occurrence.[60] Effective planning requires that top management prioritize job openings so that they can be filled in the order that best meets the needs of the business. It also requires that recruiters be fully prepared to conduct the search. To do so, recruiters must be knowledgeable about print deadlines for the placement of ads in appropriate periodicals. Also, recruiters should be knowledgeable about the availability of labor in the market place. For example, the availability of college graduates is determined by graduation dates which vary from school to school.

Time Sequence Concerns

In a successful recruitment program, the steps involved in the process are clearly defined and sequenced in a logical order. A staffing flowchart should be used to organize all components of the recruitment process. The sequence of recruitment activities has a large bearing on the time that will be required to fill job vacancies.

A very useful set of indicators for time sequence concerns is known as time-lapse statistics. These statistics provide data on the average length of time that expires between various phases in the recruitment process. Organizations should routinely collect these data in order to assist managers in planning when vacancies are to be filled.

SEARCHING

Once the recruitment planning and strategy development phases are completed, then it is time to actively conduct the search. Searching for candidates first requires the development of a message and then the selection of a medium to communicate that message. Each of these phases is considered in turn.

Communication Message

Job Requirements and Rewards Matrices

Information presented by the organization to the job applicant is essential to the decision to accept or reject a job offer.[61] The starting point for all information presented by the organization should be the job requirements and job rewards matrices (or their equivalent). These matrices may be used in all forms of communications with job applicants, including advertisements, recruitment brochures, and face-to-face discussions. The job requirements matrix communicates to the applicant what is needed to perform the job. The job rewards matrix describes what rewards are offered to the applicant for performing the job. Both pieces of information are essential to the applicant in formulating a decision whether to become an applicant, to remain an applicant, and ultimately to join an organization.

Types of Messages

Traditional Messages Information about the organization, also known as the message, varies by the amount of information presented and by the accuracy of that information.[62] With traditional recruitment procedures, the job applicant may be given relatively little concrete or accurate information. For example, it is common to see the phrase "unlimited growth opportunities" in job recruitment advertisements in the paper. This phrase may sound promising, but it is very vague and possibly misleading. Such information may cause applicants to shun the advertised position. It may also create retention problems for misled applicants who joined the organization.

Fortunately, some organizations are now presenting messages that are more specific and accurate than the traditional message. As a result, job applicants are able to make better informed decisions about their employment with an organization, and organizations gain more credibility in the eyes of the applicants.

Realistic Recruitment Message   A realistic recruitment message portrays the organization and job as it really is rather than describing what the organization thinks job applicants want to hear. Several different recruitment practices work well with this approach.

A very well-researched recruitment message is known as a realistic job preview or RJP.[63] According to this practice, job applicants are given a "vaccination" by being told verbally, in writing, or on videotape what the actual job is like.[64] An example of the attributes that might be contained in an RJP is shown in Exhibit 7.6. It shows numerous attributes for the job of elementary school teacher. Note that the attributes are quite specific, and that they are both positive and negative. Information like this "tells it like it is" to job applicants.

After receiving the vaccination, job applicants can decide whether they want to work for the organization. The hope with the RJP is that job applicants will self-select into and out of the organization. By selecting into the organization, the applicant may be more committed than otherwise to working there. By selecting out, the organization does not face the costs associated with recruiting, selecting, training, and compensating employees, only to then have them leave because the job did not meet their expectations.

The research that has been conducted to date on the effectiveness of RJPs has yielded differing interpretations.[65] What seems clear is that RJPs, like any recruit-

---

EXHIBIT 7.6   Example of Job Attributes in an RJP for Elementary School Teachers

---

Positive Job Attributes

Dental insurance is provided
Innovative teaching strategies are encouraged
University nearby for taking classes
Large support staff for teachers

Negative Job Attributes

Salary growth has averaged 2% in past three years
Class sizes are large
The length of the school day is long
Interactions with community have not been favorable

---

ment message, are more or less likely to be successful under certain conditions. These conditions will be reviewed shortly.

There are other possible ways to provide job applicants with a realistic look at their potential job. These approaches include work-site tours, work simulations or job try-outs, internships, co-op arrangements, part-time work, and summer jobs.[66] While employers may use these other recruitment practices more frequently than RJPs, they have not been explicitly developed for the purpose of communicating realism and they have not received much attention by researchers. As a result, this is a newer area of exploration for the development of realistic messages.

In developing different methods to realistically portray the job to applicants, the research is clear that applicants should spend considerable time with their potential peers during on-site visits.[67] By providing the applicant with this opportunity, the organization can benefit in two ways. First, applicants can hear what the job and organization are "really like" rather than simply hearing the "company line," which may or may not capture the reality of work in a particular location. Second, potential peers are more likely to be accepting of staffing decisions because they have an opportunity to be a part of the process.

Realism is sometimes very difficult to convey to job applicants. This is especially true when top management is reluctant to provide "full disclosure" to the applicants. Top management may fear, for example, that self-selection will be so prevalent that vacancies cannot be filled. Also, it is sometimes difficult to capture and convey certain parts of the job such as mental activity and environmental hazards. Even if the job can be adequately described, it may be changing so rapidly that it is too expensive to constantly update realism programs. Finally, people are sometimes hired for jobs that don't yet exist or for jobs that are constantly evolving. This last concern is of particular relevance to newly formed and growing organizations where people "pitch in" and do whatever it takes to make the new business successful.

Attractive Messages   An attractive message portrays the organization in a manner such that applicants are induced to interview, join, or stay with the organization before they actually become employees. For example, most employers pay travel expenses for the applicant to interview. Some organizations go much further. For example, General Mills has wined and dined MBA students from Northwestern University aboard a yacht in hopes of getting them to sign up for an interview.[68] Upon completion of the trip, General Mills also sent each prospective interviewee a Wheaties box with his or her picture and name on it.

Once interviews have been conducted, other attractive messages are used to induce the applicant to accept a job offer. Traditionally, this has meant paying for moving expenses. Some organizations go beyond moving expenses to help the person locate and pay for a new house, sell an old home, or assist a partner in finding a new job.

Organizations also try to induce job applicants to make a long-term commitment to the organization. To do so, organizations have traditionally offered basic benefits such as health care and the possibility of salary growth through merit pay. Some employers have expanded these inducements in order to be seen as family-friendly organizations. Johnson and Johnson offers family care leave and sick days, and child care. IBM offers flexible work hours, leaves of absence, work-at-home programs, and child care programs. Aetna Life and Casualty offers job sharing, part-time work, flexible hours, a school-holiday program, and a work-at-home program. Corning offers child care, part-time work, summer camps, and after-school programs.[69]

Targeted Messages   One way to improve upon matching people with jobs is to target the recruitment message to a particular audience. Different audiences may be looking for different rewards from an employer.[70] This would appear to be especially true of special applicant populations such as teenagers, older workers, welfare recipients, people with disabilities, homeless individuals, veterans, and displaced homemakers, who may have special needs. Older workers, for example, may be looking for employers who can meet their financial needs (e.g., supplement social security), security needs (e.g., retraining), and social needs (e.g., place to interact with people).[71] College students appear to be attracted to organizations that provide rewards and promotions on the basis of individual rather than group performance. Also, college students prefer to receive pay in the form of a salary rather than in the form of incentives.[72]

Choice of Messages

The four different types of messages—traditional, realistic, attractive, and targeted—are not likely to be equally effective under the same conditions. Which message to convey depends upon the labor market, vacancy characteristics, and applicant characteristics.

If the labor market is tight and applicants are difficult to come by, then realism may not be an effective message, because to the extent that applicants self-select out of the applicant pool, fewer are left for an employer to choose from during an already tight labor market. Hence, if the employment objective is simply to fill job slots in the short run and worry about turnover later, a realistic message will have counterproductive effects. Obviously then, when applicants are in abundance and turnover is an immediate problem, a realistic message is appropriate.

During a tight labor market, attractive and targeted messages are likely to be more effective in attracting job applicants. Attraction is strengthened as there are inducements in applying for a job. In addition, individual needs are more likely to be perceived as met by a prospective employer. Hence, the applicant is more motivated to apply for organizations with an attractive or targeted message than without. During loose economic times when applicants are plentiful, the attractive or targeted approaches may be more costly than necessary to attract an adequate supply of labor. Also, they may set up false expectations concerning what life will be like on the job, and thus lead to turnover.

Job applicants have better knowledge about the actual characteristics of some jobs than others.[73] For example, service sector jobs, such as cashier, are highly visible to people. For these jobs, it may be redundant to give a realistic message. Other jobs, such as an outside sales position, are far less visible to people. They may seem very glamorous (e.g., sales commissions) to prospective applicants who fail to see the less glamorous aspects of the job (e.g., heavy travel and paperwork).

Some jobs seem to be better suited to special applicant groups, and hence, a targeted approach may work well. For example, older employees may have social needs that can be met well by a job that requires lots of public contact. Organizations, then, can take advantage of the special characteristics of jobs to attract applicants.

The value of the job to the organization also has a bearing on the selection of an appropriate recruitment message. Inducements for jobs of higher value or worth to the organization are easier to justify in a budgetary sense than are jobs of lower worth. The job may be of such importance to the organization that it is willing to pay a premium through inducements to attract well-qualified candidates.

Some applicants are less likely than others to be influenced in their attitudes and behaviors by the recruitment message. In a recent study, for example, it was shown that a realistic message is less effective for those with considerable previous job experience.[74] A targeted message does not work very well if the source is seen as being not credible.[75] Inducements may not be particularly effective with applicants who do not have a family or have considerable wealth.

Communication Medium

Not only is the message itself an important part of the recruitment process, so, too, is the selection of a medium to communicate the message. The most common recruitment mediums are recruitment brochures, videos and video conferencing, advertisements, voice messages, and on-line services.

Recruitment Brochures

A recruitment brochure is usually sent or given directly to job applicants. Information in the brochure may be very detailed, and hence, the brochure may be lengthy. A brochure not only covers information about the job, but also communicates information about the organization and the location of the organization. It may include pictures in addition to written narrative in order to illustrate various aspects of the job, such as the city in which the organization is located and actual coworkers.

The advantage of a brochure is that the organization controls who receives a copy. Also, it can be more lengthy than an advertisement. A disadvantage is that it can be quite costly to develop this medium.

Developing a brochure can be done inside the organization or by outside media professionals. By developing a brochure in-house, the organization may be able to keep the cost down. However, in-house capabilities may not be very technically advanced, so that outside sources may be needed if technical advances are required.

A successful brochure possesses the following characteristics:

1. unique theme or point of view relative to other organizations in same industry
2. visual distinctiveness in terms of design and photographs
3. credibility and detailed information regarding the organization, location, position, people who hold jobs, career paths, and benefits

Videos and Videoconferencing

A video can be used along with the brochure, but should not simply replicate the brochure. The brochure should be used to communicate basic facts and information. The video should be used to communicate the culture and climate of the organization. Professional Marketing Services, Inc., in Milwaukee, helps organizations to develop a "profile" of their organization. As part of the profile they can highlight characteristics of the city that the organization resides in such as the climate, housing market, school systems, churches, performing arts, spectator sports, nightlife, and festivals. This profile can be communicated to job seekers via videocassette, diskette, CD-ROM, CD-I, and the Internet.[76] Video diskettes can also be made interactive so that the job seeker can submit an application electronically, request additional information, or even arrange an interview.

A new form of communicating with job applicants is known as videoconferencing.[77] Rather than meeting in person with applicants, organizational representatives meet with applicants in separate locations face-to-face on a television monitor. The actual image of the person in action appears on the screen, although the transmission appears to be in slow motion. The technology needed for videoconferencing is expensive, but the costs have decreased in recent years. Moreover, this technology makes it possible for the organization to screen applicants at multiple or remote locations without having to physically travel to these locations. Many college placement offices now have the equipment for videoconferencing. The equipment is also available at some Kinko's copy centers for applicants who do not have access to a college placement office.

Advertisements

Given the expense of advertising in business publications, ads are much shorter and to the point than are recruitment brochures. As a general rule, the greater the circulation of the publication, the greater the cost of advertising in it.

Ads appear in a variety of places other than business publications. Ads can be found in local, regional, and national newspapers; on television and radio; and in bargain shoppers, door hangers, direct mail, and welcome wagons. Advertisements can thus be used to reach a broad market segment. Although they are brief, there are many different types of ads:[78]

1. Classified advertisements—These ads appear in alphabetical order in the "Help Wanted" section of the newspaper. Typically, they allow for very limited type and style selection and are usually only one newspaper column in width. These ads are used most often for the purpose of quick resume solicitation for low-level jobs at a low cost.

2. Classified display ads—A classified display ad allows more discretion in the type that is used, and its location in the paper. A classified display ad does not have to appear in alphabetical order and can appear in any section of the newspaper. The cost of these ads is moderate, and they are often used as a way to announce openings for professional and managerial jobs. An example of a classified display ad is shown in Exhibit 7.7.

3. Display ads—These ads allow for freedom of design and placement in a publication. As such, they are very expensive and begin to resemble recruitment brochures. These ads are typically used when an employer is searching for a large number of applicants to fill multiple openings.

EXHIBIT 7.7   Classified Display Ad for Human Resource Generalist

---

HUMAN RESOURCE GENERALIST

ABC Health, a leader in the health care industry, currently has a position available for an experienced **Human Resource Generalist.**

This position will serve on the human resources team, which serves as a business partner with our operational departments. Our team prides itself on developing and maintaining progressive and impactful human resources policies and programs.

Qualified candidates for this position will possess a bachelor's degree in business with an emphasis on human resource management, or a degree in a related field, such as industrial psychology. In addition, a minimum of three years experience as a human resource generalist is required. This experience should include exposure to at least four of the following functional areas: compensation, employment, benefits, training, employee relations, and performance management.

In return for your contributions, we offer a competitive salary as well as comprehensive, flexible employee benefits. If you meet the qualifications and our opportunity is attractive to you, please forward your resume and salary expectations to:

Human Resource Department
ABC Health
P.O. Box 123
Pensacola, FL 12345

An Equal Opportunity/Affirmative Action Employer

---

4. Blind ad—A blind ad is one where the identity of the employer is hidden from job applicants. Resumes are solicited and sent to a post office box. In most instances, these ads are to be avoided. Readers of these ads are likely to have negative reactions to them because they have no idea where their resume is being sent. Also, some applicants may fear that their employer is advertising with a blind ad to see who is thinking of leaving the organization. Due to these perceptions, it is unlikely that blind ads draw any applicants other than those who are desperate for a job.

How to Write an Ad   The State of Wisconsin published an excellent booklet on how to write advertisements.[79] Points to consider in writing advertising copy follow:

- A good ad should draw attention, create interest, screen candidates, and provide for easy responses.
- The headline should be used to draw attention.
- The body of the ad should be based on the job requirements matrix to create interest in the job through the job description and to allow applicants to self-screen through the job specification.
- The body of the ad should also be based on the job rewards matrix to provide basic information about job rewards.
- The writing style should be natural, enthusiastic, engaging, and easy to understand.
- The ad should close with detailed information about how to apply for the job.
- The best time of week to advertise in the newspaper is on Sunday.
- Advertising around the time of major holidays is ineffective.

Voice Messages

As a result of the latest advances in the telecommunications industry, a recent development in advertising is voice messages. With this approach, the applicant hears information over the phone about job openings. The Dime National Bank of New York uses this relatively inexpensive approach.[80] At Dime Bank, calls are solicited through advertisements in the paper. Once an applicant calls, he or she is routed through the menu shown in Exhibit 7.8. Callers have access to each of the items on the menu by pressing keys on a touch-tone phone. If what they hear is of interest to them, they can leave a message in a voice mailbox. All applicants receive a return call, and if they appear to be qualified for a vacant position, they are invited in for an interview. Although the effectiveness of this procedure has not yet been researched, it appears to be a promising way to provide a more personable introduction to job applicants.

EXHIBIT 7.8   Advertising by Voice Messages

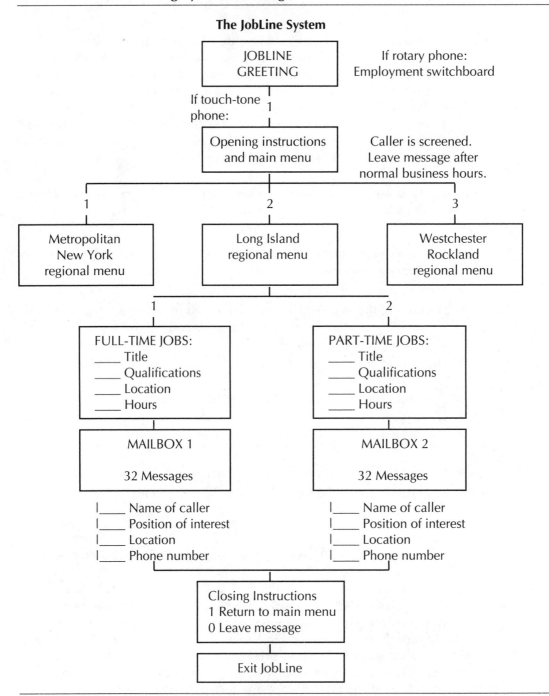

The JobLine System

JOBLINE GREETING

If rotary phone: Employment switchboard

If touch-tone phone: 1

Opening instructions and main menu

Caller is screened. Leave message after normal business hours.

1 — Metropolitan New York regional menu
2 — Long Island regional menu
3 — Westchester Rockland regional menu

1 — FULL-TIME JOBS:
____ Title
____ Qualifications
____ Location
____ Hours

2 — PART-TIME JOBS:
____ Title
____ Qualifications
____ Location
____ Hours

MAILBOX 1

32 Messages

|____ Name of caller
|____ Position of interest
|____ Location
|____ Phone number

MAILBOX 2

32 Messages

|____ Name of caller
|____ Position of interest
|____ Location
|____ Phone number

Closing Instructions
1 Return to main menu
0 Leave message

Exit JobLine

Source: A. M. Micola, "High-Tech Recruiting at Low Cost," *HR Magazine,* August 1991, pp. 49–52. Reprinted with the permission of HR Magazine (formerly Personnel Administrator) published by the Society for Human Resource Management, Alexandria, VA.

On-line Services

Organizations can directly interact with applicants on the computer.[81] In order to do so, organizations can make themselves known to applicants in two ways. The first way is to create a "home page" on the World Wide Web (WWW) which is located for applicants to see on the Internet. The Internet is the information highway that connects computer networks together around the world. The home page can provide the applicant with files to browse that describe the organization and available jobs. A home page address is identified by a uniform resource locator (URL) which lets the user know where on the Internet to look. Organizations can also list jobs in public bulletin boards on the Internet.

Organizations can also make their jobs known with on-line service groups because it is difficult for some individuals to navigate the Internet. These service groups include organizations that provide on-line job services for their members. Organizations that provide on-line job services include major on-line service companies, such as Compuserve, which have job forums, professional societies that have job banks, and global recruitment centers such as On-line Career Center, which serve as an intermediary between applicants and organizations. Because of the expense involved for job applicants, not all have access to computers; consequently, the on-line medium should be only one of several mediums used to interact with job seekers.

One of the most well-known and respected sources of advertisements and resumes is the On-line Career Center. It was started three years ago by Aetna, Alcoa, IBM, Eli Lilly, Monsanto, and P&G. It now has over 262 corporate members who pay a fee to list their vacant jobs. Job seekers can browse and display their own resumes for no fee. The address of the On-line Career Service on the Internet is http://www.careerpath.com.

Applicant Reactions

An important source of information in designing and implementing an effective recruitment system is applicant reactions to the system. Both attitudinal and behavioral reactions to components of the recruitment system are important. Components of this system that have been studied include the recruiter and the recruitment process.

Reactions to Recruiters

Considerable research has been conducted and carefully reviewed on the reactions of job applicants to the behavior and characteristics of recruiters.[82] The data that have been collected have been somewhat limited by the fact that they focus primarily on reactions to college rather than noncollege recruiters. Despite this limitation, several key themes emerge in the literature.

First, while the recruiter does indeed influence job applicant reactions, he or she does not have as much influence on them as do actual characteristics of the job. This indicates that the recruiter cannot be viewed as a substitute for a well defined and communicated recruitment message showing the actual characteristics of the job. It is not enough just to have good recruiters to attract applicants to the organization.

Second, the influence of the recruiter is more likely to be felt on the attitudes rather than the behaviors of the job applicant. That is, an applicant who has been exposed to a talented recruiter is more likely to walk away with a favorable impression of the recruiter than to accept a job on the basis of the interaction with a recruiter. This attitudinal effect is important, however, as it may lead to good publicity for the organization. In turn, good publicity may lead to a larger applicant pool to draw upon in the future.

Third, demographic characteristics of the recruiter do not have much impact on applicant reactions, with one exception. Recruiters who are human resource specialists do not fare as well in terms of applicant reactions as do line managers. Hence, the common practice of using line managers to recruit, and human resource people to coordinate recruitment activities, appears to be an appropriate strategy.

Fourth, two behaviors of the recruiter seem to have the largest influence on applicant reactions. The first behavior is the level of warmth that the recruiter shows toward the job applicant. Warmth can be expressed by being enthusiastic, personable, empathetic, and helpful in dealings with the candidate. The second behavior is being knowledgeable about the job. This can be conveyed by being well-versed with the job requirements matrix and the job rewards matrix.

Reactions to the Recruitment Process

Only some administrative components of the recruitment process have been shown to have an impact on applicant reactions.[83] First, job applicants are more likely to have favorable reactions to the recruitment process when the screening devices that are used to narrow the applicant pool are seen as job-related. That is, the process that is used should be closely related to the content of the job as spelled out in the job requirements matrix.

Second, delay times in the recruitment process do indeed have a negative effect on applicants' reactions. In particular, when long delays take place between the applicant's expression of interest and the organization's response, negative reactions are formed by the applicant. The negative impression formed by the applicant is about the organization rather than the applicant him or herself. For example, with a long delay between an on-site visit and a job offer, an applicant is more likely to believe that something is wrong with the organization rather than with his or her personal qualifications. This is especially true of the better quality candidate who is also likely to act on these feelings by accepting another job offer.

Third, simply throwing money at the recruitment process is unlikely to result in any return. There is no evidence that increased expenditures on the recruitment process result in more favorable attitudes or behaviors by job applicants. In order for expenditures to pay dividends, they need to be specifically targeted to effective recruitment practices rather than indiscriminately directed to all practices.

Fourth, the influence of the recruiter on the applicant is more likely to occur in the initial rather than the latter stages of the recruitment process. In the latter stages, actual characteristics of the job carry more weight in the applicant's decision. At the initial screening interview, the recruiter may be the applicant's only contact with the organization. Later in the process, the applicant is more likely to have additional information about the job and company. Hence, the credibility of the recruiter is most critical upon initial contact with applicants.

TRANSITION TO SELECTION

Once a job seeker has been identified and attracted to the organization, the organization needs to prepare the person for the selection process. In preparation, applicants need to be made aware of the next steps in the hiring process and what will be required of them along the way. If this transitory step is overlooked by the recruiting organization, it may lose qualified applicants who mistakenly think that delays between steps in the hiring process indicate that the organization is no longer interested in them or are fearful that they "didn't have what it takes" to successfully compete during the next steps.

The city of Columbus, Ohio has done an excellent job of preparing job seekers from external recruitment sources to become applicants for the position of firefighter. To become a firefighter, applicants must pass a series of physical ability exams which require them to go through an obstacle course, carry heavy equipment up stairs, and complete a number of other timed physical exercises. Many applicants have never encountered these types of tests before or are fearful that they don't have the physical ability to successfully complete the tests.

To prepare job seekers and applicants for these tests, videotapes have been developed showing instructions on how to take the tests, and a firefighter actually taking the tests. These tests are shown not only to those who have applied for the position, but are also shown on public access television to those job seekers who are thinking about applying for the job. The city of Columbus also provides upper body strength training, as upper body strength is a stumbling point for some job applicants in the selection process.

This example from the city of Columbus indicates that in order to successfully prepare people for the transition to selection, organizations should consider reviewing the selection method instructions with the applicants, showing them actual samples of the selection method, and providing them with practice or training if necessary. These steps should be followed for not just physical ability tests, but for all selection methods in the hiring process likely to be unfamiliar or uncomfortable to applicants.

LEGAL ISSUES

External recruitment practices are subject to considerable legal scrutiny and influence. It is through external recruitment that job applicants first establish contact with the organization and then become more knowledgeable about job requirements and rewards. During this process, there is ample room for the organization to exclude certain applicant groups (e.g., minorities, women, and people with disabilities), as well as deceive in its dealings with applicants. Various laws and regulations seek to place limits on these exclusionary and deceptive practices.

Legal issues regarding several of the practices are discussed in this section. These include definition of job applicants and disclaimers (planning), targeted recruitment (where to look), recruitment sources (how to look), job advertisements (communication medium), and fraud and misrepresentation (communication message).

Definition of Job Applicant

Exactly what and who is a job applicant? Does the definition include unsolicited resumes, applications for any job opening, casual walk-ins, phone call inquiries, anyone who fills out an application blank? Any person who is considered an applicant by the organization must be reflected in its record keeping; all such people are also potential litigants against the organization.

The organization is required to keep records on numbers of applicants and use these in the calculation of applicant flow and selection rate statistics (see Chapter 6). Presumably, the organization would like such statistics to reflect its real or serious applicants and not its casual and frivolous applicants. In a related vein, without any limitations on who is deemed an applicant, anyone who makes any effort at application might be considered legally an applicant and thus be a potential litigant in an EEO/AA case.

As these examples suggest, the organization needs to establish an explicit job applicant policy for guidance and protection in EEO/AA matters. The following are some suggestions for such a policy:[84]

1. Applicants should be accepted only when there is a job vacancy open and ready to be filled (any exception to this, such as for difficult-to-fill jobs, should also be included in the policy).
2. Applicants must specify the job being applied for.
3. There should be a limit on the number of people who will be considered applicants when there are likely to be large numbers of applicants (e.g., first 100 who apply).
4. Applications should be kept live and on file for only one year, unless there are specific legal reasons for a longer period.

5. All unsolicited applications should be returned via the mail.

6. There should be a written policy about these application procedures; it should be communicated to applicants and employees.

Applications scanned and/or received electronically via E-mail or on-line present new problems for the organization. Must it consider each such instance as an application that must be recorded? The OFCCP's position is that all resumes screened from electronic on-line data submissions must be recorded as an application. While the issue awaits more legal clarification, the prudent practice for the organization would be to count all electronic contacts as applications for record-keeping purposes.[85]

The above suggestions apply primarily to the private sector. Public sector employers by law must be more lenient in defining job applicants. The state of Wisconsin, for example, counts as an applicant anyone who completes and turns in a simple machine-scorable application blank. Because of this, the state typically has large numbers of applicants for any specific job vacancy announcement.

Targeted Recruitment

Targeted recruitment is a necessary part of EEO/AA programs designed to address problems of underutilization of minorities and women. Such recruitment refers to explicit attempts to identify and attract people from underutilized groups in areas where, and through sources from which, they are available.

Examples of targeted recruitment are numerous. Discussed previously, for example, were special availabilities of people outside the mainstream of labor force participation (teenagers, older workers, welfare recipients, and people with disabilities).

As another important example, under Revised Order No. 4 (see appendix B), federal contractors' AAPs must include targeted recruitment. The order gives contractors special recruitment sources to consider, suggests holding recruitment briefings with representatives from these sources, encourages employer use of employee referral systems for women and minority applicants, and requires active recruiting at schools with predominantly minority and female enrollment.

Other examples of targeted recruitment occur within the context of larger EEO/ AA programs at employers such as McDonald's, Kentucky Fried Chicken (KFC), the California Department of Corrections, and the U.S. Postal Service.[86] McDonald's started its McJobs program for hiring people with disabilities back in 1981, and it has hired more than 9,000 mentally and physically challenged people since then. The program is a partnership between vocational rehabilitation (VR) agencies, local school systems and workshops, and family members. Individuals are recruited from these sources and then assigned a specific VR counselor to serve as a liaison between them and the company. Recruits then embark on a six-to eight-week training program to learn job skills, both in the classroom and on the job at a McDonald's restaurant.

KFC's targeted recruitment program, called the Designates Program, is intended to identify and attract female and minority executives from other companies. It seeks to place, or promote these recruits through the managerial ranks into senior-level management positions. To do this, it uses executive search firms owned by minority group members and women, as well as white men. In a given recruiting initiative, recruiters from these three differently owned search firms (all using the same KSAO job requirements) are asked to produce three different slates of candidates—all white men, all black men, and all women (minority and white). One person is then hired from all three slates.

The California Department of Corrections hires about 2,000 correctional officers each year. It tracks the ethnic composition of its workforce to identify emergent underutilization (recently, Hispanics, Asians, Filipinos, Pacific Islanders, Native Americans, and women). Its multiracial recruitment staff then implements a variety of recruitment initiatives. These include newspaper ads, TV and radio commercials, posters and billboards, mass mailings, job information workshops, and high school and college campus visits.

The U.S. Postal Service (USPS) is undertaking substantial recruitment for Hispanic employees, who comprise 6.4% of the USPS workforce. Recruitment barriers include lack of awareness of job opportunities, misperceptions of kinds of jobs and hours of work, and lack of English skills. Strategies for recruitment include using Hispanic employees as recruiters, bilingual recruitment advertising in postal lobbies, schools, and neighborhoods, and conducting workshops on the required entrance exams.

Recruitment Sources

Use of traditional or conventional recruitment sources can create EEO/AA problems for the organization. Often, the demographic pools available through these sources lack in diversity, and this leads to underutilization in the organization's workforce.

Several conventional recruitment sources are potentially tainted with possible discrimination effects, and they should be used cautiously by the employer.[87] Employee referral systems are often suspect because employees are most likely to advise only people like themselves about job opportunities. This is also a strong possibility with nepotism systems, in which only family members of current employees may be hired. Finally, it is illegal for employment agencies and executive firms to fail, or refuse, to refer members of protected groups for employment. Despite this, it is sometimes alleged that such refusals occur.

Any recruitment source can potentially lead to discrimination. The organization should carefully track the demographics of recruits from various sources, looking for possible adverse impact in the use of those sources. Where it is found, the organization must take steps to eliminate it. This may mean a halt in the use of the source, discussions with the source to rectify the problem, a shift to more demographically neutral sources, or use of targeted recruitment sources in order to address and correct workforce imbalances.

Job Advertisements

Some of the earliest, and most blatant, examples of discrimination come from job advertisements. Newspaper employment ads were once listed under separate "Help Wanted—Male" and "Help Wanted—Female" sections and the content of the ads contained statements such as "Applicant must be young and energetic." Such types of ads would obviously discourage certain potential applicants from applying because of their sex or age.

The EEOC has issued policy statements regarding age- and sex-referent language in advertising.[88] It bans the use of explicit age- or sex-based preferences. It also addresses more subtle situations in which ads contain implicit age- or sex-based preferences, such as "junior executive," "recent college graduate," "me-termaid," and "patrolman." These are referred to in the policy statements as "trigger words," and their use may have the effect of deterring certain individuals from becoming applicants. The statements make clear that trigger words, in and of themselves in an advertisement, are not illegal. However, the total context of the ad in which trigger words appear must not be discriminatory, or the trigger words will be a violation of the law.

The EEOC provides the following as an example of an advertisement with a trigger word: "Wanted: Individuals of all ages. Day and evening hours available. Full- and part-time positions. All inquiries welcomed. Excellent source of secondary income for retirees."

Use of the trigger word "retiree" in this ad is considered permissible because the context of the ad makes it clear that applicants of all ages are welcome to apply.

Fraud and Misrepresentation

Puffery, promises, half-truths, and even outright lies are all encountered in recruitment under the guise of selling the applicant on the job and the organization. Too much of this type of selling can be legally dangerous. When it occurs, under workplace tort law, applicants may file suit claiming fraud or misrepresentation.[89] Claims may cite false statements of existing facts (e.g., the nature and profitability of the employer's business), or false promises of future events (e.g., promises about terms and conditions of employment, regarding pay, promotion opportunities, and geographic location). It does not matter if the false statements were made intentionally (fraud) or negligently (misrepresentation). Both types of statements are a reasonable basis for a claim by the applicant or newly hired employee.

To be successful in such a suit, the plaintiff must demonstrate that

1. a misrepresentation occurred;
2. the employer knew, or should have known, about the misrepresentation;
3. the plaintiff relied on the information to make a decision or take action; and
4. the plaintiff was injured because of reliance placed on the statements made by the employer.[90]

While these four requirements appear to be a stiff set of hurdles for the plaintiff, they are by no means insurmountable, as many successful plaintiffs can attest.

Avoidance of fraud and misrepresentation claims in recruitment requires straightforward action by the organization and its recruiters. First, provide applicants with copies of the job requirements matrix and the job rewards matrix. They contain a wealth of specific, truthful information about the job. Second, be truthful about the nature of the business and its profitability. Third, avoid specific promises about future events, regarding terms and conditions of employment or business plans and profitability. Finally, make sure that all recruiters follow these suggestions when they recruit job applicants.

SUMMARY

The objective of the external recruitment process is to identify and attract qualified applicants. In order to meet this objective the organization must conduct recruitment planning. At this stage, attention must be given to both organizational issues (e.g., centralized versus decentralized recruitment function) and administrative issues (e.g., size of the budget). Particular care needs to be taken in the selection, training, and rewards of recruiters.

The next stage in external recruitment is the development of a strategy. The strategy should detail where to look, how to look, and when to look. In general, an organization should consider looking at a wide range of applicant groups to attract a well-qualified applicant pool. Consideration should be given to those with special availabilities, and the search should be guided by the job requirements matrix. Multiple sources should be used to identify specific applicant populations. There are trade-offs involved in using any source to identify applicants, which should be carefully reviewed prior to using it. When to look for applicants depends upon the lead time required to fill a vacancy and the time it took to fill previous vacancies.

The next stage is to develop a message to give to the job applicants and to select a medium to convey that message. The message may be traditional, realistic, attractive, or targeted. There is no one best message; it depends upon the characteristics of the labor market, the job, and the applicants. The message should, however, be based on the job requirements matrix and the job rewards matrix. The message can be communicated through brochures, videos, advertisements, voice messages, video conferencing, or on-line services, each of which has different strengths and weaknesses.

Applicants are definitely influenced by characteristics of recruiters and of the recruitment process. Through proper attention to these characteristics, the organization can help provide applicants a favorable recruitment experience. That experience can be continued by preparing applicants carefully for the selection process.

Recruitment activities are highly visible and sensitive for employees. They raise a host of legal issues regarding potential exclusion of minority and female applicants, and truthful communication with job applicants. The organization should carefully define what it considers to be job applicants. For enhanced representation of minorities and women in the applicant pool, targeted recruitment and possible changes in use of conventional recruitment sources should be undertaken. Consistent with this, job advertisements should not openly or implicitly express preferences for or against protected demographic characteristics of applicants. Finally, the organization should be truthful with applicants about the terms and conditions of employment, as well as the overall nature of the business, in order to avoid allegations of fraud and misrepresentation in recruitment.

DISCUSSION QUESTIONS

1. List and briefly describe each of the administrative issues that needs to be addressed in the planning stage of external recruiting.

2. List ten sources of applicants that organizations turn to when recruiting. For each source, identify needs specific to the source, as well as pros and cons of using the source for recruitment.

3. In designing the communication message to be used in external recruiting, what kinds of information should be included?

4. What are the advantages of conveying a realistic recruitment message as opposed to one portraying the job in a way that the organization thinks that job applicants want to hear?

5. What nontraditional inducements are some organizations offering so that they are seen as family-friendly organizations? What result does the organization hope to realize as a result of providing these inducements?

APPLICATIONS

Improving a College Recruitment Program

The White Feather Corporation (WFC) is a rapidly growing consumer products company that specializes in the production and sales of specialty household items such as lawn furniture cleaners, spa (hot tub) accessories, mosquito and tick repellents, and stain-resistant garage floor paints. The company currently employs 400 exempt and 3,000 nonexempt employees, almost all of whom are full-time. In addition to its corporate office in Clucksville, Arkansas, the company has five plants and two distribution centers at various rural locations throughout the state.

Two years ago WFC created a corporate HR department to provide centralized direction and control for its key HR functions planning, compensation, training, and staffing. In turn, the staffing function is headed by the senior manager of staffing, who receives direct reports from three managers: the manager of nonexempt employment, the manager of exempt employment, and the manager of EEO/AA. The manager of exempt employment is Marianne Collins, who has been with WFC for ten years, and has grown with the company through a series of sales and sales management positions. She was chosen for her current position as a result of the WFC's commitment to promotion-from-within, as well as her broad familiarity with the company's products and customers. When appointed, Marianne's key area of accountability was defined as college recruitment, with 50% of her time to be devoted to it.

In her first year, Marianne developed and implemented WFC's first-ever formal college recruitment program. Working with the HR planning person, they decided there was a need for 40 college graduate new hires by the end of the year. They were to be placed in the production, distribution, and marketing functions; specific job titles and descriptions were to be developed during the year. Armed with this forecast, Marianne began the process of recruitment planning and strategy development. The result was the following recruitment process.

Recruitment was to be conducted at 12 public and private schools throughout the state. Marianne contacted the placement office(s) at each school and set up a one-day recruitment visit for each school. All visits were scheduled during the first week in May. The placement office at each school set up 30-minute interviews (16 at each school), and made sure that applicants completed and had on file a standard application form. To visit the schools and conduct the interviews, Marianne selected three young, up-and-coming managers (one each from production, distribution, and marketing) to be the recruiters. Each manager was assigned to four of the schools. Since none of the managers had any experience as a recruiter, Marianne conducted a recruitment briefing for them. During that briefing she reviewed the overall recruitment (hiring) goal, provided a brief rundown on each of the schools, and then explained the specific tasks the recruiters were to perform. Those tasks were to pick up the application materials of the interviewees at the placement office prior to the interviews, review the materials, conduct the interviews in a timely manner (they were told they could ask any questions they wanted to that pertained to qualifications for the job), and at the end of the day complete an evaluation form on each applicant. The form asked for a 1–7 rating of overall qualifications for the job, written comments about strengths and weaknesses, and a recommendation of whether or not to invite the person for a second interview in Clucksville. These forms were to be returned to Marianne, who would review them and decide which people to invite for a second interview.

After the campus interviews were conducted by the managers, problems began to surface. Placement officials at some of the schools contacted Marianne and lodged several complaints. Among those complaints were that (a) one of the managers failed to pick up the application materials of the interviewees, (b) none of the managers were able to provide much information about the nature of the jobs they were recruiting for, especially jobs outside of their own functional area, (c) the interviewers got off schedule early on, so that applicants were kept waiting and others had shortened interviews as the managers tried to make up time, (d) none of the managers had any written information describing the company and its locations, (e) one of the managers asked female applicants very personal questions about marriage plans, use of drugs and alcohol, and willingness to travel with male coworkers, (f) one of the managers talked incessantly during the interviews, so that the interviewees had little opportunity to present themselves and their qualifications to the manager, and (g) all of the managers told interviewees they did not know when they would be contacted about decisions on invitations for second interviews. In addition to these complaints, Marianne had difficulty getting the managers to complete and turn in their evaluation forms (they claimed they were too busy, especially after being away from the job for a week). Based on the reports she did receive, Marianne extended invitations to 55 of the applicants for second interviews. Of these, 30 accepted the invitation. Ultimately, 25 of these were given job offers, and 15 of them accepted the offers.

To put it mildly, the first-ever college recruitment program was a disaster for WFC and Marianne. In addition to her embarrassment, Marianne was asked to meet with her boss and the president of WFC to explain what went wrong and to receive "guidance" from them as to their expectations for the next year's recruitment program. Marianne subsequently learned that she would receive no merit pay increase for the year, and that the three managers all received above average merit increases.

In order to turn things around for the second year of college recruitment, Marianne realized that she needed to engage in a thorough process of recruitment planning and strategy development. As she began this undertaking, her analysis of past events lead her to the conclusion that one of her key mistakes was to naively assume that the three managers would actually know how to be good recruiters and be motivated to do the job effectively. Marianne first decides to use 12 managers as recruiters, assigning one to each of the 12 campuses. She also decides that she cannot send them off to the campuses with just a recruitment "briefing." So, she determines that an intensive, one-day training program must be developed and given to the managers prior to the beginning of the recruitment "season."

You are a professional acquaintance of Marianne's who works in HR at another company in Clucksville. Knowing that you have had some experience in both college recruiting and training, Marianne calls you up for some advice. She asks you if you would be willing to meet and discuss the following questions:

1. What topics should be covered in the training program?
2. What materials and training aids will be needed for the program?
3. What skills should the trainees actually practice during the training?
4. Who should conduct the training?
5. What other changes might have to be made to ensure that the training has a strong impact on the managers and that during the recruitment process they are motivated to use what they learned in training?

Recruitment Via a Mass Mailed Brochure

Family Meals, Inc. is a thriving business in a large metropolitan area of over 500,000 people. The business consists of the preparation and delivery of hot meals to families. Customers must call 24 hours in advance to select meals to be prepared and select a time for the meal to be delivered. Recently, this business has had trouble recruiting drivers to deliver the meals. The four-line advertisements in the paper no longer seem to attract the number of drivers they need. In response to this situation, Family Meals, Inc. proposes to conduct a mass mailing campaign where a recruitment brochure will be sent to each person's home in the metropolitan area by bulk mail. It is hoped that in doing so they will be able to improve upon their hiring rates for drivers.

The following job requirements and rewards exist for the driver's job. Drivers must (a) be over 18 years of age, (b) have their own automobile to use, (c) possess a valid driver's license, (d) have auto insurance, (e) have a good driving record (lost no more than three points off record in last year), (f) be able to read maps and make change, and (g) be courteous. No previous driving experience is required. The job is part-time, varying between 10 and 30 hours per week, depending on business needs. Driving occurs between 4:00 P.M. and 11:30 P.M., seven days a week. The wage is $7.00 per hour plus tips. Tips are highly variable; about 25% of customers provide no tip, 50% provide some tip, and 25% provide tips of 15 + %. Drivers are provided one week of training (they are trained by an experienced driver), after which they must pass a ride-along test conducted by the owner of Family Meals. There is a meal allowance, in which drivers may purchase any items on the menu at 50% off the menu price. The company pays for mileage at 21 cents per mile, and it pays for an oil change and lube job every 7,000 miles, as well as a car wash every week. A paid vacation (one week) is provided to drivers after accumulating 1,200 hours of work in a 52-week period. Another benefit is that drivers often hear of other job opportunities from their customers.

1. Prepare two versions of the recruitment brochure. The first should carry a realistic message, and the second should carry an attractive message. The brochure is to be a single, 8½" × 11" stiff piece of paper that will be folded in half, with one of the outside halves being used for the mailing and return addresses.

2. Prepare a brief report in which you indicate (a) which of the two brochures would likely attract more job applicants, and why; (b) whether you think either brochure would attract more applicants than the currently used newspaper ads, and why; and (c) other recommendations you have for generating more job applicants.

ENDNOTES

1. A. S. Bargerstock and G. A. Swanson, "Four Ways to Build Cooperative Recruitment Alliances," *HR Magazine*, 1991, 36(3), pp. 49–51. 79; L. S. Vines, "Recruiting Outlook," *Human Resource Executive*, 1992, 6(10), pp. 47.

2. Personnel Policies Forum, *Recruiting and Selection Procedures* (PPF Survey No. 146) (Washington: Bureau of National Affairs, Inc., 1988).

3. P. F. Wernimont, "Recruitment Policies and Practices," in D. Yoder and H. G. Heneman, Jr. (eds.), *ASPA Handbook of Personnel and Industrial Relations* (Washington, DC: Bureau of National Affairs, 1979), pp. 4–85 to 4–115.

4. J. S. Scott, "External and Internal Recruitment," in W. F. Cascio (ed.), *Human Resource Planning, Employment, and Placement* (Washington, DC: Bureau of National Affairs, 1989), pp. 2–73 to 2–134.

5. D. P. Schwab, "Recruiting and Organizational Participation," in K. M. Rowland and G. R. Ferris (eds.), *Personnel Management* (Boston: Allyn and Bacon, 1982), pp. 103–128.

6. D.P. Schwab, S. L. Rynes, and R. J. Aldag, "Theories and Research on Job Search and Choice," in K. M. Rowland and G. R. Ferris (eds.), *Research in Personnel and Human Resources Management*, 1987, 5, pp. 129–166; S. M. Bostnick and M. H. Ports, "Job Search Methods and Results: Tracking the Unemployed, 1991," *Monthly Labor Review*, Dec. 1992, pp. 29–35; M. H. Ports, "Trends in Job Search Methods, 1970–1992," *Monthly Labor Review*, 1993, Oct., pp. 63–67; A. E. Barber, C. L. Daily, G. M. Giannantonio, and J. Phillips, "Job Search Activities: An Examination of Changes over Time," *Personnel Psychology*, 1994, 47, pp. 739–765.

7. J. D. Olian and S. L. Rynes, "Organizational Staffing: Integrating Practice with Strategy," *Industrial Relations*, 1984, 23(2), pp. 170–183; "Ten Ways HR Can Take the Lead in Breaking Down Barriers to Employment," (Special Report), *Personnel Journal*, Mar. 1993, pp. 47–99.

8. "Personnel Shop Talk," *BNA Bulletin to Management*, May 23, 1991, p. 154.

9. W. L. Bainbridge and S. M. Sundre, "Employment Objectives Increasingly Linked to School/Business Partnerships," *EMA Journal*, 1991, 6(4), pp. 20–23.

10. I. J. Shaver, "Innovative Techniques Lure Quality Workers to NASA," *Personnel Journal*, Aug. 1990, pp. 100–106.

11. R. D. Gatewood, M. A. Gowen, and G. Lautenschlager, "Corporate Image, Recruitment Image,

and Initial Job Choice Decisions," *Academy of Management Journal*, 1993, 36(2), pp. 414–427.

12. Coopers and Lybrand, *Employment Policies, Turnover, and Cost-Per-Hire* (New York: Coopers and Lybrand Compensation Resources, 1992).

13. Coopers and Lybrand, *Employment Policies, Turnover, and Cost-Per-Hire.*

14. Coopers and Lybrand, *Employment Policies, Turnover, and Cost-Per-Hire.*

15. R. D. Borgeson, "Planning the Human Resources Function Program and Budget," in J. J. Famularo (ed.), *Handbook of Human Resources Administration* (New York: McGraw-Hill, 1986), pp. 7-1 to 7-17.

16. Personnel Policies Forum, *Recruiting and Selection Procedures.*

17. Department of Employment Relations, *Recruitment Planning* (Madison, WI: State Division of Personnel, 1981); R. H. Hawk, *The Recruitment Function* (New York: American Management Association, 1967).

18. J. A. Breaugh, *Recruitment: Science and Practice* (Boston: PWS-Kent, 1992); S. L. Rynes and J. W. Boudreau, "College Recruiting Practices in Large Organizations: Practice, Evaluation, and Research Implications," *Personnel Psychology*, 1986, 39(3), pp. 286–310.

19. S. L. Rynes and A. E. Barber, "Applicant Attraction Strategies: An Organizational Perspective," *Academy of Management Review*, 1990, 15(2), pp. 286–310.

20. M. S. Taylor and T. J. Bergmann, "Organizational Recruitment Activities and Applicant Reactions at Different Stages of the Recruitment Process," *Personnel Psychology*, 1987, 40, pp. 261–285.

21. Rynes and Boudreau, "College Recruiting Practices in Large Organizations: Practice, Evaluation, and Research Implications."

22. Rynes and Boudreau, "College Recruiting Practices in Large Organizations: Practice, Evaluation, and Research Implications."

23. B. J. Asch, "Do Incentives Matter? The Case of Navy Recruiters," *Industrial and Labor Relations Review*, 43 (Special Issue), pp. 89–106.

24. R. L. Heneman, *Merit Pay: Linking Pay Increases to Performance Ratings* (Reading, MA: Addison-Wesley, 1992).

25. A. S. Bargerstock, "Seven Ways to Improve Recruitment Information Systems," *EMA Journal*, 1994, Winter, pp. 8–15.

26. Employment Management Association, "Alternative Recruitment Methods Take Center at Fall Conference," *EMA Reporter*, 1992, 18(1), pp. 3–5.

27. B. Quirk, "Older Workers Prove Valuable," *Madison (Wis.) Capital Times*, Oct. 29, 1991, p. 1.

28. American Association of Retired Persons, "The Older Workforce: Recruitment and Retention, A Survey by the American Association of Retired Persons and the Society for Human Resource Management," (Washington, DC: author, 1993).

29. American Association of Retired Persons, "How to Recruit Older Workers," (Washington, DC: author, 1993).

30. B. Rogers, "From Welfare to Workforce," *HR Magazine*, 1991, 36(7), pp. 36–38, 85.

31. J. E. Peters, "How to Bridge the Hiring Gap," *Personnel Administrator*, Oct. 1989, pp. 76–85.

32. Employment Management Association, "Alternative Recruitment Centers Take Center Stage at Fall Conference."

33. "Phone Message Service Helps Homeless Find Jobs," *Columbus Dispatch*, Feb. 16, 1993, p. 5B.

34. K. E. Larson and L. Davis, "Workforce 2000 Solutions: A Partnership with Armed Services," *EMA Journal*, 1991, 6(4), pp. 2–8.

35. S. Mangum, "Transferability of Military Occupational Training in the Post Draft Era," *Industrial and Labor Relations Review*, 1989, 42(2), pp. 230–245.

36. R. D. Arvey and M. E. Begella, "Analyzing the Homemaker Job Using the PAQ," *Journal of Applied Psychology*, 1975, 60, pp. 513–517.

37. A. Bargerstock and H. Engel, "Six Ways to Boost Employee Referral Programs," *HR Magazine*, 1994 Dec., pp. 72–79; Bureau of National Affairs, *Personnel Management* (periodically updated) (Washington, DC: author) pp. 201: 68.

38. College Placement Council, *College Relations and Recruitment Sourcebook* (Bethlehem, PA: author, 1991); A. Hardin, "Small Colleges Band Together in Oregon Consortium," *Journal of Career Planning and Employment*, 1995 60(3), pp. 22–23.

39. Rynes and Boudreau, "College Recruiting in Large Organizations: Practice, Evaluation, and Research Implications"; G. H. Varma and J. W. Smither, "Selecting Colleges and Universities for On-Campus Recruiting," *Journal of Career Planning and Employment*, Spring 1990, pp. 34–40; Wernimont, "Recruitment Policies and Practices."

40. W. J. Kucker, "Marketing Your Company on Campus," *Journal of Career Planning and Employment*, Spring 1987, pp. 34–38.

41. AT&T, "Customer-Supplier Discussion Guide: 'AT&T Driving Quality on Campus' For Use by AT&T Campus Leader with Career Services Offices," July 1992.

42. M. Tynes, "How to Set Up a College Recruitment Program That Pays Off," *Recruiting and Hiring Handbook* (Waterford, CT: Prentice-Hall, 1989), pp. 14-1 to 14-12.

43. G. A. Cluff, *1990 National Cost-Per-Hire Survey* (Raleigh, NC: Employment Management Association, 1990); Coopers and Lybrand, *Employment Policies, Turnover, and Cost-Per-Hire.*

44. Deutsch, Shea, and Evans, *Human Resources Manual*, (New York: author, 1992–1993).

45. A. Bargerstock, "Low-Cost Recruiting For Quality," *HR Magazine*, 1990, 35(9), pp. 68–70.

46. U.S. Department of Labor, "National Job Bank System Launched in Time for Veterans' Day Celebration." *News*, Nov. 10, 1993.

47. U. S. Department of Labor, "Labor Department Awards $25 Million to Seven States for One-Step Implementation," *News Release*, August 10, 1995.

48. Deutsch, Shea, and Evans, *Human Resources Manual.*

49. M. S. Taylor, "Effects of College Internships on Individual Participants," *Journal of Applied Psychology*, 1988, 73(3), pp. 393–401.

50. S. E. Frank, "Taking Out the Garbage, Walking the Boss's Dog, and Other Interns' Tales," *Wall Street Journal*, July 19, 1995, p. B1; D. A. Casella and C. E. Broughham, "Work Works: Student Jobs Open Front Doors to Careers," *Journal of Career Planning and Employment*, August 1995, pp. 24–27.

51. J. Ross, "Effective Ways to Hire Contingent Personnel," *HR Magazine*, 1991, February, pp. 52–54; S. Drake, "Temporaries Are Here to Stay," *Human Resource Executive*, 1992, 6(2), pp. 27–30; J. Gonyea, *The On-Line Job Search Companion* (New York: McGraw-Hill, 1995).

52. L. Phillion and John R. Brugger, "Encore! Retirees Give Top Performance as Temporaries," *HR Magazine*, 1994, Oct., pp. 74–77.

53. "High Tech Recruitment Solutions," *HR Magazine*, Feb. 1992, p. 54.

54. T. Lee, "Alumni Go Back to School to Hunt Jobs," *Wall Street Journal*, June 11, 1991, p. B1.

55. Deutsch, Shea, and Evans, *Human Resources Manual*, p. 24.

56. American Association of Retired Persons, "How to Recruit Older Workers."

57. C. D. Fyock, "Ways to Recruit Top Talent," *HR Magazine*, 1991, 36(7), pp. 33–35.

58. G. A. Cluff, *1990 National Cost-Per-Hire Survey* (Raleigh, NC: Employment Management Association, 1990); Coopers and Lybrand, *Employment Policies, Turnover, and Cost-Per-Hire*; Bureau of National Affairs, *Personnel Policies Forum, Recruiting and Selection Procedures* (Washington, DC: author, May 1988); S. L. Rynes, "Recruitment, Job Choice and Post-Hire Decisions," in M. D. Dunnette and L. M. Hough (eds.) *Handbook of Industrial and Organizational Psychology*, Vol. 2, second ed. (Palo Alto, CA: Consulting Psychologists Press, 1991), pp. 399–444; D. P. Schwab, "Recruiting and Organizational Participation," in K. M. Rowland and G. R. Ferris (eds.) *Personnel Management* (Boston: Allyn and Bacon, 1982), pp. 103–128; D. P. Schwab, S. L. Rynes, and R. J. Aldag, "Theories and Research on Job Search and Choice," in K. M. Rowland and G.R. Ferris (eds.) *Research in Personnel and Human Resources Management*, 1987, 5, pp. 129–166; J. P. Wanous, *Organizational Entry*, second ed. (Reading, MA: Addison-Wesley, 1992); J. P. Wanous and A. Colella, "Organizational Entry Research: Current Status and Future Directions," in G. R. Ferris and K. M. Rowland (eds.) *Organizational Entry* (Greenwich, CT: JAI Press, 1990), pp. 253–313.

59. G. A. Cluff, *1990 National Cost-Per-Hire Survey.*

60. State of Wisconsin, Department of Employment Relations (WPM-Staffing-Chapter 136) "Recruitment Planning"(Madison, WI: author, September 1981); W. F. Cascio, *Applied Psychology in Personnel Management*, fourth ed. (Englewood Cliffs, NJ: Prentice Hall 1991); R. H. Hawk, *The Recruitment Function* (New York: American Management Association, 1967).

61. J. A. Breaugh, *Recruitment: Science and Practice*, (Boston: PWS-Kent, 1992); S. D. Maurer, V. Howe, and T. W. Lee, "Organizational Recruiting as Marketing Management: An Interdisciplinary Study of Engineering Graduates," *Personnel Psychology*, 1992, 45, pp. 807–833.

62. J. P. Wanous, *Recruitment, Selection, Orientation, and Socialization of Newcomers*, second ed., (Reading, MA: Addison-Wesley, 1992).

63. S. L. Premack and J. P. Wanous, "A Meta-Analysis of Realistic Job Preview Experiments," *Journal of Applied Psychology*, 1985, 70, pp. 706–719.

64. Wanous, *Recruitment, Selection, Orientation, and Socialization of Newcomers.*

65. Premack and Wanous, "A Meta-Analysis of Realistic Job Preview Experiments"; Rynes, "Recruitment, Job Choice, and Post-Hire Decisions."

66. Breaugh, *Recruitment: Science and Practice.*

67. S. L. Rynes and C. Q. Trank, "Moving Upstream in the Employment Relationship: Using Recruitment and Selection to Enhance Quality Outcomes." In S. Ghosh and D. Fedor (eds.), *Advances in the Management of Organizational Quality*, Vol. 1, JAI Press, in press.

68. J. S. Hirsch, "Companies Try Bolder Tactics to Win MBAs," *Wall Street Journal*, Nov. 29, 1989, pp. B1.

69. S. Shellenbarger, "More Job Seekers Put Family Needs First," *Wall Street Journal*, Nov. 15, 1991, p. B1.

70. K. G. Connolly and P. M. Connolly, *Competing for Employees: Proven Marketing Strategies for Keeping and Hiring Exceptional People*, (Lexington, MA: D.C. Heath, 1991); Maurer, Howe, and Lee, "Organizational Recruiting as Marketing Management: An Interdisciplinary Study of Engineering Graduates."

71. C. D. Fyock, *America's Work Force is Coming of Age*, (Lexington, MA: D.C. Heath, 1990).

72. R. H. Bretz and T. A. Judge. "The Role of Human Resource Systems In Job Applicant Decision Processes," *Journal of Management*, 1994 20, pp. 531–551; D. Cable and T. Judge. "Pay

Preferences and Job Search Decisions: A Person-Organization Fit Perspective," *Personnel Psychology*, 47, pp. 648–657.

73. Wanous, *Organizational Entry*.

74. R. J. Vandenberg and V. Scarpello, "The Matching Model: An Examination of the Processes Underlying Realistic Job Previews," *Journal of Applied Psychology*, 1990, 75(1), pp. 60–67.

75. D. R. Ilgen, C. D. Fisher, and M. S. Taylor (1979). "Consequences of Individual Feedback on Behavior in Organizations," *Journal of Applied Psychology*, 1979, 64, pp. 349–371.

76. College Placement Council, *College Relations and Recruitment Sourcebook*. College Placement Council, "Technology," *Spotlight on Career Planning, Placement, and Recruitment*, 1995, 18(1), pp. 2.

77. K. O. Magnusen and K. G. Kroeck, "Videoconferencing Maximizes Recruiting," *HR Magazine*, 1995 Aug., pp. 70–72; B. Kelley, "High-Tech Hits Recruiting," *Human Resource Executive*, 1994 April, pp. 43–45; College Placement Council, "Technology," *Spotlight on Career Planning, Placement, & Recruitment*, 1994, 17(20), p. 2.

78. P. F. Wernimont, "Recruitment Policies and Practices," in D. Yoder and H. G. Heneman Jr. (eds.), *ASPA Handbook of Personnel and Industrial Relations* (Washington, DC: Bureau of National Affairs, 1979), pp. 4-85 to 4-115.

79. State of Wisconsin, Department of Employment Relations, *Recruitment Advertising: Writing and Placing in the Print Media* (Madison, WI: Author 1980).

80. A. M. Micolo, "High-Tech Recruiting at Low Cost," *HR Magazine*, August 1991, pp. 49–52.

81. S. Overman, "Cruising Cyberspace for the Best Recruits," *HR Magazine*, 1995, Feb., pp. 52–55; J. Gonyea, *The On-line Job Search Companion*; A. Saltzman, "An Electronic Job Hunt," *US News and World Report*, March 28, 1994, pp. 72–75; E. Monsen and P.D. Weddle, "Into a Brave New World: Recruiting in Hyperspace," *EMA Journal*, 1995, 9(3), pp. 14–19; C. Allen, "Job.Search@Internet," *Journal of Career Planning and Employment*, 1995 Spring, pp. 53–55; Loeb, M, "Getting Hired by Getting Wired," *Fortune*, Nov. 13, 1995, p. 252.

82. Rynes, "Recruitment, Job Choice, and Post-Hire Decisions," pp. 399–444; Wanous, *Organizational Entry*; Scott, "Total Quality College Relations and Recruitment Programs: Students Benchmark Best Practices," *EMA Journal*, 1995 Winter, pp. 2–5.

83. S. L. Rynes, "Who's Selecting Whom? Effects of Selection Practices in Applicant Attitudes and Behaviors," in N. Schmitt, W. Borman, and Associates (eds.), *Personnel Selection in Organizations* (San Francisco: Jossey-Bass, 1993), pp. 240–276; Rynes, "Recruitment, Job Choice, and Post-Hire Decisions"; S. L. Rynes, R. D. Bretz, and B. Gerhart, "The Importance of Recruitment and Job Choice: A Different Way of Looking," *Personnel Psychology*, 1991, 44, pp. 487–521; M. S. Taylor and T. J. Bergmann, "Organizational Recruitment Activities and Applicant Reactions to Different Stages of the Recruiting Process," *Personnel Psychology*, 40, pp. 261–285.

84. J. C. Cook, "Preparing for Statistical Battles under the Civil Rights Act," *HR Focus*, May 1992, pp. 12–13; G. P. Panaro, *Employment Law Manual* (Boston: Warren Gorham Lamont, 1990), pp. I-24 to I-26; G. P. Panaro, *Employment Law Manual*, second ed. (Boston: Warren Gorham Lamont, 1993), pp. I-51 to I-57.

85. E. Shelley, "High Tech Recruiting Methods," *HR Magazine*, Sept. 1995, pp. 61–64.

86. J. L. Laabs, "Affirmative Outreach," *Personnel Journal*, 1991, 70, pp. 86–93; J. L. Laabs, "The Golden Arches Provide Golden Opportunities," *Personnel Journal*, 1991, 70, pp. 52–57; J. E. Rigdon, "PepsiCo's KFC Scouts for Blacks and Women for its Top Echelons," *Wall Street Journal*, Nov. 19,1991, p. A1; Bureau of National Affairs, "Postal Service Developing Steps to Increase Recruitment of Hispanics," *Daily Labor Report*, May 11,1994, pp. A-17 to A-18.

87. Bureau of National Affairs, *Fair Employment Practices* (Washington, D.C.: author, periodically updated), pp. 421:101–104.

88. Bureau of National Affairs, *Fair Employment Practices*, pp. 405:4027–4033; 405:6847–6848.

89. R. M. Green and R. J. Reibstein, *Employer's Guide to Workplace Torts* (Washington, DC: Bureau of National Affairs, 1992, pp. 40–61, 200, 254–255.

90. A. G. Feliu, *Primer on Individual Employee Rights*, (Washington, DC: Bureau of National Affairs, 1992), p. 270.

CHAPTER EIGHT

Internal Recruitment

The objective of the internal recruitment process is to identify and attract applicants from among individuals already holding jobs with the organization. The first step in this process is recruitment planning which addresses both organizational and administrative issues. Organizational issues include mobility paths and mobility path policies. Administrative issues include requisitions, number and types of contacts, budgets, and the recruitment guide.

The second step in the internal recruitment process is strategy development. Attention is directed here to where, when, and how to look for qualified internal applicants. Knowing where to look requires an understanding of open, closed, and targeted internal recruitment systems. Knowing how to look requires an understanding of job postings, skills inventories, nominations, employee referrals, and in-house temporary pools. Knowing when to look requires an understanding of lead time and time sequence concerns.

The third step in the process is searching for internal candidates. This step consists of the communication message and medium for notification of the job vacancy. The message can be realistic, attractive, or targeted. The medium for delivery can be a job posting, other written documents, and potential supervisors and peers.

The fourth step in the process is developing a system to make the transition to selection for job applicants. Making a transition requires a well-developed job posting system and providing applicants with an understanding of the selection process and how to best prepare for it.

The fifth step in the process is the consideration of legal issues. Specific issues to be addressed include Revised Order No. 4, bona fide seniority systems, and the glass ceiling. All three of these issues deal with mechanisms for enhancing the identification and attraction of minorities and women for higher-level jobs within the organization.

RECRUITMENT PLANNING

Prior to identifying and attracting internal applicants to vacant jobs, attention must be directed to organizational and administrative issues that facilitate the effective matching of internal applicants with vacant jobs.

Organizational Issues

Just as the external labor market can be divided into segments or strata of workers believed to be desirable job applicants, so too can the internal labor market of an organization. This division is often done inside organizations on an informal basis. For example, managers might talk about the talented pool of managerial trainees this year and refer to some of them as "high-potential employees." As another example, people in the organization talk about their "techies," an internal collection of employees with the technical skills needed to run the business.

At a more formal level, organizations must create a structured set of jobs for their employees and paths of mobility for them to follow as they advance in their careers. To do this, organizations create internal labor markets.[1] Each internal labor market has two components: mobility paths and mobility policies. Mobility paths depict the paths of mobility between jobs. Mobility policies cover the operational requirements needed to move people between jobs.

Mobility Paths

A mobility path consists of possible employee movements within the internal labor market structure. Mobility paths are determined by many factors, including workforce, organizational, labor union, and labor market characteristics.[2] Mobility paths are of two types: traditional and innovative.[3] Both types of mobility paths determine who is eligible for a new job in the organization.

Traditional Mobility Paths

Examples of traditional mobility paths are shown in Exhibit 8.1. As shown, the emphasis is primarily on upward mobility in the organization. Due to the upward nature of traditional mobility paths, they are often labeled promotion ladders. This label implies that each job is a step toward the top of the organization. Upward promotions in an organization are often seen by employees as prizes because of the promotions' desirable characteristics. Employees receive these prizes as they compete against one another for available vacancies.[4] For example, a promotion may lead to a higher rate of pay, and a transfer may result in a move to a better work location. Research has shown that these competitions may be contested, as opportunities for upward advancement are limited in most organizations.[5]

An exception to the primarily upward mobility in the promotion ladders in Exhibit 8.1 shows the lateral moves that sometimes occur for the staff member who has both generalist and specialist experiences as well as corporate and division experience. This staff member is considered more well-rounded and better able to work within the total organization. Experience as a specialist helps the person to be familiar with technical issues that arise. Experience as a generalist gives the employee a breadth of knowledge about many matters in the staff function. Corporate experience provides a policy and planning perspective, while division experience provides greater insight on day-to-day operational matters.

Traditional mobility paths make it very easy, from an administrative vantage point, to identify where to look for applicants in the organization. For promotion, one looks at the next level down in the organizational hierarchy, and over, for transfer. Although such a system is straightforward to administer, it is not very flexible and may inhibit the matching of the best person for the job. For example, the best person for the job may be at two job levels down and in another division

EXHIBIT 8.1   Traditional Mobility Paths

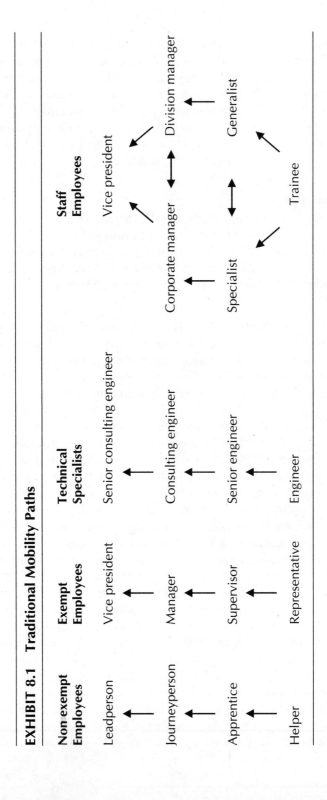

from the vacant job. It is very difficult to locate such a person under a traditional mobility path.

Innovative Mobility Paths   Examples of innovative mobility paths are shown in Exhibit 8.2. The emphasis here is no longer simply on upward mobility. Instead, movement in the organization may be in any direction, including up, down, and from side to side. Employee movement is emphasized to ensure continuous learning by employees such that each can make the greatest contribution to the organization. This is in direct contrast to the traditional promotion ladder, where the goal is for each person to achieve a position with ever-higher status. Many organizations have shifted to innovative mobility paths for two reasons: (a) There is the need to be flexible given global and technological changes, and (b) slower organizational growth has made it necessary to find alternative ways to utilize employees' talents.

Parallel tracks allow for employees to specialize in technical work or management work and advance within either. Historically, technical specialists had to shift away from technical to managerial work if they wanted to continue to receive higher-status job titles and pay. In other words, being a technical specialist was a dead-end job. Under a parallel track system, both job titles and salaries of technical specialists are elevated to be commensurate with their managerial counterparts.

With a lateral track system, there may be no upward mobility at all. The individual's greatest contribution to the organization may be to stay at a certain level of the organization for an extended period of time while serving in a variety of capacities, as shown in Exhibit 8.2.

A lattice mobility path has upward, lateral, and even downward movement. For example, a recruiter may be promoted to a recruitment supervisor position, but to continue to contribute to the organization, the person may need to take a lateral step to become knowledgeable about all the technical details in compensation. After mastering these details, the person may then become a supervisor again, this time in the compensation area rather than recruitment. From a previous company, the person may have experience in training and be ready to take the next move to training manager without training experience internal to the organization. Finally, the person may take a lateral move to manage all the human resource functions (recruitment, compensation, training) in a division as a division personnel manager.

The downside to innovative mobility paths, such as those discussed, is that they are very difficult to administer. Nice, neat categories of where to look do not exist to the same degree as with traditional mobility paths. On the positive side, however, talented inside candidates, who may not have been identified within a traditional system, are identified because the system is flexible enough to do so.

When upward mobility is limited in an organization, as with many organizations using innovative mobility paths, special steps need to be taken to ensure that work remains meaningful to employees. If steps are not taken, the organization with

EXHIBIT 8.2   Innovative Mobility Paths

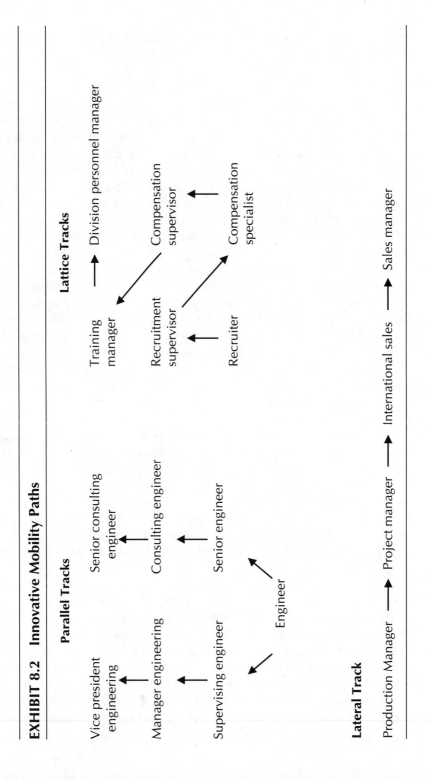

limited promotional opportunities risks turnover of good employees. Examples of steps to make work more meaningful include the following:[6]

1. Alternative reward systems—Rather than basing pay increases on promotions, pay increases can be based upon knowledge and skill acquisition and contribution to the organization as a team member and individual.

2. Team building—Greater challenge and autonomy in the workplace can be created by having employees work in teams where they are responsible for all aspects of work involved in providing a service or product, including self-management.

3. Counseling—Workshops, self-directed workbooks, and individual advising can be used by organizations to ensure that employees have a well-reasoned plan for movement in the organization.

4. Alternative Employment—Arrangements can be made for employee leaves of absence, sabbaticals, and consulting assignments to ensure that employees remain challenged and acquire new knowledge and skills.

Mobility Policies

Mobility paths show the relationship among jobs, but they do not show the rules by which people move between jobs. These rules are specified in written policies which must be developed and should specify eligibility criteria.

Development   A well-defined mobility path policy statement is needed for both traditional and innovative mobility paths and has the following characteristics:[7]

1. The intent of the policy is clearly communicated.

2. The policy is consistent with the philosophy and values of top management.

3. The scope of the policy, such as coverage by geographic region, employee groups, and so forth, is clearly articulated.

4. Employees' responsibilities and opportunities for development are clearly defined.

5. Supervisors' responsibilities for employee development are clearly stated.

6. Procedures are clearly described, such as how employees will be notified of openings, time deadlines and data to be supplied by the employee, how requirements and qualifications will be communicated, how the selection process will work, and how job offers will be made.

7. Rules regarding compensation and advancement are included.

8. Rules regarding benefits and benefit changes as they relate to advancement are included.

A well-articulated and well-executed mobility path policy is likely to be seen by employees as being fair. A poorly-developed or nonexistent policy is likely to lead to employee claims of favoritism and discrimination.

Eligibility Criteria   An important component of an effective mobility policy is a listing of the criteria by which the organization will decide who is eligible to be considered for an open vacancy in a mobility path. In essence, these criteria restrict eligibility for recruitment to certain individuals. Usually these criteria are based upon the amount of seniority, level of experience, KSAOs, or job duties required for the job. For example, to be considered for an international assignment, the applicant may be required to be with the organization a certain length of time, have experience in a functional area in which there is a vacancy, be proficient in a foreign language, and be interested in performing new duties. These criteria need to be made very clear in the policy, otherwise unqualified people will apply and be disappointed when they are not considered. Also, the organization may be flooded with the paper work and processing of applicants who were not eligible.

Administrative Issues

Not only must mobility paths and mobility policies be established as part of the planning process, but so, too, must administrative matters. Those administrative matters include requisitions, coordination, the budget, and the recruitment guide.

Requisitions

A requisition or authorization to fill a position by higher-level management is essential to the internal recruitment process. Without a formal requisition, it is far too easy for managers to make promises or "cut deals" with employees, contrary to organizational objectives. For example, managers may promote their employees into new job titles that have not been authorized by top management. In doing so, they may create perceptions of unfairness among those with similar backgrounds who were not promoted. This action thus runs contrary to the organizational goal of fair human resource systems. Formal requisitions, thus, should always be used in internal recruitment, just as they are in external recruitment.

Coordination

Internal and external recruitment efforts need to be coordinated and synchronized via the organization's staffing philosophy. If this coordination is not done, disastrous results can occur. For example, if independent searches are conducted internally and externally, then two people may be hired for one open vacancy. If only an external recruitment search is conducted, the morale of existing employees may be reduced when they feel that they have been bypassed for a promotion. If only an internal recruitment search is conducted, the person hired may not be as qualified as someone from the external market. Because of these possibilities, internal *and* external professionals must work together with the line manager to coordinate efforts before the search for candidates begins.

To coordinate activities, two steps should be taken. First, internal staffing specialist positions should be designated to ensure that internal candidates are considered in the recruitment process. External staffing specialists are called recruiters; internal staffing specialists are often known as placement or classification professionals, to acknowledge the fact that they are responsible for placing or classifying existing employees rather than bringing in or recruiting employees from outside the organization.

Second, policies need to be created that specify the number and types of candidates sought internally and the number and types of candidates sought externally. For example, at Honeywell's Systems and Research Center in Bloomington, Minnesota, a management team meets regularly as a part of the planning and development process to make these determinations.[8]

Budget

An organization's internal recruitment budgeting process should also closely mirror the budgeting process that occurs with external recruitment. The cost per hire may, however, differ between internal and external recruitment. The fact that internal recruitment targets candidates already working for the organization does not mean that the cost per hire is necessarily less than external recruitment. Sometimes internal recruitment can be more costly than external recruitment because some of the methods involved in internal recruitment can be quite costly. For example, when internal candidates are considered for the job but not hired, they need to be counseled on what to do to further develop their careers to become competitive for the position the next time it is vacant. When a candidate is rejected with external recruiting, a simple and less costly rejection letter usually suffices.

Recruitment Guide

As with external recruitment, internal recruitment activities involve the development of a recruitment guide, a formal document that details the process to be followed to attract applicants to a vacant job. Included in the plan are details such as the time, money, and staff activities required to fill the job, as well as the steps to be taken to fill the vacancy. An example of an internal recruitment guide is shown in Exhibit 8.3.

STRATEGY DEVELOPMENT

After organizational and administrative issues have been covered in the planning phase of internal recruitment, an organization must develop a strategy to locate

EXHIBIT 8.3 Internal Recruitment Guide

Position Reassignments into New Claims Processing Center

Goal: Transfer all qualified medical claims processors and examiners from one company subsidiary to the newly developed claims processing center. Terminate those who are not well qualified for the new positions and whose existing positions are being eliminated.

Assumptions: That all employees have been notified that their existing positions in company subsidiary ABC are being eliminated and they will be eligible to apply for positions in the new claims processing center.

Hiring responsibility: Manager of Claims Processing and Manager of Claims Examining.

Other resources: Entire human resource department staff.

Time frames:
Positions posted internally on April 2, 1996
Employees may apply until April 16, 1996
Interviews will be scheduled/coordinated during week of April 19, 1996
Interviews will occur during the week of April 26, 1996
Selections made and communicated by last week in May
Total number of available positions: 60

Positions available and corresponding qualification summaries:

6 claims supervisors—4-year degree with 3 years of claims experience, including 1 year of supervisory experience.

14 claims data entry operators—6 months data entry experience. Knowledge of medical terminology helpful.

8 hospital claims examiners—12 months claims data entry/processing experience. Knowledge of medical terminology necessary.

8 physician claims examiners—12 months claims data entry/processing experience. Knowledge of medical terminology necessary.

8 dental claims examiners—12 months claims data entry/processing experience and 6 months dental claims examining experience. Knowledge of dental terminology necessary.

8 mental health claims examiners—12 months claims data entry/processing experience and 6 months mental health claims experience. Knowledge of medical and mental health terminology necessary.

8 substance abuse claims examiners—12 months claims data entry/processing experience and 6 months substance abuse experience. Knowledge of medical terminology necessary.

Transfer request guidelines: Internal candidates must submit internal transfer requests and an accompanying cover page listing all positions for which they are applying, in order of preference.

Internal candidates may apply for no more than five positions.

(continued)

EXHIBIT 8.3 Continued

Transfer requests must be complete and be signed by the employee and the employee's supervisor.

Candidate qualification review process: Transfer requests from internal candidates will be reviewed on a daily basis. Those not qualified for any positions for which they applied will be notified by phone that day, due to the large volume of requests.

All transfer requests and accompanying cover pages will be filed by the position to which they refer. If internal candidates applied for more than one position, their transfer packet will be copied so that one copy is in each position folder.

Once all candidate qualifications have been received and reviewed, each candidate's transfer packet will be copied and transmitted to the managers for review and interview selection. Due to the large number of candidates, managers will be required to interview only those candidates with the best qualifications for the available positions. Managers will notify human resources with the candidates with whom they would like interviews scheduled. Whenever possible, the manager will interview the candidate during one meeting for all of the positions applied and qualified for.

Selection guidelines: Whenever possible, the best-qualified candidates shall be selected for the available positions.

The corporation has committed to attempting to place all employees whose positions are being eliminated.

Managers reserve the right to not select employees currently on disciplinary probationary periods.

Employees should be slotted in a position with a salary grade comparable to their current salary grade. Employees' salaries shall not be reduced due to the involuntary nature of the job reassignment.

Notification of nonselection: Candidates not selected for a particular position will be notified by electronic message.

Selection notifications: Candidates selected for a position will be notified in person by the human resource staff, and will be given a confirmation letter specifying starting date, position, reporting relationship, and salary.

viable internal job applicants. It must consider where to look, how to look, and when to look.

Where to Look

The strategy for where to look must be conducted within the constraints of the general eligibility criteria for mobility. Within these constraints it requires a knowledge of closed, open, and targeted systems.[9]

Closed Internal Recruitment System

Under a closed internal recruitment system, employees are not made aware of job vacancies. The only people made aware of promotion or transfer opportunities are those who oversee placement in the human resource department, line managers with vacancies, and contacted employees. The way a vacancy is typically filled under a closed system is shown in Exhibit 8.4.

A closed system is very efficient. There are only a few steps to follow, and the time and cost involved in implementing it are minimal. However, a closed system is only as good as the files showing candidates' KSAOs. If inaccurate or out-of-date files are kept, qualified candidates may be overlooked.

Open Internal Recruitment System

Under an open internal recruitment system, employees are made aware of job vacancies. Usually this is accomplished by a job posting and bidding system. The typical steps followed in filling a vacancy under an open internal recruitment system are shown in Exhibit 8.5.

An open system gives employees a chance to measure their qualifications against those required for advancement. It helps minimize the possibility of supervisors selecting only their favorite employees for promotion or transfer. Hidden talent is often uncovered.

EXHIBIT 8.4   Closed Internal Recruitment System

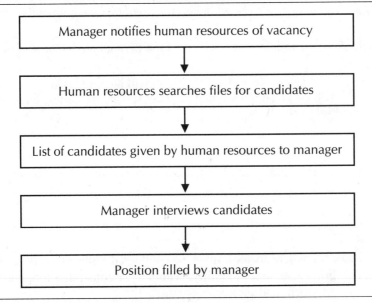

EXHIBIT 8.5   Open Internal Recruitment System

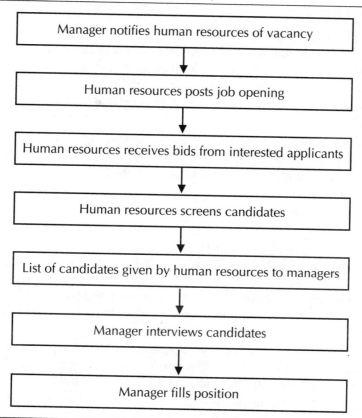

An open system may, however, create unwanted competition among employees for limited advancement opportunities. It is a very lengthy and time-consuming process to screen all candidates and provide them with feedback. Employee morale may be decreased among those who are not advanced.

Targeted System of Internal Recruitment

Under a targeted system, both open and closed steps are followed at the same time. Jobs are posted, and the human resources department conducts a search outside the job posting system. Both systems are used to cast as wide a net as possible. The large applicant pool is then narrowed down by KSAOs, seniority eligibility, demographics, and availability of applicants.

A targeted system has three advantages: a thorough search is conducted, people have equal opportunity to apply for postings, and hidden talent is uncovered. The major disadvantage with a targeted system is that it entails a very time-consuming and costly process.

Criteria for Choice of System

In an ideal world, with unlimited resources, one would choose a targeted system of internal recruitment. Resource constraints often make this choice impossible, so organizations must choose between open and closed systems. There are several criteria that need to be considered thoroughly before selecting an internal recruitment system:

1. A closed system is the least expensive in terms of search costs. However, it may lead to high legal costs if minorities and women do not have equal access to jobs. An open system is more costly; a targeted system costs the most.

2. Many managers want a person to start work immediately when they have a vacancy; a closed system offers the quickest response.

3. An open system is more likely than a closed system to identify more candidates, and hidden talent is less likely to be overlooked.

4. Some openings may require a very narrow and specialized KSAO set. A closed system may be able to identify these people quickly. An open system may be very cumbersome when only a select few meet the minimum qualifications needed to perform the job.

5. An open system may motivate migration of labor from jobs that are critical and difficult to fill. If so, then employees may create vacancies in critical areas, which in turn may create new recruitment problems.

6. A labor agreement or contract is a legally binding agreement. Whatever system is specified within must be followed.

7. An open system, where rules and regulations are known, enhances perception of fairness.

How to Look

Once it has been specified where and how in the organization individuals are likely to be found, there are several major methods that can be used to decide how to look for them: job postings, skills inventory, nominations, employee referral, and in-house temporary pool.

Job Posting

A job posting is very similar to the advertisement used in external recruitment. It spells out the duties and requirements of the job and shows how applicants can apply. Its content should be based upon the job requirements matrix. The procedures to be followed for a job posting system is shown in Exhibit 8.6. Applicants respond to job postings using a bid sheet like the one shown in Exhibit 8.7.

EXHIBIT 8.6   Recruiting and Selection Procedures—Job Posting Procedure for Small North-Central Hospital

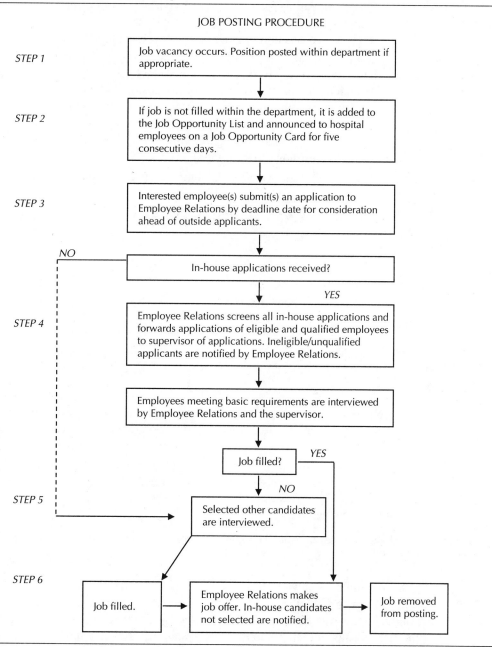

JOB POSTING PROCEDURE

STEP 1 — Job vacancy occurs. Position posted within department if appropriate.

STEP 2 — If job is not filled within the department, it is added to the Job Opportunity List and announced to hospital employees on a Job Opportunity Card for five consecutive days.

STEP 3 — Interested employee(s) submit(s) an application to Employee Relations by deadline date for consideration ahead of outside applicants.

NO — In-house applications received?   YES

STEP 4 — Employee Relations screens all in-house applications and forwards applications of eligible and qualified employees to supervisor of applications. Ineligible/unqualified applicants are notified by Employee Relations.

Employees meeting basic requirements are interviewed by Employee Relations and the supervisor.

Job filled?   YES

NO

STEP 5 — Selected other candidates are interviewed.

STEP 6 — Job filled. → Employee Relations makes job offer. In-house candidates not selected are notified. → Job removed from posting.

Source: Reprinted with permission from *Recruiting and Selection Procedures,* Personnel Policies Forum Survey No. 146, p. 34 (May 1988). Copyright 1988 by the Bureau of National Affairs, Inc. (800-372-1033).

EXHIBIT 8.7 Example of Bidding Form

INTERNAL APPLICATION FORM COVER SHEET

To apply for a posted position, interested employees should:

1. Look at the job posting notebook(s) or postings posted on the bulletin boards and choose the job or jobs that you are qualified for and interested in applying for. (Check the Qualifications section of the posting.) Make note of the deadline for applying for this position, which is indicated on the posting.

2. Complete one Internal Application Form to apply for a position or positions. This form acts as a resume/application form. Obtain your direct supervisor's signature before turning the form into human resources.

3. Indicate below the priority of the jobs for which you would like to be given consideration.

   (Priority: 1 = first choice, 2 = second choice, 3 = third choice)

Priority Job Title

_____   _____

_____   _____

_____   _____

_____   _____

_____   _____

4. Attach this cover sheet to the UHC Internal Application Form and turn both in to Karen in human resources by the application deadline appearing on the job posting.

5. Sign and date below:

_____   _____

Employee Signature   Date

Source: Reprinted with permission from United HealthCare Corporation and Physicians Health Plan of Ohio, Inc., Columbus, Ohio.

An example of a well-developed job posting system comes from National SemiConductors in Santa Clara, California.[10] Previously, at National Semi-Conductors, it was easier to find a job through external recruitment than through internal recruitment. In response to this state of affairs, a new user-friendly job posting system was developed and put on the computer for access by internal employees. Not only does the new system contain traditional job posting data for each vacant position, it shows the user how the job fits into established mobility paths and what training, education, and experience are needed to become eligible for the job. Hence, the new system communicates information about jobs and also helps to further career development planning. The system is being used currently for exempt jobs only, but plans are to use it for hourly and salaried nonexempt jobs as well.

Not all job posting systems are this advanced, and even advanced job posting systems may have some problems in administration. Examples of such difficulties include situations where employees believe that someone has been selected before the job was posted (a "bagged" job), cumbersome systems where managers and human resources personnel are overwhelmed with resumes of unqualified candidates, and criticisms that the human resources department is not doing an effective job of screening candidates for positions.[11]

Some of these problems again point to the critical importance of the job requirements matrix. A good job posting system will clearly define the requisite KSAOs needed to perform the job. By having a job requirements matrix, employees, human resources staff, and managers can do a more effective and efficient job of screening.

Another important issue with posting systems is feedback. Not only do employees need to know whether they receive the job or not, but those who do not receive the job need to be made aware of *why* they did not. Providing this feedback serves two purposes. First, it makes job posting a part of the career development system of the organization. Second, it invites future bidding on postings by candidates. If employees are not given feedback, they may be less likely to bid again for a job because they feel that their bidding attempts are futile.

An empirical study shows the characteristics of job posting systems that lead to high satisfaction by users.[12] Key characteristics include the adequacy of job descriptions, the adequacy of job notification procedures, the treatment received during the interview, the helpfulness of counseling, and the fairness of the job posting system. These characteristics should be treated as requirements of a good job posting policy.

As indicated, job posting can be done traditionally by physically posting job openings in a convenient location. Such an approach, however, can be very slow, inefficient, and create a large amount of paperwork. A faster and more efficient way to post jobs is to put them on personal computers, which also gives employees 24-hour-a-day access to job postings. Phones can be used when not all employees have access to personal computers.[13]

Skills Inventory

KSAOs that are used in making advancement decisions are stored in a skills inventory. The inventory consists of manual files or computer files for each employee. Examples of computer file screens for employees are shown in Exhibit

EXHIBIT 8.8 Sample Elements in Skills Inventory

Screen 1: Current employee data

Name:
SS #:
Department:
Position:
Supervisor:
Date in position:
Date of hire:

Screen 2: Education data

	School Attended	Degree	Major	GPA	Year(s)
High school:					
Undergrad:					
Graduate:					
Doctorate:					

Additional course work:
Certifications/licenses:
Additional training:
Company training:

Additional training recommended:

Screen 3: Company employment data

	Title	Date in Job	Performance Ratings/Dates
Present position:			
Previous positions:			

Positions in company qualified for:

Screen 4: Previous employment data

	Company	Title	From	To	Reference Quality
Prev. Empl.					
Prev. Empl.					
Prev. Empl.					
Prev. Empl.					

Screen 5: Express interests/goals

Areas of company:
Positions:
Additional training/education:

8.8. Unfortunately, many skills inventories are plagued by problems that make their usefulness suspect. One such problem is the very careful and tedious record keeping required to keep them up to date and useful. Maintenance of these files is key. Qualified candidates may be bypassed if current files are not maintained. Another problem is that too much information is sometimes recorded. Variables having little relevance to advancement decisions are included, making them redundant with other files (e.g., payroll). Managers are often overwhelmed by the sheer volume in files and, as a result, may be resistant to using a skills inventory.

A final problem that must be confronted in maintaining a skills inventory is that files must be user-friendly. Files must be understood and accepted by system users. Doing so requires the participation of users in deciding which variables are to be retained. A user-friendly data base should also have the following attributes:[14]

- simplicity of format for data collection
- easy method for updating basic information on a scheduled basis
- reasonable and efficient techniques for extracting information from the data base
- provisions for varied formats for output
- capability for statistical analysis using relational data bases
- confidentiality of information
- representativeness of data provided
- accuracy of data by audit and verification procedures
- simplicity in querying data bank
- inclusive but not unwieldy detail
- integration with other human resource files

Nominations

Nominations for internal candidates to apply for open positions can be solicited from potential supervisors and peers. They may be an excellent source of names of internal candidates as they have a great deal of familiarity with what is required to be successful in the position. They can help establish the criteria for eligibility and then, through their contacts in the organization, search for eligible candidates. Self nominations are also very useful in that they ensure that qualified candidates are not inadvertently overlooked using other applicant searching methods. This self nomination is an especially important consideration in the internal recruitment of minorities and women.

Employee Referral

Using employees to refer potential hires to the organization is a very common method of looking for candidates in external recruitment. Unfortunately, it does not appear to be used much in internal recruitment. It would seem to be an excellent method of internal recruitment, especially for larger organizations where talented employees may "slip through the cracks." As with external recruitment, employee referral programs used internally may need to rely upon formal programs with recognition for participation to get employees actively participating in making referrals. Moreover, they need to be educated on eligibility requirements to ensure that qualified personnel are referred.

In-House Temporary Pools

In-house temporary pools are not only important to the temporary staffing of organizations as the temporary need for personnel arises periodically, they are also an excellent source of permanent internal employment. From the perspective of the organization, they are a "known" commodity and require less orientation to the organization than would external hires. From the perspective of the applicant, in-house temporary employees are more likely to have realistic expectations regarding the organization and the job than external candidates. Policies must be clearly established in the organization to govern the movement of in-house temporary employees into more permanent positions. For example, accommodations must be made to replace the in-house temporary who has accepted a permanent assignment in a timely manner. Otherwise, the organization may face a shortage of temporaries to fill temporary assignments.

When to Look

A final strategic consideration an organization must make is when to look for internal candidates. As with external recruitment, consideration involves calculation of lead time and time sequence concerns.

Lead Time Concerns

A major difference between internal and external recruitment is that internal recruitment not only fills vacancies, but creates them as well. Each time a vacancy is filled with an internal candidate, a new vacancy is created in the spot vacated by the internal candidate.

As a result of this difference, it is incumbent upon the organization to do human resource planning along with internal recruitment. This human resource planning involves elements of succession planning (see Chapter 4). Such planning is essential for effective internal recruitment.[15]

Time Sequence Concerns

As previously noted, it is essential that internal and external recruitment activities be coordinated properly. This proper coordination is especially true with the timing and sequencing of events that must be laid out carefully for both recruitment and placement personnel. Many organizations start with internal recruitment followed by external recruitment to fill a vacancy. Issues that need to be addressed include how long the internal search will take place, whether external recruitment can be done concurrently with internal recruitment, and who will be selected if both an internal and external candidate are identified with relatively equal KSAOs.

SEARCHING

Once the planning and strategy development phases are conducted, then it is time to conduct the search. As with external recruitment, the search for internal recruits is activated with a requisition. Once the requisition has been approved, then the message and medium must be developed to communicate the vacancy to applicants.

Communication Message

As with external recruitment, the message to be communicated can be traditional, realistic, targeted, or attractive. A traditional message provides the applicant with little concrete or accurate information. A realistic message portrays the job as it really is including positive and negative aspects. A targeted message is one that points out how the job matches the needs of the applicant. An attractive message provides the applicant with monetary and nonmonetary inducements for accepting the invitation to interview and eventually accept a job.

Realistic messages can be communicated using a technique like a realistic job preview (RJP). This technique needs to be applied carefully for internal recruitment because as a result of their already being a member of the organization, applicants may have an accurate picture of the job.[16] Hence, an RJP may not be needed. It should not, however, be automatically assumed that all internal candidates have accurate information about the job and organization. Hence, RJPs are appropriate for internal applicants when they move to an unknown job, a newly created job, or a new geographic area including an international assignment.

Targeted messages along with inducements are likely to attract experienced internal employees. Targeted messages about the desirability of a position and the actual rewards should come directly from the job rewards matrix. Clearly, it is the information in the job rewards matrix that needs to be communicated by the hiring manager who hopes to catch an experienced employee, rather than offers of elaborate promises that the manager may not be able to keep.

Communication Medium

The actual method or medium used to communicate job openings internally may be a job posting, other written documents, potential supervisors and peers, and informal systems. An example of a very well developed job posting is shown in Exhibit 8.9. As can be seen in this posting, the duties and requirements of the job

EXHIBIT 8.9   Job Posting Form

ANNOUNCEMENT NO.: 92-25   OPENING DATE 12-14-92   CLOSING DATE:
APPLICATION MUST BE
POSTMARKED BY:

POSITION: Loan Specialist (Commercial)
              GS-1165-9/11 (1 position)

SALARY: GS-9 = $26,798–$34,835 per annum
              GS-11 = $32,423–$42,152 per annum

LOCATION: Small Business Administration, 477 Michigan Ave., Room 515
              Detroit, MI

AREA OF CONSIDERATION: Regionwide

COMPETITIVE STATUS REQUIRED: _____ Yes _X_ No

DUTIES: Incumbent performs loan processing activities such as interviewing and counseling of loan applicants, screening loan applications for eligibility, and processing applications. Makes professional analysis of loan applications and accompanying financial statements to assess the risk of granting the loan and the assurance of repayment. Determines eligibility and most beneficial type of assistance. Prescribes corrective financial or management changes to be accomplished by applicant as a prerequisite to loan approval. Prepares report of loan analysis including pro forma balance sheet, with recommendation for approval or decline. Analyzes requests for modification to loan authorizations on undisbursed loans and prepares report, with recommendation for appropriate actions. Screens applications on basis of eligibility, completeness and credit sufficiency. Counsels small business firms on SBA programs and requirements, financial needs, purchasing, profit margin, etc. Explains financing program requirements to financial institutions.

OTHER PERTINENT FACTS: This position has promotion potential to the GS-12 level. Applicants who are considered under SBA merit promotion plan procedures are subject to time-in-grade requirements. Applicants who meet the time-in-grade requirements within 45 days of the closing date will be considered. No written test is required. PAYMENT OF RELOCATION EXPENSES IS NOT AUTHORIZED.

QUALIFICATIONS: Applicant must possess one year of experience demonstrating competence in commercial loan making. Experience may have been gained in such work as reviewing and passing upon applications for commercial loans; servicing a loan portfolio of a bank or other loan association; or performing financial analysis of commercial concerns for investment purposes. Experience must be of a scope and quality sufficient to give him/her the ability to handle technical assignments commensurate with the duties of the position.

SUBSTITUTION OF EDUCATION FOR EXPERIENCE: Two full academic years of graduate level education or master's or equivalent graduate degree or LL.B. or J.D. may be substituted for experience at the GS-9 level. Three full academic years of graduate level education or Ph.D. or

(continued)

EXHIBIT 8.9   Continued

---

equivalent doctoral degree may be substituted for experience at the GS-11 level. Education may be substituted provided major study was finance, business administration, economics, accounting, mathematics, banking and credit, law, real estate operations, statistics, or other fields related to the position.

KNOWLEDGE, SKILLS, AND ABILITIES (KSA'S) USED IN THE RATING PROCESS:

To aid us in more closely matching your work experience and/or education with the actual job requirements, provide a narrative self-assessment as a supplement to your SF-171, concisely describing work you have performed which addresses the knowledge, skills and abilities described below. Include relevant paid or volunteer public or private sector experience and the dates. Do not send position descriptions, manuscripts, personal endorsements or other unsolicited materials. Please address each KSA in the following order:

1) Skill in analyzing business-related financial statements such as statements of assets and liabilities, statements of earning for the purpose of determining repayment risks.

2) Knowledge of laws and customs governing negotiable instruments, transfer of title to chattels and realty, contracts and assignment of collateral.

3) Knowledge of economic-related factors and trends and their impact on business.

4) Knowledge of business financial structures and management practices.

APPLICANTS WILL BE EVALUATED ON THE FOLLOWING CRITERIA:

1. Experience Documented on Application

2. Narrative Self-assessment of KSA's Listed Above

3. Education (Merit promotion procedures only)

4. Training (within last 5 years) (Merit promotion procedures only)

5. Awards (within last 5 years) (Merit promotion procedures only)

6. Annual Performance Appraisal (Merit promotion procedures only)

APPLICATION REQUIREMENTS

Applicants should submit the following materials:

1. Standard Form 171—Application for Federal Employment

2. Narrative response to knowledge, skills and abilities listed above

3. Copy of last appraisal under an annual performance rating system (only for consideration under merit promotion procedures)

4. Standard Form 15—Application for 10-Point Veteran Preference, if applicable (only for consideration under competitive examining procedures)

Candidates will NOT routinely be contacted to provide missing information concerning their experience, education, veteran's preference, citizenship, etc. Application materials will be retained in the merit promotion file or competitive examining case file and will not be returned to applicant.

(continued)

EXHIBIT 8.9 Continued

The evaluation procedures used to evaluate applications depend upon whether or not the applicant has competitive status. Applicants who have competitive status (current Federal employees serving on career or career-conditional appointments, or former employees eligible for reinstatement to the federal service) may be considered under both government-wide competitive examining procedures and SBA merit promotion plan procedures. Applicants with competitive status who wish to be considered under both procedures MUST submit two complete applications. When only one application is received from a status applicant, it will be considered under SBA merit promotion procedures only, unless a clear and unequivocal statement is received from the applicant that he or she wishes to be considered under competitive examining procedures only.

COMPLETED APPLICATION MATERIALS SHOULD BE SUBMITTED TO:

U.S. Small Business Administration
230 S. Dearborn Street, Room 580
Chicago, IL 60604
ATTN: Kay Yount

For information call (312) 353-4695.

IMPORTANT INFORMATION—READ CAREFULLY.

The use of U.S. Government postage-paid envelopes for the filing of job applications is a violation of the Office of Personnel Management and Postal Service regulations. Penalties include fines of up to $300 and/or disciplinary action under SBA regulations.
The Defense Authorization Act of 1986 requires all males born after 12/31/59 to register under the Military Selective Service Act. Failure to register may prohibit appointment in this agency.

Any individual eligible for consideration under special hiring authorities, e.g., handicapped, and VRA, etc. may apply for this position. Please indicate on SF 171 if you are in one of these categories.

SBA—AN EQUAL OPPORTUNITY EMPLOYER

SBA FORM 534 (1-90)

Source: U.S. Small Business Administration, Chicago, 1993.

are clearly defined as are the eligibility requirements. To insure consistency and fair treatment, job postings are usually coordinated by the human resources department.

Other written documents used to communicate a vacancy may include a description of the organization and location as well as a description of the job. A brochure, videocassette, or diskette can be created to actually show, as well as describe, what the organization and the location of the organization is really like. This message may be of critical importance to the applicant who may, for example, be asked to relocate to a new geographic area or to accept an international assignment.

Potential supervisors and peers can be used to describe to the internal applicant how the position they are considering fits into the larger organizational picture. Supervisors will have knowledge about how the position fits with the strategic direction of the organization. Hence, they can communicate information regarding the expansion or contraction of the business unit within which the organization resides. Moreover, supervisors can convey the mobility paths and requirements for future movement by the applicants within the business unit should they be hired. Peers can be used to supplement these supervisory observations to give candidates a realistic look at what actually happens by way of career development.

Informal systems exist in organizations where organizational members communicate with one another about job vacancies to be filled internally in the absence of verifiable information. The problem with "word of mouth," the "grapevine," and "hall talk" is that it can be a highly selective, inaccurate, and haphazard method of communicating information. It is selective because, by accident or design, not all employees hear about vacant jobs. Talented personnel, including minorities and women, may thus be overlooked. It is inaccurate because it relies on second- or thirdhand information, and important details, such as actual job requirements and job rewards, are omitted or distorted as they are passed from person to person. Informal methods are also haphazard in that there is no regular communication channel specifying set times for communicating job information. As a result of these problems, informal systems are not to be encouraged.

APPLICANT REACTIONS

A glaring omission in the research literature is a lack of attention paid to studying the reactions of applicants to the internal recruitment process. This lapse stands in stark contrast to the quantity of research conducted on reactions to the external recruitment process. One notable exception in the internal recruitment process is the study of perceived fairness. Given limited opportunities for promotion and transfer, issues of fairness often arise over mobility decisions within an organization. Issues of fairness can be broken down into the categories of distributive and procedural justice.[17] Distributive justice refers to how fair the employee perceives the actual decision to be (e.g., promote or not promote). This particular aspect of fairness is very salient today because there are a large number of baby boomers competing for the few positions at the top of organizational hierarchies. At the same time, many organizations are eliminating middle management positions. Procedural justice refers to how fair the employee perceives the process (e.g., policies and procedures) that leads to the promotion or transfer decision to be.[18] Reviews of the evidence suggest that procedures may be nearly as great a source of dissatisfaction to employees as are decisions.[19] In some organizations, dissatisfaction arises as a result of the fact that there is no formal policy regarding promotion and transfer opportunities. In other organizations, there may be a formal policy, but it may not be followed. In yet other organizations, it may be who you know, rather than what you know, that serves as the criterion that determines advancement. Finally, in some organizations there is outright discrimination against women and minorities. All of these examples are violations of procedural justice and likely to be seen as unfair.

The concepts of procedural and distributive justice indicate that organizations should routinely survey the reactions of organizational members to determine the effectiveness of the internal recruitment process. An example of such a study examining applicants' reactions to job posting, is shown in Exhibit 8.10. The first step in this study was to generate a list of questionnaire items showing characteristics of a job posting system. As can be seen, these items closely mirror the concepts of procedural and distributive justice. Next, the questionnaire items were

EXHIBIT 8.10 Evaluation of a Job Posting System

Item	N	Applicants' Response (Percent)		
		Favorable	Neutral	Unfavorable
Adequacy of job description	382	39.7	35.9	24.3
Adequacy of job notification procedures	390	42.0	36.9	21.0
Difficulty of completing application	197	87.3	9.1	3.5
Quality of handbook	155	76.8	18.7	4.5
Treatment during interview	152	61.8	18.4	19.7
How well reasons for nonacceptance were explained	87	23.0	17.2	59.8
How well job requirements match those in job description	79	60.8	24.1	15.2
How well worker met job demands	76	94.8	3.9	1.3
Helpfulness of counseling	52	28.8	26.9	44.2
Effect on job mobility	362	65.2	24.9	9.9
Fairness of job posting system	367	35.8	28.0	34.6
Satisfaction with job posting system	378	28.8	26.9	36.2
Was handbook read?	403	38.6	—	61.4
Did applicant receive a job offer?	173	44.5	—	55.5
Was counseling sought?	403	12.5	—	87.5
Was applicant considered for position?	183	82.5	—	17.5
Average number of times interviewed	153 Mean = 1.83			

Source: L. W. Kleinman and K. J. Clark, "Users' Satisfaction With Job Posting," *HR Magazine,* 1984, 29(9) pp. 104–110. Reprinted with the permission of HR Magazine (formerly Personnel Administrator) published by the Society for Human Resource Management, Alexandria, VA.

passed out to employees to gather their reactions. These reactions were tallied and summarized, as shown in Exhibit 8.10, according to the percentage of employees who had "favorable," "neutral," or "unfavorable" reactions to each of the characteristics of the job posting system. It can be seen that applicants had diverse reactions to the system. Though not shown, applicants' reactions to characteristics of the job posting system were also correlated with overall satisfaction with the system. The three largest correlations with satisfaction involved the fairness of the job posting system, effect on job mobility, and treatment during the interview.

This exhibit is a good illustration of how applicant reactions can be measured for job posting. The same steps can be followed to evaluate applicant reactions to other steps in the internal recruitment process.

TRANSITION TO SELECTION

As with external recruitment, once a job seeker has been identified and attracted to a new job, the organization needs to prepare the person for the selection process. It should not be assumed that just because job seekers come from inside the organization they will automatically know and understand the selection procedures. With the rapid advances being made in selection methods, the applicant may be unaware of new selection methods being used that are different from those used previously to hire the applicant to a previous job. Even if the same selection methods are being used, the applicant may need to be "refreshed" on the process, as a considerable period of time may have transpired between the current and previous selection decisions.

An example of an organization that has done an excellent job of preparing internal job seekers to become applicants is the Public Works Agency for the County of Sacramento, California.[20] The county uses a panel of interviewers together, rather than a series of individual interviews, to make selection decisions. For many lower-level employees in the maintenance department this approach was a first-time experience. Consequently, they were apprehensive about this process because they had no previous experience with the internal selection process. In response to this situation, the human resources group initially conducted classroom training classes to describe the process to applicants. However, this was a very time-consuming process for the staff so they replaced the classroom training with videos. One major component of the video was the preparation required prior to the panel interview. Instructions here included appropriate dress and materials to review. Another major component of the video depicted what happens to the applicant during the panel interview. This component included instructions on types of questions to be asked, the process to be followed, and do's and don't's in answering the panel interview questions. A final component of the video was testimonials from previous exam takers who have become managers. They explain from an organizational perspective what the organization is looking for, as well as study tips and strategies.

LEGAL ISSUES

The mobility of people within the organization, particularly upward, has long been a matter of EEO/AA concern. The workings of the internal labor market rely heavily on internal recruitment activities. As with external recruitment, internal recruitment activities can operate in exclusionary ways, resulting in unequal promotion opportunities, rates, and results for certain groups of employees, particularly women and minorities. Revised Order No. 4 specifically addresses internal recruitment as a part of the federal contractor's AAP. Seniority systems are likewise subject to legal scrutiny, particularly regarding the determination of what constitutes a bona fide system under the law. More recently, promotion systems have been studied as they relate to the "glass ceiling" effect and the kinds of barriers that have been found to stifle the rise of minorities and women upward in organizations.

Revised Order No. 4

Revised Order No. 4 (see Appendix B) treats internal recruitment as a part of an AAP in some detail, since an AAP addresses both seniority systems and promotion. Regarding seniority systems, the order requires the organization to make an in-depth analysis of several facets of HR programs that may lead to underutilization. One such facet is seniority practices and seniority provisions in labor contracts and applies to all seniority-based internal staffing systems, regardless of whether or not they are governed by the provisions of a labor contract. Unfortunately, the order is silent on what constitutes an in-depth examination of a seniority system.

For promotion systems specifically, the order is explicit in its suggestions for the organization. Most of these pertain to recruitment, though some also spill over into selection. According to the order, the contractor should ensure that minority and female employees are given equal opportunity for promotion. Suggestions for achieving this result include:

- Post or otherwise announce promotion opportunities
- Make an inventory of current minority and female employees to determine academic, skill, and experience level of individual employees
- Initiate necessary remedial job training and workstudy programs
- Develop and implement formal employee evaluation programs
- Make certain "worker specifications" have been validated on job performance–related criteria (neither minority nor female employees should be required to possess higher qualifications than those of the lowest qualified incumbent)

- When apparently qualified minority or female employees are passed over for upgrading, require supervisory personnel to submit written justification

- Establish formal career counseling programs to include attitude development, education aid, job rotation, buddy systems and similar programs

- Review seniority practices and seniority clauses in union contracts to ensure such practices or clauses are nondiscriminatory and do not have a discriminatory effect.

As can be seen, the order contains a broad range of suggestions for reviewing and improving promotion systems. In terms of recruitment itself, the order appears to favor developing KSAO-based information about employees as well as an open promotion system characterized by job posting and cautious use of seniority as a basis for governing upward mobility.

Bona Fide Seniority Systems

The law (see Chapter 3) explicitly permits the use of "bona fide" seniority systems, as long as they are not the result of an intention to discriminate. This position confronts the organization with a serious dilemma. Past discrimination in external staffing may have resulted in a predominantly white male workforce. A change to a nondiscriminatory external staffing system may increase the presence of women and minorities within an organization, but they will have less seniority there than the white males. If eligibility for promotion is based on seniority and/or if seniority is an actual factor considered in promotion decisions, then those with less seniority will have a lower incidence of promotion. Thus, the seniority system will have an adverse impact on women and minorities, even though there is no current intention to discriminate. Is such a seniority system a bona fide one?

Two points are relevant here. First, the law never defines the term seniority system. Generally, however, any practice that uses length of employment as a basis for making decisions, such as promotion decisions, is interpreted as a seniority system. Thus, seniority systems can and do occur outside the context of a collective bargaining agreement.[21]

Second, current interpretation is that, in the absence of a discriminatory intent, virtually any seniority system is likely to be bona fide, even if it causes adverse impact.[22] This interpretation creates an incentive for the organization not to change its current seniority-based practices or systems. Other pressures, such as Revised Order No. 4 or a voluntary AAP, create an incentive to change in order to eliminate the occurrence of adverse impact in promotion. The organization thus must carefully consider exactly what its posture will be toward seniority practices and systems within the context of its overall AAP.

The Glass Ceiling

The glass ceiling is a term used to characterize strong but invisible barriers for women and minorities to promotion in the organization, particularly to the highest levels. Evidence demonstrating the existence of a glass ceiling is substantial. The composition of the U.S. labor force is approximately 54.5% male and 45.5% female, and 79% white and 21% minority. In the Fortune 2,000 industrial and service companies, however, only 5% of the senior level managers are women, and of that 5% virtually all are white. In the Fortune 500 companies, 97% of senior managers are white, and 95% are male.

As one goes down the hierarchy or looks across specific industries, however, a more mixed pattern of evidence is found. Across all executive, administrative, and managerial occupations, 52% are held by males (40% white and 12% minority), and 48% are held by females (36% white and 12% minority); in these occupations the percentage of white males ranges from 75% in construction to 42% in retail to 16% in health services and social services.[23] Thus, the closer to the top of the hierarchy, the thicker is the glass in the ceiling. At lower levels, the glass becomes much thinner. There are substantial variations in this pattern, though, across industries.

Even within industries there appear to be large differences in prevalence of a glass ceiling. In the financial sector, for example, 66% of officials and managers at Wells Fargo are women, as opposed to 17% at Loews. For the technology sector at AT&T, 45% of officials and managers are women, while 9% are at Raytheon.[24]

Where glass ceilings exist, there are two important questions to ask. What are the reasons for a lack of upward mobility and representation for minorities and women at higher levels of the organization? What changes need to be made, especially staffing-related ones, to help shatter the glass ceiling?

Barriers to Mobility

The Federal Glass Ceiling Commission conducted a four-year study of glass ceiling issues, including barriers to mobility. It identified three sets of barriers:[25]

- societal—access to educational opportunities; stereotyping, prejudice, and bias related to race, gender, ethnicity
- governmental—weakness in collection and dissemination of glass ceiling information; lack of vigorous and consistent monitoring and law enforcement
- internal—lack of outreach recruitment practices, management training, mentoring, tailor training and job assignments in revenue-producing areas, access to critical developmental assignments on committees and task forces; initial selection and placement on jobs in staff and professional jobs outside the upward pipeline to top jobs; biased rating and testing systems; little access to informal networks of communication; counter productive behavior and harassment by colleagues

An instructive illustration of these barriers, particularly the internal ones, comes from a 21-company study of men and women in sales careers.[26] The study found that 41% of women and 45% of men were eager to move into management, but the women were much less optimistic of their chances of getting promoted. While the sales forces studied were 26% female, only 14% of sales managers were female. The study portrayed "a survivalist culture where career paths are more like obscure jungle trails and where most women say they experience sexual harassment." The study also found "recruiters' use of potentially discriminatory screening tests, managers' negative stereotypes about women, women's lack of access to career-boosting mentors and networks, and difficulty entertaining customers in traditional ways such as fishing and golf outings." Saleswomen were also highly dependent on their mostly male managers for job and territory assignments, which were often based on stereotypes about willingness to travel, relocate and work long hours.

Overcoming Barriers

The Federal Glass Ceiling Commission also studied in-depth the practices found in many organizations that were successfully changing themselves to overcome barriers to upward advancement for women and minorities. They concluded that such glass ceiling initiatives had the following characteristics in common:[27]

- They have CEO support.
- They are part of the strategic business plan.
- They are specific to the organization.
- They are inclusive; they do not exclude white non-Hispanic men.
- They address preconceptions and stereotypes.
- They emphasize and require accountability for promoting women and minorities.
- They track progress.
- They are comprehensive.

Based upon their findings and deliberations, the Commission issued a set of 12 recommendations for eliminating the glass ceiling. A summary of those recommendations is provided in Exhibit 8.11.

In terms of specific staffing practices that are desirable for eliminating the glass ceiling, we offer the following suggestions. Barriers to upward mobility can be addressed and removed, at least in part, through internal recruitment activities. Internal recruitment planning needs to involve the design and operation of internal labor markets that facilitate the identification and flows of people to jobs throughout the organization. This may very well conflict with seniority-based practices or seniority systems, both of which are likely to be well-entrenched. Organizations simply have to make hard and clear choices about the role(s) that seniority will play in promotion systems.

Exhibit 8.11 Summary of Glass Ceiling Commission Recommendations

For Business

- Demonstrate CEO commitment
- Include diversity in all strategic business plans; hold line managers accountable for results
- Select and promote qualified individuals; expand recruitment pools; seek candidates from noncustomary sources, backgrounds and experiences
- Use Affirmative Action
- Prepare minorities and women for senior positions; enhance developmental experiences; provide mentoring
- Provide training throughout the organization to improve sensitivity to gender, racial and ethnic differences
- Adopt policies that accommodate the balance between work and family responsibilities
- Adopt workplace practices that emphasize high performance

For Government

- Be a leader in eliminating own glass ceilings
- Strengthen enforcement of antidiscrimination laws
- Improve data collection about women and minorities in the workforce and organizations
- Provide for public disclosure of diversity data, especially for senior positions

---

Source: Federal Glass Ceiling Commission, Washington, D.C., 1995.

In terms of recruitment strategy, where to look for employees looms as a major factor in potential change. The organization must increase its scanning capabilities and horizons to identify candidates to promote throughout the organization. In particular, this requires looking across functions for candidates, rather than merely promoting within an area (from sales to sales manager to district manager, for example). Candidates should thus be recruited through both traditional and innovative career paths.

Recruitment sources have to be more open and accessible to far-ranging sets of candidates. Informal, word-of-mouth, and "good old boy" sources do not suffice. Job posting and other recruitment strategies that encourage openness of vacancy notification and candidate application will become necessary.

The timing of internal recruitment has to be carefully integrated with overall business plans. Promotions may have to be speeded up or slowed down in order to fit the business plan. With business downturns, for example, care must be taken to ensure that the upward mobility of women and minorities is not thwarted.

Finally, it should be recognized, and acted upon, that recruitment activities do not suffice to bring about the desired changes. They must be supported by a myriad of other HR activities, especially in the compensation, and training and development, areas. In addition, the organization has to make its managers responsible and accountable for the desired demographics in promotion results.

As organizations seek to change their staffing practices along the lines suggested above, they should be mindful of both sticks and carrots for tackling the problem. The sticks are the threat of legal inspection and sanction. For example, the OFCCP reached an out-of-court settlement with Georgia Power that involved $132,000 in back pay and $79,500 in salary adjustments to 23 women and minorities; an additional $108,000 was earmarked for diversity training and recruitment. The OFCCP alleged that Georgia Power had discriminated against women and minorities by placing them in lower pay grades than men doing comparable work, overlooking qualified women and minorities by not following its own selection procedures, and promoting several nonminority men whose names did not appear on either the job posting or career search lists.[28]

On the carrot side, there are many organizations making great strides forward in eliminating glass ceilings. Their experiences should encourage and reinforce the positive aspects of change for other organizations. Just as it provides a stick, the OFCCP also provides a carrot in the form of EVE (Exemplary Voluntary Efforts) awards to federal contractors for their leadership in creating programs to enhance diversity and shatter the glass ceiling. Brief descriptions of some of these awards are shown in Exhibit 8.12.

SUMMARY

The steps involved in the internal recruitment process closely parallel those in the external recruitment process. These steps include planning, strategy development, and communication. With internal recruitment, the search is conducted inside rather than outside the organization. Where both internal and external searches are conducted, they need to be coordinated with one another.

The planning stage requires that the applicant population be identified. To do so requires an understanding of mobility paths in the organization and mobility path policies. To get access to the internal applicant population, attention must be devoted in advance of the search to requisitions, number and type of contacts, the budget, and development of a recruitment guide.

In terms of strategy development, a closed, open, or targeted system can be used to decide where to look. How to look requires a knowledge of job postings, skills inventories, nominations, employee referrals, and in-house temporary pools. When to look requires consideration of lead time and time sequence concerns.

When searching for candidates, the message to be communicated can be traditional, realistic, targeted, or attractive. Which approach is best to use depends upon the applicants, job, and organization. The message is usually communicated with a job posting. It should, however, be supplemented with other mediums including other written documents, and potential peers' and supervisors' input. In-

---

Exhibit 8.12   Examples of Award Winning Programs to Increase Diversity and Eliminate the Glass Ceiling

---

CBS, INC., New York, N.Y., is recognized for its extraordinary efforts in achieving broad-based minority and female representation and for its executive development programs and overall employment programs that support affirmative action and diversity. CBS was cited for its history of employing a large number of women and minorities for professional and technical jobs in the newsroom during the past two decades. CBS employs 64,000 nationwide.

MOBIL CORPORATION, Fairfax, Va., the nation's second largest oil company, employs 58,000 individuals worldwide. It is being recognized for its many programs that support affirmative action and equal employment opportunity, for its career and management development programs, and its work-and-family-life programs.

SEATTLE FIRST NATIONAL BANK, Seattle, Wash., is being recognized both for a pilot program that addresses the needs of Native Americans in the state and a long-term employment and education program for high school students.

THE LAW COMPANY, Wichita, Kan., a construction company with 135 employees, is being recognized for its outreach efforts to joint-venture and subcontract with minority and disadvantaged vendors, and for providing free technical and legal assistance to nonprofit organizations.

ATLANTA REGIONAL LIAISON GROUP (ARLG), founded in 1989, has a membership of 40 companies. The group has strengthened relationships with OFCCP and contractors through a public education program which keeps members informed about various issues and concerns. Since its founding, ARLG has coordinated conferences on diversity in the workplace, glass ceiling issues, and training and support of senior citizens.

Source: U.S. Department of Labor, *News*, Sept. 13, 1995.

---

formal communication methods without information that cannot be verified are to be discouraged.

The organization needs to provide the applicant with assistance for the transition to selection. This assistance requires that the applicant be made fully aware of the selection process and how to best prepare for it. Taking this step, along with providing well-developed job postings and clearly articulated mobility paths and policies in the organization, should help applicants to see the internal recruitment system as a fair one.

Internal recruitment activities have been the object of close legal scrutiny. Beginning with Revised Order No. 4, which contains specific provisions about seniority-based practices and labor contract provisions, as well as several suggestions regarding promotion systems, the relevant laws permit "bona fide" seniority systems, as long as they are not intentionally used to discriminate. Seniority systems may have the effect of impeding promotions for women and minorities because these groups have not had the opportunity to accumulate an equivalent amount of seniority to that of white males. The glass ceiling refers to invisible barriers to upward advancement, especially to the top levels, for minorities and women. Studies of promotion systems indicate that internal recruitment practices contribute to this barrier. As a portion of an overall strategy to shatter the glass ceiling, changes are now being experimented with for opening up internal recruitment

DISCUSSION QUESTIONS

1. Traditional career paths emphasize strict upward mobility within an organization. How does mobility differ in organizations with innovative career paths? List three innovative career paths discussed in this chapter, describing how mobility occurs in each.
2. A sound policy regarding promotion is important. List the characteristics necessary for an effective promotion policy.
3. Compare and contrast a closed internal recruitment system with an open internal recruitment system.
4. What information should be included in the targeted internal communication message?
5. Applicant reactions and perceptions of the fairness of the internal recruitment process are an important consideration when evaluating the effectiveness of the process. Describe the two categories of fairness discussed in this chapter.
6. For each of the recommendations from the Glass Ceiling Commission (Exhibit 8.11), what are specific examples of how organizations could change in order to remove barriers to mobility?

APPLICATIONS

Recruitment in a Changing Internal Labor Market

Mitchell Shipping Lines is a distributor of goods on the Great Lakes in the United States. Not only does it distribute goods, but it also manufactures shipping containers used to store the goods while in transit. The name of the subsidiary that manufactures those containers is Mitchell-Cole Manufacturing, and the president and chief executive officer is Zoe Brausch.

Brausch is in the midst of converting the manufacturing system from an assembly line to autonomous work teams. Each team will be responsible for producing a separate type of container, and each team will have different tools, machinery, and manufacturing routines for its particular type of container. Members of each team will have the job title "assembler," and each team will be headed by a permanent "leader." Brausch would like all leaders to come from the ranks of current employees, both in terms of the initial set of leaders, and leaders in the future as vacancies arise. In addition, she wants employee movement across teams to be discouraged in order to build team identity and cohesion. The current internal labor market, however, presents a formidable potential obstacle to her internal staffing goals.

Based on a long history at the container manufacturing facility, employees are treated like union employees even though the facility is nonunion. Such treatment was desired many years ago as a strategy to remain nonunion. It was management's belief that if employees were treated like union employees, there should be no need for employees to vote for a union. A cornerstone of the strategy is use of what everyone in the facility calls the "blue book." The blue book looks like a typical labor contract, and it spells out all terms and conditions of employment. Many of those terms apply to internal staffing, and are very typical of traditional mobility systems found in unionized work settings. Specifically, internal transfer and promotions are governed by a facility-wide job posting system. A vacancy is posted throughout the facility and remains open for 30 days; an exception to this is identified entry-level jobs that are filled only externally. Any employee with two or more years of seniority is eligible to "bid" for any posted vacancy; employees with less seniority may also bid, but they are considered for positions only if no two-year-plus employees apply or are chosen. Internal applicants are assessed by the hiring manager and a representative from the HR department. They review applicants' seniority, relevant experience, past performance appraisals, and other special KSAOs. The blue book requires that the most senior employee who meets the desired qualifications should receive the transfer or promotion. Thus, seniority is weighted heavily in the decision.

Brausch is worried about this current internal labor market, especially for recruiting and choosing team leaders. These leaders will likely be required to have many KSAOs that are more important than seniority, and KSAOs likely to not even be positively related to seniority. For example, team leaders will need to have advanced computer, communication, and interpersonal skills. Brausch thinks these skills will be critical for team leaders to have, and that they will more likely be found among junior rather than senior employees. Brausch is in a quandary. She asks for your responses to the following questions:

1. Should seniority be eliminated as an eligibility standard for bidding on jobs—meaning no longer giving the two-year-plus employees priority?

2. Should the job posting system simply be eliminated? If so, what should it be replaced with?

3. Should a strict promotion-from-within policy be maintained? Why or why not?

4. How could career mobility paths be developed that would allow across-team movement without threatening team identity and cohesion?

5. If a new internal labor market system is to be put in place, how should it be communicated to employees?

Creating a Computerized Skills Inventory

Many organizations are now in the process of taking employees' personnel files and putting them on the computer, thus creating a computerized skills inventory. Attention must be devoted in advance to which data needs to be put on the computer and why. To make these decisions, one needs to be concerned about how each set of data entered into the computer will be used for making human resource decisions. The purpose of this application is to have you confront two major issues involved in creating a computerized skills inventory. Specifically:

1. What are the steps in a process you would use to determine which employee data, especially KSAO data, should be contained in the skills inventory?
2. What are examples, in general, of the kinds of data you would likely include in the skills inventory?

ENDNOTES

1. P. M. Osterman, "Internal Labor Markets in a Changing Environment: Models and Evidence," in D. Lewin, O. S. Mitchell, and P. Sherer (eds.), *Research Frontiers in Industrial Relations and Human Resources* (Madison, WI: Industrial Relations Research Association), pp. 273–308; P. D. Sherer, "Labor Market Balkanization Revisited: Variation in Internal Labor Markets and Employment Arrangements," *IRRA Proceedings*, 1990, Washington DC, pp. 458–466; M. L. Wachter and R. D. Wright, "The Economics of Internal Labor Markets," *Industrial Relations*, 1990, 29(2), pp. 240–262; P. Osterman (ed.) *International Labor Markets* (Cambridge, MA: The MIT Press, 1984); P. Doeringer and M. Piore, *Internal Labor Markets and Manpower Analysis* (Lexington: Health, 1971); R. P. Althauser and A. L. Kalleberg, "Firms, Occupations, and the Structure of Labor Markets," in I. Berg (ed.), *Sociological Perspectives on Labor Markets* (New York: Academic Press, 1981), pp. 119–149; L. T. Pinfield and M. F. Berner, "Employment Systems: Toward a Coherent Conceptualization of Internal Labor Markets," in G. Ferris (ed.) *Research in Personnel and Human Resources Management*, Vol. 12 (Greenwich, CT: JAI Press, 1994), pp. 41–78; W. E. Halal, "From Hierarchy to Enterprise: Internal Markets are the New Foundation of Management," *Academy of Management Executive*, 1994, 8(4), pp. 69–83.

2. J. C. Anderson, G. T. Milkovich, and A. Tsui, "A Model of Intra-organizational Mobility," *Academy of Management Review*, 1981, 6(4), pp. 529–538; J. N. Baron, "Organizational Perspectives on Stratification," in R. F. Turner and J. F. Short, Jr. (eds.), *Annual Review of Sociology* (Palo Alto, CA: Annual Reviews, 1985), pp. 37–69.

3. C. Harkin, "Boost Morale to Gain Productivity: Lattice Rather Than Ladder Career Paths Keep Morale High in Flatter Organizations," *HR Magazine*, Feb. 1993, pp. 46–49; G. Fuchsberg, "Parallel Lines: Companies Create New Ways to Promote Employees without Making Them Bosses," *Wall Street Journal*, Apr. 21, 1993, pp. R4–R7; R. W. Goddard, "Lateral Moves Enhance Careers," *HR Magazine*, Dec. 1990, pp. 69–74; S. Shellenberger, "Allowing Fast Trackers to Stay in One Place," *Wall Street Journal*, Jan. 7, 1992, p. B1; B. Nussbaum, "A Career Survival Kit," *Business Week*, Oct. 7, 1991, pp. 98–99.

4. J. E. Rosenbaum, "Tournament Mobility: Career Patterns in a Corporation," *Administrative Science Quarterly*, 1979, 24, pp. 220–241.

5. W. T. Markham, S. L. Harlan, and E. J. Hackett, "Promotion Opportunity in Organizations: Causes and Consequences," in K. M. Rowland and G. R. Ferris (eds.), *Research in Personnel and Human Resources Management*, 1987, 5, pp.223–287.

6. Farewell, Fast Track: Promotions and Raises Are Scarcer: So What Will Energize Managers?" *Business Week*, Dec. 10, 1990, pp. 192–198.

7. F. K. Foulkes, *Personnel Policies in Large Nonunion Companies* (Englewood Cliffs, NJ: Prentice-Hall, 1980); R. D. Connor and R. L. Fjersted, "Internal Personnel Maintenance," in D. Yoder and H. G. Heneman Jr. (eds.), ASPA Handbook of Personnel and Industrial Relations (Washington, DC: Bureau of National Affairs, 1979), pp. 4-203 to 4-234.

8. National Foreman's Institute, "The Need for Hiring: A Second Look," *Employee Relations and Human Resources Bulletin* (Waterford, CT: author), Feb. 21, 1993, Report No. 1778, Section 1, p. 7.

9. L. E. Albright, "Staffing Policies and Strategies," in D. Yoder and H. G. Heneman, Jr. (eds.), *ASPA Handbook of Personnel and Industrial Relations* (Washington, DC: Bureau of National Affairs, 1979), pp. 4-1 to 4-34; Foulkes, *Personnel Policies in Large Nonunion Companies*.

10. M. Moravec, "Effective Job Posting Fills Dual Needs," *HR Magazine*, Sept. 1990, pp. 76–80.

11. Foulkes, *Personnel Policies in Large Nonunion Companies*.

12. L. W. Kleinman and K. J. Clark, "Users' Satisfaction with Job Posting," *Personnel Administrator*, 1984, 29(9), pp. 104–110.

13. R. D. Connor and R. L. Fjersted, "Internal Personnel Maintenance"; W. C. DeLone, "Telephone Job Posting Cuts Costs," *Personnel Journal*, Apr. 1993, pp. 115–118.

14. Foulkes, *Personnel Policies in Large Nonunion Companies*; Connor and Fjersted, "Internal Personnel Maintenance."

15. C. Borwick, "Integrating Succession Planning and Employment: A Necessary Step," *EMA Journal*, 1992, 7(4), pp. 24–29.

16. R. J. Vanderberg and V. Scarpello, "The Matching Model: An Examination of the Processes Underlying Realistic Job Previews," *Journal of Applied Psychology*, 1990, 75(1) pp. 60–67.

17. J. Greenberg, "A Taxonomy of Organizational Justice Theories," *Academy of Management Review*, 1987, 12, pp. 9–22.

18. R. Folger and J. Greenberg, "Procedural Justice: An Interpretive Analysis of Personnel Systems," in K. M. Rowland and G. R. Ferris (eds.), *Research in Personnel and Human Resources Management*, (Greenwich, CT: JAI Press, 1985), pp. 141–183.

19. F. K. Foulkes, *Personnel Policies in Large Nonunion Companies*, (Englewood Cliffs, NJ: Prentice-Hall, 1980); M. London and S. A. Stumpf, *Managing Careers* (Reading, MA: Addison Wesley, 1982); Markham, Harlan, and Hackett, "Promotion Opportunity in Organizations: Causes and Consequences"; S. A. Stumpf and M. London, "Management Promotions: Individual and Organizational Factors Influencing the Decision Process," *Academy of Management Review*, 1981, 6(4), pp. 539–549.

20. "Panic or Pass—Preparing for Your Oral Board Review," *IPMA News*, July 1995, p. 2.

21. Bureau of National Affairs, *Fair Employment Practices* (Washington, DC: author, periodically updated), pp. 421:161–166.

22. Bureau of National Affairs, *Fair Employment Practices*, pp. 421:161–166.

23. Federal Glass Ceiling Commission, "Good For Business: Making Full Use of the Nation's Human Capital—Fact-Finding Report of the Federal Glass Ceiling Commission," *Daily Labor Report*, Bureau of National Affairs, March 17, 1995, Special Supplement.

24. "Corporate Rankings: The First and the Last," *Wall Street Journal* March 24, 1994, p. A8.

25. Federal Glass Ceiling Commission, "Good For Business: Making Full Use of the Nation's Human Capital," p. S6.

26. S. Shellenberger, "Sales Offers Women Fairer Pay, But Bias Lingers," *Wall Street Journal*, Jan. 24, 1995, p. B1.

27. Federal Glass Ceiling Commission, "Good For Business: Making Full Use of the Nation's Human Capital," p. S19.

28. U.S. Department of Labor, "Settlements of Glass Ceiling Reviews to Provide $473,674 in Back Pay, Salary Adjustments to 68 Women and Minorities," *News*, Sept. 15, 1994, p. 1.

STAFFING ORGANIZATIONS MODEL

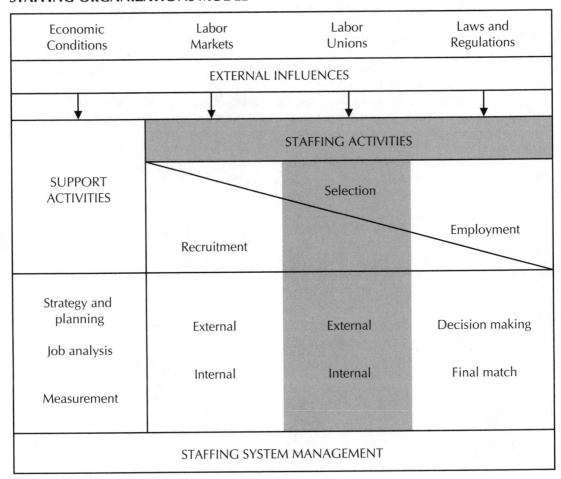

PART FOUR

Staffing Activities: Selection

CHAPTER NINE

External Selection I

Preliminary Issues
The Logic of Prediction
The Nature of Predictors
Development of the Selection Plan
Selection Sequence

Initial Assessment Methods
Resumes and Cover Letters
Application Blanks
Biographical Information
Reference Reports
Handwriting Analysis
Literacy Testing
Genetic Screening
Initial Interview
Choice of Initial Assessment Methods

Legal Issues
Disclaimers
Reference Checks
Preemployment Inquiries
Bona Fide Occupational Qualifications

Summary

Discussion Questions

Applications

External selection refers to the assessment and evaluation of external job applicants. A variety of different assessment methods are used. Preliminary issues that guide the use of these assessment methods will be discussed. These issues include the logic of prediction, the nature of predictors, development of the selection plan, and the selection sequence.

Initial assessment methods are used to select candidates from among the initial job applicants. The initial assessment methods that will be reviewed are resumes and cover letters, application blanks, biographical information, reference reports (which include letters of recommendation, reference checks, and background testing), handwriting analysis, literacy testing, genetic screening, and initial interviews. The factors that should guide the choice of initial assessment methods will be reviewed. These factors are frequency of use, cost, reliability, validity, utility, applicant reactions, and adverse impact.

The use of assessment methods also requires a firm understanding of legal issues. One method of preventing legal difficulties, the use of disclaimers as a means of protecting employer rights, is described. Due to myriad legal issues surrounding their use, reference reports and preemployment inquires require special attention to numerous details in using these methods of initial assessment. The most important of these details will be reviewed. Finally, bona fide occupational qualifications have particular relevance to initial assessment because such qualifications are usually assessed during the initial stages of selection. The legal issues involved in establishing such qualifications will be reviewed.

PRELIMINARY ISSUES

Many times, selection is equated with one event, namely, the interview. Nothing could be further from the truth if the best possible person/job match is to be made. In order for the best possible match to take place, a series of well-thought-out activities need to take place. Hence, selection is a process rather than an event. It is guided by a logic that determines the steps that need to be taken. The logic applies to all predictors that might be used, even though they differ in terms of several characteristics. Actual implementation of the logic of prediction requires that predictors be chosen through development of a selection plan. Implementation also requires creation of a selection sequence, which is an orderly flow of people through the stages of applicant, candidate, finalist, and offer receiver.

The Logic of Prediction

In Chapter 1, the selection component of staffing was defined as the process of assessing and evaluating people for purposes of determining the likely fit between the person and the job. This process is based on the logic of prediction, which holds that indicators of a person's degree of success in past situations should be predictive of how successful he or she will likely be in new situations. Application of this logic to selection is illustrated in Exhibit 9.1.

A person's KSAOs and motivation are the product of experiences of past job, current job, and nonjob situations. During selection, samples of these KSAOs and motivation are identified, assessed, and evaluated by the organization. The results constitute the person's overall qualifications for the new situation or job. These qualifications are then used to predict how successful the person is likely to be in that new situation or job as regards the HR outcomes. The logic of prediction works in practice if the organization accurately identifies and measures qualifications relative to job requirements, and if those qualifications remain stable over time so that they are carried over to the new job and used on it.

An example of how this logic can be followed in practice comes from a national communications organization with sales volume in the billions of dollars.[1] They were very interested in improving upon the prediction of job success (sales volume) for their sales people, whose sales figures had stagnated. To do so, they constructed what they labeled a "sales competency blueprint," or selection plan, to guide development of a new selection process. The blueprint depicted the KSAOs that needed to be sampled from previous jobs in order to predict sales success in a telemarketing sales job. The blueprint was established on the basis of a thorough job analysis in which subject matter experts identified the KSAOs thought necessary to be a successful telemarketer (e.g., knowledge of the product, how it was developed, and how it compared to the competitors' products). Then a structured interview was developed to sample the extent to which applicants for sales jobs in telemarketing had acquired the necessary KSAOs. In turn, the interview was used in selection to predict the likely success of applicants for the job.

The logic of prediction shown in Exhibit 9.1 demonstrates how critical it is to carefully scrutinize the applicant's past situation when making selection decisions. For example, in selecting someone for a police officer position, the successfulness of the applicant in a previous security guard position might be considered a relevant predictor of the likelihood that the applicant will succeed in the new police

---

EXHIBIT 9.1   The Logic of Prediction

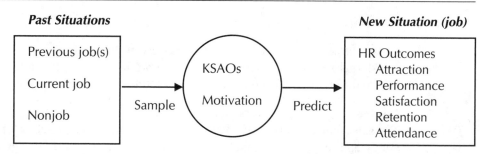

officer position. Alternatively, the fact that the person was previously successful as a homemaker might be viewed as totally irrelevant to the job of police officer. Surprisingly, considering the homemaker role to be irrelevant might well be an incorrect assessment. A study showed that there is a close correspondence between the homemaker and the police officer position.[2] Specifically, thorough job analysis showed that both jobs rely heavily upon troubleshooting and emergency handling skills. Hence, in the absence of a sound job analysis, many qualified applicants may inadvertently be overlooked even though they have some of the characteristics needed to perform the job. Nonjob experience in the home, in the community, and in other institutions may be as valuable or more valuable than previous employment experiences.

Job titles, such as homemaker, are not nearly specific enough for making selection decisions. Similarly, the fact that someone has a certain number of years of experience usually does not provide sufficient detail to make selection decisions. What counts, and what is revealed through job analysis, is the specific types of experiences required and the level of successfulness at each. Similarly, the fact that someone was paid or not paid for employment is not relevant. What counts is the quality of the experience as it relates to success on the new job. Thus, for example, someone who volunteered to serve as an arbitrator of disputes in the community may have more relevant experience for the position of labor relations representative than someone who was paid as a bookkeeper. In short, the logic of prediction indicates that a point-to-point comparison needs to be made between requirements of the job to be filled and the qualifications that applicants have acquired from a variety of past situations.

Not only is the logic of prediction important to selection, but it is important to recruitment as well. A recent study shows that applicant reactions to selection procedures are determined in part by the job-relatedness of the selection procedure. If applicants see the selection process as job related, which should occur if the logic of prediction is used, then they are more likely to view the selection process as being fair.[3] It would be expected that applicants who view the selection procedure as fair are more likely to accept a job offer and/or encourage others to apply for a job in the organization.

The Nature of Predictors

As will be seen shortly, there is a wide variety of different types of predictors used in external selection, ranging from interviews to genetic screening. These types can be differentiated from one another in terms of their content and their form.

Content

The substance or content of what is being assessed with a predictor varies considerably and may range from a sign to a sample to a criterion.[4] A sign is a predisposition of the person that is thought to relate to performance on the job. Personality as a predictor is a good example here. If personality is used as a predictor, the prediction is that someone with a certain personality (e.g., "abrasive") will demonstrate certain behaviors (e.g., "rude to customers") leading to certain results on the job (e.g., "failure to make a sale"). As can be seen, a sign is very distant from the actual on-the-job results. A sample is closer than a sign to actual on-the-job results. Observing a set of interactions between a sales applicant and customer to see if sales are made provides an example of a sample. The criterion is very close to the actual job performance, such as sales during a probationary period for a new employee.

Form

The form or design of the predictor may vary along a number of different lines.

Speed versus Power A person's score on some predictors is based upon the number of responses completed within a constrained time frame. One event in a physical abilities test may, for example, be the number of bench presses completed in a given period of time. This is known as a speed test. A power test, on the other hand, presents individuals with items of increasing difficulty. For example, a power test of numerical ability may begin with addition and subtraction, move on to multiplication and division, and conclude with complex problem-solving questions. A speed test is used when speed of work is an important part of the job, and a power test is used when the correctness of the response is essential to the job.[5] Of course, some tests (see the *Wonderlic Personnel Test* in Chapter 10) can be both speed and power tests, in which case few individuals would finish.

Paper and Pencil versus Performance Many predictors are of the paper-and-pencil variety; applicants are required to fill out a form, write out an answer, or complete multiple choice items. Other predictors are performance tests where the applicant is asked to manipulate an object or equipment. Testing running backs for the NFL on their time in the 40-yard dash is a performance test. Paper-and-pencil tests are frequently used when psychological abilities are required to perform the job, and performance tests are used when physical and social skills are required to perform the job.[6]

Objective versus Essay An objective paper-and-pencil predictor is one where multiple choice questions or true/false questions are used. These tests should be used to measure specific knowledge in specific areas. Another form of a predictor is an essay, where a written answer is required of the respondent. Essays are best used to assess written communication, problem solving, and analytical skills.[7]

Oral versus Written versus Computer Responses to predictor questions can be spoken, written, or entered into the computer. For example, when conducting interviews, some organizations listen to oral responses, read written responses, or read computer printouts of typed-in responses to assess applicants. As with all predictors, the appropriate form depends upon the nature of the job. If the job requires a high level of verbal skill, then oral responses should be solicited. If the job requires a large amount of writing, then written responses should be required. If the job requires constant interaction with the computer, then applicants should enter their responses into the computer.[8]

Development of the Selection Plan

In order to translate the results of a job analysis into the actual predictors to be used for selection, a selection plan must be developed. A selection plan describes which predictor(s) will be used to assess the KSAOs required to perform the job. The recommended format for a selection plan and an example of such a plan for the job of secretary is shown in Exhibit 9.2. In order to establish a selection plan, three steps are followed. First, a listing of KSAOs is written in the left-hand column. This list comes directly from the job requirements matrix. Second, for each KSAO, a "yes" or "no" is written to show whether this KSAO needs to be assessed in the selection process. Sometimes the answer is no because it is a KSAO the applicant will acquire once on the job (e.g., knowledge of company policies and procedures). Third, possible methods of assessment are listed for the required KSAOs, and the specific method to be used for each of these KSAOs is then indicated.

Although costly and time-consuming to develop, organizations are increasingly finding that the benefits of developing a selection plan outweigh the cost. As a result, it is and should be a required step in the selection process. For example, a selection plan or "niche testing" was used to select tellers and customer service representatives by Barnett Bank in Jacksonville, Florida.[9] They found that an essential KSAO for both positions is the ability to make judgments when interacting with the public. For this KSAO, a niche test was developed in which applicants watch actual dealings with the public on video and then decide on the appropriate course of action. Their responses are graded and used to predict their likelihood of success in either position.

Selection Sequence

Usually a series of decisions is made about job applicants before they are selected. These decisions are depicted in Exhibit 9.3. The first decision that is reached is whether initial applicants who have applied for the job become candidates or are rejected. A candidate is someone who has not yet received an offer but who possesses the minimum qualifications to be considered for further assessment. Initial assessment methods are used to choose candidates. These will be discussed later in this chapter. The second decision made is which candidates become finalists.

EXHIBIT 9.2 Selection Plan Format and Example for Secretarial Position

Major KSAO Category	Necessary for Selection? (Y/N)	Method of Assessment								
		WP	CT	DB	LTR	TEF	ML	EM	TM	Interview
1. Ability to follow oral directions/ listening skills	Y							X	X	
2. Ability to read and understand manuals/guidelines	Y	X	X	X	X	X	X	X		
3. Ability to perform basic arithmetic operations	Y			X		X				
4. Ability to organize	Y						X			
5. Judgments/priority setting/decision making ability	Y			X		X		X		
6. Oral communication skills	Y									X
7. Written communication skills	Y		X					X	X	
8. Interpersonal skills	Y									X
9. Typing skills	Y	X	X		X					
10. Knowledge of word processing, graphics, database, and spreadsheet software	Y	X	X	X	X	X				
11. Knowledge of company policies and procedures	N									
12. Knowledge of basic personal computer operations	Y	X	X	X	X	X		X		
13. Knowledge of how to use basic office machines	N									
14. Flexibility in dealing with changing job demands	Y						X	X	X	
15. Knowledge of computer software	Y	X	X	X	X		X	X		
16. Ability to attend to detail and accuracy	Y	X	X	X	X	X	X	X	X	

WP = Word processing test, CT = Correction test, DB = Data base exam, LTR = Letter, TEF = Travel expense form, ML = Mail log, EM = Electronic mail messages, and TM = Telephone messages.

Source: Adapted from N. Schmitt, S. Gilliland, R. S. Landis, and D. Devine, "Computer-Based Testing Applied to Selection of Secretarial Positions," *Personnel Psychology*, 1993, 46, pp. 149–165.

EXHIBIT 9.3   Assessment Methods by Applicant Flow Stage

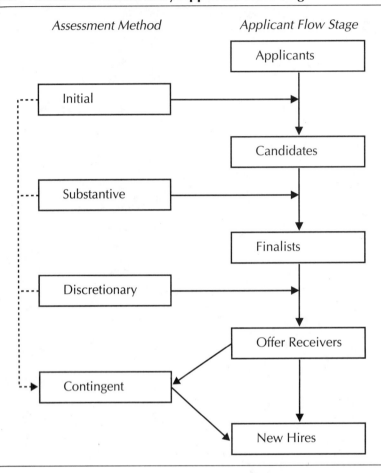

Assessment Method   *Applicant Flow Stage*

A finalist is someone who meets all the minimum qualifications and whom the organization considers fully qualified for the job. Substantive assessment methods are used to select finalists. These methods will be discussed in the next chapter. The third decision made is which finalist receives the actual job offer. Offer receivers are those finalists to whom the organization extends an offer of employment. Discretionary methods are used to select finalists and also will be described in the next chapter. Contingent methods are sometimes used, meaning the job offer is subject to certain qualifications, such as passing a medical exam or drug test, before the offer receiver can become a new hire. Use of contingent methods, in particular drug testing and medical exams, will be reviewed in the next chapter. Finally, some offer receivers become new hires when they decide to join the organization.

INITIAL ASSESSMENT METHODS

In this section, initial assessment methods are covered. These methods are also referred to as preemployment inquiries and are used to minimize the costs associated with substantive assessment methods by reducing the number of people assessed. Predictors typically used to screen candidates from applicants include application blanks, biographical information, reference reports, handwriting analysis, literacy testing, genetic screening, and initial interviews. Each of these initial assessment methods will be described in turn. Using meta-analysis results, the average validity (i.e., $\bar{r}$) of each method is also provided if possible. Then, a general evaluation will be presented to help guide decisions about which initial assessment methods to use.

Resumes and Cover Letters

The first introduction of the applicant to the organization is often a cover letter and resume. This introduction is controlled by the applicant as to the amount, type, and accuracy of information provided. As a result, resumes and cover letters always need to be verified with other predictors such as application blanks to ensure that there is accurate and complete data across all job applicants with which to make informed selection decisions.

One major issue with resumes as a selection tool is the volume of resumes that organizations must process. It is very difficult for many organizations to store resumes for any extended period of time and to read them accurately. Fortunately, the computer has resolved this issue.[10] For example, resumes from previous searches can be stored on disk so that when a new vacancy arises, a new recruitment search does not have to take place. Also, optical scanners now make it possible to machine read resumes. For example, the Clinton Administration used Resumix to screen applicants for the 4,000 jobs that needed to be filled in the early days of the administration.[11] In positions such as these that generate strong interest from applicants, the advantages offered by computerized searches are particularly important.

A well-documented problem with resumes and cover letters is fraud.[12] Consider the extreme case of Eugene Roscoe.[13] Not only did Eugene lie about his degree and experiences, but he also lied in his cover letter about interviews. He made over $100,000 in reimbursements for expenses incurred during interviews that he never made. Although most cases are not nearly this extreme, the falsification of credentials does occur.

A computer does not guard against the falsification of credentials. Resumes need to be verified by other predictors and carefully reviewed. Warnings that should throw up a red flag include gaps in employment dates, a lack of any employment history, a preponderance of former employers listed who are out of business, and a lack of location for previous employers.[14] Vague expressions that sound impressive may not be. Phrases to be on guard for include "was thoroughly involved in . . . ," "steered the company through . . . ," "worked closely with . . . ," "had deep involvement in . . . ," "was active in the planning and implementation of . . . ," and "quickly responded to . . . "[15] Obviously, these types of statements are not fraudulent per se, but they are so vague and general that they should be judged with caution.

Almost no research exists on resumes and cover letters. We do not know their validity or reliability. Nor is there information on their costs or adverse impact. This situation is unfortunate given their pervasive use in certain types of jobs, especially entry-level management, professional, and technical positions. Thus, organizations using resumes and cover letters in selection should carefully evaluate their effectiveness.

Application Blanks

Most application blanks request in written form the applicant's background with regard to educational experiences, training, and job experiences. This information is also often on the resume and may seem unnecessarily duplicated. This is not the case. An application can be used to verify the data presented on the resume and also can be used to obtain data omitted on the resume, such as employment dates. The major advantage of application blanks over resumes is that the organization, rather than the applicant, dictates what information is presented. As a result, information critical to success on the job is less likely to be omitted by the applicant or overlooked by the reviewer of the resume. The major issue with application blanks is to make sure that information requested is critical to job success, following the logic of prediction discussed earlier.

A sample application blank is provided in Exhibit 9.4. As with most application blanks, the major sections of the application are personal information, employment desired, educational background, special interests and abilities, work experience, and suggested references. The only information sought from the application blank should be KSAOs that can be demonstrated as job relevant. This not only avoids wasting the organization's and the applicant's time, but also protects the employer from charges of unfair discrimination (also see Legal Issues at the end of this chapter). It is important to take note of the statement at the bottom of the application blank, known as a disclaimer statement. It provides certain legal protections to the organization, discussed under the Legal Issues section at the end of this chapter. Asking applicants to sign a disclaimer also may decrease the incentive to distort and falsify information.

Educational Requirements

Special care needs to be taken in wording items on an application blank when soliciting information about educational experiences and performance.[16] Following are discussed several particularly important areas pertaining to educational requirement information on application blanks.

EXHIBIT 9.4   Application for Employment

PERSONAL INFORMATION

DATE _____

SOCIAL SECURITY
NUMBER _____

NAME _____
        LAST   FIRST   MIDDLE

PRESENT ADDRESS _____
                  STREET   CITY   STATE   ZIP

PERMANENT ADDRESS _____
                    STREET   CITY   STATE   ZIP

PHONE NO. _____ ARE YOU 18 YEARS OR OLDER?   Yes ☐   No ☐

ARE YOU PREVENTED FROM LAWFULLY BECOMING EMPLOYED
IN THIS COUNTRY BECAUSE OF VISA OR IMMIGRATION STATUS?   Yes ☐   No ☐

EMPLOYMENT DESIRED

POSITION _____ DATE YOU
                     CAN START _____ SALARY
                                           DESIRED _____

ARE YOU EMPLOYED NOW? _____ IF SO MAY WE INQUIRE
                                  OF YOUR PRESENT EMPLOYER? _____

APPLIED TO THIS COMPANY BEFORE? _____ WHERE? _____ WHEN? _____

REFERRED BY _____

EDUCATION

	NAME AND LOCATION	NO. OF YEARS ATTENDED	DID YOU GRADUATE?	SUBJECTS STUDIED
GRAMMAR SCHOOL				
HIGH SCHOOL (GED)				
COLLEGE				
OTHER				

(continued)

EXHIBIT 9.4   Continued

GENERAL

SUBJECTS OF SPECIAL STUDY

SPECIAL SKILLS

ACTIVITIES: (CIVIC, ATHLETIC, ETC.)

U.S. MILITARY OR
NAVAL SERVICE   RANK

PRESENT MEMBERSHIP IN
NATIONAL GUARD OR RESERVES

FORMER EMPLOYERS (LIST BELOW LAST 3 EMPLOYERS, STARTING WITH THE LAST ONE FIRST)

DATE	NAME & ADDRESS	SALARY	POSITION	REASON FOR LEAVING
FROM				
TO				
FROM				
TO				
FROM				
TO				

REFERENCES (GIVE THE NAMES OF 3 PERSONS NOT RELATED TO YOU)

	NAME	ADDRESS	BUSINESS	YEARS ACQUAINTED
1				
2				
3				

"I certify that all the information submitted by me on this application is true and complete, and I understand that if any false information, omissions, or misrepresentations are discovered, my application may be rejected and, if I am employed, my employment may be terminated at any time. In consideration of my employment, I agree to conform to the company's rules and regulations, and I agree that my employment and compensation can be terminated, with or without cause, and with or without notice, at any time, at either my or the company's option. I also understand and agree that the terms and conditions of my employment may be changed, with or without cause, and with or without notice, at any time by the company. I understand that no company representative, other than its president, and only when in writing and signed by the president, has any authority to enter into any agreement for employment for any specific period of time, or to make any agreement contrary to the foregoing."

DATE   SIGNATURE

Level of Education   Level of education or degree is one element of educational performance used to predict job performance. Often, level of education is measured by the attainment of a degree. The degree should be assessed in conjunction with other educational requirements. A high-level degree from a nonaccredited school may be an indication of a lesser accomplishment than a lower-level degree from an accredited school. Research indicates that level of education is weakly related to job performance ($\bar{r}$ = .13).[17]

Furthermore, a recent report indicates that the high school degree may no longer be as good a predictor as it once was, because the attainment of a GED (high school equivalency) is often used as a substitute for a diploma on an application form, and does not predict as well.[18] Hence, in designing the application form, an item separate from high school degree should be used for high school equivalency.

Grade Point Average   Classroom grades are measured using a grade point average (GPA). Care should be exercised in the interpretation of GPA information. For example, a GPA in one's major in college may be different (usually higher) than one's GPA for all classes. Grades also vary widely by field (e.g., grades in engineering tend to be lower than in other fields). Further, a GPA of 3.5 may be good at one school, but not at another. For example, GPAs are calculated on a 4-point scale at some schools, while they are calculated on a 5-point scale at other schools. Some schools do not report GPAs. Some schools (especially colleges) have grade inflation (e.g., at Princeton University 80 percent of undergraduates receive As and Bs).[19] Graduate students receive higher grades on average than do undergraduates.[20] In short, GPA may be influenced by many factors in addition to the applicant's KSAOs and motivation. Meta-analyses have suggested that the validity of GPA in predicting job performance ranges from $\bar{r}$ = .17 to $\bar{r}$ = .20.[21] College grades appear to be no more valid than high school grades. In part, this may be due to grade inflation as described above.

Quality of School   In recent times, much has been said and written about the quality of various educational programs. For example, *U.S. News and World Report* annually publishes the results of a survey showing ratings of school quality. A more comprehensive source on school quality is the *Gourman Report*.[22] The *Gourman Report* assigns numerical scores (ranging from 1.00 = unacceptable to 5.00 = perfect) to virtually every degree-granting university in the U.S. on the basis of 18 criteria (e.g., faculty qualifications, admission standards, curriculum, quality of instruction). The *Gourman Report* includes ratings for undergraduate and graduate programs in many fields. Although educational quality has not been related to job performance, a recent study indicated that managers whose highest degree was from a school rated as "1" on the *Gourman Report* earned $16,070 less per year than managers whose school was rated as "4" or "5."[23] (Results suggested prestige was even more important than quality, though. Graduates of Ivy League schools enjoyed a $32,000 pay advantage even taking school quality into account.)

While this evidence suggests that quality of school matters (at least to the labor market), care should be taken to critically examine on what basis school quality ratings are made and their relevance to the job for which selection is to occur.

Major Field of Study   The more specialized the knowledge requirements of a particular position, the more important is an applicant's major field of study likely to be as a predictor. An English major may do very well as an editor, but may be unsuccessful as a physician. It should also be noted that a major does not guarantee that a certain number or type of classes have been taken. The number and type of classes needed for a major or minor varies from school to school and needs to be carefully scrutinized to ensure comparability across majors. The relationship between field of study and job performance is very difficult to assess and therefore no conclusive validity evidence is available.[24]

Extracurricular Activities   The usefulness of extracurricular activities as a predictor depends upon the job. Being an ice or field hockey player may have little relevance to being a successful manager. However, being elected captain of a hockey team may be a sign of leadership qualities needed to be a successful manager. Information about extracurricular activities taken from an application blank must be relevant to the job in question. As with field of study, there is insufficient basis to draw any conclusions about the relationship between extracurricular activities and job performance.

Training and Experience Requirements

Many past experiences predictive of future performance do not take place in a classroom. Instead, these experiences come from life experiences in other institutions which, fortunately, also can be captured on an application blank. A great deal of weight is often put on training and experience requirements on the theory that "actions speak louder than words." The drawback of putting too much emphasis on previous work experience, however, is that the amount of experience and training an applicant has may be overstated. Also, applicants with high potential may be overlooked because they have not had the opportunity to gain the training or experience needed.

Various methods can be used to measure training and experience. Since training and experience information is not directly equivalent across applicants, all methods require the judgment of selection decision makers. These decision makers render judgments about how to classify and weight different levels of experience. An approach termed the behavioral consistency method has shown the highest degree of validity because it focuses on determining the quality of an applicant's previous training and experience. One of the means through which the behavioral consistency method determines quality is by asking applicants to complete a supplemental application where they describe their most significant accomplishments relative to a list of key job behaviors. Due to their involved nature, however, behavioral consistency ratings are time consuming and expensive to administer, and they require the applicant to possess some degree of analytical ability and writing skills. Thus, the choice of weighting methods rests on a trade-off between accuracy, and ease and cost of administration.[25]

Licensing, Certification, and Job Knowledge

Many professions and occupations require or encourage people to demonstrate mastery of a certain body of knowledge. A license is required of people by law to perform an activity, whereas a certification is voluntarily acquired.[26] The purpose of a license is to protect the public interest, while the purpose of a certification is to identify those people who have met a minimum standard of proficiency. Licensing exams and certification exams are usually developed by subject matter experts in conjunction with testing specialists.

Approximately 800 occupations in the United States are regulated by state government boards. Many others are monitored by professional associations. For example, in human resources, there are seven certifications offered by five certifying agencies. Certifications offered are the Professional in Human Resources, Senior Professional in Human Resources, Certified Compensation Professional, Certified Employee Benefit Specialist, Associate Safety Professional, Certified Safety Professional, and Occupational Health and Safety Technologist.[27]

Certification helps guard against the misuse of job titles in human resource selection. For example, anyone could adopt the title of safety consultant, but a certification from the Board of Certified Safety Professionals and/or American Board of Industrial Hygiene guarantees that the person has mastered a certain amount of technical knowledge in the safety area.

As was mentioned earlier, licensing and certification requirements can be used either as an initial or contingent assessment method. When used as an initial method, licensing and certification requirements are used to eliminate applicants who fail to possess these credentials. For example, a car repair shop electing to hire only certified mechanics might initially screen out individuals who fail to have the proper certification. When used as a contingent method, the selection process proceeds on the assumption that the applicant has the requisite credential (or will have it by the time of hire). This is then verified after an initial offer decision is made. For example, rather than verifying that each applicant for a nursing position possesses a valid state license, a hospital may assess applicants based on the assumption they have a valid license and then verify this assumption after a tentative hiring decision has been made. Thus, the difference between using licensing and certification requirements as initial or contingent assessment methods depends on when the information is considered in the selection process.

While licensure and certification demonstrate mastery of a general body of knowledge applicable to many organizations, job knowledge tests assess a specific body of knowledge within a particular organization. Job knowledge tests are usually used in the public sector as an initial screening device. In the private sector, they are used primarily for promotion purposes. Although mentioned here, job knowledge tests will be covered in detail in Chapter 10.

Weighted Application Blanks

Not all of the information contained on an application blank is of equal value to the organization in making selection decisions. Depending on the organization and job, some information better predicts success on the job than other information. Procedures have been developed that help to weight application blank information by the degree to which the information differentiates between high- and low-performing individuals.[28] This scoring methodology is referred to as a weighted application blank (WAB) and is useful not only in making selection decisions, but also in developing application blanks as well. The statistical procedures involved help the organization to discern which items should be retained for use in the application blank and which should be excluded, on the basis of how well they predict performance.

Evaluation of Application Blanks

Evidence suggests that scored evaluations of the unweighted application blank are not particularly valid predictors of job performance (average validity ranges from $\bar{r} = .10$ to $\bar{r} = .20$).[29] This is not surprising given the rudimentary information that is collected in application blanks. Another factor that may undermine the validity of application blanks is distortion. A study of the National Credential Verification Service found that about one-third of the investigations into the background of applicants suggested that misrepresentation occurred on the application blank. Subsequent studies have suggested that the most common questions that are misrepresented include past salary, education, tenure on previous job, and reasons for leaving previous job. Some individuals even go beyond misrepresentation to invention. One study revealed that 15 percent of supposedly previous employers of applicants indicated that the individual never worked for them.[30] Thus, application information which is given heavy weight in selection decisions should be verified.

The validity evidence for weighted application blanks is much more positive.[31] In a sense, this would almost have to be true since items in the weighted application blank are scored and weighted based on their ability to predict job performance. Thus, as long as *some* of the items are predictive, the scoring and weighting schemes embedded in the weighted application blank will ensure that the overall score is predictive. Because the process used to develop the weighted application blank is time consuming and expensive, more cost-benefit studies need to be conducted on the weighted application blank. Is the validity worth the cost? Unfortunately, there is little recent research on the weighted application blank, so answers to this question are difficult to come by.

The relatively poor validity of unweighted application blanks also should not be taken as indication that they are useless in selection decisions. Unweighted application blanks are a very inexpensive means of collecting basic information on job applicants. Most organizations use unweighted application blanks only for initial screening decisions (to rule out applicants who are obviously unqualified for the job). Thus, it is not necessarily appropriate to condemn unweighted application blanks based on a criterion for which they are rarely used (i.e., used by themselves to make substantive selection decisions about applicants). As long as application blanks are used in this context (and not relied on to a significant degree in making substantive hiring decisions), they can be a useful method of making initial decisions about applicants.

Biographical Information

Biographical information, often called biodata, is personal history information on an applicant's background and interests. Basically, results from a biodata survey formulate a general description of a person's life history. The principal assumption behind the use of biodata is the axiom "The best predictor of future behavior is past behavior." These past behaviors may reflect ability or motivation. Biodata inventories are thought to measure applicant motivation that can be inferred from past choices. However, research also suggests that many ability items are included in biodata inventories.[32]

Like application blanks, biographical information blanks ask applicants to report on their background. Responses to both of these questionnaires can provide useful information in making initial selection decisions about applicants. Unlike application blanks, however, biographical information can also be fruitfully used for substantive selection decisions. In fact, if scores on a biodata inventory are predictive of subsequent job performance (which, as we will see, is often the case), it may be somewhat limiting to use biodata scores only for initial assessment decisions. Thus, although biographical information is as much a substantive as an initial assessment method because it shares many similarities with application blanks, we have included it in this section. Nevertheless, it should also be considered in deliberations about which substantive assessment methods are to be used.

Biographical information also has similarities and differences with background tests (see the section on reference reports). Biodata and background tests are similar in that both look into an applicant's past. However, the two types of selection methods differ in a number of important ways:[33] (1) background checks are used primarily when screening applicants for positions in which integrity and emotional adjustment are necessary (e.g., law enforcement, private security, etc.), while biodata inventories are used to screen applicants in many jobs; (2) background information is obtained through interviews and conversations with references, while biodata information is usually collected by survey; (3) the criterion by which background information is validated is typically behavioral reliability (attendance, integrity, etc.), while performance is the principal criterion against which biodata scores are validated. Thus, biodata inventories and background checks are distinct methods of selection that require that they be considered separately.

The type of biographical information collected varies a great deal from inventory to inventory and often depends on the job. For example, a biographical survey for executives might focus on career aspirations, accomplishments, and disappointments.[34] A survey for blue-collar workers might focus on training and work experience.[35] A biodata inventory for federal government workers might focus on school and educational experiences, work history, skills, and interpersonal relations.[36] As can be seen from these examples, most biodata surveys consider individual accomplishments, group accomplishments, disappointing experiences, and stressful situations.[37] The domains in which these attributes are studied often vary from job to job but can range from childhood experiences to educational or early work experiences to current hobbies or family relations.

Measures

Typically, biographical information is collected in a questionnaire that applicants complete. Exhibit 9.5 provides example biodata items. As can been seen, the items are quite diverse. It has been suggested that each biodata item can be classified according to ten criteria: *history* (does the item describe an event that has occurred in the past, or a future or hypothetical event?), *externality* (does the item address an observable event or an internal event such as values or judgments?), *objectivity* (does the item focus on reporting factual information or subjective interpretations?), *firsthandedness* (does the item seek information that is directly available to the applicant rather than an evaluation of the applicant's behavior by others?), *discreteness* (does the item pertain to a single, unique behavior or a simple count of events as opposed to summary responses?), *verifiability* (can the accuracy of the response to the item be confirmed?), *controllability* (does the item address an event that was under the control of the applicant?), *equal accessibility* (are the events or experiences expressed in the item equally accessible to all applicants?), *job relevance* (does the item solicit information closely tied to the job?), and *invasiveness* (is the item sensitive to the applicant's right to privacy?).[38] Exhibit 9.6 provides example items that fall into each of these categories. This categorization has important implications for deciding how to construct biodata inventories, as will be discussed shortly.

Most selection tests simply score items in a predetermined manner and add the scores to arrive at a total score. These total scores then form the basis of selection decisions made about the applicants. With most biodata inventories, the process of making decisions on the basis of responses to items is considerably more complex. The traditional recommended approach to the development of a biodata survey is as follows:[39]

Choosing or Developing the Criterion   Generally, the criterion is job performance. Because the items included in the biodata inventory may depend on the nature of the job, great care must be taken to ensure that the measure of job

---

EXHIBIT 9.5   Examples of Biodata Items

---

1. In college, my grade point average was:
   a. I did not go to college or completed less than two years
   b. less than 2.50
   c. 2.50 to 3.00
   d. 3.00 to 3.50
   e. 3.50 to 4.00

2. In the past five years, the number of different jobs I have held is:
   a. more than five
   b. three–five
   c. two
   d. one
   e. none

3. The kind of supervision I like best is:
   a. very close supervision
   b. fairly close supervision
   c. moderate supervision
   d. minimal supervision
   e. no supervision

4. When you are angry, which of the following behaviors most often describes your reaction:
   a. reflect on the situation for a bit
   b. talk to a friend or spouse
   c. exercise or take a walk
   d. physically release the anger on something
   e. just try to forget about it

5. Over the past three years, how much have you enjoyed each of the following (use the scale at right below):

a. ____ Reading	1 = Very much
b. ____ Watching TV	2 = Some
c. ____ Home improvements	3 = Very little
d. ____ Music	4 = Not at all
e. ____ Outdoor recreation	

6. In most ways is your life close to ideal?
   a. agree
   b. disagree
   c. undecided or neutral

EXHIBIT 9.6   A Taxonomy of Biodata Items

Historical
How old were you when you got your first paying job?

Future or Hypothetical
What position do you think you will be holding in 10 years?

External
Did you ever get fired from a job?

Internal
What is your attitude toward friends who smoke marijuana?

Objective
How many hours did you study for your real-estate exam?

Subjective
Would you describe yourself as shy?

Firsthand
How punctual are you about coming to work?

Secondhand
How would your teachers describe your punctuality?

Discrete
At what age did you get your driver's license?

Summative
How many hours do you study during an average week?

Verifiable
What was your grade point average in college?

Nonverifiable
How many fresh vegetables do you eat every day?

Controllable
How many tries did it take you to pass the CPA exam?

Noncontrollable
How many brothers and sisters do you have?

Equal Access
Were you ever class president?

Nonequal access
Were you captain of the football team?

Job Relevant
How many units of cereal did you sell during the last calendar year?

Not job relevant
Are you proficient at crossword puzzles?

Noninvasive
Were you on the tennis team in high school?

Invasive
How many young children do you have at home?

Source: F. A. Mael, "A Conceptual Rationale for the Domain and Attributes of Biodata Items," *Personnel Psychology*, 1991, 44, pp. 763–792. Used by permission.

performance reflects the most important job behaviors. Obviously, this is the goal of job analysis. Other criteria beyond job performance may be valued, including length of service, attendance, and advancement.

Identifying Criterion Groups   Empirical keys for biodata generally are developed on the basis of how well they separate different criterion groups (e.g., high vs. low performers, low-absenteeism vs. high-absenteeism employees, stayers vs.

leavers, etc.). With criterion measures such as performance ratings, one method that has been developed to accomplish this is to take the upper 27 percent and lower 27 percent of performers (e.g., in a sample of 500 this would translate into the 135 highest performers and 135 lowest performers).[40] The 27 percent figure achieves a compromise between maximizing the difference between the criterion groups and maintaining a reasonably large sample size for each criterion group.

Selecting Items to Be Analyzed Generally, a large number of items (perhaps as many as 200) are administered to current employees. The items can be obtained from consulting firms or from compendia of biodata items.[41] In deciding which items to include, it is helpful to return to the earlier classification of biodata items into ten categories (Exhibit 9.6). When using biodata inventories in selection, they are likely to be more useful when the items are characterized by the left-hand side attributes in Exhibit 9.6. Otherwise, the items are likely to be transparent, unverifiable, or may add little validity over other selection measures such as personality tests. In many cases, items are selected based on their ability to separate the criterion groups (e.g., how well they predict job performance). Often, the items that are selected are the ones that display strong differences between high and low performers (thus suggesting that this item will do a good job of forecasting job performance). Naturally, the ability of a particular item to separate criterion groups may vary from job to job. For example, the item, "Have you ever built a model airplane that flew?" is probably invalid for most jobs but may be predictive in selecting airline pilots, mechanics, or engineers. Thus, although the initial set of items in the biodata inventory may be quite large, many of these items usually end up being excluded because they are not a valid means of separating high and low performers in a particular job.

Specifying Item Response Alternatives As can be seen from Exhibit 9.5, most biodata items are in a multiple-choice format. In many cases, there is not a clear "right" response, which helps ensure that responses are not socially desirable. Often, response options are determined to be those that do the best job of separating high and low performers. For example, rather than asking applicants for an international assignment if they have ever traveled outside of the country and posing a yes/no response alternative (most have), the item might do a better job if individuals were allowed to respond by indicating how many international trips they have taken. As another example, it might be found that response option *(d)* to question 3 in Exhibit 9.5 displays more difference between high and low performers than response option *(e)*. In such a case, option *(e)* could be eliminated or given less weight in scoring the question.

Weighting Items Unlike most selection tests, biodata items generally are not given an equal weight in computing the total score. The traditional approach to weighting responses to biodata inventories is to use the "empirical key" approach.

The empirical key approach weights items according to their ability to separate criterion groups. Those items that do the best job of separating high and low performers, for example, are given the highest weight. It is important to note that in order for these weighting schemes to be stable (i.e., generalize from one group of applicants to the next), a large sample is required.[42] Generally, the sample should consist of at least five to ten persons for each item or response option.

Cross Validating   Cross validation (or validating the initial items and weights with another sample) is especially important in developing empirically keyed biodata items because the process of scoring weights based on a sample will, to some degree, capitalizes on sample-specific factors. For example, a question that does a good job of separating good and poor *employees* may not be as effective in separating good and poor *applicants*. If this holds true across many items, the weighting scheme based on current employees will have no validity. The degree to which this process is a problem can be investigated only through the process of cross validation.

Developing Cutoff Scores   The last step in using biodata for selection is to establish a minimum score that maximizes the number of persons correctly classified on the criterion. For example, if the criterion is job performance, a cutoff score may be set at the point at which the best separation occurs between high and low performers. As is the case with all selection methods, there are numerous specific means of setting cut scores (also see Chapter 12).

The preceding discussion assumes that the process of developing biodata items is completely based on empirical-keying responses to maximize prediction. This empirical-key approach has been criticized, however, because it limits generalizability of biodata inventories and detracts from understanding the validity of the biodata construct. As a result, some have argued for a "rational" approach to developing and validating biodata inventories. Rational approaches involve generating biodata items based on logical hypotheses (often based on job analysis results) about how a particular item should be related to the criterion (usually job performance) as judged by subject matter experts. Thus, in the rational-key approach, both item selection and item weighting are based on theory or expert judgment as opposed to the empirical-key approach of using the data to reveal how well each item or weight separates high and low performers.[43] While rational-keying approaches do permit greater understanding of the nature of the biodata construct, empirical- and rational-key approaches have been found to have similar levels of predictive validity.[44] In practice, each method has advantages, so compromise methods between the two have been developed.[45]

Accomplishment Records

A selection method that can be considered a form of a biographical information survey is the accomplishment record, sometimes termed an achievement history questionnaire or retrospective life essay.[46] Accomplishment records survey the past accomplishments of job candidates as they relate to dimensions of work that are part of performing effectively at a particular job. Information that is solicited from each candidate includes a written statement of the accomplishment, when it took place, any recognition for the accomplishment, and verification of the accomplishment.[47] The emphasis is on achievements rather than activities only, and it is in this regard that accomplishment records differ from application blanks that solicit data on activities. Interestingly, this procedure may replace the traditional paper-and-pencil tests used by the federal government to select new college graduates.[48]

An example of an accomplishment record scoring key, developed to select attorneys, is shown in Exhibit 9.7. Specifically, it is used to evaluate the candidate's research and investigation skills. The scale is used to score the accomplishment record submitted by the candidate. Similar scales are used to score other aspects of the candidate's skills. The scale is anchored with behavioral benchmarks. These benchmarks are illustrative of what candidates would have to present in their essay to earn a certain score, which can range from 1 to 6. Research has suggested impressive validity for accomplishment records although further study is needed.

EXHIBIT 9.7   Scoring Key Excerpt for an Accomplishment Record

---

Dimensions: Researching/Investigating

General Definition: Obtaining all information, facts, and materials that are important, relevant, or necessary for a case, project, or assignment; gathering accurate information from all possible sources (i.e., persons both within and outside, interviews, journals, publications, company records, etc.); being thorough and overcoming all obstacles in gathering the required information.

Guidelines for Ratings: In RESEARCHING/INVESTIGATING, accomplishments at the lower levels are characterized by projects which require a minimal amount of research or research that is mundane in nature, e.g., routine interviews or journal reviews. At progressively higher levels, the accomplishments describe information gathered from multiple sources or information that would require considerable expertise to collect. The research projects may be part of a case or procedure which is novel or of substantial import. The projects generally demand increasingly complex interpretation of the information gathered. At the highest levels of achievement, awards or commendations are likely.

Scale:

6 =   I assumed major responsibility for conducting an industry-wide investigation of the industry and for preparation of a memorandum in support of complaints against the three largest members of the industry. A complaint was issued unanimously by the Commission and a consent settlement was

(continued)

EXHIBIT 9.7 Continued

---

obtained subsequently from all three respondents. I obtained statistical data from every large and medium industry in the U.S. and from a selection of small ones. I obtained and negotiated subpoenas with, and obtained statistical information from numerous other members of the industry. I deposed *many* employees of manufacturers and renters. I received a Meritorious Service award.

5 = I obtained crucial evidence in Docket, which was used as the basis for obtaining consent orders against more than 25 companies. I personally conducted more than 30 Investigational Hearings by subpoena. I did much outside research and reading to become familiar with technology. I handled all investigational and research work in the Northeastern United States. I obtained documentary material from many sources and obtained the files upon which the matter was finally based.

4 = As a lead attorney in a major investigation at the _____ , I performed all of the tasks described in this category. I supervised the investigation and brought it to its ultimate conclusion, which was to recommend that the matter be closed with no official action. I interviewed witnesses, including interviews on official record, subpoenaed documents from target sources, and spoke with numerous experts about scientific and technical information related to the case.

3 = In the investigation, I helped to develop and gather the evidence necessary to pursue litigation. I prepared several complex subpoenas and negotiated them with industry counsel from three major corporations. The subpoenas requested detailed information on activities of major _____ .

2 = I interviewed potential witnesses and compiled evidence that was relevant to the case against Corporation. I analyzed documents submitted pursuant to subpoenas, interviewed witnesses, and wrote admission of fact.

1 = My research involved checking reference books, LEXIS, and telephone interviews with various people—individuals, state officials, etc.

Source: L. M. Hough, M. A. Keyes, and M. D. Dunnette, "An Evaluation of Three 'Alternative' Selection Procedures," *Personnel Psychology*, 1983, 36, p. 265. Used by permission.

Evaluation of Biodata

Research that has been conducted on the reliability and validity of biodata is quite positive.[49] Responses tend to be reliable (test-retest coefficients range from .77 to .90). More importantly, past research suggests that biodata inventories are some of the most valid predictors of job performance. A number of meta-analyses have been conducted and the average validity has ranged from $\bar{r} = .32$ to $\bar{r} = .37$.[50]

Because biodata inventories are developed and scored on the basis of a particular job and sample, it has commonly been argued that the validity of a particular inventory in one organization is unlikely to generalize to another organization. However, one study demonstrated that biodata inventories can be constructed in a way that will lead to generalizability across organizations.[51] In this study, items to be included in the biodata inventory were selected based on two criteria: (1) their job relevance (based on job analysis data), and (2) their ability to generalize across organizations (whether the item was a valid predictor of job performance in at least four of the six organizations studied). Scores were computed for the retained items and then tested on a sample of other organizations. The cross-validation effort resulted in a validity coefficient of .33. Thus, this research suggests that biodata inventories can generalize across organizations when constructed in an appropriate manner. It remains to be seen, however, whether organizations that use biodata will adopt this approach.

While biographical inventories do have predictive validity, it is not clear exactly what these inventories assess. Some have argued that biographical information represents personality and, in fact, many biographical items are indistinguishable from personality items. For example, questions about academic interest may reflect openness to experience, questions about past accomplishments may reflect conscientiousness, and so on.[52] If biodata inventories are, in part, measures of personality, it is important to show that they demonstrate incremental validity over personality measures because they are much more costly to develop. Unfortunately, such investigations are lacking in the literature.

One of the more important issues in evaluating the usefulness of biodata is the issue of faking. Because responses to most biodata items are difficult if not impossible to verify (e.g., "Did you collect coins or stamps as a child?"), it is conceivable applicants distort their responses in order to tell prospective employers what they want to hear. In fact, research clearly shows that faking does occur. Research also suggests, though, that faking can be reduced in a number of ways:

1. Use less "fakable" items. Using the typology of biodata items in Exhibit 9.6, one study found that the least-fakable items were more historical, objective, discrete, verifiable, external, and *less* job relevant.[53]

2. Warn applicants against faking. One study found that warning applicants that faking could be detected and would reduce their score (even if faking could not actually be detected) reduced the faking of transparent items, that is, where the desirable response was clear (e.g., "I hate to see people suffer.").[54]

3. Use option-keyed scoring. Option-keyed items refer to analyzing each response separately and scoring only those responses that separate criterion groups or correlate with the criterion. Assume, for example, that of the five responses to item 3 in Exhibit 9.5, only responses *(b)* and *(e)* help separate high and low performers. Using option-keyed scoring, only those two re-

sponses would be scored. Option-keyed items are a contrast to those that are item-keyed, where each response is scored in a predetermined manner. For example, an item-keyed scoring strategy for item 3 might entail assigning 0 points to response *(a)*, 1 point to response *(b)*, 2 points to response *(c)*, and so on. Option-keyed formats are hard to fake because the "right" answer is difficult to guess. For example, responses that are circled by nearly everyone (suggesting some degree of faking) will not do a good job of discriminating between high and low performers and therefore will not be scored. In fact, one study suggests that option-keyed formats are less susceptible to faking.[55]

4. Validate responses using applicant samples. One study found that it may not be a good idea to key items based on concurrent validity designs (i.e., using employees) because the cross-validity in predicting performance based on a concurrent design was .08 for item-keyed responses and .09 for option-keyed responses. One of the suggested reasons for this lack of convergence was social desirability.[56]

While the steps outlined above may reduce the degree of faking present in biodata inventories, it is important to keep in mind that the substantial validities of biodata were found in past research without systematic attempts to control faking. Thus, while the above steps may make biodata inventories even more valid, faking apparently has not undermined the validity of biodata information.[57]

Finally, only a few studies have looked at applicant reactions to biodata inventories. In general, research suggests that biodata inventories are not viewed favorably by applicants. One study found that biodata inventories were viewed as the least valid of 14 specific selection measures examined; another study found that biodata was seen as the least valid of five selection measures studied (the other four were interviews, personality tests, cognitive ability tests, and drug tests).[58] Thus, applicants do not seem to react well to biodata inventories. The likely reason for this is because applicants do not seem to believe that items contained in most biographical inventories bear little similarity to job content (see items in Exhibit 9.5). In this regard, accomplishment records may do better. For example, one study found that accomplishment records were viewed as among the *most* job-related selection methods (only interviews and work samples were viewed as more job-related).[59] Since accomplishment records are work-related biographical inventories, this suggests that using items in biodata inventories that are seen as related to job performance (as is the case with accomplishment records or achievement history questionnaires) likely will generate more favorable applicant reactions.

Reference Reports

Background information about job applicants can come not only from the applicant, but also from people familiar with the applicant in previous situations (e.g., employers, creditors, neighbors).[60] Organizations often solicit this information on their own or use the services of agencies that specialize in investigating applicants. Background information solicited from others is called a reference report and consists of letters of recommendation, reference checks, and background testing. Reference reports can be used to verify information presented by the applicant on the resume, application form, and biographical information survey.

Letters of Recommendation

A very common selection procedure in some settings (e.g., academic institutions) is to ask applicants to have letters of recommendation written for them. There are two major problems with this approach. First, these letters may do little to help the organization discern more qualified from less qualified applicants. The reason for this is that only very poor applicants are unable to arrange for positive letters about their accomplishments. Second, most letters are not structured or standardized. What this means is that the organization receives data from letter writers that are not consistent across organizations. For example, a letter about one applicant may concern the applicant's educational qualifications, while a letter about another applicant may focus on the applicant's work experience. Comparing the qualifications of applicants A and B under these circumstances is like comparing apples and oranges.

The problem with letters of recommendation is demonstrated dramatically in one study that showed there was a stronger correlation between two letters written by one person for two different applicants than between two different people writing letters for the same person.[61] This finding indicates that letters of recommendation have more to do with the letter writer than the person being written about.[62]

Such problems indicate that organizations should downplay the weight given to letters unless a great deal of credibility and accountability can be attached to the letter writer's comments. Also, a structured form should be provided so that each writer provides the same information about each applicant.

Another way to improve upon letters of recommendation is to use a standardized scoring key. An example of one is shown in Exhibit 9.8. Using this method, categories of KSAOs are established and become the scoring key (shown at the bottom of the exhibit). Then the adjectives in the actual letter are underlined and classified into the appropriate category. The number of adjectives used in each category constitute the applicant's score.

Reference Checks

With this form of reference report, a check is made on the applicant's background. Usually the person contacted is the immediate supervisor of the applicant or is in the human resource department of current or previous organizations with which the applicant has had contact. A recent survey of 1,331 human resource managers provided some helpful information about the use of reference checks in organizations.[63] Eighty percent of organizations check references with every applicant.

EXHIBIT 9.8 Scoring Letters of Recommendation

Dear Personnel Director:

Mr. John Anderson asked that I write this letter in support of his application as assistant manager and I am pleased to do so. I have know John for six years as he was my assistant in the accounting department.

John always had his work completed accurately and promptly. In his years here, he never missed a deadline. He is very detail oriented, alert in finding errors, and methodical in his problem solving approach. Interpersonally, John is a very friendly and helpful person.

I have great confidence in John's ability. If you desire more information, please let me know.

MA 0   CC 2   DR 6   U 0   V 0

Dear Personnel Director:

Mr. John Anderson asked that I write this letter in support of his application as assistant manager and I am pleased to do so. I have know John for six years as he was my assistant in the accounting department.

John was one of the most popular employees in our agency as he is a friendly, outgoing, sociable individual. He has a great sense of humor, is poised, and is very helpful. In completing his work, he is independent, energetic, and industrious.

I have great confidence in John's ability. If you desire more information, please let me know.

MA 0   CC 2   DR 0   U 5   V 3

Key MA = mental ability
CC = consideration-cooperation
DR = dependability-reliability
U = urbanity
V = vigor

Source: M. G. Aumodt, D. A. Bryan, and A. J. Whitcomb, "Predicting Performance with Letters of Recommendation," *Public Personnel Management*, 1993, 22, pp. 81–90. Reprinted with permission of *Public Personnel Management*, published by the International Personnel Management Association.

The most common person to be contacted in a reference check is the applicant's former supervisor. In the vast majority of cases (81%), references are checked over the phone. The most commonly sought data are dates of employment (96%), eligibility for rehire (65%), qualifications for prospective job (56%), overall impression of applicant (49%), and reason for leaving job (47%). In 89% of the cases, applicants are asked to sign a waiver against taking legal action against either the past or prospective employer as a consequence of checking references. Exhibit 9.9 provides a sample reference request. Although this reference request

EXHIBIT 9.9 Sample Reference Request

TO BE COMPLETED BY APPLICANT

NAME (PRINT):	SOCIAL SEC. NUMBER:

I HAVE MADE APPLICATION FOR EMPLOYMENT AT THIS COMPANY. I REQUEST AND AUTHORIZE YOU TO RELEASE ALL INFORMATION REQUESTED BELOW CONCERNING MY EMPLOYMENT RECORD, REASON FOR LEAVING YOUR EMPLOY, OR MY EDUCATION. I HEREBY RELEASE MY PERSONAL REFERENCES, MY FORMER EMPLOYERS AND SCHOOLS, AND ALL INDIVIDUALS CONNECTED THEREWITH, FROM ALL LIABILITY FOR ANY DAMAGE WHATSOEVER FOR FURNISHING THIS INFORMATION.

SIGNATURE _____ DATE _____

SCHOOL REFERENCE

DATES ATTENDED

FROM: TO: GRADUATED?   YES ☐   NO ☐
DEGREE AWARDED:

EMPLOYMENT REFERENCE

POSITION HELD: EMPLOYMENT DATES:

IMMEDIATE SUPERVISOR'S NAME

REASON FOR LEAVING

          DISCHARGED ☐   RESIGNED ☐   LAID OFF ☐

FORMER EMPLOYER OR SCHOOL—Please complete the following. Thank you.

IS THE ABOVE INFORMATION CORRECT?

          YES ☐   NO ☐   If not, give correct information:

_____
_____
_____

PLEASE CHECK

	EXCEL.	GOOD	FAIR	POOR	COMMENTS:
ATTITUDE	____	____	____	____	
QUALITY OF WORK	____	____	____	____	
COOPERATION	____	____	____	____	
ATTENDANCE	____	____	____	____	

WOULD YOU RECOMMEND FOR EMPLOYMENT?   YES ☐   NO ☐

ADDITIONAL COMMENTS

_____
_____
_____

SIGNATURE OF EMPLOYER OR SCHOOL REPRESENTATIVE   TITLE was developed for checking references by mail, the questions contained in the request could easily be adapted for use in checking references via telephone.

Both of the problems that occur with letters of recommendation take place with reference checks as well. An even more significant concern, however, is the reluctance of organizations to give out the requested information because they fear a lawsuit due to invasion of privacy or defamation of character.[64] Recall the survey results reported above indicating that 80% of employers always check references. The same survey indicated that 63% of employers *refuse* to provide reference information for fear of being sued. As one executive stated, "There's a dire need for better reference information but fear of litigation keeps employers from providing much more than name, rank, and serial number."[65] As a result of the reluctance to provide reference information, reference checkers claim to receive inadequate information roughly half of the time. To a large degree, this concern over providing even rudimentary reference information is excessive (see Legal Issues section at the end of this chapter). It is important to remember that if every organization refuses to provide useful reference information, a potentially important source of applicant information would lose any of its potential value.

Background Testing

How would you feel if you found out that the organization you had hoped to join was having your court record and moral character investigated? How would you feel if an organization did *not* investigate the court record and moral character of guards to be selected for the gun storage depot of the U.S. military base near your home?

Although it may seem to be a very invasive procedure, background investigations are routinely conducted on matters such as these and are sometimes needed to protect the public's interests. Some organizations do background testing on their own, while others employ agencies such as Pinkerton to do so.[66] As with any predictor, the reasonableness of this procedure depends upon how related the factors being investigated are to the requirements of the job.[67]

At a general level, background testing is concerned with the reliability of applicants' behavior, integrity, and personal adjustment. These factors are often used as requirements for the selection of people in occupations such as law enforcement, private security, and nuclear power, and in positions requiring government-issued security clearances.[68]

Measures used include criminal history (convictions), civil litigation (both plaintiff and defendant history), financial history (credit reports, bankruptcies, tax liens, civil judgments, and defaults), driving record (citations, accidents, and DUIs), education (degree awarded), earnings history, and workers' compensation claims.[69] Extreme care needs to be taken in the use of such measures because of the limited validity reports available to date, as well as legal constraints on pre-employment inquiries (see Legal Issues at the end of this chapter).

Evaluation of Reference Reports

The empirical data that does exist on the validity of reference checks is not all that positive. A meta-analysis of a number of studies revealed that the validity coefficients of reference data ranged from $\bar{r} = .16$ to $\bar{r} = .26$. To some degree, the validity depends on who is providing the information. If it is the personnel officer, coworker, or relative, the information is not very valid. On the other hand, reference reports from supervisors and acquaintances are somewhat more valid. The validity of personnel officers may be less valid because they are less knowledgeable about the applicant (their past employee); the reports of coworkers and relatives probably are less valid because these individuals are positively biased toward the applicant.

Although references do not have high validity, we need to take a cost-benefit approach. In general the quality of the information may be low but in the few cases where reference information changes a decision, the payoff can be significant. An executive with the U.S. Postal Service once told one of the authors that many of the acts of violence by Postal Service employees would have been avoided if a thorough background check had been conducted. Thus, since references are a relatively cheap method of collecting information on applicants, screening out the occasional unstable applicant or in a few cases learning something new and important about an applicant may make reference checks a good investment. As with unweighted application blanks, though, using reference checks requires employers to turn elsewhere to obtain information suitable for making final decisions about applicants.

Handwriting Analysis

An extremely distant sign of job performance is handwriting analysis or graphology.[70] Yet, some employers use this type of analysis to predict job performance. In fact, graphology is widely used in western Europe (particularly France) and Israel as a selection method.[71] While the process of obtaining handwriting samples from applicants is virtually costless, the process of analyzing the samples is not. Estimates are that handwriting assessments cost about $75 per applicant.[72]

The theory behind graphology as a selection device is that handwriting is a measure of personality. So, for example, the height of the bar used to cross one's *t*'s is a measure of one's approach to achievement. The higher the bar used to cross lowercase *t*'s, the stronger the willpower. Individuals who write a sentence on a blank piece of paper that slants upward are thought to be optimists while those whose sentences slant downward are thought to be pessimists. In turn, these signs of personality are believed to have an impact on job performance.

One of the very few advantages of this predictor over other predictors measuring personality is that it is difficult to fake. The problem with this approach is that the link between handwriting, personality, and HR outcomes is tenuous at best. One would expect to find virtually no relationship between handwriting analysis and a distant outcome such as job performance and, in fact, that is exactly what has been found. A well-conducted study of real estate brokers found no relationship between graphologist ratings of handwriting and any measure of job performance (sales volume, supervisor ratings of job performance, or self ratings of performance).[73] Another well-controlled study reported similarly weak findings.[74] Thus, although little research has been conducted on the validity of graphology, the evidence that is available suggests organizations would be best advised to avoid this selection method.

Literacy Testing

Most jobs require that employees possess reading and writing skills. In some jobs, the need for these skills is obvious. In others, while the need is not obvious, these skills are nevertheless critical to successful on-the-job performance. A good example is the position of custodian. Reading skills do not at first seem important for this position. However, reading skills may be very important for custodians, as witnessed by the authors of this book in a small school district in Ohio, where an illiterate night custodian mistakenly used what he thought was a cleaning compound for toilets. The substance turned out to have a large amount of an acid compound, as shown on the label. He then used it to clean the toilet seats. Fortunately, no one was hurt in this incident. The incident emphasizes the importance of carefully identifying all relevant KSAOs when developing the job requirements matrix and selection plan.

Illiteracy is a big problem in our country. It is estimated that over 30 million Americans are functionally illiterate. Historically, this was not a selection issue in industries where people's physical skills were much more important than their mental skills. Today, all that has changed. Ford, Chrysler, and GM claim to have invested almost $100 million dollars in literacy programs.[75] These dollars have gone toward providing training for those presently employed workers who cannot read or write up to the standards required by new jobs in the auto industry.

Another way for employers to address the issue of illiteracy is to select in advance those people who already have the required reading and writing skills. A great deal of theory and research has gone into developing standardized reading tests.[76] In addition, companies are developing their own tests. For example, Southern California Gas Company has developed a writing test for its sales position that assesses writing mechanics, written content, and ability to follow exercise directions.[77] It has been well received by the company and by the union as well, because of the detailed feedback it gives to applicants.

Genetic Screening

Due to advances in medical technology, it is now possible for employers to screen people on the basis of their genetic code. The testing is done to screen out people who are susceptible to certain diseases (e.g., sickle-cell anemia) due to exposure to toxic substances at work.[78] Screening out susceptible people is one way to ensure that workers do not become ill. Another way to do so is to eliminate the toxic substances. Although the use of genetic screening is not widespread, companies such as Du Pont and Dow Chemical experimented with it to protect their employees.[79] Organizations also experimented with genetic screening because of the huge costs associated with work-related diseases and illnesses.[80] However, a recent court decision has ruled that genetic screening is prohibited under the Americans with Disabilities Act.[81] Therefore, employers should avoid the use of genetic screening as a selection method.

Initial Interview

The initial interview occurs very early in the initial assessment process, and is often the applicant's first personal contact with the organization and its staffing system. At this point, applicants are relatively undifferentiated to the organization in terms of KSAOs. The initial interview will begin the process of necessary differentiation, a "rough cut" of sorts.

The purpose of the initial interview is, and should be, to screen out the most obvious cases of person/job mismatches. To do this, the interview should focus on an assessment of KSAOs that are absolute requirements for the applicant. Examples of such minimum levels of qualifications for the job include certification and licensure requirements, and necessary (not just preferred) training and experience requirements.

These assessments may be made on the basis of information gathered from written means (e.g., application blank or resume), as well as the interview per se. Care should be taken to ensure that the interviewer focuses on only this information as a basis for decision making. Evaluations of personal characteristics of the applicant (e.g., race, sex), as well as judgments about an applicant's personality (e.g., she seems so outgoing and just "right" for this job), are to be avoided. Indeed, to ensure that this focus happens, some organizations (e.g., civil service agencies) have basically eliminated the initial interview altogether and make the initial assessment only on the basis of written information provided by the applicant.

One of the limitations with the initial interview is that it is perhaps the most expensive method of initial assessment. Given that the validity evidence for such types of interview is not particularly impressive, the payoff of using the initial interview relative to other methods of initial assessment is questionable.

Video and Computer Interviews

One means of reducing the costs of initial interviews is to use video interviews. Video interviews can take at least one of two forms.[82] One form of the video interview is to link the applicant and recruiter via remote video access. This sort of video-conferencing allows the applicant and recruiter to see each other on a monitor and, in some cases, even exchange documents. Viewnet of Madison, Wis. has sold their video interview technology to more than 70 colleges to use as an alternative selection device. A variant of this type of video interview is to hire a consulting firm to conduct the video interviews for the organization. Under this approach, the organization identifies the candidates (perhaps after screening their applications or resumes), and submits their names to the consulting firm. The firm then videotapes the interviews and submits the tapes to the organization. Another example of a firm that provides this type of service is the Corporate Interviewing Network, Inc. (CNI). The benefits that CNI promotes are reduced costs per hire, compressed time frame (on average, videotaped interviews are delivered to organizations within a week), and saved management time interviewing applicants. In general, one of the advantages of video-based interviews is that they can dramatically lower the cost of initial interviews. This is particularly true for employers who may wish to interview only a few applicants at a given location. Another advantage of these interviews is that they can be arranged on short notice (no travel and no schedule rearrangements). Of course, a disadvantage of these interviews is that they do not permit face-to-face contact. The effect of this limitation on validity and applicant reactions is unknown.

Another form of video interviews takes the process even a step further. Computer-based interviews utilize software that asks applicants questions (e.g., "Have you ever been terminated for stealing?") or presents realistic scenarios (e.g., present an irate customer on the screen), all the while recording applicants' responses. These responses are then forwarded to selection decision makers for use in making initial screening decisions. The software can also be configured to inform applicants about job duties and requirements. It can even track how long it takes an applicant to answer each question. As with video interviews, computer-based interviews can offer dramatic costs savings (although start-up costs to customize programs can be high). As before, though, the accuracy of these high-tech interviews as compared to the old standby person-to-person variety, is unclear. The same holds true for how applicants will react to these relatively impersonal methods.

Evaluation of Initial Interview

Whether high-tech or traditional, the interview has its benefits and its limitations. Nearly all of the research evaluating the interview in selection has considered it as a substantive method (see Structured Interview section in Chapter 10). Thus, there is little evidence about the usefulness of the initial interview. However, organizations using the initial interview in selection are likely to find it more useful by following a few guidelines such as the following:

1. Ask questions that assess the most basic KSAOs identified by job analysis. This requires separating what is required from what is preferred.

2. Stick to basic, qualifying questions suitable for making rough cuts (e.g., "Have you completed the minimum certification requirements to qualify for this job?") rather than subtle, subjective questions more suitable for substantive decisions (e.g., "How would this job fit within your overall career goals?"). Remember, the purpose of the initial interview is closer to cutting with a saw than operating with a scalpel. Ask only the most fundamental questions now and leave the fine-tuning for later.

3. Keep interviews brief. Most interviewers make up their minds quickly and, given the limited usefulness and the type of information collected, a long (e.g., 45–60 minutes) interview is unlikely to add much over a shorter (15–30 minutes) one.

4. As with all interviews, the same questions should be asked of all applicants, and EEO compliance must be monitored.

Choice of Initial Assessment Methods

As has now been described, there is a wide range of initial assessment methods available to organizations to help reduce the applicant pool to bona fide candidates. A range of formats is available as well. Fortunately, with so many choices available to organizations, research results are available to help guide choices of methods to use. This research has been reviewed many times and is summarized in Exhibit 9.10.[83] In Exhibit 9.10, each initial assessment method is rated according to several criteria. Each of these criteria will be discussed in turn.

Use

Use refers to how frequently surveyed organizations use each predictor. Use is probably an "overused" criterion in deciding which selection measures to adopt. Benchmarking—basing human resource decisions on what other companies are doing—is a predominant method of decision making in all areas of human resources, including staffing. However, is this a good basis on which to make decisions about selection methods? Although it is always comforting to do what other organizations are doing, relying on information from other organizations assumes that they know what they are doing. Just because many organizations use a selection measure does not make it a good idea for a particular organization. Circumstances differ from organization to organization. Perhaps more importantly, many organizational decision makers (and HR consultants) either lack knowledge about the latest findings in human resources research or have decided that such findings are inapplicable to their organization. It also is difficult to determine whether a successful organization that uses a particular selection method is successful because it uses this method or if it will be as successful in the future. Thus, from a research standpoint, there may be real strategic advantage in relying on

EXHIBIT 9.10   Evaluation of Initial Assessment Methods

Predictors	Use	Cost	Reliability	Validity	Utility	Reactions	Adverse Impact
Level of education	High	Low	Moderate	Low	Low	?	Moderate
Grade point average	Moderate	Low	Moderate	Low	?	?	?
Quality of school	?	Low	Moderate	Low	?	?	Moderate
Major field of study	?	Low	Moderate	Moderate	?	?	?
Extracurricular activity	?	Low	Moderate	Moderate	?	?	?
Training and experience	High	Low	High	Moderate	Moderate	?	Moderate
Licensing and certification	Moderate	Low	?	?	?	?	?
Weighted application blanks	Low	Moderate	Moderate	Moderate	Moderate	?	?
Biographical data	Low	High	High	High	High	Negative	Moderate
Letters of recommendation	Moderate	Low	?	Low	?	?	?
Reference checks	High	Moderate	Low	Moderate	Moderate	Mixed	Low
Background testing	Low	High	?	?	?	Mixed	Moderate
Resumes and cover letters	Moderate	Low	Moderate	?	?	?	?
Initial interview	High	Moderate	Low	Low	?	Positive	Moderate
Handwriting analysis	Low	Moderate	Low	Low	?	Negative	?
Genetic screening	Low	High	Moderate	?	?	?	High
Literacy testing	Low	Moderate	?	Low	?	?	?

"effectiveness" criteria (e.g., validity, utility, adverse impact) rather than worrying about the practices of other organizations.

Another reason to have a healthy degree of skepticism about the use criterion is that there is a severe lack of broad (i.e., coverage of many industries and regions in the United States) and timely surveys of selection practices. The Bureau of National Affairs (BNA) has conducted broad surveys of selection practices but the most recent survey was in 1988. Other surveys of selection practices are available, but they generally cover only a single selection practice (e.g., drug testing) or lack adequate scope or breadth. In providing conclusions about use of various selection methods in organizations, we are forced to make judgment calls concerning which survey to rely upon. In the case of some selection measures (e.g., application blanks), there is little reason to believe the BNA figures have changed much. With other predictors, the use figures have shown a fair degree of volatility and change from year to year. Thus, in classifying the use of assessment methods, we rely on the most recent surveys that achieve some degree of breadth. For purposes of classifying the predictors, high use refers to use by more than two-thirds of organizations, moderate is use by one-third to two-thirds of organizations, and low use refers to use by less than one-third of organizations.

Having issued these caveats about the use criterion, Exhibit 9.10 reveals clear differences in the use of different methods of initial assessment. The most frequently used methods of initial assessment are education level, training and experience, reference checks, and initial interview. These methods are considered, to some degree, in selection decisions for most types of positions. Licensing and certification requirements, letters of recommendation, and resumes and cover letters have moderate levels of use. All three of these methods are widely used in filling some types of positions but infrequently used in filling many others. The least widely used initial assessment methods are weighted application blanks, biographical information, background testing, handwriting analysis, genetic screening, and literacy testing. It is relatively unusual for organizations to use these methods for initial screening decisions. There are no reliable figures on the use of quality of school, major field of study, and extracurricular activity in initial selection decisions; thus their use could not be estimated.

Cost

Cost refers to expenses incurred in using the predictor. Although most of the initial assessment methods may seem relatively cost free since the applicant provides the information on his or her own time, this is not so. For most initial assessment methods, the major cost associated with each selection measure is administration. Consider an application blank. It is true that applicants complete application blanks on their own time, but someone must be present to hand out applications, answer inquiries in person and over the phone about possible openings, and collect, sort, and forward applications to the appropriate person. Then the selection decision maker must read each application, perhaps make notes and weed out the clearly unacceptable applicants, and then make decisions about candidates. Thus, even for the least expensive methods of initial assessment, costs associated with their use are far from trivial.

On the other hand, utility research has suggested that costs do not play a large part in evaluating the financial benefit of using particular selection methods. This becomes readily apparent when one considers the costs of hiring a poor performer. For example, a secretary who performs one standard deviation below average (16th percentile, if performance is normally distributed) may cost the organization $8,000 in lost productivity per year. And this person is likely to remain on the job for more than one year, multiplying the costs. Considered in this light, spending an extra few hundred dollars to accurately identify good secretaries is an excellent investment. Thus, although costs need to be considered in evaluating assessment methods, more consideration should be given to the fact that valid selection measures pay off handsomely and will return many times their cost.

As can be seen in Exhibit 9.10, the least costly initial assessment methods include information that can obtained from application blanks (level of education, grade point average, quality of school, major field of study, extracurricular activity, training and experience, licensing and certification) and other applicant-provided information (letters of recommendation, resumes and cover letters). Initial assessment methods of moderate cost include weighted applicant blanks, reference checks, initial interviews, handwriting analysis, and literacy testing. Biographical information, background testing, and genetic screening are relatively expensive assessment methods.

Reliability

Reliability refers to consistency of measurement. As was noted in Chapter 6, reliability is a bound for validity so it would be very difficult for a predictor with low reliability to have high validity. By the same token, it is unlikely that a valid predictor would have low reliability. Unfortunately, the reliability information on many initial assessment methods is lacking in the literature. Some researchers have investigated distortion of applicant-reported information (application blanks and resumes). One study found that nearly half of the items on application blanks were distorted by 20% of the applicants. Other studies have suggested that one-third of application blanks contain some inaccuracies.[84] Thus, it is probably reasonable to infer that applicant-supplied information in application blanks and resumes is of moderate reliability. The reliability of reference checks appears to be relatively low. In terms of training and experience evaluations, while distortion can occur if the applicant supplies training and experience information, interrater agreement in evaluating this information is quite high.[85] Biographical information also generally has high reliability. The initial interview, like most unstructured interviews, probably has a relatively low level of reliability. Handwriting analysis has a moderate degree of reliability.

Validity

Validity refers to the strength of the relationship between the predictor and job performance. Low validity refers to validity in the range of about .00 to .15. Moderate validity corresponds to validity in the range of about .16 to .30, and high validity is .31 and above. As might be expected, most initial assessment methods have moderate to low validity because they are used only for making "rough cuts" among applicants rather than for final decisions. Perhaps the two most valid initial assessment methods are biodata and training and experience requirements; their validity can range from moderate to high. Among the least valid initial methods are the initial interview and handwriting analysis.

Utility

Utility refers to the monetary return associated with using the predictor, relative to its cost. According to researchers and decision makers, when comparing the utility of selection methods, validity appears to be the most important consideration.[86] In short, it would be very unusual for a valid selection method to have low utility. Thus, as can be seen in Exhibit 9.10, high, moderate, and low validities tend to directly correspond to high, moderate, and low utility values, respectively. Question marks predominate this column in the exhibit because relatively few studies have directly investigated the utility of these methods. However, based on the argument that validity should be directly related to utility, it is likely that high validity methods also will realize large financial benefits to organizations that choose to use them. Research does indicate that training and experience requirements have moderate (or even high) levels of utility, and reference checks have moderate levels of utility.

Applicant Reactions

Reactions refers to the favorability of applicants' reactions to the predictor. Applicant reactions are an important evaluative criterion because research has indicated that applicants who feel positively about selection methods and the selection process report higher levels of satisfaction with the organization, are more likely to accept a position with the organization, and are more likely to recommend the organization to others.[87]

Research suggests that selection measures that are perceived as job related, present applicants with an opportunity to perform, are administered consistently, and provide applicants with feedback about their performance, are likely to generate favorable applicant reactions.[88] (We will have more to say on this issue in Chapter 14.) Unfortunately, though, very little research has investigated applicant reactions to specific assessment methods. One study suggested that background checks are viewed neutrally by applicants, and handwriting analysis is viewed negatively.[89] We are aware of no research on the other initial assessment methods.

Adverse Impact

Adverse impact refers to the possibility that a disproportionate number of protected class members may be rejected using this predictor. Several initial assessment methods have moderate degrees of adverse impact against women and/or minorities, including level of education, quality of school, training and experience, biographical information, and the initial interview. Genetic screening may have a high degree of adverse impact while reference checks appear to have little adverse impact.

LEGAL ISSUES

Initial assessment methods are subject to numerous laws, regulations, and other legal considerations. Four major matters of concern pertain to using disclaimers, conducting reference checks, making preemployment inquiries, and making bona fide occupational qualifications claims.

Disclaimers

During the initial stages of contact with job applicants, it is important for the organization to protect itself legally by clearly identifying rights it wants to maintain for itself. This involves the use of disclaimers. Disclaimers are statements (usually written) that provide or confer explicit rights to the employer as part of the employment contract, and that are shown to job applicants. The organization needs to decide (or reevaluate) which rights it wants to retain and how these will be communicated to job applicants.

Three areas of rights are usually suggested for possible inclusion in a disclaimer policy. These are (a) employment-at-will (right to terminate the employment relationship at any time, for any reason); (b) verification consent (right to verify information provided by the applicant); and (c) false statement warning (right to not hire, terminate, or discipline prospective employee for providing false information to the employer). Examples of disclaimer statements in these three areas are shown in Exhibit 9.4. Usually, it is recommended that the organization have all three of these disclaimers as part of its planned policy toward job applicants.[90]

To communicate disclaimers, it is advisable that they be shown in writing to job applicants (often on the application blank), reviewed with the applicant if possible, and then signed by the applicant. It should be remembered that signed disclaimer statements will become part of the employment contract for those applicants who accept a job offer. Care should thus be exercised in the development and communication of disclaimers.

Reference Checks

Reference checking creates a legal quagmire for the organization. Current or former employers of the job applicant may be reluctant to provide a reference (especially one with negative information about the applicant) because they fear the applicant may file a defamation suit against them. Hence, the organization may view requesting references to be rather fruitless. On the other hand, failure to conduct a reference check opens up the organization to the possibility of a negligent hiring suit, in which it is claimed that the organization hired a person it should have known would cause harm to its other employees or customers. To deal with such problems and obtain thorough, accurate information, the following suggestions are offered.

First, gather as much information as possible directly from the applicant, along with a verification consent. In this way, use of reference providers and information demands on them are minimized.

Second, be sure to obtain written authorization from the applicant to check references. To do so, the applicant should sign a blanket consent form. Also, the organization could prepare a request-for-reference form that the applicant would give to person(s) being asked to provide a reference. That form would authorize the person(s) to provide requested information, release the person from any liability for providing the information, and be signed by the applicant (see Exhiit 9.9).

Third, specify the types of information being requested of the reference provider. That information should be specific, factual, and job related in content. Finally, limit access to the reference information to only those who will actually be participating in the selection decision.[91]

It is also important to check relevant state laws regarding permissible and impermissible reference check practices, since these vary among the states. Also, several states have reference immunity laws. In general, these laws provide immunity from civil liability to organizations that in good faith provide information about the job performance and professional conduct of its former or current employees. In these states, organizations should be particularly willing to both request and provide reference information.

Preemployment Inquiries

The term preemployment inquiry (PI), as used here, pertains to both content and method of assessment. Regarding content, PI refers to applicants' personal and background data. These data cover such areas as demographics (race, color, religion, sex, national origin, age), physical characteristics (disability, height, weight), family and associates, residence, economic status, and education. The information could be gathered by any method; most frequently, it will be gathered with an initial assessment method, particularly the application blank, biodata questionnaire, or preliminary interview. At times, PIs may also occur as part of an unstructured interview.

PIs have been singled out for particular legal (EEO/AA) attention at both the federal and state levels. The reason for this is that PIs have great potential for use in a discriminatory manner early on in the selection process.[92] Moreover, research continually finds that organizations make inappropriate and illegal PIs. One study, for example, found that out of 46 categories of application blank items, there was an average of 7.4 inadvisable items used by employers on their application blanks.[93] It is thus critical to understand the laws and regulations surrounding the use of PIs.

Federal Laws and Regulations

The laws and their interpretation indicate that it is illegal to use PI information that has a disparate impact based on a protected characteristic (race, color, etc.), unless such disparate impact can be shown to be job related and consistent with business necessity. The emphasis here is on the potentially illegal use of the information, rather than its collection per se.

The EEOC makes the following points generally about PIs:[94]

1. It is reasonable to assume that all information on an application form or in a pre-employment interview are for some purpose and that selection or hiring decisions are being made on the basis of the answers given. In an investigation of charges of discrimination, the burden of proof is on the employer to show that answers to all questions on application forms or in oral interviews are not used in making hiring and placement decisions in a discriminatory manner prohibited by law.

2. To seek information other than that which is essential to effectively evaluate a person's qualifications for employment is to make oneself vulnerable to charges of discrimination and consequent legal proceedings.

3. It is, therefore, in an employer's own self-interest to carefully review all procedures used in screening applicants for employment, eliminating or altering any not justified by business necessity.

These principles are reflected in two sets of regulations and guidelines.

EEOC Guide to Preemployment Inquiries   This guide provides the principles just given above. It then provides specific guidance (dos and don'ts) on PIs regarding the following: race, color, religion, sex, national origin, age, height and weight, marital status, number of children, provisions for child care, English language skill, educational requirements, friends or relatives working for the employer, arrest records, conviction records, discharge from military service, citizenship, economic status, and availability for work on weekends or holidays.[95]

ADA Regulations   These regulations (see Appendix C) prohibit PIs or preemployment medical examinations in order to determine if an applicant is disabled, or the nature or severity of a disability. Despite this seemingly strict prohibition, the regulations also specifically permit PIs as follows:

> Acceptable pre-employment inquiry—A covered entity may make pre-employment inquiries into the ability of an applicant to perform job-related functions, and/or ask an applicant to describe or to demonstrate how, with or without reasonable accommodation, the applicant will be able to perform job-related functions.
>
> Employment entrance examination—A covered entity may require an inquiry (such as a medical exam) after making an offer of employment to a job applicant and before the applicant begins his or her employment duties, and may condition an offer of employment on the results of such inquiry, if all employees in the same job category are subjected to such an inquiry regardless of disability.

There appears to be a fine line between permissible and impermissible information that may be gathered, and between appropriate and inappropriate methods for gathering it, under the ADA. To help employers, the EEOC has developed specific enforcement guidance on these matters.[96]

The general thrust of the guidance is that the organization may not ask disability-related questions and may not conduct medical examinations until after it makes a conditional job offer to a person. Once that offer is made, however, the organization may ask disability-related questions and conduct medical examinations, so long as this is done for all entering employees in the job category. When such questions or exams screen out a person with a disability, the reason for rejection must be job related and consistent with business necessity. A person may be rejected for safety reasons if the person provides a direct threat of substantial harm to him/herself or others. We will have more to say about the legality of medical examinations in the next chapter.

More specific guidance is provided for the preoffer stage as follows. Disability-related questions cannot be asked, meaning questions (a) whether a person has a disability, (b) that are likely to elicit information about a disability, or (c) that are closely related to disability. Along with these general prohibitions, it is impermissible to ask applicants whether they will need reasonable accommodation to perform the functions of the job or can perform major life activities (e.g., lifting, walking), to ask about lawful use of drugs, to ask about workers' compensation history, and to ask third parties (e.g., former employers, references) questions that cannot be asked of the applicant.

Alternatively, preoffer it is permissible to ask:

- if the applicant can perform the job, with or without reasonable accommodation

- the applicant to describe or demonstrate how they would perform the job (including any needed reasonable accommodation)
- if the applicant will need reasonable accommodation for the hiring process (unless there is an obvious disability or the applicant discloses a disability)
- the applicant to provide documentation of a disability if requesting reasonable accommodation for the hiring process
- if the applicant can meet the organization's attendance requirement
- the applicant for certifications and licenses
- about the applicant's current illegal use of drugs (but not past addiction)
- about the applicant's drinking habits (but not alcoholism)

State Laws and Regulations

There is a vast cache of state laws and regulations pertaining to PIs.[97] These requirements vary substantially among the states. They are often more stringent and inclusive than federal laws and regulations. The organization thus must become familiar with and adhere to the laws for each state in which it is located.

An example of Ohio state law regarding PIs is shown in Exhibit 9.11. Notice how the format of the example points out both lawful and unlawful ways of gathering PI information.

EXHIBIT 9.11 Ohio Pre-Employment Inquiry Guide

INQUIRIES BEFORE HIRING	LAWFUL	UNLAWFUL*
1. NAME	Name	Inquiry into any title which indicates race, color, religion, sex, national origin, handicap, age or ancestry.
2. ADDRESS	Inquiry into place and length at current address.	Inquiry into any foreign addresses which would indicate national origin.
3. AGE	Any inquiry limited to establishing that applicant meets any minimum age requirement that may be established by law.	A. Requiring birth certificate or baptismal record before hiring. B. Any inquiry which may reveal the date of high school graduation. C. Any other inquiry which may reveal whether applicant is at least 40 and less than 70 years of age.

(continued)

EXHIBIT 9.11   Continued

INQUIRIES BEFORE HIRING	LAWFUL	UNLAWFUL*
4. BIRTHPLACE, NATIONAL ORIGIN, OR ANCESTRY		A. Any inquiry into place of birth. B. Any inquiry into place of birth of parents, grandparents or spouse. C. Any other inquiry into national origin or ancestry.
5. RACE OR COLOR		Any inquiry which would indicate race or color.
6. SEX		A. Any inquiry which would indicate sex. B. Any inquiry made of members of one sex, but not the other.
7. HEIGHT AND WEIGHT	Inquiries as to ability to perform actual job requirements.	Being a certain height or weight will not be considered to be a job requirement unless the employer can show that no employee with the ineligible height or weight could do the work.
8. RELIGION—CREED		A. Any inquiry which would indicate or identify religious denomination or custom. B. Applicant may not be told any religious identity or preference of the employer. C. Request pastor's recommendation or reference.
9. HANDICAP	Inquiries necessary to determine applicant's ability to substantially perform specific job without significant hazard.	A. Any inquiry into past or current medical conditions not related to position applied for. B. Any inquiry into Worker's Compensation or similar claims.

(continued)

EXHIBIT 9.11 Continued

INQUIRIES BEFORE HIRING	LAWFUL	UNLAWFUL*
10. CITIZENSHIP	A. Whether a U.S. citizen B. If not, whether applicant intends to become one. C. If U.S. residence is legal. D. If spouse is citizen. E. Require proof of citizenship after being hired. F. Any other requirement mandated by the Immigration Reform and Control Act of 1986, as amended.	A. If native-born or naturalized. B. Proof of citizenship before hiring. C. Whether parents or spouse are native-born or naturalized.
11. PHOTOGRAPHS	May be required after hiring for identification.	Require photograph before hiring.
12. ARREST AND CONVICTIONS	Inquiries into *conviction* of specific crimes related to qualifications for the job applied for.	Any inquiry which would reveal arrests without convictions.
13. EDUCATION	A. Inquiry into nature and extent of academic, professional or vocational training. B. Inquiry into language skills such as reading and writing of foreign languages, if job related.	A. Any inquiry which would reveal the nationality or religious affiliation of a school. B. Inquiry as to what mother tongue is or how foreign language ability was acquired.
14. RELATIVES	Inquiry into name, relationship, and address of person to be notified in case of emergency.	Any inquiry about a relative which would be unlawful if made about the applicant.
15. ORGANIZATIONS	Inquiry into membership in professional organizations and offices held, excluding any organization, the name or character of which indicates the race, color, religion, sex, national origin, handicap, age, or ancestry of its members.	Inquiry into every club and organization where membership is held.

(continued)

EXHIBIT 9.11   Continued

INQUIRIES BEFORE HIRING	LAWFUL	UNLAWFUL*
16. MILITARY SERVICE	A. Inquiry into service in U.S. Armed Forces when such service is a qualification for the job. B. Require military discharge certificate after being hired.	A. Inquiry into military service in armed service of any country but U.S. B. Request military service records. C. Inquiry into type of discharge.
17. WORK SCHEDULE	Inquiry into willingness or ability to work required work schedule.	Any inquiry into willingness or ability to work any particular religious holidays.
18. MISCELLANEOUS	Any question required to reveal qualifications for the job applied for.	Any non-job related inquiry which may elicit or attempt to elicit any information concerning race, color, religion, sex, national origin, handicap, age, or ancestry of an applicant for employment or membership.
19. REFERENCES	General personal and work references which do not reveal the race, color, religion, sex, national origin, handicap, age, or ancestry of the applicant.	Request references specifically from clergymen or any other persons who might reflect race, color, religion, sex, national origin, handicap, age, or ancestry of applicant.

I. Employers acting under bona fide Affirmative Action Programs or acting under orders of Equal Employment law enforcement agencies of federal, state, or local governments may make some of the prohibited inquiries listed above to the extent that these inquiries are required by such programs or orders.

II. Employers having Federal defense contracts are exempt to the extent that otherwise prohibited inquiries are required by Federal Law for security purposes.

III. Any inquiry is prohibited although not specifically listed above, which elicits information as to, or which is not job related and may be used to discriminate on the basis of, race, color, religion, sex, national origin, handicap, age, or ancestry in violation of law.

*Unless bona fide occupational qualification is certified in advance by the Ohio Civil Rights Commission.

Source: Ohio Civil Rights Commission, 1989.

Bona Fide Occupational Qualifications

Title VII of the Civil Rights Act explicitly permits discrimination on the basis of sex, religion, or national origin (but not race or color) if it can be shown to be a bona fide occupational qualification (BFOQ) "reasonably necessary to the normal operation" of the business. The ADEA contains a similar provision regarding age. These provisions thus permit outright rejection of applicants because of their sex, religion, national origin, or age, as long as the rejection can be justified under the "reasonably necessary" standard. Exactly how have BFOQ claims by employers fared? When are BFOQ claims upheld as legitimate? Several points are relevant to understanding the BFOQ issue.

The burden of proof is on the employer to justify any BFOQ claim, and it is clear that the BFOQ exception is to be construed narrowly. Thus, it does not apply to the following:[98]

- refusing to hire women because of a presumed difference in comparative HR outcomes (e.g., women are lower performers, have higher turnover rates)
- refusing to hire women because of personal characteristic stereotypes (e.g., women are less aggressive than men)
- refusing to hire women because of the preferences of others (customers or fellow workers)

To amplify on the above points, an analysis of BFOQ claims involving sex reveals four types of justifications usually presented by the employer. These involve inability to perform the work, personal contact with others requires the same sex, customers have a preference for dealing with one sex, and pregnancy or fertility protection concerns.[99]

Inability to Perform

The general employer claim here is that one sex (usually women) is unable to perform the job due to job requirements such as lifting heavy weight, being of a minimum height, or long hours of work. The employer must be able to show that the inability holds for most, if not all, members of the sex. Moreover, if it is possible to test the required abilities for each person, then that must be done rather than having a blanket exclusion from the job based on sex.

Same-Sex Personal Contact

Due to a job requirement of close personal contact with other people, the employer may claim that employees must be the same sex as those people with whom they have contact. This claim has often been made, but not always successfully defended, for the job of prison guard. Much will depend on an analysis of just how inhospitable and dangerous the work environment is (e.g., minimum security versus maximum security prisons). Same-sex personal conflict claims have been made successfully for situations involving personal hygiene, health care, and rape victims. In short, the permissibility of these claims depends on a very specific analysis of the job requirements matrix (including the job context portion).

Customer Preference

Organizations may argue that customers prefer members of one sex, and this preference must be honored in order to serve and maintain the continued patronage of the customer. This claim might occur, for example, for the job of salesperson in women's sportswear. Usually, customer preference claims cannot be successfully defended by the employer.

Pregnancy or Fertility

Nonpregnancy could be a valid BFOQ claim, particularly in jobs where the risk of sudden incapacitation due to pregnancy poses threats to public safety (e.g., airline attendant). Threats to fertility of either sex generally cannot be used as a basis for sustaining a BFOQ claim. For example, an employer's fetal protection policy that excluded women from jobs involving exposure to lead in the manufacture of batteries was held to not be a permissible BFOQ.[100]

The discussion and examples here should make clear that BFOQ claims involve complex situations and considerations. The organization should remember that the burden of proof is on it to defend BFOQ claims. BFOQ provisions in the law are and continue to be construed very narrowly. The employer thus must have an overwhelming preponderance of argument and evidence on its side in order to make and successfully defend a BFOQ claim.

SUMMARY

This chapter reviews the processes involved in external selection and focuses specifically on methods of initial assessment. Before candidates are assessed, it is important to base assessment methods on the logic of prediction and to use selection plans. The logic of prediction focuses on the requisite correspondence between elements in applicants' past situations and KSAOs critical to success on the job applied for. The selection plan involves the process of detailing the required KSAOs and indicating which selection methods will be used to assess each KSAO. The selection sequence is the means by which the selection process is used to narrow down the size of the initial applicant pool to candidates, then finalists, and, eventually, job offer receivers.

Initial assessment methods are used during the early stages of the selection sequence to reduce the applicant pool to candidates for further assessment. The methods of initial assessment were reviewed in some detail. The methods include resumes and cover letters, application blanks, biographical data, reference reports, handwriting analysis, literacy testing, genetic screening, and initial interviews. Initial assessment methods differ widely in their usefulness. The means by which these methods can be evaluated for potential use include frequency of use, cost, reliability, validity, utility, applicant reactions, and adverse impact.

Legal issues need to be considered in making initial assessments about applicants. The use of disclaimers as a protective mechanism is critical. Also, three areas of initial assessment that require special attention are reference checking, preemployment inquiries, and bona fide occupational qualifications.

DISCUSSION QUESTIONS

1. A selection plan describes which predictor(s) will be used to assess the KSAOs required to perform the job. What are the three steps to follow in establishing a selection plan?

2. In what ways are the following three initial assessment methods similar and in what ways are they different: application blanks, biographical information, and reference reports?

3. Describe the criteria by which initial assessment methods are evaluated. Are some of these criteria more important than others?

4. Some methods of initial assessment appear to be more useful than others. If you were starting your own business, which initial assessment methods would you use and why?

5. How can organizations avoid legal difficulties in the use of preemployment inquiries in initial selection decisions?

APPLICATIONS

Determining Initial Assessment Methods

Claud and Maude Cornfield farm 2,500 acres of grain crops (mostly corn and soybeans) and 200 head of cattle in Garwin, Iowa. The Cornfield's farm operation has expanded dramatically from 800 acres of row crops and 100 cattle only five years ago. As a result of the rapid expansion of the farm operation, the Cornfields used informal methods, such as experience and "word of mouth" recommendations from fellow farmers, to hire farm hands. Many of the Cornfield's hiring decisions have not turned out well. Last fall during the harvest, one of the Cornfield's employees, Filmore Bins, misread the brake fluid level on one of the grain trucks. As it turned out, the fluid level was low and as Filmore was driving to the grain elevator with a full load of corn, the brakes failed and Filmore crashed the truck into the town tavern. Several years ago, another former employee, John D. Steel, drove a $100,000 tractor into a ditch while attempting to steal it. (Fortunately, only Steel was seriously hurt.)

Recently, the Cornfield's neighbor, Moe Weeds, was forced to sell out his 750-

acre farm. As it turns out, Moe and Maude are second cousins, twice removed. As a result of their kinship, Moe offered the Cornfields first bid on the farm. As Claud and Maude were weighing the decision, one of their hesitations was their past difficulty in hiring good, reliable help. As Maude commented to Claud, "There's got to be a better way to find help. We offer the farm hands a good salary, good benefits, and a chance to work with us. And we have lots of people interested. But we just can't seem to find the right types of people. It makes no sense to take over Moe's farm unless we can get good people to help. We're short of help already. Is there a better way to go about this?"

The Cornfields are short two farm hands already. If they were to buy or rent Moe's farm, they figure they would need another two hands. The farm hands must perform a number of different activities, depending on the season. The most important activities are the following:

- operating complex farm equipment with minimal direction
- possessing good communication skills (following directions with little explanation required, reading instructions for equipment operation, and understanding Claud's hand signals)
- lifting and carrying moderately heavy objects such as seed sacks, fertilizer bags, and fencing materials
- displaying dependability and honesty in all activities (e.g., showing up for work on time, not stealing tractors or other things, not driving machinery into buildings)
- working long hours when required, particularly in the spring planting season and the fall harvest season

If you were advising the Cornfields, how would you answer Maude's questions:

1. Is there a better process for selecting their farm hands?
2. How would you advise them to develop their selection process?
3. What specific initial assessment methods would you advise that they use?
4. How can they evaluate whether your suggestions produce better results than their previous methods?

Developing a Lawful Application Blank

The Consolidated Trucking Corporation, Inc. (CTCI) is a rapidly growing short-haul (local) firm within the greater Columbus, Ohio area. It has grown primarily through the acquisitions of numerous small, family-owned trucking companies. As of now it has a fleet of 150 trucks and over 250 full-time drivers. Most of the drivers were hired initially by the firms that CTCI acquired, and they accepted generous offers from CTCI to become members of the CTCI team. CTCI's expansion plans are very ambitious, but they will be fulfilled primarily from internal growth rather than additional acquisitions. Consequently, CTCI is now faced with the need to develop an external staffing system that will be geared up to hire 75 new truckers within the next two years.

Terry Tailgater is a former truck driver for CTCI who was promoted to truck maintenance supervisor, a position he has held for the past five years. Once CTCI's internal expansion plans become finalized, the firm's HR Director (and sole member of the HR department) Harold Hornblower decided he needed a new person to handle staffing and employment law duties. Terry Tailgater was promoted by Harold to the job of Staffing Manager. One of Terry's major assignments was to develop a new staffing system for truck drivers.

One of the first projects Terry undertook was to develop a new, standardized application blank for the job of truck driver. To do this, Terry looked at the many different application blanks the current drivers had completed for their former companies. (These records were given to CTCI at the time of acquisition.) The application blanks showed that a large amount of information was requested, and that the specific information sought varied among the application forms. Terry scanned the various forms and made a list of all the "questions" the forms contained. He then decided to evaluate each question in terms of its probable lawfulness under federal and state (Ohio) law. Terry wanted to identify and use only lawful questions on the new form he is developing.

Shown below is the list of the "questions" Terry developed, along with columns labeled "probably lawful" and "probably unlawful." Assume that you are Terry, and are deciding on the lawfulness of each question. Place a check mark in the appropriate column for each question. For each question, prepare a justification for its mark as "probably lawful" or probably unlawful."

Questions Terry is Considering Including on Application Blank

Question About	Probably Lawful	Probably Unlawful
Birthplace	————	————
Previous arrests	————	————
Previous felony convictions	————	————
Distance between work and residence	————	————
Domestic responsibilities	————	————
Height	————	————
Weight	————	————
Previous work experience	————	————

(continued)

Question About	Probably Lawful	Probably Unlawful
Educational attainment	_____	_____
High school favorite subjects	_____	_____
Grade point average	_____	_____
Received workers' compensation in past	_____	_____
Currently receiving workers' compensation	_____	_____
Child care arrangements	_____	_____
Length of time on previous job	_____	_____
Reason for leaving previous job	_____	_____
Age	_____	_____
Sex	_____	_____
Home ownership	_____	_____
Any current medical problems	_____	_____
History of mental illness	_____	_____
OK to seek references from previous employer	_____	_____
Have you provided complete/truthful information	_____	_____
Native language	_____	_____
Willing to work on Easter and Christmas	_____	_____
Get recommendation from pastor/priest	_____	_____

ENDNOTES

1. G. J. Myszkowski and S. Sloan, "Hiring by Blueprint," *HR Magazine,* May 1991, pp. 55–58.
2. R. D. Arvey and M. E. Begella, "Analyzing the Homemaker Job Using the Position Analysis Questionnaire (PAQ)," *Journal of Applied Psychology,* 1975, 60, pp. 513–517.
3. J. W. Smither, R. R. Reilly, R. E. Millsap, K. Pearlman, and R. Stoffey, "Applicant Reactions to Selection Procedures," *Personnel Psychology,* 1993, 46, pp. 49–76.
4. P. F. Wernimont and J. P. Campbell, "Signs, Samples, and Criteria," *Journal of Applied Psychology,* 1968, 52, pp. 372–376.
5. P. M. Muchinsky, *Psychology Applied to Work,* third ed. (Pacific Grove, CA: Brook/Cole, 1990).
6. P. M. Muchinsky, *Psychology Applied to Work.*
7. State of Wisconsin, Chapter 134, *Evaluating Job Content for Selection,* Undated.
8. State of Wisconsin, *Evaluating Job Content for Selection.*
9. B. Kelley, "The Right Niche," *Human Resource Executive,* Jan. 1993, pp. 32–34.
10. M. Mannix, "Writing a Computer-Friendly Resume," *U.S. News and World Report,* Oct. 26, 1992, pp. 90–93; G. A. Cluff, "To Scan or Not to Scan," *The EMA Journal,* 1992, 7, pp. 2–3;

L. Stevens, "Resume Scanning Simplifies Tracking," *Personnel Journal*, Apr. 1993, pp. 77–79; J. Perry, "Resume-Sorting Computer Helps Clinton Team Screen Thousands Seeking Administrative Jobs," *Wall Street Journal*, Jan. 11, 1993, p. B1.

11. J. M. Perry, "Resume-Sorting Computer Helps Clinton Team Screen Thousands Seeking Administration Jobs," *Wall Street Journal*.

12. J. E. Rigdon, "Deceptive Resumes Can Be Door-Openers, But Can Become an Employee's Undoing," *Wall Street Journal*, July 17, 1992, pp. B1, B11; A. A. Sloane, "Countering Resume Fraud Within and Beyond Banking: No Excuse for Not Doing More," *Labor Law Journal*, May 1991, pp. 303–310; W. Yu, "Firms Tighten Resume Checks of Applicants," *Wall Street Journal*, Aug. 20, 1985, p. 27.

13. C. Harlan, "He Apparently Succeeded Better Than Most of Us at Avoiding Work," *Wall Street Journal*.

14. M. Brown, "Checking the Facts on a Resume," *Human Resource Measurements* (Supplement to the January 1993 *Personnel Journal*), pp. 6–7.

15. K. W. Moore, "The Most Important Things to Know About an Applicant," *Recruiting and Hiring Handbook* (Waterford, CT: Prentice Hall, 1989), pp. 4–1 to 4–8.

16. A. Howard, "College Experiences and Managerial Performance," *Journal of Applied Psychology*, 1986, 71, pp. 530–552; R. Merritt-Halston and K. Wexley, "Educational Requirements: Legality and Validity," *Personnel Psychology*, 1983, 36, pp. 743–753.

17. R. T. Schneider, *The Rating of Experience and Training: A Review of the Literature and Recommendations on the Use of Alternative E & T Procedures* (Alexandria, VA: International Personnel Management Association, 1994).

18. Wonderlic Personnel Testing, Inc., "New Employment Standards Needed as Meaning of Diploma Changes," *Human Resource Measurements*, Fall 1992, pp. 1–2.

19. S. Alexander, "Trophy Transcript Hunters are Finding Professors Have Become an Easy Mark," *Wall Street Journal*, Apr. 27, 1993, pp. B1, B10.

20. L. E. Briggs, "Administrators Disagree Over Role of Grades," *Ohio State University Lantern Commencement Issue*, June 2, 1993, p. 16.

21. R. T. Schneider, *The Rating of Experience and Training: A Review of the Literature and Recommendations on the Use of Alternative E & T Procedures*.

22. J. Gourman, *The Gourman Report* (Los Angeles: National Education Standards, 1994).

23. T. A. Judge, D. M. Cable, J. W. Boudreau, and R. D. Bretz, "An Empirical Investigation of the Predictors of Executive Career Success," *Personnel Psychology*, 1995, 48, pp. 485–519.

24. R. T. Schneider, *The Rating of Experience and Training: A Review of the Literature and Recommendations on the Use of Alternative E & T Procedures*.

25. R. A. Ash, "A Comparative Study of Behavioral Consistency and Holistic Judgment Methods of Job Applicant Training and Work Experience Evaluation," *Public Personnel Management*, 1984, 13, pp. 157–172; M. A. McDaniel, F. L. Schmidt, and J. E. Hunter, "A Meta-Analysis of the Validity of Methods for Rating Training and Experience in Personnel Selection," *Personnel Psychology*, 1988, 41, pp. 283–314; R. T. Schneider, *The Rating of Experience and Training: A Review of the Literature and Recommendations on the Use of Alternative E & T Procedures*.

26. B. Shimberg, "Testing for Licensure and Certification," *American Psychologist*, 1981, 36, pp. 1138–1146.

27. C. Wiley, "The Certified HR Professional," *HR Magazine*, Aug. 1992, pp. 77–84.

28. G. W. England, *Development and Use of Weighted Application Blanks* (Dubuque, IA: W. M. C. Brown, 1961).

29. J. E. Hunter and R. F. Hunter, "Validity and Utility of Alternative Predictors of Job Performance," *Psychological Bulletin*, 1984, 96, pp. 72–98.

30. I. L. Goldstein, "The Application Blank: How Honest Are the Responses?" *Journal of Applied Psychology*, 1974, 59, pp. 491–494.

31. G. W. England, *Development and Use of Weighted Application Blanks* (revised ed.) (Minneapolis: University of Minnesota Industrial Relations Center, 1971).

32. B. K. Brown and M. A. Campion, "Biodata Phenomenology: Recruiters' Perceptions and Use of Biographical Information in Resume Screening," *Journal of Applied Psychology*, 1994, 79, pp. 897–908.

33. M. A. McDaniel, "Biographical Constructs for Predicting Employee Suitability," *Journal of Applied Psychology*, 1989, 74, pp. 964–970.

34. C. J. Russell, "Selection of Top Corporate Leaders: An Example of Biographical Information," *Journal of Management*, 1990, 16, pp. 71–84.

35. R. Pannone, "Blue Collar Selection," in G. S. Stokes, M. D. Mumford, and W. A. Owens (eds.), *Biodata Handbook* (Palo Alto, CA: CPP Books, 1994), pp. 261–273.

36. J. A. Gandy, D. A. Dye and C. N. MacLane, "Federal Government Selection: The Individual Achievement Record," in G. S. Stokes, M. D. Mumford and W. A. Owens (eds.), *Biodata Handbook* (Palo Alto, CA: CPP Books, 1994), pp. 275–309.

37. C. J. Russell, J. Mattson, S. E. Devlin and D. Atwater, "Predictive Validity of Biodata Items Generated from Restrospective Life Experience Essays," *Journal of Applied Psychology*, 1990, 75, pp. 569–580.

38. F. A. Mael, "A Conceptual Rationale for the Domain and Attributes of Biodata Items," *Personnel Psychology*, 1991, 44, pp. 763–792.

39. J. B. Hogan, "Empirical Keying of Background Data Measures," in G. S. Stokes, M. D. Mumford, and W. A. Owens (eds.), *Biodata Handbook* (Palo Alto, CA: CPP Books, 1994), pp. 69–107.

40. E. E. Ghiselli, J. P. Campbell and S. Zedeck, *Measurement Theory for the Behavioral Sciences* (San Francisco: W. H. Freeman, 1981).

41. J. R. Glennon, L. E. Albright, and W. A. Owens, *A Catalog of Life History Items* (Greensboro, NC: The Richardson Foundation, 1968).

42. F. L. Schmidt, "The Reliability of Differences Between Linear Regression Weights in Applied Differential Psychology," *Educational and Psychological Measurement*, 1972, 32, 879–886.

43. L. Hough and C. Paullin, "Construct-Oriented Scale Construction," in G. S. Stokes, M. D. Mumford, and W. A. Owens (eds.), *Biodata Handbook* (Palo Alto, CA: CPP Books, 1994), pp. 109–145.

44. M. D. Mumford and W. A. Owens, "Methodology Review: Principles, Procedures, and Findings in the Application of Background Data Measures," *Applied Psychological Measurement*, 1987, 11, 1–31.

45. F. A. Mael and A. C. Hirsch, "Rainforest Empiricism and Quasi-Rationality: Two Approaches to Objective Data," *Personnel Psychology*, 1993, 46, pp. 719–738.

46. L. M. Hough, M. A. Keyes and M. D. Dunnette, "An Evaluation of Three 'Alternative' Selection Procedures," *Personnel Psychology*, 1983, 36, pp. 261–276; S. Landers, "PACE to be Replaced with Biographical Test," *The APA Monitor*, 1989, 20(4), p. 14; C. J. Russell, J. Mattson, S. E. Devlin, and D. Atwater, "Predictive Validity of Biodata Items Generated from Retrospective Life Experience Essays."

47. F. L. Schmidt, J. R. Caplan, S. E. Bemis, R. Decuir, L. Dunn, and L. Antone, *The Behavioral Consistency Method of Unassembled Testing* (Washington, DC: U.S. Office of Personnel Management, 1979).

48. S. Landers, "PACE to be Replaced with Biographical Test."

49. see M. D. Mumford and G. S. Stokes, "Developmental Determinants of Individual Action: Theory and Practice in Applying Background Measures," in M. D. Dunnette and L. M. Hough

(eds.), *Handbook of Industrial and Organizational Psychology* (second ed., vol. 3) (Palo Alto, CA: Consulting Psychologists Press, 1993), pp. 61–138.

50. J. E. Hunter and R. F. Hunter, "Validity and Utility of Alternative Predictors of Job Performance"; R. R. Reilly and G. T. Chao, "Validity and Fairness of Some Alternative Selection Procedures," *Personnel Psychology*, 1982, 35, pp. 1–62.

51. H. R. Rothstein, F. L. Schmidt, F. W. Erwin, W. A. Owens and C. P. Sparks, "Biographical Data in Employment Selection: Can Validities Be Made Generalizable?" *Journal of Applied Psychology*, 1990, 75, pp. 175–184.

52. F. A. Mael, "A Conceptual Rationale for the Domain and Attributes of Biodata Items"; M. L. Tenopyr, "Big Five, Structural Modeling, and Item Response Theory," in G. S. Stokes, M. D. Mumford and W. A. Owens (eds.), *Biodata Handbook* (Palo Alto, CA: CPP Books, 1994), pp. 519–533.

53. T. E. Becker and A. L. Colquitt, "Potential Versus Actual Faking of a Biodata Form: An Analysis Along Several Dimensions of Item Type," *Personnel Psychology*, 1992, 45, pp. 389–406.

54. A. N. Kluger and A. Colella, "Beyond the Mean Bias: The Effect of Warning Against Faking on Biodata Item Variances," *Personnel Psychology*, 1993, 46, pp. 763–780.

55. A. N. Kluger, R. R. Reilly and C. J. Russell, "Faking Biodata Tests: Are Option-Keyed Instruments More Resistant?" *Journal of Applied Psychology*, 1991, 76, pp. 689–896.

56. G. S. Stokes, J. B. Hogan and A. F. Snell, "Comparability of Incumbent and Applicant Samples for the Development of Biodata Keys: The Influence of Social Desirability," *Personnel Psychology*, 1993, 46, pp. 739–762.

57. G. S. Stokes, J. B. Hogan and A. F. Snell, "Comparability of Incumbent and Applicant Samples for the Development of Biodata Keys: The Influence of Social Desirability."

58. T. A. Judge, D. Blancero, D. M. Cable, and D. E. Johnson, "Effects of Selection Systems on Job Search Decisions," Paper presented at the Tenth Annual Conference of the Society for Industrial and Organizational Psychology, 1995, Orlando, FL.; J. W. Smither, R. R. Reilly, R. E. Millsap, K. Pearlman, and R. Stoffey, "Applicant Reactions to Selection Procedures."

59. D. A. Kravitz, V. Stinson and T. L. Chavez, "Evaluations of Tests Used for Making Selection and Promotion Decisions," *International Journal of Selection and Assessment*, in press.

60. P. M. Muchinsky, "The Use of Reference Reports in Personnel Selection: A Review and Evaluation," *Journal of Occupational Psychology*, 1979, 52, pp. 287–297.

61. J. C. Baxter, B. Brock, P. C. Hill and R. M. Rozelle, "Letters of Recommendation: A Question of Value," *Journal of Applied Psychology*, 1981, 66, pp. 296–301.

62. M. G. Aamodt, D. A. Bryan and A. J. Whitcomb, "Predicting Performance with Letters of Recommendation," *Public Personnel Management*, 1993, 22, pp. 81–90; S. H. Peres and J. R. Garcia, "Validity and Dimensions of Descriptive Adjectives Used in Reference Letters for Engineering Applicants," *Personnel Psychology*, 1962, 15, pp. 279–296.

63. J. Click, "SHRM Survey Highlights Dilemmas of Reference Checks," *HR News*, July 1995, p. 13.

64. C. S. White and L. S. Kleiman, "The Cost of Candid Comments," *HR Magazine*, Aug. 1991, pp. 54–56.

65. J. Click, "SHRM Survey Highlights Dilemmas of Reference Checks."

66. Pinkerton Investigation Services, *Pinkerton Reference Guide to Investigation Services* (Atlanta: Pinkerton Information Resources Center, 1995).

67. J. M. Hahn, "Pre-Employment Information Services: Employers Beware?" *Employee Relations Law Journal*, 1991, 17(1), pp. 45–69.

68. M. A. McDaniel, "Biographical Construct for Predicting Employee Suitability," *Journal of Applied Psychology*, 1989, 74, pp. 964–970.

69. M. S. Olson, "Security Issues of the 90's Addressed at San Diego Conference," *EMA Reporter*, 1992, 18, p. 4.

70. "Handwriting Analysis," *Bulletin to Management* (Washington, DC: Bureau of National Affairs, May 8, 1986).

71. R. Cohen, "In France, It's How You Cross the t's," *New York Times*, Oct. 19, 1993, p. D1–D2.

72. "Hiring: Voodoo Job Screening," *Inc.*, 1994, 16, p. 133.

73. A. Rafaeli and R. Klimoski, "Predicting Sales Success Through Handwriting Analysis: An Evaluation on the Effects of Training and Handwriting Sample Content," *Journal of Applied Psychology*, 1983, 68, pp. 212–217.

74. G. Ben-Shakhar, M. Bar-Hillel, Y. Bilu, E. Ben-Abba, and A. Flug, "Can Graphology Predict Occupational Success? Two Empirical Studies and Some Methodological Ruminations," *Journal of Applied Psychology*, 1986, 71, pp. 645–653.

75. K. Miller, "At GM, the Three R's Are the Big Three," *Wall Street Journal*, July 3, 1992, p. D1.

76. S. Schwartz (ed.), *Measuring Reading Competence: A Theoretical Prescriptive Approach* (New York: Praeger, 1985).

77. "Assessing Writing Skills," *The Industrial/Organizational Psychologist*, 1992, 30, pp. 27–28.

78. Office of Technology Assessment, *Genetic Monitoring and Screening in the Workplace* (Washington, DC: U.S. Congress, 1990).

79. S. Dentzer, B. Cohn, G. Raine, G. Carroll, and V. Quade, "Can You Pass This Job Test?" *Newsweek*, May 5, 1986, pp. 46–53.

80. J. D. Olian, "Genetic Screening for Employment Purposes," *Personnel Psychology*, 1984, 37, pp. 423–438.

81. V. Kiernan, "US Bans Gene Prejudice at Work," *New Scientist*, 1995, 146, p. 4.

82. W. M. Bulkeley, "Replaced by Technology: Job Interviews," *Wall Street Journal* (Aug. 22, 1994), p. B1-B4; "College Interviews Going Remote," *The Vancouver Sun* (Aug. 4, 1995), p. D12.

83. R. D. Arvey and R. H. Faley, *Fairness in Selecting Employees*, second ed. (Reading, MA: Addison-Wesley, 1988); E. Bean, "More Firms Use 'Attitude Tests' to Keep Thieves Off the Payroll," *Wall Street Journal*, Feb. 27, 1987, p. 33; G. Ben-Shakhar, M. Bar-Hillel, Y. Bilu, E. Ben-Abba, and A. Flug, "Can Graphology Predict Occupational Success? Two Empirical Studies and Some Methodological Ruminations"; J. A. Cox, D. W. Schlueter, K. K. Moore, and D. Sullivan, "A Look Behind Corporate Doors," *Personnel Administrator*, Mar. 1989, pp. 56–59; R. M. Guion and W. M. Gibson, "Personnel Selection and Placement," *Annual Review of Psychology*, 39, pp. 349–374; "Handwriting Analysis," *Bulletin to Management* (Washington, DC: Bureau of National Affairs, May 8, 1986); A. Howard, "College Experiences and Managerial Performance;" J. E. Hunter and R. F. Hunter, "Validity and Utility of Alternative Predictors of Job Performance"; C. W. Langdon and W. P. Galle, Jr., ". . . And What Was the Reason for Departure?" *Personnel Administrator*, 1989, 34, pp. 62–70; V. R. Lindquist, "The Northwestern Lindquist-Endicott Report-1991," *The Placement Center of Northwestern University* (Evanston, IL: Northwestern University, 1991); M. A. McDaniel, "Biographical Constructs for Predicting Employee Suitability," *Journal of Applied Psychology*, 1989, 74, pp. 964–970; R. Meritt-Halston and K. N. Wexley, "Educational Requirements: Legality and Validity," *Personnel Psychology*, 1983, 36, pp. 743–753; Office of Technology Assessment, *Genetic Monitoring and Screening in the Workplace*, (Washington: U.S. Congress, 1990); J. D. Olian, "Genetic Screening for Employment Purposes"; Bureau of National Affairs, *Personnel Policies Forum, Recruiting and Selection Procedures* (Washington, DC: author, May 1988); R. R. Reilly and G. T. Chao, "Validity and Fairness of Some Alternative Selection Procedures"; P. M. Rowe, M. C. Williams, and A. L. Day, "Selection Procedures in North America," *International Journal of Selection and Assessment*, 1994, 2, pp. 74–79; P. R. Sackett, L. R. Burris, and C. Callahan, "Integrity Testing for Personnel Selection: An Update," *Personnel Psychology*, 42, pp. 491–529; P. R. Sackett and M. M. Harris, "Honesty Testing for Personnel Selection: A Review and Critique," *Personnel Psychology*, 1984, 37, pp. 221–245; P. R. Sackett and M. M. Harris, "Honesty Testing

for Personnel Selection: A Review and Critique," in H. J. Bernardin and D. A. Bownas (eds.), *Personality Assessment in Organizations* (New York: Praeger, 1985), pp. 236–276; F. L. Schmidt, D. S. Ones, and J. E. Hunter, "Personnel Selection," *Annual Review of Psychology*, 43, 627–670; N. Schmitt, R. Z. Gooding, R. A. Noe, and M. Kirsch, "Meta-Analyses of Validity Studies Between 1964 and 1982 and the Investigation of Study Characteristics," *Personnel Psychology*, 1984, 37, pp. 407–422; M. S. Singer and C. Bruhns, "Relative Effect of Applicant Work Experience and Academic Qualifications on Selection Interview Decisions: A Study of Between-Sample Generalizability," *Journal of Applied Psychology*, 1991, 76, pp. 550–559; "Testing Report," *HR Magazine*, 1992, 6, pp. 46–47; J. William Townsend, "Is Integrity Testing Useful?" *HR Magazine*, July 1992, p. 96; D. S. Ones, C. Viswesvaran, and F. L. Schmidt, "Comprehensive Meta-Analysis of Integrity Test Validities: Findings and Implications for Personnel Selection and Theories of Job Performance," *Journal of Applied Psychology*, 1993, 78, pp. 531–537.

84. I. L. Goldstein, "The Application Blank: How Honest Are the Responses?"; W. Keichel, "Lies on the Resume," *Fortune*, Aug. 23, 1982, pp. 221–222, 224; J. N. Mosel and L. W. Cozan, "The Accuracy of Application Blank Work Histories," *Journal of Applied Psychology*, 1952, 36, pp. 365–369.

85. R. A. Ash and E. L. Levine, "Job Applicant Training and Work Experience Evaluation: An Empirical Comparison of Four Methods," *Journal of Applied Psychology*, 1985, 70, pp. 572–576.

86. G. P. Latham and G. Whyte, "The Futility of Utility Analysis," *Personnel Psychology*, 1994, 47, pp. 31–46.

87. J. W. Smither, R. R. Reilly, R. E. Millsap, K. Pearlman and R. Stoffey, "Applicant Reactions to Selection Procedures."

88. S. W. Gilliland, "Fairness from the Applicant's Perspective: Reactions to Employee Selection Procedures," *International Journal of Selection and Assessment*, 1995, 3, pp. 11–19.

89. D. A. Kravitz, V. Stinson and T. L. Chavez, "Evaluations of Tests Used for Making Selection and Promotion Decisions."

90. G. P. Panaro, *Employment Law Manual*, second ed. (Boston: Warren Gorham Lamont, 1993), pp. 1–29 to 1–42.

91. G. P. Panaro, *Employment Law Manual*, 1993, pp. 2–101 to 2–106.

92. R. D. Arvey and R. H. Faley, *Fairness in Selecting Employees*, pp. 251–310.

93. S. J. Vodanovich and R. H. Lowe, "They Ought to Know Better: The Incidence and Correlates of Inappropriate Application Blank Inquiries," *Public Personnel Management*, 1992, 21, pp. 363–370.

94. Bureau of National Affairs, "EEOC Guide to Pre-Employment Inquiries," *Fair Employment Practices* (Washington DC: author, periodically updated), pp. 443:65–80.

95. Bureau of National Affairs, "EEOC Guide to Pre-Employment Inquiries," pp. 443:65–80.

96. Equal Employment Opportunity Commission, *ADA Enforcement Guidance: Pre-Employment Disability Related Questions and Medical Examinations* (Washington, D.C.: author, 1995).

97. Bureau of National Affairs, *Fair Employment Practices*, 454: whole section.

98. Bureau of National Affairs, *Fair Employment Practices* (Washington, DC: author, periodically updated), pp. 421:352–356.

99. N. J. Sedmak and M. D. Levin-Epstein, *Primer on Equal Employment Opportunity* (Washington, DC: Bureau of National Affairs, 1991), pp. 36–40.

100. Bureau of National Affairs, *Fair Employment Practices*, pp. 405:6941–6943.

CHAPTER TEN

External Selection II

Substantive Assessment Methods
    Personality Tests
    Ability Tests
    Job Knowledge Tests
    Performance Tests and Work Samples
    Integrity Tests
    Interest, Values, and Preference Inventories
    Structured Interview
    Constructing a Structured Interview
    Assessment for Team and Quality Environments
    Clinical Assessments
    Choice of Substantive Assessment Methods

Discretionary Assessment Methods

Contingent Assessment Methods
    Drug Testing
    Medical Exams

Collection of Assessment Data

Legal Issues
    Uniform Guidelines on Employee Selection Procedures
    Selection under the Americans with Disabilities Act
    Drug Testing

Summary

Discussion Questions

Applications

T he previous chapter reviewed preliminary issues surrounding external staffing decisions made in organizations, including the use of initial assessment methods. This chapter continues the discussion of external selection by discussing in some detail substantive assessment methods. The use of discretionary and contingent assessment methods, collection of assessment data, and legal issues also will be considered.

While initial assessment methods are used to reduce the applicant pool to candidates, substantive assessment methods are used to reduce the candidate pool to finalists for the job. Thus, the use of substantive methods is often more involved than using initial methods. Numerous substantive assessment methods will be discussed in depth, including various tests (personality, ability, job knowledge, performance/work samples, integrity), interest, values, and preference inventories, structured interviews, assessment for team and quality environments, and clinical assessments. The average validity (i.e., $\bar{r}$) of each method, and the criteria used to choose among methods will be reviewed.

Discretionary assessment methods are used in some circumstances to separate those who receive job offers from the list of finalists. The applicant characteristics that are assessed when using discretionary methods are sometimes quite subjective. Several of the characteristics most commonly assessed by discretionary methods will be reviewed.

Contingent assessment methods are used to make sure that tentative offer recipients meet certain qualifications for the job. Although any assessment method can be used as a contingent method (e.g., licensing/certification requirements, background checks), perhaps the two most common contingent methods are drug tests and medical exams. These procedures will be reviewed.

All forms of assessment decisions require the collection of assessment data. The procedures used to make sure this process is properly conducted will be reviewed. In particular, several issues will be discussed, including support services, training requirements in using various predictors, maintaining security and confidentiality, and the importance of standardized procedures.

Finally, many important legal issues surround the use of substantive, discretionary, and contingent methods of selection. The most important of these issues will be reviewed. Particular attention will be given to the Uniform Guidelines on Employee Selection Procedures and staffing requirements under the Americans with Disabilities Act.

SUBSTANTIVE ASSESSMENT METHODS

Organizations use initial assessment methods to make "rough cuts" among applicants—weeding out the obviously unqualified. Conversely, substantive assessment methods are used to make more precise decisions about applicants—among those who meet minimum qualifications for the job, which are the most likely to be high performers if hired? Because substantive methods are used to make fine distinctions among applicants, the nature of their use is somewhat more involved than initial assessment methods. As with initial assessment methods, however, substantive assessment methods are developed using the logic of prediction outlined in Exhibit 9.1 and the selection plan shown in Exhibit 9.2. Predictors typically used to select finalists from the candidate pool include personality tests, ability tests, job knowledge tests, performance tests and work samples, interest, values and preference inventories, structured interviews, team/quality assessments, and clinical assessments. Each of these predictors is described next in some detail.

Personality Tests

Until recently, personality tests were not seen as a valid selection method. Historically, most studies estimated the validity of personality tests to be between .10 and .15, which would rank them among the poorest predictors of job performance and only marginally better than a coin toss.[1] Starting with the publication of an influential review in the 1960s, personality tests were not viewed favorably, nor were they widely used.[2]

There are several reasons why personality tests had such a dismal record of success. Perhaps the most important factor was that there was no accepted taxonomy of personality for use in selection. Thus, some studies related personality measures to job performance when there was no reason to believe the measure was suited to predict job performance. Perhaps the best example of this is the *Minnesota Multiphasic Personality Inventory* (MMPI), which until relatively recently was the most common personality test used for selection decisions. The use of the MMPI to predict job performance always was (and still is) an inappropriate application for nearly all jobs.[3] The MMPI was never intended to be used as a selection tool. Rather, it was developed and validated as an instrument to diagnose severe psychological disorders (e.g. schizophrenia), as the items readily illustrate ("I often feel as if one of my limbs will fall off," "There are persons who try to steal my thoughts and ideas"). In short, the MMPI does a good job of measuring mental imbalance, but screening out the few (if any) individuals in the applicant pool who suffer from say, psychopathic deviance, is unlikely to be a useful means of making selection decisions. Thus, when inappropriate measures are used to assess traits generally unrelated to job performance, the results are (predictably) very poor.

Recent advances, however, have suggested much more positive conclusions about the role of personality tests in predicting job performance. Mainly, this is due to the widespread acceptance of a major taxonomy of personality, often termed the Big Five. The Big Five is used to describe behavioral (as opposed to emotional or cognitive) traits that may capture up to 75% of an individual's personality. The Big Five factors are *neuroticism* (disposition to experience negative affects such as fear, anger, depression, anxiety, and guilt—sometimes defined by its opposite, emotional adjustment), *extraversion* (tendency to be sociable, assertive, active, upbeat, and talkative), *openness to experience* (tendency to be imaginative, attentive to inner feelings, have intellectual curiosity and independence of judgment), *agreeableness* (tendency to be altruistic, trusting, sympathetic, and cooperative), and *conscientiousness* (tendency to be purposeful, determined, dependable, and attentive to detail). The Big Five are a reduced set of many more specific traits. The Big Five are very stable over time and there is even research to suggest a strong genetic basis of the Big Five traits (up to 50% of the variance in the Big Five traits may be inherited).[4] Because job performance is a broad concept that comprises many specific behaviors, it will be best predicted by broad dispositions such as the Big Five. In fact, some research evidence supports this proposition.[5]

Measures of Personality

Measures of personality traits can be surveys, projective techniques, or interviews. Most personality measures used in personnel selection are surveys. There are several survey measures of the Big Five traits that are used in selection. The *Personal Characteristics Inventory* (PCI) is a self-report measure of the Big Five that asks applicants to report their agreement or disagreement (using a "strongly disagree" to "strongly agree" scale) with 150 sentences.[6] The measure takes about 30 minutes to complete and has a 5th- to 6th-grade reading level. Exhibit 10.1 provides sample items from the PCI. Another commonly used measure of the Big Five is the *NEO Personality Inventory,* of which there are several versions that have been translated into numerous languages.[7] A third alternative is the *Hogan Personality Inventory* (HPI), which also is based on the Big Five typology. Responses to the HPI can be scored to yield measures of employee reliability and of service orientation.[8] All three of these measures have shown validity in predicting job performance in various occupations.

Although surveys are the most common means of assessing personality, other methods have been used, such as projective tests and interviews. However, with few exceptions (e.g., the *Miner Sentence Completion Scale* has shown validity in predicting managerial performance[9]), the reliability and validity of projective tests and interviews as methods of personality assessment are questionable at best.[10] Thus, survey measures in general, and the Big Five measures in particular, are the most reliable and valid means of personality testing for selection decisions.

Evaluation of Personality Tests

Many comprehensive reviews of the validity of personality tests have been published. Nearly all of the recent reviews focus on the validity of the Big Five. Although there has been a debate over inconsistencies in these studies,[11] the largest-scale study revealed the following:[12]

1. Conscientiousness predicted performance across all occupational groupings studied.

EXHIBIT 10.1   Sample Items for Personal Characteristics Inventory

Conscientiousness
I can always be counted on to get the job done.
I am a very persistent worker.
I almost always plan things in advance of work.

Extraversion
Meeting new people is enjoyable to me.
I like to stir up excitement if things get boring.
I am a "take charge" type of person.

Agreeableness
I like to help others who are down on their luck.
I usually see the good side of people.
I forgive others easily.

Emotional Stability
I can become annoyed at people quite easily (reverse-scored).
At times I don't care about much of anything (reverse-scored).
My feelings tend to be easily hurt (reverse-scored).

Openness to Experience
I like to work with difficult concepts and ideas.
I enjoy trying new and different things.
I tend to enjoy art, music, or literature.

Source: M. K. Mount and M. R. Barrick, *Manual for the Personal Characteristics Inventory* (December, 1995). Reprinted by permission of the Wonderlic Personnel Test, Inc.

2. Some traits predicted performance for certain types of jobs (e.g., extraversion for managers), but in most cases validities for the other four traits were not significant.

3. Openness to experience and extraversion predicted training performance.

More recent evidence further supports the validity of conscientiousness in predicting job performance. A recent update to the original findings suggested that the validity of conscientiousness in predicting overall job performance is $\bar{r} = .31$, and it seems to predict many specific facets of performance (training proficiency, reliability, quality of work, administration).[13] The conclusion that conscientiousness is a valid predictor of job performance across all types of jobs and organizations studied is significant. Previously, researchers believed that personality was valid only for *some* jobs in *some* situations. These results suggest that conscientiousness is important to job performance whether the job is working on an assembly line or selling automotive parts or driving trucks.

Why is conscientiousness predictive of performance? Exhibit 10.2 provides some possible answers.[14] When employees have autonomy, research shows that conscientious employees set higher work goals for themselves and are more committed to achieving the goals they do set. Also, conscientiousness is an integral part of integrity, and two of the key components of conscientiousness, achievement and dependability, are related to reduced levels of irresponsible job behaviors (e.g., absenteeism, insubordination, use of drugs on job). Conscientiousness also predicts work effort and is associated with ambition. Further, conscientious individ-

EXHIBIT 10.2   Possible Factors Explaining the Importance of Conscientiousness in Predicting Job Performance

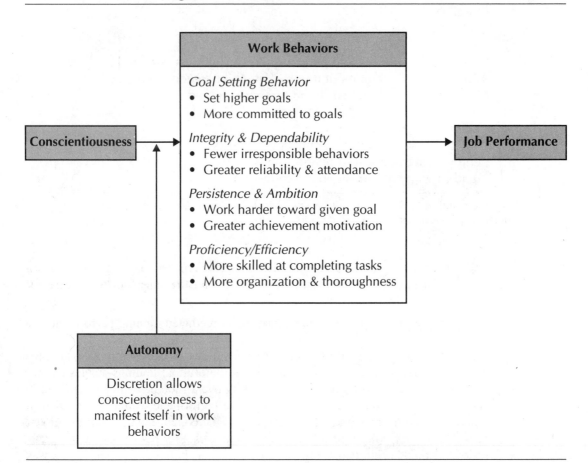

uals are more technically proficient in their jobs and more organized and thorough. Thus, conscientiousness predicts job performance well because it is associated with a range of attitudes and behaviors that are important to job success.

Beyond conscientiousness, is there a role for the other Big Five traits in selection? In general, the other four traits are not valid predictors of job performance. In considering the validity of other elements of the Big Five, it is possible they are too broad and that in order to predict specific work behaviors, more fine-grained traits are necessary.[15] When predicting criteria more specific than overall job performance, this is undoubtedly true. For example, measures of compliance, trust, and dutifulness (all are subfacets of the NEO) might do a better job of predicting attendance than any of the five general traits. Similarly, the tendency to fantasize or be original or be creative may better predict creative work behaviors than the general openness to experience factor. Furthermore, even among the Big Five, each of the traits is likely predictive of performance in certain types of jobs. For example, agreeableness may be an important trait in predicting the performance of customer service representatives, but the same level of agreeableness might actually be a liability for a bill collector! Openness to experience might be important for artists, inventors, or those in advertising, while it has been argued that conscientiousness might be a liability in these types of jobs.[16] Thus, the key is to match traits, both in terms of type and level of generality, to the criteria that are being predicted. Research indicates that such strategies make personality tests quite valid methods of selection.[17] One method of matching traits to dimensions of job performance was recently developed.[18] Termed the *Personality-Related Position Requirements Form* (PPRF), it bases the collection of job analysis data on the Big Five so that once a job analysis is completed, the Big Five traits can be easily matched to dimensions of job performance. While the PPRF is a promising way to ensure that personality–job performance linkages are relevant, it is as yet untested.

While personality testing is in much better standing in selection research, some limitations need to be kept in mind. First, there is some concern that applicants may distort their responses.[19] This concern is apparent when one considers the items (see Exhibit 10.1) and the nature of the traits. Few individuals would want to describe themselves as disagreeable, neurotic, closed to new experiences, and unconscientious. Furthermore, since answers to these questions are nearly impossible to verify (e.g., imagine trying to verify whether an applicant really prefers reading a book to watching television), the possibility of "faking good" is quite real. In fact, research suggests that applicants can enhance or even fake their responses if they are motivated to do so. Given that a job is on the line when applicants complete a personality test, the tendency to enhance is undeniable. Although applicants do try to look good by enhancing their responses to personality tests, it seems clear that such enhancement does not significantly detract from the validity of the tests.[20] Thus, it has yet to be shown that faking undermines the validity of personality tests in selection.

Finally, it is important to evaluate personality tests not only in terms of their validity, but also from the applicant's perspective. From an applicant's standpoint, the subjective and personal nature of the questions asked in these tests may cause questions about their validity and concerns about invasiveness. In fact, the evidence that is available concerning applicants' perceptions of personality tests suggests that they are viewed negatively. One study reported that 46% of applicants had no idea how a personality test could be interpreted by organizations, and 31% could not imagine how qualifications could be assessed with a personality inventory.[21] Similarly, another study found that newly hired managers perceived personality tests as the 13th least-valid predictor of job performance of 14 selection tools.[22] Other studies suggest that applicants believe personality tests are invasive and unnecessary for companies to make accurate selection decisions.[23] Thus, while personality tests—when used properly—do have validity, this validity does not seem to translate into favorable applicant perceptions. More research is needed into the ways that these tests could be made more acceptable to applicants.

Ability Tests

Ability tests are measures that assess an individual's capacity to function in a certain way. There are two major types of ability tests: aptitude and achievement. Aptitude tests look at a person's innate capacity to function, while achievement tests assess a person's learned capacity to function. In practice, these types of abilities are often difficult to separate. Thus, it is not clear this is a productive, practical distinction for ability tests used in selection.

Surveys reveal that between 15% and 20% of organizations use some sort of ability test in selection decisions.[24] Organizations that use ability tests do so because they assume the tests assess a key determinant of employee performance. Without a certain level of ability, be it innate or learned, performance is unlikely to be at an acceptable level, regardless of motivation. Someone may try extremely hard to do well in a very difficult class (e.g., calculus), but will not succeed unless they have the ability to do so (e.g., mathematical aptitude).

There are four major classes of ability tests: cognitive, psychomotor, physical, and sensory/perceptual.[25] As these ability tests are quite distinct, each will be considered separately below. Because most of the research attention—and public controversy—has focused on cognitive ability tests, they are discussed below in considerable detail.

Cognitive Ability Tests

Cognitive ability tests refer to measures that assess abilities involved in thinking, including perception, memory, reasoning, verbal and mathematical abilities, and the expression of ideas. Is cognitive ability a general construct or does it have a number of specific aspects? Research shows that measures of specific cognitive abilities, such as verbal, quantitative, reasoning, and so on, appear to reflect general intelligence (sometimes referred to as IQ or 'g').[26] One of the facts that best illustrates this finding is the relatively high correlations between scores on measures of specific facets of intelligence. Someone who scores well on a measure of one specific ability is more likely to score well on measures of other specific abilities. In other words, it is general intelligence that causes individuals to have similar scores on measures of specific abilities.[27]

Measures of Cognitive Ability There are many cognitive ability tests that measure both specific cognitive abilities and general mental ability. Many test publishers offer an array of tests. For example, The Psychological Corporation sells the *Employee Aptitude Survey*, a test of ten specific cognitive abilities (e.g., verbal comprehension, numerical ability, numerical and verbal reasoning, word fluency, etc.). Each of these specific tests is sold separately and each takes no more than five minutes to administer to applicants. Each of the 10 specific tests is sold in packages of 25 for roughly $44 per package. The Psychological Corporation also sells the *Wonderlic Personnel Test*, perhaps the most widely used test of general mental ability for selection decisions. The Wonderlic is a 12-minute, 50-item test. Items range in type from spatial relations to numerical problems to analogies. Exhibit 10.3 provides examples of items from one of the forms of the Wonderlic. In addition to being a speed (timed) test, the Wonderlic also is a power test where the items get harder as the test progresses (very few individuals complete all 50 items). The Wonderlic has been administered to more than 2.5 million applicants and normative data are available from a database of more than 450,000 individuals. Cost of the Wonderlic ranges from approximately $1.50 to $3.50 per applicant, depending on whether the organization scores the test itself. Costs of other cognitive ability tests are similar. While cognitive ability tests are not costless, they are among the least expensive of any substantive assessment method.

There are many other tests and test publishers in addition to those reviewed above. Before deciding which test to use, organizations should seek out a reputable testing firm. An association of test publishers has been formed with the bylaws to help ensure this process.[28] It is also advisable to seek out the advice of researchers or testing specialists. Many of these individuals are members of the American Psychological Association or the American Psychological Society. Guidelines are available that can serve as a guide in deciding which test to use.[29]

Evaluation of Cognitive Ability Tests

The findings regarding general intelligence have had profound implications for personnel selection. A number of meta-analyses have been conducted on the validity of cognitive ability tests. Although the validities found in these studies have fluctuated to some extent, the most comprehensive reviews have estimated the "true" validity of measures of general cognitive ability to be roughly $\bar{r} = .50$.[30] The conclusions from these meta-analyses are dramatic:

EXHIBIT 10.3 Sample Cognitive Ability Test Items

Look at the row of numbers below. What number should come next?

| 8 | 4 | 2 | 1 | 1/2 | 1/4 | ? |

Assume the first 2 statements are true. Is the final one: (1) true, (2) false, (3) not certain?

The boy plays baseball. All baseball players wear hats. The boy wears a hat.

One of the numbered figures in the following drawing is most different from the others. What is the number in that drawing?

A train travels 20 feet in 1/5 second. At this same speed, how many feet will it travel in three seconds?

How many of the six pairs of items listed below are exact duplicates?

3421	1243
21212	21212
558956	558956
10120210	10120210
612986896	612986896
356471201	356571201

The hours of daylight and darkness in SEPTEMBER are nearest equal to the hours of daylight and darkness in

(1) June   (2) March   (3) May   (4) November

Source: Reprinted with permission from C. F. Wonderlic Personnel Test, Inc. *1992 Catalog: Employment Tests, Forms, and Procedures* (Libertyville, IL: Author—Charles F. Wonderlic, 1992).

1. Cognitive ability tests are among the most valid, if not *the* most valid, methods of selection.
2. Cognitive ability tests appear to generalize across all organizations, all job types, and all types of applicants; thus, they are likely to be valid in virtually any selection context.
3. Organizations using cognitive ability tests in selection enjoy large economic gains compared to organizations that fail to use them.[31]

These conclusions are not simply esoteric speculations from the Ivory Tower. They are based on hundreds of studies of hundreds of organizations employing hundreds of thousands of workers. Thus, whether an organization is selecting engineers, customer service representatives, or meat cutters, general mental ability is likely the single most valid method of selecting among applicants. A large-scale quantitative review of the literature suggested relatively high average validities for many occupational groups:[32]

- manager, $\bar{r} = .53$
- clerk, $\bar{r} = .54$
- salesperson, $\bar{r} = .61$
- protective professional, $\bar{r} = .42$
- service worker, $\bar{r} = .48$
- trades and crafts, $\bar{r} = .46$
- elementary industrial worker, $\bar{r} = .37$
- vehicle operator, $\bar{r} = .28$
- sales clerk, $\bar{r} = .27$.

These results show that cognitive ability tests have some degree of validity for all types of jobs. The validity is particularly high for complex jobs (i.e., manager, engineer), but even for simple jobs the validity is positive.[33] The same review also revealed that cognitive ability tests have very high degrees of validity in predicting training success ($\bar{r} = .37$ for vehicle operators to $\bar{r} = .87$ for protective professionals). This is due to the substantial learning component of training and the obvious fact that smart people learn more.[34]

While cognitive ability tests are more valid for jobs of medium (e.g., police officers, salespersons) and high (e.g., computer programmers, pilots) complexity, they are valid even for jobs of relatively low complexity (e.g., bus driver, factory worker). Why are cognitive ability tests predictive even for relatively simple jobs where intelligence would not appear to be an important attribute? The fact is that, when you think about it, some degree of intelligence is important for *any* type of job. The validity of cognitive ability tests even seems to generalize to performance on and of athletic teams (see Exhibit 10.4). In addition to performance as a professional football player, one study also found that college basketball teams high in cognitive ability performed better than teams low in cognitive ability.[35] Thus, cognitive ability may be unimportant to performance in some jobs but, if this is true, we have yet to find them.

Take the example of the job of garbage collector in Tallahassee, Florida. In Tallahassee, the city supplies each household with a large garbage can that residents normally place in their backyard. Rather than asking residents to place this garbage can curbside prior to collection, garbage collectors are required to locate each garbage can, haul it to the truck, and replace it when finished. This practice continued until one day a new employee figured out that the workload could be cut nearly in half by hauling the last household's emptied garbage can into the next household's back yard, replacing this household's full garbage can with the last household's empty one, and continuing this procedure for each household.[36] The economic benefit to the city of Tallahassee of this action is undoubtedly substantial. It is likely that this intelligent action was the product of an intelligent

EXHIBIT 10.4   Cognitive Ability Testing in the National Football League

Lest you think cognitive ability testing is used only to select applicants for unimportant jobs such as rocket scientists or nuclear engineers, completing the *Wonderlic Personnel Test* is an important part of the selection process in the National Football League (NFL). In fact, use of the Wonderlic in the NFL has been likened to use of the SAT or ACT among universities. The NFL uses the Wonderlic as one component in its physical and mental screening of potential draft picks. Most teams rely on Wonderlic scores, to varying degrees, in making draft decisions. Which teams rely most heavily on the Wonderlic? Among the Wonderlic's biggest supporters are Carmen Policy, President of the San Francisco 49ers, Carl Peterson, General Manager of the Kansas City Chiefs, and Cincinnati Bengals General Manager Mike Brown. The major justification for use of these tests is a belief that players need intelligence to understand the increasingly complex NFL playbooks. NFL officials believe this to be particularly true for positions that rely heavily on the playbook, namely quarterback and offensive lineman.

The Chicago Bears, conversely, pay little attention to the results. One cannot help but note, though, the 14 score (2nd percentile of college graduates) of punter Todd Sauerbrun, whom coach Dave Wannstedt had indicated would be replaced for 1996. (Sauerbrun's punting average was one of the poorest in the NFL during the 1995–1996 season.) Maybe next year the Bears plan on paying more attention to the Wonderlic scores.

The average NFL draftee score is 20 compared to 21 for the population as a whole. Quarterbacks and centers score the highest of players in all positions. Offensive players tend to do better than defensive players. Some teams even have cutoff scores for different positions. For example, one team used to require quarterbacks to score 25 on the Wonderlic compared to a cutoff of only 12 for wide receivers. Cutoffs seem to be highest for quarterbacks and offensive linemen.

So how do the players feel about these tests? Taking the Wonderlic caught former Michigan Heisman Trophy candidate Ki-Jana Carter by surprise. (Carter scored average [20] and is now playing with a multi-million dollar contract in hand.) Penn State Quarterback Kerry Collins, who scored a 30 and was one of the first players taken in the draft by Carolina, took a somewhat different view. Collins commented that the key to scoring well on the Wonderlic was skipping questions and only answering those that were readily apparent.

Of course, like all selection methods, cognitive ability tests have their limits. George Young, General Manager of the New York Giants, was the individual responsible for convincing the NFL to use the Wonderlic. He recalls a game where a defensive lineman with an IQ of 90 went up against an offensive lineman with a 150 IQ. According to Young, "The defensive lineman told the offensive lineman, 'Don't worry. After I hit you a few times, you'll be just as dumb as I am.' "

Source: Adapted from R. Hofer, "Get Smart", *Sports Illustrated*, Sept. 5, 1994; B. Plaschke and E. Almond, "Has NFL Draft Become Thinking Man's Game?" *Los Angeles Times*, April 21, 1995.

person. This example illustrates how intelligence can be a critical performance factor in even the most seemingly cognitively simple jobs.

Why do cognitive ability tests work so well in predicting job performance? Research has shown that most of the effect of cognitive ability tests is due to the fact that intelligent employees have greater job knowledge.[37] Another important issue in understanding the validity of cognitive ability tests is the nature of specific versus general abilities. As was noted earlier, measures of specific abilities are available and continue to be used in selection. These specific measures will likely have some validity in predicting job performance, but this is simply because these tests measure general mental ability. Research has suggested, rather conclusively, that specific abilities do not explain additional variance in job performance over and above that explained by measures of general cognitive ability.[38] One recent study found that the average validity of general mental abilities tests, for various types of jobs, was $\bar{r} = .46$. The average incremental validity of a composite of specific abilities (i.e., controlling for general mental ability) was only .02.[39] In fact, in many cases, the validity of a combination of specific cognitive abilities is lower than that for general ability.[40] Thus, in most cases, organizations would be better served by using a measure of general cognitive ability than measures of specific abilities.

Some researchers have argued that cognitive ability tests measure only academic knowledge and that while such tests may be somewhat predictive of job performance, other types of intellectual abilities may be relevant as well. In particular, it has been argued that common sense (termed tacit knowledge or practical intelligence) can be an important predictor of job performance because practical knowledge is important to the performance of any job.[41] It is argued, for example, that a carpenter or nurse or lawyer can have all the intelligence in the world, but without common sense, these people will not be able to adequately perform their jobs. Accordingly, measures of tacit knowledge have been developed. An example is provided in Exhibit 10.5 for a sales manager. In this example, examinees rate the quality of each piece of advice on a 1 (low) to 9 (high) scale. Research suggests that the correlation between scores on a tacit knowledge measure and job performance ranges from .3 to .4. Such measures have modest relations with intelligence but it has been argued that such measures simply reflect job knowledge.[42] If this is true, the importance of distinguishing common sense from general intelligence is called into serious question. (We will have more to say about the utility of job knowledge tests in the next section.) In short, arguing that practical intelligence is anything other than job knowledge, without further data, could be likened to "putting old wine in a new bottle."[43]

Potential Limitations

If cognitive ability tests are so valid and cheap, you might be thinking, why aren't more organizations using them? One of the principal reasons is concern over the adverse impact and fairness of these tests. In terms of adverse impact, regardless of the type of measure used, cognitive ability tests have such severe adverse impact

---

EXHIBIT 10.5   Sample Measure of Tacit Knowledge

You have just learned that detailed weekly reports of sales-related activities will be required of employees in your department. You have not received a rationale for the reports. The new reporting procedure appears cumbersome and it will probably be resisted strongly by your group. Neither you nor your employees had input into the decision to require the report, nor in decisions about its format. You are planning a meeting of your employees to introduce them to the new reporting procedures. Rate the quality of the following things you might do:

- Emphasize that you had nothing to do with the new procedure.
- Have a group discussion about the value of the new procedure and then put its adoption to a vote.
- Promise to make your group's concerns known to the supervisors, but only after the group has made a good faith effort by trying the new procedure for six weeks.
- Since the new procedure will probably get an unpleasant response anyway, use the meeting for something else and inform them about it in a memo.
- Postpone the meeting until you find out the rationale for the new procedure.

Source: R. J. Sternberg, "Tacit Knowledge and Job Success," in N. Anderson and P. Herriot (eds.), *Assessment and Selection in Organizations* (Chichester, England: Wiley, 1994), pp. 27–39. © 1994 John Wiley & Sons. Reprinted by permission of John Wiley & Sons, Limited.

against blacks that only 10% of blacks score above the average score for whites.[44] Historically, this lead to close scrutiny—and sometimes rejection—of cognitive ability tests by the courts. The issue of fairness of cognitive ability tests has been hotly debated and heavily researched. One way to think of fairness is in terms of accuracy of prediction of a test. If a test predicts job performance with equal accuracy for two groups, such as whites and blacks, then most people would say the test is a "fair" one. The problem is that even though the test is equally accurate for both groups, the average test score may be different between the two groups. When this happens, use of the test will cause some degree of adverse impact. This causes a dilemma: should the organization use the test because it is an accurate and unbiased predictor, or should it not be used because it would cause adverse impact?

Research shows that cognitive ability tests are equally accurate predictors of job performance for various racial and ethnic groups.[45] But research also shows that blacks and Hispanics score lower on such tests than whites. Thus, the dilemma noted above is a real one for the organization. It must decide whether to (a) use cognitive ability tests, and experience the positive benefits of using an accurate predictor; (b) not use the cognitive ability test in order to avoid adverse impact, and substitute a different measure that has less adverse impact; or (c) use the cognitive ability test in conjunction with other predictors that do not have adverse impact, thus lessening adverse impact overall. Although each organization must weigh the costs and benefits of each of these choices, research does support option (c) in that using cognitive ability tests in conjunction with other selection measures that do not have adverse impact (e.g., personality and integrity tests, work samples, etc.) will lower the adverse impact of cognitive ability tests appreciably.[46]

Another aspect of using cognitive ability tests in selection is concern over applicant reactions. Research on how applicants react to cognitive ability tests is scant and somewhat mixed. One study suggested that 88% of applicants for managerial positions perceived the Wonderlic as job related.[47] Another study, however, demonstrated that applicants thought companies had little need for information obtained from a cognitive ability test.[48] Perhaps one explanation for these conflicting findings is the nature of the test. One study characterized eight cognitive ability tests as either concrete (vocabulary, mathematical word problems) or abstract (letter sets, quantitative comparisons) and found that concrete cognitive ability test items were viewed as job related while abstract test items were not.[49] Thus, while applicants may have mixed reactions to cognitive ability tests, concrete items are less likely to be objectionable.

Other Types of Ability Tests

In the following section we consider tests that measure other types of abilities. Following the earlier classification of abilities into cognitive, psychomotor, physical, and sensory/perceptual, and having just reviewed cognitive ability tests, we now consider the other types of ability tests: psychomotor, physical, and sensory/perceptual.

Psychomotor Ability Tests Psychomotor ability tests measure the correlation of thought with bodily movement. Involved here are processes such as reaction time, arm-hand steadiness, control precision, and manual and digit dexterity. An example of testing for psychomotor abilities is a test used by the city of Columbus, Ohio, to select firefighters. The test mimics coupling a hose to a fire hydrant, and it requires a certain level of processing with psychomotor abilities to achieve a passing score. Some tests of mechanical ability are psychomotor tests. For example, the *MacQuarrie Test for Mechanical Ability* is a 30-minute test that measures manual dexterity. Seven subtests require tracing, tapping, dotting, copying, and so on.

Physical Abilities Tests Physical abilities tests measure muscular strength, cardiovascular endurance, and movement quality.[50] An example of a test that requires all three again comes from the city of Columbus. The test mimics carrying firefighting equipment (e.g., hose, fan, oxygen tanks) up flights of stairs in a building. Equipment must be brought up and down the stairs as quickly as possible in the test. The equipment is heavy, so muscular strength is required. The climb is taxing under limited breathing, so cardiovascular endurance is necessary. The trips up and around the flights of stairs, in full gear, require high degrees of flexibility and balance.

Physical abilities tests may be necessary for EEO reasons.[51] Although female applicants typically score 1.5 standard deviations lower than male applicants on a physical abilities test, the distributions of scores for male and female applicants overlap considerably. Therefore, all applicants must be given a chance to pass requirements and not be judged as a class. Another reason to use physical abilities tests for appropriate jobs is to avoid injuries on the job. Well-designed tests will screen out applicants who have applied for positions poorly suited to their physical abilities. Thus, fewer injuries should result. In fact, one study found, using a concurrent validation approach on a sample of railroad workers, that 57% of all injury costs were due to the 26% of current employees who failed the physical abilities test.[52]

When carefully conducted for appropriate jobs, physical abilities tests can be highly valid. One comprehensive study reported average validities of $\bar{r} = .39$ for warehouse workers to $\bar{r} = .87$ for enlisted army men.[53] Applicant reactions to these sorts of tests are unknown.

Sensory/Perceptual Abilities Tests Sensory/perceptual abilities tests assess the ability to detect and recognize environmental stimuli. An example of a sensory/perceptual ability test is a flight simulator that is used as part of the assessment process for airline pilots. Some tests of mechanical and clerical ability can be considered measures of sensory/perceptual ability, although they take on characteristics of cognitive ability tests. For example, the most commonly used mechanical ability test is the *Bennett Mechanical Comprehension Test*, which contains 68 items that measure an applicant's knowledge of the relationship between physical forces and mechanical objects (e.g., how a pulley operates, how gears function, etc.). In terms of clerical tests, the most widely known is the *Minnesota Clerical Test*. This timed test consists of 200 items in which the applicant is asked to compare names or numbers to identify matching elements. For example, an applicant might be asked (needing to work under time constraints) to check the pair of number series that is the same:

109485 _____ 104985
456836 _____ 456836
356823 _____ 536823
890940 _____ 890904
205837 _____ 205834

These tests of mechanical and clerical ability, and others like them, have reliability and validity data available that suggests they are valid predictors of performance within their specific area.[54] The degree to which these tests add validity over general intelligence, however, is not known.

Computer Testing

The development of computer technology and its widespread application to the workplace has resulted in an ever-increasing number of ability tests being administered via computer. Allstate Insurance administers a battery of computerized ability tests for certain positions at all 230 of its learning centers nationwide. For example, for the job of claims representative, applicants complete a test on customer service skills and verbal and mathematical abilities.[55] Computerized tests have the advantage of being easy to administer (automatic timing of speed tests, computer self-scores the tests). One computerized test, named *QUIZ*, actually assesses applicants' computer skills. Employers can customize the computer skills they want assessed (Microsoft Excel, Word, WordPerfect, DOS, etc.).[56] Other computerized tests include direct measures of cognitive ability, clerical ability, spatial ability, and so on.[57]

Research on computerized testing is only beginning to be published.[58] A recent meta-analysis suggests that computerized and paper-and-pencil ability tests have similar levels of validity when they are power tests, but speed versions of these tests are not always the same.[59] In any event, given the proliferation of computers in life and at work, the use of computers in selection, both to assess computer skills and as a medium to assess other abilities, is likely to increase.

Job Knowledge Tests

Job knowledge tests attempt to directly assess an applicant's comprehension of job requirements. Job knowledge tests can be one of two kinds. One type asks questions that directly assess knowledge of the duties involved in a particular job. For example, an item from a job knowledge test for an oncology nurse might be, "Describe the five oncological emergencies in cancer patients." The other type of job knowledge test focuses on the level of experience with, and corresponding knowledge about, critical job tasks and tools/processes necessary to perform the job. For example, the State of Wisconsin uses an *Objective Inventory Questionnaire* (OIQ) to evaluate applicants on the basis of their experience with tasks, duties, tools, technologies, and equipment that are relevant to a particular job.[60] OIQs ask applicants to evaluate their knowledge about and experience using skills, tasks, tools, and so forth, by means of a checklist of specific job statements. Applicants can rate their level of knowledge on a scale ranging from "have never performed the task" to "have trained others and evaluated their performance on the task." An example of an OIQ is provided in Exhibit 10.6. An advantage of OIQs is that they are fast and easy to process and can provide broad content coverage. A disadvantage of an OIQ is that applicants can easily falsify information. Thus, if job knowledge is an important prerequisite for a position, it is necessary to verify this information independently.

EXHIBIT 10.6 An Example Objective Inventory Questionnaire

For each of the following tasks, indicate your level of proficiency using the following codes. Use the one code that best describes your proficiency.

A = I have not performed the task or activity.
B = I have not performed the task independently but have assisted others in performing it.
C = I have performed the task independently, without assistance, and am fully proficient.
D = I have led or trained others in performing this task.

_____ compiled Database (DB2) tables in production
_____ rebuilt a master catalog
_____ installed a tape input system

Source: *Developing Wisconsin State Civil Service Examinations and Assessment Procedures* (Madison, WI: Wisconsin Department of Employment Relations, 1994).

Evaluation

There has been less research on the validity of job knowledge tests than most other selection measures. A recent study, however, provided relatively strong support for the validity of job knowledge tests. A meta-analytic review of 502 studies indicated that the "true" validity of job knowledge tests in predicting job performance is .45. These validities were found to be higher for complex jobs and when job and test content was similar.[61]

As was discussed when reviewing the literature on cognitive ability tests, scores on cognitive ability tests are highly correlated with measures of job knowledge. Typically, this relationship has been interpreted as evidence that intelligence allows employees to process job information more quickly so that they learn more about their job.[62] A question that becomes relevant, however, is the following, "Given the high correlation between scores on a test of general mental ability and a measure of job knowledge, do job knowledge tests explain any additional level of job performance beyond cognitive ability tests?" Numerous studies have found that measures of job knowledge add little to the prediction of job performance over the prediction due to cognitive ability. In fact, most studies have been quite consistent in finding that job knowledge or specific ability measures add an average increase in predictiveness of only .02.[63] These results suggest that while job knowledge plays an important role in understanding how cognitive ability is predictive of job performance, using job knowledge tests in selection will contribute very little to the prediction of job performance beyond that provided by cognitive ability tests. As one research team wrote, "This suggests that given competition for resources, testing of *g* may yield greater gains and should take precedence over testing for prior job knowledge."[64]

Performance Tests and Work Samples

These tests are mechanisms to assess actual performance rather than underlying capacity or disposition. As such, they are more akin to samples rather than signs of work performance. For example, at Domino's Pizza Distribution, job candidates for the positions of dough maker, truck driver, and warehouse worker are given performance tests to ensure that they can safely perform the job.[65] This sample is taken rather than using drug testing as a sign, because candidates may not be able to safely perform the job for a variety of reasons in addition to drug and alcohol abuse. Exhibit 10.7 provides examples of performance tests and work samples for a variety of jobs. As can be seen in the exhibit, the potential uses of these selection measures is quite broad in terms of job content and skill level.

Types of Tests

Performance Test versus Work Sample A performance test measures what the person actually does on the job. The best examples of performance tests are internships, job tryouts, and probationary periods. A work sample is designed to capture parts of the job, for example, a drill press test for machine operators and a programming test for computer programmers.[66] A performance test is more costly to develop than a work sample, but it is usually a better predictor of job performance.

Motor versus Verbal Work Samples A motor work sample test involves the physical manipulation of things. Examples include a driving test and a clothes-making test. A verbal work sample test involves a problem situation requiring language skills and interaction with people. Examples include role-playing tests that simulate contacts with customers, and an English test for foreign teaching assistants.[67]

High- versus Low-Fidelity Tests A high-fidelity test uses very realistic equipment and scenarios to simulate the actual tasks of the job. As such, they elicit actual responses encountered in performing the task.[68] A good example of a high-fidelity test is one being developed to select truck drivers in the petroleum industry. The test is on the computer and mimics all the steps taken to load and unload fuel from a tanker to a fuel reservoir at a service station.[69] It is not a test of perfect high fidelity, because fuel is not actually unloaded. It is, however, a much safer test because the dangerous process of fuel transfer is simulated rather than performed.

A low-fidelity test is one that simulates the task in a written or verbal description and elicits a written or verbal response rather than an actual response.[70] An example of a low-fidelity test is describing a work situation to job applicants and asking them what they would do in that particular situation. This was done in writing in a study by seven companies in the telecommunications industry for the position of manager.[71] Low-fidelity work samples bear many similarities to some

---

EXHIBIT 10.7   Examples of Performance Tests and Work Samples

---

Professor
　Teaching a class while on a campus interview
　Reading samples of applicant's research
Mechanic
　Repairing a particular problem on a car
　Reading a blueprint
Clerical
　Typing test
　Proofreading
Cashier
　Operating cash register
　Counting money and totaling balance sheet
Manager
　Performing a group problem solving exercise
　Reacting to memos and letters
Airline Pilot
　Pilot simulator
　Rudder control test
Taxi Cab Driver
　Driving test
　Street knowledge test
TV Repair Person
　Repairing broken television
　Finger and tweezer dexterity test
Police Officer
　Check police reports for errors
　Shooting accuracy test
Computer Programmer
　Programming and debugging test
　Hardware replacement test

---

types of structured interviews, and in some cases they may be indistinguishable (see Structured Interview section).

Computer Interaction Performance Tests versus Paper-and-Pencil Tests   As with ability testing, the computer has made it possible to measure aspects of work not possible to measure with a paper-and-pencil test. The computer can capture the complex and dynamic nature of work. This is especially true in work where perceptual and motor performance is required.[72]

An example of how the computer can be used to capture the dynamic nature of service work comes from Connecticut General Life Insurance Company. Fact-based scenarios, such as processing claims, are presented to candidates on the computer. The candidates' reactions to the scenarios, both mental (e.g., comprehension, coding, calculation) and motor (e.g., typing speed and accuracy), are assessed.[73]

The computer can also be used to capture the complex and dynamic nature of management work. On videotape, AccuVision shows the candidate actual job situations likely to be encountered on the job. In turn, the candidate selects a behavioral option in response in each situation. The response is entered in the computer and scored according to what it demonstrates of the skills needed to successfully perform as a manager.[74]

Evaluation

Research indicates that performance or work sample tests have a high degree of validity in predicting job performance. One meta-analysis of a large number of studies suggested that the average validity was $\bar{r} = .54$ in predicting job performance.[75] Because performance tests measure the entire job, and work samples measure a part of the job, they also have a high degree of content validity. Thus, when one considers the high degree of empirical and content validity, work samples are perhaps the most valid method of selection for many types of jobs.

Performance tests and work samples have other advantages as well. Research indicates that these measures are widely accepted by applicants as being job related.[76] One study found that no applicants complained about performance tests when 10% to 20% complained about other selection procedures.[77] Another study of American workers in a Japanese automotive plant concluded that work sample tests are best able to accommodate cross-cultural values and therefore are well-suited for selecting applicants in international joint ventures.[78] Another important advantage of performance tests and work samples is that they have low degrees of adverse impact.

Work samples do have several limitations. The costs of the realism embedded in work samples are high. The closer a predictor comes to simulating actual job performance, the more expensive it becomes to use it. Actually having people perform the job, as with an internship, may require paying a wage. Using videotapes and computers adds cost as well. As a result, performance tests and work samples are among the most expensive means of selecting workers. The costs of performance tests and work samples are amplified when one considers the lack of generalizability of such measures. Probably more than any other selection method, performance tests and work samples are tied to the specific job at hand. This means that a different test, based on a thorough analysis of the job, will need to be developed for each job. While their validity may well be worth the cost, in some circumstances the costs of work samples may be prohibitive. One means of mitigating the administrative expense associated with performance tests or work samples is to use a two-stage selection process whereby the full set of applicants is reduced by using relatively inexpensive tests. Once the initial cut is made, then performance tests or work samples can be administered to the smaller group of applicants who demonstrated minimum competency levels on the first-round tests.[79]

The importance of safety must also be considered as more realism is used in the selection procedure. If actual work is performed, care must taken so that the candidate's and employer's safety are ensured. When working with dangerous objects or procedures, the candidate must have the knowledge to follow the proper procedures. For example, in selecting nurse's aides for a long-term health care facility, it would not be wise to have candidates actually move residents in and out of their beds. Both the untrained candidate and resident may suffer physical harm if proper procedures are not followed.

Finally, most performance tests and work samples assume that the applicant already possesses the KSAOs necessary to do the job. If substantial training is involved, applicants will not be able to perform the work sample effectively, even though they could be high performers with adequate training. Thus, if substantial on-the-job training is involved and some or many of the applicants would require this training, work samples simply will not work.

Integrity Tests

Integrity tests attempt to assess an applicant's honesty and moral character. There are two major types of integrity tests: clear purpose (sometimes also called overt) and general purpose (sometimes called veiled purpose). Exhibit 10.8 provides examples of items from both types of measures. Clear purpose tests directly assess employee attitudes toward theft. Such tests often consist of two sections: (1) questions of anti-theft attitudes (see items 1–5 in Exhibit 10.8), and (2) questions about the frequency and degree of involvement in theft or other counterproductive activities (see items 6–10 in Exhibit 10.8).[80] General or veiled purpose integrity tests assess employee personality with the idea that personality influences dishonest behavior (see items 11–20 in Exhibit 10.8). There are many integrity tests that are commercially available. A report issued by the American Psychological Association (APA) has issued guidelines for using integrity tests.[81] Organizations considering adopting such tests must consider the validity evidence offered for the measure. The APA report identified 46 publishers of integrity tests, only 30 of which complied with the task force's request.[82] Thus, it cannot be assumed that all tests being marketed are in good scientific standing.

The use of integrity tests in selection decisions has grown dramatically in the past decade. Estimates are that several million integrity tests are administered to applicants each year.[83] There are numerous reasons why employers are interested in testing applicants for integrity, but perhaps the biggest factor is the high cost

---

EXHIBIT 10.8   Sample Integrity Test Questions

Clear Purpose or Overt Test Questions

1. Do you think most people would cheat if they thought they could get away with it?
2. Do you believe a person has a right to steal from an employer if he or she is unfairly treated?
3. What percentage of people take more than $5.00 per week (in cash or supplies) from their employer?
4. Do you think most people think much about stealing?
5. Are most people too honest to steal?
6. Do you ever gamble?
7. Did you ever write a check knowing there was not enough money in the bank?
8. Did you make a false insurance claim for personal gain?
9. Have you ever been in serious indebtedness?
10. Have you ever stolen anything?

Veiled Purpose or Personality-Based Test Questions

11. Would you rather go to a party than read a newspaper?
12. How often do you blush?
13. Do you almost always make your bed?
14. Do you like to create excitement?
15. Do you like to take chances?
16. Do you work hard and steady at everything you do?
17. Do you ever talk to authority figures?
18. Are you more sensible than adventurous?
19. Do you think taking chances makes life more interesting?
20. Would you rather "go with the flow" than "rock the boat"?

---

of employee theft in organizations. Although such estimates vary widely, most place the cost of employee theft to the U.S. economy at from $15 to $50 billion per year.[84] One-third of all employees have admitted to stealing something from their employers.[85] Thus, the major justification for integrity tests is to select employees who are less likely to steal or engage in other undesirable behaviors at work. Integrity tests are most often used for clerks, tellers, cashiers, security guards, police officers, and high-security jobs.

The construct of integrity is still not well understood. Presumably, the traits that these tests attempt to assess include reliability, conscientiousness, adjustment, and sociability. In fact, some recent evidence indicates that several of the Big Five personality traits are related to integrity test scores, particularly conscientiousness.[86] One study found that conscientiousness correlated significantly with scores on two integrity tests.[87] It appears that applicants who score high on integrity tests also tend to score high on conscientiousness, low on neuroticism, and high on agreeableness.[88] It has been suggested that integrity tests might measure a construct even more broad than those represented by the Big Five traits.[89] More work on this important issue is needed, particularly the degree to which integrity is related to, but distinct from, more established measures of personality.

Measures

The most common method of measuring employee integrity is paper-and-pencil measures. Some employers had previously used polygraph ("lie detector") tests, but for most employers these tests are now prohibited by law. Another approach has been to try to detect dishonesty in the interview. However, research tends to suggest that the interview is a very poor means of detecting lying. In fact, in a study of interviewers who should be experts at detecting lying (members of Secret Service, CIA, FBI, National Security Agency, Drug Enforcement Agency, California police detectives, and psychiatrists), only the Secret Service performed significantly better than chance.[90] Thus, paper-and-pencil measures are the most feasible for assessing integrity for selection decisions.

Evaluation

Until recently, the validity of integrity tests was poorly studied. However, a recent meta-analysis of more than 500,000 people and more than 650 individual studies was recently published.[91] The principal findings from this study are the following:

1. Both clear and general purpose integrity tests are valid predictors of counterproductive behaviors (actual and admitted theft, dismissals for theft, illegal activities, absenteeism, tardiness, workplace violence). The average validity for clear purpose measures ($\bar{r} = .55$) was higher than for general purpose ($\bar{r} = .32$).

2. Both clear and general purpose tests were valid predictors of job performance ($\bar{r} = .33$ and $\bar{r} = .35$, respectively).

3. The average correlation between scores on an integrity test and detection of theft was $\bar{r} = .32$.

4. Integrity tests were more valid predictors of counterproductive behaviors for high-complexity jobs ($\bar{r} = .68$) than low-complexity jobs ($\bar{r} = .43$).

5. Integrity tests have no adverse impact against women or minorities and are relatively uncorrelated with intelligence. Thus, integrity tests demonstrate incremental validity over cognitive ability tests and reduce the adverse impact of cognitive ability tests.

Results from this comprehensive study suggest that organizations would benefit from using integrity tests for a wide array of jobs. Since most of the individual studies included in the meta-analysis were conducted by test publishers (who have an interest in finding good results), however, organizations using integrity tests should consider conducting their own validation studies.

One of the most significant concerns with the use of integrity tests is obviously the possibility that applicants may fake their responses. Consider answering the questions in Exhibit 10.8. Now consider answering these questions in the context of applying for a job that you desire. It seems more than plausible that applicants might distort their responses in such a context (particularly given that most of the answers would be impossible to verify). This possibility becomes a real concern when one considers the prospect that the individuals most likely to "fake good" (people behaving dishonestly) are exactly the type of applicants organizations would want to weed out.

Only recently has the issue of faking been investigated in the research literature. One study found that subjects who were asked to respond as if they were applying for a job had 8% more favorable scores than those who were instructed to respond truthfully. Subjects who were specifically instructed to "fake good" had 24% more favorable scores than those who were told to respond truthfully.[92] A more recent study found some enhancement in completing an integrity test, but the degree of distortion was relatively small and did not undermine the validity of the test.[93] These results are consistent with the meta-analysis results reported earlier in the sense that if faking were pervasive, integrity test scores would either have no validity in predicting performance from applicant scores, or the validity would be *negative* (honest applicants reporting worse scores than dishonest applicants). The fact that validity was positive for applicant samples suggests that if faking does occur, it does not severely impair the predictive validity of integrity tests. It has been suggested that dishonest applicants do not fake more than honest applicants because they believe that everyone is dishonest and therefore they are reporting only what everyone else already does.

Objections to Integrity Tests and Applicant Reactions

Integrity tests have proven to be controversial. There are many reasons for this. Perhaps the most fundamental concern is misclassification of truly honest applicants as being dishonest. For example, the results of one study that was influential in a government report on integrity testing is presented in Exhibit 10.9. In this study, it has been claimed that 93.3% of individuals who failed the test were misclassified because no thefts were detected among 222 of the 238 individuals who failed the test. However, this ignores the strong possibility that some of the 222 individuals who failed the test and for whom no theft was detected may have stolen without being caught.[94] In fact, the misclassification rate is unknown and, most likely, unknowable. (After all, if all thefts were detected there would be no

---

EXHIBIT 10.9   Integrity Test Results and Theft Detections

Theft category	Failed test	Passed test	Total
No theft detected	222	240	462
Theft detected	16	1	17
Total	238	241	479

Source: U.S. Congress, Office of Technology Assessment, *The Use of Integrity Tests for Preemployment Screening*, OTA-SET-442 (Washington, DC: U.S. Government Printing Office, 1990).

---

demand for integrity tests!) Also, all selection procedures involve misclassification of individuals because all selection methods are imperfect (have validities less than 1.0). Perhaps a more valid concern is the stigmatization of applicants who are thought to be dishonest based on their test scores,[95] but these problems can be avoided with proper procedures for maintaining the confidentiality of test scores.

There has been little research on how applicants react to integrity tests. Research suggests that applicants view integrity tests less favorably than most selection practices; they also see them as more invasive.[96] Thus, although the evidence is scant, it appears that applicants do not view integrity tests favorably. Whether these negative views affect their willingness to join an organization, however, is unknown.

Interest, Values, and Preference Inventories

Interest, values, and preference inventories attempt to assess the activities individuals prefer to do both on and off the job. This is in comparison with predictors that measure whether the person can do the job. However, just because a person can do a job does not guarantee success on the job. If the person does not want to do the job, that individual will fail regardless of ability. Although interests seem important, they have not been used very much in human resource selection.

Standardized tests of interests, values, and preferences are available. Many of these measure vocational interests (e.g., the type of career that would motivate and satisfy someone) rather than organizational interests (e.g., the type of job or organization that would motivate and satisfy someone). The two most widely used interest inventories are the *Strong Vocational Interest Blank* (SVIB) and the *Myers-Briggs Type Inventory* (MBTI). Rather than classify individuals along continuous dimensions (e.g., someone is more or less conscientious than another), both the SVIB and MBTI classify individuals into distinct categories based on their responses to the survey. With the MBTI, individuals are classified in 16 types that have been found to be related to the Big Five personality characteristics discussed earlier.[97] Example interest inventory items are provided in Exhibit 10.10. The SVIB classifies individuals into six categories (realistic, investigative, artistic, social, enterprising, and clerical) that match jobs that are characterized in a corresponding manner. Both of these inventories are used extensively in career counseling in high school, college, and trade schools.[98]

Past research has suggested that interest inventories are not valid predictors of job performance. The average validity of interest inventories in predicting job performance appears to be roughly $\bar{r} = .10$.[99] This does not mean that interest inventories are invalid for all purposes. Research clearly suggests that when individuals' interests match those of their occupation, they are happier with their jobs and are more likely to remain in their chosen occupation.[100] Thus, while interest inventories fail to predict job performance, they do predict occupational choices and job satisfaction levels. Undoubtedly one of the reasons why vocational interests are poorly related to job performance is because the interests are tied to the occupation rather than the organization or the job.

EXHIBIT 10.10 Sample Items from Interest Inventory

---

1. Are you usually:
    (a) a person who loves parties
    (b) a person who prefers to curl up with a good book?
2. Would you prefer to:
    (a) run for President
    (b) fix a car?
3. Is it a higher compliment to be called:
    (a) a compassionate person
    (b) a responsible person?
4. Would you rather be considered:
    (a) someone with much intuition
    (b) someone guided by logic and reason?
5. Do you more often:
    (a) do things on the "spur of the moment"
    (b) plan out all activities carefully in advance?
6. Do you usually get along better with:
    (a) artisitic people, or
    (b) realistic people?
7. With which statement do you most agree:
    (a) Learn what you are, and be such.
    (b) Ah, but a man's reach should exceed his grasp, or what's a heaven for?
8. At parties and social gatherings, do you more often:
    (a) introduce others, or
    (b)   get introduced?

Research suggests that while interest inventories play an important role in vocational choice, their role in organizational selection decisions is limited. However, a more promising way of considering the role of interests and values in the staffing process is to focus on person-organization fit.[101] As was discussed in Chapter 1, person-organization fit argues that it is not the applicants' characteristics alone that influence performance, but rather the interaction between the applicants' characteristics and those of the organization. For example, an individual with a strong interest in social relations at work may perform well in an organization that emphasizes cooperation and teamwork but the same individual might do poorly in an organization whose culture is characterized by independence or rugged individualism. An assessment process that considers applicant values from the perspective of person-organization fit recently has been developed. A modified version of this assessment tool is provided in Exhibit 10.11.[102] This measure, termed the *Organizational Culture Profile* (OCP), assesses applicant values by asking them to rank the importance of various organizational values. Applicants' responses to the OCP have been found to be relatively stable even after they have joined an organization. Although the development of this measure is relatively recent, research has shown that congruence between applicant values (as expressed in the OCP) and those emphasized within the organization predicts applicant job choice decisions and organizational selection decisions. Employee-organizational value congruence as defined by the OCP is predictive of employee satisfaction, commitment, and turnover decisions. Furthermore, as opposed to other interest inventories, interests or values congruence as defined by the OCP appears to predict job performance.[103] Thus, in considering the relationship of interests, values, and preferences with job performance, it seems necessary to also consider how well those characteristics match the culture of the organization. There are other ways in which person-organization fit can be assessed in selection decisions although the ability of these measures to predict job performance has not been established.[104] Because organizations pursuing a quality strategy provide employees greater control over their work, person-organization fit may be a particularly important selection factor in quality environments.[105]

Structured Interview

The structured interview is a very standardized, job-related method of assessment. It requires careful and thorough construction, as described in the sections that follow. It is instructive to compare the structured job interview with an unstructured or psychological interview. This comparison will serve to highlight the difference between the two.

A typical unstructured interview has the following sorts of characteristics:

● It is relatively unplanned (e.g., just sit down and "wing it" with the candidate) and often "quick and dirty" (e.g., 10–15 minutes).

EXHIBIT 10.11 Modified Organizational Culture Profile

Below you will find 40 characteristics that could be used to describe your preferred organization. Please consider each characteristic according to the question: To what degree is this a characteristic of an organization in which you would like to work? Then, place each characteristic in an appropriate box, which range from most characteristic to least characteristic. Each box receives only one attribute. For example, only 2 items may be "most characteristic" of this organization while 12 items may be "neither characteristic nor uncharacteristic" of the organization. You can write the number in the box rather than the words. It may be easiest to first read through the entire list of characteristics looking for extremes.

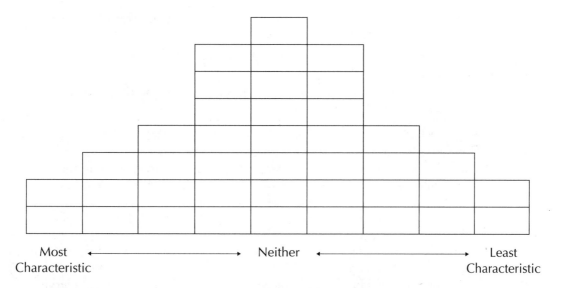

| Most | | Neither | | Least |
| Characteristic | | | | Characteristic |

1. Adaptability
2. Stability
3. Being reflective
4. Being innovative
5. Quickly seize on opportunities
6. Taking individual responsibility
7. Risk taking
8. Chances for professional growth
9. Autonomy
10. Being rule oriented
11. Being analytical
12. Paying attention to detail
13. Confronting conflict directly
14. Being team oriented
15. Sharing information freely
16. Being people oriented
17. Fairness
18. Not being constrained by rules
19. Tolerance
20. Informality

21. Decisiveness
22. Being competitive
23. Being highly organized
24. Achievement orientation
25. Having a clear guiding philosophy
26. Being results oriented
27. High performance expectations
28. Being aggressive
29. High pay for good performance
30. Security of employment
31. Praise for good performance
32. Being supportive
33. Being calm
34. Developing friends at work
35. Being socially responsible
36. Enthusiasm for the job
37. Working long hours
38. Having a good reputation
39. An emphasis on quality
40. Being distinctive/different

Source: Adapted by D. M. Cable from C. A. O'Reilly III, J. Chatman and D. F. Caldwell, "People and Organizational Culture: A Profile Comparison Approach to Assessing Person-Organization Fit," *Academy of Management Journal*, 1991, 34, pp. 487–516. Used by permission.

- Rather than being based on the requirements of the job, questions are based on interviewer "hunches" or "pet questions" in order to psychologically diagnose applicant suitability.
- It consists of casual, open-ended, or subjective questioning (e.g., "Tell me a little bit about yourself").
- It has obtuse questions (e.g., "What type of animal would you most like to be, and why?").
- It has highly speculative questions (e.g., "Where do you see yourself ten years from now?").
- The interviewer is unprepared (e.g., forgot to review job description and specification before the interview).
- The interviewer makes a quick, and final, evaluation of the candidate (e.g., often in the first couple of minutes).

Interviews are the most commonly used selection practice, and the unstructured interview is the most common form of interview in actual interview practice.[106] Research shows that organizations clearly pay a price for the use of the unstructured interview, namely lower reliability and validity.[107] Interviewers using the unstructured interview (a) are unable to agree among themselves in their evaluation of job candidates, and (b) cannot predict the job success of candidates with any degree of consistent accuracy.

Fortunately, research has begun to unravel the reasons why the unstructured interview works so poorly and what factors need to be changed in order to improve reliability and validity. Sources of error or bias in the unstructured interview include the following:

1. There is low reliability between interviewers regarding what questions should be asked of applicants and how applicants are evaluated.
2. Applicant appearance, including facial attractiveness, cosmetics, and attire, has consistently been shown to predict interviewer evaluations. A recent experiment found that moderately obese applicants (especially female applicants) were much less likely to be recommended for employment, even controlling for job qualifications.[108]
3. Nonverbal cues (eye contact, smiling, etc.) have been found to be related to interview ratings.[109]
4. Negative information receives more weight than positive in the interview. Research suggests it takes more than twice as much positive as negative information to change an interviewer's initial impression of an applicant. As a result, the unstructured interview has been labeled a "search for negative evidence."[110]
5. There are primacy effects, where information obtained prior to the interview or during its early stages, dominates interviewer judgments. An early study

suggested that on average, interviewers reached final decisions about applicants after only *four* minutes of a half-hour interview. These first impressions are particularly influential because interviewers engage in hypothesis confirmation strategies that are designed to confirm their initial impressions. Interviewers with positive first impressions sell the applicants more on the company, do more recruiting, and tell them more about the company.[111] One study showed that the same candidate was described by different interviewers as "Alert, enthusiastic, responsible, intelligent, can express himself well, well-rounded, reliable, and generally capable of handling himself well" versus "Nervous, quick to object to the interviewer's assumptions, and doesn't have enough self-confidence." What caused these opposite conclusions? The first group of interviewers was given positive information about the candidate before the interview while the latter group of interviewers was given negative information about the candidate before the interview.[112]

6. There are similarity effects, where applicants who are similar to the interviewer with respect to race, gender, or other characteristics receive higher ratings, also seem to exist.[113]

7. Poor recall by interviewers often plagues unstructured interviews. One study demonstrated this by giving managers an exam based on factual information after watching a 20-minute videotaped interview. Some managers got all 20 questions correct, but the average manager only got half right.[114]

Thus, the unstructured interview is not very valid and research has identified the reasons why this is so. The structured interview is an attempt to eliminate the biases inherent in unstructured formats by standardizing the process.

Types of Structured Interviews

There are two principal types of structured interviews: situational and experience-based. Situational interviews assess an applicant's ability to project what his or her behavior would be in future, hypothetical situations.[115] The assumption behind the use of the situational interview is that the goals or intentions individuals set for themselves are good predictors of what they will do in the future.

Experienced-based or job-related interviews assess past behaviors that are linked to the prospective job. The assumption behind the use of experienced-based interviews is the same as that for the use of biodata—past behavior is a good predictor of future behavior. It is assumed that applicants who are likely to succeed have demonstrated success with past job experiences similar to the experiences they would encounter in the prospective job. An example of an experienced-based interview is the *Patterned Behavior Description Interview*, which collects four types of experiential information during the interview: (1) *credentials* (objective verifiable information about past experiences and accomplishments); (2) *experience descriptions* (descriptions of applicants' normal job duties, capabilities, and responsibilities); (3) *opinions* (applicants' thoughts about their strengths, weaknesses, and self-perceptions); (4) *behavior descriptions* (detailed accounts of actual events from the applicants' job and life experiences).[116]

Situational and experienced-based interviews have many similarities. Generally, both are based on the critical incidents approach to job analysis where job behaviors especially important to (as opposed to typically descriptive of) job performance are considered. Also, both approaches attempt to assess applicant *behaviors* rather than feelings, motives, values, or other psychological states. Finally, both methods have substantial reliability and validity evidence in their favor.

On the other hand, situational and experienced-based interviews have important differences. The most obvious difference is that situational interviews are future oriented ("what *would* you do if?"), while experienced-based interviews are past oriented ("what *did* you do when?"). Also, situational interviews are more standardized in that they ask the same questions of all applicants while many experienced-based interviews place an emphasis on discretionary probing based on responses to particular questions. Presently, there is little basis to guide decisions about which of these two types of structured interviews should be adopted. However, one factor to consider is that experienced-based interviews may only be relevant for individuals who have had significant job experience. In other words, it does not make much sense to ask applicants what they did in a particular situation if they have never been in that situation. Some recent interview formats strike a balance between past- and future-oriented questions.[117]

Evaluation

Traditionally, the employment interview was thought to have a low degree of validity. Recently, however, evidence for the validity of structured (and even unstructured) interviews has been much more positive. A recent meta-analysis suggested the following conclusions:[118]

1. The average validity of interviews was found to be $\bar{r} = .26$. This figure increased to $\bar{r} = .37$ when estimates were corrected for range restriction, which is not without controversy.[119] To be conservative, the estimates reported here are those uncorrected for range restriction.

2. Structured interviews were more valid ($\bar{r} = .31$) than unstructured interviews ($\bar{r} = .23$).

3. Situational interviews were more valid ($\bar{r} = .35$) than experienced-based interviews ($\bar{r} = .28$).

4. Panel interviews were *less* valid ($\bar{r} = .22$) than individual interviews ($\bar{r} = .31$).

It is safe to say that these values are higher than researchers had previously thought. Even unstructured interviews were found to have moderate degrees of validity. One of the reasons the validity may have been higher than previously thought is because in order to validate unstructured interviews, each interview must be given a numerical score. Assigning numerical scores to an interview imposes some degree of structure (interviewees are rated using the same scale), so it might be best to think of the unstructured interviews included in this analysis as semistructured rather than purely unstructured. Therefore, the estimated validity for "unstructured" interviews included in the meta-analysis is probably higher than that of the typical unstructured interview.

Future Uses of the Structured Interview

While the meta-analysis reviewed above has offered a comprehensive summary of the literature on the validity of the interview, some of the most important questions in evaluating the usefulness of the interview have not been answered by past research. One potentially important use of the interview involves consideration of the issue of employee value. Without a doubt, performance or productivity is the central aspect of employee value to the organization. But it surely is not the only criterion. Other important criteria that should be used to evaluate the selection process include applicant reactions, employee attendance and retention, "citizenship" behaviors, and fit within the organization. Thus, a valuable employee is not only a good performer, but also is helpful to others, reliable, pleasant to be around, thinks in ways compatible with others, and otherwise contributes to the interpersonal climate of the organization. Clearly there is value in this. Whether one considers sports teams or business enterprises, organizations filled with individual contributors working in a hostile organizational climate are unlikely to succeed in the long run. Thus, the interpersonal orientation of the employee is important beyond its ability to contribute to productivity, and some selection measures, like the interview, are valuable for their ability to predict "nonperformance" aspects of employee value.

Consider the concept of person-organization match (see Chapter 1). Researchers have distinguished between person-*job* match, matching the KSAOs of the applicant to the technical requirements of the job, from person-*organization* match, matching the goals, values, and interpersonal skills of the applicant to the culture of the organization.[120] Thus, if selecting applicants who fit the organization's culture requires assessment of their goals, values, and interpersonal skills, the interview would seem better suited than other selection measures to assess these subjective elements. In fact, interviewers distinguish between interpersonal skills and objective qualifications, and interviews predict subjective performance better than objective measures of productivity.[121]

What implications do these arguments have for the interview? An "alternative" model of selection decisions is presented in Exhibit 10.12. As the model shows, hiring decisions are based not only on the match between applicant KSAOs and job requirements, but also on the basis of how the applicant will fit with the goals, values, and culture of the organization. While some selection methods are suitable for judging technical qualifications (e.g., ability and personality tests, work samples, biodata, and so on), the interview may be ideally suited to assess applicant goals, values, and interpersonal skills.

EXHIBIT 10.12   An Alternative Model of the Use of the Interview in Selection Decisions

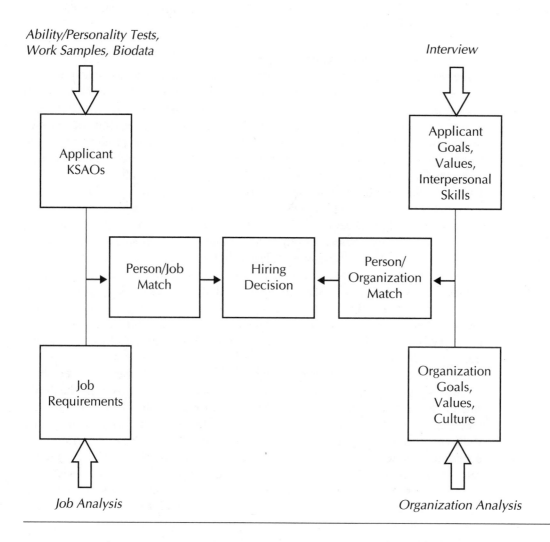

This model is untested and therefore it can only be offered tentatively. However, it does suggest dramatic changes to the use of the interview in selection decisions. The typical approach to the structured interview is to make it a close approximation of the skill and ability requirements of the job. However, a consequence of structured interviews is that they are highly correlated with cognitive ability tests. In fact, one study found that scores on the structured interview were more highly correlated with scores on cognitive ability tests than they were with job performance.[122] Other studies have found that structured interviews do not add validity in predicting job performance beyond cognitive ability tests.[123] In fact, the meta-analysis of interviews reviewed earlier found that when cognitive ability test scores were available to interviewers prior to the interview, the validity of structured interviews dropped to $\bar{r} = .16$ (this incremental validity was even lower than for unstructured interviews). As a result of the strong linkage between structured interview performance and cognitive ability, some have termed structured interviews as nothing more than "verbal cognitive ability tests." Thus, structuring interviews around KSAOs may cause them to lose their unique contribution to selection decisions—the ability to assess applicant goals, values, and interpersonal skills. If we are correct in our reasoning, the proper use of the interview is not to return to unstructured interviewing. Rather, the key question becomes: structure the interview around *what*? Under our reasoning, the interview would become structured around those elements of employee value that it is uniquely suited to predict, namely person/organization match.

Another important factor to consider in evaluating the employment interview is that it serves other goals besides identifying the best candidates for the job. One of the most important uses of the interview is recruitment. The interview is the central means through which applicants learn about important aspects of the job and the organization. This information can be very useful to applicants for making decisions about organizations. A recent study suggested that the goals of recruitment and selection in the interview are not complementary ones. Interviews that are focused solely on recruitment lead applicants to learn more about the job and the organization than interviews that are dual purpose (recruitment and selection).[124] The more information applicants acquire during an interview, the more likely they are to think highly of an organization and thus accept an offer from the organization.

In fact, applicants tend to react very favorably to the interview. Research suggests that most applicants believe the interview is an essential component of the selection process and most view the interview as the most suitable measure of relevant abilities.[125] As a result, the interview has been rated by applicants as more job related than any other selection procedure.[126] One study estimated that use of the interview in the selection process resulted in a 6% increase in the probability of offer acceptance.[127] Why do applicants react so favorably to the interview? One model of applicant reactions to selection procedures suggested that selection methods that are perceived as controllable by the candidate, obvious in purpose, providing task relevant information, and offering a means of feedback are considered the most socially valid or acceptable.[128] The interview would appear to offer all of these components. As a result, applicants may perceive the interview as a mutual exchange of relevant information predictive of future performance, and therefore job related. Thus, the interview generates very positive applicant reactions and can serve an important role in recruitment.

Regardless of what information the interview is structured around, the process of structuring an interview requires that organizations follow a systematic and standardized process. Next, the process of constructing a structured interview is described. For purposes of illustration, we describe development of a situational interview.

Constructing a Structured Interview

The structured interview is one that, by design and conduct, standardizes and controls for sources of influence on the interview process and the interviewer. The goal here is to improve interview reliability and validity beyond that of the unstructured interview. Research shows that this goal can be achieved. Doing so requires following each of these steps: consult the job requirements matrix, develop the selection plan, develop the structured interview plan, select and train interviewers, and evaluate effectiveness. Each of these steps is elaborated upon next.

The Job Requirements Matrix
The starting point for the structured interview is the job requirements matrix. It identifies the tasks and KSAOs that define the job requirements around which the structured interview is constructed and conducted.

The Selection Plan
As previously described, the selection plan flows from the KSAOs identified in the job requirements matrix. The selection plan addresses which KSAOs it is necessary to assess during selection, and whether the structured interview is the preferred method of assessing them.

Is the KSAO Necessary?   Some KSAOs must be brought to the job by the candidate, and others can be acquired on the job (through training and/or job experience). The bring-it/acquire-it decision must be made for each KSAO. This decision should be guided by the importance indicator(s) for the KSAOs in the job requirements matrix.

Is the Structured Interview the Preferred Method?   It must be decided if the structured interview is the preferred method of assessing each KSAO necessary for selection. Several factors should be considered when making this decision. First, job knowledges are usually best assessed through other methods, such as a written ability or job knowledge test or specific training and experience requirements. The structured interview thus should focus more on skills and abilities. Second, many alternative methods are available for assessing these skills and abilities, as discussed throughout this chapter. Third, the structured interview is probably best suited for assessing only some of these skills and abilities, such as verbal, interpersonal, adaptability, and flexibility skills and abilities.

An example of a selection plan for the job of sales associate in a retail clothing store is shown in Exhibit 10.13. While there were five task dimensions for the job in the job requirements matrix (customer service, use of machines, use of customer service outlets, sales and departmental procedures, cleaning and maintenance), the selection plan is shown only for the dimension customer service.

Note in the exhibit that the customer service dimension has several required KSAOs. However, only some of these will be assessed during selection, and only some of those will be assessed by the structured interview. The method of assessment is thus carefully targeted to the KSAO to be assessed.

The Structured Interview Plan

Development of the structured interview plan proceeds along three sequential steps: construction of interview questions, construction of benchmark responses for the questions, and weighting of the importance of the questions. The output of this process for the sales associate job is shown in Exhibit 10.14, and is referred to in the discussion that follows.

Constructing Questions   One or more questions must be constructed for each KSAO targeted for assessment by the structured interview. Many different types of questions have been experimented with and researched, including situational interviewing, behavior description interviewing, job content interviewing, and structured behavioral interviewing.[129] Despite differences, there is a major underlying characteristic common to all.

That characteristic is sampling of the candidate's behavior, as revealed by past situations and what the candidate reports would be his or her behavior in future situations. The questions ask in essence, "What have you done in this situation?" and "What would you do if you were in this situation?"

EXHIBIT 10.13   Partial Selection Plan for Job of Retail Store Sales Associate

---

Task Dimension: Customer Service

KSAO	Necessary for Selection?	Method of Assessment
1. Ability to make customer feel welcome	Yes	Interview
2. Knowledge of merchandise to be sold	Yes	Written test
3. Knowledge of location of merchandise in store	No	– – – –
4. Skill in being cordial with customers	Yes	Interview
5. Ability to create and convey ideas to customers	Yes	Interview

EXHIBIT 10.14 Structured Interview Questions, Benchmark Responses, Rating Scale, and Question Weights

Job: Sales Associate
Task Dimension: Customer Service

	Rating Scale					Rating	X	Weight	= Score
	1	2	3	4	5				

Question No. One (KSAO 1)

A customer walks into the store. No other salespeople are around to help the person, and you are busy arranging merchandise. What would you do if you were in this situation?

Keep on arranging merchandise		Keep working but greet the customer		Stop working, greet customer, and offer to provide assistance

Rating 5 X Weight 1 = Score 5

Question No. Two (KSAO 4)

A customer is in the fitting room and asks you to bring her some shirts to try on. You do so, but by accident bring the wrong size. The customer becomes irate and starts shouting at you. What would you do if you were in this situation?

Tell customer to "keep her cool"		Go get correct size		Apologize, go get correct size

Rating 3 X Weight 1 = Score 3

Question No. Three (KSAO 5)

A customer is shopping for the "right" shirt for her 17-year-old granddaughter. She asks you to show her shirts that you think would be "right" for her. You do this, but the customer doesn't like any of them. What would you do if you were in this situation?

Tell customer to go look elsewhere		Explain why you think your choices are good ones		Explain your choices, suggest gift certificate as alternative

Rating 5 X Weight 2 = Score 10

18

The key to constructing both types of questions is to create a scenario relevant to the KSAO in question and to ask the candidate to respond to it by way of answering a question. Situations may be drawn from past job experiences, as well as nonjob experiences. Inclusion of nonjob experiences is important for applicants who have not had similar previous job experience, or have not had any previous job experience at all.

The "what would you do if" type questions should be constructed around important scenarios or events that the person is likely to encounter on the job. The candidate may draw upon both previous job and nonjob situations, as well as more general behavioral intentions, in fashioning a response.

Exhibit 10.14 shows three questions for the KSAOs to be assessed by the interview, as determined by the initial selection plan for the job of sales associate in a retail store. As can be seen, all three questions present very specific situations that a sales associate is likely to encounter. The content of all three questions is clearly job relevant, a logical outgrowth of the process that began with the development of the job requirements matrix.

Benchmark Responses and Rating Scales   The interviewer must somehow evaluate or judge the quality of the candidates' response to the interview questions. Prior development of benchmark responses and corresponding rating scales is the method for providing firm guidance to the interviewer in doing this task. Benchmark responses represent qualitative examples of the types of candidate response that the interviewer may encounter. They are located on a rating scale (usually 1–5 or 1–7 rating scale points) to represent the level or "goodness" of the response.

Exhibit 10.14 contains benchmark responses, positioned on 1–5 rating scales, for each of the three interview questions. Note that all the responses are quite specific, and they clearly suggest that some answers are better than others. These responses represent judgments on the part of the organization as to the desirability of behaviors its employees could engage in.

Weighting Responses   Each candidate will receive a total score for the structured interview. It thus must be decided whether each question is of equal importance in contributing to the total score. If so, the candidate's total interview score is simply the sum of the scores on the individual rating scales.

If some questions are more important than others in assessing candidates, then those questions receive greater weight. The more important the question, the greater its weight relative to the other questions.

Exhibit 10.14 shows the weighting decided upon for the three interview questions. As can be seen, the first two questions receive a weight of 1, and the third question receives a weight of 2. The candidate's assigned ratings are multiplied by their weights and then summed to determine a total score for this particular task dimension. In the exhibit, the candidate receives a score of 18

$(5 + 3 + 10 = 18)$ for customer service. The candidate's total interview score would be the sum of the scores on all the dimensions.

Selection and Training of Interviewers

Some interviewers are more accurate in their judgments than others. In fact, several studies have found significant differences in interviewer validity.[130] Thus, rather than asking, "How valid is the interview?" it might be more appropriate to ask, "Who is a valid interviewer?"[131] Answering this question requires selecting interviewers based on characteristics that will enable them to make accurate decisions about applicants. Little research is available regarding the factors that should guide selection of interviewers. Perhaps not surprisingly, cognitive ability has been linked to accuracy in evaluating others. It also would be possible to design an interview simulation where prospective interviewers are asked to analyze jobs to determine applicant KSAOs, preview applications, conduct hypothetical interviews, and evaluate the applicants.[132] Thus, selecting interviewers who are intelligent and who demonstrate effective interviewing skills in interview simulations likely will improve the validity of the interviewing process.

Training of interviewers is another means of increasing the validity of structured interviews. It is likely that interviewers will need training in the structured interview process. The process is probably quite different from what they have encountered and/or used, and training becomes a way of introducing them to the process. Logical program content areas to be covered as part of the training are:

- problems with the unstructured interview
- advantages of the structured interview
- development of the structured interview
- use of probe questions and note taking
- elimination of rating errors
- actual practice in conducting the structured interview

While research suggests that interviewers are generally receptive to training attempts, it is not clear that such efforts are successful. As one review concluded, the evidence regarding the ability of training programs to reduce rating errors showed that these programs "have achieved at best mixed results."[133] This makes it even more important to accurately select effective interviewers as a means of making the interview process more accurate.

Evaluating Effectiveness

As with any assessment device, there is a constant need to learn more about the reliability, validity, and utility of the structured interview. This is particularly so because of the complexity of the interview process. Thus, evaluation of the structured interview's effectiveness should be built directly into the process itself.[134]

Assessment for Team and Quality Environments

In order to be responsive to a rapidly changing business environment, some organizations are decentralizing decision making and putting increased emphasis on quality. In many cases, these business strategies have resulted in total quality management (TQM) programs and the development of team-based jobs. The process of selection in quality and team environments may be different than in the more traditional context. This necessitates consideration of how these new work arrangements may affect staffing processes and decisions. Accordingly, assessment in quality and team environments is considered in turn.

Selection in Quality Environments

Interestingly, organizations with TQM missions often seem to ignore selection systems. One study of Malcolm Baldrige Award winners found that only one had fundamentally altered its selection processes to make them more compatible with a TQM strategy, and it has been noted that the Baldrige Award criteria barely mention selection.[135] In an effort to bring selection activities into closer alignment with quality objectives, it has been suggested that organizations with a strategy of quality enhancement or TQM may need to revise their selection policies in a number of important ways.[136]

1. The types of skills assessed in quality organizations may be different. Quality organizations require that employees demonstrate customer service skills, self-direction and self-development, and team-development skills. As a result, three of the Big Five personality characteristics—conscientiousness, openness to experience, and agreeableness—may be particularly important to performance in quality organizations.[137] Conscientious individuals are dependable, organized, and persistent. Therefore, they may perform better in quality environments due to the emphasis on control, reliability, and decreased errors. Open individuals are flexible, creative, and autonomous. Openness may an important characteristic in quality organizations given that TQM requires autonomy, willingness to experiment, taking risks, and continuous learning. Finally, agreeableness may be important because quality organizations emphasize customer relations, cooperation, and collaboration.

2. Specificity of skills assessed may be different in a quality environment. Quality organizations embrace change and emphasize flexibility in production processes and environmental response. Since this requires that employees be flexible and competent in numerous work roles, emphasis on job-spanning KSAOs as opposed to narrow job-specific skills may be warranted. General mental ability is perhaps the most generalized skill an employee can have; thus, it may be particularly important in adapting to the rapid changes and flexible processes of quality environments.

3. The processes by which selection decisions are made may need to be different. Quality organizations rely more heavily on employee discretion and autonomy to make decisions about work processes, and more work is team-based in quality organizations. Therefore, it would be appropriate for selection in quality organizations to be based on peer (as opposed to manager) decisions.

There is virtually no research on staffing in quality environments, therefore it is even more important than in traditional cases that quality organizations validate their selection processes prior to full implementation.

Selection in Team Environments

As with selection for quality environments, the first step in understanding the proper steps for selection in team-based environments is to understand the requirements of the job. A recent analysis of the KSAOs for teamwork is presented in Exhibit 10.15. Identified in the exhibit are 2 major categories of KSAs for teamwork, 5 subcategories, and 14 specific KSAs (the "other" category was not considered in the study). Thus, in order to be effective in a teamwork assignment, an employee needs to demonstrate *interpersonal KSAs* (consisting of conflict resolution, collaborative problem solving, and communication KSAs) and *self-management KSAs* (consisting of goal setting and performance management KSAs and planning and task coordination KSAs). The implication of this framework for selection is that existing selection processes and methods may need to be revamped to incorporate these KSAs.

One means of incorporating team-based KSAs into the existing selection process has been developed.[138] Exhibit 10.16 provides some sample items from the 35-item test. This test has been validated against three criteria (teamwork performance, technical performance, and overall performance) in two studies.[139] The teamwork test showed substantial validity in predicting teamwork and overall performance in one of the studies but no validity in predicting any of the criteria in the other study. (It is not clear why the teamwork test worked well in one study yet not in the other.) Another important finding was that while general cognitive ability was a valid predictor of technical and overall job performance, it did not predict teamwork performance. It should be noted that tests are not the only method of measuring teamwork KSAs. Other methods of assessment that some leading companies have used in selecting team members include structured interviews, assessment centers, personality tests, and biographical inventories.[140] For example, the PCI personality test described earlier has a special scale that is designed to predict team performance. It is also important to remember that because teams serve different functions, the assessment process may need to depend on the type of team that is being staffed.[141] This is another reason to begin the process of team member selection with a thorough job analysis of teamwork activities.

EXHIBIT 10.15   Knowledge, Skill, and Ability (KSA) Requirements for Teamwork

I. INTERPERSONAL KSAs
A. Conflict Resolution KSAs
1. The KSA to recognize and encourage desirable, but discourage undesirable, team conflict.
2. The KSA to recognize the type and source of conflict confronting the team and to implement an appropriate conflict resolution strategy.
3. The KSA to employ an integrative (win-win) negotiation strategy rather than the traditional distributive (win-lose) strategy.

B. Collaborative Problem-Solving KSAs
4. The KSA to identify situations requiring participative group problem solving and to utilize the proper degree and type of participation.
5. The KSA to recognize the obstacles to collaborative group problem solving and implement appropriate corrective actions.

C. Communication KSAs
6. The KSA to understand communication networks, and to utilize decentralized networks to enhance communication where possible.
7. The KSA to communicate openly and supportively, that is, to send messages which are: (1) behavior- or event-oriented, (2) congruent, (3) validating, (4) conjunctive, and (5) owned.
8. The KSA to listen nonevaluatively and to appropriately use active listening techniques.
9. The KSA to maximize consonance between nonverbal and verbal messages, and to recognize and interpret the nonverbal messages of others.
10. The KSA to engage in ritual greetings and small talk, and a recognition of their importance.

II. SELF-MANAGEMENT KSAs
D. Goal Setting and Performance Management KSAs
11. The KSA to help establish specific, challenging, and accepted team goals.
12. The KSA to monitor, evaluate, and provide feedback on both overall team performance and individual team member performance.

E. Planning and Task Coordination KSAs
13. The KSA to coordinate and synchronize activities, information, and task interdependencies between team members.
14. The KSA to help establish task and role expectations of individual team members, and to ensure proper balancing of workload in the team.

Source: M. J. Stevens and M. A. Campion, "The Knowledge, Skill, and Ability Requirements for Teamwork: Implications for Human Resource Management," *Journal of Management*, 1994, 20, pp. 503–530. Used by permission.

EXHIBIT 10.16   Example Items Assessing Teamwork KSAs

1. Suppose that you find yourself in an argument with several coworkers about who should do a very disagreeable, but routine task. Which of the following would likely be most effective way to resolve this situation?
   A. Have your supervisor decide, because this would avoid any personal bias.
   B. Arrange for a rotating schedule so everyone shares the chore.
   C. Let the workers who show up earliest choose on a first-come, first-served basis.
   D. Randomly assign a person to do the task and don't change it.

2. Your team wants to improve the quality and flow of the conversations among its members. Your team should:
   A. Use comments that build upon and connect to what others have said.
   B. Set up a specific order for everyone to speak and then follow it.
   C. Let team members with more to say determine the direction and topic of conversation.
   D. Do all of the above.

3. Suppose you are presented with the following types of goals. You are asked to pick one for your team to work on. Which would you choose?
   A. An easy goal to ensure the team reaches it, thus creating a feeling of success.
   B. A goal of average difficulty so the team will be somewhat challenged, but successful without too much effort.
   C. A difficult and challenging goal that will stretch the team to perform at a high level, but attainable so that effort will not be seen as futile.
   D. A very difficult, or even impossible goal so that even if the team falls short, it will at least have a very high target to aim for.

Source: M. J. Stevens and M. A. Campion, "The Knowledge, Skill, and Ability Requirements for Teamwork: Implications for Human Resource Management," *Journal of Management*, 1994, 20, pp. 503–530. Used by permission.

Another important decision in team member selection is who should make the hiring decisions. In many cases, team assessments are made by members of the self-directed work team in deciding who becomes a member of the group. An example of an organization following this procedure is South Bend, Indiana–based I/N Tek, a billion-dollar steel-finishing mill established in a joint venture between the United States' Inland Steel and Japan's Nippon Steel. Employees in self-directed work teams, along with managers and human resource professionals, interview candidates as a final step in the selection process. This approach is felt to lead to greater satisfaction with the results of the hiring process because employees have a say in which person is selected to be part of the team.[142]

Thus, staffing processes and methods in team and quality environments require modifications from the traditional approaches to selection. Before organizations go to the trouble and expense of modifying these procedures, however, it would be wise to examine whether the team and quality initiatives are likely to be successful. Many teams fail because they are implemented as an isolated practice, and many quality initiatives also do not succeed.[143] Thus, before overhauling selection practices in an effort to build teams and implement quality initiatives, care must be taken to ensure that the context is proper for these environments in the first place.

Clinical Assessments

A clinical assessment is a mechanism whereby a trained psychologist makes a judgment about the suitability of a candidate for a job. Typically, such assessments are used for selecting people for middle- and upper-level management positions. A typical assessment takes about half a day. Judgments are formed on the basis of an interview, personal history form, ability tests, and personality tests. Feedback to the organization usually includes a narrative description of the candidate, with or without a stated recommendation.[144]

Scott Paper Company has taken this approach in an effort to improve its selection for 50 management positions in the manufacturing operations of the company. In particular, Scott was very interested in shifting the orientation of its management staff away from an autocratic, hierarchical system of decision making to one where the participation and the development of subordinates was emphasized. To do so, selection of individuals with this management style was emphasized as opposed to the training of managers to acquire this style. Clinical assessments were made to ensure that this selection procedure worked.[145] This example nicely demonstrates the role that clinical assessments can play in the selection process. They can be useful when making decisions about criteria in the job requirements matrix that are difficult to quantify. In the case of many companies, as with Scott, management style is one such KSAO. Clinical assessments have the limitation of being unstandardized, however, and very little validity evidence is available.

Choice of Substantive Assessment Methods

As with the choice of initial assessment methods, there has been a large amount of research conducted on substantive assessment methods that can help guide organizations on the appropriate methods to use. Reviews of this research, using the same criteria that were used to evaluate initial assessment methods, are shown in Exhibit 10.17.[146] Specifically, the criteria are use, cost, reliability, validity, utility, applicant reactions, and adverse impact.

Use

As can be seen in Exhibit 10.17, there are no widely used (at least two-thirds of all organizations) substantive assessment methods. Job knowledge tests, structured interviews, and performance tests and work samples have moderate degrees of use.

EXHIBIT 10.17 Evaluation of Substantive Assessment Methods

Predictors	Use	Cost	Reliability	Validity	Utility	Reactions	Adverse Impact
Personality tests	Low	Low	Moderate	Moderate	?	Negative	Low
Ability tests	Low	Low	High	High	High	Negative	High
Performance tests and work samples	Moderate	High	High	High	High	Positive	Low
Interest, value, and preference inventories	Low	Low	High	Low	?	?	Low
Structured interviews	Moderate	High	Moderate	High	?	Positive	Mixed
Clinical assessments	Low	High	Moderate	Low	?	?	?
Team/Quality assessments	Low	Moderate	?	?	?	Positive	?
Job knowledge tests	Moderate	Moderate	High	High	?	Neutral	?
Integrity tests	Low	Low	High	High	High	Negative	Low

The other substantive methods are only occasionally or infrequently used by organizations.

Cost

The cost of substantive assessment methods vary widely. Some methods can be purchased from vendors quite inexpensively (personality tests, ability tests, interest, value, and preference inventories, integrity tests)—often for less than $2 per applicant. (Of course, the costs of administering and scoring the tests must be factored in.) Some methods, such as job knowledge tests or team/quality assessments, can vary in price depending on whether the organization develops the measure itself or purchases it from a vendor. Other methods, such as structured interviews, performance tests and work samples, and clinical assessments, generally require extensive time and resources to develop, thus, these measures are the most expensive substantive assessment methods.

Reliability

The reliability of all of the substantive assessment methods is moderate or high. Generally, this is true because many of these methods have undergone extensive development efforts by vendors. However, whether an organization purchases an assessment tool from a vendor or develops it independently, the reliability of the method must be investigated. Just because a vendor claims a method is reliable does not necessarily mean it will be so within a particular organization.

Validity

Like cost, the validity of substantive assessment methods varies a great deal. Some methods, such as interest, value, and preference inventories and clinical assessments, have demonstrated little validity in past research. As was noted when reviewing these measures, however, steps can be taken to increase their validity. Some methods, such as personality tests and structured interviews, have at least moderate levels of validity. Some structured interviews have high levels of validity, but the degree to which they add validity beyond cognitive ability tests remains in question. Finally, ability tests, performance tests and work samples, job knowledge tests, and integrity tests, have high levels of validity. As with many structured interviews, while the validity of job knowledge tests is high, the degree to which job knowledge is important in predicting job performance beyond cognitive ability is suspect. Integrity tests are moderate to high predictors of job performance; their validity in predicting other important job behaviors (counterproductive work behaviors) appears to be quite high.

Utility

As with initial assessment methods, the utility of most substantive assessment methods is unknown. A great deal of research has shown that the utility of ability tests (in particular, cognitive ability tests) is quite high. Performance tests and work samples and integrity tests also appear to have high levels of utility.

Applicant Reactions

Research is just beginning to emerge concerning applicant reactions to substantive assessment methods. From the limited research that has been conducted, however, applicants' reactions to substantive assessment methods appear to depend on the particular method. Relatively abstract methods that require an applicant to answer questions not directly tied to the job (i.e., questions on personality tests, most ability tests, and integrity tests) seem to generate negative reactions from applicants. Thus, research tends to suggest that personality, ability, and integrity tests are viewed unfavorably by applicants. Methods that are manifestly related to the job for which applicants are applying appear to generate positive reactions. Thus, research suggests that applicants view performance tests and work samples and structured interviews favorably. Job knowledge tests, perhaps because they are neither wholly abstract nor totally experiential, appear to generate neutral reactions.

Adverse Impact

A considerable amount of research has been conducted on adverse impact of some substantive assessment methods. In particular, research suggests that personality tests, performance tests and work samples, and integrity tests have little adverse impact against women or minorities. In the past, interest, value, and preference inventories had substantial adverse impact against women, but this problem has been corrected. Conversely, ability tests have a high degree of adverse impact. In particular, cognitive ability tests have substantial adverse impact against minorities, while physical ability tests have significant adverse impact on women. The adverse impact of structured interviews was denoted as mixed. While evidence suggests that many structured interviews have little adverse impact against women or minorities, other evidence suggests some adverse impact. Furthermore, since even structured interviews have an element of subjectivity to them, the potential always exists for interviewer bias to enter into the process. There is too little data to draw conclusions about the adverse impact of clinical assessments and job knowledge tests.

A comparison of Exhibits 9.10 and 10.17 is instructive. In general, both the validity and the cost of substantive assessment procedures are higher than those of initial assessment procedures. As with the initial assessment procedures, the economic and social impact of substantive assessment procedures is not well understood. Many initial assessment methods are widely used while most substantive assessment methods have moderate or low degrees of use. Thus, many organizations rely upon initial assessment methods to make substantive assessment decisions. This is unfortunate because, with the exception of biographical data, the validity of substantive assessment methods is higher. This is especially true of the initial interview relative to the structured interview. At a minimum, organizations need to supplement the initial interview with structured interviews. Better yet, organizations should strongly consider using ability, performance, personality, and work sample tests along with either interview.

DISCRETIONARY ASSESSMENT METHODS

Discretionary assessment methods are used to separate those who receive job offers from the list of finalists. Sometimes discretionary methods are not used because all finalists may receive job offers. When used, discretionary assessment methods are typically very subjective and rely heavily on the intuition of the decision maker. Thus, factors other than KSAOs per se may be assessed. Organizations intent on maintaining strong cultures may wish to consider assessing the person/organization match at this stage of the selection process. As was indicated earlier, two promising means of doing this are the *Organizational Culture Profile* and revisions to the traditional interviewing process (see Exhibit 10.12).

Another interesting method of discretionary assessment that focuses on person/organization match is the selection of people on the basis of likely organizational citizenship behavior.[147] With this approach, finalists not only must fulfill all of the requirements of the job, but also are expected to fulfill some roles outside the requirements of the job, called organizational citizenship behaviors. These behaviors include things like doing extra work, helping others at work, covering for a sick coworker, and being courteous.

Discretionary assessments should involve use of the organization's staffing philosophy regarding EEO/AA commitments. Here, the commitment may be to enhance the representation of minorities and women in the organization's workforce, either voluntarily or as part of an organization's affirmative action plan. At this point in the selection process, the demographic characteristics of the finalists may be given weight in the decision about to whom the job offer will be extended. Regardless of how the organization chooses to make its discretionary assessments, they should never be used without being preceded by initial and substantive methods.

CONTINGENT ASSESSMENT METHODS

As was shown in Exhibit 9.3, contingent methods are not always used, depending on the nature of the job and also legal mandates. Virtually any selection method can be used as a contingent method. For example, a health clinic may verify that an applicant for a nursing position possesses a valid license after a tentative offer decision has been made. Similarly, a defense contractor may perform a security clearance check on applicants once initial, substantive, and discretionary methods have been exhausted. While these methods may be used as initial or contingent methods, depending on the preferences of the organization, two selection methods, drug testing and medical exams, should be used exclusively as contingent assessment methods for legal compliance. When drug testing and medical exams are used, considerable care must be taken in their administration and evaluation.

Drug Testing

The cost of alcohol and drug abuse in our country is estimated to be $60 billion per year.[148] Additionally, substance abuse leads to higher utilization of benefits, such as sick time and health care. One comprehensive study found that from 1975 to 1986, approximately 50 train accidents were attributed to workers under the influence of drugs or alcohol. These accidents resulted in 37 people being killed, 80 injured, and the destruction of property valued at $34 million.[149] A National Transportation Safety Board study found that 31% of all fatal truck accidents were due to alcohol or drugs.[150] A study of drug abuse at work found that the average drug user was 3.6 times more likely to be involved in an accident, received 3 times the average level of sick benefits, was 5 times more likely to file a workers' compensation claim, and missed 10 times as many work days as nonusers.[151] Substance abuse is also associated with psychological (e.g., daydreaming, spending work time on personal matters) and physical (e.g., falling asleep at work, extra long lunch and rest breaks, theft) withdrawal behaviors while employees are at work.[152] As a result of the manifold problems caused by drug use, drug testing is used by 87% of major U. S. corporations, according to a study of nearly 800 human resource managers.[153] Drug testing has increased dramatically in the last decade. Drug testing among the *Fortune 500* has grown from one in twenty companies in 1983 to nearly eighteen of twenty today.

Drug testing is a procedure used by organizations to assess those who abuse alcohol and drugs. By identifying abusers, employers can potentially select them out of the organization before they engage in negative work behaviors and jeopardize the safety of others or, worse yet, cost the organization large sums of money. Typical substances that are screened for by employers include alcohol, cocaine, amphetamines, marijuana, heroin, and PCP. Screening usually takes place at a laboratory away from the company premises.[154]

As drug testing has become more widespread, more and more is being learned about the process under which it is used, as well as its effectiveness. A recent survey of vice presidents of human resources in *Fortune 1000* companies revealed the following:[155]

- Applicants were twice as likely to be tested for drug use as alcohol use.
- Most of the alcohol tests were "for cause" (e.g., cases when applicants were suspected of alcohol abuse), while most drug testing of applicants was universal (all applicants were tested).
- The vice presidents reported considerable consistency in use of testing across business units within a company.

- Corporations are less likely to make exclusionary decisions following positive tests for alcohol than for drugs.
- Industries where exposure/risk was apparent (industrial manufacturing, transportation, construction) were more likely to test for drugs and alcohol.
- Lower-level employees are more likely to be tested than upper-level employees.
- Drug and alcohol testing is *more* prominent in unionized industries.
- Large organizations are more likely to test for drugs than small organizations.

Types of Tests

There are a variety of tests to ascertain substance abuse. The major categories of tests are:[156]

1. Body fluids—Both urine and blood tests can be used. Urine tests are by far the most frequently used method of detecting substance abuse.[157] There are different types of measures for each test. For example, urine samples can be measured using the enzyme-multiplied immunoassay technique or the gas chromatography/spectrometry technique.[158]

2. Hair analysis—Samples of hair are analyzed using the same techniques as are used to measure urine samples. Chemicals remain in the hair as it grows, so it can provide a longer record of drug use.

3. Pupillary reaction test—The reaction of the pupil to light is assessed. Applicants' pupils will react differently when under the influence of drugs than when drug free.

4. Performance tests—Hand-eye coordination is assessed to see if there is impairment compared with the standard drug-free reactions. One of the limitations of performance tests in a selection context is that there may be no feasible means of establishing a baseline against which performance is compared. Thus, performance tests are usually more suitable for testing employees than applicants.

5. Psychological tests—Many integrity tests contain a section that asks applicants about drug use. The section on substance abuse often includes 20 or so items that inquire about past and present drug use ("I only drink at work when things get real stressful") as well as attitudes toward drug use (e.g., "How often do you think the average employee smokes marijuana on the job?").[159]

Administration

In order for the results of drug tests to be accurate, precautions must be taken in their administration. When collecting samples to be tested, care must be exercised to ensure that the sample is authentic and not contaminated. To do so, the U.S.

Department of Health and Human Services has established specific guidelines to be followed.[160]

The testing itself must be carefully administered as well. Labs may process up to 3,000 samples per day. Hence, human error can occur in the detection process. Also, false-positive results can be generated due to cross-reactions. What this means is that a common compound (e.g., poppy seeds) may interact with the antibodies and mistakenly identify a person as a substance abuser. Prescription medications may also affect drug test results.

In order for the testing to be carefully administered, two steps need to be taken. First, care must be taken in the selection of a reputable drug testing firm. Various certification programs, such as the College of American Pathologists and the National Institute for Drug Abuse (NIDA), exist to ensure that accurate procedures are followed. More than 50 drug testing laboratories have been certified by NIDA. Second, positive drug tests should always be verified by a second test to ensure reliability.

What would a well-conducted drug testing program look like? Samples are first submitted to screening tests, which are relatively inexpensive ($10 to $20 per applicant) but yield many false positives (test indicates drug use when none occurred) due to the cross-reactions described above. Confirmatory tests are then used, which are extremely accurate but are more expensive ($60 per applicant). The average total cost per applicant has been estimated to be $41. Error rates for confirmatory tests with reputable labs are very low. It should be noted that in order to avoid false positives, most companies have nonzero cutoff levels for most drugs. Thus, if a mistake does occur, it is much more likely to be a false negative (testing negative when in fact drug use did occur) than a false positive.[161] Thus, some applicants who occasionally use drugs may pass a test but it is very rare for an individual who has never used the drug to fail the test—assuming the two-step process described above is followed. Exhibit 10.18 outlines the steps involved in a well-designed drug testing program. In this example:

- Applicants are advised in advance of testing.
- All applicants are screened by urine testing.
- Prescreening is done in-house; positives are referred to independent lab.
- A strict chain of custody is followed.
- Verified positive applicants are disqualified.
- Disqualified applicants cannot reapply for two years.

Smoking

Some employers are beginning to ban smokers from hiring consideration. A recent study estimated that about 6% of employers will not hire smokers (urinalysis also picks up nicotine). Such policies are usually aimed at cutting insurance costs (smoking costs employers $27 billion annually), absence rates (smokers' absence

---

EXHIBIT 10.18   Example of an Organizational Drug Testing Program

---

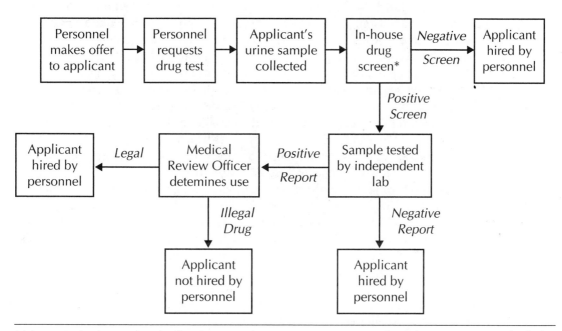

* Most organizations screen for five drugs: amphetamines, cocaine, cannabinoids (e.g., marijuana, hashish), opiates (morphine, heroin), phencyclidine (PCP).

---

rates are 50% higher than those of nonsmokers), and potential liability due to the dangers of secondary smoke. However, about half the states have passed laws prohibiting discrimination against off-the-job smoking. Thus, while some employers may wish to screen out smokers to lower health care costs, the myriad legal and ethical issues make it a risky selection practice.

Evaluation

It is commonly believed that drug testing results in a large number of false positives. In fact, if the proper procedures are followed (as already outlined), drug test results are extremely accurate and error rates are very low. Accuracy of the test, however, is not the same as its validity in predicting important job criteria. The most accurate drug test in the world will be a poor investment if it cannot be established that substance abuse is related to employee behaviors such as accidents, absenteeism, tardiness, impaired job performance, and so on. One of the factors that may bear on the utility of the drug testing program is the number of individuals detected. A 1991 study of 38 federal agencies put the positive rate at only 0.5%, which translated into a testing cost of $77,000 for each positive.[162]

Although more research on the validity of drug testing programs is needed, some organizations are conducting research on the deleterious effects of substance abuse. The U.S. Postal Service recently conducted an evaluation of their drug testing program using applicants who applied for positions in 21 sites over a six-month period.[163] A quality-control process revealed that the drug testing program was 100% accurate (zero false positives and false negatives). Ten percent of applicants tested positive for drug use (for the purposes of the study, applicants were hired without regard to their test scores). Of those positive tests, 65% were for marijuana, 24% for cocaine, and 11% were for other drugs. They found higher absenteeism for drug users and higher dismissal rates for cocaine users. Drug use was not related to accidents or injuries. A cost-benefit analysis suggested that full implementation of the program would save the Postal Service several million dollars per year in lower absenteeism and turnover rates.

The validity of performance and psychological drug tests is not well established. London House completed a study on applicants for conductor and ticket agent positions at the Chicago Transit Authority (CTA) and found that 77% of those not recommended for employment based on their psychological test scores were disciplined for excessive absenteeism, while the discipline rate for other applicants was 41% (obviously the CTA has an absenteeism problem). Another London House study found that psychological and medical drug tests had the same results for 84% of applicants.[164] As with integrity tests, a major concern is faking, but an advantage of psychological drug tests is that they are likely to be perceived as less intrusive by applicants. However, a 1993 survey suggested that relatively few organizations rely on physical (2%) or psychological (9%) drug tests.[165]

In considering the validity of drug tests, one should not assume that the logical criterion against which the tests are validated is job performance. Typically, the criterion of job performance is central to evaluating the validity of most selection measures, yet drug tests have not been validated against job performance. Thus, it is far from clear that drug tests do a good job of discerning good from poor performers. Drug tests do appear to predict other work behaviors, however, including absenteeism, accidents, and other counterproductive behaviors. For the purposes for which they are suited, then, validity of drug tests can be concluded to be high.

Finally, as with other assessment methods, two other criteria against which drug testing should be evaluated are adverse impact and applicant reactions. The adverse impact of drug testing is not universally accepted but the Postal Service study indicated that drug testing programs did have a moderate to high degree of adverse impact against black and Hispanic applicants.[166] Research on applicant reactions to drug tests has revealed inconsistent results.[167] Research does tend to show that if applicants perceive a need for drug testing, they are more likely to find such a program acceptable.[168] Thus, organizations that do a good job explaining the reasons for the tests to applicants are more likely to find that applicants react favorably to the program.

Recommendations for Effective Drug Testing Programs

Due to the recent upturn in drug use among individuals entering the workforce, and improved methods of detecting drug use, drug testing is likely to continue as one of the most commonly used selection methods. In an effort to make organizations' drug testing program as accurate and effective as possible, six recommendations concerning use of drug testing programs are outlined as follows:

1. Emphasize drug testing in safety-sensitive jobs as well as positions where the link between substance abuse and negative outcomes (e.g., as was the case with the Postal Service study described earlier) has been documented.
2. Use only reputable testing laboratories and ensure that strict chain of custody is maintained.
3. Ask applicants for their consent and inform them of test results; provide rejected applicants with the opportunity to appeal.
4. Use retesting to validate positive samples from the initial screening test.
5. Ensure that proper procedures are followed to maintain the applicant's right to privacy.
6. Review program and validate the results against relevant criteria (accidents, absenteeism, turnover, job performance); conduct a cost-benefit analysis of the program, as a very small number of detections may cause the program to have low utility.

Medical Exams

Medical exams are often used to identify potential health risks in job candidates. Care must be taken to ensure that medical exams are used only when a compelling reason to use them exists. This is to ensure that individuals with disabilities unrelated to job performance are not screened out. As a result of these sorts of potential abuses, the use of medical exams is strictly regulated by the Americans with Disabilities Act (discussed later in this chapter).

Although many organizations use medical exams, they are not particularly valid because the procedures performed vary from doctor to doctor.[169] Also, medical exams are not always job related.[170] Finally, the emphasis is usually on short-term rather than long-term health.[171] A promising new development has recently taken place in medical exams. This development is known as job-related medical standards.[172] Under this procedure, physical health standards have been developed that are highly job related. Physicians' manuals have been developed that provide information on the specific diseases and health conditions that prohibit adequate functioning on specific jobs or clusters of tasks. Not only should this procedure improve content validity because it is job related, but it should also improve reliability because it standardizes diagnosis across physicians. Along with the manuals, useful data-gathering instruments have been developed to properly assess applicants' actual medical conditions. Again, this helps to standardize assessments by physicians, which should improve reliability.

COLLECTION OF ASSESSMENT DATA

Any of the predictors discussed requires the collection of data about people. Several issues must be addressed to ensure that the data are properly and fairly collected and used.

If a predictor is purchased, then support services are needed as well. Helpful support, especially for smaller organizations, includes computerized scoring of tests and quick turnaround time. Also necessary is legal support to ensure compliance with laws and regulations. Validity studies are important to ensure the effectiveness of the tests. Training on how to administer the predictor is also needed.

Predictors cannot always be purchased by any firm that wants to use them; many test publishers require the purchaser to have certain expertise to properly use the test. For example, they may require the user to hold a Ph.D. in a field of study related to the test and its use. For smaller organizations, this means that they need to hire the consulting services of a specialist in order to use a particular test.

Care must be taken to ensure that correct answers for predictors are not shared with job applicants in advance of administration of the predictor. Any person who has access to the predictor answers should be fully trained and sign a predictor security agreement. Also, a regular inventory procedure needs to be established to ensure that predictor materials are not inappropriately dispersed. Should a breach of security take place, use of the predictor should be abandoned and a new one should be used.

Not only should the predictor itself be kept secure, but so, too, should the results of the predictor in order to ensure the privacy of the individual. The results of the predictor should be used only for the intended purposes and by persons qualified to interpret them. While feedback can be given to the candidate concerning results, the individual should not be given a copy of the predictor or the scoring key.

Finally, it is imperative that all applicants be assessed with standardized procedures. This means that not only should the same or a psychometrically equivalent predictor be used, but individuals should take the test under the same circumstances. The purpose of the predictor should be explained to applicants, and they should be put at ease, held to the same time requirements to complete the predictor, and take the predictor in the same location. Standardization is important when collecting information about applicant reactions to the assessment process. Many selection decision makers might feel they have a good sense of how applicants react to the selection process, but in order to move beyond subjective "hunches" to objective data, it is important that standardized procedures are followed when collecting information on applicant reactions (see Chapter 14).

LEGAL ISSUES

This section discusses three major legal issues. The first of these is the Uniform Guidelines on Employee Selection Procedures (UGESP), a document that addresses the need to determine if a selection procedure is causing adverse impact, and if so, the validation requirements for the procedure. The second issue is selection in conformance with the ADA as pertains to reasonable accommodation to job applicants and the use of medical tests. The final issue is that of drug testing for job applicants.

Uniform Guidelines on Employee Selection Procedures

The UGESP is a comprehensive set of federal regulations specifying requirements for the selection systems of organizations covered under the Civil Rights Acts and under E.O. 11246 (see Appendix A for the full text of the UGESP). There are four major sections to the UGESP, namely, general principles, technical standards, documentation of impact and validity evidence, and definitions of terms. Each of these sections is summarized next. An excellent review of the UGESP in terms of court cases and examples of acceptable and unacceptable practices is available and should be consulted.[173]

General Principles

1. Summary—The organization must keep records that allow it to determine if its selection procedures are causing adverse impact in employment decisions. If no adverse impact is found, the remaining provisions of the UGESP generally do not apply. If adverse impact is found, the organization must either validate the selection procedure(s) causing the adverse impact or take steps to eliminate the adverse impact (such as using an alternative selection procedure that has less adverse impact).

2. Scope—The scope of the UGESP is very broad in that the guidelines apply to selection procedures that are used as the basis for any employment decisions. Employment decisions include hiring, promotion, demotion, and retention. A selection procedure is defined as "any measure, combination of measures, or procedure used as a basis for any employment decision." The procedures include "the full range of assessment techniques from traditional paper and pencil tests, performance tests, training programs, or probationary periods and physical, educational, and work experience requirements through informal or casual interviews and unscored application forms."

3. Discrimination defined—In general, any selection procedure that has an adverse impact is discriminatory unless it has been shown to be valid. There is a separate section for procedures that have not been validated.

4. Suitable alternative selection procedures—When a selection procedure has adverse impact, consideration should be given to the use of any suitable alternative selection procedures that may have lesser adverse impact.

5. Information on adverse impact—The organization must keep impact records by race, sex, and ethnic group for each of the job categories shown on the EEO-1 form (see Chapter 14).

6. Evaluation of selection rates—For each job or job category, the organization should evaluate the results, also known as the "bottom line," of the total selection process. The purpose of the evaluation is to determine if there are differences in selection rates that indicate adverse impact. If adverse impact is not found, the organization usually does not have to take additional compliance steps, such as validation of each step in the selection process. If overall adverse impact is found, the individual components of the selection process should be evaluated for adverse impact.

7. Adverse impact and the four-fifths rule—To determine if adverse impact is occurring, the organization should compute and compare selection rates for race, sex, and ethnic groups. A selection rate that is less than four-fifths (or 80%) of the rate for the group with the highest rate is generally regarded as evidence of adverse impact. There are exceptions to this general rule, based on sample size (small sample) considerations, and on the extent to which the organization's recruitment practices have discouraged applicants disproportionately on grounds of race, sex, or ethnic group.

8. General standards for validity studies—There are three types of acceptable validity studies: criterion-related, content, and construct. There are numerous provisions pertaining to standards governing these validity studies, as well as the appropriate use of selection procedures.

9. Procedures that have not been validated—This section discusses the use of alternative selection procedures to eliminate adverse impact. It also discusses instances in which validation studies cannot or need not be performed.

10. Affirmative Action—Use of validated selection procedures does not relieve the employer of any affirmative action obligation it may have. The employer is encouraged to adopt and implement voluntary affirmative action plans.

Technical Standards

This section contains a lengthy specification of the minimum technical standards that should be met when conducting a validation study. There are separate standards given for each of the three types of validity (criterion-related, content, construct) studies.

Documentation of Impact and Validity Evidence

For each job or job category, the employer is required to keep detailed records on adverse impact, and where adverse impact is found, evidence of validity. Detailed record keeping requirements are provided.

There are two important exceptions to these general requirements. First, a small employer (fewer than 100 employees) does not have to keep separate records for each job category, but only for its total selection process across all jobs. Second, records for race or national origin do not have to be kept for groups constituting less than 2% of the labor force in the relevant labor area.

Definitions

This section provides definitions of terms (25 total) used throughout the UGESP.

In totality, the UGESP makes substantial demands of an organization and its staffing systems. Those demands exist to ensure organizational awareness of the possibility of adverse impact in employment decisions. When adverse impact is found, the UGESP provides mechanisms (requirements) for coping with it. The UGESP thus should occupy a place of prominence in any covered organization's EEO/AA policies and practices.

Selection under the Americans With Disabilities Act (ADA)

The Americans With Disabilities Act (ADA), as interpreted by the EEOC, creates substantial requirements (Appendix C) and suggestions for compliance pertaining to external selection.[174] The general nature of these is identified and commented upon next.

General Principles

There are two major, overarching principles pertaining to selection. The first principle is that it is unlawful to screen out individuals with disabilities, unless the selection procedure is job related and consistent with business necessity. The second principle is that a selection procedure must accurately reflect the KSAOs being measured, and not impaired sensory, manual, or speaking skills, unless those impaired skills are the ones being measured by the procedure.

The first principle is obviously very similar to principles governing selection generally under federal laws and regulations. The second principle is important because it cautions the organization to be sure that its selection procedures do not inadvertently and unnecessarily screen out applicants with disabilities.

Access to Job Application Process

The organization's job application process must be accessible to individuals with disabilities. Reasonable accommodation must be provided to enable all persons to apply, and applicants should be provided assistance (if needed) in completing the application process. Applicants should also be told about the nature and content of the selection process. This allows them to request reasonable accommodation to testing, if needed, in advance.

Reasonable Accommodation to Testing

In general, the organization may use any kind of test in assessing job applicants. These tests must be administered consistently to all job applicants for any particular job.

A very important provision of testing pertains to the requirement to provide reasonable accommodation, if requested, by an applicant to take the test. The purpose of this requirement is to ensure that the test accurately reflects the KSAO being measured, rather than an impairment of the applicant. Reasonable accommodation, however, is not required for a person with an impaired skill if the purpose of that test is to measure that skill. For example, the organization does not have to provide reasonable accommodation on a manual dexterity test to a person with arthritis in the fingers and hands, if the purpose of the test is to measure manual dexterity.

There are numerous types of reasonable accommodation that can be made, and there is organizational experience and research in providing reasonable accommodation.[175] Examples of what might be done to provide reasonable accommodation include substituting an oral test for a written one (or vice versa), providing extra time to complete a test, scheduling rest breaks during a test, and administering tests in large print, in Braille, or by reader.

Medical Examinations

There are substantial regulations surrounding medical exams, both before and after a job offer. Prior to the offer, the organization may not make medical inquiries or require medical exams of an applicant. The job offer, however, may be conditional, pending the results of a medical exam.

Postoffer, the organization may conduct a medical exam. The exam must be given to all applicants for a particular job, not just individuals with a known or suspected disability. While the content of the exam is not restricted to being only job related, the reasons for rejecting an applicant on the basis of the exam must be job related. A person may also be rejected if exam results indicate a direct threat to the health and safety of others. Results of medical exams are to be kept confidential, held separate from the employee's personnel file, and released only under very specific circumstances.

It is difficult to determine whether something is a medical examination, and thus subject to the above requirements surrounding their use. The EEOC defines a medical examination as "a procedure or test that seeks information about an individual's physical or mental impairments or health."[176] The following factors are suggestive of a selection procedure that would be considered a medical examination:

- It is administered by a health care professional and/or someone trained by such a professional.
- It is designed to reveal an impairment of physical or mental health.
- It is invasive (e.g., requires drawing blood, urine, or breath).
- It measures the applicant's physiological responses to performing a task.
- It is normally given in a medical setting, and/or medical equipment is used.
- It tests for alcohol consumption.

Though closely allied with medical examinations, several types of tests fall outside the bounds of medical examinations; and these may be used preoffer. These include physical agility tests, physical fitness tests, vision tests, drug tests for current illegal use of controlled substances, and tests that measure honesty, tastes, and habits.

A gray area involves the use of psychological tests, such as personality tests. They are considered medical if they lead to identifying a medically recognized mental disorder or impairment, such as those in the American Psychiatric Association's *Diagnostics and Statistical Manual of Mental Disorders*. Future regulations and court rulings may help clarify which types of psychological tests are medical exams.

Drug Testing

Drug testing is permitted to detect the use of illegal drugs. The law, however, is neutral as to its encouragement.

UGESP

The UGESP do not apply to the ADA or its regulations. This means that the guidance and requirements for employers' selection systems under the Civil Rights Act may or may not be the same as those that end up being required for compliance with the ADA.

Drug Testing

Drug testing is surrounded by an amalgam of laws and regulations at the federal and state levels.[177] The organization should seek legal and medical advice to determine if it should do drug testing, and if so, what the nature of the drug testing program should be. Beyond that, the organization should require and administer drug tests on a contingency (postoffer) basis only to avoid the possibility of obtaining and using medical information illegally. For example, positive drug test results may occur because of the presence of a legal drug, and using these results preoffer to reject a person would be a violation of the ADA.

SUMMARY

This chapter continues discussion of proper methods and processes to be used in external selection. Specifically, substantive, discretionary, and contingent assessment methods are discussed, as well as collection of assessment data and pertinent legal issues.

Most of the chapter discusses various substantive methods, which are used to separate out finalists from candidates. As with use of initial assessment methods, use of substantive assessment methods should always be based on the logic of prediction and the use of selection plans. The substantive methods that are reviewed include personality tests, ability tests, job knowledge tests, performance tests and work samples, integrity tests, interest, values, and preference inventories, structured interview, assessment for team and quality environments, and clinical assessments. As with initial assessment methods, the criteria used to evaluate the effectiveness of substantive assessment methods are frequency of use, cost, reliability, validity, utility, applicant reactions, and adverse impact. In general, substantive assessment methods show a marked improvement in reliability and validity over initial assessment methods. This is probably due to the stronger relationship between the sampling of the applicant's previous situations with the requirements for success on the job.

Discretionary selection methods are somewhat less formal and more subjective than other selection methods. When discretionary methods are used, two judgments are most important: will the applicant be a good organization "citizen" and do the values and goals of this applicant match those of the organization?

While discretionary methods are subjective, contingent assessment methods typically involve decisions about whether applicants meet certain objective requirements for the job. The two most common contingent methods are: drug testing and medical exams. Particularly in the case of drug testing, the use of contingent methods is relatively complex from an administrative and legal standpoint.

Regardless of predictor type, attention must be given to the proper collection and use of predictor information. In particular, support services need to be established, administrators with the appropriate credentials need to be hired, data need to be kept private and confidential, and administration procedures must be standardized.

Along with administrative issues, legal issues need to be considered as well. Particular attention must be paid to regulations that govern permissible activities by organizations. Regulations include those in the Uniform Guidelines on Employee Selection Procedures and the Americans with Disabilities Act.

DISCUSSION QUESTIONS

1. Describe the similarities and differences between personality tests and integrity tests. When is each warranted in the selection process?

2. How would you advise an organization considering adopting a cognitive ability test for selection?

3. Describe the structured interview. What are the characteristics of structured interviews that improve upon the shortcomings of unstructured interviews?

4. What are the selection implications for an organization that has recently adopted a total quality management program?

5. What are the most common discretionary and contingent assessment methods? What are the similarities and differences between the use of these two methods?

6. How should organizations apply the general principles of the Uniform Guidelines on Employee Selection Procedures to practical selection decisions?

APPLICATIONS

Assessment Methods for the Job of Human Resources Director

Nairduwel, Inoalot, and Imslo (NII) is a law firm specializing in business law. Among other areas, they deal in equal employment opportunity law, business litigation, and workplace torts. The firm has more than 50 partners and approximately 120 employees. They do business in three states and have law offices in two major metropolitan areas. The firm has no federal contracts.

NII has plans to expand into two additional states with two major metropolitan areas. One of the primary challenges accompanying this ambitious expansion plan is how to staff, train, and compensate individuals who will fill the positions in the new offices. Accordingly, the firm wishes to hire a human resources director to oversee the recruitment, selection, training, performance appraisal, and compensation activities accompanying the business expansion, as well as supervise the human resource activities in the existing NII offices. The newly created job description for the human resource director is listed in the accompanying exhibit.

The firm wishes to design and then use a selection system for assessing applicants that will achieve two objectives: (1) create a valid and useful system that will do a good job of matching applicant KSAOs to job requirements; (2) be in compliance with all relevant federal and state employment law.

The firm is considering numerous selection techniques for possible use. For each method listed below, decide whether you would probably use it or not in the selection process and state exactly why.

1. job knowledge test specifically designed for human resource professionals that focuses on an applicant's general knowledge of human resource management

2. medical examination and drug test at the beginning of the selection process in order to determine if applicants are able to cope with the high level of stress and frequent travel requirements of the job and are drug free

3. paper-and-pencil integrity test
4. a structured, behavioral interview that will be specially designed for use in filling only this job
5. general cognitive ability test
6. Personal Characteristics Inventory
7. a set of interview questions that the firm typically uses for filling any position:
    (a) Tell me about a problem you solved on a previous job.
    (b) Do you have any physical impairments that would make it difficult for you to travel on business?
    (c) Have you ever been tested for AIDS?
    (d) Are you currently unemployed, and if so, why?
    (e) This position requires fresh ideas and energy. Do you think you have those qualities?
    (f) What is your definition of success?
    (g) What kind of sports do you like?
    (h) How well do you work under pressure? Give me some examples.

Exhibit

Job Description for Human Resources Director

JOB SUMMARY

Performs responsible administrative work managing personnel activities. Work involves responsibility for the planning and administration of HRM programs, including recruitment, selection, evaluation, appointment, promotion, compensation, and recommended change of status of employees, and a system of communication for disseminating information to workers. Works under general supervision, exercising initiative and independent judgment in the performance of assigned tasks.

TASKS

1. Participates in overall planning and policy making to provide effective and uniform personnel services.
2. Communicates policy through organization levels by bulletin, meetings, and personal contact.
3. Supervises recruitment and screening of job applicants to fill vacancies. Supervises interviewing of applicants, evaluation of qualifications, and classification of applications.
4. Supervises administration of tests to applicants.

continued

5. Confers with supervisors on personnel matters, including placement problems, retention or release of probationary employees, transfers, demotions, and dismissals of permanent employees.

6. Initiates personnel training activities and coordinates these activities with work of officials and supervisors.

7. Establishes effective service rating system, trains unit supervisors in making employee evaluations.

8. Supervises maintenance of employee personnel files.

9. Supervises a group of employees directly and through subordinates.

10. Performs related work as assigned.

JOB SPECIFICATIONS

1. *Experience and Training*
   Should have considerable experience in area of HRM administration. Six year minimum.

2. *Education*
   Graduation from a four-year college or university, with major work in human resources, business administration, or industrial psychology. Master's degree in one of these areas is preferable.

3. *Knowledge, Skills, and Abilities*
   Considerable knowledge of principles and practices of HRM, including staffing, compensation, training, and performance evaluation.

4. *Responsibility*
   Supervises the human resource activities of six office managers, one clerk, and one secretary.

Choosing among Finalists for the Job of Human Resources Director

Assume that Nairduwel, Inoalot, and Imslo (NII), after weighing their options, decided to use the following selection methods to assess applicants for the HR Director job: Resume, cognitive ability test, job knowledge test, structured interview, and questions *(f)* and *(g)* from the list of generic interview questions.

NII advertised for the position extensively, and out of a pool of 23 initial applicants, they were able to come up with a list of three finalists. Shown in the accompanying exhibit are the results from the assessment of the three finalists using these selection methods. In addition, information from an earlier resume screen is included for possible consideration. For each finalist, you are to decide whether or not you would be willing to hire the person and why.

Exhibit
Results of Assessment of Finalists for Human Resource Director Position

	Finalist 1— Lola Vega	Finalist 2— Sam Fein	Finalist 3— Shawanda Jackson
Resume	GPA 3.9/Cornell University B.S. Human Resource Mgmt.	GPA 2.8/SUNY Binghamton B.B.A. Finance	GPA 3.2/Auburn University B.B.A. Business and English
	Five years' experience in HRM • 4 years in recruiting	20 years' experience in HRM • Numerous HR assignments • Certified HR professional	Eight years' experience in HRM • 3 years HR generalist • 4 years compensation analyst
	No supervisory experience	15 years' supervisory experience	Five years' supervisory experience
Cognitive ability test	90% correct	78% correct	84% correct
Knowledge test	94% correct	98% correct	91% correct
Structured Int. (out of 100 pts)	85	68	75
Question (f)	Ability to influence others	To do things you want to do	Promotions and earnings
Question (g)	golf, shuffleboard	spectator sports	basketball, tennis

ENDNOTES

1. L. M. Hough, ''The 'Big Five' Personality Variables—Construct Confusion: Description Versus Prediction,'' *Human Performance*, 1992, 5, 139–155; J. E. Hunter and R. F. Hunter, ''Validity and Utility of Alternative Predictors of Job Performance,'' *Psychological Bulletin*, 1984, 96, pp. 72–98.

2. R. M. Guion and R. F. Gottier, ''Validity of Personality Measures in Personnel Selection,'' *Personnel Psychology*, 1965, 18, pp. 135–164; F. J. Landy and L. J. Shankster, ''Personnel Selection and Placement,'' *Annual Review of Psychology*, 1994, 45, pp. 261–296.

3. For other reviews on the use of the MMPI in selection, see J. M. Cortina, M. L. Doherty, N. Schmitt, G. Kaufman, and R. G. Smith, ''The 'Big Five' Personality Factors in the IPI and MMPI: Predictors of Police Performance,'' *Personnel Psychology*, 1992, 45, pp. 119–140; R.

T. Hogan, "Personality and Personality Measurement," in M. D. Dunnette and L. M. Hough (eds.), *Handbook of Industrial and Organizational Psychology,* vol. 2, (Palo Alto, CA: Consulting Psychologists Press, 1991), pp. 873–919.

4. P. T. Costa, Jr. and R. R. McCrae, "Four Ways Five Factors Are Basic," *Personality and Individual Differences,* 1992, 13, pp. 653–665.

5. D. S. Ones and C. Viswesvaran, "Bandwidth-Fidelity Dilemma in Personality Measurement for Personnel Selection," *Journal of Organizational Behavior,* in press; D. S. Ones, F. L. Schmidt, and C. Viswesvaran, "Do Broader Personality Variables Predict Job Performance with Higher Validity?" Paper Presented at the 1994 Conference of the Society for Industrial and Organizational Psychology, Nashville, TN.

6. M. K. Mount and M. R. Barrick, *Manual for the Personal Characteristics Inventory* (Iowa City, Iowa: author, 1995).

7. P. T. Costa, Jr. and R. R. McCrae, *Revised NEO Personality Inventory (NEO-PI-R) and NEO Five-Factor (NEO-FFI) Inventory Professional Manual* (Odessa, FL: Psychological Assessment Resources, 1992).

8. J. Hogan and R. Hogan, "How to Measure Employee Reliability," *Journal of Applied Psychology,* 1989, 74, pp. 273–279.

9. J. B. Miner, "The Miner Sentence Completion Scale: A Reappraisal," *Academy of Management Journal,* 1978, 21, pp. 283–294.

10. H. J. Kinslinger, "Application of Projective Techniques in Personnel Psychology Since 1940," *Psychological Bulletin,* 1966, 66, 134–149; For a challenge of this conclusion see E. T. Cornelius III, "The Use of Projective Techniques in Personnel Selection," in K. M. Rowland and G. R. Ferris (eds.), *Research in Personnel and Human Resources Management* (Greenwich, CT: JAI Press), 1993.

11. D. S. Ones, M. K. Mount, M. R. Barrick, and J. E. Hunter, "Personality and Job Performance: A Critique of the Tett, Jackson, & Rothstein (1991) Meta-Analysis," *Personnel Psychology,* 1994, 47, pp. 147–156; R. P. Tett, D. N. Jackson, and M. Rothstein, "Personality Measures as Predictors of Job Performance: A Meta-Analytic Review," *Personnel Psychology,* 1991, 44, pp. 703–742; R. P. Tett, D. N. Jackson, M. Rothstein, and J. R. Reddon, "Meta-Analysis of Personality–Job Performance Relations: A Reply to Ones, Mount, Barrick, and Hunter (1994)," *Personnel Psychology,* 1994, 47, pp. 157–172.

12. M. R. Barrick and M. K. Mount, "The Big Five Personality Dimensions and Job Performance: A Meta-Analysis," *Personnel Psychology,* 1991, 44, pp. 1–26.

13. M. K. Mount and M. R. Barrick, "The Big Five Personality Dimensions: Implications for Research and Practice in Human Resources Management," in G. R. Ferris (ed.), *Research in Personnel and Human Resources Management,* vol. 13, (Greenwich, CT: JAI Press), pp. 153–200.

14. M. R. Barrick and M. K. Mount, "Autonomy as a Moderator of the Relationships Between the Big Five Personality Dimensions and Job Performance," *Journal of Applied Psychology,* 1993, 78, pp. 111–118; M. R. Barrick, M. K. Mount, and J. P. Strauss, "Conscientiousness and Performance of Sales Representatives: Test of the Mediating Effects of Goal Setting," *Journal of Applied Psychology,* 1993, 78, pp. 715–722; L. M. Hough, "The 'Big Five' Personality Variables—Construct Confusion: Description Versus Prediction"; M. K. Mount and M. R. Barrick, "The Big Five Personality Dimensions: Implications for Research and Practice in Human Resources Management"; K. R. Murphy and S. L. Lee, "Personality Variables Related to Integrity Test Scores: The Role of Conscientiousness," *Journal of Business and Psychology,* 1994, 9, pp. 413–424.

15. L. M. Hough, "The 'Big Five' Personality Variables—Construct Confusion: Description Versus Prediction"; M. J. Schmit and S. L. Hammer, "Personnel Selection and the Big Five: Bandwidth and Fidelity Explorations," Paper presented at the Ninth Annual Conference of the Society for Industrial and Organizational Psychology, 1994.

16. B. Azar, "Which Traits Predict Job Performance?" *APA Monitor,* July 1995, pp. 30–31.

17. I. T. Roberston, "Personality Assessment and Personnel Selection," *European Review of Applied Psychology,* 1993, 43, pp. 187–194; R. P. Tett, D. N. Jackson and M. Rothstein, "Personality Measures as Predictors of Job Performance: A Meta-Analytic Review."

18. M. J. Schmit, R. M. Guion, and P. H. Raymark, *Development of an Instrument to Identify Personality-Related Position Requirements*, Working paper, Department of Management, University of Florida, 1995.

19. See M. K. Mount and M. R. Barrick, "The Big Five Personality Dimensions: Implications for Research and Practice in Human Resources Management," for a thorough discussion of response distortion.

20. M. R. Barrick and M. K. Mount, "Effects of Impression Management and Self-Deception on the Predictive Validity of Personality Constructs," *Journal of Applied Psychology*, in press; N. D. Christiansen, R. D. Goffin, N. G. Johnston, and M. G. Rothstein, "Correcting the 16PF for Faking: Effects on Criterion-Related Validity and Individual Hiring Decisions," *Personnel Psychology*, 1994, 47, pp. 847–860; L. M. Hough, N. E. Eaton, M. D. Dunnette, J. D. Kamp, and R. A. McCloy, "Criterion-Related Validities of Personality Constructs and the Effect of Response Distortion of Those Validities," *Journal of Applied Psychology* (Monograph), 1990, 75, pp. 581–595; M. K. Mount, M. R. Barrick, and J. P. Strauss, "Validity of Observer Ratings of the Big Five Personality Factors," *Journal of Applied Psychology*, 1994, 79, pp. 272–280; D. S. Ones, C. Viswesvaran, and A. D. Reiss, "Response Distortion and Social Desirability in Personality Testing and Personnel Selection," Symposium conducted at the Tenth Annual Meeting of the Society for Industrial and Organizational Psychology, Orlando, FL, 1995; M. J. Schmit and A. M. Ryan, "The Big Five in Personnel Selection: Factor Structure in Applicant and Nonapplicant Populations," *Journal of Applied Psychology*, 1993, 78, pp. 966–974; M. J. Schmit and A. M. Ryan, "Test-Taking Dispositions: A Missing Link?" *Journal of Applied Psychology*, 1992, 77, pp. 629–637.

21. H. Schuler, "Social Validity of Selection Situations: A Concept and Some Empirical Results," in H. Schuler, J. L. Farr and M. Smith (eds.), *Personnel Selection and Assessment: Individual and Organizational Perspectives* (Hillsdale, NJ: Erlbaum, 1993), pp. 11–26.

22. J. W. Smither, R. R. Reilly, R. E. Millsap, K. Pearlman and R. W. Stoffey, "Applicant Reactions to Selection Procedures," *Personnel Psychology*, 1993, 46, pp. 49–76.

23. J. G. Rosse, J. L. Miller, and M. D. Stecher, "A Field Study of Job Applicants' Reactions to Personality and Cognitive Ability Testing," *Journal of Applied Psychology*, 1994, 79, pp. 987–992; S. L. Rynes and M. L. Connerley, "Applicant Reactions to Alternative Selection Procedures," *Journal of Business and Psychology*, 1993, 7, pp. 261–277.

24. Bureau of National Affairs, *Personnel Policies Forum, Recruiting and Selection Procedures* (Washington, DC: author, May 1988); P. M. Rowe, M. C. Williams, and A. L. Day, "Selection Procedures in North America," *International Journal of Selection and Assessment*, 1994, 2, pp. 74–79.

25. E. A. Fleishman and M. E. Reilly, *Handbook of Human Abilities* (Palo Alto, CA: Consulting Psychologists Press, 1992).

26. A. R. Jensen, *Bias in Mental Testing* (New York: The Free Press, 1980); M. J. Ree and J. A. Earles, "The Stability of Convergent Estimates of g," *Intelligence*, 1991, 15, pp. 271–278.

27. A. R. Jensen, *Bias in Mental Testing*.

28. F. Wonderlic, Jr., "Test Publishers Form Association," *Human Resource Measurements* (Supplement to the January 1993 *Personnel Journal*), p. 3.

29. B. Azar, "Could 'Policing' Test Use Improve Assessments?" *APA Monitor*, June, 1994, p. 16.

30. L. S. Gottfredson, "Societal Consequences of the *g* Factor in Employment," *Journal of Vocational Behavior*, 1986, 29, pp. 379–410.

31. J. E. Hunter and R. F. Hunter, "Validity and Utility of Alternative Predictors of Job Performance"; F. L. Schmidt, J. E. Hunter, and K. Pearlman, "Assessing the Economic Impact of Personnel Programs on Work Force Productivity," *Personnel Psychology*, 1982, 35, pp. 333–347.

32. J. E. Hunter, "Cognitive Ability, Cognitive Aptitudes, Job Knowledge, and Job Performance," *Journal of Vocational Behavior*, 1986, 29, 340–362.

33. D. S. Ones, C. Viswesvaran, and F. L. Schmidt, "Comprehensive Meta-Analysis of Integrity Test Validities: Findings and Implications for Personnel Selection and Theories of Job Performance," *Journal of Applied Psychology* (monograph), 1993, 78, pp. 531–537.

34. M. J. Ree and J. A. Earles, "Predicting Training Success: Not Much More Than *g*," *Personnel Psychology*, 1991, 44, pp. 321–332.

35. P. M. Wright, G. McMahan, and D. Smart, "Team Cognitive Ability as a Predictor of Performance: An Examination of the Role of SAT Scores in Determining NCAA Basketball Team Performance." Working paper, Department of Management, Texas A&M University.

36. R. J. Sternberg, R. K. Wagner, W. M. Williams, and J. A. Horvath, "Testing Common Sense," *American Psychologist*, 1995, 50, pp. 912–927.

37. J. E. Hunter, "Cognitive Ability, Cognitive Aptitudes, Job Knowledge, and Job Performance"; F. L. Schmidt and J. E. Hunter, "Development of a Causal Model of Processes Determining Job Performance," *Current Directions in Psychological Science*, 1992, 1, pp. 89–92.

38. J. J. McHenry, L. M. Hough, J. L. Toquam, M. A. Hanson, and S. Ashworth, "Project A Validity Results: The Relationship Between Predictor and Criterion Domains," *Personnel Psychology*, 1990, 43, 335–354.

39. M. J. Ree, J. A. Earles, and M. S. Teachout, "Predicting Job Performance: Not Much More than *g*," *Journal of Applied Psychology*, 1994, 79, pp. 518–524.

40. J. E. Hunter, "Cognitive Ability, Cognitive Aptitudes, Job Knowledge, and Job Performance".

41. R. J. Sternberg, et al., "Testing Common Sense"; R. J. Sternberg, "Tacit Knowledge and Job Success," in N. Anderson and P. Herriot (eds.), *Assessment and Selection in Organizations* (Chichester, England: Wiley, 1994), pp. 27–39.

42. F. L. Schmidt and J. E. Hunter, "Tacit Knowledge, Practical Intelligence, General Mental Ability, and Job Knowledge," *Current Directions in Psychological Science*, 1992, 1, pp. 8–9.

43. F. J. Landy and L. J. Shankster, "Personnel Selection and Placement".

44. P. R. Sackett and S. L. Wilk, "Within-Group Norming and Other Forms of Score Adjustment in Preemployment Testing," *American Psychologist*, 1994, 49, pp. 929–954.

45. R. D. Arvey and R. H. Faley, *Fairness in Selecting Employees* (Reading, MA: Addison-Wesley, 1988); R. D. Arvey and P. R. Sackett, "Fairness in Selection: Current Developments and Perspectives," in N. Schmitt, W.C. Borman, and Associates (eds.), *Personnel Selection in Organizations* (San Francisco: Jossey-Bass, 1993), pp. 171–202; L. S. Gottfredson, "Societal Consequences of the *g* Factor in Employment"; J. E. Hunter, F. L. Schmidt, and J. Rauschenberger, "Methodological, Statistical, and Ethical Issues in the Study of Bias in Psychological Tests," in C. R. Reynolds, and R. T. Brown (eds.), *Perspectives on Bias in Mental Testing*

(New York: Plenum, 1984), pp. 41–99; F. L. Schmidt, "The Problem of Group Differences in Ability Test Scores in Employment Selection," *Journal of Vocational Behavior*, 1988, 33, pp. 272–292.

46. D. S. Ones, C. Viswesvaran, and F. L. Schmidt, "Comprehensive Meta-Analysis of Integrity Test Validities: Findings and Implications for Personnel Selection and Theories of Job Performance."

47. T. A. Judge, D. Blancero, D. M. Cable, and D. E. Johnson, "Effects of Selection Systems on Job Search Decisions," Paper presented at the Tenth Annual Conference of the Society for Industrial and Organizational Psychology, 1995, Orlando, FL.

48. S. L. Rynes and M. L. Connerley, "Applicant Reactions to Alternative Selection Procedures."

49. J. W. Smither, et al., "Applicant Reactions to Selection Procedures."

50. J. C. Hogan, "Physical Abilities," in M. D. Dunnette and L. M. Hough (eds.), *Handbook of Industrial and Organizational Psychology*, vol. 2 (Palo Alto, CA: Consulting Psychologists Press, 1991), pp. 753–831.

51. M. A. Campion, "Personnel Selection for Physically Demanding Jobs: Review and Recommendations," *Personnel Psychology*, 36, 527–550.

52. T. A. Baker, *The Utility of a Physical Test in Reducing Injury Costs*, Paper Presented at the Ninth Annual Meeting of the Society for Industrial and Organizational Psychology, Nashville, TN, 1995.

53. R. D. Arvey, T. E. Landon, S. M. Nutting, and S. E. Maxwell, "Development of Physical Ability Tests for Police Officers: A Construct Validation Approach," *Journal of Applied Psychology*, 77, pp. 996–1009; B. R. Blakley, M. A. Quinones, M. S. Crawford, and I A. Jago, "The Validity of Isometric Strength Tests," *Personnel Psychology*, 47, pp. 247–274; E. A. Fleishman, "Some New Frontiers in Personnel Selection Research," *Personnel Psychology*, 1988, 41, pp. 679–701; J. C. Hogan, "Physical Abilities."

54. E. F. Ghiselli, "The Validity of Aptitude Tests in Personnel Selection," *Personnel Psychology*, 1973, 61, pp. 461–467.

55. V. C. Smith, "An Upgrade for Testing," *Human Resource Executive*, 1995, 8, pp. 41–43.

56. Wonderlic Personnel Test, Inc., *QUIZ Skills Evaluation System* (Northfield, IL: author, undated).

57. F. Drasgow, J. B. Olson, P. A. Keenan, P. Moberg, and A. D. Mead, "Computerized Assessment," in G. R. Ferris and K. M. Rowland (eds.), *Research in Personnel and Human Resources Management* (Greenwich, CT: JAI Press, 1993), pp. 163–206.

58. For a general review of this area, see M. J. Burke, "Computerized Psychological Testing: Impacts on Measuring Predictor Constructs and Future Job Behavior," in N. Schmitt, W.C. Borman, and Associates (eds.), *Personnel Selection in Organizations* (San Francisco: Jossey-Bass, 1993), pp. 203–239.

59. A. D. Mead and F. Drasgow, "Equivalence of Computerized and Paper-and-Pencil Cognitive Ability Tests: A Meta-Analysis," *Psychological Bulletin*, 1993, 114, pp. 449–458.

60. Wisconsin Department of Employment Relations, *Developing Wisconsin State Civil Service Examinations and Assessment Procedures* (Madison, WI: author, 1994).

61. D. A. Dye, M. Reck, and M. A. McDaniel, "The Validity of Job Knowledge Measures," *International Journal of Selection and Assessment*, 1993, 1, pp. 153–157.

62. J. E. Hunter, "Cognitive Ability, Cognitive Aptitudes, Job Knowledge, and Job Performance."

63. J. J. McHenry, L. M. Hough, J. L. Toquam, M. A. Hanson, and S. Ashworth, "Project A Validity Results: The Relationship Between Predictor and Criterion Domains"; M. J. Ree, J. A. Earles,

and M. S. Teachout, "Predicting Job Performance: Not Much More than *g*" M. M. Olea and M. J. Ree, "Predicting Pilot and Navigator Criteria: Not Much More than *g*," *Journal of Applied Psychology*, 1994, 79, pp. 845–851.

64. M. J. Ree, T. R. Carretta, and M. S. Teachout, "Role of Ability and Prior Job Knowledge in Complex Training Performance," *Journal of Applied Psychology*, 1995, 80, pp. 721–730.

65. L. McGinley, "Fitness Exams Help to Measure Worker Activity," *Wall Street Journal*, Apr. 21, 1992, p. B1.

66. J. J. Asher and J. A. Sciarrino, "Realistic Work Sample Tests: A Review," *Personnel Psychology*, 1974, 27, pp. 519–533.

67. J. J. Asher and J. A. Sciarrino, "Realistic Work Sample Tests: A Review."

68. S. J. Motowidlo, M. D. Dunnette, and G. Carter, "An Alternative Selection Procedure: A Low-Fidelity Simulation," *Journal of Applied Psychology*, 1990, 75, pp. 640–647.

69. W. Arthur, Jr., G. V. Barrett, and D. Doverspike, "Validation of an Information Processing-Based Test Battery Among Petroleum-Product Transport Drivers," *Journal of Applied Psychology*, 1990, 75, pp. 621–628.

70. S. J. Motowidlo, et al., "An Alternative Selection Procedure: A Low-Fidelity Simulation."

71. S. J. Motowidlo, et al., "An Alternative Selection Procedure: A Low-Fidelity Simulation."

72. E. A. Fleishman, "Some New Frontiers in Personnel Selection Research," *Personnel Psychology*, 1988, 41, pp. 679–699.

73. S. Sillup, "Applicant Screening Cuts Turnover Costs," *Personnel Journal*, May 1992, pp. 115–116.

74. Electronic Selection Systems Corporation, *AccuVision: Assessment Technology for Today, Tomorrow, and Beyond* (Maitland, FL: author, 1992).

75. J. E. Hunter and R. F. Hunter, "Validity and Utility of Alternative Predictors of Job Performance," *Psychological Bulletin*, 1984, 96, pp. 72–98.

76. F. Schmidt, A. Greenthol, J. Hunter, J. Berner, and F. Seaton, "Job Sample vs. Paper-and-Pencil Trade and Technical Tests: Adverse Impact and Examiner Attitudes," *Personnel Psychology*, 1977, 30, pp. 187–197.

77. W. Cascio and W. Phillips, "Performance Testing: A Rose Among Thorns?" *Personnel Psychology*, 1979, 32, pp. 751–766.

78. K. G. Love, R. C. Bishop, D. A. Heinisch, and M. S. Montei, "Selection Across Two Cultures: Adapting the Selection of American Assemblers to Meet Japanese Job Performance Dimensions," *Personnel Psychology*, 1994, 47, pp. 837–846.

79. K. A. Hanisch and C. L. Hulin, "Two-Stage Sequential Selection Procedures Using Ability and Training Performance: Incremental Validity of Behavioral Consistency Measures," *Personnel Psychology*, 1994, 47, pp. 767–785.

80. P. R. Sackett, "Integrity Testing for Personnel Selection."

81. L. R. Goldberg, J. R. Grenier, R. M. Guion, L. B. Sechrest, and H. Wing, *Questionnaires Used in the Prediction of Trustworthiness in Pre-Employment Selection Decisions: An APA Task Force Report* (Washington, DC: American Psychological Association, 1991).

82. W. J. Camera and D. L. Schneider, "Integrity Tests: Facts and Unresolved Issues," *American Psychologist*, 49, pp. 112–119.

83. P. R. Sackett, "Integrity Testing for Personnel Selection," *Current Directions in Psychological Science*, 1994, 3, 73–76.

84. M. R. Cunningham, D. T. Wong, and A. P. Barbee, "Self-Presentation Dynamics on Overt Integrity Tests: Experimental Studies of the Reid Report," *Journal of Applied Psychology*, 79, 1994, pp. 643–658.

85. R. C. Hollinger and J. P. Clark, *Theft by Employees* (Lexington, MA: Lexington Books, 1983).

86. D. S. Ones, "The Construct Validity of Integrity Tests," Unpublished Doctoral Dissertation, University of Iowa, Iowa City, Iowa, 1993.

87. K. R. Murphy and S. L. Lee, "Personality Variables Related to Integrity Test Scores: The Role of Conscientiousness," *Journal of Business and Psychology*, 1994, 9, pp. 413–424.

88. D. S. Ones, C. Viswesvaran, F. L. Schmidt, and A. D. Reiss, "The Validity of Honesty and Violence Scales of Integrity Tests in Predicting Violence at Work," Paper Presented at the Academy of Management Annual Meetings, Dallas, TX, Aug. 1994.

89. D. S. Ones, F. L. Schmidt, and C. Viswesvaran, "Do Broader Personality Variables Predict Job Performance with Higher Validity?"; D. S. Ones, C. Viswesvaran, and F. L. Schmidt, "Integrity Tests: Overlooked Facts, Resolved Issues, and Remaining Questions," *American Psychologist*, 1995, 50, pp. 456–460.

90. P. Ekman and M. O'Sullivan, "Who Can Catch a Liar?" *American Psychologist*, 1991, 46, pp. 913–920.

91. D. S. Ones, C. Viswesvaran, and F. L. Schmidt, "Comprehensive Meta-Analysis of Integrity Test Validities: Findings and Implications for Personnel Selection and Theories of Job Performance."

92. A. M. Ryan and P. R. Sackett, "Preemployment Honesty Testing: Fakability, Reactions of Test Takers, and Company Image," *Journal of Business and Psychology*, 1987, 1, pp. 248–256.

93. M. R. Cunningham, D. T. Wong and A. P. Barbee, "Self-Presentation Dynamics on Overt Integrity Tests: Experimental Studies of the Reid Report," *Journal of Applied Psychology*, 79, 1994, pp. 643–658.

94. P. R. Sackett, "Integrity Testing for Personnel Selection."

95. S. O. Lilienfeld, G. Alliger, and K. Mitchell, "Why Integrity Testing Remains Controversial," *American Psychologist*, 1995, 50, pp. 457–458; M. L. Rieke and S. J. Guastello, "Unresolved Issues in Honesty and Integrity Testing," *American Psychologist*, 1995, 50, pp. 458–459.

96. S. W. Gilliland, "Fairness from the Applicant's Perspective: Reactions to Employee Selection Procedures," *International Journal of Selection and Assessment*, 1995, 3, pp. 11–19; D. A. Kravitz, V. Stinson, and T. L. Chavez, "Evaluations of Tests Used for Making Selection and Promotion Decisions," *International Journal of Selection and Assessment*, in press.

97. P. T. Costa, Jr., R. R. McCrae, and J. L. Holland, "Personality and Vocational Interests in an Adult Sample," *Journal of Applied Psychology*, 1984, 69, pp. 390–400; R. R. McCrae and P. T. Costa, Jr., "Reinterpreting the Myers-Briggs Type Indicator from the Perspective of the Five-Factor Model of Personality," *Journal of Personality*, 1989, 57, pp. 17–40.

98. R. V. Dawis, "Vocational Interests, Values, and Preferences," in M. D. Dunnette and L. M. Hough (eds.), *Handbook of Industrial and Organizational Psychology* (Palo Alto, CA: Consulting Psychologists Press, 1991), pp. 833–871.

99. L. M. Hough, "The 'Big Five' Personality Variables—Construct Confusion: Description Versus Prediction."

100. M. Assouline and E. I. Meir, "Meta-Analysis of the Relationship Between Congruence and Well-Being Measures," *Journal of Vocational Behavior*, 1987, 31, pp. 319–332.

101. See B. Schneider, H. W. Goldstein, and D. B. Smith, "The ASA Framework: An Update," *Personnel Psychology*, 1995, 48, pp. 747–773.

102. D. M. Cable, "The Role of Person-Organization Fit in Organizational Entry." Unpublished Doctoral Dissertation, Cornell University, 1995.

103. D. M. Cable and T. A. Judge, *Person-Organization Fit, Job Choice Decisions, and Organizational Entry*. Working paper, Georgia Institute of Technology 1996; D. F. Caldwell and C. A. O'Reilly III, "Measuring Person-Job Fit With a Profile Comparison Process," *Journal of Applied Psychology*, 1990, 75, pp. 648–657; J. A. Chatman, "Matching People to Organizations: Selection and Socialization in Public Accounting Firms," *Administrative Science Quarterly*, 1989, 36, pp. 459–484; C. A. O'Reilly III, J. Chatman, and D. F. Caldwell, "People and Organizational Culture: A Profile Comparison Approach to Assessing Person-Organization Fit," *Academy of Management Journal*, 1991, 34, pp. 487–516.

104. R. J. Karren and L. M. Karren, "Assessing Person-Organization Fit in Personnel Selection: Evaluation of Alternative Approaches." Paper presented at the Academy of Management Meetings, Miami, FL, 1991.

105. S. L. Rynes and C. Q. Trank, "Moving Upstream in the Employment Relationship: Using Recruitment and Selection to Enhance Quality Outcomes," in S. Ghosh and D. Fedor (eds.), *Advances in the Management of Organizational Quality* (Greenwich, CT: JAI Press, 1996).

106. A. M. Ryan and P. R. Sackett, "A Survey of Individual Assessment Practices by I/O Psychologists," *Personnel Psychology*, 1987, 40, pp. 455–488.

107. R. L. Dipboye, *Selection Interviews: Process Perspectives* (Cincinnati, OH: South-Western, 1992), pp. 150–180; R. L. Dipboye and B. B. Gaugler, "Cognitive and Behavioral Processes in the Selection Interview," in N. Schmitt, W. C. Borman, and Associates (eds.), *Personnel Selection in Organizations* (San Francisco: Jossey-Bass, 1993), pp. 135–170; R. D. Gatewood and H. S. Feild, *Human Resource Selection*, second ed. (Chicago: Dryden, 1990), pp. 461–504; S. J. Motowidlo, G. W. Carter, M. D. Dunnette, N. Tippins, S. Werner, J. R. Burnett, and M. J. Vaughn, "Studies of the Structured Behavioral Interview," *Journal of Applied Psychology*, 1992, 77, pp. 571–587.

108. R. Pingatore, B. L. Dugoni, R. S. Tindale, and B. Spring, "Bias Against Overweight Job Applicants in a Simulated Employment Interview," *Journal of Applied Psychology*, 1994, 79, pp. 909–917.

109. R. L. Dipboye, *Selection Interviews: Process Perspectives*.

110. P. M. Rowe, "Unfavorable Information and Interview Decisions," in R. W. Eder and G. R. Ferris (eds.), *The Employment Interview: Theory, Research, and Practice* (Newbury Park, CA: Sage, 1989), pp. 77–89.

111. T. W. Dougherty, D. B. Turban, and J. C. Callender, "Confirming First Impressions in the Employment Interview: A Field Study of Interviewer Behavior," *Journal of Applied Psychology*, 1994, 79, pp. 659–665.

112. R. L. Dipboye, C. S. Stramler, and G. A. Fontanelle, "The Effects of the Application on Recall of Information from the Interview," *Academy of Management Journal*, 1984, 27, pp. 561–575.

113. T. R. Lin, G. H. Dobbins, and J. L. Farh, "A Field Study of Race and Age Similarity Effects on Interview Ratings in Conventional and Situational Interviews," *Journal of Applied Psychology*, 1992, 77, pp. 363–371.

114. R. E. Carlson, P. W. Thayer, E. C. Mayfield, and D. A. Peterson, "Improvements in the Selection Interview," *Personnel Journal*, 1971, 50, pp. 268–275.

115. G. P. Latham, L. M. Saari, E. D. Pursell, and M. A. Campion, "The Situational Interview," *Journal of Applied Psychology*, 1980, 65, pp. 422–427; G. P. Latham, "The Reliability, Va-

lidity, and Practicality of the Situational Interview,'' in R. W. Eder and G. R. Ferris (eds.), *The Employment Interview: Theory, Research, and Practice* (Newbury Park, CA: Sage, 1989), pp. 169–182.

116. T. Janz, ''The Patterned Behavior Description Interview: The Best Prophet of the Future is the Past,'' in R. W. Eder and G. R. Ferris (eds.), *The Employment Interview: Theory, Research, and Practice* (Newbury Park, CA: Sage, 1989), pp. 158–168.

117. M. A. Campion, E. D. Pursell, and B. K. Brown, ''Structured Interviewing: Raising the Psychometric Properties of the Employment Interview,'' *Personnel Psychology*, 1988, 41, pp. 25–42; S. J. Motowidlo, G. W. Carter, M. D. Dunnette, N. Tippins, S. Werner, J. R. Burnett, and M. J. Vaughan, ''Studies of the Structured Behavioral Interview,'' *Journal of Applied Psychology*, 1992, 77, pp. 571–587.

118. M. A. McDaniel, D. L. Whetzel, F. L. Schmidt, and S. D. Maurer, ''The Validity of Employment Interviews: A Comprehensive Review and Meta-Analysis,'' *Journal of Applied Psychology*, 1994, 79, pp. 599–616.

119. L. R. James, R. G. Demaree, S. A. Mulaik, and R. T. Ladd, ''Validity Generalization in the Context of Situational Models, *Journal of Applied Psychology*, 1992, 77, pp. 3–14.

120. T. A. Judge and G. R. Ferris, ''The Elusive Criterion of Fit in Human Resources Staffing Decisions,'' *Human Resource Planning*, 1992, 15, pp. 47–68.

121. J. E. Hunter and R. F. Hunter, ''Validity and Utility of Alternative Predictors of Job Performance''; S. Rynes and B. Gerhart, ''Interviewer Assessments of Applicant ''Fit'': An Exploratory Investigation,'' *Personnel Psychology*, 1990, 43, pp. 13–22.

122. M. A. Campion, J. E. Campion, and J. P. Hudson, ''Structured Interviewing: A Note on Incremental Validity and Alternative Question Types,'' *Journal of Applied Psychology*, 1994, 79, pp. 998–1002.

123. M. A. Campion, E. D. Pursell, and B. K. Brown, ''Structured Interviewing: Raising the Psychometric Properties of the Employment Interview''; L. C. Walters, M. R. Miller, and M. J. Ree, ''Structured Interviews for Pilot Selection: No Incremental Validity,'' *International Journal of Aviation Psychology*, 1993, 3, pp. 25–38; for an exception see E. D. Pulakos and N. Schmitt, ''Experience-Based and Situational Interview Questions: Studies of Validity,'' *Personnel Psychology*, 1995, 48, pp. 289–308.

124. A. E. Barber, J. R. Hollenbeck, S. L. Tower, and J. M. Phillips, ''The Effects of Interview Focus on Recruitment Effectiveness: A Field Experiment,'' *Journal of Applied Psychology*, 1994, 79, pp. 886–896.

125. G. N. Powell, ''Applicant Reactions to the Initial Employment Interview: Exploring Theoretical and Methodological Issues,'' *Personnel Psychology*, 1991, 44, pp. 67–83; S. Rynes and B. Gerhart, ''Interviewer Assessments of Applicant 'Fit': An Exploratory Investigation''; H. Schuler, ''Social Validity of Selection Situations: A Concept and Some Empirical Results.''

126. S. L. Rynes and M. L. Connerley, ''Applicant Reactions to Alternative Selection Procedures.''; J. W. Smither, et al., ''Applicant Reactions to Selection Procedures.''

127. T. A. Judge, D. Blancero, D. M. Cable, and D. E. Johnson, ''Effects of Selection Systems on Job Search Decisions.''

128. H. Schuler, ''Social Validity of Selection Situations: A Concept and Some Empirical Results.''

129. See the references in endnote 82.

130. T. W. Dougherty, D. B. Turban, and J. C. Callender, ''Confirming First Impressions in the Employment Interview: A Field Study of Interviewer Behavior.''; G. F. Dreher, R. A. Ash, and P. Hancock, ''The Role of the Traditional Research Design in Underestimating the Validity

of the Employment Interview," *Personnel Psychology*, 1988, 41, pp. 315–327; L. M. Graves and R. J. Karren, "Interviewer Decision Processes and Effectiveness: An Experimental Policy-Capturing Investigation," *Personnel Psychology*, 1992, 45, pp. 313–340; A. J. Kinicki, C. A. Lockwood, P. W. Hom, and R. W. Griffeth, "Interviewer Predictions of Applicant Qualifications and Interviewer Validity: Aggregate and Individual Analyses," *Journal of Applied Psychology*, 1990, 75, pp. 477–486.

131. R. L. Dipboye, *Selection Interviews: Process Perspectives*.

132. R. L. Dipboye, *Selection Interviews: Process Perspectives*.

133. R. L. Dipboye, *Selection Interviews: Process Perspectives*; see also M. M. Harris, "Reconsidering the Employment Interview: A Review of Recent Literature and Suggestions for Future Research," *Personnel Psychology*, 1989, 42, pp. 691–726.

134. R. L. Dipboye, *Selection Interviews: Process Perspectives*, pp. 150–179.

135. R. Blackburn and B. Rosen, "Total Quality and Human Resources Management: Lessons Learned from Baldrige Award-Winning Companies," *Academy of Management Executive*, 1992, 7, 49–66; S. L. Rynes and C. Q. Trank, "Moving Upstream in the Employment Relationship: Using Recruitment and Selection to Enhance Quality Outcomes."

136. R. Blackburn and B. Rosen, "Total Quality and Human Resources Management: Lessons Learned from Baldrige Award-Winning Companies."; S. L. Rynes and C. Q. Trank, "Moving Upstream in the Employment Relationship: Using Recruitment and Selection to Enhance Quality Outcomes."

137. S. L. Rynes and C. Q. Trank, "Moving Upstream in the Employment Relationship: Using Recruitment and Selection to Enhance Quality Outcomes."

138. M. J. Stevens and M. A. Campion, "The Knowledge, Skill, and Ability Requirements for Teamwork: Implications for Human Resource Management," *Journal of Management*, 1994, 20, pp. 503–530.

139. M. J. Stevens, Staffing Work Teams: Testing for Individual-Level Knowledge, Skill, and Ability Requirements for Teamwork. Unpublished Doctoral Dissertation, Purdue University, 1993.

140. R. S. Wellens, W. C. Byham and G. R. Dixon, *Inside Teams* (San Francisco: Jossey-Bass, 1995).

141. R. Klimoski and R. G. Jones, "Staffing for Effective Group Decision Making: Key Issues in Matching People and Teams," in R. A. Guzzo and E. Salas (eds.), *Team Effectiveness and Decision Making in Organizations* (San Francisco: Jossey-Bass, 1995), pp. 291–332.

142. M. Levinson, "When Workers Do the Hiring," *Newsweek*, June 21, 1993, p. 48; S. M. Colarelli and A. L. Boos, "Sociometric and Ability-Based Assignment to Work Groups: Some Implications for Personnel Selection," *Journal of Organizational Behavior Management*, 1992, 13, pp. 187–196.

143. B. Dumaine, "The Trouble with Teams," *Fortune*, Sept. 5 1994, pp. 86–92.

144. A. M. Ryan and P. R. Sackett, "A Survey of Industrial Assessment Practices by I/O Psychologists."

145. R. J. Stahl, "Succession Planning Drives Plant Turnaround," *Personnel Journal*, Sept. 1992, pp. 67–70.

146. R. D. Arvey and R. H. Faley, *Fairness in Selecting Employees*; M. R. Barrick and M. K. Mount, "The Big Five Personality Dimensions and Job Performance: A Meta-Analysis"; M. A. Campion, "Personnel Selection for Physically Demanding Jobs: Review and Recommendations"; E. T. Cornelius III, "The Use of Projective Tests in Personnel Selection," in G. R. Ferris and K. M. Rowland (eds.), *Organizational Entry* (Greenwich, CT: JAI Press, 1990), pp.

73–114; J. A. Cox, D. W. Schlueter, K. K. Moore, and D. Sullivan, ''A Look Behind Corporate Doors,'' *Personnel Administrator*, Mar. 1989, pp. 56–59; R. V. Dawis, ''Vocational Interests, Values, and Preferences''; ''Employee Drug Testing Escalates,'' *BNA Bulletin to Management*, May 23, 1991, p. 154; R. M. Guion and W. M. Gibson, ''Personnel Selection and Placement,'' *Annual Review of Psychology*, 39, pp. 349–374; J. C. Hogan, ''Physical Abilities''; R. T. Hogan, ''Personality and Personality Measurement''; R. T. Hogan, B. N. Carpenter, S. R. Briggs, and R. O. Hansson, ''Personality Assessment and Personnel Selection,'' in H. J. Bernardin and D. A. Bounds (eds.), *Personality Assessment in Organizations* (New York: Praeger, 1985), pp. 21–52; L. M. Hough, M. A. Keyes, and M. D. Dunnette, ''An Evaluation of Three 'Alternative' Selection Devices,'' *Personnel Psychology*, 1983, 36 pp. 261–277; J. E. Hunter and R. F. Hunter, ''Validity and Utility of Alternative Predictors of Job Performance''; V. R. Lindquist, ''The Northwestern Lindquist-Endicott Report-1991,'' *The Placement Center of Northwestern University* (Evanston, IL: Northwestern University, 1991); K. R. Murphy, G. C. Thornton III, and D. H. Reynolds, ''College Students' Attitudes Towards Drug Testing Programs''; J. Normand, S. D. Salyards, and J. J. Mahoney, ''An Evaluation of Preemployment Drug Testing''; M. R. Potsfall and N. R. Feimer, ''The Role of Person-Environment Fit in Job Performance and Satisfaction,'' in H. J. Bernardin and D. A. Bownas (eds.), *Personality Assessment in Organizations* (New York: Praeger, 1985), pp. 53–81; ''Pay Now, Fly Later,'' *Newsweek*, Nov. 1991; Bureau of National Affairs, *Personnel Policies Forum, Recruiter and Selection Procedures* (Washington, DC: author, May 1988); R. R. Reilly and G. T. Chao, ''Validity and Fairness of Some Alternative Selection Procedures,'' *Personnel Psychology*, 1982, 35, pp. 1–62; S. L. Rynes, ''Who's Selecting Whom? Effects of Selection Practices on Applicant Attitudes and Behaviors''; P. R. Sackett, L. R. Burris, and C. Callahan, ''Integrity Testing for Personnel Selection: An Update,'' *Personnel Psychology*, 42, pp. 491–529; ''Satisfaction With the Quality of New Hires is 50% Higher for Companies who Test,'' *Human Resource Measurements* (Northfield, IL: Wonderlic Personnel Test, Inc., Spring 1992), pp. 1–2; F. L. Schmidt, D. S. Ones and J. E. Hunter, ''Personnel Selection,'' *Annual Review of Psychology*, 1992, 43, 627–670; N. Schmitt, R. Z. Gooding, R. A. Noe, and M. Kirsch, ''Meta-Analyses of Validity Studies Between 1964 and 1982 and the Investigation of Study Characteristics,'' *Personnel Psychology*, 1984, 37, pp. 407–422; R. T. Tett, D. N. Jackson, and M. Rothstein, ''Personality Measures as Predictors of Job Performance: A Review''; S. Zedeck and W. F. Cascio, ''Psychological Issues in Personnel Decisions,'' *Annual Review of Psychology*, 1984, 35, pp. 461–518; S. M. Colarelli and A. L. Boos, ''Sociometric and Ability-Based Assignment to Work Groups: Some Implications for Personnel Selection,'' *Journal of Organizational Behavior*, 1992, 13, pp. 187–196.

147. W. C. Borman and S. J. Motowidlo, ''Expanding the Criterion Domain to Include Elements of Contextual Performance,'' in N. Schmitt, W. Borman, and Associates (eds.), *Personnel Selection in Organizations* (San Francisco: Jossey-Bass, 1993) pp. 71–98; D. Organ, *Organizational Citizenship Behavior: The Good Soldier Syndrome* (Lexington, MA: D.C. Heath, 1988).

148. S. Dentzer, B. Cohn, G. Raine, G. Carroll, and V. Quade, ''Can You Pass This Job Test?'' *Newsweek*, May 5, 1986, pp. 46–53.

149. Smithers Institute, ''Drug Testing: Cost and Effect,'' *Cornell/Smithers Report*, (Ithaca, NY: Cornell University, 1992), 1, pp. 1–5.

150. ''Drug Testing: Cost and Effect.''

151. ''Drug Testing: Cost and Effect.''

152. W. E. K. Lehman and D. D. Simpson, ''Employee Substance Abuse and On-the-Job Behaviors,'' *Journal of Applied Psychology*, 1992, 77, pp. 309–321.

153. "More Major U.S. Firms Test Workers for Drugs," *Daily Labor Report*, April 8 1994, p. A-4.

154. V. C. Smith, "Fighting Back," *Human Resource Executive*, Sept. 1992, pp. 38–39.

155. J. P. Guthrie and J. D. Olian, "Drug and Alcohol Testing Programs: Do Firms Consider Their Operating Environment?" *Human Resource Planning*, 1992, 14, pp. 221–232.

156. J. A. Segal, "To Test or Not To Test," *HR Magazine*, Apr. 1992, pp. 40–43.

157. V. C. Smith, "Fighting Back."

158. J. Normand, S. D. Salyards, and J. J. Mahoney, "An Evaluation of Pre-employment Drug Testing."

159. S. L. Martin and D. J. DeGrange, "How Effective Are Physical and Psychological Drug Tests?" *EMA Journal*, Fall 1993, pp. 18–22.

160. M. D. Urich, "Are You Positive the Test is Positive?" *HR Magazine*, Apr. 1992, pp. 44–48.

161. S. L. Martin and D. J. DeGrange, "How Effective Are Physical and Psychological Drug Tests?"

162. "Drug Testing: Cost and Effect."

163. J. Normand, S. D. Salyards and J. J. Mahoney, "An Evaluation of Preemployment Drug Testing," *Journal of Applied Psychology*, 1990, 75, pp. 629–639.

164. S. L. Martin and D. J. DeGrange, "How Effective Are Physical and Psychological Drug Tests?"

165. J. Michaelis, "Waging War," *Human Resource Executive*, Oct. 1993, pp. 39–42.

166. J. Normand, S. D. Salyards, and J. J. Mahoney, "An Evaluation of Preemployment Drug Testing."

167. T. A. Judge, D. Blancero, D. M. Cable, and D. E. Johnson, "Effects of Selection Systems on Job Search Decisions"; S. L. Rynes and M. L. Connerley, "Applicant Reactions to Alternative Selection Procedures."

168. J. M. Crant and T. S. Bateman, "An Experimental Test of the Impact of Drug-Testing Programs on Potential Job Applicants' Attitudes and Intentions," *Journal of Applied Psychology*, 1990, 75, pp. 127–131; K. R. Murphy, G. C. Thornton III, and D. H. Reynolds, "College Students' Attitudes Toward Employee Drug Testing Programs," *Personnel Psychology*, 1990, 43, pp. 615–631.

169. E. A. Fleishman, "Some New Frontiers in Personnel Selection Research."

170. M. A. Campion, "Personnel Selection for Physically Demanding Jobs: Review and Recommendations," *Personnel Psychology*, 1983, 36, pp. 527–550.

171. J. C. Hogan, "Physical Abilities," in M. D. Dunnette and L. M. Hough (eds.), *Handbook of Industrial & Organizational Psychology*, second ed. (Palo Alto, CA: Consulting Psychologists Press, 1991), pp. 753–832.

172. E. A. Fleishman, "New Research Frontiers in Personnel Selection."

173. G. P. Panero, *Employment Law Manual*, second ed. (Boston: Warren Gorham Lamont, 1993), pp. 3–28 to 3–82.

174. See Appendix C; Equal Employment Opportunity Commission, *Technical Assistance Manual of the Employment Provisions (Title 1) of the Americans With Disabilities Act* (Washington, DC: author, 1992), pp. 51–88; J. G. Frierson, *Employer's Guide to the Americans With Disabilities Act* (Washington, DC: Bureau of National Affairs, 1992).

175. L. Daley, M. Dolland, J. Kraft, M. A. Nester, and R. Schneider, *Employment Testing of Persons With Disabling Conditions* (Alexandria, VA: International Personnel Management Association,

1988); L. D. Eyde, M. A. Nester, S. M. Heaton, and A. V. Nelson, *Guide for Administering Written Employment Examinations to Persons With Disabilities* (Washington, DC: U.S. Office of Personnel Management, 1994).

176. Equal Employment Opportunity Commission, *ADA Enforcement Guidance: Preemployment Disability Related Questions and Medical Examinations* (Washington, DC: author, 1995).

177. A. G. Feliu, *Primer on Employee Rights* (Washington, DC: Bureau of National Affairs, 1992); J. A. Segal, "Urine or You're Out," *HR Magazine*, Dec. 1994, pp. 30–38.

CHAPTER ELEVEN

Internal Selection

Preliminary Issues
   The Logic of Prediction
   Types of Predictors
   Evolving Nature of Internal Selection Decisions
   Selection Plan

Initial Assessment Methods
   Skills Inventory
   Peer Assessments
   Self Assessments
   Managerial Sponsorship
   Informal Discussions and Recommendations
   Career Concepts
   Choice of Initial Assessment Methods

Substantive Assessment Methods
   Seniority and Experience
   Job Knowledge Tests
   Performance Appraisal
   Promotability Ratings
   Assessment Centers
   Interview Simulations
   Promotion Panels and Review Boards
   Choice of Substantive Assessment Methods

Discretionary Assessment Methods

Applicant Reactions

Collection of Assessment Data

Legal Issues
   Uniform Guidelines on Employee Selection Procedures
   The Glass Ceiling

Summary

Discussion Questions

Applications

Internal selection refers to the assessment and evaluation of employees from within the organization as they move from job to job via transfer and promotion systems. Many different assessment methods are used to make internal selection decisions. Preliminary issues we will discuss to guide the use of these assessment methods include the logic of prediction, the nature of predictors, the changing nature of internal selection decisions, and the development of a selection plan.

Initial assessment methods are used to select internal candidates from among the internal applicants. Initial assessment methods that will be reviewed include skills inventories, peer and self assessments, managerial sponsorship, informal discussions and recommendations, and career concepts. The criteria that should be used to choose among these methods will be discussed.

Substantive assessment methods are used to select internal finalists from among internal candidates. Various methods will be reviewed, including seniority and experience, job knowledge tests, performance appraisal, promotability ratings, assessment centers, interview simulations, and promotion panels and review boards. The criteria used to choose among the substantive assessment methods will be discussed.

Discretionary assessment methods are used to select offer recipients from among the finalists. The factors upon which these decisions are based, such as EEO/AA concerns, whether the finalist had previously been a finalist, and second opinions about the finalist by others in the organization, will be considered.

All of these assessment methods require the collection of a large amount of data. Accordingly, attention must be given to support services, the required expertise needed to administer and interpret predictors, security, privacy and confidentiality, and the standardization of procedures. Since candidates for internal selection decisions are usually valued employees, employee reactions to the selection process will also be discussed.

The use of internal selection methods requires a clear understanding of legal issues. In particular, the Uniform Guidelines on Employee Selection Procedures and the glass ceiling are reviewed.

PRELIMINARY ISSUES

The Logic of Prediction

The logic of prediction described in Chapter 9 is equally relevant to the case of internal selection. Specifically, indicators of internal applicants' degree of success in past situations should be predictive of their likely success in new situations. Past situations importantly include previous jobs, as well as the current one, held by the applicant with the organization. The new situation is the internal vacancy the applicant is seeking via the organization's transfer or promotion system.

There also may be similarities between internal and external selection in terms of the effectiveness of selection methods. As you may recall from Chapters 9 and 10, three of the most valid external selection measures are biographical data, cognitive ability tests, and work samples. These methods also have validity in internal selection decisions. Biographical information has been found to be a valid predictor in selecting top corporate leaders. Research indicates that cognitive ability is strongly predictive of long-term job performance and advancement. Finally, work samples are valid predictors of advancement.[1] In this chapter we focus on processes and methods of selection that are unique to promotion and transfer decisions. However, in considering these methods and processes, it should be kept in mind that many of the techniques of external selection may be relevant as well.

Although the logic of prediction and the likely effectiveness of selection methods are similar for external and internal selection, in practice there are several potential advantages of internal over external selection. In particular, the data collected on internal applicants in their previous jobs often offer greater depth, relevance, and verifiability than the data collected on external applicants. This is because organizations usually have much more detailed and in-depth information about internal candidates' previous job experiences. In this age of computers, where organizations can store large amounts of data on employees' job experiences, this is especially true. It is far more difficult to access data in a reliable manner when external candidates are used. As indicated in Chapter 9 previous employers are often hesitant to release data on previous employees due to legal concerns, such as potential invasion of privacy. As a result, employers often have to rely upon reports by external candidates of their previous experiences, and the candidates may not always present the whole picture or an accurate picture of their past experiences.

In terms of the relevance of past experiences, organizations may also have better data with which to make selection decisions on internal than external candidates. The experiences of insiders may more closely mirror the experiences likely to be encountered on the new job than the experiences of outsiders. For example, organizations often worry about whether some candidate will be willing to live in a certain geographic area. The answer may be obvious with an internal candidate who already lives in that location. As another example, organizations often wonder about the transferability of skills learned in another organization to their own. Hence, when a new CEO is brought to a computer company from a tobacco company, many will comment on whether he will make it in this new environment.

Along with depth and relevance, another positive aspect of the nature of predictors for internal selection is verifiability. Rather than simply relying on the opinion of one person as to the suitability of an internal candidate for the job, multiple assessments may be solicited. Opinions about the suitability of the candidate also can be solicited from other supervisors and peers as well. By pooling opinions, it is possible to get a more complete and accurate picture of a candidate's qualifications.

Types of Predictors

The distinctions made between types of predictors used in external selection are also applicable to types of internal predictors. One important difference to note between internal and external predictors pertains to content. There is usually greater depth and relevance to the data available on internal candidates. As a result, greater emphasis can be placed on samples and criteria rather than signs in selection. This is possible because the data on previous situations are more readily available with internal candidates. That is, the organization can go to their own files or managers to get reports on the applicants' previous experiences.

Evolving Nature of Internal Selection Decisions

The nature of internal staffing decisions has changed dramatically in the last decade. Because of slower organizational growth, trends toward flatter organizational structures, and dramatic downsizing efforts, fewer and fewer promotions are being made. As a result, organizations increasingly have turned to lateral moves, job rotations, and transfers to fill positions within an organization. To some degree, this change in the nature of internal staffing decisions does not (and should not) alter the appropriate methods of internal selection. A selection method that does a good job of identifying capabilities to perform a higher-level job with new responsibilities also should do a good job of identifying capabilities to perform a same-level job with new responsibilities.

The changing nature of internal staffing decisions raises another issue. Despite fewer promotion opportunities available in organizations, most workers continue to expect continual advancement in the organization. Thus, there may be a conflict between employee expectations and the current realities of organizational promotions systems. In fact, most employees continue to describe themselves in terms of a linear career model which equates continual ascendance up the organizational ladder with career success.[2] To avoid high levels of career dissatisfaction, a burden is placed on organizations to socialize employees away from a linear model to more realistic career models. Given the inherent difficulties in orienting employees away from their dominant career concept, however, organizations also may want to consider assessing an individual's career concept as a criterion for future internal selection decisions. This issue will be taken up later in the chapter when discussing initial assessment methods. More broadly, the recent redefinition of career systems illustrates how staffing decisions are not made in isolation—the broader organizational context must be considered.

Selection Plan

Often it seems that internal selection is done on the basis of who you know rather than relevant KSAOs. Managers tend to rely heavily upon the subjective opinions of previous managers who supervised the internal candidate for a job. When asked why they rely on these subjective assessments, the answer is often, "Because the candidate has worked here for a long time and I trust his supervisor's feel for the candidate."

Decision errors often occur when relying upon subjective feelings for internal selection decisions. For example, in selecting managers to oversee engineering and scientific personnel in organizations, it is sometimes felt that those internal job candidates with the best technical skills will be the best managers. This is not always the case. Some technical wizards are poor managers and vice versa. Sound internal selection procedures need to be followed to guard against this error. A sound job analysis will show that both technical and managerial skills need to be assessed with well-crafted predictors.

Feel, hunch, gut instinct, intuition, and the like do not substitute for well-developed predictors. Relying solely on others' "feelings" about the job may result in the lowering of hiring standards for some employees, discrimination against protected class employees, and decisions with low validity. As a result, it is imperative that a selection plan be used for internal as well as external selection. As described in Chapter 9, a selection plan lists the predictors to be used for assessment of each KSAO.

INITIAL ASSESSMENT METHODS

The internal recruitment process may generate a large number of applications for vacant positions. This is especially true when an open rather than closed recruitment system is used—where jobs are posted for employees to apply. Given the time and cost of rigorous selection procedures, organizations use initial assessment methods to screen out applicants who do not meet the minimum qualifications needed to become a candidate. Initial assessment methods for internal recruitment typically include the following predictors: skills inventories, peer evaluations, self-assessments, managerial sponsorship, informal discussions and recommendations, and career concepts. Each of these predictors will be described in turn, followed by a general evaluation of them all.

Skills Inventory

An immediate screening device in applicant assessment is to rely upon existing data on employee skills. These data can be found in personnel files, which are usually on the computer in larger organizations and in file drawers in smaller organizations. The level of sophistication of the data kept by organizations varies considerably, depending upon the method used. Methods used include traditional skills inventories, upgraded skills inventories, and customized skills assessments.

Traditional Skills Inventory

A traditional skills inventory is a listing of the KSAOs held by each employee in the organization. Usually the system records a small number of skills listed in generic categories such as education, experience, and supervisory training received. A sound traditional system should be systematically updated on a periodic basis by the human resources group. Unfortunately, the maintenance of the database is often a low-priority project, and, as a result, traditional skills inventories often do not reflect current skills held by employees.

Upgraded Skills Inventory

In an upgraded skills inventory, managers systematically enter the latest skills acquired by employees into the database as soon as they occur. The system may also include a listing of the skill sets held by external job candidates who were not hired. Members of the human resources group systematically record and enter the skills of people whose resume they receive. Thus, even though some individuals were not hired for an initial position, their resumes can be drawn upon for future positions where they match the qualifications. In essence, human resources is enlarging the existing internal applicant pool with external applicants' files.

Customized Skill Inventory

Both the traditional and upgraded skills inventory rely upon broadly defined skill categories. As has been indicated repeatedly throughout the book, the more specific the KSAOs required for the job, the more likely is a good person/job match. A customized skills assessment (CSA) moves in this direction.[3] With a CSA, specific skill sets are recorded for specific jobs. Skills are not included simply because they are relevant to all jobs or because they happen to match a particular computer software package. Instead, subject matter experts (e.g., managers and experienced job incumbents) identify skills that are critical to job success.

An example of a customized skills inventory is shown in Exhibit 11.1. As can be seen, each job requires increasing numbers of KSAOs. The associate position requires technical skills only; the team leader position requires technical skills plus coaching, counseling, and teamwork skills. The manager position requires all of these skills plus strategic management skills as well. An inventory like this is kept for each employee. As the person gains skills, they are entered into the appropriate boxes. Once a column of boxes is completed, the person then becomes eligible for the appropriate position when a vacancy exists.

Peer Assessments

Assessments by peers or coworkers can be used to evaluate the promotability of an internal applicant. A variety of methods can be used, including peer ratings,

EXHIBIT 11.1   Customized Skill Inventory

Name: _____

Skills Required for Future Position

KSAO Dimension	Associate	Team Leader	Manager
Technical knowledge	1. ___ 2. ___ 3. ___	1. ___ 2. ___ 3. ___	1. ___ 2. ___ 3. ___
Coaching, counseling, teamwork		1. ___ 2. ___ 3. ___	1. ___ 2. ___ 3. ___
Strategic management			1. ___ 2. ___ 3. ___

peer nominations, and peer rankings.[4] Examples of all three are shown in Exhibit 11.2.

As can be seen in Exhibit 11.2, while peers are used to make promotion decisions in all three methods of peer assessments, the format of each is different. With peer ratings, readiness to be promoted is assessed for each peer using a rating scale. The person with the highest ratings is deemed most promotable. On the other hand, peer nominations rely on voting for the most promotable candidates.

EXHIBIT 11.2   Peer Assessments Methods

Peer Rating

Please consider each of the following employees and rate them using the following scale for the position of manager described in the job requirements matrix:

	Not Promotable		Promotable in One Year		Promotable Now
	1	2	3	4	5
Jean	1	2	3	4	5
John	1	2	3	4	5
Andy	1	2	3	4	5
Herb	1	2	3	4	5

Peer Nominations

Please consider each of the following employees and mark an X for the one employee who is most promotable to the position of manager as described in the job requirements matrix:

Jeff   _____
Carolyn   _____
Jeffrey   _____
Shelly   _____
Renee   _____

Peer Ranking

Please rank order the following employees from the most promotable (1) to the least promotable (5) for the position of manager as described in the job requirements matrix:

Ila   _____
Karen   _____
Phillip   _____
Rebecca   _____
Buster   _____

Peers receiving the greatest number of "votes" are the most promotable. Finally, peer rankings rely upon a rank ordering of peers. Those peers with the highest rankings are the most promotable.

Peer assessments have been used extensively in the military over the years and to a lesser degree in industry. A virtue of peer assessments is that they rely upon raters who presumably are very knowledgeable of the applicants' KSAOs due to their day-to-day contact with them. A possible downside to peer assessments, however, is that they may encourage friendship bias. Also, they may undermine morale in a work group by fostering a very competitive environment.

Another possible problem with peer assessment is that the criteria by which assessments are made are not always made clear. For peer assessments to work, care should be taken in advance to carefully spell out the KSAOs needed for successful performance in the position the peer is being considered for. In order to do so, a job requirements matrix should be used.

A probable virtue of peer assessments is that peers are more likely to feel that the decisions reached are fair ones, because they had an input into the decision. The decision is thus not seen as a "behind the backs" maneuver by management. As such, peer assessments are used more often with open rather than closed systems of internal recruitment.

Self Assessments

Job incumbents can be asked to evaluate their own skills as a basis for determining promotability. This procedure is sometimes used with open recruitment systems. An example of this approach is shown in Exhibit 11.3. Caution must be exercised in using this process for selection as it may raise the expectations of those rating themselves that they will be selected. Also, this approach should be coupled with other internal selection procedures as employees may have a tendency to overrate themselves.

Managerial Sponsorship

Increasingly, organizations are relying upon higher-ups in the organization to identify and develop the KSAOs of those at lower levels in the organization. Historically, the higher-up has been the person's immediate supervisor. Today, however, the higher-up may be a person at a higher level of the organization who does not have direct responsibility for the person being rated. Higher-ups are sometimes labeled coaches, sponsors, or mentors, and their roles are defined in Exhibit 11.4. In some organizations, there are formal mentorship programs where employees are assigned coaches, sponsors, and mentors. In other organizations, these matches may just naturally occur, often progressing from coach to sponsor to mentor as

EXHIBIT 11.3   Self Assessment Form Used for Application in Job Posting System

SUPPLEMENTAL QUESTIONNAIRE

This supplemental will be the principle basis for determining whether or not you are highly qualified for this position. You may add information not identified in your SF-171 or expand on that which is identified. You should consider appropriate work experience, outside activities, awards, training, and education for each of the items listed below.

1. Knowledge of the Bureau of Indian Affairs' mission, organization, structure, policies, and functions, as they relate to Real Estate.
2. Knowledge of technical administrative requirements to provide technical guidance in administrative areas, such as personnel regulations, travel regulations, time and attendance requirements, budget documents, Privacy Act, and Freedom of Information Act, etc.
3. Ability to work with program directors and administrative staff and ability to apply problem solving techniques and management concepts; ability to analyze facts and problems and develop alternatives.
4. Ability to operate various Computer programs and methodology in the analysis and design of automated methods for meeting the information and reporting requirements for the Division.
5. Knowledge of the Bureau Budget process and statistical Profile of all field operations that impact in the Real Estate Services program.

On a separate sheet of paper, address the above items in narrative form. Identify the vacancy announcement number across the top. Sign and date your Supplemental Questionnaire.

Source: Department of the Interior, Bureau of Indian Affairs. Form BIA-4450 (4/22/92).

the relationship matures. Regardless of the formality of the relationship, these individuals are often given considerable weight in promotion decisions. Their weight is due to their high organizational level and in-depth knowledge of the employee's KSAOs. Not only is the judgment of these advocates important, but so, too, are their behaviors. Mentors, for example, are likely to put employees in situations where they receive high visibility. That visibility may increase the applicants' chances of promotion.

Informal Discussions and Recommendations

Not all promotion decisions are made on the basis of formal human resource policy and procedures. Much of the decision process occurs outside normal channels through informal discussions and recommendations. These discussions are difficult to characterize because some are simply idle hall talk, while others are directly

---

EXHIBIT 11.4   Employee Advocates

Coach

- Provides day to day feedback
- Diagnoses and resolves performance problems
- Creates opportunities for employees using existing training programs and career development programs

Sponsor

- Actively promotes person for advancement opportunities
- Guides person's career rather than simply informing them of opportunities
- Creates opportunities for people in decision making capacities to see the skills of the employee (e.g., lead a task force)

Mentor

- Becomes personally responsible for the success of the person
- Available to person on and off the job
- Lets person in on "insider" information
- Solicits and values person's input

Source: Reprinted with permission from Dr. Janina Latack, PhD, Nelson O'Connor & Associates/ Outplacement International, Phoenix/Tucson.

job related. For example, a lawyer who is expected to be a rainmaker (someone who brings in clients and possible revenue) may be assessed by his contacts in the community. An assessment of the person's qualifications for rainmaking may be done by an informal conversation between a senior partner and a previous client of the supposed rainmaker at a board meeting. Unfortunately, many informal discussions are suspect in terms of their relevance to actual job performance.

Career Concepts

Career concepts are the basic assumptions people hold about their careers. Research suggests that most individuals possess one of four career concepts and that once individuals have settled on a dominant concept, it is very difficult to socialize them away from it. Exhibit 11.5 provides a definition of the four career concepts. Although most individuals may find several career types relevant to them, usually one career type predominates.

These career concepts have been measured with the *Career Concepts Questionnaire*. Exhibit 11.6 is a sample from the *Career Concepts Questionnaire*. In this portion of the questionnaire, individuals for whom a Type 1 career is most descriptive are characterized as *Spirals*; those for whom a Type 2 career is most descriptive are *Linears*; those for whom a Type 3 career is most descriptive are

---

EXHIBIT 11.5   General Career Concepts

Linear Concept

The Linear concept places great importance on rapid movement "up the ladder" to positions of increasing responsibility and authority. Staying in one job or at one level in an organization is seen as very undesirable. This is a fairly traditional way of thinking about career success—particularly in America with its heavy cultural emphasis on upward mobility. To people who wish to have Linear careers, this pattern often is the *only* real definition of career success. Many business executives and politicians think about careers in Linear terms.

Expert Concept

This is a very traditional way of describing a career. According to this concept, a person makes a choice of career field and then sticks to it for the long term. Typically, the choice is a lifelong vocation or commitment to a single area of expertise. People who pursue Expert careers often develop strong feelings of personal identity with a particular occupation or profession. For example, a person comes to think of himself or herself as *being* an engineer, a doctor, or a carpenter.

Spiral Concept

This is a much less traditional way of describing a career, and it differs in some very basic ways from the Expert and Linear concepts. The Spiral career is one that consists of major changes in career field. These changes take place every five to ten years. Usually, the changes involve moving from one field into another that allows a person to use his or her previously developed skills while opening the door to the development of new skills and knowledge.

Transitory Concept

The Transitory concept is even less traditional than the Spiral concept. However, it accurately describes the careers of many people. It is marked by a great deal of change—in jobs and career fields. As a pattern, the Transitory career has been called a "consistent pattern of inconsistency." People whose careers are Transitory tend to make major changes in jobs or even in career fields every two to four years. The direction of movement in these changes is just as likely to be lateral as it is up or down.

Source: M. J. Driver and K. R. Brousseau, *The Driver-Brousseau Career Concept Model* (Los Angeles, CA: Decision Dynamics Corporation). Adapted with permission.

EXHIBIT 11.6   Sample Items from Career Concepts Questionnaire

DIRECTIONS: The following paragraphs describe very different types of careers. After reading the paragraphs, consider how well each specific pattern describes your ideal career.

Type 1 Career: Major functional career changes typically every five to ten years. These changes involve moves to different but related skill areas and activities (i.e., the new skills built upon existing skills). These changes may involve either lateral or upward movement.

Type 2 Career: Staying in one general career area and continually moving up to higher levels in the organization or occupational group. Positions not representing upward movement are desirable only if they provide the basis for later upward movement.

Type 3 Career: Staying in one chosen area or field. The principal activities involve exercising or refining skills and capabilities in that career area, rather than moving on to different career areas or even higher levels in an organization.

Type 4 Career: Major changes in career area typically every one to four years. These changes do not necessarily involve movement to higher levels in an organization or occupational group, but involve getting into completely new areas or fields that require distinctly different skills and activities unrelated, for the most part, to previous career areas.

Using the scales presented below, rate the extent to which each of the above patterns describes your preferred career (assuming no limitations).

	Very little	Some	Moderate	Considerable	Very Great
Type 1	1	2	3	4	5
Type 2	1	2	3	4	5
Type 3	1	2	3	4	5
Type 4	1	2	3	4	5

Note: Adapted from K. R. Brousseau and M. J. Driver, *Career Concept Questionnaire*, version 2.0 Ideal (Decisions Dynamics Corporation, 1981). Adapted with permission. For valid use, the entire questionnaire may be obtained from Decision Dynamics, Inc., 30423 Canwood Street, Suite 116, Angora Hills, CA 91301.

Experts; and individuals for whom a Type 4 career is most descriptive are characterized as *Transitories*. This is only a sample from the questionnaire but it illustrates how career concepts can be measured for internal assessment purposes.

Although the *Career Concepts Questionnaire* has had limited applicability to internal selection decisions, it may be an important tool for initial assessment decisions. For internal selection decisions, career concepts have three potential applications.

First, the organization could consider initially screening internal candidates for openings based on their career concepts, with the idea of screening out internal applicants whose career concept is inconsistent with the strategy of the business. It has been argued that Linears are most compatible with a business strategy of expansion, Experts are most compatible with a maintenance or quality business strategy, Spirals are most compatible with diversification and new ventures strategies, and Transitories are most compatible with opportunistic (e.g., takeover) or novel (e.g., new product development) strategies.

Second, applicants could be matched to career cultures on the basis of their career concepts. Individuals are most likely to be happy and motivated by career systems that match their self-concept. Accordingly, Linears are most likely to thrive in tall, pyramidal organizations where upward movement is emphasized. Experts should be happy with and motivated by well-defined jobs and rules where quality and reliability are rewarded. Spiral career types are most likely to function well in matrix or open organizational designs and where creativity and developing others is expected. Transitories thrive in ad-hoc assignments where immediate results are expected.

Third, career concepts could be used to make assignments in transforming or high-change environments. We have conducted a study of managers in a transforming organization and found that Transitory career types dealt much better with change than Linears or Spirals, while Expert career types dealt much worse with change.

The career concepts approach is a relatively novel (and thus untested) approach to internal selection. Thus, organizations using this approach must make an effort to ensure that it has validity for its intended use. However, such efforts may be worthwhile, as the approach can help remedy the ever-increasing problem of placing employees into assignments that do not match their career concepts.

Choice of Initial Assessment Methods

As was discussed, there are several formal and informal methods of initial assessment available to screen internal applicants in order to produce a list of candidates. Research has been conducted on the effectiveness of each method, which will now be presented to help determine which initial assessment methods should be used.[5] The reviews of this research are summarized in Exhibit 11.7.

In Exhibit 11.7, the same criteria are applied to evaluating the effectiveness of these predictors as were used to evaluate the effectiveness of predictors for external selection. Cost refers to expenses incurred in using the predictor. Reliability refers to the consistency of measurement. Validity refers to the strength of the relationship between the predictor and job performance. Low validity refers to validity in the range of about .00 to .15, moderate validity corresponds to validity in the range of about .16 to .30, and high validity is .31 and above. Utility refers to the monetary

EXHIBIT 11.7   Evaluation of Initial Assessment Methods

Predictors	Use	Cost	Reliability	Validity	Utility	Reactions	Adverse Impact
Self-nominations	Low	Low	Moderate	Moderate	?	Mixed	?
Skills inventories	High	High	Moderate	Moderate	?	?	?
Peer assessments	Low	Low	High	High	?	Negative	?
Managerial sponsorship	Low	Moderate	?	?	?	Positive	?
Informal methods	High	Low	?	?	?	Mixed	?
Career concepts	Low	Low	High	?	?	?	?

return, minus costs, associated with using the predictor. Adverse impact refers to the possibility that a disproportionate number of women and minorities are rejected using this predictor. Finally, reaction refers to the likely impact on applicants.

Two points should be made about the effectiveness of initial internal selection methods. First, skills inventories and informal methods are used extensively. This suggests that many organizations continue to rely upon closed rather than open internal recruitment systems. Certainly this is a positive procedure when administrative ease is of importance. However, it must be noted that these approaches may result in the overlooking of talented applicants for candidate status. Also, there may be a discriminatory impact on women and minorities.

The second point to be made is that peer assessment methods are very promising in terms of reliability and validity. They are not frequently used, but need to be given more consideration by organizations as a screening device. Perhaps this will take place as organizations continue to decentralize decision making and empower employees to make business decisions historically made only by the supervisor.

SUBSTANTIVE ASSESSMENT METHODS

The internal applicant pool is narrowed down to candidates using the initial assessment methods. A decision as to which internal candidates will become finalists is usually made using the following substantive assessment methods: seniority and experience, job knowledge tests, performance appraisal, promotability ratings, assessment centers, interview simulations, and review boards. After each of these methods is discussed, an evaluation is made.

Seniority and Experience

At first blush the concepts of seniority and experience may seem the same. In fact, they may be quite different. Seniority typically refers to length of service or tenure with the organization, department, or job. For example, company seniority is measured as length of continuous employment in an organization and is operationalized as the difference between the present date of employment and the date of hire. Thus, seniority is a purely quantitative measure that has nothing to do with the type or quality of job experiences.

Conversely, experience generally has a broader meaning. While seniority may be one aspect of experience, experience also reflects *type* of experience. Two employees working in the same company for 20 years may have the same level of seniority but very different levels of experience if one employee has performed a number of different jobs, worked in different areas of the organization, enrolled in various training programs, and so on. Thus, experience includes not only length of service in the organization or in various positions in the organization, but also the kinds of activities employees have undertaken in those positions. Thus, although seniority and experience are often considered to be synonymous, they are quite different and—as we will see in the following discussion—these differences have real implications for internal selection decisions.

Use and Evaluation

Seniority and experience are among the most prevalent methods of internal selection. In most unionized companies, heavy reliance is placed on seniority over other KSAOs for advancement.[6] Between two-thirds and four-fifths of union contracts stipulate that seniority be considered in promotion decisions, and about 50% mandate that it be the determining factor. In policy, nonunion organizations claim to place less weight on seniority than other factors in making advancement decisions. In practice, however, at least one study showed that regardless of the wording in policy statements, heavy emphasis is still placed on seniority in nonunion settings.[7] Research has shown that seniority is more likely to be used for promotions in small, unionized, and capital-intensive companies.[8] Although little data are available, there is reason to be believe that experience also is frequently considered in internal selection decisions.

There are various reasons why seniority and experience are so widely used as methods of internal selection decisions. First, organizations believe that direct experience in a job content area reflects an accumulated stock of KSAOs necessary to perform the job.[9] In short, experience may be content valid because it reflects on-the-job experience. Second, seniority and experience information is easily and cheaply obtained. Furthermore, unions believe that reliance on objective measures such as seniority and experience protects the employee from capricious treatment and favoritism. Finally, promoting experienced or senior individuals is socially acceptable because it is seen as rewarding loyalty. In fact, it has been found that most decision makers feel that negative repercussions would result if a more junior employee is promoted over a more senior employee.

In evaluating seniority and experience as methods of internal selection, it is important to return to our earlier distinction between the two concepts. Several studies have found that seniority is unrelated to job performance.[10] In fact, one study of unionized plants found that 97% of the promotions went to the most senior employee, yet in nearly half the cases this person was not the highest performer. Thus, seniority does not seem to be a particularly valid method of internal selection. In fact, the "Big Three" automakers cite abandoning seniority for promotions as a reason for their improved performance in the mid-1990s.[11]

As compared to seniority, evidence for the validity of experience is somewhat more positive. Several large-scale studies have shown that experience is moderately related to job performance.[12] Research suggests that experience is predictive of job performance in the short run, followed by a plateau during which experience loses its ability to predict job performance. It appears that most of the effect of experience on performance is due to the fact that experienced employees have greater job knowledge. However, while seniority may result in increased performance due to greater job knowledge, it does not remedy performance difficulties due to low ability; initial performance deficits of low-ability employees are not remedied by increased experience over time.[13] Thus, while experience is more likely to be related to job performance than seniority, neither ranks among the most valid predictors for internal selection decisions.

Based on the research evidence, several conclusions about the use of seniority and experience in internal selection decisions seem appropriate:

1. Experience is a more valid method of internal selection than seniority (although unionized employers may have little choice but to use seniority).
2. Experience is better suited to predict short-term rather than long-term potential.
3. Experience is more likely to be content valid if the past or present jobs are similar to the future job.
4. Employees seem to expect that promotions will go to the most senior or experienced employee, so using seniority or experience for promotions may yield positive reactions from employees.
5. Experience is unlikely to remedy initial performance difficulties of low-ability employees.

Job Knowledge Tests

Job knowledge measures one's mastery of the concepts needed to perform certain work. Job knowledge is a complex concept that includes elements of both ability (capacity to learn) and seniority (opportunity to learn). It is usually measured with a paper-and-pencil test. In order to develop a paper-and-pencil test to assess job knowledge, the content domain from which test questions will be constructed must be clearly identified. For example, a job knowledge test used to select sales managers from among salespeople must identify the specific knowledges necessary for being a successful sales manager.

An innovative video-based job knowledge test to be used as part of the promotion system was developed by Federal Express Corporation.[14] Federal Express developed the interactive video test to assess employees' ability to deal with customers. The test is based on job analysis data derived from the critical tasks necessary to deliver high levels of customer service. The test, termed QUEST (Quality Using Electronic Systems Training), presents employees with a menu of modules on CD-ROM (e.g., delivering packages, defensive driving, etc.). A 90% competency level on the test is established as the expectation for minimum performance—and subsequent promotability. This suggests that such assessments could fruitfully be used in internal selection decisions when promoting employees into customer-sensitive positions. The greater the portfolio of customer skills employees have, the better able they should be to help Federal Express meet its customer service goals.

Although job knowledge is not a well-researched method of either internal or external employee selection, it holds great promise as a predictor of job performance. This is because it reflects an assessment of previous experiences of an applicant and an important KSAO, namely cognitive ability.[15]

Performance Appraisal

One possible predictor of future job performance is past job performance. This assumes, of course, that elements of the future job are similar to the past job. Data on employees' previous performance is routinely collected as a part of the performance appraisal process and thus available for use in internal selection.

One advantage of performance appraisals over other internal assessment methods is that they are readily available in many organizations. Another desirable feature of performance appraisals is that they likely capture both ability and motivation. Hence, they offer a very complete look at the person's qualifications for the job. Care must still be taken in using performance appraisals because there is not always a direct correspondence between the requirements of the current job and the requirements of the position applied for. Performance appraisals should only be used as predictors when job analysis indicates a close relationship between the current job and position applied for.

For example, performance in a highly technical position (e.g., scientist, engineer) may require certain skills (e.g., quantitative skills) that are required in both junior- and senior-level positions. As a result, using the results of the performance appraisal of the junior position is appropriate in predicting the performance in the senior position. It is not, however, appropriate to use the results of the performance appraisal for the junior-level technical job to predict performance in a job, such as manager, requiring a different set of skills (e.g., planning, organizing, staffing).

Although there are some advantages to using performance appraisal results for internal selection, they are far from perfect predictors. They are subject to many influences that have nothing to do with the likelihood of success in a future job.[16]

The well-known "Peter Principle"—that individuals rise to their lowest level of incompetence—illustrates another limitation with using performance appraisal as a method of internal staffing decisions.[17] The argument behind the Peter Principle is that if organizations promote individuals on the basis of their past performance, the only time that people stop being promoted is when they are poor performers at the job into which they were last promoted. Thus, over time, organizations will have internally staffed positions with individuals who are incompetent. In fact, the authors have data from a *Fortune 100* company showing that less than one-fifth of the variance in an employee's current performance rating can be explained by their previous three year's performance ratings. Thus, although past performance may have some validity in predicting future performance, the relationship may not be overly strong.

This is not to suggest that organizations should abandon using performance ratings as a factor in internal staffing decisions. Rather, the validity of using performance appraisal as an internal selection method may depend on a number of considerations. Exhibit 11.8 provides several questions that should be used in deciding how much weight to place on performance appraisal as a means of making internal selection decisions. Affirmative answers to these questions suggest that past performance may be validly used in making internal selection decisions.

Promotability Ratings

In many organizations, an assessment of promotability (assessment of potential for higher-level job) is made at the same time that performance appraisals are conducted. An example of a form to be used for such an assessment is shown in Exhibit 11.9.

Promotability ratings are useful not only from a selection perspective, but from a recruitment perspective as well. By discussing what is needed to be promotable, employee development may be encouraged as well as coupled with organizational sponsorship of the opportunities needed to develop. In turn, the development of new skills in employees increases the internal recruitment pool for promotions.

Caution must be exercised in using promotability ratings as well. If employees receive separate evaluations for purposes of performance appraisal, promotability, and pay, the possibility exists of mixed messages going out to employees that may be difficult for them to interpret. For example, it is difficult to understand why one receives an excellent performance rating and a solid pay raise, but at the same time is rated as not promotable. Care must be taken to show employees the relevant judgments that are being made in each assessment. In the example presented, it must be clearly indicated that promotion is based not only upon past performance, but is also based on skill acquisition and opportunities for advancement.

EXHIBIT 11.8   Questions to Ask in Using Performance Appraisal as a Method of Internal Staffing Decisions

---

- Is the performance appraisal process reliable and unbiased?
- Is future job content representative of present job content?
- Have the KSAOs required for performance in the future job(s) been acquired and demonstrated in the previous job(s)?
- Is the organizational or job environment stable such that what lead to past job success will lead to future job success?

EXHIBIT 11.9   Promotability Rating Form

Form BIA-4450	DEPARTMENT OF THE INTERIOR	44 BIAM335
(4/22/92)	BUREAU OF INDIAN AFFAIRS	Illustration 4
		Page 1 of 2

SUPERVISORY APPRAISAL OF DEMONSTRATED
PERFORMANCE OF POTENTIAL

ANNOUNCEMENT NO. CO-92-125

PLEASE HAVE THIS APPRAISAL COMPLETED BY YOUR
SUPERVISOR AND SUBMIT WITH YOUR APPLICATION.
SF-171 (If the appraisal is submitted directly by the
Supervisor, the Applicant will be permitted to review
and/or obtain a copy of the appraisal upon request.)

Name of Applicant: _____   Position: Program Specialist _____

Basis of Appraisal					Level of Performance			
Check One					Check as appropriate:			
Outside Activities	On-the-job Performance	Formal Training	Unable to Appraise	RANKING FACTORS (Knowledge, Skills, Abilities, and Personal Characteristics)	4 – Exceptional 3 – Above average 2 – Average/Satisfactory 1 – Rarely Satisfactory			
					4	3	2	1
				1. Knowledge of the Bureau of Indian Affairs' mission, organizaton, structure, policies, and functions, as they relate to Real Estate.				
				2. Knowledge of technical administrative requirements to provide technical guidance in administrative areas, such as personnel regulations, travel regulations, time and attendance requirements, budget documents, Privacy Act, and Freedom of Information Act, etc.				
				3. Ability to work with program directors and administrative staff and ability to apply problem solving techniques and management concepts; ability to analyze facts and problems and develop alternatives.				
				4. Ability to operate various Computer programs and methodology in the analysis and design of automated methods for meeting the information and reporting requirements for the Division.				
				5. Knowledge of the Bureau Budget process and statistical Profile of all field operations that impact in the Real Estate Services program.				

44 BIAM, 335, REL. 127, 4/22/92   *(continued)*

EXHIBIT 11.9 Continued

Form BIA-4450   DEPARTMENT OF THE INTERIOR   44 BIAM 335
(Rev. 4/22/92)   BUREAU OF INDIAN AFFAIRS   Illustration 4
                                                          Page 2 of 2

SUPERVISORY APPRAISAL OF DEMONSTRATED
PERFORMANCE OF POTENTIAL

ANNOUNCEMENT NO.: CO-92-125

NARRATIVE: BRIEFLY EVALUATE THE CANDIDATE'S OVERALL ABILITY TO PERFORM THE DUTIES AND RESPONSIBILITIES OF THE POSITION. NARRATIVE COMMENTS ARE REQUIRED FOR ALL EVALUATIONS.

IN WHAT CAPACITY ARE YOU MAKING THIS APPRAISAL? (Please ✓ as appropriate)

( ) Present Immediate Supervisor   ( ) Present 2nd Level Supervisor   ( ) Other
                                                                          (Specify)
( ) Former Immediate Supervisor   ( ) Former 2nd Level Supervisor

---

Period during which you supervised the Applicant:
                              From: To:

Appraiser:

          (Signature)   (Date)   (Phone No.)

Source: Department of the Interior, Bureau of Indian Affairs, Form BIA-4450 (4/22/92).

Assessment Centers

An elaborate method of employee selection, primarily used internally, is known as an assessment center. An assessment center is a collection of predictors used to forecast success, primarily in higher-level jobs. It is used for higher-level jobs because of the high costs involved in conducting the center. The assessment center can be used to select employees for lower-level jobs as well, though this is rarely done.

The theory behind assessment centers is relatively straightforward. Concern is with the prediction of an individual's behavior and effectiveness in critical roles, usually managerial ones. Since these roles require complex behavior, multiple KSAOs will predict those behaviors. Hence, there is a need to carefully identify and assess those KSAOs. This will require multiple methods of assessing the KSAOs, as well as multiple assessors. The result should be higher validity than could be obtained from a single assessment method or assessor.

As with any sound selection procedure, the assessment center predictors are based on job analysis to identify KSAOs and aid in the construction of content valid methods of assessment for those KSAOs. As a result, a selection plan must be developed when using assessment centers. An example of such a selection plan is shown in Exhibit 11.10.

Characteristics of Assessment Centers

While specific characteristics vary from situation to situation, assessment centers generally have some common characteristics.[18] Job candidates usually participate in an assessment center for a period of days rather than hours. Most assessment centers last two to three days, but some may be as long as five days. Exhibit 11.11 is an example of a 3-day assessment center (exercises are defined below). Participants take part in a series of simulations and work sample tests known as exercises. The participants may also be assessed with other devices, such as interviews, personality and ability tests, and biographical information blanks. As they participate in the exercises, trained assessors evaluate participants' performance. Assessors are usually line managers, but sometimes psychologists are used as well. The average ratio of assessors to assessees ranges from 1:1 to 4:1.

The participants in the center are usually managers who are being assessed for higher-level managerial jobs. Normally, they are chosen to participate by other organizational members, such as their supervisor. Often selection is based on an employee's current level of job performance.

At the conclusion of the assessment center, the participants are evaluated by the assessors. Typically, this involves the assessor examining all of the information gathered about each participant. The information is then translated into a series of ratings on several dimensions of managerial jobs. Typical dimensions assessed include communications (written and oral), leadership and human relations, and planning, problem solving, and decision making. In evaluating these dimensions,

EXHIBIT 11.10   Selection Plan for an Assessment Center

KSAO	Writing Exercise	Speech Exercise	Analysis Problem	In-Basket Tent.	In-Basket Final	Leadership Group Discussion Management Problems	Leadership Group Discussion City Council
Oral communications					X	X	X
Oral presentation		X				X	
Written communications	X		X	X	X		
Stress tolerance				X	X	X	
Leadership					X	X	
Sensitivity			X	X	X	X	X
Tenacity				X	X	X	
Risk taking			X	X	X	X	X
Initiative			X	X	X	X	X
Planning & organization			X	X	X	X	X
Management control			X	X	X		
Delegation				X	X		
Problem analysis			X	X	X	X	X
Decision making			X	X	X	X	X
Decisiveness			X	X	X	X	X
Responsiveness			X	X	X	X	X

Source: Department of Employment Relations, State of Wisconsin.

EXHIBIT 11.11   Assessment Center Program Schedule

Sunday	P.M.	Candidates arrive for social hour, orientation, meeting, and discussion.
Monday	A.M.	Leaderless group discussion. The candidates were divided into two groups of five to discuss a possible business investment. Each group was observed by three assessors who took notes on the total activity and the individual participants.
	P.M.	1. Individual interview with clinical psychologist.
		2. Psychological testing with candidates for assessment information and research purposes.
Tuesday	A.M.	Individual exercise (in-basket).
	P.M.	1. Interview regarding in-basket performance.
		2. Additional testing.
		3. Group exercise.
Wednesday	A.M.	Case analysis.
	P.M.	1. Assessors write two to three page narrative reports based on observation of participants.
		2. Candidates are notified of their overall assessment.

---

assessors are trained to look for critical behaviors that represent highly effective or ineffective responses to the exercise situations in which participants are placed. There may also be an overall assessment rating (OAR) that represents the bottom-line evaluation for each participant. Exhibit 11.12 provides a sample rating form.

A variety of different exercises are used at a center, but those most frequently used are the in-basket exercise, leaderless group discussions, and case analysis. Each of these exercises will be briefly described.

In-Basket Exercise   An element common to most higher-level positions is an in-basket. The in-basket usually contains memoranda, reports, phone calls, and letters that require a response. In an assessment center, a simulated in-basket is presented to the candidate. The candidate is asked to respond to the paperwork in the in-basket by prioritizing items, drafting memos, scheduling meetings, and so forth. It is a timed exercise, and usually the candidate has two to three hours to respond. Even when used alone, the in-basket exercise seems to forecast ascendancy, one of the key criteria of assessment centers.[19]

Leaderless Group Discussion   In a leaderless group discussion, a small group of candidates is given a problem to work on. The problem is one they would likely

---

EXHIBIT 11.12   Sample Assessment Center Rating Form

Participant Name: _____

Personal Qualities:

    1. Energy   _____

    2. Risk-taking   _____

    3. Tolerance for ambiguity   _____

    4. Objectivity   _____

    5. Reliability   _____

Communication Skills:

    6. Oral   _____

    7. Written   _____

    8. Persuasion   _____

Human Relations:

    9. Teamwork   _____

    10. Flexibility   _____

    11. Awareness of social environment   _____

Leadership Skills:

    12. Impact   _____

    13. Autonomy   _____

Decision-Making Skills:

    14. Decisiveness   _____

    15. Organizing   _____

    16. Planning   _____

Problem-Solving Skills:

    17. Fact-Finding   _____

    18. Interpreting information   _____

Overall Assessment Rating:

Indication of potential to perform
effectively at the next level is:

    Excellent   _____

    Good   _____

    Moderate   _____

    Low   _____

---

encounter in the higher-level position for which they are applying. As a group, they are asked to resolve the problem. As they work on the problem, assessors sit around the perimeter of the group and evaluate how each candidate behaves in an unstructured setting. They look for skills such as leadership and communication.

Case Analysis   Cases of actual business situations can also be presented to the candidates. Each candidate is asked to provide a written analysis of the case, describing the nature of the problem, likely causes, and recommended solutions. Not only are the written results evaluated, but the candidate's oral report is scored as well. The candidates may be asked to give an oral presentation to a panel of managers and to respond to their questions, comments, and concerns.

Validity and Effective Practices

In a study of 50 different assessment centers, their average validity was very favorable ($\bar{r} = .37$). This study showed that the validity of the assessment center was higher when multiple predictors were used, when assessors were psychologists rather than managers, and when peer evaluations as well as assessor evaluations were used. The latter results question the common practice of using only managers as assessors. It suggests that multiple assessors be used, including psychologists and peers as well as managers. Such usage provides a different perspective on participants' performance, one which may be overlooked by managers.[20]

There are some problems with past assessment center research.[21] One of the most commonly cited problems is the "crown prince or princess" syndrome. Here, it is alleged, decision makers may know how people did on the assessment center and therefore promote those who did well versus those who did not do well. Thus, assessment centers could be a self-fulfilling prophecy—they are valid only because decision makers think they are. However, research indicates that assessment centers are valid even when the results of the assessment center are "blind" to decision makers. Thus, due to the validity of assessment centers, they should be seriously considered in making promotion decisions—if they can be afforded.

There is little research that has examined participant reactions to assessment centers. However, it is commonly noted that while assessment centers are stressful to participants, they generate positive reactions for assessors and assesses. This probably is partly due to the fact that they are seen as valid by participants. Furthermore, they may result in increased self-confidence for participants, even for those who are not promoted as a result of the assessment center. The positive effects of assessment centers on employee attitudes and self-confidence may be relatively fleeting, however, as one study of British managers found.[22] Thus, it is possible that the positive impact of assessment centers on assessees wanes over time.

Interview Simulations

An interview simulation simulates the oral communication required on the job. It is sometimes used in an assessment center, but it is used less frequently than in-baskets, leaderless group discussions, and case analysis. It is also used as a predictor separate from the assessment center. There are several different forms of interview simulations.[23]

Role-Play

With a role-play, the job candidate is placed in a simulated situation where she must interact with a person at work, such as the boss, a subordinate, or a customer. The interviewer or someone else plays one role, and the job candidate plays the role of the person in the position for which she has applied. So, for example, in selecting someone to be promoted to a supervisory level, the job candidate may be asked to role-play dealing with a difficult employee.

Fact Finding

In a fact-finding interview, the job candidate is presented with a case or problem with incomplete information. It is the job of the candidate to solicit from the interviewer or a resource person the additional facts needed to resolve the case. If one was hiring someone to be an equal employment opportunity manager, one might present him with a case where adverse impact is suggested, and then evaluate the candidate according to what data he solicits to confirm or disconfirm adverse impact.

Oral Presentations

In many jobs, presentations need to be made to customers, clients, or even boards of directors. To select someone to perform this role, an oral presentation can be required. This approach would be useful, for example, to see what sort of "sales pitch" a consultant might make or to see how an executive would present his or her proposed strategic plan to a board of directors.

Given the importance of interpersonal skills in many jobs, it is unfortunate that not many organizations use interview simulations. This is especially true with internal selection where the organization knows if the person has the right credentials (e.g., company experiences, education, and training), but may not know if the person has the right interpersonal "chemistry" to fit in with the work group. Interview simulations allow for a systematic assessment of this chemistry rather than relying upon the instinct of the interviewer. To be effective, these interviews need to be structured and evaluated according to observable behaviors identified in the job analysis as necessary for successful performance.

Promotion Panels and Review Boards

In the public sector, it is a common practice to use a panel or board of people to review the qualifications of candidates. Frequently, a combination of both internal and external candidates are being assessed. Typically, the panel or board consists of job experts, human resource professionals, and representatives from constituencies in the community that the board represents. Having a board such as this hire public servants, such as school superintendents or fire and police officials, offers two advantages. First, as with assessment centers, there are multiple assessors with which to ensure a complete and accurate assessment of the candidate's qualifications. Second, by participating in the selection process, constituents are likely to be more committed to the decision reached. This "buy-in" is particularly important for community representatives with whom the job candidate will interact. It is hoped that by having a voice in the process, they will be less likely to voice objections once the candidate is hired.

Choice of Substantive Assessment Methods

Along with research on initial assessment methods, there has also been research conducted on substantive assessment methods.[24] The reviews of this research are summarized in Exhibit 11.13. The same criteria are applied to evaluating the effectiveness of these predictors as were used to evaluate the effectiveness of initial assessment methods.

An examination of Exhibit 11.13 indicates that there is no one best method of narrowing down the candidate list to finalists. What is suggested, however, is that some predictors are more likely to be effective than are others. In particular, job knowledge, promotability ratings, and assessment centers have a strong record in terms of reliability and validity in choosing candidates. A very promising development for internal selection is use of job knowledge tests. The validity of these tests appears to be substantial, but, unfortunately, few organizations use them for internal selection purposes.

The effectiveness of several internal selection predictors (case analysis, interview simulations, panels and review boards) is not known at this stage. Interview simulations appear to be a promising technique for jobs requiring public contact skills. All of them need additional research. Other areas in need of additional research are the utility, reactions, and adverse impact associated with all of the substantive assessment methods.

DISCRETIONARY ASSESSMENT METHODS

Discretionary methods are used to narrow down the list of finalists to those who will receive job offers. Sometimes all finalists will receive offers, but other times, there may not be enough positions to fill for each finalist to receive an offer. As with external selection, discretionary assessments are sometimes made on the basis of organizational citizenship behavior and staffing philosophy regarding EEO/AA.

There are two areas of discretionary assessment that differ from external selection and need to be considered in deciding job offers. First, previous finalists who

EXHIBIT 11.13 Evaluation of Substantive Assessment Methods

Predictors	Use	Cost	Reliability	Validity	Utility	Reactions	Adverse Impact
Seniority	High	Low	High	Low	?	?	High
Experience	High	Low	High	Moderate	High	Positive	Mixed
Job knowledge tests	Low	Moderate	High	High	?	?	?
Performance appraisal	Moderate	Moderate	?	Moderate	?	?	?
Promotability ratings	Low	Low	High	High	?	?	?
Assessment center	Low	High	High	High	High	?	?
In-basket exercise	Low	Moderate	Moderate	Moderate	High	Mixed	Mixed
Leaderless group discussion	Low	Low	Moderate	Moderate	?	?	?
Case analysis	Low	Low	?	Moderate	?	?	?
Interview simulations	Low	Low	?	?	?	?	?
Panels and review boards	Low	?	?	?	?	?	?

do not receive job offers do not disappear. They may remain with the organization in hopes of securing an offer next time the position is open. At the margin, this may be a factor in decision making because being bypassed a second time may create a disgruntled employee. As a result, a previous finalist may be given an offer over a first-time finalist, all other things being equal.

Second, multiple assessors are generally used with internal selection. That is, not only can the hiring manager's opinion be used to select who will receive a job offer, but so can the opinions of others (e.g., previous manager, top management) who are knowledgeable about the candidate's profile and the requirements of the current position. As a result, in deciding which candidates will receive job offers, evaluations by people other than the hiring manager may be accorded substantial weight in the decision-making process.

APPLICANT REACTIONS

While applicant reactions to an external staffing process are an important part of its evaluation, such reactions are likely to be even more important for internal candidates. Organizations are likely to be more reticent to use a negatively perceived selection measure for internal than external applicants. While it may be understandable to leave external *applicants* unhappy with the selection process, the consequences of causing a valued *employee* to be dissatisfied are even more serious. While there is little research on applicant reactions to internal selection processes, one experiment conducted in a large service company in Israel found that nonpromoted candidates reported greater feelings of inequity, lower commitment to the organization, and heightened levels of absenteeism.[25] Thus, organizations must realize that internal promotions may carry with them negative consequences for the employees who are not selected.

Research also suggests that employees who feel unfairly treated by an organization restore equity ("get even") with a variety of behaviors ranging from reducing work effort to stealing.[26] This suggests that employees who feel unfairly treated in the selection process may behave in ways that are likely to be seen as undesirable by organizations. Any useful selection process will lead to the rejection of some employees and thus it is impossible to make everyone happy with the results of internal selection decisions. However, research has suggested that beliefs that the process is unfair are more important in influencing subsequent attitudes and behaviors than negative feelings resulting from rejection. Thus, organizations who ensure that the internal process is fair will mitigate many of the negative consequences of rejecting internal applicants.

COLLECTION OF ASSESSMENT DATA

As with external selection, the careful administration of internal selection predictors is crucial for measurement, legal, and motivation reasons. Attention must be given to support services, required expertise, security, privacy and confidentiality, and standardization (see Chapter 10). With internal selection, a premium must be placed on security. Unlike with external selection, where applicants are physically outside the organization, applicants in internal selection are physically inside the organization. As a result, internal applicants potentially have far greater access to private and confidential selection materials. Computer files regarding internal selection must be carefully set up so that only authorized personnel have access to them. Clerks, secretaries, and anyone having access to manual files must be trained and held accountable to procedures designed to safeguard manual files.

LEGAL ISSUES

From a legal perspective, methods and processes of internal selection are to be viewed in the same ways as external selection ones. The laws and regulations make no major distinctions between them. Consequently, most of the legal influences on internal selection have already been treated in Chapters 9 and 10. There are, however, some brief comments to be made about internal selection legal influences. Those influences are the Uniform Guidelines on Employee Selection Procedures (UGESP), and the glass ceiling.

Uniform Guidelines on Employee Selection Procedures

It should be remembered that the UGESP (see Appendix A) defines a "selection procedure" in such a way that virtually any selection method, be it used in an external or internal context, is covered by the requirements of the UGESP. It should also be remembered that the UGESP applies to any "employment decision," which explicitly includes promotion decisions.

When there is adverse impact in promotions, the organization is given the option of justifying it through the conduct of validation studies. These are primarily criterion-related or content validity studies. Ideally, criterion-related studies with predictive validation designs will be used, as has been partially done in the case of assessment centers. Unfortunately, this places substantial administrative and research demands on the organization that are difficult to fulfill most of the time. Consequently, content validation appears a better bet for validation purposes.

Many of the methods of assessment used in internal selection attempt to gauge KSAOs and behaviors directly associated with a current job that are felt to be related to success in higher-level jobs. Examples include seniority, performance appraisals, and promotability ratings. These are based on current, as well as past, job content. Validation of these methods, if necessary legally, likely occurs along content validation lines. The organization thus should pay particular and close attention to the validation and documentation requirements for content validation in the UGESP.

The Glass Ceiling

In Chapter 8, the nature of the glass ceiling was discussed, as well as staffing steps to remove it from organizational promotion systems. Most of that discussion centered on internal recruitment and supporting activities that could be undertaken. Surprisingly, selection methods used for promotion assessment are rarely mentioned in literature on the glass ceiling.

This is a major oversight. While the internal recruitment practices recommended may enhance the identification and attraction of minority and women candidates for promotion, effectively matching them to their new jobs requires application of internal selection processes and methods. What might this require of an organization committed to shattering the glass ceiling?

The first possibility is for greater use of selection plans. As discussed in Chapter 9, these plans lay out the KSAOs required for a job, which KSAOs are necessary to bring to the job (as opposed to being acquired on the job), and of those necessary, the most appropriate method of assessment for each. Such a plan forces an organization to conduct job analysis, construct career ladders or KSAO lattices, and consider alternatives to many of the traditional methods of assessment used in promotion systems.

A second suggestion is for the organization to back away from use of these traditional methods of assessment as much as possible, in ways consistent with the selection plan. This means a move away from casual, subjective methods, such as supervisory recommendation, typical promotability ratings, quick reviews of personnel files, and informal recommendations. In their place should come more formal, standardized, and job-related assessment methods. Examples here include assessment centers, promotion review boards or panels, and interview simulations.

A final suggestion is for the organization to pay close attention to the types of KSAOs necessary for advancement, and undertake programs to impart these KSAOs to aspiring employees. These developmental actions might include key job and committee assignments, participation in conferences and other networking opportunities, mentoring and coaching programs, and skill acquisition in formal training programs. Internal selection methods would then be used to assess proficiency on these newly acquired KSAOs, in accordance with the selection plan.

SUMMARY

The selection of internal candidates follows a process very similar to the selection of external candidates. The logic of prediction is applied and a selection plan is developed and implemented.

One important area where internal and external selection methods differ is in the nature of the predictor. Predictors used for internal selection tend to have greater depth and more relevance, and are better suited for verification. As a result, there are often different types of predictors used for internal than for external selection decisions.

Initial assessment methods are used to narrow down the applicant pool to a qualified set of candidates. Approaches used are skills inventories, peer assessments, self-assessments, managerial sponsorship, informal discussions and recommendations, and career concepts. Of these approaches, no one approach is particularly strong in predicting future performance. Hence, consideration should be given to using multiple predictors to verify the accuracy of any one method. These results also point to the need to use substantive as well as initial assessment methods in making internal selection decisions.

Substantive assessment methods are used to select finalists from the list of candidates. Predictors used to make these decisions include seniority and experience, job knowledge tests, performance appraisals, promotability ratings, the assessment center, interview simulations, and panels and review boards. Of this set of predictors, ones that work well are job knowledge tests, promotability ratings, and assessment centers. Organizations need to give greater consideration to the latter three predictors to supplement traditional seniority and experience.

Although very costly, the assessment center seems to be very effective. The reason that it is so effective is that it is grounded in behavioral science theory and the logic of prediction. In particular, samples of behavior are analyzed, multiple assessors and predictors are used, and predictors are developed on the basis of job analysis.

Internal job applicants have the potential for far greater access to selection data than do external job applicants due to their physical proximity to the data. As a result, procedures must be implemented to ensure that manual and computer files with sensitive data are kept private and confidential.

Two areas of legal concern for internal selection decisions are the Uniform Guidelines on Employee Selection Procedures (UGESP), and the glass ceiling. In terms of the UGESP, particular care must be taken to ensure that internal selection methods are valid if adverse impact is occurring. In order to minimize glass ceiling effects, organizations should make greater use of selection plans and more objective internal assessment methods, as well as help impart the KSAOs necessary for advancement.

DISCUSSION QUESTIONS

1. Explain how internal selection decisions differ from external selection decisions.

2. What are the differences between peer ratings, peer nominations, and peer rankings?

3. Explain the theory behind assessment centers.

4. Describe the three different types of interview simulations.

5. Evaluate the effectiveness of seniority, assessment centers, and job knowledge as substantive internal selection procedures.

6. What steps should be taken by an organization that is committed to shattering the glass ceiling?

APPLICATIONS

Changing a Promotion System

Bioglass Inc. specializes in sales of a wide array of glass products. One area of the company, the Commercial Sales Division (CSD), specializes in the selling of high-tech mirrors and microscope and photographic lenses. Sales associates in CSD are responsible for selling the glass products to corporate clients. In CSD there are four levels of sales associates, ranging in pay from $28,000 to $76,000 per year. There are also four levels of managerial positions in CSD; those positions range in pay from $76,000 to $110,000 per year (that's what the division president makes).

Tom Caldwell has been a very effective sales associate. He has consistently demonstrated good sales techniques in his 17 years with Bioglass and has a large and loyal client base. Over the years, Tom has risen from the lowest level of sales associate to the highest. He has proven himself successful at each stage. An entry- (first-) level management position in CSD opened up last year and Tom was the natural candidate. Although several other candidates were given consideration, Tom was the clear choice for the position.

However, once in the position, Tom had a great deal of difficulty being a manager. He was not accustomed to delegating, and rarely provided feedback or guidance to the people he supervised. Although he set goals for himself, he never set performance goals for his workers. Morale in Tom's group was low, and group performance suffered. The company felt that demoting Tom back to sales would be disastrous to Tom and present the wrong image to other employees, and firing such a loyal employee was considered unacceptable. Therefore, Bioglass decided to keep Tom where he was but never promote him again. They were also considering enrolling Tom in some expensive managerial development programs to enhance his management skills.

Meanwhile, Tom's replacement, although successful at the lower three levels of sales associate positions, was having a great deal of difficulty with the large corporate contracts that the highest-level sales associates must service. Two of Tom's biggest clients had recently left Bioglass for a competitor. CSD was confused about how such a disastrous situation had developed when they seemed to make all the right decisions.

Based on this application and your reading of this chapter, answer the following questions:

1. What is the likely cause of CSD's problems?
2. How might CSD, and Bioglass more generally, make better promotion decisions in the future? Be specific.
3. In general, what role should performance appraisals play in internal selection decisions? Are there some cases in which they are more relevant than others? Explain.

Making a Promotion Decision

Animal Butchering Cooperative (ABC) is a cooperative association of pork processing plants headquartered in Swine City, Iowa. In the last 15 years, ABC has gone through a painful series of expansions and contractions corresponding to the ups and downs of pork consumption in the United States. These contractions and expansions have put ABC on a revolving door of hiring and firing from one year to the next. This hire-fire roller coaster causes ABC to incur costs that put them at a competitive disadvantage relative to other pork producers and processors of competing animal products (especially beef and chicken).

Six months ago, Bernie Bovine, CEO of ABC, attended a trade show in Bratisvlava, Slovakia and noticed the consistently strong demand for pork in the Czech and Slovak Republics. Bernie came back from the conference convinced that ABC could acquire several small-scale pork producers in the Czech and Slovak Republics and thereby smooth out demand for its pig products. In fact, this is exactly what ABC did. They formed a joint venture with Veprové Československé (VC), a medium-sized pork processing company with plants in Pilsen, Brno, Nové Město, and Bratislava. ABC has formally acquired the plants but VC continues to manage them. Although so far the joint venture has gone smoothly, due to language and cultural barriers, ABC feels it should have one of their managers oversee the VC operation. Recently, ABC internally posted the position for consideration of all ABC middle managers. ABC would consider the position a promotion, and accompanying the promotion is a considerable pay increase along with generous fringe benefits (relocation allowance, transportation allowance, etc.). Five managers applied for the assignment and ABC proceeded to administer several selection measures to the candidates. These selection measures consisted of the *Career Concepts Questionnaire,* a cognitive ability test, and a personality test of openness to experience (see Ch. 10). Additionally, ABC asked each candidate, using a 1 = poor to 5 = good scale, to rate his or her own ability to deal with change. The results from this assessment process, along with career and personal data (company tenure, most recent performance rating, family status), are presented in the exhibit.

In order to help ABC make this internal selection decision, answer the following questions:

1. Is the logic of prediction relevant to ABC's internal selection decision? Explain why or why not.
2. Rank order the candidates in terms of your recommendation for the VC assignment. What factors did you weigh most heavily in your decision and why?
3. What other information do you feel might be important to make a good decision? How would you obtain that information—what predictors would you use?
4. If ABC had this decision to make over again, would you collect all of the assessment data for all five candidates at once? Explain why or why not.

Exhibit
Scores of Finalists for Manager of VC Operations

	Candidate				
	Dunbar	Fisher	Earhart	Hempy	Weaver
	Assessment Data				
Career concept	Linear	Spiral	Transitory	Expert	Transitory
Cognitive ability test (% items correct)	84%	76%	85%	89%	91%
Openness to experience (1 = low to 10 = high)	5	7	8	2	10
Self assessment of change (1 = poor to 5 = good)	4	5	5	4	5
	Career Data				
Tenure at ABC	2 years	16 years	4 years	6 years	25 years
Performance rating (1 = low to 5 = high)	3	3	4	5	4
Family status	Single no children	Married 2 children	Divorced 2 children	Married no children	Married 4 children

ENDNOTES

1. A. Howard and D. W. Bray, "Predictions of Managerial Success Over Long Periods of Time: Lessons from the Management Progress Study," in K. E. Clark and M. B. Clark (eds.), *Measures of Leadership* (West Orange, NJ: Leadership Library of America, 1990), pp. 113–130; C. J. Russell "Selecting Top Corporate Leaders: An Example of Biographical Information," *Journal of Management*, 1990, 16, pp. 73–86; J. S. Schippman and E. P. Prien, "An Assessment of the

Contributions of General Mental Ability and Personality Characteristics to Management Success," *Journal of Business and Psychology*, 1989, 3, pp. 423–437.

2. M. J. Driver, "Demographic and Societal Factors Affecting the Linear Career Crisis," *Canadian Journal of Administrative Science*, 1985, 2, pp. 245–263; M. J. Driver, "Careers: A Review of Personal and Organizational Research," in C. I. Cooper and I. Robertson (eds.), *International Review of Industrial and Organizational Psychology*, vol. 3 (Chichester, England: Wiley, 1988), pp. 245–277.

3. K. Ludwan, "Customized Skills Assessments," *HR Magazine,* July 1991, pp. 67–69, 85.

4. J. J. Kane and E. E. Lawler, "Methods of Peer Assessment," *Psychological Bulletin,* 1978, 85, 555–586.

5. R. R. Reilly and G. T. Chao, "Validity and Fairness of Some Alternative Selection Procedures," *Personnel Psychology,* 1982, 35, pp. 1–62.

6. Bureau of National Affairs, *Basic Patterns in Union Contracts*, (Washington, DC: author, 1995); R. D. Connor and R. L. Fjersted, "Internal Personnel Maintenance," in D. Yoder and H. G. Heneman, Jr. (eds.), *ASPA Handbook of Personnel and Industrial Relations* (Washington, DC: Bureau of National Affairs, 1979), pp. 203–234; D. Q. Mills, "Seniority Versus Ability in Promotion Decisions," *Industrial and Labor Relations Review*, 1985, 38, pp. 421–425.

7. F. K. Folkes, *Personnel Policies in Large Non-Union Companies* (Englewood Cliffs, NJ: Prentice-Hall, 1985).

8. J. F. Schnell, "An Ordered Choice Model of Promotion Rules," *Journal of Labor Research*, 1987, 8, pp. 159–178; C. Ichniowski, J. T. Delaney and D. Lewin, "The New Resource Management in US Workplaces: Is It Really New and Is It Only Nonunion?" *Industrial Relations*, 1989, 44, pp. 97–119.

9. R. D. Arvey and R. H. Faley, *Fairness in Selecting Employees*, second ed. (Reading, MA: Addison-Wesley, 1988); Mills, "Seniority Versus Ability in Promotion Decisions."

10. K. G. Abraham and J. L. Medoff, "Length of Service and Promotions in Union and Nonunion Work Groups," *Industrial and Labor Relations Review*, 1985, 38, pp. 408–420; M. E. Gordon and W. J. Fitzgibbons, "An Empirical Test of the Validity of Seniority as a Factor in Staffing Decisions," *Journal of Applied Psychology*, 1982, 67, pp. 311–319; M. E. Gordon and W. A. Johnson, "Seniority: A Review of Its Legal and Scientific Standing," *Personnel Psychology*, 1982, 35, pp. 255–280.

11. A. Lienert, "From Rust to Riches," *Management Review*, 1994, 83, pp. 10–14.

12. B. J. Avolio, D. A. Waldman, and M. A. McDaniel, "An Examination of Age and Cognitive Test Performance Across Job Complexity and Occupational Types," *Academy of Management Journal*, 1990, 33, pp. 407–422; D. A. Hoffman, R. Jacobs, and S. J. Gerras, "Mapping Individual Performance Over Time," *Journal of Applied Psychology*, 1992, 77, pp. 185–193; J. E. Hunter and R. F. Hunter, "Validity and Utility of Alternative Predictors of Job Performance," *Psychological Bulletin*, 1984, 96, pp. 72–98; R. Jacobs, D. A. Hoffman, and S. D. Kriska, "Performance and Seniority," *Human Performance*, 1990, 3, pp. 107–121; M. A. McDaniel, F. L. Schmidt, and J. E. Hunter, "Job Experience Correlates of Job Performance," *Journal of Applied Psychology*, 1988, 73, pp. 327–330; M. P. McEnrue, "Length of Experience and the Performance of Managers in the Establishment Phase of Their Careers," *Academy of Management Journal*, 1988, 31, pp. 175–185; F. L. Schmidt, J. E. Hunter, and A. N. Outerbridge, "Impact of Job Experience and Ability on Job Knowledge, Work Sample Performance, and Supervisory Ratings of Job Performance," *Journal of Applied Psychology*, 1986, 71, pp. 432–439.

13. F. L. Schmidt, J. E. Hunter, and A. N. Outerbridge, "Joint Relation of Experience and Ability with Job Performance: Test of Three Hypotheses," *Journal of Applied Psychology*, 1988, 73, pp. 46–57.

14. W. Wilson, "Video Training and Testing Supports Customer Service Goals," *Personnel Journal*, 1994, 73, pp. 47–51.

15. F. L. Schmidt and J. E. Hunter, "Development of a Causal Model of Processes Determining Job Performance," *Current Directions in Psychological Science*, 1992, 1, pp. 89–92.

16. K. R. Murphy and J. M. Cleveland, *Performance Appraisal: An Organizational Perspective* (Boston: Allyn and Bacon, 1991).

17. L. J. Peter and R. Hull, *The Peter Principle* (New York: William Morrow, 1969).

18. S. B. Keel, D. S. Cochran, K. Arnett, and D. R. Arnold, "AC's are not Just for the Big Guys," *Personnel Administrator*, May 1989, pp. 100–101; G. C. Thornton, *Assessment Centers in Human Resource Management* (Reading, MA: Addison-Wesley, 1992).

19. J. J. Turnage and P. M. Muchinsky, "A Comparison of the Predictive Validity of Assessment Center Evaluations Versus Traditional Measures in Forecasting Supervisory Job Performance: Interpretative Implications of Criterion Distortion for the Assessment Paradigm," *Journal of Applied Psychology*, 69, pp. 595–602.

20. B. B. Gaugler, D. B. Rosenthal, G. C. Thornton, III, and C. Bentson, "Meta-Analysis of Assessment Center Validity," *Journal of Applied Psychology*, 1987, 72, pp. 493–511.

21. Gaugler et al., "Meta-Analysis of Assessment Center Validity"; A. Howard, "An Assessment of Assessment Centers," *Academy of Management Journal*, 1974, 17, pp. 115–134; R. Klimoski and M. Brickner, "Why Do Assessment Centers Work? The Puzzle of Assessment Center Validity," *Personnel Psychology*, 1987, 40, pp. 243–260; P. R. Sackett, "A Critical Look at Some Common Beliefs About Assessment Centers," *Public Personnel Management*, pp. 140–146.

22. C. Fletcher, "Candidates' Reactions to Assessment Centres and Their Outcomes: A Longitudinal Study," *Journal of Occupational Psychology*, 1991, 64, pp. 117–127.

23. G. C. Thornton, *Assessment Centers*, 1992.

24. R. D. Arvey and R. H. Faley, *Fairness in Selecting Employees*, second ed.; B. B. Gaugler, D. B. Rosenthal, G. C. Thornton III, and C. Bentson, "Meta-Analysis of Assessment Center Validity,"; J. R. Hinrichs, "An Eight-year Follow-up of a Management Assessment Center," *Journal of Applied Psychology*, 1978, 63(5), pp. 596–601; J. E. Hunter and R. F. Hunter, "Validity and Utility of Alternative Predictors of Job Performance,"; S. B. Keel, D. S. Cochran, K. Arnett, and D. R. Arnold, "AC's are not Just for the Big Guys," *Personnel Administrator*, May 1989, pp. 98–100; R. C. Liden and G. M. Kromm, "Testing Standards in Grievance Arbitration: A Case Review and Critique," *Employee Relations Law Journal*, 13, pp. 287–303; J. E. Pynes and H. J. Bernardin, "Predictive Validity of an Entry-Level Police Officer Assessment Center," *Journal of Applied Psychology*, 1989, 74(5), 831–833; R. R. Reilly and G. T. Chao, "Validity and Fairness of Some Alternative Selection Procedures,"; J. S. Schippman, E. P. Prien, and J. A. Katz, "Reliability and Validity of In-Basket Performance Measures," *Personnel Psychology*, 1990, 43, pp. 837–859; F. L. Schmidt, D. S. Ones, and J. E. Hunter, "Personnel Selection," *Annual Review of Psychology*, 1992, 43, 627–670; F. L. Schmidt, J. E. Hunter, A. N. Outerbridge, and S. Goff, "Joint Relation of Experience and Ability with Job Performance: Test of Three Hypotheses,"; F. L. Schmidt and J. E. Hunter, "Development of a Causal Model of Processes Determining Job Performance," *Current Directions in Psychological Science*, 1992, 1(3), pp. 89–92; N. Schmitt, R. Z. Gooding, R. A. Noe, and M. Kirsch, "Meta-Analyses of Validity Studies Between 1964 and 1982 and the Investigation of Study Characteristics," *Personnel*

Psychology, 1984, 37, pp. 407–422; J. Schwarzwald, M. Koslowsky, & B. Shalit, "A Field Study of Employees' Attitudes and Behaviors After Promotion Decisions," *Journal of Applied Psychology,* 1992, 77(4), pp. 511–514; G. C. Thornton, *Assessment Centers in Human Resource Management* (Reading, MA: Addison-Wesley, 1992).

25. J. Schwarzwald et al., "A Field Study of Employees' Attitudes and Behaviors After Promotion Decisions."

26. J. Greenberg, "Employee Theft as a Reaction to Underpayment Inequity: The Hidden Costs of Pay Cuts," *Journal of Applied Psychology,* 1990, 75, pp. 561–568; J. Greenberg, "Stealing in the Name of Justice: Informational and Interpersonal Moderators of Theft Reactions to Underpayment Treatment," *Organizational Behavior and Human Decision Processes,* 1993, 54, pp. 81–103.

STAFFING ORGANIZATIONS MODEL

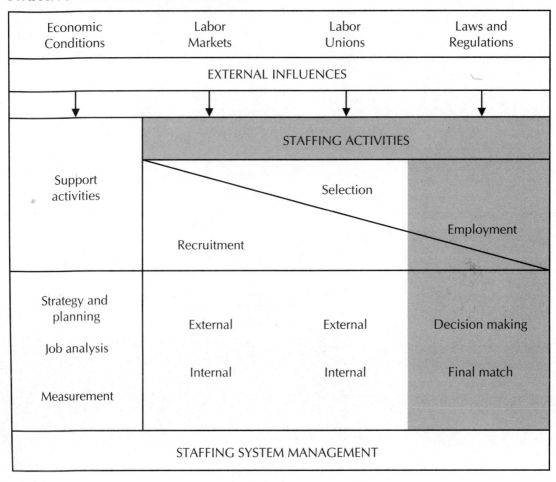

PART FIVE

Staffing Activities: Employment

CHAPTER TWELVE

Decision Making

Choice of Assessment Method
    Validity Coefficient
    Correlation with Other Predictors
    Adverse Impact
    Utility
    Applicant Reactions

Determining Assessment Scores
    Single Predictor
    Multiple Predictors

Hiring Standards and Cut Scores
    Description of the Process
    Consequences of Cut Scores
    Methods to Determine Cut Scores
    Professional Guidelines

Methods of Final Choice
    Random Selection
    Ranking
    Grouping

Decision Makers
    Human Resource Professionals
    Managers
    Employees

Legal Issues
    Uniform Guidelines on Employee Selection Procedures
    Choices Among Finalists

Summary

Discussion Questions

Applications

Individuals flow through the staffing process, passing through several stages: applicant, candidate, finalist, offer receiver, and new hire. To implement and manage this flow, the key decisions that must be made in several areas will be discussed. First, the factors that determine the choice of assessment methods to be used will be reviewed. Discussion will focus on the important considerations of validity, the correlation of one assessment method with other methods, likely adverse impact, the utility of the method, and applicant reactions.

Once assessment data have been collected from applicants, decisions must be made about how to determine assessment scores. The process of translating predictor scores into assessment scores will be discussed for using single predictors and multiple predictors. In the case of multiple predictors, methods to combine predictor scores will be considered. Methods that will be reviewed are a compensatory model, multiple hurdles, and a combined approach. Each has distinct strengths and weaknesses.

Hiring standards and cut scores must be established to determine passing levels for the assessment scores. The process used to determine cut scores will be described, as well as the consequences of cut scores, and methods to determine cut scores. Methods that will be discussed are minimum competency, top-down, and banding. Professional guidelines for determining cut scores also will be reviewed.

Methods of final choice must be considered to determine who from among the finalists will receive a job offer. Methods of final choice that will be reviewed include random selection, ranking, and grouping. Each method may be advantageous, depending upon one's objectives.

For all of the preceding decisions, consideration must be given to who should be involved in the decision process. The role of various potential decision makers will be discussed, including human resource professionals, line managers, and employees. In general, decisions about the staffing procedures to be followed are determined by HR professionals. Actual hiring decisions are usually made by managers. Increasingly, employees are being involved in both decisions.

Finally, legals issues should also guide the decision making. Particular consideration will be given to the Uniform Guidelines on Employee Selection Procedures. Of special concern are the use of cutoff scores, and choices from among finalists.

CHOICE OF ASSESSMENT METHOD

In our discussions of external and internal selection methods, we listed multiple criteria to consider when deciding which method(s) to use (e.g., validity, utility). Some of these criteria require more amplification, specifically validity, correlation with other predictors (newly discussed here), adverse impact, utility, and applicant reactions.

Validity Coefficient

Validity refers to the relationship between predictor and criterion scores. Often this relationship is assessed using a correlation (see Chapter 6). The correlation between predictor and criterion scores is known as a validity coefficient. For example, the validity coefficient for an ability test may be $r = .40$ when scores on the test (predictor) are correlated with performance ratings (criterion). The usefulness of a predictor is determined on the basis of the practical significance and statistical significance of its validity coefficient. As was noted in Chapter 6, reliability is a necessary condition for validity. Selection measures with questionable reliability will have questionable validity. This reinforces the need to use only those selection measures that are standardized and have proven reliability.

Practical Significance

Practical significance refers to the extent to which the predictor adds value to the prediction of job success. It is assessed by examining the sign and the magnitude of the validity coefficient.

Sign   The sign of the validity coefficient refers to the direction of the relationship between the predictor and criterion. A useful predictor is one where the sign of the relationship is positive or negative and is consistent with the logic or theory behind the predictor.

A positive or negative sign in and of itself, however, says nothing about the usefulness of a predictor. A positive sign does not mean a good predictor and a negative sign does not mean a poor predictor. The signs should not be considered independent of the theory because a positive sign may be desirable in one situation, but not another. A useful predictor is one where the sign is consistent with the theory. For example, if an ability test is used to predict job performance, then the test would probably be most useful when there is a positive sign. This is because theory suggests that ability is positively related to how well people perform on the job.

Magnitude   The magnitude of the validity coefficient refers to the size of the coefficient. It can range from 0 to 1.00, with a coefficient of 0 being the least desirable and a coefficient of 1.00 being the most desirable. The closer the validity coefficient is to 1.00, the more useful is the predictor. Predictors with validity coefficients of 1.00 are not to be expected given the inherent difficulties in predicting human behavior. Instead, as shown in Chapters 9 and 10, validity coefficients for current assessment methods range from 0 to about .60. Any validity coefficient above 0 is better than random selection and may be somewhat useful. Validities above .15 are of moderate usefulness and validities above .30 are of high usefulness.

Statistical Significance

Statistical significance, as assessed by probability or p values (see Chapter 6) is another factor that should be used to interpret the validity coefficient. If a validity coefficient has a reasonable p value, it indicates that chances are good that, if the same predictor were used with different sets of job applicants, it would yield a similar validity coefficient. That is, a reasonable p value indicates that the method of prediction rather than chance produced the observed validity coefficient.

Convention has it that a reasonable level of significance is $p<.05$. This means there are fewer than 5 chances in 100 of concluding there is a relationship in the population of job applicants, when, in fact, there is not. In most cases, this is a reasonable level of certainty indicating that the validity coefficient is statistically significant. Other times, a smaller p value, such as .001, is chosen for statistical significance. This may be the case, for example, when selecting people for a hazardous occupation, such as firefighting, and using a nonvalid predictor may have many disastrous and expensive consequences.

It should be pointed out that caution must be exercised in using statistical significance as a way to gauge the usefulness of a predictor. Research has clearly shown that nonsignificant validity coefficients may simply be due to the small samples of employees used to calculate the validity coefficient. Rejecting the use of a predictor solely on the basis of a small sample may lead to the rejection of a predictor that would have been quite acceptable had a larger sample of employees been used to test for validity.[1] These concerns over significance testing have led some researchers to recommend the use of "confidence intervals," for example, showing that one can be 90% confident that the true validity is no less than .30 and no greater than .40.[2]

Correlation with Other Predictors

If a predictor is to be considered useful, it must add value to the prediction of job success. In order to add value, it must add to the prediction of success above and beyond the forecasting powers of current predictors. In general, a predictor is more useful the smaller the correlation it has with other predictors and the higher the correlation it has with the criterion.

In order to assess whether the predictor adds anything new to forecasting, a matrix showing all the correlations between the predictors and the criteria should always be generated. If the correlations between the new predictor and existing predictors are higher than the correlations between the new predictor and criterion, then the new predictor is not adding much that is new. There are also relatively straightforward techniques such multiple regression which take the correlation among predictors into account.[3]

Predictors are likely to be highly correlated with one another when their domain of content is similar. For example, both biodata and application blanks may focus on previous training received. Thus, using both biodata and application blanks as predictors may be redundant, and neither one may augment the other much in predicting job success.

Adverse Impact

A predictor discriminates between people in terms of the likelihood of their success on the job. A predictor may also discriminate by screening out a disproportionate number of minorities and women. To the extent that this happens, the predictor has adverse impact and it may result in legal problems. As a result, when the validity of alternative predictors is the same and one predictor has less adverse impact than the other predictor, then the predictor with less adverse impact should be used.

A very difficult judgment call arises when one predictor has high validity and high adverse impact while another predictor has low validity and low adverse impact. From the perspective of accurately predicting job performance, the former predictor should be used. From an EEO/AA standpoint, the latter predictor is preferable. Balancing the trade-offs is difficult and requires use of the organization's staffing philosophy regarding EEO/AA.[4] One of the suggested solutions to this trade-off is banding, which is discussed later in this chapter.

Utility

Utility refers to the expected gains to be derived from using a predictor. Expected gains are of two types: hiring success and economic.

Hiring Success Gain

Hiring success refers to the proportion of new hires who turn out to be successful on the job. Hiring success *gain* refers to the increase in the proportion of successful new hires that is expected to occur as a result of adding a new predictor to the selection system. If the current staffing system yields a success rate of 75% for new hires, how much of a gain in this success rate will occur by adding a new predictor to the system? The greater the expected gain, the greater the utility of the new predictor. This gain is influenced not only by the validity of the new predictor (as already discussed), but also by the selection ratio and base rate.

Selection Ratio   The selection ratio is simply the number of people hired divided by the number of applicants (sr = number hired/number of applicants). The lower the selection ratio, the more useful the predictor. When the selection ratio is low, the organization is more likely to be selecting successful employees.

If the selection ratio is low, then the denominator is large or the numerator is small. Both conditions are desirable. A large denominator means that the organization is reviewing a large number of applicants for the job. The chances of identifying a successful candidate are much better in this situation than when an organization hires the first available person or only reviews a few applicants. A small numerator indicates that the organization is being very stringent with its hiring standards. The organization is hiring people likely to be successful rather than hiring anyone who meets the most basic requirements for the job; it is using high standards to ensure that the very best are selected.

Base Rate   The base rate is defined as the proportion of current employees who are successful on some criterion or HR outcome (br = number of successful employees/number of employees). A high base rate is desired for obvious reasons. A high base rate may come about from the organization's staffing system alone, or in combination with other HR programs such as training and compensation.

When considering possible use of a new predictor, one issue is whether the proportion of successful employees (i.e., the base rate) will increase as a result of using the new predictor in the staffing system. This is the matter of hiring success gain. Dealing with it requires simultaneous consideration of the organization's current base rate and selection ratio, as well as the validity of the new predictor.

The Taylor-Russell tables provide the necessary assistance for addressing this issue.[5] An excerpt from the Taylor-Russell tables is shown in Exhibit 12.1.

The Taylor-Russell table shows in each of its cells the percentage of new hires who will turn out to be successful. This is determined by a combination of the

EXHIBIT 12.1   Excerpts from the Taylor-Russell Tables

A.

Validity	Base Rate = .30 Selection Ratio	
	.10	.70
.20	43%	33
.60	77	40

B.

Validity	Base Rate = .80 Selection Ratio	
	.10	.70
.20	89%	83
.60	99	90

Source: H. C. Taylor and J. T. Russell, "The Relationship of Validity Coefficients to the Practical Effectiveness of Tests in Selection," *Journal of Applied Psychology*, 1939, 23, pp. 565–578.

validity coefficient for the new predictor, the selection ratio, and the base rate. The top matrix (A) shows the percentage of successful new hires when the base rate is low (.30), the validity coefficient is low (.20) or high (.60), and the selection ratio is low (.10) or high (.70). The bottom matrix (B) shows the percentage of successful new hires when the base rate is high (.80), the validity coefficient is low (.20) or high (.60), and the selection ratio is low (.10) or high (.70). Two illustrations show how these tables may be used.

The first illustration has to do with the decision whether or not to use a new test to select computer programmers. Assume that the current test used to select programmers has a validity coefficient of .20. Also assume that a consulting firm has approached the organization with a new test that has a validity coefficient of .60. Should the organization purchase and use the new test?

At first blush, the answer might seem to be affirmative, since the new test has a substantially higher level of validity. This initial reaction, however, must be gauged in the context of the selection ratio and the current base rate. If the current base rate is .80 and the current selection ratio is .70, then, as can be seen in the lower matrix (B) of Exhibit 12.1, the new selection procedure will only result in a hiring success gain from 83% to 90%. The organization may already have a very high base rate due to other facets of human resource management it does quite well (e.g., training, rewards). Hence, even though it has validity of .20, the base rate of its current predictor is already .80.

On the other hand, if the existing base rate of the organization is .30 and the existing selection ratio is .10, then it should strongly consider use of the new test. As shown in the top matrix (A) in Exhibit 12.1, the hiring success gain will go from 43% to 77% with the addition of the new test.

A second illustration using the Taylor-Russell tables has to do with recruitment in conjunction with selection. Assume that the validity of the organization's current predictor, a cognitive ability test, is .60. Also assume that a new college recruitment program has been very aggressive. As a result, there is a large swell in the number of applicants, and the selection ratio has decreased from .70 to .10. The decision the organization faces is whether to continue this new college recruitment program.

An initial reaction may be that the program should be continued because of the large increase in applicants generated. As shown in the top matrix of Exhibit 12.1, this answer would be correct if the current base rate is .30. By decreasing the selection ratio from .70 to .10, the hiring success gain increases from 40% to 77%. On the other hand, if the current base rate is .80, the correct decision may be to not continue the program. The hiring success increases from only 90% to 99%, which may not justify the very large expense associated with aggressive college recruitment campaigns.

The point of these illustrations is that when confronted with the decision whether or not to use a new predictor, the decision depends upon the validity coefficient, base rate, and selection ratio. They should not be considered independent of one another. Human resource professionals should carefully record and monitor base rates and selection ratios. Then, when asked by management whether they should be using a new predictor, they can respond appropriately. Fortunately, the Taylor-Russell tables are for any combination of validity coefficient, base rate, and selection ratio values. The values shown in Exhibit 12.1 are excerpts for illustration only. When other values need to be considered, then the original tables should be consulted to provide the appropriate answers.

Economic Gain

(es) Higher more productive as well as less productive empes.

Economic gain refers to the bottom line or monetary impact of a predictor on the organization. A predictor is more useful the greater the economic gain it produces. Considerable work has been done over the years on assessing the economic gain associated with predictors.[6] The basic utility formula used to estimate economic gain is shown in Exhibit 12.2.

At a general level, the economic gain formula shown in Exhibit 12.2 works as follows. Economic gains derived from using a valid predictor versus random selection (the left-hand side of the equation) depend upon two factors (the right-hand side of the equation). The first factor (the entry before the subtraction sign) is the revenue generated by hiring productive employees using the new predictor. The second factor (the entry after the subtraction sign) is the costs associated with using the new predictor. Positive economic gains are achieved when revenues are maximized and costs are minimized. Revenues are maximized by using the most valid selection procedures. Costs are minimized by using the predictors with the least costs. In order to estimate actual economic gain, values are entered into the equation for each of the variables shown. Values are usually generated by experts

---

EXHIBIT 12.2   Economic Gain Formula

$\Delta U = N_s TrSDy\bar{Z}_s - NC$

Where:

ΔU = expected dollar value increase to the organization using the predictor versus random selection

T = tenure of selected group

N_s = number of applicants selected

r = correlation between predictor and job performance

SDy = standard deviation of job performance

$\bar{Z}_s$ = average standard predictor score of selected group

N = number of applicants

C = cost per applicant

Source: Wayne F. Cascio, *Applied Psychology in Personnel Management*, 4e, © 1991, p. 300. Adapted by permission of Prentice-Hall, Englewood Cliffs, NJ.

in human resource research relying upon the judgments of experienced line managers.

Several variations on the economic gain (utility) formula shown in Exhibit 12.2 have been developed. For the most part, these variations require consideration of additional factors, such as assumptions about tax rates and applicant flows. In all of these models, the most difficult factor to estimate is the standard deviation of job performance (SDy), which represents the difference between productive and nonproductive employees in dollar value terms. A variety of methods have been proposed to measure SDy, ranging from manager estimates of employee value to percentages of compensation (usually 40% of base pay).[7] Despite this difficulty, economic gain formulas represent a significant way of estimating the economic gains that may be anticipated with the use of a new (and valid) predictor.

Limitations with Utility Analysis

While utility analysis can be a powerful method to communicate the bottom-line implications of using valid selection measures, it is not without its limitations. Perhaps the most fundamental concern among researchers and practitioners is that utility estimates lack realism because:

1. Virtually every organization uses multiple selection measures, yet existing utility models assume that the decision is whether to use a single selection measure rather than selecting applicants by chance alone.[8]

2. There are many important variables missing from the model, such as EEO/AA concerns.[9]

3. The utility formula is based on many assumptions that are probably overly simplistic, including that validity does not vary over time,[10] that nonperformance criteria such as attendance, trainability, applicant reactions, and fit are irrelevant,[11] and that applicants are selected in a top-down manner and that all job offers are accepted.[12]

Perhaps as a result of these limitations, several factors indicate that utility analysis may have a limited effect on managers' decisions about selection measures. For example, a recent survey of managers who have discontinued use of utility analysis found that 40% did so because they felt that utility analysis was too complicated, while 32% discontinued use because they believed that the results were unbelievable.[13] Another study found that reporting simple validity coefficients was more likely to persuade human resource decision makers to adopt a particular selection method than was reporting utility analysis results.[14]

These criticisms should not be taken as arguments that organizations should ignore utility analysis when evaluating selection decisions. However, decision makers are much less likely to become disillusioned with utility analysis if they are informed consumers and realize some of the limitations inherent in such analyses. Researchers have the responsibility of better embedding utility analysis in the strategic context in which staffing decisions are made, while human resource decision makers have the responsibility to use the most rigorous methods possible to evaluate their decisions.[15] By being realistic about what utility analysis can and cannot accomplish, the potential to fruitfully inform staffing decisions will increase.[16]

Applicant Reactions

Another factor relevant to the choice of assessment methods is how applicants react to the selection methods. Research has shown that applicants who feel unfairly treated in the selection process are less likely to accept a job offer, are more likely to sue an organization for unfair discrimination, have lower motivation to perform well on other selection measures, and even if hired, are more likely to have negative attitudes toward the organization.[17] The importance of applicant perceptions becomes even more apparent when one considers the fact that the most desirable applicants (e.g., high ability applicants) are likely to be the ones most likely to refuse job offers based on their reactions since they have more alternatives.[18] Thus, applicant reactions to a selection process affect its utility and contribution to organizational effectiveness.

Although applicant reactions to selection procedures have been studied only recently, some initial conclusions appear warranted. First, the process by which selection measures are administered appears to be critical. One important process factor is explaining the reason for rejection to applicants. Rejected applicants are more likely to recommend the organization to others when they are given an explanation for their rejection.[19] Other potentially important process factors are ensuring that the applicant has the proper opportunity to demonstrate his or her true level of ability, consistency and sensitivity of administration (particularly important in the case of invasive selection procedures such as drug tests), and proper feedback and the opportunity to appeal.[20]

Research also suggests that the content of selection procedures influences applicant reactions. In particular, selection procedures that are seen as difficult, unrelated to job performance, and provide little feedback on how well the applicant did, are likely to be viewed negatively by applicants.[21] More generally, research suggests that selection measures that sample job content (such as work samples and assessment centers) are more likely to be seen as valid and fair by applicants than paper-and-pencil tests (such as personality tests or abstract ability tests).[22]

To some extent, research has suggested that the selection methods that have the highest empirical validity are often seen least favorably by applicants.[23] For example, cognitive ability tests, biodata inventories, and personality tests all have substantial validity yet (particularly in the case of abstractly worded tests) have the lowest degree of perceived validity among applicants. Conversely, unstructured employment interviews are among the least valid selection procedures, yet are perceived to be among the most valid selection measures.[24] Perhaps the best solution to this apparent paradox is not to abandon valid (and objectively fair) selection measures such as these, but to concentrate on the process factors noted above that may have more of an influence on applicant reactions than the particular selection measure used.

DETERMINING ASSESSMENT SCORES

Single Predictor

Using a single predictor in selection decisions makes the process of determining scores easy. In fact, scores on the single predictor *are* the final assessment scores. Thus, concerns over how to combine assessment scores are not relevant when a single predictor is used in selection decisions. Although using a single predictor has the advantage of simplicity, there are some obvious drawbacks. First, few employers would feel comfortable hiring applicants on the basis of a single attribute. In fact, almost all employers use multiple methods in selection decisions. A second and related reason for using multiple predictors is that utility increases as the number of valid predictors used in selection decisions increases. In most cases, using two valid selection methods will result in more effective selection decisions than using a sole predictor. For these reasons, while basing selection decisions on a single predictor is a simple way to make decisions, it is rarely the best one.

Multiple Predictors

Given the less-than-perfect validities of predictors, most organizations use multiple predictors in making selection decisions. With multiple predictors, decisions must be made about combining the resultant scores. These decisions can be addressed through consideration of compensatory, multiple hurdles, and combined approaches.

Compensatory Model

With a compensatory model, scores on one predictor are simply added to scores on another predictor to yield a total score. What this means is that high scores on one predictor can compensate for low scores on another predictor. For example, if an employer is using an interview and grade point average (GPA) to select a person, an applicant with a low GPA, who does well in the interview, may still get the job.

The advantage of a compensatory model is that it recognizes that people have multiple talents and that many different constellations of talents may produce success on the job. The disadvantage to a compensatory model is that, at least for some jobs, level of proficiency for specific talents cannot be compensated for by other proficiencies. For example, a firefighter requires a certain level of strength that cannot be compensated for by intelligence.

In terms of making actual decisions using the compensatory model, there are four procedures that may be followed: clinical prediction, unit weighting, rational weighting, and multiple regression. The four methods differ from one another in terms of the manner in which predictor scores (raw or standardized) are weighted before being added together for a total or composite score.

The following example will be used to illustrate these procedures. In all four procedures, raw scores are used to determine a total score. Standard scores (see Chapter 6) may need to be used rather than raw scores if each predictor variable uses a different method of measurement or is measured under different conditions.[25] Differences in weighting methods are shown in part A of Exhibit 12.3. In Part B of Exhibit 12.3, there is a selection system consisting of interviews, application blanks, and recommendations. For simplicity, assume that scores on each predictor range from 1 to 5. Scores on these three predictors are shown for three applicants.

Clinical Prediction   Returning to Exhibit 12.3, note that with a clinical prediction, managers use their expert judgment to arrive at a total score for each applicant. That final score may or may not be a simple addition of the three predictor scores shown in Exhibit 12.3. Hence, applicant A may be given a higher total score than applicant B even though simple addition shows that applicant B had one point more ($4 + 3 + 4 = 11$) than did applicant A ($3 + 5 + 2 = 10$).

The advantage to this approach is that it draws upon the expertise of managers to weight and combine predictor scores. In turn, managers may be more likely to accept the selection decisions than if a mechanical scoring rule (e.g., add up the points) were used. The problem with this approach is that the reasons for the weightings are known only to the manager. Also, clinical predictions have generally been shown to be less accurate than mechanical decisions.[26]

Unit Weighting   With unit weighting, each predictor is weighted the same at a value of 1.00. What this means is shown in Exhibit 12.3 (Part A): the predictor scores are simply added together to get a total score. So, in Exhibit 12.3 (Part B), the total scores for applicants A, B, and C are 10, 11, and 12, respectively. The advantage to unit weighting is that it is a simple and straightforward process to follow and makes the importance of each predictor explicit to decision makers. The problem with this approach is that it assumes that each predictor contributes equally to the prediction of job success, which often will not be the case.

Rational Weighting   With rational weighting, each predictor receives a differential rather than equal weighting. Managers and other subject matter experts establish the weights for each predictor according to degree to which each is

---

EXHIBIT 12.3   Four Compensatory Model Procedures for Three Predictors

---

A. Models
Clinical Prediction

$P_1 \rightarrow P_2 \rightarrow P_3 \rightarrow$ Total Score

Unit Weighting

$P_1 + P_2 + P_3 =$ Total Score

Rational Weighting

$w_1 P_1 + w_2 P_2 + w_3 P_3 =$ Total Score

Multiple Regression

$a + b_1 P_1 + b_2 P_2 + b_3 P_3 =$ Total Score

Where: P = predictor score
w = rational weight
a = intercept
b = statistical weight

B. Raw Scores for Applicants on Three Predictors

	Predictors		
Applicant	**Interview**	**Application Blank**	**Recommendation**
A	3	5	2
B	4	3	4
C	5	4	3

---

believed to predict job success. These weights (w) are then multiplied times each raw score (P) to yield a total score as shown in Exhibit 12.3 (Part A).

For example, the predictors in Exhibit 12.3 (Part B) may be weighted .5, .3, and .2 for the interview, application blank, and recommendation. Each applicant's raw score in Exhibit 12.3 (Part B) is multiplied times the appropriate weight to yield a total score. For example, the total score for applicant A is (.5) 3 + (.3) 5 + (.2) 2 = 3.4.

The advantage to this approach is that it considers the relative importance of each predictor and makes this assessment explicit. The downside, however, is that it is an elaborate procedure that requires managers and subject matter experts to agree upon the differential weights to be applied.

Multiple Regression   Multiple regression is similar to rational weighting in that the predictors receive different weights. With multiple regression, however, the weights are established on the basis of statistical procedures rather than on the basis of judgments by managers or other subject matter experts. The statistical weights are developed on the basis of (a) the correlation of each predictor with the criterion, and (b) the correlations among the predictors.[27] As a result, regression weights provide optimal weights in the sense that the weights are those that will yield the highest total validity.

The calculations result in a multiple regression formula like the one shown in Exhibit 12.3 (Part A). A total score for each applicant is obtained by multiplying the statistical weight (b) for each predictor by the predictor (P) score, and summing these along with the intercept value (a). As an example, assume the statistical weights are .9, .6, and .2 for the interview, application blank, and recommendation, respectively, and that the intercept is .09. Using these values, the total score for applicant A is $.09 + (.9)3 + (.6)5 + (.2)2 = 6.19$.

Multiple regression offers the possibility of a much higher degree of precision in the prediction of criterion scores than do the other methods of weighting. Unfortunately, this level of precision is realized only under a certain set of circumstances. In particular, for multiple regression to be more precise than unit weighting, there must be a small number of predictors, low correlations between predictor variables, and a large sample.[28] Many selection settings do not meet these criteria, so in these cases consideration should be given to unit or rational weighting instead. In situations where these conditions are met, however, multiple regression weights can produce higher validity and utility than the other weighting schemes.

Choice among Weighting Schemes The choice from among different weighting schemes is important because how various predictor combinations are weighted is critical in determining the usefulness of the selection process. To illustrate, Exhibit 12.4 provides the changes in validity and utility that occur when supplementing the most empirically valid method of selection (cognitive ability tests) with another selection method. The first column shows that change in validity by unit weighting scores on the cognitive ability test with the specified selection measure. For example, the validity of a cognitive ability test, when used by itself to predict job performance, has been estimated to be .50. Past research suggests that the validity of an integrity test, when used by itself to predict job performance, is .41. When scores on the cognitive ability and integrity test are combined by weighting them equally, the total validity increases to .65, an increase of 27.6% over the validity of the cognitive ability test alone. When scores are weighted according to multiple regression, however, the increase in validity becomes 28.2%. In fact, the exhibit shows that when supplementing cognitive ability tests with additional selection procedures, using multiple regression to establish weights always yields higher validity than unit weighting. Furthermore, when using selection methods that have moderate or low levels of validity in conjunction with cognitive ability tests, unit weighted combinations often provide lower levels of validity than using only cognitive ability tests.

EXHIBIT 12.4 Effects of Unit Weighting and Multiple Regression Weighting on the Validity and Utility of Cognitive Ability Tests

Additional Selection Method	Unit-Weighted Composite	Regression-Weighted Composite
Integrity Test	27.6%	28.2%
Structured Interview	27.0%	27.1%
Work Sample	23.9%	24.1%
Conscientiousness	13.7%	17.1%
Job Knowledge Test	12.8%	12.9%
Unstructured Interview	10.8%	12.8%
Reference Check	6.8%	12.2%
Assessment Center	−1.5%	2.8%
Biodata	−2.6%	2.4%
Job Experience	−4.3%	6.1%
Interest Inventory	−15.4%	2.0%
Handwriting Analysis	−26.5%	0.0%

Columns show the change in validity and utility by adding specified selection method to cognitive ability tests (general mental ability test) in predicting job performance.

Source: Adapted from D. S. Ones, F. L. Schmidt, and K. Yoon, "Validity of an Equally-Weighted Composite of General Mental Ability and a Second Predictor" and "Predictive Validity of General Mental Ability Combined with a Second Predictor Based on Standardized Multiple Regression." Working Papers, (University of Iowa, Iowa City, Iowa: author, 1996). Used by permission.

These results do not prove that multiple regression weighting is a superior method in all circumstances. In fact, limitations of regression-based weighting schemes were noted above. What this example does help illustrate, though, is that the choice of the best weighting scheme is a consequential one, and one that is likely to depend on answers to the most important questions about clinical, unit, rational, and multiple regression schemes (in that order):

- Do selection decision makers have considerable experience and insight into selection decisions, and is managerial acceptance of the selection process important?

- Is there reason to believe that each predictor contributes relatively equally to job success?

- Are there adequate resources to use relatively involved weighting schemes such as rational weights or multiple regression?

- Are the conditions under which multiple regression is superior (relatively small number of predictors, low correlations among predictors, large sample) satisfied?

Answers to these questions—and the importance of the questions themselves—will go a long way toward deciding which weighting scheme to use.

Multiple Hurdles Model

With a multiple hurdles approach, an applicant must earn a passing score on each predictor before advancing in the selection process. Such an approach is taken when each requirement measured by a predictor is critical to job success. Passing scores are set using the methods to determine cut scores discussed in the next section. With multiple hurdles, unlike the compensatory model, a high score on one predictor cannot compensate for a low score on another predictor. An example of a multiple hurdles approach is shown in Exhibit 12.5 for the position of pyrotechnician.

As can be seen in Exhibit 12.5, a pyrotechnician must pass a multiple set of hurdles to be hired. A pyrotechnician is the person responsible for the demolition of high-powered explosives and fireworks. This is a highly hazardous endeavor, and false positive errors must be absolutely minimized. If this is not done, then the safety of the public may be jeopardized. For example, at the annual Fourth of July celebrations in Columbus or Boston, tons of explosives are detonated in fairly close proximity to hundreds of thousands of spectators. A misdirected explosive could result in a disaster. To adequately perform this job, one must be well versed in many areas, including computers. The timing and detonation of the explosives, as well as modeling of the entire program, is done by computer.

Multiple hurdles are used to prevent false positive errors. They are costly and time consuming to set up. As a result, they are used to select people for jobs where the occupational hazards are great (e.g., astronaut) or the consequences of poor performance have a great impact upon the public at large (e.g., police officers and firefighters).

Combined Model

For jobs where some, but not all requirements, are critical to job success, a combined method may be used in which the compensatory and multiple hurdles models are combined together. The process starts with the multiple hurdles and ends with the compensatory method.

An example of the combined approach for the position of recruitment manager is shown in Exhibit 12.6. The selection process for recruitment manager starts with two hurdles that must be passed, in succession, by the applicant. These are the application blank and the job knowledge test. Failure to clear either hurdle results in rejection. Having passed them, applicants take an interview and have their references checked. Information from the interview and the references is combined in a compensatory manner. Those who pass are offered the job, and those who do not pass are rejected.

EXHIBIT 12.5   Multiple Hurdles for Pyrotechnician Position

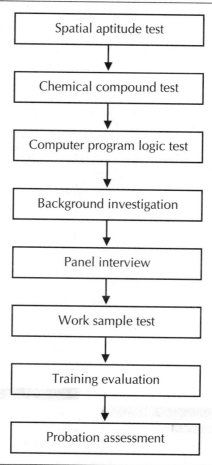

HIRING STANDARDS AND CUT SCORES

Hiring standards or cut scores address the issue of what constitutes a passing score. The score may be a single score from a single predictor, or a total score from multiple predictors. To address this, a description of the process and the consequences of cut scores are presented. Then, methods that may be used to establish the actual cut score are described.

Description of the Process

Once one or more predictors have been chosen for use, a decision must be made as to who advances further in the selection process. This decision requires that

EXHIBIT 12.6   Combined Model for Recruitment Manager

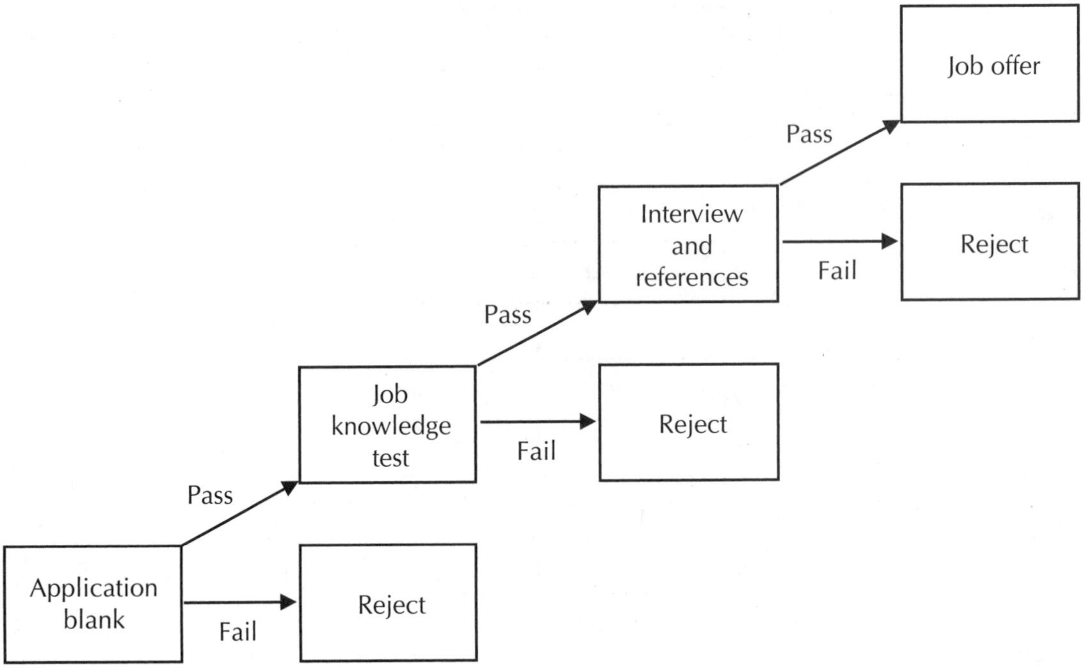

one or more cut scores be established. A cut score is the score that separates those who advance further in the process (e.g., applicants who become candidates) from those who are rejected. For example, assume a test is used on which scores may range from 0 to 100 points. A cut score of 70 would mean that those applicants with a 70 or more would advance, while all others would be rejected for employment purposes.

Consequences of Cut Scores

The setting of a cut score is a very important process as it has consequences for the organization and the applicant. The consequences of cut scores can be shown using Exhibit 12.7, which contains a summary of a scatter diagram of predictor and criterion scores. The horizontal line shows the criterion score at which the organization has determined whether an employee is successful or unsuccessful—for example, a 3 on a 5-point performance appraisal scale where 1 is the low performance and 5 is the high performance. The vertical line is the cut score for the predictor—for example, a 3 on a 5-point interview rating scale where 1 reveals no chance of success and 5 a high chance of success.

EXHIBIT 12.7   Consequences of Cut Scores

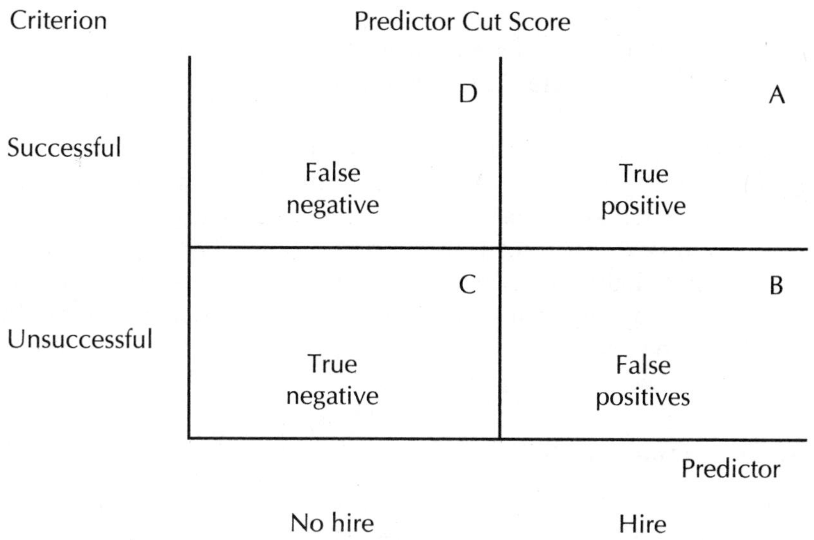

Criterion	Predictor Cut Score	
	D	A
Successful	False negative	True positive
	C	B
Unsuccessful	True negative	False positives
		Predictor
	No hire	Hire

The consequences of setting the cut score at a particular level are shown in each of the quadrants. Quadrants A and C represent correct decisions, which have positive consequences to the organization. Quadrant A applicants are called true positives because they were assessed as having a high chance of success using the predictor and would have succeeded if hired. Quadrant C applicants are called true negatives because they were assessed as having little chance for success and, indeed, would not be successful if hired.

Quadrants D and B represent incorrect decisions, which have negative consequences to the organization and affected applicants. Quadrant D applicants are called false negatives because they were assessed as not being likely to succeed, but had they been hired, they would have been successful. Not only was an incorrect decision reached, but a person who would have done well was not hired. Quadrant B applicants are called false positives. They were assessed as being likely to succeed, but would have ended up being unsuccessful performers. Eventually, these people would need to receive remedial training, be transferred to a new job, or even be terminated.

How high or low a cut score is set has a large impact on the consequences shown in Exhibit 12.7, and trade-offs are always involved. Compared with the moderate cut score in Exhibit 12.7, a high cut score results in fewer false positives, but a larger number of false negatives. Is this a good, bad, or inconsequential set of outcomes for the organization? The answer depends upon the job open for selection and the costs involved. If the job is an astronaut position for NASA, then it is essential that there be no false positives. The cost of a false positive may be the loss of a human life.

Now consider the consequences of a low cut score, relative to the one shown in Exhibit 12.7. There are fewer false negatives and more true positives, but more false positives are hired. In organizations that gain competitive advantage in their industry by hiring the very best, this set of consequences may be unacceptable. Alternatively, for EEO/AA purposes it may be desirable to have a low cut score so that the number of false negative minorities and women are minimized.

In short, when setting a cut score, attention must be given to the consequences. As indicated, these consequences can be very serious. As a result, different methods of setting cut scores have been developed to guide decision makers. These will now be reviewed.[29]

Methods to Determine Cut Scores

There are three different methods that may be used to determine cut scores: minimum competency, top-down, and banding. Each of these is described below, along with professional guidelines for setting cutoff scores.

Minimum Competency

Using the minimum competency method, the cut score is set on the basis of the minimum qualifications deemed necessary to perform the job. Subject matter experts are usually used to establish a minimum competency score. This approach is often needed in situations where the first step in the hiring process is the demonstration of minimum skill requirements. Exhibit 12.8 provides an illustration of the use of cut scores in selection. The exhibit lists the scores of 25 applicants on a particular test. Using the minimum competency method, the cut score is set at the level at which applicants who score below the line are deemed unqualified for the job. In this case, a score of 75 was determined to be the minimum competency level necessary to perform the job. Thus, all applicants who scored below 75 are deemed unqualified and rejected and all applicants who scored 75 or above are deemed at least minimally qualified. Finalists and ultimately offer receivers can then be chosen among these qualified applicants on the basis of other criteria.

Top-Down

Another method of determining at what level the cut score should be set is to simply examine the distribution of predictor scores for applicants and set the cut score at the level that best meets the demands of the organization. Demands of the organization may include the number of vacancies to be filled and EEO/AA requirements. This top-down method of setting cut scores is illustrated in Exhibit 12.8. As the exhibit shows, under top-down hiring, cut scores are established by

EXHIBIT 12.8   Use of Cut Scores in Selection Decisions

Rank	Test Scores	Minimum Competency		Top Down			Banding*
1.	100	100 ⌐		100	1st	choice	100 ⌐
2.	98	98		98	2nd	choice	98
3.	97	97		97	3rd	choice	97
4.	96	96		96	4th	choice	96
T5.	93	93		93	5th	choice	93
T5.	93	93		93	5th	choice	93 ⌐
7.	91	91		91	"		91 ⌐
T8.	90	90		90	"		90 ⌐
T8.	90	90		90	"		90
10.	88	88	Qualified	88	"		88
11.	87	87		87	"		87
T12.	85	85		85	"		85
T12.	85	85		85	"		85
14.	83	83		83	"		83
15.	81	81		81	"		81 ⌐
16.	79	79		79	"		79 ⌐
T17.	77	77		77	"		77
T17.	77	77		77	"		77
19.	76	76		76	"		76
20.	75	75 ⌐	Min. competency	75	"		75
21.	74	74 ⌐		74	21st	choice	74
22.	71	71		71	22nd	choice	71 ⌐
23.	70	70	Unqualified	70	23rd	choice	70 ⌐
24.	69	69		69	24th	choice	69
25.	65	65 ⌐		65	25th	choice	65 ⌐

*All scores within brackets treated as equal; choice of applicants within brackets (if necessary) can be made on the basis of other factors, such as EEO/AA considerations.

the number of applicants that need to be hired. Once that number has been determined, applicants are selected from the top based on the order of their scores until the number desired is reached. The advantage of this approach is that it is a system that is easy to administer. It also minimizes judgment required because the cut score is determined on the basis of the demand for labor. The big drawback to this approach is that validity has often not been established prior to the use of the predictor. Also, there may be overreliance on the use of a single predictor and cut score, while other potentially useful predictors are ignored.

A well-known example of a top-down method is the Angoff method.[30] According to this approach, subject matter experts are used to set the minimum cut scores needed to proceed in the selection process. These experts go through the content of the predictor (e.g., test items) and determine which items the minimally qualified person should be able to pass. Usually seven to ten subject matter experts (e.g., job incumbents, managers) are used who must agree upon the items to be passed. The cutoff score is the sum of the number of items that must be answered correctly.

There are several problems with this particular approach and subsequent modifications to it. First, it is a time-consuming procedure. Second, the results are dependent upon the subject matter experts. It is a very difficult matter to get members of the organization to agree upon who are "the" subject matter experts. Which set of subject matter experts are selected may have a bearing on the actual cut scores developed. Finally, it is unclear how much agreement there must be among subject matter experts when they evaluate test items. There also may be judgmental errors and biases in how cutoff scores are set.[31]

Banding

The traditional selection cut score method is the top-down approach. For both external hiring and internal promotions, the top-down method will yield the highest validity and utility. This method has been criticized, however, for ignoring the possibility that small differences between scores are due to measurement error. The top-down method also has been criticized for its ability to yield socially undesirable outcomes. Particularly in the area of cognitive ability testing, top-down decisions are likely to exclude substantial numbers of minorities. As a result, the selection measures are likely to have adverse impact against minorities. The magnitude of the adverse impact is such that, on a standard cognitive ability test, if half the white applicants are hired, only 16% of the black applicants would be expected to be hired.[32]

One suggestion that has been made for reducing the adverse impact of top-down hiring is using different norms for minority and majority groups; thus, hiring decisions are based on normatively defined (rather than absolute) scores. For example, a black employee who achieved a score of 75 on a test where the mean of all black applicants was 50 could be considered to have the same normative score as a white applicant who scored a 90 on a test where the mean for white applicants was 60. However, this "race-norming" of test scores, which was a common practice in the civil service and among some private employers, is expressly forbidden by the Civil Rights Act. As a result, another approach, termed "banding," is being considered.

Banding refers to the procedure whereby applicants who score within a certain score range or band are considered to have scored equivalently. A simple banding procedure is provided in Exhibit 12.8. In this example, using a 100-point test, all applicants who score within the band of 10-point increments are considered to have scored equally. For example, all applicants who score 91 and above could be assigned a score of 9, those who score 81–90 are given a score of 8, and so on. (In essence, this is what is done when letter grades are assigned based on exam scores.) Hiring within bands then could be done at random or, more typically, based on race or sex in conjunction with other factors (e.g., seniority, experience, etc.). Banding might reduce the adverse impact of selection tests because such a procedure tends to reduce differences between higher- and lower-scoring groups (as is the case with whites and minorities on cognitive ability tests). In practice, band widths are usually calculated on the basis of the standard error of measurement.

Research suggests that banding procedures do result in substantial decreases in the adverse impact of cognitive ability tests while, under certain conditions, the losses in terms of utility are relatively small.[33] Various methods of banding have been proposed, but the differences between these methods are relatively unimportant.[34] As a result of the positive implications of banding for reducing adverse impact, the use of banding has been sanctioned, for the time being, by the scientific affairs committee of the largest professional association of industrial psychologists.[35]

While banding does have considerable social appeal in terms of increasing diversity and reducing the adverse impact of selection processes, numerous limitations are evident. One limitation is that decreases in validity and utility resulting from banding become significant when even moderately reliable tests are used. Because the standard error of the difference between test scores is partly a function of the reliability of the test, when test reliability is low, band widths are wider than when the reliability of the test is high. For example, if the reliability of a test is .80, at a reasonable level of confidence, nearly half the scores on a test can be considered equivalent.[36] Obviously, taking scores on a 100-point test and lumping applicants into only two groups wastes a great deal of important information on applicants (it is very unlikely that an applicant who scores a 51 on a valid test will perform the same on the job as an applicant who scores 99). Therefore, if the reliability of a test is even moderately high, the validity and utility decrements that result from banding become quite severe.

Another limitation of banding is that while it will always be expected to yield lower utility, using banding and random selection within bands may not reduce the adverse impact of cognitive ability tests.[37] Given the adverse impact of cognitive ability tests, too few minorities may be placed into the upper bands. Thus, even if selection from the upper bands is done at random, there may not be enough minorities in these bands to prevent adverse impact. As a result, banding may require more drastic modifications to ensure that the desired result (less adverse impact) is achieved.

The scientific merits of test banding is hotly debated.[38] It is unlikely that we could resolve here the myriad ethical and technical issues underlying their use. Organizations considering the use of banding in personnel selection decisions must weigh the pros and cons carefully. However, it should be noted that, when using cognitive ability tests in selection, the goals of validity and diversity may not be complementary ones. If organizations decide to use banding as a means of promoting diversity, they do so at some potential cost to the validity and utility of their selection process. Given that banding results in validity and utility losses, perhaps a better solution to the sometimes conflicting goals of utility and diversity is to supplement the use of cognitive ability tests with other valid selection measures that have less (or no) adverse impact. In this way, validity and diversity can be increased concomitantly. For example, one comprehensive study found that supplementing cognitive ability tests with integrity tests (and weighting them equally) reduces the adverse impact of cognitive ability tests by 58% while raising total validity by 46%.[39]

Professional Guidelines

Much more research is needed on systematic procedures that are effective in setting optimal cut scores. In the meantime, a sound set of professional guidelines for setting cut scores is shown in Exhibit 12.9.

METHODS OF FINAL CHOICE

The discussion thus far has been on decision rules that can be used to narrow down the list of people to successively smaller groups who advance in the selection process from applicant to candidate to finalist. How can the organization now choose from among the finalists to decide which of them will receive job offers?

EXHIBIT 12.9   Professional Guidelines for Setting Cutoff Scores

---

1. It is unrealistic to expect that there is a single "best" method of setting cutoff scores for all situations.
2. The process of setting a cutoff score (or a critical score) should begin with a job analysis that identifies relative levels of proficiency on critical knowledge, skills, abilities, or other characteristics.
3. The validity and job relatedness of the assessment procedure are crucial considerations.
4. How a test is used (criterion-referenced or norm-referenced) affects the selection and meaning of a cutoff score.
5. When possible, data on the actual relation of test scores to outcome measures of job performance should be considered carefully.
6. Cutoff scores or critical scores should be set high enough to ensure that minimum standards of job performance are met.
7. Cutoff scores should be consistent with normal expectations of acceptable proficiency within the workforce.

Source: W. F. Cascio, R. A. Alexander, and G. V. Barrett, "Setting Cutoff Scores: Legal, Psychometric, and Professional Issues and Guidelines," *Personnel Psychology*, 1988, 41, pp. 21–22. Used by permission.

Discretionary assessments about the finalists must be converted into final choice decisions. The methods of final choice are the mechanisms by which discretionary assessments are translated into job offer decisions.

Methods of final choice include random selection, ranking, and grouping. Examples of each of these methods of final choice are shown in Exhibit 12.10 and are discussed here.

Random Selection

With random selection, each finalist has an equal chance of being selected. The only rationale for the selection of a person is the "luck of the draw." For example, the six names from Exhibit 12.10 could be put in a hat and the finalist drawn out. The one drawn out would be the person selected and made a job offer. This approach has the advantage of being quick. Also, with random selection, one cannot be accused of favoritism because everyone has an equal chance of being selected. The disadvantage to this approach is that discretionary assessments are simply ignored.

Ranking

With ranking, finalists are ordered from the most desirable to the least desirable based on results of discretionary assessments. As shown in Exhibit 12.10, the person ranked 1 (Goldie) is the most desirable, and the person ranked 6 (Harold) is the least desirable. It is important to note that desirability should be viewed in the context of the entire selection process. When this is done, persons with lower levels of desirability (e.g., ranks of 3, 4, 5) should not be viewed necessarily as

EXHIBIT 12.10   Methods of Final Choice

Random	Ranking	Grouping
Casey	1. Goldie	Goldie, Roxie — Top choices
Goldie	2. Roxie	
Buster	3. Buster	
Abby — Pick one	4. Abby	Buster, Abby — Acceptable
Roxie	5. Casey	
Harold	6. Harold	Casey, Harold — Last resorts

failures. Job offers are extended to people on the basis of their rank ordering, with the person ranked 1 receiving the first offer. Should that person turn down the job offer, or suddenly withdraw from the selection process, then the finalist ranked 2 receives the offer, and so on.

The advantage to ranking is that it provides an indication of the relative worth of each finalist for the job. It also provides a set of backups should one or more of the finalists withdraw from the process.

It should be remembered that backup finalists may decide to withdraw from the process to take a position elsewhere. Although ranking does give the organization a cushion should the top choices withdraw from the process, it does not mean that the process of job offers can proceed at a leisurely pace. Immediate action needs to be taken with the top choices in case they decide to withdraw and there is a need to go to backups. This is especially true in tight labor markets where there is a strong demand for the services of people on the ranking list.

Grouping

With the grouping method, finalists are banded together into rank-ordered categories. For example, in Exhibit 12.10, the finalists are grouped according to whether they are top choices, acceptable, or last resorts. The advantage of this method is that it permits ties among finalists, thus avoiding the need to assign a different rank to each person. The disadvantage is that choices still have to be made from among the top choices. These might be made on the basis of factors such as probability of each person accepting the offer.

DECISION MAKERS

A final consideration in decision making for selection is who should participate in the decisions. That is, who should determine the process to be followed (e.g., establishing cut scores) and who should determine the outcome (e.g., who gets the job offer)? The answer is that both human resource professionals and line managers must play a role. Although the two roles are different, both are critical to the organization. Employees may play certain roles as well.

Human Resource Professionals

As a general rule, human resource professionals should have a high level of involvement in the processes used to design and manage the selection system. They should be consulted in matters such as which predictors to use and how to use them best. In particular, they need to orchestrate the development of policies and procedures in the staffing areas covered. These professionals have or know where to find the technical expertise needed to develop sound selection decisions. Also, they have the knowledge to ensure that relevant laws and regulations are being followed. Finally, they can also represent the interests and concerns of employees to management.

Although the primary role to be played by human resource professionals is in terms of process, they should also have some involvement in determining who receives job offers. One obvious area where this is true is with staffing the human resource function. A less obvious place where human resource professionals can play an important secondary role is in terms of providing input into selection decisions made by managers.

Human resource professionals may be able to provide some insight on applicants that is not always perceived by line managers. For example, they may be able to offer some insight on the applicants' people skills (e.g., communications, teamwork). Human resource professionals are sensitive to these issues because of their training and experience. They may have data to share on these matters as a result of their screening interviews, knowledge of how to interpret paper-and-pencil instruments (e.g., personality test), and interactions with internal candidates (e.g., serving on task forces with the candidates).

The other area where human resource professionals may make a contribution to outcomes is in terms of initial assessment methods. Many times, human resource professionals are and should be empowered to make initial selection decisions such as who gets invited into the organization for administration of the next round of selection. Doing so they save managers time to carry out their other responsibilities. Also, human resource professionals can ensure that minorities and women applicants are actively solicited and not excluded from the applicant pool for the wrong reasons.

Managers

As a general rule, a manager's primary involvement in staffing is in determining who is selected for employment. Managers are the subject matter experts of the business, and, thus, they are held accountable for the success of the people hired. They are far less involved in determining the processes followed to staff the organization because they often do not have the time or expertise to do so.

Although they may not play a direct role in establishing process, managers can and should periodically be consulted by human resource professionals on process issues. They should be consulted because they are the consumers of human resource services. As such, it is important to provide them input into the staffing process to ensure that it is meeting their needs in making the best possible person/job matches.

There is an additional benefit to allowing management a role in process issues. As a result of their involvement, managers may develop a better understanding of why certain practices are prescribed by human resource professionals. When they are not invited to be a part of the process to establish staffing policy and procedures, line managers may view human resource professionals as an obstacle to hiring the right person for the job.

It should also be noted that the degree of managers' involvement usually depends on the type of assessment decisions made. Decisions made using initial assessment methods are usually delegated to the human resource professional, as just discussed. Decisions made using substantive assessment methods usually involve some degree of input from the manager. Decisions made using discretionary methods are usually the direct responsibility of the manager. As a general rule, the extent of managerial involvement in determining outcomes should only be as great as management's knowledge of the job. If managers are involved in hiring decisions for jobs with which they are not familiar, then legal, measurement, and morale problems are likely to be created.

Employees

Traditionally, employees are not considered part of the decision-making process in staffing. Slowly this tradition is changing. For example, in team assessment approaches (see Chapter 9), employees may have a voice in both process and outcomes. That is, they may have ideas about how selection procedures are established and make decisions about or provide input into who gets hired. Employee involvement in the team approach is encouraged because it may give a sense of ownership of the work process and help employees to better identify with organizational goals. Also, it may result in the selection of members who are more compatible with the goals of the work team. In order for employee involvement to be effective, employees need to be provided with staffing training just as managers do (see Chapter 10).

LEGAL ISSUES

The legal issue of major importance in decision making is that of cutoff scores or hiring standards. These scores or standards regulate the flow of individuals from applicant to candidate to finalist. Throughout this flow, adverse impact may occur. When it does, the Uniform Guidelines on Employee Selection Procedures (UGESP) come into play. At the finalist stage, decisions about to whom to offer the job are made, and the UGESP has less direct relevance.

Uniform Guidelines on Employee Selection Procedures

If there is no adverse impact in decision making, the UGESP (see Appendix A) are essentially silent on the issue of cutoff scores. The discretion being exercised by the organization as it makes its selection decisions is thus unconstrained legally.

If there is adverse impact occurring, however, then the UGESP become directly applicable to decision making.

Recall that under conditions of adverse impact, the UGESP requires the organization to either eliminate its occurrence or justify it through the conduct of validity studies. As part of the general standards for such validity studies, the UGESP says the following about cutoff scores:

> Where cutoff scores are used, they should normally be set as to be reasonable and consistent with normal expectations of acceptable proficiency within the workforce. Where applicants are ranked on the basis of properly validated selection procedures and those applicants scoring below a higher cutoff score than appropriate in light of such expectations have little or no chance of being selected for employment, the higher cutoff score may be appropriate, but the degree of adverse impact should be considered.

This provision suggests that the organization should be cautious in general about setting cutoff scores that are above those necessary to achieve acceptable proficiency among those hired. In other words, even with a valid predictor, the organization should be cautious that its hiring standards are not so high that they create needless adverse impact. This is particularly true with ranking systems. Use of random, or to a lesser extent grouping, methods would help overcome this particular objection to ranking systems.

Whatever cutoff score procedure is used, the UGESP also requires that the organization be able to document its establishment and operation. Specifically, the UGESP says that "if the selection procedure is used with a cutoff score, the user should describe the way in which normal expectations of proficiency within the workforce were determined and the way in which the cutoff score was determined."

The preceding validation and cutoff score approach is one option for dealing with problems of adverse impact. The UGESP also suggests two other options, both of which seek to eliminate adverse impact rather than justify it as in the validation and cutoff score approach. The next option is the "alternative procedures" one. Here, the organization must consider using an alternative selection procedure that causes less adverse impact (e.g., work sample instead of a written test), but has roughly the same validity as the procedure it replaces.

The final selection option is that of affirmative action. The UGESP do not relieve the organization of any affirmative action obligations it may have. Also, the UGESP strive to "encourage the adoption and implementation of voluntary affirmative action programs" for organizations that do not have any affirmative action obligations.

Choices Among Finalists

Where there is more than one finalist for a job, a decision must be made as to which will receive the job offer. There is little legal influence on this finalist decision. Presumably, if the steps in the selection process leading up to this point have been within legal bounds, the finalist choice is a legal matter of relative indifference. Despite this, the organization should once again review its EEO/AA commitments, policies, and results to date. Such a review may prove instructive as final choices are made. It represents the organization's "last chance" concerning selection, and the organization should be sure that its decision is consistent with its affirmative action objectives.

SUMMARY

The selection component of a staffing system requires that decisions be made in several areas. The critical concerns are deciding which predictors (assessment methods) to use, determining assessment scores and setting cut scores, making final decisions about applicants, considering who within the organization should help make selection decisions, and complying with legal guidance.

In deciding which assessment methods to use, consideration should be given to the validity coefficient, correlation with other predictors, adverse impact, utility, and applicant reactions. Ideally, a predictor would have a validity coefficient with large magnitude and significance, low correlations with other predictors, little adverse impact, high utility, and be perceived favorably by applicants. In practice, this ideal situation is hard to achieve, so decisions about trade-offs are necessary.

How assessment scores are determined depends on whether a single predictor or multiple predictors are used. In the case of a single predictor, assessment scores are simply the scores on the predictor. With multiple predictors, a compensatory, multiple hurdles, or combined model must be used. A compensatory model allows a person to compensate for a low score on one predictor with a high score on another predictor. A multiple hurdles model requires that a person achieve a passing score on each predictor. A combined model uses elements of both the compensatory and multiple hurdles models.

In deciding who earns a passing score on a predictor or combination of predictors, cut scores must be set. When doing so the consequences of setting different levels of cut scores should be considered, especially those of assessing some applicants as false positives and false negatives. Approaches to determining cutoff scores include minimum competency, top-down, and banding methods. Professional guidelines are reviewed on how best to set cut scores.

Methods of final choice involve determining, from among those who have passed the initial hurdles, who will receive job offers. Several methods of making these decisions are reviewed, including random selection, ranking, and grouping. Each has advantages and disadvantages.

Multiple individuals may be involved in selection decision making. Human resource professionals play a role primarily in determining the selection process to be used and in making selection decisions based on initial assessment results.

Managers play a role primarily in deciding whom to select during the final choice stage. Employees are becoming part of the decision-making process, especially in team assessment approaches. A basic legal issue is conformance with the Uniform Guidelines on Employee Selection Procedures. The UGESP provide guidance on how to set cut scores in ways that help minimize adverse impact and allow the organization to fulfill its EEO/AA obligations.

DISCUSSION QUESTIONS

1. Your boss is considering using a new predictor. The base rate is high, the selection ratio is low, and the validity coefficient is high for the current predictor. What would you advise your boss and why?

2. What are the positive consequences associated with a high predictor cutoff score? What are the negative consequences?

3. Under what circumstances should a compensatory model be used? When should a multiple hurdles model be used?

4. What are the advantages of ranking as a method of final choice over random selection?

5. What roles should human resource professionals play in staffing decisions? Why?

6. What guidelines do the Uniform Guidelines on Employee Selection Procedures offer to organizations when it comes to setting cutoff scores?

APPLICATIONS

Utility Concerns in Choosing an Assessment Method

Randy May is a 32-year-old airplane mechanic for a small airline based in Nantucket Island, Massachusetts. Recently, Randy won $2 million in the New England Lottery. Because Randy is relatively young, he decided to invest his winnings in a business to create a future stream of earnings. After weighing many investment decisions, Randy opted to open up a chain of ice cream shops in the Cape Cod area. (As it turns out, Cape Cod and the nearby islands are short of ice cream shops.) Based on his own budgeting, Randy figured he had enough cash to open shops on each of the two islands (Nantucket and Martha's Vineyard), and two shops in small towns on the Cape (Falmouth and Buzzards Bay). Randy contracted with a local builder and the construction/renovation of the four shops is well under way.

The task that is occupying Randy's attention now is how to staff the shops. Two weeks ago, he placed advertisements in three area newspapers. So far, he has received 100 applications. Randy has done some informal human resource planning and figures he needs to hire 50 employees to staff the four shops. Being a novice at this, Randy is unsure how to select the 50 people he needs to hire. Randy consulted his friend, Mary, who owns the lunch counter at the airport. Mary advised Randy that she used the interview to get "the most knowledgeable people possible," and recommended it to Randy because her people had "generally worked out well." While Randy greatly respected Mary's advice, upon reflection several questions came to mind. Does Mary's use of the interview mean that it meets Randy's requirements? How could Randy determine whether his chosen method of selecting employees was effective or ineffective?

Confused, Randy also sought the advice of Professor Ray Higgins, from whom Randy took a human resource management course while getting his business degree. After learning of his situation, and offering his consulting services, Professor Higgins suggested that Randy choose between one of two selection methods (after paying Professor Higgins' consulting fees, he cannot afford to use both methods). The two methods Professor Higgins recommended are, like Mary, the interview and also a work sample test that entails scooping ice cream and serving it to the customer. Randy estimates that it would cost $100 to interview an applicant and $150 per applicant to administer the work sample. Professor Higgins has told Randy that the validity of the interview is $r = .30$ while the validity of the work sample is $r = .50$. Professor Higgins also informed Randy that if the selection ratio is .50, the average score on the selection measure of those applicants selected is $z = .80$ (.80 standard deviations above the mean). Randy plans to offer employees a wage of $6.00 per hour. (Over the course of a year, this would amount to a $12,000 salary.)

Based on the information presented above, Randy would really appreciate it if you could help him answer the following questions:

1. How much money would Randy save using each selection method?
2. If Randy can use only one method, which should he use?
3. If the number of applicants increases to 200 (more applications are coming in every day), how would your answers to questions 1 and 2 change?
4. What limitations are inherent in the estimates you have made?

Choosing Entrants into a Management Training Program

Come As You Are, a convenience store chain headquartered in Fayetteville, Arkansas, has developed an assessment program to promote nonexempt employees into its management training program. The minimum entrance requirements into the program are five years of company experience, a college degree from an accredited university, and a minimum acceptable job performance rating (3 or higher on their 1–5 scale). Any interested applicant into the program can enroll in the half-day assessment program, where the following assessments are made:

1. cognitive ability test
2. handwriting test
3. integrity test
4. signed permission for background test
5. brief (30-minute) interview by various members of the management team
6. drug test

At the Hot Springs store, 11 applicants have applied for openings in the management training program. The selection information on the candidates is provided in the following exhibit. (The scoring key is provided at the bottom of the exhibit.) It is estimated that there are three slots in the program available for qualified candidates from the Hot Springs location. Given this information and what you know about external and internal selection, as well as staffing decision making, answer the following questions:

1. How would you go about the process of making decisions about who to select for the openings? In other words, without providing your decisions for the individual candidates, describe how you would weigh the various selection information in order to reach a decision.
2. Using the decision-making process from the previous question, who would you select into the training program? Explain your decisions.
3. Although the data provided in the exhibit reveals that all selection measures were given to all 11 candidates, would you advise Come As You Are to continue to administer all the predictors at one time during the half-day assessment program? Or, should the predictors be given in a sequence so that a multiple hurdles or combined approach could be used? Explain your recommendation.

EXHIBIT

Predictor Scores for Eleven Applicants to Management Training Program

Name	Company Experience	College Degree	Performance Rating	Cognitive Ability Test	Handwriting Test	Integrity Test	Background Test	Interview Rating	Drug Test
Peter	4	Yes	4	9	3	6	OK	6	P
Paul	12	Yes	3	3	9	6	OK	8	P
Mary	9	Yes	4	8	1	5	Arrest '95	4	P
Harry	5	Yes	4	5	4	5	OK	4	P
Sally	14	Yes	5	7	6	8	OK	8	P
Ginger	7	No	3	3	7	4	OK	6	P
Fred	6	Yes	4	7	7	8	OK	2	P
Felix	9	Yes	5	2	10	5	OK	7	P
Oscar	10	Yes	4	10	3	9	OK	3	P
Sonny	18	Yes	3	3	8	7	OK	6	P
Cher	11	Yes	4	7	4	6	OK	5	P
Scale	*Years*	*Yes–No*	*1–5*	*1–10*	*1–10*	*1–10*	*OK–Other*	*1–10*	*P–F*

ENDNOTES

1. F. L. Schmidt and J. E. Hunter, "Moderator Research and the Law of Small Numbers," *Personnel Psychology,* 1978, 31, pp. 215–232.

2. J. Cohen, "The Earth Is Round (p < .05)," *American Psychologist*, 1994, 49; pp. 997–1003; F. L. Schmidt, "Quantitative Methods and Cumulative Knowledge in Psychology: Implications for the Training of Researchers," Paper presented at the meeting of the American Psychological Association, Los Angeles, CA, 1994.

3. L. G. Grimm and P. R. Yarnold, *Reading and Understanding Multivariate Statistics* (Washington, DC: American Psychological Association, 1995).

4. L. Gottfredson and J. C. Sharf (eds.), "Fairness in Employment Testing," *A Special Issue of the Journal of Vocational Behavior,* 1988, 33, pp. 225–490.

5. H. C. Taylor and J. T. Russell, "The Relationship of Validity Coefficients to the Practical Effectiveness of Tests in Selection," *Journal of Applied Psychology,* 1939, 23, pp. 565–578.

6. H. E. Brogden, "When Testing Pays Off," *Personnel Psychology,* 1949, 2, pp. 171–183; L. J. Cronbach and G. C. Gleser, *Psychological Tests and Personnel Decisions,* second ed. (Urbana, IL: University of Illinois Press, 1965); F. L. Schmidt, J. E. Hunter, R. C. McKenzie, and T. W. Muldrow, "Impact of Valid Selection Procedures on Work-Force Productivity," *Journal of Applied Psychology,* 1979, 64, pp. 609–626; J. W. Boudreau and C. J. Berger, "Decision Theoretic Utility Analysis Applied to Employee Separations and Acquisitions," *Journal of Applied Psychology,* 1985, 70, pp. 581–612.

7. J. W. Boudreau, "Utility Analysis for Decisions in Human Resource Management," in M. D. Dunnette and L. M. Hough (eds.), *Handbook of Industrial and Organizational Psychology*, vol. 2 (Palo Alto, CA: Consulting Psychologists Press), pp. 621–745.

8. M. C. Sturman and T. A. Judge, "Utility Analysis for Multiple Selection Devices and Multiple Outcomes" (Working paper, Cornell University, 1994).

9. J. Hersch, "Equal Employment Opportunity Law and Firm Profitability," *Journal of Human Resources*, 1991, 26, pp. 139–153.

10. G. V. Barrett, R. A. Alexander, and D. Doverspike, "The Implications for Personnel Selection of Apparent Declines in Predictive Validities Over Time: A Critique of Hulin, Henry, and Noon," *Personnel Psychology*, 1992, 45, pp. 601–617; C. L. Hulin, R. A. Henry, and S. L. Noon, "Adding a Dimension: Time as a Factor in Predictive Relationships," *Psychological Bulletin*, 1990, 107, pp. 328–340.

11. J. W. Boudreau, M. C. Sturman, and T. A. Judge, "Utility Analysis: What Are the Black Boxes, and Do They Affect Decisions?" in N. Anderson and P. Herriot (eds.), *Assessment and Selection in Organizations* (Chichester, England: Wiley, 1994), pp. 77–96.

12. K. M. Murphy, "When Your Top Choice Turns You Down," *Psychological Bulletin*, 1986, 99, pp. 133–138; F. L. Schmidt, M. J. Mack, and J. E. Hunter, "Selection Utility in the Occupation of US Park Ranger for Three Modes of Test Use," *Journal of Applied Psychology*, 1984, 69, pp. 490–497.

13. T. H. Macan and S. Highhouse, "Communicating the Utility of Human Resource Activities: A Survey of I/O and HR Professionals," *Journal of Business and Psychology*, 1994, 8, pp. 425–436.

14. G. P. Latham and G. Whyte, "The Futility of Utility Analysis," *Personnel Psychology*, 1994, 47, pp. 31–46.

15. C. J. Russell, A. Colella and P. Bobko, "Expanding the Context of Utility: The Strategic Impact of Personnel Selection," *Personnel Psychology*, 1993, 46, pp. 781–801.

16. W. F. Cascio, "Assessing the Utility of Selection Decisions: Theoretical and Practical Considerations," in N. Schmitt and W. Borman (eds.), *Personnel Selection in Organizations* (San Francisco: Jossey-Bass, 1993), pp. 310–340.

17. R. D. Arvey and P. R. Sackett, "Fairness in Selection: Current Developments and Perspectives," in N. Schmitt and W. Borman (eds.), *Personnel Selection in Organizations* (San Francisco: Jossey-Bass, 1993), pp. 171–202; R. Cropanzano, "The Justice Dilemma in Employee Selection: Some Reflections on the Trade-Offs Between Fairness and Validity," *Industrial/Organizational Psychologist*, pp. 90–93; S. L. Rynes, "Who's Selecting Whom? Effects of Selection Practices on Applicant Attitudes and Behavior," in N. Schmitt and W. C. Borman (eds.), *Personnel Selection in Organizations* (San Francisco: Jossey-Bass, 1993), pp. 240–274; J. W. Smither, R. R. Reilly R. E. Millsap, K. Pearlman, and R. W. Stoffey, "Applicant Reactions to Selection Procedures," *Personnel Psychology*, 1993, 46, pp. 49–76.

18. K. M. Murphy "When Your Top Choice Turns You Down."

19. S. W. Gilliland, "Effects of Procedural and Distributive Justice on Reactions to a Selection System," *Journal of Applied Psychology*, 1994, 79, pp. 691–701.

20. S. W. Gilliland, "The Perceived Fairness of Selection Systems: An Organizational Perspective," *Academy of Management Review*, 1993, 18, pp. 694–734.

21. A. N. Kluger and H. R. Rothstein, "The Influence of Selection Test Type on Applicant Reactions to Employment Testing," *Journal of Business and Psychology*, 1993, 8, pp. 3–25; S. L. Rynes, "Who's Selecting Whom? Effects of Selection Practices on Applicant Attitudes and Behavior"; S. L. Rynes and M. L. Connerley, "Applicant Reactions to Alternative Selection Procedures," *Journal of Business and Psychology*, 1993, 7, pp. 261–277; H. Schuler, "Social Validity of Selection Situations: A Concept and Some Empirical Results," in H. Schuler, J. L. Farr, and M. Smith (eds.), *Personnel Selection and Assessment: Individual and Organizational Perspectives* (Hillsdale, NJ: Erlbaum), pp. 11–26.

22. J. W. Smither, R. R. Reilly, R. E. Millsap, K. Pearlman, and R. W. Stoffey, "Applicant Reactions to Selection Procedures," I. T. Robertson, P. A. Iles, L. Gratton, and D. Sharpley, "The Impact of Personnel Selection and Assessment Methods on Candidates," *Human Relations*, 1994, 44, pp. 963–982; S. L. Rynes and M. L. Connerly, M. L., "Applicant Reactions to Alternative Selection Procedures."

23. R. Cropanzano, "The Justice Dilemma in Employee Selection: Some Reflections on the Trade-Offs Between Fairness and Validity."

24. T. A. Judge, D. Blancero, D. M. Cable, and D. E. Johnson, "Effects of Selection Systems on Job Search Decisions," Paper presented at the Tenth Annual Conference of the Society for Industrial and Organizational Psychology, 1995 Orlando, FL.

25. E. E. Ghiselli, J. P. Campbell, and S. Zedeck, *Measurement Theory for the Behavioral Sciences* (San Francisco: W. H. Freeman, 1981).

26. J. Sawyer, "Measurement and Predictions, Clinical and Statistical," *Psychological Bulletin*, 1966, 66, pp. 178–200.

27. N. W. Schmitt and R. J. Klimoski, *Research Methods in Human Resources Management* (Cincinnati: South-Western, 1991).

28. F. L. Schmidt, "The Relative Efficiency of Regression and Sample Unit Predictor Weights in Applied Differential Psychology," *Educational and Psychological Measurement*, 1971, 31, pp. 699–714.

29. W. F. Cascio, R. A. Alexander, and G. V. Barrett, "Setting Cutoff Scores: Legal, Psychometric, and Professional Issues and Guidelines," *Personnel Psychology*, 1988, 41, pp. 1–24.

30. W. H. Angoff, "Scales, Norms, and Equivalent Scores," in R. L. Thorndike (ed.), *Educational Measurement* (Washington, DC: American Council on Education, 1971), pp. 508–600; R. E. Biddle, "How to Set Cutoff Scores for Knowledge Tests Used in Promotion, Training, Certification, and Licensing," *Public Personnel Management,* 1993, 22, pp. 63–79.

31. J. P. Hudson, Jr. and J. E. Campion, "Hindsight Bias in an Application of the Angoff Method for Setting Cutoff Scores," *Journal of Applied Psychology*, 1994, 79, pp. 860–865.

32. P. R. Sackett and S. L. Wilk, "Within-Group Norming and Other Forms of Score Adjustment in Preemployment Testing," *American Psychologist*, 1994, 49, pp. 929–954.

33. W. F. Cascio, J. Outtz, S. Zedeck, and I. L. Goldstein, "Statistical Implications of Six Methods of Test Score Use in Personnel Selection," *Human Performance*, 1991, 4, pp. 233–264; P. R. Sackett and L. Roth, "A Monte Carlo Examination of Banding and Rank Order Selection Methods of Test Score Use in Personnel Selection," *Human Performance*, 1991, 4, pp. 279–296.

34. K. R. Murphy, K. Osten, K. and B. Myors, "Modeling the Effects of Banding in Personnel Selection," *Personnel Psychology*, 1995, 48, pp. 61–84.

35. "An Evaluation of Banding Methods in Personnel Selection: A Report of the Scientific Affairs Committee," *The Industrial-Organizational Psychologist*, 1995, 32, pp. 80–86.

36. K. R. Murphy, "Potential Effects of Banding as a Function of Test Reliability," *Personnel Psychology*, 1994, 47, pp. 477–495.

37. P. R. Sackett and S. L. Wilk, "Within-Group Norming and Other Forms of Score Adjustment in Preemployment Testing."

38. W. F. Cascio, I. L. Goldstein, J. Outtz and S. Zedeck, "Twenty Issues and Answers about Sliding Bands," *Human Performance*, 1995, 8, pp. 227–242; W. F. Cascio, S. Zedeck, I. L. Goldstein and J. Outtz, "Selective Science or Selective Interpretation?" *American Psychologist*, 1995, 50, pp. 881–882; L. S. Gottfredson, "The Science and Politics of Race-Norming," *American Psychologist*, 1994, 4, pp. 955–963; K. R. Murphy and B. Myors, "Evaluating the Logical Critique of Banding," *Human Performance*, 1995, 8, pp. 191–201; F. L. Schmidt, "Why All Banding Procedures in Personnel Selection Are Logically Flawed," *Human Performance*, 1991, 4, pp. 265–277; F. L. Schmidt and J. E. Hunter, "The Fatal Internal Contradiction in Banding: Its Statistical Rationale Is Logically Inconsistent with Its Operational Procedures," *Human Performance*, 1995, 8, pp. 203–214; S. Zedeck, J. Outtz, W. F. Cascio, and I. L. Goldstein, "Why Do 'Testing Experts' Have Such Limited Vision?" *Human Performance*, 1991, 4, pp. 297–308.

39. D. S. Ones, C. Viswesvaran, and F. L. Schmidt, "Comprehensive Meta-Analysis of Integrity Test Validities: Findings and Implications for Personnel Selection and Theories of Job Performance," *Journal of Applied Psychology*, 1993, 78, pp. 679–703.

CHAPTER THIRTEEN

Final Match

Employment Contracts
> Requirements for an Enforceable Contract
> Parties to the Contract
> Form of the Contract
> Disclaimers
> Contingencies
> Reneging
> Other Employment Contract Sources

Job Offers
> Applicant Attraction Strategies
> Job Offer Content

Job Offer Process
> Formulation of the Job Offer
> Presentation of the Job Offer
> Job Offer Acceptance and Rejection
> Reneging

New Employee Orientation and Socialization
> Orientation
> Socialization

Legal Issues
> Authorization to Work
> Negligent Hiring
> Employment-at-Will

Summary

Discussion Questions

Applications

In the previous chapter, the focus was on organizational aspects of decision making regarding the likely match or fit between an individual and an organization. The emphasis was on reducing the initial applicant pool to a smaller set of candidates, and identifying one or more job finalists from that candidate set to whom to offer employment.

A final match occurs when the offer receiver and the organization have determined that the probable overlap between the person's KSAOs/motivation and the job's requirements/rewards is sufficient to warrant entering into the employment relationship. Once this decision has been made, the organization and the individual seek to become legally bound to each other through mutual agreement on the terms and conditions of employment. They thus enter into an employment contract, and each expects the other to abide by the terms of the contract. Failure to do so constitutes a breach of contract, which may lead to litigation between the parties as well as potential recovery of damages for the breach.

The formation of, and agreement upon, the employment contract occurs in both external and internal staffing. Any time the matching process is set in motion, either through external or internal staffing, the goal is establishment of a new employment relationship.

Knowledge of employment contract concepts and principles is central to understanding the final match. This chapter begins with an overview of such material, emphasizing the essential requirements for establishing a legally binding employment contract, as well as some of the nuances in doing so. Then major components of a job offer, and points to address in it, are suggested. As is apparent, staffing organizations effectively demands great skill and care by the employer as it enters into employment contracts. The employer and offer receiver are accorded great freedom in the establishment of terms and conditions of employment; both parties have much to decide and agree upon pertaining to job offer content.

Through the job offer process, these terms and conditions are proposed, discussed, negotiated, modified, and, ultimately, agreed upon. The job offer process thus is frequently complex, requiring planning by those responsible for it. Elements and considerations in this process are discussed next.

Once agreement on the terms and conditions of employment has been reached, the final match process is completed, and the formal employment relationship is established. In a sense, staffing activities end at this point. In another sense, however, it is important to phase these activities into initial postemployment activities that help the new employee adapt and adjust to the new job. Employee orientation and socialization activities are discussed as ways to facilitate this.

The chapter concludes with a discussion of specific legal issues that pertain not only to the establishment of the employment contract, but to potential long-run consequences of that contract that must be considered at the time it is established.

EMPLOYMENT CONTRACTS

The establishment and enforcement of employment contracts is a very complex and constantly changing undertaking. Touched on next are some very basic, yet subtle, issues associated with this undertaking. It is crucial to understand the elements that comprise a legally enforceable contract and to be able to identify the parties to the contract (employees or independent contractors, third-party representatives), the form of the contract (written, oral), disclaimers, fulfillment of other conditions, reneging on an offer or acceptance, and other sources (e.g., employee handbooks) that may also constitute a portion of the total employment contract.

Requirements for an Enforceable Contract

There are three basic elements required for a contract to be legally binding and enforceable: offer, acceptance, and consideration.[1] If any one of these is missing, there is no binding contract.

Offer

The offer is usually made by the employer. It is composed of the terms and conditions of employment desired and proposed by the employer. The terms must be clear and specific enough to be acted on by the offer receiver. Vague statements and offers are unacceptable (e.g., "Come to work for me right now; we'll work out the details later"). The contents of newspaper ads for the job, and general written employer material such as a brochure describing the organization, probably are also too vague to be considered offers. Both the employer and the offer receiver should have a definite understanding of the specific terms being proposed.

Acceptance

To constitute a contract, the offer must be accepted on the terms as offered. Thus, if the employer offers a salary of $25,000 per year, the offer receiver must either accept or reject that term. Acceptance of an offer on a contingency basis does not constitute an acceptance. If the offer receiver responds to the salary offer of $25,000 by saying, "Pay me $27,500, and I'll come to work for you," this is not an acceptance. Rather it is a counteroffer, and the employer must now either formally accept or reject it.

The offer receiver must also accept the offer in the manner specified in the offer. If the offer requires acceptance in writing, for example, the offer receiver must accept it in writing. Or, if the offer requires acceptance by a certain date, it must be accepted by that date.

Consideration

Consideration entails the exchange of something of value between the parties to the contract. Usually, it involves an exchange of promises. The employer offers or promises to provide compensation to the offer receiver in exchange for labor, and the offer receiver promises to provide labor to the employer in exchange for compensation. The exchange of promises must be firm and of value, which is usually quite straightforward. Occasionally, consideration can become an issue. For example, if the employer makes an offer to a person that requires a response by a certain date, and then does not hear from the person, there is no contract, even though the employer thought that they "had a deal."

Parties to the Contract

Two issues arise regarding the parties to the contract: whether the employer is entering into a contract with an "employee" or with an "independent contractor,"[2] and whether an outsider or "third party" can execute or otherwise play a role in the employment contract.[3]

Employee or Independent Contractor

Individuals are acquired by the organization as either employees or independent contractors. Both of these terms have definite legal meaning that should be reviewed (see Chapter 3) prior to entering into a contractual relationship. The organization should be clear in its offer whether the relationship being sought is that of employer–employee or employer–independent contractor. Care should be taken to avoid misclassifying the offer receiver as an independent contractor when in fact the receiver will be treated practically as an employee (e.g., subject to specific direction and control by the employer). Such a misclassification can result in substantial tax and other legal liability problems for the organization.

Third Parties

Often times, someone other than the employer or offer receiver speaks on their behalf in the establishment or modification of employment contracts. These people serve as agents for the employer and offer receiver. For the employer, this may mean the use of outsiders such as employment agencies, executive recruiters, or search consultants; it also usually means the use of one or more employees, such as the HR department representative, the hiring manager, higher-level managers, and other managers within the organization. For the offer receiver, it may mean the use of a special agent, such as a professional agent for a sports player or executive. These possibilities raise three important questions for the employer.

First, who if anyone speaks for the offer receiver? This is usually a matter of checking with the offer receiver as to whether any given person is indeed authorized by the offer receiver to be a spokesperson, and what, if any, limits have been placed on that person regarding terms that may be discussed and agreed upon with the employer.

Second, who is the spokesperson for the employer? In the case of its own employees, the employer must recognize that, from a legal standpoint, any of them could be construed as speaking for the employer. Virtually anyone could thus suggest and agree to contract terms, knowingly or unknowingly. This means that the employer should formulate and enforce explicit policies as to who is authorized to speak on its behalf.

Third, exactly what is that person authorized to say? Here, the legal concept of apparent authority is relevant. If the offer receiver believes that a person has the authority to speak for the employer, and there is nothing to indicate otherwise, that person has the apparent authority to speak for the employer. In turn, the employer may be bound by what that person says and agrees to, even if the employer did not grant express authority to do so to this person. It is thus important for the organization to clarify to both the offer receiver and designated spokespersons what the spokesperson is authorized to discuss and agree to without approval from other organizational members.

Form of the Contract

Employment contracts may be written, oral, or even a combination of the two.[4] All may be legally binding and enforceable. Within this broad parameter, however, are numerous caveats and considerations.

Written Contracts

As a general rule, the law favors written contracts over oral ones. This alone should lead an organization to use only written contracts whenever possible.

A written contract may take many forms, and all may be legally enforceable. Examples of a written document that may be construed as a contract include a letter of offer and acceptance (the usual example), a statement on a job application blank (such as an applicant voucher to the truthfulness of information provided), internal job posting notices, and statements in employee handbooks or other personnel manuals. The more specific the information and statements in such documents, the more likely they are to be considered employment contracts.

Unintended problems may arise with these documents. They may become interpreted as enforceable contracts even though that was not their intent (perhaps the intent was merely informational). Or, statements on a given term or condition of employment may contradict each other in various documents.

An excellent illustration of these kinds of problems involves the issue of employment-at-will. Assume an employer wishes to be, as a matter of explicit policy, a strict at-will employer. That desire may be unintentionally undercut by written documents that imply something other than an employment-at-will relationship. For example, correspondence with an applicant may talk of "continued employment after you complete your probationary period." This statement might be legally interpreted as creating something other than a strict at-will employment relationship. To further muddy the waters, the employee handbook may contain an explicit at-will statement, thus contradicting the policy implied in the correspondence with the applicant.

Care must thus be taken to ensure that all written documents accurately convey only the intended meanings regarding terms and conditions of employment. To this end, the following suggestions should be heeded:[5]

1. Before putting anything in writing, ask, Does the company mean to be held to this?
2. Choose words carefully; where appropriate avoid using words that imply binding commitment.
3. Make sure all related documents are consistent with each other.
4. Always have a second person review what another has written.
5. Form the habit of looking at the entire hiring procedure and consider any writings within that context.

Oral Contracts

While oral contracts may be every bit as binding as written contracts, there are two notable exceptions that support placing greater importance on written contracts.

The first exception is the one-year rule, which comes about in what is known as the statute of frauds.[6] Under this rule, a contract that cannot be performed or fulfilled within a one-year interval is not enforceable unless it is in writing. Thus, oral agreements for any length greater than one year are not enforceable. Because of this rule, the organization should not make oral contracts that are intended to last more than one year.

The second exception involves the concept of parole evidence, which pertains to oral promises that are made about the employment relationship.[7] Legally, parole evidence (e.g., the offer receiver's claim that "I was promised that I wouldn't have to work on weekends") may not be used to enforce a contract if it is inconsistent with the terms of a written agreement. Thus, if the offer receiver's letter of appointment explicitly stated that weekend work was required, the oral promise of not having to work weekends would not be enforceable.

Note, however, in the absence of written statements to the contrary, oral statements may indeed be enforceable. In the preceding example, if the letter of appointment was silent on the issue of weekend work, then the oral promise of no weekend work might well be enforceable.

More generally, oral statements are more likely to be enforceable as employment contract terms[8]

1. when there is no written statement regarding the term (e.g., weekend work) in question;

2. when the term is quite certain ("You will not have to work on weekends," as opposed to, "Occasionally, we work weekends around here");

3. when the person making the oral statement is in a position of authority to do so (e.g., the hiring manager as opposed to a coworker);

4. the more formal the circumstances in which the statement was made (the manager's office as opposed to around the bar or dinner table as part of a recruiting trip); and

5. the more specific the promise ("You will work every other Saturday from 8:00 to 5:00," as opposed to, "You may have to work from 8:00 to the middle of the afternoon on the weekends, but we'll try to hold that to a minimum").

As this discussion makes clear, from the legal perspective, oral statements are a potential minefield in establishing employment contracts. They obviously cannot be avoided (employer and applicant have to speak to each other), and they may serve other legitimate and desired outcomes such as providing realistic recruitment information to job applicants. Nonetheless, the organization should use oral statements with extreme caution, and alert all members to its policies regarding their use. As further protection, the organization should include in its written offer that, by accepting the offer, the employee agrees the organization has made no other promises than those contained in the written offer.

Disclaimers

A disclaimer is a statement (oral or written) that explicitly limits an employee right and reserves that right for the employer.[9] Disclaimers are often used in letters of appointment, job application blanks, and employee handbooks.

A common, and increasingly important, employee "right" that is being limited through the use of disclaimer is that of job security. Here, through its policy of employment-at-will, the employer explicitly makes no promise of any job security and reserves the right to terminate the employment relationship at its own will. The following is an example of such a disclaimer that survived legal challenge:

> In consideration of my employment, I agree to conform to the rules and regulations of Sears, Roebuck and Company, and recognize that employment and compensation can be terminated, with or without cause, and with or without notice, at any time, at the option of either the company or myself. I understand that no store manager or representative of Sears, Roebuck and Company, other than the president or vice-president of the company, has any authority to enter into any agreement for employment for any specified period of time, or to make any agreement contrary to the foregoing.[10]

An employment-at-will disclaimer should appear on the application blank, along with two other disclaimers (see Chapter 9). First, there should be a statement of consent by the applicant for the organization to check provided references, along with a waiver of the right to make claims against them for anything they said. Second, there should be a so-called false statement warning, indicating that any false statement, misleading statement, or material omission may be grounds for dismissal.

Disclaimers are generally enforceable. They can thus serve as an important component of employment contracts. Their use should be guided by the following set of recommendations:[11]

1. They should be clearly stated and conspicuously placed in appropriate documents.
2. The employee should acknowledge receipt and review of the document and the disclaimer.
3. The disclaimer should state that it may be modified only in writing, and by whom.
4. The terms and conditions of employment, including the disclaimer, as well as limits on their enforceability, should be reviewed with offer receivers and employees.

It would be wise to obtain legal counsel for drafting language for all disclaimers.

Contingencies

Often, the employer may wish to make a job offer that is contingent upon certain other conditions being fulfilled by the offer receiver.[12] Examples of such contingencies include (a) passage of a particular test, such as a licensure exam (e.g., CPA or bar exam); (b) passage of a medical exam, including alcohol/drugs/screening tests; (c) satisfactory background and reference checks; and (d) proof of employability under the Immigration Reform and Control Act.

While contingencies to a contract are generally enforceable, contingencies to an employment contract (especially those involving any of the preceding examples) are exceedingly complex and may be made only within defined limits. For this reason, contingencies should not be used in employment contracts without prior legal counsel.

Reneging

At times, the employer may wish to withdraw an offer that has already been made to an offer receiver. Or, the offer receiver may wish to withdraw from an offer that has already been extended and accepted. These withdrawals are known as reneging. Though reneging is usually an unfortunate event, and one that may invoke ill feelings, it generally may be done without legal recourse or penalty by either party. This is a logical extension of the employment-at-will concept.

An important exception to this conclusion regarding reneging involves the doctrine of promissory estoppel.[13] This doctrine covers the situation where the offer receiver relied on the employer's job offer with good faith, the offer was subsequently withdrawn by the employer, and the withdrawal had a detrimental effect on the offer receiver. Examples of these effects include resigning from one's current employer, passing up other job opportunities, relocating geographically, and incurring expenses associated with the job offer. When the offer receiver experiences such detrimental reliance, the person may sue the employer for damages; actual hiring of the offer receiver is rarely sought or required in such suits.

Other Employment Contract Sources

As alluded to previously, employment contract terms may be established through multiple sources, not just the letters of job offer and acceptance. Such establishment may be the result of both intentional and unintentional acts by the employer. Moreover, these terms may come about not only when the employment relationship is first established, but also during the course of the employment relationship.[14]

The employer thus must constantly be alert to the fact that terms and conditions of employment may come into being, and be modified, through a variety of employment contract sources. Sources worth reiterating here are employee handbooks (and other written documents) and oral statements made by employer representatives. Job advertisements and job descriptions are generally not considered employment contracts.

In the case of employee handbooks, the employer must consider whether statements in them are legally enforceable or merely informational. While there is legal opinion on both sides of this question, handbooks are being considered increasingly as a legally enforceable part of the employment contract. To avoid this occurrence, the employer may wish to place an explicit disclaimer in the handbook that states the intent to provide only information to employees, and that it will not be bound by any of the statements contained in the handbook.

In the case of oral statements, their danger and the need for caution in their use has already been addressed. It should be remembered that oral statements may present legal problems and challenges when made not only at the time of the initial employment contract, but throughout the course of the employment relationship as well. Of particular concern here are oral promises made to employees regarding future events such as job security ("Don't worry, you will always have a place with us") or job assignments ("After training, you will be assigned as the assistant manager at our new store"). With oral statements, there is thus a constant need to be careful regarding the messages being delivered to employees, as well as who delivers those messages.

JOB OFFERS

A job offer is an attempt by the organization to induce the offer receiver into the establishment of an employment relationship. Assuming that the offer is accepted and that consideration is met, the organization and offer receiver will have established their relationship in the form of a legally binding employment contract. That contract is the culmination of the staffing process. The contract also signifies that the person/job match process has concluded and that the person/job match is now about to become a reality. That reality, in turn, becomes the start of, and foundation for, subsequent employee effectiveness on the various HR outcomes. For these reasons, the content and extension of the job offer become critical final parts of the overall staffing process.

This section discusses job offers as part of an overall applicant attraction strategy, and it relates the job rewards matrix to the making of job offers. Also, the content of job offers is discussed, with a dual emphasis on what is normally required by way of content, and some of the complexities often associated with determining job offer content.

Applicant Attraction Strategies

A basic theme of this book has been that applicants are exposed and subjected to numerous forces throughout the staffing process. These forces include labor markets, laws and regulations, recruitment and selection activities, and knowledge of likely job requirements and rewards. The job offer is the final confluence of these forces and must be crafted and extended within them. It is the organization's attempt to "make it all happen"—to realize the person/job match within this set of forces. Doing this requires thinking of the job offer in strategic terms.

A helpful model for these purposes is the applicant attraction strategy model shown in Exhibit 13.1.[15] This model shows that there are three basic attraction strategy components: recruitment activities, inducements, and applicant pools. The inducements component is of most interest here, for it represents the job rewards (pecuniary or extrinsic, nonpecuniary or intrinsic) that become part and parcel of the job offer. Recruitment activities and applicant pool characteristics are also important components.

The three attraction strategy components combine to influence pre- and postemployment outcomes. The preemployment outcomes are those that occur either before or at the point of job offer acceptance. They include applicant quantity (e.g., number of applicants, percent of vacancies filled), applicant quality (e.g., KSAOs), and spillover effects (e.g., applicants' reports of their recruitment experiences to other people, such as customers or potential future applicants).

Postemployment outcomes represent long-term effects of the attraction strategy, and are also expressed in terms of quantity, quality, and spillover. A quantity indicator might be the one-year retention rate for new hires. For quality, indicators

EXHIBIT 13.1   Model of the Applicant Attraction Process

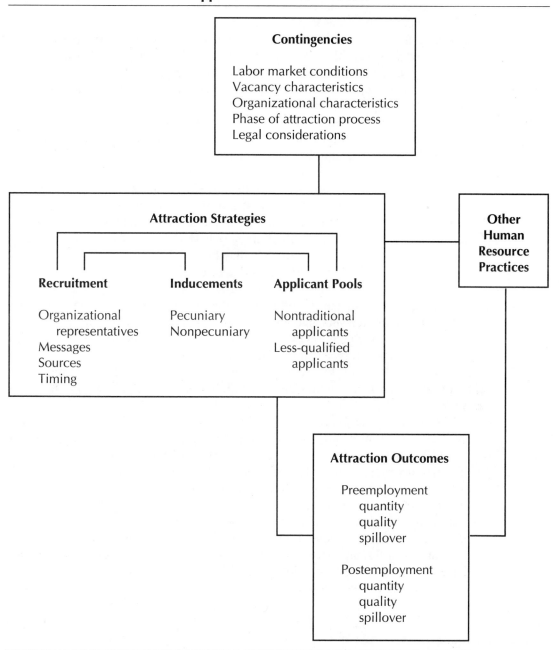

Source: S. L. Rynes and A. E. Barber, "Applicant Attraction Strategies: An Organizational Perspective," *Academy of Management Review*, 1990, 15, pp. 286–310.

might be such things as KSAOs of new hires, their success in entry-level training programs, their performance ratings, and their promotion rates over time. Spillover effects might include the impact of the new hires on other employees, such as their socialization with other employees and acceptance into work groups.

The model suggests that the three recruitment strategy components have definite links to or impact upon the attraction outcomes. These linkages are conditioned, however, by various contingencies such as labor markets and legal influences. The linkages also depend on the operation and effectiveness of other HR activities, such as training and compensation.

The applicant attraction strategy model thus shows that job offers (inducements) do not occur in a vacuum, but in a much broader strategic context. This means that job offers must be synchronized and meshed with other attraction activities and external forces for purposes of achieving effectiveness on the attraction outcomes. For example, the desirability of job offers from the offer receiver's perspective may depend upon the credibility of the organizational representative who delivers it. Or, the content of job offers may have to vary according to characteristics of the recipients. Higher salaries may have to be offered to certain persons, for example, because of their higher levels of qualifications.

Despite these interactions of the job offer content with other forces, it is ultimately the content of the job offer itself that is likely the most important force influencing offer receivers and, thus, determines the effectiveness of the attraction process. It is through the job offer, more than anything else, that the organization seeks to provide the types and amounts of rewards that are sufficient to induce acceptance of the offer by the offer receiver. A "yes" to an offer is explicit recognition by the receiver that the person/job match is sufficiently promising to warrant formally entering into it via an employment contract.

The nature of the job rewards matrix was discussed in Chapter 5. The matrix specifies the extrinsic and intrinsic rewards associated with the job. For each such reward it also shows three reward characteristics: its level or amount, the amount of variability present in the reward among employees, and the reward's stability or frequency of change. Such information is extremely important to communicate to applicants as part of a realistic recruitment campaign (see Chapters 7 and 8). The matrix, however, should not be construed or presented by the organization as part of a job offer to anyone. Rather, it should be emphasized to each person that the matrix is informational only, and that the terms and conditions that count are those contained in the formal job offer. Failure to do this may mean that the job rewards matrix becomes interpreted as part of the actual employment contract.

Job Offer Content

The organization has considerable latitude in the terms and conditions of employment that it may offer to people. That latitude, of course, should be exercised within the organization's particular applicant attraction strategy, as well as the rewards generally available and shown in the job rewards matrix.

With some degree of latitude in terms and conditions offered for almost any job, it is apparent that job offers should be carefully constructed. There are definite rewards that can, and for the most part should, be addressed in any job offer. Moreover, the precise terms or content of the offer to any given finalist requires careful forethought. What follows is a discussion of the types of rewards to address, as well as some of their subtleties and complexities.

Starting Date

Normally, the organization desires to control when the employment relationship begins. To do so, it must provide a definite starting date in its offer. If it does not, acceptance and consideration of the offer occurs at the time the new hire actually begins work. Normally, the starting date is one that allows the offer receiver at least two weeks to provide notification of the resignation date to a current employer.

Duration of Contract

As noted in Chapter 3, employment contracts may be of a fixed term (i.e., have a definite ending date) or indeterminate term (i.e., have no definite ending date). The decision about duration is intimately related to the employment-at-will issue.

A fixed-term contract provides certainty to both the new hire and organization regarding the length of the employment relationship. Both parties decide to and must abide by an agreed-upon term of employment. The organization can then (according to common law) terminate the contract prior to its expiration date for "just cause" only. Determination and demonstration of just cause can be a complicated legal problem for the organization.[16]

Most organizations are unwilling to provide such employment guarantees. They much prefer an employment-at-will relationship in which either party may terminate the employment relationship at any time without having to demonstrate just cause.[17] Should the organization decide to have indeterminate-term employment contracts, it should carefully state in its written offer that the duration is indeterminate, and that it may be terminated by either party at any time, for any reason. Because of the overriding importance of this issue, all wording should be approved at the highest organizational level.

Compensation

Compensation is the most important reward that the organization has to offer in its attraction strategy. It is a multifaceted reward that may be presented to the offer receiver in many forms. Sometimes that may consist of a standard pay rate and benefit package which must be simply accepted or rejected. Other times the offer may be a more tailor-made one, often negotiated in advance.

It should be remembered that job seekers carry with them a set of pay preferences and expectations that shape how they respond to the compensation components of the job offer. For example, a study of engineering and hotel administration soon-to-graduate job seekers found that they would respond more favorably to a pay package that had (a) a high, fixed rate of pay that was not contingent on the success of the organization, (b) pay pegged to a particular job, rather than the number of skills they possessed, (c) pay raises based on individual, rather than group, performance, and (d) a flexible, as opposed to standard, benefits package.[18]

The compensation portion of the job offer should thus be carefully thought out and planned in advance. This pertains to starting pay, incentive or bonus pay, and benefits.

Starting Pay: Flat Rate   In flat rate job offers, all persons are offered an identical rate of pay, and variance from this is not permitted. Starting pay is thus offered on a "take it or leave it" basis.

Use of flat rates is appropriate in many circumstances. Examples of these include:

1. jobs for which there is a plentiful supply of job applicants
2. where applicants are of quite similar KSAO quality
3. where there is a desire to avoid creating potential inequities in starting pay among new employees

It should also be noted that under some circumstances use of flat rates may be mandatory. Examples here include pay rates under many collective bargaining agreements, and for many jobs covered by civil service laws and regulations.

Starting Pay: Differential Rates   Organizations often opt out of flat rates, despite their simplicity, and choose differential starting pay rates. In general, this occurs under two sets of circumstances.

First, there are situations where the organization thinks there are clear qualitative (KSAO) differences among finalists. Some finalists are thus felt to be worth more than others, and starting pay differentials are used in recognizing this. A good example here involves new college graduates. Research clearly shows that differences in major and previous work experience lead to starting pay differentials among them.[19]

The second situation occurs when the organization is concerned about attraction outcomes, almost regardless of applicant KSAO differences. Here, the organization is under intense pressure to acquire new employees and fill vacancies promptly. To accomplish these outcomes, flexibility in starting pay rate offers is used to be responsive to finalists' demands, to sweeten offers, and otherwise impress applicants with an entrepreneurial spirit of wheeling and dealing. Hence, the organization actively seeks to strike a bargain with the offer receiver, and differential starting pay rates are a natural part of the attraction package.

Whenever differential rates of starting pay are to be used, there is the need for the organization to carefully consider what is permissible and within bounds. At times, the organization may choose to provide minimal guidance to managers making the offers. Often, however, there is a need for some constraints on managers. These constraints may specify when differential starting pay offers may be made, and where within a pay range starting pay rates must fall. Exhibit 13.2 contains examples of such starting pay policies.

Pay Incentives and Bonuses   Pay incentives and bonuses may be available on jobs, and, if so, the organization should address this in the job offer.

Prior to the job offer itself, the organization should give serious thought to whether there should be an incentive or bonus plan in the first place. This is a major issue that far transcends staffing per se, but it does have important implications for the likely effectiveness of staffing activities.

Consider an organization with sales jobs, a classic example of a situation in which incentive or commission pay systems might be used. The mere presence/absence of such a pay plan will likely affect the motivation/job rewards part of the matching process. Such likely effects will carry over to the staffing processes of the organization. Retailers such as Sears and Dayton-Hudson, for example, are cutting back on the use of sales commission plans because of difficulties in attracting and retaining employees. These difficulties come from employees' desire for a straight salary, a revulsion for the pressure of commission selling, a lack of

---

EXHIBIT 13.2   Example of Starting Pay Policies

The Wright Company

The following policies regarding starting pay must be adhered to:

1. No person is to be offered a salary that is below the minimum, or above the midpoint, of the salary range for the job.
2. Generally, persons with reasonable qualifications should be offered a salary within the first quartile (bottom 25%) of the salary range for the job.
3. Salary offers above the first quartile, but not exceeding the midpoint, may be made for exceptionally well-qualified persons, or when market conditions dictate.
4. Salary offers should be fair in relation to other offers made and to the salaries paid to current employees.
5. Salary offers below the first quartile may be made without approval; offers at or above the first quartile must be approved in advance by the Manager of Compensation.
6. Counteroffers may not be accepted without approval of the Manager of Compensation.

training to provide them the KSAOs necessary for selling success, and a lack of promotion into the managerial ranks for successful salespeople.[20] In short, different "breeds of cat" may be attracted to jobs providing incentive plans as opposed to those that do not.

If there are to be incentive or bonus pay plans, the organization should communicate this in the offer letter. Beyond that, the organization should give careful consideration to how much detail about such plans, including payout formulas and amounts, it wants to include in the job offer. The more specific the information, the less flexibility the organization will have in the operation or modification of the plan.

Benefits Normally there is a fixed benefit package for a job, and it is offered as such to all offer receivers. Occasionally, however, differential benefit packages and/or custom-made benefit packages enter into the job offer picture. The classic example here involves the pay package for high-level executives, which normally has a detailed benefit component to it. That component is usually tailored to the individual executive, and it arises from negotiations as to its contents. The issues involve both regular benefits as well as perquisites (or "perks") to be provided. These run the gamut from life insurance to kidnapping insurance, severance packages (also called "golden parachutes") to stock option plans, country club memberships to corporate planes, and so forth.

Less rarified and more recent examples of benefits that are being offered on a personalized basis are what is generically referred to as "stuff."[21] What is stuff made up of? The answer is a vast list of perks, goodies, and assorted services. Examples include a car phone, personal computer and fax machine, take-home food from the company cafeteria, adoption assistance, and student loan assistance. Some recent MBA graduates not only received average salary offers in excess of $100,000 annually, but also stuff such as interest-free loans, tuition reimbursements, and free cars.[22]

In terms of job offers, both executive perks and stuff raise questions about whether, and how, they should be represented in the content of the offer. By not mentioning them, the organization does not commit itself to formally providing them as a term and condition of employment. Doing this, however, may diminish the potential recruitment and attraction value of stuff. Conversely, mentioning them in the job offer heightens awareness of them, but also commits the organization to providing them over the course of the contract. Also, the offer receiver may insist that the offer deal with these items, and then the organization may have little choice but to do so. This is particularly the case with executive perks, and may well become the case with certain stuff that has high perceived value to the offer receiver.

Hours

Statements regarding hours of work should be carefully thought out and worded. For the organization, such statements will affect staffing flexibility and cost. In terms of flexibility, a statement such as, "Hours of work will be as needed and scheduled," provides maximum flexibility. Designation of work as part-time, as opposed to full-time, may affect cost because the organization may provide restricted, if any, benefits to part-time employees.

Factors other than just number of hours may also need to be addressed in the job offer. If there are to be any special, tailor-made hours of work arrangements, these need to be clearly spelled out. Examples include "Weekend work will not be required of you," and "Your hours of work will be from 7:30 to 11:30 A.M., and 1:30 to 5:30 P.M."

Special Hiring Inducements

At times, the organization may want or need to offer special inducements to increase the likelihood that an offer will be accepted. Two common examples of these inducements are hiring bonuses and relocation assistance.

Hiring Bonuses   Hiring, signing, or "up-front" bonuses are one-time payments offered and subsequently paid upon acceptance of the offer. Typically, the bonus is in the form of an outright cash grant; the bonus may also be in the form of a cash advance against future expected earnings.

One example of hiring bonuses is that employed by brokerage firms, who have long used them as a way of luring applicants away from competitors. Bonuses up to $100,000 are not uncommon. The bonus is usually a combination of cash grant and cash advance against future sales commissions.[23]

Another example is the use of hiring bonuses for new bachelor's and master's degree graduates. A survey of employers found 23% of them were paying hiring bonuses, from $1,471 to $3,200 for bachelor's degrees and $4,500 to $8,474 for master's degrees.[24]

Relocation Assistance   Acceptance of the offer may require a geographic move and entail relocation costs for the offer receiver. The organization may want to provide assistance to conduct the move, as well as totally or partially defray moving costs. Thus, a relocation package may include assistance with house hunting, guaranteed purchase of the applicant's home, a mortgage subsidy, and actual moving cost reimbursement.

A survey of employers hiring recent graduates found that 79% of them provided relocation assistence, at an average cost of $4,749. Almost all of the employers paid for the travel expense of the new hire and partner, moving of personal and household goods, auto transportation, and temporary housing. Only one-third, however, paid for a trip to look for housing.[25]

Recently, relocation has become even more difficult in dual career circumstances.[26] With both people working, it may be necessary to move both the offer receiver and the accompanying partner. Such a move may entail employing both people, or providing job search assistance to the accompanying partner. The problem is likely to grow in magnitude.

Other Terms and Conditions

Job offers are by no means restricted to the terms and conditions discussed so far. Virtually any terms and conditions may be covered and presented in a job offer, provided they are legally permissible. Hence, the organization should carefully and creatively think of other terms it may wish to offer. None of these other possible terms should be offered, however, unless the organization is truly willing to commit itself to them as part of a legally binding contract.

The organization should also give careful thought to the possible use of contingencies, which, as mentioned previously, are terms and conditions that the applicant must fulfill before the contract becomes binding (e.g., passage of a medical exam). As was noted, inclusion of these contingencies should not be done without prior knowledge and understanding of their potential legal ramifications (e.g., in the case of a medical exam, potential factors to consider under the Americans with Disabilities Act).

Acceptance Terms

The job offer should specify terms of acceptance required of the offer receiver. For reasons previously noted regarding oral contracts, acceptances should normally be required in writing only. The receiver should be required to accept or reject the offer in total, without revision. Any other form of acceptance is not an acceptance, but merely a counteroffer. Finally, the offer should specify the date, if any, by which it will lapse. A lapse date is recommended so that certainty and closure are brought to the offer process.

Sample Job Offer Letter

A sample job offer letter is shown in Exhibit 13.3 that summarizes and illustrates the previous discussion and recommendations regarding job offers. This letter should be read and analyzed for purposes of becoming familiar with job offer letters, as well as gaining an appreciation for the many points that need to be addressed in such a letter. Remember that, normally, whatever is put in the job offer letter, once accepted by the receiver, becomes a binding employment contract.

JOB OFFER PROCESS

Besides having a knowledge of the types of issues to address in a job offer, it is equally important to have an understanding of the total job offer process. The content of any specific job offer must be formulated within a broad context of considerations. Once these have been taken into account, the specific offer must be developed and presented to the finalist. Following this, there will be matters to address in terms of either acceptance or rejection of the offer. Finally, there will be an occasional need to deal with the unfortunate issue of reneging, either by the organization or by the offer receiver.

EXHIBIT 13.3   Example of Job Offer Letter

The Wright Company

Mr. Laverne Markowski
152 Legion Lane
Clearwater, Minnesota

Dear Mr. Markowski:

We are pleased to offer you the position of Human Resource Specialist, beginning March 1, 1996. Your office will be located here in our main facility at Silver Creek, Minnesota.

This offer is for full-time employment, meaning you will be expected to work a minimum of 40 hours per week. Weekend work is also expected, especially during peak production periods.

Your starting pay will be $2,100 per month. Should you complete one year of employment, you will then participate in our managerial performance review and merit pay process.

Should you choose to relocate to the Silver Creek area, we will reimburse you for one house/apartment hunting trip for up to $1,000. We will also pay reasonable and normal moving expenses up to $7,500, with receipts required.

It should be emphasized that we are an employment-at-will employer. This means that we, or you, may terminate our employment relationship at any time, for any reason. Only the president of the Wright Company is authorized to provide any modification to this arrangement.

This offer is contingent upon (a) your receiving certification as a Professional in Human Resources (PHR) from the Human Resource Certification Institute prior to March 1, 1996, and (b) your passing a company-paid and -approved medical exam prior to March 1, 1996.

We must have your response to this offer by February 1, 1996, at which time the offer will lapse. If you wish to accept our offer as specified in this letter, please sign and date at the bottom of the letter and return it to me (a copy is enclosed for you). Should you wish to discuss these or any other terms prior to February 1, 1996, please feel free to contact me.

Sincerely yours,

Mary Kaiser
Senior Vice President, Human Resources

I accept the employment offer, and its terms, contained in this letter. I have received no promises other than those contained in this letter.

_____   _____
Signed   Date

Formulation of the Job Offer

When the organization puts together a job offer, several factors should be explicitly considered. These factors are knowledge of the terms and conditions offered by competitors, applicant truthfulness about KSAO and reward information provided, the receiver's likely reaction to the offer, and policies on negotiation of job offer content with the offer receiver.

Knowledge of Competitors

As discussed in Chapter 2, the organization competes for labor within labor markets. The job offer must be sensitive to the labor demand and supply forces operating, for these forces set the overall parameters for job offers to be extended.

On the demand side, this requires becoming knowledgeable about the terms and conditions of job contracts offered and provided by competitors. Here, the organization must confront two issues: exactly who are the competitors, and exactly what terms and conditions are they offering for the type of job for which the hiring organization is staffing?

Assume the hiring organization is a national discount retailer, and it is hiring recent (or soon-to-be) college graduates for the job of management trainee. It may identify as competitors other retailers at the national level (e.g., Sears), as well as national discount retailers (e.g., Target, Wal-Mart, and Kmart). There may be fairly direct competitors in other industries as well (e.g., banking, insurance) that typically place new college graduates in training programs.

Once such competitors are identified, the organization needs to determine, if possible, what terms and conditions they are offering. This may be done through formal mechanisms such as performing salary surveys, reading competitors' ads, or consulting with trade associations. Information may be gathered informally as well, such as through telephone contacts with competitors, and conversations with actual job applicants who have firsthand knowledge of competitors' terms.

Through all of these mechanisms, the organization becomes "marketwise" regarding its competitors. Invariably, however, the organization will discover that, for any given term or condition, there will be a range of values offered. For example, starting pay might range from $24,000 per year to $34,500, and the length of the training program may vary from three months to two years. The organization will thus need to determine where within these ranges it wishes to position itself in general, as well as for each particular offer receiver.

On the labor supply side, the organization will need to consider its needs concerning both labor quantity and quality (KSAOs and motivation). In general, offers need to be attractive enough that they yield the head count required. Moreover, offers need to take into account the KSAOs each specific receiver possesses, and what these specific KSAOs are worth in terms and conditions offered the person. This calculation is illustrated in Exhibit 13.2, which shows an example of an organization's policies regarding differential starting pay offers among offer receivers. Such differential treatment, and all the issues and questions it raises, applies to virtually any other term or condition as well.

Applicant Truthfulness

Throughout the recruitment and selection process, information about KSAOs and other factors (e.g., current salary) is being provided by the applicant. Initially, this information is gathered as part of the assessment process, whose purpose is to determine which applicants are most likely to provide a good fit with job requirements and rewards. For applicants who pass the hurdles and are to receive job offers, the information that has been gathered may very well be used to decide the specific terms and conditions to include in a job offer. Just how truthful or believable is this information? The content and cost of job offers depends on how the organization answers this question.

There is little solid evidence on the degree of applicant truthfulness. However, there are some anecdotal indications that lack of truthfulness by applicants may be a problem.

Consider the case of starting pay. Quite naturally, the organization may wish to base its starting pay offer on knowledge of what the offer receiver's pay is currently. Will the person be truthful or deceitful in reporting current salary? Indications are that deceit may be common. People may embellish or enhance not only their reported salaries, but their KSAOs as well, in order to provide an artificially high base or starting point for the organization as it prepares its job offer. A production analyst earning $55,000 did this and obtained a new job at $150,00, with a company car and a country club membership also included in the package.[27]

To combat such deceit by applicants, organizations are becoming increasingly prone to pursue verification of all applicant information, including salary, and may go to extremes to do so. At the executive level, for example, some organizations now require people to provide copies of their W-2 income forms that are used for reporting to the Internal Revenue Service. The organization should not act on finalist-provided information in the preparation of job offers unless it is willing to assume, or has verified, that the information is accurate.

Likely Reactions of Offer Receivers

Naturally, the terms and conditions to be presented in an offer should be based on some assessment of the receiver's likely reaction to it. Will the receiver jump at it or laugh at it, or something in between?

One way to gauge likely reactions to the offer is to gather information about various preferences from the offer receiver during the recruitment/selection process. Such preliminary discussions and communications will help the organization construct an offer that is likely to be acceptable. At the extreme, the process may lead to almost simultaneous presentation and acceptance of the offer.

Another way to assess likely reactions to offers from offer receivers is to conduct research on why they accept or decline job offers. An example of this is a study of finalists for entry-level jobs in a broad range of occupations (e.g., accounting, mathematics, biology, immigration inspection) in the federal civil service.[28] While all finalists had been certified as qualified and thus eligible to receive a job offer, some accepted the offer and others declined to even receive the offer. Results of the study are shown in Exhibit 13.4.

The results show that several terms and conditions were responsible for the split between accepters and decliners. The most important were starting pay and cost of living in the relevant location. Also important were other extrinsic and intrinsic rewards, such as opportunities for advancement and quality of work (i.e., utilization of KSAOs). Note also that, rewards aside, the excessive length of the recruitment process itself also played a role in decliners' decisions.

EXHIBIT 13.4   Comparison of Job Offer Accepters and Decliners in Federal Government

---

A.   SURVEY METHODOLOGY

We obtained hiring data from the Office of Personnel Management for June through November 1990. This data was the most recent available. During this period, 78 people accepted offers and were hired for entry-level professional and administrative positions from OPM job registers; 132 people declined those same jobs.

Because of the limited hiring and timing period, the conclusions that can be drawn from our survey data are limited. The data represent only the 52 accepters and 94 decliners who responded to our survey questionnaires. Nevertheless, we believe the information is important because it sheds light on some of the reasons for the government's recruiting difficulties.

B.   SURVEY RESULTS

Financial considerations dominated the decliners' reasons for their decisions. Two-thirds or more said low salaries or the high cost of living in the job locations caused them to lose interest in federal employment. A comment one of the decliners wrote on her questionnaire reflected a typical concern: "To the best of my knowledge, this job offered below $20,000 per year. With the cost of living anywhere, much less New York City, I don't know how anyone could make it."

Two-thirds of the 61 decliners who were in permanent jobs or self-employed said they would have suffered pay cuts if they had taken the federal jobs. For 24 decliners (39 percent), the loss would have been more than $6,000 a year.

In contrast, most of the accepters said salaries were not the driving force behind their decisions. Over three-fourths said opportunities for career advancement or a chance to apply their education and skills were of great or very great importance in selecting federal employment. Sixteen accepters (31 percent) said salary was an important factor. The location of the job was influential with about half of the accepters.

Unlike the decliners, the majority of the 19 accepters who were self-employed or in permanent jobs said they received pay increases when they joined the government. For five accepters, the increase was more than $6,000.

(continued)

EXHIBIT 13.4 Continued

Another important difference between accepters and decliners related to their employment status. Compared to the decliners, a larger proportion of accepters were unemployed at the time they were offered a federal job. Thus, the need for a better paying job, or a job of any kind, appears to have been a major factor in many of the accepters' decisions.

Fifty-six decliners (65 percent) said the location of the job was a great or very great factor in their decisions to reject federal employment.

The next highest factors related to the decliners' perceptions of the nature and quality of federal work. Thirty-nine decliners (45 percent) thought they would be unable to apply their education and skills, while the same number thought there would be few opportunities for career advancement.

The length of the hiring process was a great or very great consideration to 35 decliners (42 percent). In fact, 47 decliners (56 percent) said they had accepted other jobs while waiting to hear the results of their federal job applications. One candidate wrote the following in her questionnaire:

"... I declined because it was too far to travel for an interview and I had already found a full-time job. However, I have applied for several other federal government jobs and the hiring process is worse than any I have encountered. . . . In the length of time it takes to start, I imagine that most of the good candidates have already found other jobs."

Thirty-three decliners (38 percent) said they turned down federal employment because they believed the work would not be challenging.

Source: U.S. Government Accounting Office, "Survey of Applicants Who Accepted or Declined Federal Job Offers" (Washington, D.C.: author, March 20, 1992, B-243207).

How would such results be used in the formulation of job offers? There seems to be a clear need for higher starting pay to be offered. This may not only address low pay and high cost of living issues, but help compensate for deficiencies in intrinsic rewards. Steps will also have to be taken to shorten the recruitment process. More generally, there is probably a need to examine the total applicant attraction strategy used (i.e., recruitment practices, extrinsic and intrinsic rewards, and applicant pools). Once this examination has been completed, then the narrower issue of job offer formulation can be more thoughtfully addressed.

Policies on Negotiations and Initial Offers

Prior to making job offers, the organization should decide whether or not it will negotiate on them. In essence, the organization must decide whether its first offer to a person will also be its final offer.

Several considerations should be borne in mind when formulating strategies and policies for making job offers. First, remember that job offers occur for both external and internal staffing. For external staffing, the job offer is intended to convert the offer receiver into a new hire. For internal staffing, the job offer is being made to induce the employee to accept a new job assignment or to attempt to retain the employee by making a counteroffer to an offer the employee has received from another organization. These separate types of job offers (new hires, new assignment, retention) will likely require separate job offer strategies and policies.

Second, consider fully the costs of not having a job offer be accepted by the offer receiver. Are there other equally qualified individuals available as "backup" offer receivers? How long can the organization afford to let a position remain vacant? How will current employees feel about job offers being rejected—will they, too, feel rejected, or that something they are unaware of is amiss in the organization? Will those next in line to receive an offer feel like second-class citizens or choices of desperation and last resort? Answers to such questions will often suggest it may be desirable to negotiate (up to a point) with the offer receiver.

Third, recognize that many people to whom you will be making offers may in turn be seeking and receiving counteroffers from their current employer. Anecdotal evidence suggests that counteroffers are being used much more frequently in attempts to retain increasingly less loyal employees. ("People are jumping jobs so frequently these days that U.S. business is beginning to look like a French bedroom farce. The new morality says that you have to be more loyal to your career than to your company, and the new math adds, if you are typical, you'll have about ten employers during your working life. So even if you're not hopping around now, you may soon be."[29]) Shortages of qualified replacements and the high cost of hiring replacements also contribute to the counteroffer wave. Hence, the organization should recognize that any offer it makes may lead to a bidding war of sorts with other organizations.

Fourth, a currently employed offer receiver normally incurs costs for leaving and will expect a "make whole" offer from the organization. Often these costs can amount to 20–30% of the offer receiver's current base pay. In addition to relocation or higher commuting costs, the offer receiver may forfeit employer contribution to a retirement plan, vacation time and holidays, various perks, and so forth. In addition, there may be waiting periods before the offer receiver would be eligible for various benefits, leading to opportunity costs of lost coverage and possibly paying the costs (e.g., health insurance premiums) out of pocket until coverage begins.

Finally, job seekers are often quite sophisticated in formulating and presenting their demands to the organization. They will know what it truly costs them to leave their current job and frame their demands accordingly. They will be aware of the particular KSAOs that they uniquely have to offer, make these acutely known to the organization, and demand a high price for them. The terms demanded (or more politely, "proposed") may focus not only on salary, but myriad other possibilities including vacation time, a flexible work schedule to help balance work and family pressures, guaranteed expenditures on training and development, higher employer matching to a 40l(k) retirement plan, and so on. In short, unless it is illegal, it is negotiable, and the organization must be prepared to handle demands from job seekers on virtually every term and condition of employment.

Presumably, each term or condition contained in an offer is a mini-offer itself. For each term or condition, therefore, the organization must decide

1. whether it will negotiate on this term or condition; and
2. if it negotiates, what are its lower and (especially) upper bounds.

Once these questions have been answered, the organization may determine its posture regarding the presentation of the initial offer to the receiver. There are three basic strategies to choose from: lowball, competitive, and best shot.

Lowball   This strategy involves offering the lower bounds of terms and conditions to the receiver. Advantages to this strategy include getting acceptances from desperate or unknowledgeable receivers, minimizing initial employment costs, and leaving plenty of room to negotiate upward. Dangers to the lowball strategy are failing to get any acceptances, driving people away from and out of the finalist pool, developing an unsavory reputation among future potential applicants, and creating inequities and hard feelings that the reluctant accepter may carry into the organization, which may then influence postemployment attraction outcomes, such as retention.

Competitive   With a competitive strategy, the organization prepares an offer that it feels is "on the market," neither too high nor too low. The competitive strategy should yield a sufficient number of job offer acceptances overall, though not all of the highest-quality (KSAO) applicants. This strategy leaves room for subsequent negotiation, should that be necessary. Competitive offers are unlikely to either offend or excite the receiver, and they probably will not have negative consequences for postemployment outcomes.

Best Shot   With this strategy, the organization "goes for broke" and gives a high offer, one right at the upper bounds of feasible terms and conditions. Accompanying this offer is usually a statement to the receiver that this is indeed the organization's "best shot," thus leaving little or no room for negotiation. These offers should enhance both preemployment attraction outcomes (e.g., filling vacancies quickly) and postemployment outcomes (e.g., job satisfaction). Best-shot offers obviously increase employment costs. They also leave little or no room for negotiation or for "sweetening" the offer. Finally, they may create feelings of inequity or jealousy among some current employees.

None of these initial offer strategies is inherently superior. But the organization does need to make some choices as to which to generally use. It could also choose to tailor-make a strategy to fit the finalist pursued, as well as other circumstances. For example, the best-shot strategy may be chosen (a) for high-quality finalists,

(b) when there are strong competitive hiring pressures from competitors, (c) when the organization feels great pressure to fill vacancies quickly, and (d) as part of an aggressive EEO/AA recruitment program.

Presentation of the Job Offer

Presentation of the offer may proceed along many different paths. The precise path chosen depends upon the content of the offer, as well as factors considered in formulating the offer. To illustrate, two extreme approaches to presenting the job offer—the mechanical and the sales approaches—are detailed.

Mechanical Approach

The mechanical approach is a dry, sterile one that relies on simple one-way communication from the organization to the offer receiver. Little more than a standard, or "form," written offer is sent to the person. The organization then awaits a response. Little or no input about the content of the offer is received from the person, and after the offer has been made, there is no further communication with the person. If the person rejects the offer, another form letter acknowledging receipt of the rejection is sent. Meanwhile, the offer process is repeated anew, without modification, for a different receiver.

Sales Approach

The sales approach treats the job offer as a product that must be developed and sold to the customer (i.e., receiver). There is active interaction between the organization and the receiver as the terms and conditions are developed and incorporated into an offer package. There is informal agreement that unfolds between the receiver and organization, and reduction of that agreement into an actual job offer is a mere formality. After the formal offer has been presented, the organization continues to have active communication with the receiver. In this way, the organization can be alert to possible glitches that occur in the offer process, and continue to sell the job to the receiver.

An excellent example of the sales approach is shown in Exhibit 13.5. This example is based on two premises:

1. The offer is not a gift. Instead, it must be sold to the receiver. Extending the job offer is a sales job and should be treated as such.
2. If possible, an offer should not be left open awaiting a response, since this generally precludes making an offer to another person.[30]

As the mechanical and sales approaches to job offer presentation make clear, the organization has considerable discretion in choosing how it delivers the offer. When it develops its job offer presentation process, it should be ever mindful of the applicant attraction strategy (Exhibit 13.1), and its emphasis on both the re-

EXHIBIT 13.5   Example of a Sales Approach to Job Offers

Steps in the Hiring Process

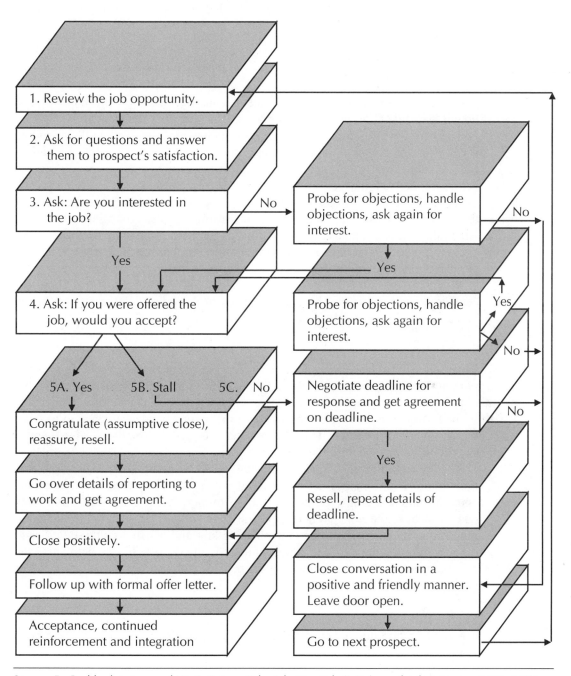

Source: R. Goddard, J. Fox, and W. E. Patton, "The Job-Hire Sale," *Personnel Administrator,* 1989, 34(6), p. 121. Reprinted with the permission of HR Magazine (formerly Personnel Administrator) published by the Society for Human Resource Management, Alexandria, VA.

cruitment process and job offer content, as factors affecting applicant attraction outcomes.

Job Offer Acceptance and Rejection

Ultimately, of course, job offers are accepted and rejected. How this happens, and how it is handled, are often as important as the outcomes themselves.

There is very little solid data about how organizations actually handle the ending stage of the final match process. An exception to this involves college recruiting. Survey data reveal some indications about the acceptance and rejection process for new college graduates.[31] Results of that survey are shown in Exhibit 13.6.

It is clear from the exhibit that the surveyed companies differ in how they handle the acceptance/rejection process. As an interesting exercise, the reader should examine those results and ask two questions about them. First, why do these differences in practice exist? Second, how might these differences in practice affect the attraction outcomes?

Provided next are some general suggestions and recommendations about acceptances and rejections. These are intended to serve as advice about additional practices and issues involved in the job offer process.

Acceptance

When the offer receiver accepts a job offer, the organization should do two important things. First, it should check the receiver's actual acceptance to ensure that it has been accepted as required in the offer. Thus, the acceptance should not come in the form of a counteroffer or with any other contingencies attached to it. Also, the acceptance should occur in the manner required (normally, writing), and it should arrive on or before the date specified.

The second thing the organization must do is maintain contact with the new hire. Initially, this means acknowledging receipt of the acceptance. Additional communication may also be appropriate to further "cement the deal" and build commitment to the new job and organization. Examples of such continued communication include soon-to-be coworkers calling and offering congratulations to the new hire, sending work materials and reports to the new hire to help phase the person into the new job, and inviting the new hire to meetings and other activities prior to that person's starting date.

Rejection

The organization may reject the finalist, and the finalist may reject the organization.

By the Organization Depending on the decision-making process used, the acceptance of an offer by one person means that the organization will now have to

---

EXHIBIT 13.6   College Recruitment Practices Regarding Job Offers

---

Process: Rejection to Acceptance

. . . The campus interviewee is notified of your interest or rejection:

at the close of the campus interview 2%

later by letter or telephone 91%

only notified if company is interested by phone or letter 7%

. . . The second or follow-up interview is usually conducted:

the same day or in next few days on campus 4%

later at a corporate office or plant 95%

later by a third-party contractor off campus 1%

. . . After the campus interview, the second interview will likely occur:

within two weeks 5%

within one month 44%

within three months 23%

any time that is mutually convenient 28%

. . . If the candidate is rejected after the second interview is completed, she/he will be notified:

on-site—in person and immediately 2%

later by letter or phone 98%

. . . If an offer of employment is extended, it will usually be made:

after the first interview, by the on-campus interviewer in person 0%

after a single on-campus interview, but later by letter or phone 1%

after a second on-campus interview 1%

in person at the conclusion of the second interview(s) conducted on-site 5%

after the second on-site interview and usually within:

one week	40%	within 3 days	5%
one month	35%	later	5%

. . . Once a job offer is extended, the candidate is usually expected to accept or reject it:

immediately	2%	within 3 days	4%
within 1 week	15%	within 2 weeks	24%
within 1 month	15%	within 2 months	3%
within the quarter or semester	3%	at candidate's convenience	1%
open—but mutually agreeable	33%		

. . . Do you think your procedures are "forcing" the candidate into an early decision?

Yes	3%	No	97%

. . . Do you feel that you as a recruiter are under pressure, given present market conditions, to meet your hiring goals early?

Yes, significantly 5%

Yes, some 37%

Not at all 58%

Source: V. R. Lindquist, *Trends in the Employment of College and University Graduates in Business and Industry,* 1992, p. 10. The Lindquist-Endicott Report-1992 by Victor R. Lindquist, Published by The Northwestern University Placement Center, Evanston, IL.

reject others. This should be done promptly and courteously. Moreover, the organization should keep records of those it rejects. This is necessary for legal purposes (e.g., applicant flow statistics), and for purposes of building and maintaining a pool of potential applicants that the organization may wish to contact about future vacancies.

The content of the rejection message (usually a letter) is up to the discretion of the organization. Most organizations opt for short and vague content that basically mentions a lack of fit between applicant and job characteristics. Providing more specific reasons for rejection should only be done with caution. The reasons provided should be candid and truthful, and they should match with the reasons recorded and maintained on other documents by the organization.

By the Offer Receiver   When the receiver rejects the job offer, the organization must first decide whether it wants to accept the rejection or extend a new offer to the person. If the organization's position on negotiations has already been determined, as ideally it should, then there is little reason to reconsider the position chosen on negotiations.

When the rejection is accepted, it should be done so promptly and courteously. Moreover, records should also be kept of these rejections, for the same reasons they are kept when rejection by the organization occurs.

Reneging

Occasionally, and unfortunately, reneging occurs. Organizations renege on offers extended, and receivers renege on offers accepted. Solid evidence on reneging, and exactly why it occurs, is lacking.

Some feeling for reneging is available from studies of college recruitment. One survey of 489 employers of college graduates found that a total of 1,159 students had reneged on acceptances in one year. These same employers also reported there were 379 instances in which they had reneged on job offers they had made to graduating students.[32]

Another recent survey of college recruiting practices and experiences also studied the reneging phenomenon. Results of that study are shown in Exhibit 13.7.[33]

Sometimes reneging is unavoidable. The organization may experience a sudden downturn in business conditions, so that planned-on jobs evaporate. Or, the offer receiver may experience sudden changes in circumstances requiring reneging, such as a change in health status. For the most part, however, reneging is probably avoidable, and steps should be taken by both parties to minimize its occurrence.

The organization should maintain high ethical standards regarding the extension of job offers. First and foremost, this requires extending offers only for positions that are known to exist and are vacant. Second, the organization should ensure that it has done a thorough and satisfactory assessment of all applicants, including

---

EXHIBIT 13.7   Organization Experiences with College Student Reneging on Job Offers

---

Student Reneging

. . . . . Has your organization experienced any "student reneging" on accepted employment offers?

Yes . . . . . 49%   No 51%

. . . . . Do you think this has increased in the last couple of years?

Yes . . . . . 22%   No . . . . . 44%   About same 34%

Comments:

"Students are placed in the undesirable position of feeling pressure to accept an offer before they have completed their selection process. Firms that force an early decision are making a mistake."

"Most is based on pressure from company to make an early decision to fill needs."

"Some companies continue to make offers to students even with the knowledge that they have accepted other positions."

"This has gone up a little, but it is not unexpected."

"Placement Centers should conduct programs on ethics for students."

"Companies are starting to renege so students must protect themselves. Ethics have deteriorated on both sides. If a company pressured me unrealistically, I would accept and make my decision later."

Source: V. R. Lindquist, *Trends in the Employment of College and University Graduates in Business and Industry,* 1992, p. 11. The Lindquist-Endicott Report-1992 by Victor R. Lindquist, Published by The Northwestern University Placement Center, Evanston, IL.

---

verification of necessary applicant information. In this way, hidden surprises about offer receivers will be minimized. Finally, the organization should have a review procedure in which decisions to renege are subject to approval by higher levels of management.

For the offer receiver, high ethical standards are also required. The receiver should not be frivolous, just going through the application process "for the experience." Nor should the receiver accept an offer as a way of extracting a counteroffer out of his or her current employer. Indeed, organizations should be aware of the fact that some of the people to whom they make job offers will receive such counteroffers, and this should be taken into account during the time the offer is initially formulated and presented. Finally, the receiver should do a careful assessment of probable fit for the person/job match prior to accepting an offer.

NEW EMPLOYEE ORIENTATION AND SOCIALIZATION

Establishment of the employment relationship through final match activities does not end a concern with the person/job match. Rather, that relationship must now be nurtured and maintained over time to ensure that the intended match becomes and remains an effective one. The new hires become newcomers, and their initial entry into the job and organization should be guided by orientation and socialization activities.[34]

Orientation

Orientation of newcomers should start immediately upon the beginning of the employment relationship.[35] The overall focus of the orientation should be on both the person/job and person/organization matches and making them become an effective reality.

It should be remembered that the newcomer is entering a situation of uncertainties and unknowns. While these may have been lessened through a realistic recruitment program, there will remain much to be communicated and resolved. Hence, orientation is a natural extension of the organization's searching component (communication medium and message) of its recruitment efforts. Both requirements and rewards must be communicated and understood during orientation.

Orientation requires considerable advanced planning in terms of topics to cover, development of materials for the newcomer, and scheduling of the myriad activities that contribute to an effective orientation program. Often, the HR department is responsible for the design and conduct of the orientation, and it will seek close coordination of actual orientation activities and schedules with the newcomer's supervisor.

The message portion of orientation involves determining and providing key "need to know" information to the newcomer. Spacing out of the information is also usually necessary to avoid information overload. As with any realistic recruitment, the information should be accurate and broad in scope; usually, multiple media should be used: written, interpersonal, and audiovisual.

Exhibit 13.8 contains a far-ranging set of suggested topics of information for an orientation program, delivery of which is accomplished via written materials, training programs, meetings with various people, and visual inspection. Note that these activities are spaced out rather than concentrated in just the first day at work for the newcomer. Also, the orientation program begins even before the newcomer starts work, as a way of both getting the newcomer gradually "up to speed" and making the newcomer feel welcome. The newcomer's supervisor is expected to play a critical role in all aspects of orientation, particularly past the starting dates when orientation becomes appropriately focused on job performance–related issues. In team-based environments, these supervisory actions would be the responsibility of the team leader and team members.

An excellent example of an orientation program is the one provided at the Dupont Merck Pharmaceutical Company. Designed by consultants, the program involves three tiers (stages) of newcomer introduction (called "orienteering") to

EXHIBIT 13.8   New Employee Orientation Program Suggestions

Preemployment

    Prepare supervisor and review orientation responsibilities

    Send information to new hire about:

- work area or unit, organization, products, and services
- community and surrounding area
- important contact people and phone numbers

    Put name on internal mailing lists and begin delivery to new employee

    Have supervisor and coworkers contact and welcome new hire

Starting Day(s)

    Introduce newcomer to coworkers

    Meet with HR department representative

    Conduct work-site tour

    Have work station or office ready and waiting

    Provide information regarding:

- policies and procedures (work rules, personal conduct, payroll, use of equipment and supplies, time sheets and time clocks)
- locations
- communications (phone and voice mail, E-mail, fax, internal mail directory, business cards, cellular phone, pager, network)
- security (identification, keys, off-limit areas, passwords)
- parking and transportation
- safety and medical

    Schedule meeting with supervisor

    Conduct formal orientation program

    Provide employee handbook and obtain acknowledgement of receipt

Subsequent Days

    Have supervisor meetings with newcomer to:

- review job requirements matrix and related information
- discuss performance standards and expectations
- discuss performance appraisal/management system
- identify and remove performance obstacles
- identify training and development needs
- discuss adaptation to job, organization, coworkers
- listen to employee questions and concerns
- review job rewards matrix and related information

    Conduct additional orientation training covering:

- organization philosophy and values
- products and services
- customers
- general skills (interpersonal, communication, customer service)

    Provide sponsor, buddy, or mentor for newcomer

    Introduce newcomer to, and meet with, key people

their work unit, division, and organization. There is an orienteering kit containing posters illustrating the company's mission and vision, a checklist summarizing the many actions and steps (similar to those shown in Exhibit 13.8) to be taken during orientation, and guidelines for putting together and implementing an orienteering team. During the first tier, the newcomer receives work unit orienteering from a team made up of the supervisor, a "sponsor," work unit members, and an administrative coordinator. The team seeks to provide the newcomer a sense of direction, define objectives, identify resources, and assist the newcomer in assimilating company values. During the second tier (30 to 90 days later), a half-day company orienteering program is attended by the newcomer. A welcome from top management, a review of the company's culture and products, and distribution of informational materials by HR managers are elements of this tier. The third tier occurs 30 to 90 days later and focuses on division orienteering. The intent is to bring company goals into focus, explain division objectives, and help align these goals and objectives with those of the newcomer.[36]

Socialization

Socialization of the newcomer is a natural extension of orientation activities. Like orientation, the goal of socialization is to achieve effective person/job and person/ organization matches. While orientation focuses on the initial and immediate aspects of newcomer adaptation, socialization emphasizes helping the newcomer fit into the job and organization over time. The emphasis is on the "long haul," seeking to gain newcomers' adaptation in ways that will make them want to be successful, long-term contributors to the organization.[37] There are two key issues to address in developing and conducting an effective socialization process. First, what are the major elements or contents of socialization that should occur? Second, how can the organization best deliver those elements to the newcomer?

Content

While the content of the socialization process should obviously be somewhat job- and organization-specific, there are several components that are likely candidates for inclusion. From the newcomer's perspective these are:[38]

- People—meeting and learning about coworkers, key contacts, informal groups and gatherings, and networks; becoming accepted and respected by these people as "one of the gang"
- Performance proficiency—becoming very familiar with job requirements; mastering tasks; having impacts on performance results; and acquiring necessary KSAOs for proficiency in all aspects of the job
- Organization goals and values—learning of the organization's goals; accepting these goals and incorporating them into my "line of sight" for performance proficiency; learning about values and norms of desirable behavior (e.g., working late and on weekends; making suggestions for improvements)

- Politics—learning about how things "really work"; becoming familiar with "key players" and their quirks; taking acceptable shortcuts; schmoozing and networking
- Language—learning special terms, buzzwords, and acronyms; knowing what not to say; learning the jargon of people in my trade or profession
- History—learning about the origins and growth of the organization; becoming familiar with customs, rituals, and special events; understanding the origins of my work unit and the backgrounds of people in it

Many of the above topics overlap with the possible content of an orientation program, suggesting that orientation and socialization programs be developed in tandem with each other so that they are synchronized and "seamless" as the newcomer passes from orientation into socialization.

Delivery

Delivery of socialization to the newcomer should be the responsibility of several people. First, it should be the responsibility of the newcomer's supervisor to personally socialize the newcomer, particularly in terms of performance proficiency and organization goals and values. The supervisor is intimately familiar with and the "enforcer" of these key elements of socialization. It is well that the newcomer and supervisor communicate directly, honestly, and formally about these elements.

Peers in the newcomer's work unit or team are promising candidates for assisting in socialization. They can be most helpful in terms of politics, language, and history, drawing upon and sharing their own accumulated experiences with the newcomer. They can also make their approachability and availability known to the newcomer when the newcomer wants to ask questions or raise issues in an informal manner.

To provide a more formal information and support system to the newcomer, but one outside of a chain of command, a mentor or sponsor may be assigned to (or chosen by) the newcomer. The mentor functions as an identifiable "point of contact" for the newcomer, as well as someone who actively interacts with the newcomer to provide the inside knowledge, savvy, and personal contacts that will help the newcomer "settle in" to the current job and prepare for future job assignments. Mentors can also play a vital role in helping shatter the glass ceiling of the organization.

Finally, the HR department can be very useful to the socialization process. Its representatives can help establish formal, organization-wide socialization activities such as mentoring programs, special events, and informational presentations. Also, representatives may undertake development of training programs on socialization topics for supervisors and mentors. Representatives might also work closely, but informally, with supervisors as coaches for them in how to become a successful socializer of their own newcomers.

LEGAL ISSUES

The employment contract establishes the actual employment relationship and the terms and conditions that will govern it. In the process of establishing it, there are certain obligations and responsibilities that the organization must reckon with. These pertain to (a) employing only those people who meet the employment requirements under the Immigration Reform and Control Act (IRCA), (b) avoiding the negligent hiring of individuals, and (c) maintaining the organization's posture toward employment-at-will. Each of these is discussed in turn.

Authorization to Work

Under the IRCA (see Chapter 3), the organization is prohibited from hiring or continuing to employ an alien who is not authorized to work in the United States. Moreover, the organization must verify such authorization for any person hired (after November 6, 1986, only), and it must not discriminate against individuals on the basis of national origin or citizenship status. There are specific federal regulations detailing the requirements and methods of compliance.[39]

Compliance with these means the following for the organization.[40] First, the organization must verify the employability status of each new employee (not just aliens). This is accomplished through the completion of the I-9 verification form, which in turn requires documents that verify the new employee's identity and eligibility. Both identity and eligibility must be verified. Some documents (e.g., U.S. passport) verify both identity and eligibility; other documents verify only identity (e.g., state-issued driver's license or ID card) or employment eligibility (e.g., original social security card or birth certificate).

Second, verification must occur within three days of being hired. Note, therefore, that verification need not have occurred at the time of the extension of the job offer. Offers extended without verification should contain a contingency clause making the offer contingent upon satisfactory employment verification.

Finally, to avoid possible national origin or citizenship discrimination, it is best not to ask for proof of employment eligibility prior to making the offer. The reason for this is that many of the identity and eligibility documents contain personal information that pertain to national origin and citizenship status, and such personal information might be used in a discriminatory manner. As a further matter of caution, the organization should not refuse to make a job offer to a person based on that person's foreign accent or appearance.

Negligent Hiring

Negligent hiring is a workplace torts issue (see Chapter 3) involving claims by an injured plaintiff (e.g., customer or employee) that the plaintiff was harmed by an unfit employee who was negligently hired by the organization. The employer is claimed to have violated its common-law duty to protect its employees and customers from injury by hiring an employee it knew (or should have known) posed a threat of risk to them.[41] For example, a newly hired drug addict who subsequently attacks other employees or steals money from them may cause those employees to become plaintiffs in a negligent hiring lawsuit against the employer. Punitive monetary penalties may be levied against the employer if the plaintiffs are successful in their suit.

To have a successful suit, there are several things that the plaintiff must prove:

1. The person was, in fact, an employee of the organization.
2. The employee was, in fact, incompetent, as opposed to being a competent employee who acted in a negligent manner.
3. The employer knew, or should have known, of the employee's incompetence.
4. The employer had a legal duty to select competent employees.
5. The injury or harm was a foreseeable consequence of hiring the unfit employee.
6. The hiring of the unfit employee was the proximate cause of the injury or harm.

Examples of negligent hiring cases abound, particularly extreme ones involving violence, bodily injury, physical damage, and death. There is some suggestion that the incidence of such cases, along with the monetary damages awarded plaintiffs, is increasing. Accordingly, the organization should seek to ensure that its new hires will not become negligent hires.

Doing this, however, is no small task. There are many intricacies to consider, far too numerous to cover here. Despite this, there are several straightforward recommendations that can be made on the basis of staffing concepts discussed throughout this book. First, staffing any job should be preceded by a thorough job analysis that identifies all the KSAOs required by the job. Failure to identify or otherwise consider KSAOs prior to the final match is not likely to be much of a defense in a negligent hiring lawsuit.

Second, particular attention should be paid to the *O* part of KSAOs, such as licensure requirements, criminal records, references, unexplained gaps in employment history, and alcohol and illegal drug usage. Of course, these should be derived separately for each job, rather than applied identically to all jobs.

Third, methods for assessing these KSAOs that are valid and legal must be used. This is difficult to do in practice because of lack of knowledge about the validity of some predictors, or their relatively low levels of validity. Also, difficulties arise because of legal constraints on the acquisition and use of pre-employment inquiries, as explained in Chapter 9.

Fourth, require all applicants to sign disclaimer statements allowing the employer to check references and otherwise conduct background investigations. In addition, have the applicant sign a statement indicating that all provided information is true, and that the applicant has not withheld requested information.

Fifth, apply utility analysis to determine whether it is worthwhile to engage in the preceding recommendations in order to try to avoid the (usually slight) chance of a negligent hiring lawsuit. Such an analysis will undoubtedly indicate great variability among jobs in terms of how many resources the organization wishes to invest in negligent hiring prevention.

Finally, when in doubt about a finalist and whether to extend a job offer, do not extend it until those doubts have been resolved. Acquire more information from the finalist, verify more thoroughly existing information, and seek the opinions of others on whether or not to proceed with the job offer.

Employment-at-Will

As discussed in this chapter and Chapter 3, employment-at-will involves the right of either the employer or employee to unilaterally terminate the employment relationship at any time, for any legal reason. In general, the employment relationship is an at-will one, and usually the employer wishes it to remain that way. Hence, during the final match (and even before) the employer must take certain steps to ensure that its job offers in fact clearly establish the at-will relationship. These steps are merely a compilation of points already made regarding employment contracts and employment-at-will.

The first thing to be done is ensure that job offers are for an indeterminate time period, meaning that they have no fixed term or specific ending date. Second, include in the job offer a specific disclaimer stating that the employment relationship will be strictly at will. Third, review all written documents (e.g., employee handbook, application blank) to ensure that they do not contain any language that implies anything but a strictly at-will relationship. Finally, take steps to ensure that organizational members do not make any oral statements or promises that would serve to create something other than a strictly at-will relationship.[42]

SUMMARY

During the final match, the offer receiver and the organization move toward each other through the job offer/acceptance process. They seek to enter into the employment relationship and become legally bound to each other through an employment contract.

Knowledge of employment contract principles is central to understanding the final match. The most important principle pertains to the requirements for a legally enforceable employment contract (offer, acceptance, and consideration). Other important principles focus on the identity of parties to the contract, the form of the contract (written or oral), disclaimers by the employer, contingencies, reneging by the organization or offer receiver, and other sources (e.g., employee handbooks) that may also specify terms and conditions of employment.

Job offers are designed to induce the offer receiver to join the organization. Offers should be viewed and used in the context of an applicant attraction strategy by the organization. In that strategy, job offers, recruitment activities, and applicant characteristics all interact to exert forces on applicants that will have positive impacts on recruitment outcomes (preattraction, postattraction, and spillover). Use of the job rewards matrix may be helpful in the preparation and communication of the job offer.

Job offers may contain virtually any legal terms and conditions of employment. Generally, the offer addresses terms pertaining to starting date, duration of contract, compensation, hours, special hiring inducements (if any), other terms such as contingencies, and acceptance of the offer.

The process of making job offers can be a complicated one, involving a need to think through multiple issues prior to the making of formal offers. Offers should take into account the content of competitors' offers, potential problems with applicant truthfulness, likely reactions of the offer receiver, and the organization's policies on negotiating offers. Presentation of the offer can range from a mechanical process all the way to a major sales job. Ultimately, offers are accepted and rejected, and all offer receivers should receive prompt and courteous attention during these events. Steps should be taken to minimize reneging by either the organization or the offer receiver.

Acceptance of the offer marks the beginning of the employment relationship. To help ensure that the initial person/job match starts out and continues to be an effective one, the organization should undertake both orientation and socialization activities for newcomers.

From a legal perspective, the organization must be sure that the offer receiver is employable according to provisions of the Immigration Reform and Control Act. Both identity and eligibility for employment must be verified. The potential negligent hiring of individuals who, once on the job, cause harm to others (employees or customers) is also of legal concern. Those so injured may bring suit against the organization. There are certain steps the organization can take in an attempt to minimize the occurrence of negligent hiring lawsuits. There are limits on these steps, however, such as other legal constraints on the gathering of background information about applicants. Finally, the organization should have its posture, policies, and practices regarding employment-at-will firmly developed and aligned. There are numerous steps that can be taken to help achieve this.

DISCUSSION QUESTIONS

1. If you were the HR staffing manager for an organization, what guidelines might you recommend regarding oral and written communication with job applicants by members of the organization?

2. Using the applicant attraction strategy model (Exhibit 13.1), what are some examples of how the same job offer has different effects on pre- and post-attraction outcomes?

3. What are the advantages and disadvantages to the sales approach in the presentation of the job offer?

4. What are examples of orientation experiences you have had as a new hire that have been particularly effective (or ineffective) in helping to make the person/job match happen?

5. What are the steps an employer should take to develop and implement its policy regarding employment-at-will?

APPLICATIONS

Making a Job Offer

Clean Car Care (3Cs) is located within a western city of 175,000 people. The company owns and operates four full-service car washes in the city. The owner of 3Cs, Arlan Autospritz, has strategically cornered the car wash market, with his only competition being two coin-operated car washes on the outskirts of the city. The unemployment rate in the city and surrounding area is 3.8%, and it is expected to go somewhat lower.

Arlan has staffed 3Cs by hiring locally and paying wage premiums (above market wages) to induce people to accept job offers and to remain with 3Cs. Hiring occurs at the entry level only, for the job of washer. If they remain with 3Cs, washers have the opportunity to progress upward through the ranks, going from washer to shift lead person to assistant manager to manager of one of the four car wash facilities. Until recently, this staffing system worked well for Arlan. He was able to hire high-quality people, and a combination of continued wage premiums and promotion opportunities meant he had relatively little turnover (under 30% annually). Every manager at 3Cs, past or present, had come up through the ranks. But that is now changing with the sustained low unemployment and new hires who just naturally seem more turnover prone. The internal promotion pipeline is thus drying up, since few new hires are staying with 3Cs long enough to begin climbing the ladder.

Arlan has a vacancy for the job of manager at the north-side facility. Unfortunately, he does not think that any of his assistant managers are qualified for the job, and he reluctantly concluded that he has to fill the job externally.

A vigorous three-county recruitment campaign netted Arlan a total of five applicants. Initial assessments resulted in four of those being candidates, and two candidates became finalists. Jane Roberts is the number one finalist, and the one to whom Arlan has decided to extend the offer. Jane is excited about the job and told Arlan she will accept an offer if the terms are right. Arlan is quite certain Jane will get a counteroffer to his offer from her company. Jane has excellent supervisory experience in fast-food stores and a light manufacturing plant. She is willing to relocate, a move of about 45 miles. She will not be able to start for 45 days, due to preparing for the move and the need to give adequate notice to her present employer. As a single parent, Jane wants to avoid work on either Saturday or Sunday each week. The number two finalist is Betts Cook. Though she lacks the supervisory experience that Jane has, Arlan views her as superior to Jane in customer service skills. Jane has told Arlan she needs to know quickly if she is going to get the offer, since she is in line for a promotion at her current company and she wants to begin at 3Cs before being offered and accepting the promotion.

Arlan is mulling over what kind of an offer to make to Jane. His three managers make between $28,000 and $35,000, with annual raises based on a merit review conducted by Arlan. The managers receive one week's vacation the first year, two weeks of vacation for the next four years, and three weeks of vacation after that. They also receive health insurance (with a 20% employee co-pay on the premium). The managers work five days each week, with work on both Saturday and Sunday frequently occurring during peak times. Jane currently makes $31,500, receives health insurance with no employee co-pay, and one week's vacation (she is due to receive two weeks shortly, after completing her second year with the company). She works Monday through Friday, with occasional work on the weekends. Betts earns $34,500, receives health insurance fully paid by her employer, and has one week of vacation (she is eligible for two weeks in another year). Weekend work, if not constant, is acceptable to her.

Arlan is seeking input from you on how to proceed. Specifically, he wants you to:

1. Recommend whether Jane should receive a best-shot, competitive, or lowball offer, and why.
2. Recommend other inducements beyond salary, health insurance, vacation, and hours schedule that might be addressed in the job offer, and why.
3. Draft a proposed job offer letter to Jane, incorporating your recommendations in points (1) and (2) above, as well as other desired features that should be part of a job offer letter.

Designing an Orientation Program for New Employees

Consider the job you currently hold, or a job that you have held in the past. Assume you are currently the manager responsible for the hiring and supervising of holders of that job. Design and write up a proposed orientation program that you, as manager, would use for newly hired employees into that job. Your proposal should address the following questions:

1. What are the specific contents of the program?
2. What are the specific timing and steps you would follow in conducting the program?
3. How would you use the new employee's peers, and a representative of the HR department, when designing and conducting the program?

ENDNOTES

1. C. J. Bakaly, Jr. and J. M. Grossman, *The Modern Law of Employment Relationships* (Englewood Cliffs, NJ: Prentice-Hall, 1992), pp. 25–43; A. G. Feliu, *Primer on Individual Employee Rights* (Washington, D.C.: Bureau of National Affairs, 1992), pp. 9–13; G. P. Panaro, *Employment Law Manual* (Boston, MA: Warren, Gorham and Lamont, 1993), pp. 4-2 to 4-4.

2. C. J. Bakaly, Jr. and J. M. Grossman, *The Modern Law of Employment Relationships,* pp. 15–23; G. C. Pierson, "Independent Contractor v. Employees: Guess Who's Coming to Work," *SHRM Legal Report,* Summer 1993, pp. 1–4.

3. G. P. Panaro, *Employment Law Manual,* pp. 4-61 to 4-63.

4. C. J. Bakaly, Jr. and J. M. Grossman, *The Modern Law of Employment Relationships,* pp. 61–74; A. G. Feliu, *Primer on Individual Employee Rights,* pp. 37–38; G. P. Panaro, *Employment Law Manual,* pp. 4-5 to 4-60.

5. G. P. Panaro, *Employment Law Manual,* pp. 4-18 to 4-19.

6. C. J. Bakaly, Jr. and J. M. Grossman, *The Modern Law of Employment Relationships,* pp. 61–74; A. G. Feliu, *Primer on Individual Employee Rights,* pp. 23–25; G. P. Panaro, *Employment Law Manual,* pp. 4-30 to 4-31.

7. A. G. Feliu, *Primer on Individual Employee Rights,* pp. 25–26.

8. A. G. Feliu, *Primer on Individual Employee Rights,* pp. 43–47.

9. A. G. Feliu, *Primer on Individual Employee Rights,* pp. 20–23.

10. A. G. Feliu, *Primer on Individual Employee Rights,* pp. 21–22.

11. A. G. Feliu, *Primer on Individual Employee Rights,* p. 23.

12. G. P. Panaro, *Employment Law Manual,* pp. 4-66 to 4-136.

13. A. G. Feliu, *Primer on Individual Employee Rights,* pp. 15–17.

14. C. J. Bakaly, Jr. and J. M. Grossman, *The Modern Law of Employment Relationships,* pp. 47–60; A. G. Feliu, *Primer on Individual Employee Rights,* pp. 39–50.

15. S. L. Rynes and A. E. Barber, "Applicant Attraction Strategies: An Organizational Perspective," *Academy of Management Review,* 1990, 15, pp. 286–310.

16. A. G. Feliu, *Primer on Individual Employee Rights,* pp. 52–55.

17. C. J. Bakaly, Jr. and J. M. Grossman, *The Modern Law of Employment Relationships,* pp. 141–182.

18. D. M. Cable and T. A. Judge, "Pay Preferences and Job Search Decisions: A Person–Organization Fit Perspective," *Personnel Psychology,* 1994, 47, pp. 317–348.

19. V. R. Lindquist, *Trends in the Employment of College and University Graduates in Business and Industry* (Evanston, IL: Northwestern University Placement Center, 1992); S. L. Rynes and

J. W. Boudreau, "College Recruiting in Large Organizations: Practice, Evaluation, and Research Implications," *Personnel Psychology,* 1986, 39, pp. 729–757.

20. G. A. Patterson, "Distressed Shoppers, Disaffected Workers Prompt Stores to Alter Sales Commission," *Wall Street Journal,* July 1, 1992, p. B1.

21. G. Fuchsberg, "What is Pay, Anyway?", *Wall Street Journal,* April 22, 1993, p. R3.

22. L. Bongiorno and J. A. Byrne, "Is There an MBA Glut? If You Answered No, You Pass," *Business Week,* October 24, 1994, pp. 71–72.

23. W. Power and M. Siconolfi, "Wall Street Sours on Up-Front Bonuses," *Wall Street Journal,* June 13, 1991, p. C1.

24. V. R. Lindquist, *Employment Trends for College Graduates in Business* (Evanston, IL: Northwestern University Placement Center, 1994), p. 10.

25. V. R. Lindquist, *Employment Trends for College Graduates in Business,* p. 9.

26. J. S. Lubin, "As More Men Become 'Trailing Spouses,' Firms Help Them Cope," *Wall Street Journal,* April 13, 1993, p. A1.

27. J. A. Lopez, "The Big Lie," *Wall Street Journal,* April 21, 1993, pp. R6–R8.

28. U.S. Government Accounting Office, "Survey of Applicants Who Accepted or Declined Federal Job Offers" (Washington, D.C.: author, 1992, B-243207).

29. M. Loeb, "The Smart Way to Change Jobs," *Fortune,* Sept. 4, 1995, p. 139; G. McWilliams, "To Have and To Hold," *Business Week,* June 19, 1995, p. 43; B. Kelley, "Is Your Counter Productive?" *Human Resource Executive,* April 1995, pp. 57–61.

30. R. Goddard, J. Fox, and W. E. Patton, "The Job-Hire Sale," *The Personnel Administrator,* 1989, 34(6), pp. 119–122.

31. V. R. Lindquist, *Trends in the Employment of College and University Graduates in Business and Industry.*

32. L. P. Scheetz, *Recruiting Trends 1989–90* (East Lansing, MI: Michigan State University, Career Development and Placement Services, 1990).

33. V. R. Lindquist, *Trends in the Employment of College and University Graduates in Business and Industry.*

34. J. P. Wanous, *Organizational Entry,* second ed. (Reading, MA: Addison-Wesley, 1992), pp. 155–234.

35. Bureau of National Affairs, "Induction and Orientation," in *Personnel Management* (Washington, DC: author, periodically updated), pp. 201:401 to 201:428.

36. C. S. Klein and J. Taylor "Employee Orientation Is an Ongoing Process at the DuPont Merck Pharmaceutical Company," *Personnel Journal,* 1994, 73, 5, p. 67.

37. C. L. Adkins, "Pervious Work Experience and Organizational Socialization: A Longitudinal Examination," *Academy of Management Journal,* 1995, 38, pp. 839–862.

38. G. T. Chao, A. M. O'Leary-Kelly, S. Wolf, H. J. Klein, and P. D. Gardner, "Organizational Socialization: Its Content and Consequences," *Journal of Applied Psychology,* 1994, 79, pp. 730–743.

39. Bureau of National Affairs, *Fair Employment Practices Manual* (Washington, D.C.: author, periodically updated), pp. 403:5937–5941, 6169–6191.

40. G. P. Panaro, *Employment Law Manual*, pp. 1–48 to 1–54.

41. A. G. Feliu, *Primer on Individual Employee Rights,* pp. 258–263; R. M. Green and R. J. Reibstein, *Employers Guide to Workplace Torts* (Washington, D.C.: Bureau of National Affairs,

1992), pp. 1–18, 198–200, 245–250; A. M. Ryan and M. Lasek, "Negligent Hiring and Defamation: Areas of Liability Related to Preemployment Inquiries," *Personnel Psychology,* 1991, 44, pp. 293–319; W. J. Woska, "Negligent Employment Practices," *Labor Law Journal,* 1991, pp. 603–610.

42. N. K. Kubasek and M. Neil Browne, "Recruiter Beware: The Oral Promise of Lifetime Employment May Be More Than a Mere Inducement," *Labor Law Journal,* 1991, pp. 273–285; S. Jackson and A. Loftin, "Proactive Practices Avoid Negligent Hiring Claims," *HR News,* Sept. 1995, p. 9.

STAFFING ORGANIZATIONS MODEL

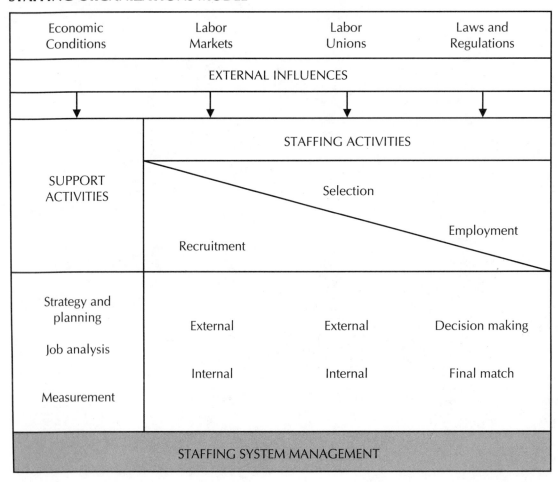

PART SIX

Staffing System Management

CHAPTER FOURTEEN
Staffing System Management

CHAPTER FOURTEEN

Staffing System Management

Administration of Staffing Systems
Organizational Arrangements
Jobs in Staffing
Policies and Procedures
Information Systems
Outsourcing

Evaluation of Staffing Systems
Staffing Validity
Staffing Process Standardization
Staffing Process Results
Staffing Costs
Customer Satisfaction

Legal Issues
Records and Reports
Audits
Managing Legal Compliance

Summary

Discussion Questions

Applications

S taffing support and functional activities involve complex processes and decisions that require organizational direction, coordination, and evaluation. Most organizations must create mechanisms for managing their staffing system and its components. Such management of staffing systems requires consideration of both administration and evaluation, as well as legal issues.

Regarding administration, this chapter shows how the staffing (employment) function is one of the key areas within the HR department. It provides illustrations of typical organizational arrangements for the staffing function. Various jobs held by people in the staffing function are also described. The role and nature of staffing policies and procedures in administering the staffing function is explained, as is the use of HR information systems to enhance efficient operation of staffing systems. Finally, the outsourcing of specific staffing activities to other organizations is described as a way for streamlining the staffing function.

Presented next is a discussion of ways to evaluate the effectiveness of the staffing function. This begins by emphasizing the importance of validity of selection procedures and the need to conduct validation studies of them. Then, evaluation of how standardized the staffing process is, and various results of the staffing process, are described as additional ways to gauge the effectiveness of staffing systems. Compilation and analysis of staffing system costs are also suggested as an evaluation technique. Last, assessment of customer (hiring managers, applicants) satisfaction is presented as a new, innovative approach to the evaluation of staffing systems.

Legal issues, as always, surround the management of staffing systems. Partly, this involves matters of compiling various records and reports, and of conducting legal audits of staffing activities. Increasingly, however, legal issues are raising the need for the development of more formal mechanisms for managing the totality of legal compliance. The chapter concludes with a discussion of all of these issues.

ADMINISTRATION OF STAFFING SYSTEMS

Organizational Arrangements

Staffing activities are usually placed and conducted within a separate unit or functional area of the organization's HR department. An example of this organizational arrangement for a multiplant manufacturing organization is shown in Exhibit 14.1. At the corporate level, the HR department is headed by the vice president (VP) of Human Resources. Reporting to the VP are directors of Employment and EEO/ AA, Compensation and Benefits, Training and Development, Labor Relations, and HR Information Systems. These directors, along with the vice president, formulate and coordinate HR strategy and policy, as well as manage their own functional units.

EXHIBIT 14.1 Example of HR Department and Employment (Staffing) Function

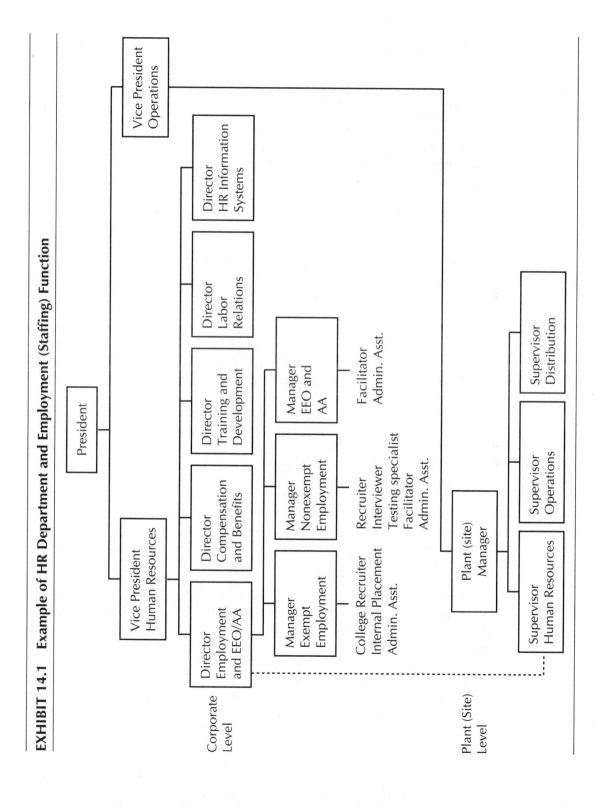

The director of Employment and EEO/AA has three direct reports: the managers of exempt, nonexempt, and EEO/AA employment areas. Each manager, in turn, is responsible for the supervision of specialists and assistants. The manager of exempt employment, for example, handles external and internal staffing for managerial and professional jobs. There are two specialists in this unit, college recruiter and internal placement specialist, plus an administrative assistant. The manager of nonexempt employment is responsible for external and internal staffing for hourly-paid employees. Reporting to this manager are four specialists (recruiter, interviewer, testing specialist, and facilitator) plus two administrative assistants. The EEO/AA manager has a facilitator plus an administrative assistant as direct reports. The facilitator specialists are individuals who serve in liaison roles with the line managers of units throughout the organization when hiring is occurring. Functioning as internal customer service representatives to these managers, the facilitators help the managers understand corporate employment policies and procedures, determine specific staffing needs, handle special staffing problems and requests, and answer questions.

At the plant level, there is a single HR supervisor, plus an administrative assistant, who perform all HR activities, including staffing. This HR supervisor is a true generalist and works closely with the plant manager on all plant issues involving people concerns. As regards staffing, the dotted line shows that the HR supervisor has an indirect reporting relationship to the director of Employment and EEO/AA (as well as the other corporate-level HR directors, not shown). Very importantly, these directors will work with the HR supervisor to develop policies and programs (including staffing) that are consistent with corporate strategy, while at the same time tailor-made to the particular needs and workforce of the plant.

The above example shows staffing to be a critical area within the HR department, and research confirms this importance accorded staffing. For example, a survey of 628 organizations found that "employment and recruitment are considered core HR department functions by most organizations, with virtually all responding companies assigning sole or partial responsibility for these activities to human resources."[1] Also, as noted in Chapter 1, another survey of HR practices found that the typical HR department allocates more of its budget to staffing than to any other HR function.[2]

Those employed within the staffing function must work closely with members of all the other functional HR areas. For example, staffing members must coordinate their activities with the compensation and benefits staff in developing policies on the economic components of job offers, such as starting pay, hiring bonuses, and special perquisites. Staffing activities must also be closely coordinated with the training and development function. This will be needed to identify training needs for external, entry-level new hires, as well as for planning transfer and promotion-enhancing training experiences for current employees. The director of Labor Relations will work with the staffing area to determine labor contract language pertaining to staffing issues (e.g., promotions and transfers), and to help resolve grievances over staffing procedures and decisions. Record keeping and applicant flow statistics requirements will be worked out with the director of HR Information Systems.

It should also be noted that while staffing activities are concentrated within the HR department, members of any specific organizational unit for which staffing is occurring will (and should) also play a role in the overall staffing process. The unit manager will submit the hiring authorization request, work closely with HR in developing KSAOs required/preferred for the vacant position and actively participate in making discretionary assessments and job offers. Other members of the unit may provide input to the unit manager on KSAOs sought, formally meet and interact with candidates for recruiting and attracting purposes, and provide inputs to the unit manager on their preferences about who should receive the job offer. In team-based work units, team members may play an even more active role in all phases of the staffing process.[3]

Each organization needs to work out for itself the organizational arrangements for staffing that best fit its own staffing strategy and preferences of organizational members. This will involve deciding how much emphasis and resources to commit to staffing activities within the HR department, and deciding the specific roles and responsibilities that will be played by the staffing function, individual unit managers, and unit members.

Jobs in Staffing

Jobs in staffing are quite varied. In the private sector, most are housed within the HR department (corporate and plant or office site level). In the public sector, they are found within the central personnel or HR office, as well as in various specified agencies such as transportation or human services. Also, staffing jobs in temporary help agencies are becoming increasingly common.

The types and scope of tasks and responsibilities in staffing jobs is also varied. Some jobs are quite specific, involving a functional specialty such as interviewing, recruiting, or college relations. These are often entry-level jobs as well. Other jobs may have a more generalist flavor to them, particularly in smaller organizations or smaller units (plant or office) of a larger organization. In such units, one person may handle all staffing-related activities. At higher organizational levels, both specialist and generalist jobs are found. Examples of specialist positions include test development and validation, executive assessment, and affirmative action. Generalists usually have broader managerial responsibilities that cut across specialties; the job of employment manager is one example. Exhibit 14.2 provides job titles, duties (tasks) and necessary KSAOs for four jobs in staffing at CompuServe.

Entry into staffing jobs normally occurs at the specialist rank in the areas of recruiting and interviewing, in both private and public organizations. And many new entry-level jobs in these two areas are opening up in temporary help agencies.

EXHIBIT 14.2　Staffing Jobs at CompuServe

---

1. EMPLOYMENT MANAGER (CORPORATE)

Summary: Manages company-wide employment program, including overseeing recruitment and selection of candidates, developing, implementing and communicating goals and strategic plans and assisting with compliance of employment laws and regulations. Supports Diversity Affairs program.

Example of Duties:

- Develops and/or participates in development of goals and strategic plans for company-wide employment program. Reviews and evaluates new and existing programs and recommends enhancements. Implements and communicates new and revised program goals and plans.

- Manages company-wide employment program, including overseeing recruitment and selection of candidates, ensuring equitable pay practices, assisting with compliance of employment laws and regulations and monitoring maintenance of employment records.

- Establishes, implements and communicates department policies, procedures and guidelines.

- Recruits, interviews and screens candidates for selected positions.

- Supports Diversity Affairs program by ensuring that candidates are included in applicant pool and by providing input on available recruitment resources and compensation, recruitment and selection practices.

- Interacts with communities, businesses and professional organizations to promote CompuServe's employment and Diversity Affairs programs.

- Develops and implements department budget and operating plan, and monitors expenditures to ensure operation within budget.

  Knowledge, Skills, Abilities: Thorough knowledge of employment programs and practices. Thorough knowledge of selection interviewing and recruitment practices. Thorough knowledge of employment laws and regulations. Good presentation and negotiation skills. Excellent verbal and written communication skills. Ability to interact diplomatically with a variety of individuals on all levels. Ability to identify, analyze and resolve issues and problems. Ability to manage, plan and direct activities and associates. Ability to make and execute immediate decisions. Ability to travel. Ability to work non standard hours.

  Education: BA/BS degree in human resources, business administration or equivalent education and experience.

Experience: Five years human resources experience, including two years of supervisory experience dealing with recruitment and selection of candidates, problem resolution and development of programs.

2. EMPLOYMENT SUPERVISOR (DIVISION)

Summary: Supervises recruitment practices and leads employment-related projects and activities for an assigned division. Identifies sources, recruits, interviews and extends employment offers to mid- and senior-level professional, technical, managerial and executive applicants. Ensures employment programs and processes comply with employment-related laws and regulations. Identifies and participates in development of employment programs and activities to secure qualified applicants.

Examples of Duties:

- Supervises recruitment practices for assigned division. Recruits, interviews and extends employment offers to mid- and senior-level professional, technical, managerial and executive positions. Evaluates applicant's qualifications and recommends applicants for further review and consideration by hiring manager. Recommends cash compensation package and ensures internal equity within guidelines (e.g., base salary, incentive compensation and relocation expenses).

- Leads employment-related activity within assigned division, including consulting with senior management to develop recruitment goals and strategic plans for division. Reviews, evaluates and recommends revisions to existing programs and communicates and implements goals and plans.

- Supports Diversity Affairs program by educating managers on goals and objectives. Ensures applicants are included in applicant pool and provides input on available recruitment sources, compensation, recruitment and selection practices. Researches and incorporates new Diversity Affairs resources in recruitment plan.

- Leads and/or coordinates projects with company-wide impact, including conducting employment-related training programs and evaluating and recommending employment related practices (e.g., testing alternatives, employment literature and applicant source alternatives).

continued

EXHIBIT 14.2   Continued

- Ensures and maintains on-going relationships with multiple external recruitment sources. Participates in career fairs, open houses and other large scale recruitment activities. Represents CompuServe at selected community and professional organizations.
- Participates in reviewing, evaluating and recommending vendors. Evaluates and oversees maintenance of applicant tracking and other human resource management systems.

Knowledge, Skills, Abilities: Thorough knowledge of interviewing and recruitment practices. Thorough knowledge of employment laws, regulations, practices and policies. Knowledge of CompuServe products and services. Knowledge of applicant tracking and other human resource management information systems. Very strong negotiation skills. Good presentation skills. Excellent verbal and written communication skills. Ability to diplomatically interact with a variety of individuals on all levels. Ability to supervise associates and plan and delegate work assignments. Ability to lead multiple projects simultaneously. Ability to identify, analyze, evaluate, provide recommendations and communicate escalated issues and problems to executive level. Ability to maintain confidential information.

Education: BA/BS degree in human resource management, business administration or related field or equivalent education and experience.

Experience: Three years experience recruiting professional, technical and/or managerial exempt-level positions and one year project leadership experience.

3. EMPLOYMENT REPRESENTATIVE II

Summary: Identifies sources, recruits, interviews and extends employment offers to applicants for mid- and senior-level professional, technical and/or managerial positions within assigned departments and divisions. Ensures programs and processes comply with employment related laws and regulations. Participates in development of employment programs and activities to secure qualified applicants.

Examples of Duties:

- Recruits, interviews and extends employment offers for mid- and senior-level professional, technical and/or managerial applicants in assigned departments and divisions. Evaluates applicants' qualifications

and recommends applicants for further review and consideration by hiring manager. Recommends cash compensation package and ensures internal equity within guidelines (e.g., base salary, incentive compensation and relocation expenses).

- Consults with hiring managers regarding employment needs and participates in strategic recruitment plan development for assigned area(s), including identifying sources for recruiting applicants (e.g., classified advertising, employment agencies, executive search firms and career fairs).
- Supports Diversity Affairs program by educating managers on goals and objectives. Ensures applicants are included in applicant pool and provides input on available recruitment sources, compensation and recruitment and selection practices.
- Ensures adherence to employment laws. Administers and recommends revisions to CompuServe's policies and practices.
- Identifies and recommends new recruitment sources (e.g., schools, career fairs and community organizations). Represents and/or conducts company presentations at schools, career fairs and community programs.
- Participates in reviewing, evaluating and recommending vendors. Assists in administering applicant tracking and other human resource management systems.
- Recommends measurements to evaluate employment-related activities. Analyzes data and provides input to management for continuous employment process improvement.
- Contributes heavily to segments of large projects or coordinates and/or leads medium size projects and/ or project teams.
- Conducts employment-related training programs and trains new department associates.

Knowledge, Skills and Abilities: Strong knowledge of selection interviewing and recruitment practices. Very good knowledge of employment-related laws and regulations. Very good knowledge of CompuServe's policies and practices. Very good knowledge of products and services in assigned department or division. Knowledge of CompuServe's products and services. Knowledge of applicant tracking and other human resource management systems. Very good presentation skills. Very good negotiation skills. Very strong verbal, written and interpersonal communication skills.

continued

EXHIBIT 14.2   Continued

Ability to interact diplomatically with a wide variety of individuals on all levels. Ability to identify, research and resolve issues and problems. Ability to exercise initiative and sound judgment. Ability to maintain confidential information.

Education: BA/BS degree in human resource management, business administration or related field or equivalent education and experience.

Experience: Two years experience interviewing and selecting nonexempt and/or exempt-level professional or technical positions.

4. EMPLOYMENT REPRESENTATIVE I

Summary: Identifies sources, recruits, interviews and extends employment offers to applicants for entry- and mid-level positions within assigned departments and divisions. Ensures compliance with employment laws, regulations, policies and practices. Participates in employment programs and activities to secure qualified applicants.

Examples of Duties:

- Recruits, interviews, screens and extends employment offers to applicants for entry- and mid-level positions within assigned departments and divisions. Evaluates applicants' qualifications and recommends applicants for review and consideration by hiring manager. Recommends cash compensation package and ensures internal equity within guidelines (e.g., base salary, incentive compensation and relocation expenses).

- Consults with hiring managers regarding a variety of employment needs and develops basic recruitment plan for assigned area(s), including identifying sources for recruiting applicants (e.g., classified advertising, employment agencies and career fairs).

- Administers applicant tracking and other human resource management systems.

- Supports Diversity Affairs program by educating managers on goals and objectives. Ensures applicants are included in applicant pool and provides input on available recruitment sources, compensation and recruitment and selection practices.

- Identifies and recommends new recruitment sources (e.g., schools, career fairs and community organizations). Represents and/or conducts company presentations at schools, career fairs and community programs.

- Ensures adherence to employment laws. Administers and recommends revisions to CompuServe's policies and practices.

- Participates in conducting employment-related training programs and trains new department associates.

- Participates in preparing segments of large projects or coordinates small projects, including developing and compiling employment-related statistics and preparing reports.

Knowledge, Skills, Abilities: Knowledge of employment laws, regulations, practices and policies. Knowledge of selection interviewing and recruitment practices and procedures. Knowledge of applicant tracking and other human resource management systems. Knowledge of CompuServe's products and services. Strong verbal and written communication skills. Ability to interact diplomatically with individuals up to mid-level management. Ability to identify, research and resolve issues and problems. Ability to exercise initiative and sound judgment. Ability to plan and organize work activities. Ability to maintain confidential information.

Education: BA/BS degree in human resource management, business administration or related field or equivalent education and experience.

Experience: Six months related human resources experience.

Source: Compliments of CompuServe, Columbus, OH. Used by permission.

Staffing of these jobs may come from the new hire ranks of the organization. It may also come from an internal transfer from a management training program, from a line management job, or from another HR function. In short, there is no fixed point or method of entry into staffing jobs.

Mobility within staffing jobs may involve both traditional and nontraditional career tracks. In a traditional track, the normal progression is from entry-level specialist up through the ranks to employment manager, with assignments at both the corporate and operating unit level. A nontraditional track might involve entry into a staffing specialist job, lateral transfer after a year to another functional HR area, rotation from there into an entry-level supervisory position, advancement within the supervisory ranks, and then promotion to the job of employment manager. In short, there is often no established mobility track upward. One should expect the unexpected.

If a person advances beyond or outside of the staffing function, this will usually serve the person well for advancement to the highest HR levels (director or vice president). At these levels, job occupants have typically held varied assignments, including working outside of HR in managerial or professional capacities. Interestingly, though, a majority of high-level HR executives have experience as a specialist, and employment and recruiting is the most frequent specialty experience, followed by compensation and labor relations.[4]

It should be noted that jobs in staffing (and other areas of HR) are becoming increasingly more customer focused and facilitative in nature.[5] As staffing activities become more decentralized and subject to line management control, holders of staffing jobs will exist to provide requested services and act as consultants to the service requesters. This will be a challenge since many of those newly responsible for staffing (line managers and team leaders) will be untrained and inexperienced in staffing matters. It will be the responsibility of those in staffing jobs within the HR department to impart to such individuals the KSAOs they will need to make effective and legal person/job matches.

Policies and Procedures

It is highly desirable to have written policies and procedures to guide the administration of staffing systems. Understanding the importance of policies and procedures first requires definition of these terms.

A policy is a selected course or guiding principle. It is an objective to be sought through appropriate actions. For example, the organization might have a promotion-from-within policy as follows: It is the intent of XXX organization to fill from within all vacancies above the entry level, except in instances of critical, immediate need for a qualified person unavailable internally. This policy makes it clear that promotion-from-within is the desired objective; the only exception is the absence of an immediately available qualified current employee.

A procedure is a prescribed routine or way of acting in similar situations. It provides the rules that are to govern a particular course of action. To carry out the promotion-from-within policy, for example, the organization may have specific procedures to be followed for listing and communicating the vacancy, identifying eligible applicants, and assessing the qualifications of the applicants.

Policies and procedures thus indicate desirable courses of action and the steps to be taken to carry out the action. Without staffing policies and procedures, staffing becomes an ad hoc, casual, whimsical process. Such a process is fraught with possibilities of hurried and catch-up recruiting, nonstandardized and nonvalid assessments of applicants, decision making based on non-job-related qualification considerations such as personal or political preferences, and job offers that exceed allowable limits on salary (and other terms) and create internal equity problems between the new hires and job incumbents. Lack of policies and procedures may also lead to practices that may foster negative applicant reactions, as well as run afoul of applicable laws and regulations.

The scope of staffing actions and practices is large, ranging across a broad spectrum of recruitment, selection, and employment issues, both external and internal. Consequently, the organization's staffing policies and procedures also need to be broad in scope. To illustrate this, Exhibit 14.3 provides an overview of the content of CompuServe's staffing policies. The total statement of these policies, and accompanying procedures, consume more than 20 pages in CompuServe's policies and procedures manual.

Information Systems

Staffing activities generate and use considerable information, often in paper form. Job descriptions, application materials, resumes, correspondence, applicant profiles, applicant flow and tracking, and reports are examples of the types of information that are necessary ingredients for the operation of a staffing system. Naturally, problems regarding what types of information to generate, and how to file, access, and use it, will arise when managing a staffing system. Addressing and solving these problems has important implications for paperwork burdens, administrative processing costs, and speed in filling job vacancies. Thus, management of a staffing system involves management of an information system.

For many organizations, the information system will continue to be a primarily paper-based and manual system. This will most likely occur in smaller organizations, single-site organizations, and organizations where there is a limited amount of staffing activity (few vacancies to fill) in a given time period. For such systems, a careful scrutiny should be done to determine if they are requiring excessive and duplicative paper documents, as well as unnecessary files and logs.

As organizations increase in size, complexity (e.g., multiple sites), and level of staffing activity, the paperwork, paper flows, and manual handling become expensive and burdensome. Moreover, the number of individuals needed to operate the staffing system and its paper become excessive. These problems cause the organization to seek staffing system efficiencies through improvements in its information systems. Many times these changes come about as part of a larger organizational reengineering effort designed to improve the speed and effectiveness of business processes generally. Since staffing systems have a process orientation underlying them, they are natural candidates for reengineering.

EXHIBIT 14.3   Staffing Topics in CompuServe's HR Policy Manual

---

Affirmative Action
Affirmative Action Plan
Americans with Disabilities Act
Associate Status
    Exempt/Nonexempt
    Full-time/Part-time
    Independent Contractor
    Internship
    Temporary Agencies
Balanced Workforce
Charges of Discrimination
Confidential Information
Diversity
Employment Agencies
Employment-at-Will
Equal Employment and Affirmative
    Action
Essential Functions of the Job
External Recruiting
Flextime
Immigration
Internal Moves
Internal Recruiting
Interviews
Job Descriptions
Job Posting
Letter of Recommendation
Offers of Employment
Outreach Programs: EEO/AA

Performance Reviews
Personnel Records and Files
Procedures
    Internal Moves
    Job Descriptions
    Promotion
    Recruiting and Selecting
    Transfer
Promotion
Reasonable Accommodation
Recruiting and Selecting
    Associate Referrals
    Classified Advertising
    Employment Agencies
    Former Associates
    Interviews
    Relatives
    Screening
    Targeted Selection
    Testing
Reference Checks
Release of Information: Personnel Files
Relocation
Right to Privacy
Secondary Job
Selection of Candidates
Temporary Agencies
Testing
Valuing Diversity
Visa Status

Source: Compliments of CompuServe, Columbus, OH. Used by Permission.

The primary improvements come about through a combination of conversion to electronic information and automation of staffing tasks and processes. A central feature is the creation of electronic databases of applicant and employee information. For staffing purposes, the database should contain all potentially relevant KSAO information about each individual. Broad-based KSAO data will allow applicants and employees to be considered for a potentially wide variety of jobs throughout the organization. Computer systems (PC and or mainframe) will also be needed to provide data entry, access, and manipulation. Also, relevant software will need to be developed or purchased commercially through vendors. These information system requirements naturally mean that HR information system specialists will need to work closely with members of the staffing function.

Armed with the above ingredients, a myriad of staffing tasks can be performed.[6] A suggestive listing of these tasks is provided in Exhibit 14.4. As can be seen, the tasks run the full gamut of staffing activities.

Scores of vendors and consultants are available to provide hardware, software, and system design and installation services to the organization. One example is Resumix, a high-tech organization offering an array of capabilities through its software programs.[7] With Resumix 4.1 software, applicant resumes are scanned with OCR (optical character recognition) to capture the exact on-line image of the resume. Key KSAO information is then extracted from the resume and used to create a resume summary database, which may be accessed instantly. The resume summary includes contact information, education data, working history, and up to 80 job skills. A manager with a vacancy to fill can then create an electronic job order that specifies KSAO requirements (both necessary and preferred). The system then automatically conducts searches among the resume summaries, yielding one or more person/job matches that are rank ordered based on the number of successful matching criteria. Another feature is that a recruiter can look up and identify all currently unfilled job orders, so that a candidate the recruiter is working with can then be matched against all such job orders. Also, as new resume summaries are entered into the database they are automatically matched against all open job orders and "flagged" for recruiter attention if there is a potential match. Other features of Resumix 4.1 are generation of standard letters (acknowledgments, interview invitation, etc.), preparation of reports, shipment of resumes and resume summaries to interested parties via fax and E-mail, creation of an em-

EXHIBIT 14.4 Computerized Staffing Tasks

- Forecasting workforce supply and demand
- Employee succession planning
- Applicant/employee database
- Job requisition database
- Job posting reports
- Applicant logs, status, and tracking reports
- Correspondence with applicants
- New hire reports (numbers, qualifications, assignments)
- Employment activity (vacancies, requisitions, positions filled)
- EEO data analysis and reports (EEO-1 form)
- Person/job matching
- Electronic resume routing
- Applicant flow and adverse impact analysis

ployment folder that adds documents (e.g., interviewer's notes) to the resume summary, and operation of a job posting system.

Outsourcing

Outsourcing refers to contracting out work to a vendor or third-party administrator (TPA). Use of temporary help agencies is a common staffing example of outsourcing. Outsourcing of HR functions and services generally is on the rise. A survey of HR departments in 121 organizations of all sizes found that 91% of them outsourced one or more HR functions or tasks, with contracts usually less than $100,000, though some were in excess of $1,000,000.[8] Respondents also indicated they would probably be expanding their use of outsourcing in the future. The following were outsourced, in descending order of frequency: outplacement, training, relocation, salary surveys, preemployment testing, benefits, organizational development, recruitment and staffing, safety and security, and HR information services.

As these data suggest, the HR department and its traditional activities, including staffing, are being selectively parceled out to HR service providers. Why? The above survey found that, in order of decreasing importance, the major reasons were to use the expertise of specialists, save time and money, save administrative costs, and be able to focus more on core HR functions. Thus, the decision to outsource was a strategic one, driven by not only a search for cost reduction, but flexibility and service quality. Many comments from respondents suggested the HR departments wanted to focus their limited resources on what they do best— their core HR competencies.

Within the staffing domain, another survey has studied the specific staffing tasks that are being outsourced.[9] In addition to the seeking of temporary employees, other tasks respondents indicated that they outsourced included recruiting for specific vacancies, checking references, relocating new hires, administering skill/aptitude tests, updating affirmative action plans, coordinating job fairs, and maintaining applicant databases.

The above study also provided case examples. One example of a staffing service provided by a vendor was the screening of applicants for positions in accounting and warehousing operations. Applicants call an 800 number, select the specific position they are interested in, and listen to a recorded description of the job. Then, a recorded voice asks for specific biodata, which is provided by the applicant on the telephone key pad. The biodata are then scored and passed along to the employing organization, which then conducts the remainder of the staffing process. Another example is a full-service vendor that received applicant inquiries to ads, scanned and entered biodata and resume data into a database, and processed the data. The vendor then provided these data and a software package to the employing organization that would allow it to complete the search, generate reports (e.g., EEO/AA), and manage job requisitions on the PC.

Entering into an outsourcing arrangement should be preceded by a careful, strategic analysis of which tasks and services (if any) are best provided by a third party. Following identification of them, it is important to become knowledgeable about alternative providers in terms of specific services, costs, the transition to use of them, how to monitor their performance, and the likely "chemistry" that will be established in the partnership.[10] Choice of providers, thus, should carefully parallel suggestions made specifically for choice of temporary help agencies and independent contractors (Chapter 4).

EVALUATION OF STAFFING SYSTEMS

Staffing Validity

The overriding goal of all staffing activities is to have effective person/job matches occur. A major portion of that match is the successful alignment of people's KSAOs with the requirements of the job. Staffing validity is the degree to which selection techniques being used by the organization accurately match peoples' qualifications to job requirements. Ideally, the organization will conduct validation studies on selection techniques and then use only those techniques with demonstrated validity (see Chapter 6). Unfortunately, organizational practice falls far short of this ideal.

Research clearly shows that the norm is to not conduct validation studies. For example, in one survey it was found that only 24% of organizations conducted either criterion-related or content validation studies.[11] In another survey it was found that only 10% of organizations conducted validation studies, and only 24% of organizations even thought it was important to do so.[12] Regarding usage of valid techniques, research indicates that the most valid techniques are not the most widely used.[13] For example, mental ability tests and biodata are highly valid techniques on average, but their rate of usage is quite low. Alternatively, the typical, unstructured employment interview is of dubious validity but almost universal use. On average, therefore, organizations appear to avoid investigating the validity of selection techniques, and to ignore validity evidence when choosing selection techniques for use.

In addition to unawareness of validation concepts and procedures, the presumed excessive cost of validation is also often offered as an explanation for why validation seems to be on a distant back burner in most organizations. While sound cost estimates for conducting validation studies are almost nonexistent, their cost may be less than is commonly assumed. One experienced consultant, for example, estimates that the average cost of conducting a job-specific content validation study is $10,000 for a consultant or $2,500 for an internal HR staff member. For a criterion-related validation study, the respective estimates are $20,000 and $5,000. Also, most tests do not need to be revalidated every year since job requirements do not change that much. Thus, the cost of the validation study can be amortized over a number of years, which effectively lowers validation costs.[14]

The tools and techniques for conducting validation studies are well established (Chapter 6), and the costs of doing these studies is usually low enough to be manageable. Any evaluation of a staffing system can and should begin with an assessment of the validity of its selection techniques. Failure to do so means the organization will not know how well it is matching people to jobs, or how it might improve the matching process. Failure to conduct validation also means the organization will lack evidence to support the job relatedness of their staffing systems if those systems' legality are challenged.

Staffing Process Standardization

Standardization refers to the consistency of operation of the organization's staffing system. Use of standardized staffing systems is desirable for several reasons. First, standardization ensures that the same KSAO information is gathered from all job applicants which, in turn, is a key requirement for reliably and validly measuring these KSAOs (see Chapter 6). Second, standardization ensures that all applicants receive the same information about job requirements and rewards. Thus, all applicants can make equally informed evaluations of the organization. Third, standardization will enhance applicants' perceptions of the procedural fairness of the staffing system and of the decisions made about them by the organization. Having applicants feel they were treated fairly and got a "fair shake" can reap substantial benefits for the organization. Applicants will speak favorably of their experience and the organization to others, they may seek employment with the organization in the future (even if rejected), they may be more likely to say "yes" to job offers, and they may become organizational newcomers with a very upbeat frame of mind as they begin their new jobs. Finally, standardized staffing systems are less likely to generate legal challenges by job applicants, and if they are challenged, they are more likely to successfully withstand the challenge.

Conducting an evaluation of staffing system standardization should proceed along the following lines. First, map out a flowchart of the staffing process used for a particular job category or cluster (see Chapter 4). Second, develop a list of the set of steps followed and actions taken throughout that process. For example, during recruitment note such steps and actions as acknowledging receipt of an application, conducting prescreening, providing information to job applicants, and informing applicants of whether they will progress forward in the staffing process. For selection, indicate when the various predictors are used sequentially, what the time limits are for tests or interviews, whether there are scoring keys available for determining applicants' scores on assessment devices, and so forth. For employment activities, take note of how cutoff scores are set, how accept-reject decisions are made, how job offers and rejections are communicated, and the content of job offers. After these two steps are completed, there will be a detailed specification of the staffing process in flow terms, along with specific actions and events that occur over the course of the process. This represents the staffing process that should be operating for the organization.

Once the staffing process has been mapped out, the next step is to check for deviations from it that have actually occurred. This will require an analysis of some past staffing "transactions" with job applicants, following what was done and what actions were taken as the applicants entered and flowed through the staffing system. All identified deviations should be recorded.

The next step is to analyze all discovered deviations and determine the reason(s) for their occurrence. For example, perhaps it is noted that some applicants receive 30 minutes to take a mental ability test and others are allowed up to 60 minutes for completion of the test. This is a serious deviation, one that could drastically affect the test scores that applicants receive. Why were applicants given differing amounts of time to take the test? Possible reasons might include: applicants were not monitored and timed when they took the test, the test administrator routinely gave applicants more time if they requested it, or the organization was attempting to provide a "reasonable accommodation" to test takers with disabilities in accordance with ADA requirements.

The final step in the evaluation is to determine what types of changes (if any) in the staffing system should be made to reduce deviations and enhance standardization. In the test time limit example above, steps could be taken to ensure that all test takers are given the test by a trained administrator, and that the administrator is carefully instructed to only allow 30 minutes for all test takers, without exception. For those applicants requesting a reasonable accommodation for taking the test, such as an extended time limit, the organization may seek professional assistance from a trained psychologist and legal counsel to help determine how to handle such requests.

Staffing Process Results

Over the course of the staffing process it is possible to develop quantitative indicators that show how effectively and efficiently the staffing system is operating. For example, how many applicants does a given vacancy attract, on average? Or, what percentage of job offers are accepted? What is the average number of days it takes to fill a vacancy? What percentage of new hires remain with the organization for one year post-hire? Answers to such questions can be determined by a tracking and analysis of applicant flows through the staffing pipeline.

Exhibit 14.5 shows the required layout for this tracking and analysis, as well as some staffing process results that may be easily calculated. In the upper part (A) of the exhibit the steps in the staffing process start with announcement of a vacancy and run through a sequential flow of selection, job offer, offer acceptance,

EXHIBIT 14.5   Evaluation of Staffing Process and Results: Example

A. Staffing Process Example

No. of vacancies filled = 25

| Process step | Vacancy announced (1) | Applicants (2) | Candidates (3) | Finalists (4) | Offer receiver (5) | Offer acceptance (6) | Start as new hire (7) | On the job | |
								Six months (8)	One Year (9)
No. of people	0	1000	200	125	30	25	25	20	13
Process time Avg. no of days	0	14	21	28	35	42	44		

B. Staffing Process Results

Applicants/Vacancy = 1000/25 = 40

Yield ratio: candidates/applicant = 20%; new hires/applicant = 2.5%; offers accepted/received = 83.3%

Time Lapse: avg. days to offer = 35; avg. days to start = 44 (cycle time)

Retention rate: $\dfrac{\text{on job six months}}{\text{new hires}}$ = 80% for six months; $\dfrac{\text{on job one year}}{\text{new hires}}$ = 52% for first year start as new hire, and retention. Also shown is a timeline, in average number of days, for completion of each step. For illustration purposes, it is assumed there are 25 vacancies that have been filled, and that these vacancies attracted 1,000 applicants who then proceeded through the staffing process. Ultimately, all 25 vacancies were filled, and these new hires were then tracked to see how many of them remained with the organization for six months and one year post-hire.

At the bottom (B) of Exhibit 14.5 are staffing process results indicators, along with calculations of them for the example. The first indicator is applicants per vacancy, which averaged 40. This is an indication of the effectiveness of recruitment activities to attract people to the organization. The second indicator is the yield ratio; it indicates the percentage of people who moved on to one or more next steps in the staffing process. For example, the percentage of applicants who became candidates is 20%; the percentage of job offers accepted is 83.3%. The third indicator, time lapse (or cycle time), shows the average amount of time lapsed between each step in the staffing process. It can be seen that the average days to fill a vacancy is 44. The final indicator is retention rate; for the new hires it can be seen that the six-month retention rate was 80%, and the one-year rate fell to 52%.

These types of indicators are very useful barometers for gauging the pulse of the staffing flow. They have an objective, "bottom line" nature that can be readily communicated to managers and others in the organization. These types of data are also very useful for comparative purposes. For example, the relative effectiveness and efficiency of staffing systems in two different units of the organization could be assessed by comparing their respective yield ratios and so forth. Another comparison could be the same staffing system compared to itself over time. Such time-based comparisons are useful for tracking trends in effectiveness and efficiency. These comparisons are also used to help judge how well changes in staffing practices have actually worked to improve staffing process performance. For example, a newly implemented program of targeted recruitment might be expected to yield fewer applicants per vacancy, but a higher proportion of candidates to applicants (more of the applicants are qualified and, thus, pass initial assessments), and a higher acceptance rate (only highly qualified people were made job offers, and the offers were very "sweet" in order to successfully land these offer receivers). Ideally, these new hires would have higher retention rates as well, due to better person/ job matches. Comparisons of results before and after the targeted recruitment program would thus help demonstrate its likely effectiveness in improving staffing system performance.

Organizations often desire to compare their own staffing process results to those of others. One source of such data comes form the Saratoga Institute. It annually collects and compiles staffing results information from approximately 800 organizations. Some examples of the data are shown in Exhibit 14.6 for average days to fill (applicant to offer accepted) and average days to start (applicant to first day on the job). The data are for exempt and nonexempt jobs combined. It can be seen

---

EXHIBIT 14.6   Staffing Process Results: National Survey

Company Size (employees)	Average Days to Fill	Average Days to Start
1– 500	41	49
501– 1,000	46	45
1,001– 2,000	47	53
2,001– 5,000	48	60
5,001–10,000	46	60
Over 10,000	53	NA[a]
All	46	54

---

[a] Not available.

Source: Saratoga Institute, *HR Financial Report*, 1994, pp. 318, 337. Used by permission of the Saratoga Institute, Santa Clara, CA.

that average days to fill was 46, and that average days to start was 54. These results did not vary significantly by company size.

Additional comparative survey data on staffing results are reported annually by the Employment Management Association (EMA). Combining results across exempt and nonexempt jobs, the EMA reports average days to fill to be 44, and average days to start to be 59. The EMA also reports that average recruiter workload was 22 vacant positions being handled at once, and the average job offer acceptance rate was 90%.[15]

Staffing Costs

While staffing costs are an obviously important concern for evaluating staffing activities, actually deriving the cost estimates is difficult. There is no commonly used way of costing out the staffing process. One suggested way for doing so is provided by the EMA.[16]

The EMA conducts an annual survey of staffing costs among a sample of companies. The respondents are required to compile and report their cost data according to a cost estimate format provided on the survey. The cost categories used and representative cost data from the survey are shown in Exhibit 14.7. It can be seen that the average cost per hire for exempt employees was $6,359, and for nonexempt employees it was $1,388.

Customer Satisfaction

Staffing systems, by their very nature, influence users of them. Such users can be thought of as customers of the system. Two of the key customers are managers and job applicants. Managers look to the staffing system to provide them the right numbers

EXHIBIT 14.7 National Cost Per Hire Estimates

A. **Cost Categories**
- Employment/recruiting office expenses (salaries and benefits of recruiters and office staff; travel, lodging and entertainment for staff, administrative expenses)
- Other recruiters expenses (same as above, but for non-HR staff, such as managers and other professionals)
- Applicants' expenses (travel, lodging, meals; interviewing time; cost for interviewers)
- Direct fees (advertising, job fairs, agency fees, executive search fees, employee referral cash awards, college recruiting)
- Relocation expenses (total cost of relocating new hire)

B. **Cost Per Hire (CPH) Data**

Category	Exempt Employees		Nonexempt Employees	
	CPH	% CPH	CPH	% CPH
Emp./Rec. Office Expenses	$2,543	40.0	$818	59.0
Other Recruiters Expenses	203	3.1	17	1.2
Applicants' Expenses	693	10.9	275	19.8
Direct Fees	1,342	21.2	253	18.2
Relocation Expenses	1,577	24.8	25	1.8
Total	$6,359	100%	$1,388	100%

Source: Employment Management Association, National Cost Per Hire Survey, 1994. Used by permission of the Employment Management Association, Raleigh, NC.

and types of new hires to meet their own staffing needs. Job applicants expect the staffing system to recruit, select, and make employment decisions about them in ways that are fair and legal. For both sets of customers, therefore, it is important to know how satisfied they are with the staffing systems that serve them. Detection of positive satisfaction can serve to reinforce the usage of current staffing practices. Discovering areas of dissatisfaction, alternatively, may serve as a trigger for needed changes in the staffing system, and help pinpoint the nature of those changes.

Customer satisfaction with staffing systems is of very recent origin as an organizational concern. Rarely were managers and job applicants even thought of as customers, and rarer yet were systematic attempts made to measure their customer satisfaction as a way of evaluating the effectiveness of staffing systems. Recently that has begun to change. Described next are two innovative studies that successfully developed measures of customer satisfaction, one for managers and one for job applicants.

Managers

The State of Wisconsin Department of Employment Relations houses the Division of Merit Recruitment and Selection (DMRS), which is the central agency responsible for staffing the state government. Annually, it helps the 40 state agencies to fill about 4,000 vacancies through hiring and promoting. Managers within these agencies, thus, are customers of the DMRS and its staffing systems.

To help identify and guide needed staffing system improvements, the DMRS decided to develop a survey measure of managers' satisfaction with staffing services. Through the use of focus groups, managers' input on the content of the survey were solicited. The final survey had 53 items on it, grouped into five areas: communication, timeliness, candidate quality, test quality, and service focus. Examples of the survey items are shown in Exhibit 14.8.

The survey was administered via internal mail to 645 line and HR managers throughout the agencies. Statistical analyses provided favorable psychometric evidence supporting usage of the survey. Survey results served as a key input to implementation of several initiatives to improve staffing service delivery. These initiatives lead to increases in the speed of filling vacancies, elimination of paperwork, higher reported quality of job applicants, and positive applicant reactions to the staffing process.[17]

Job Applicants

Researchers sought to develop the Selection Fairness Survey (SFS) that could be used to assess the satisfaction of job applicants with the staffing process. The SFS contained 40 items, all designed to tap perceptions about the fairness of the selection phases of staffing. The items were grouped into 10 categories. These categories, and sample SFS items, are shown in Exhibit 14.9. The survey was administered to over 300 recent college graduates who had searched for and found a job. Statistical analysis of their responses to the SFS showed it had favorable psychometric properties.[18]

LEGAL ISSUES

Records and Reports

In staffing systems, substantial information is generated, used, recorded, and disclosed. There are numerous legal constraints and requirements surrounding staffing information. These pertain to the creation and maintenance of records, privacy concerns, and preparation of reports.

Creation and Maintenance of Records

A wide range of information is created by the organization during staffing and other HR activities. Examples include personal data (name, address, date of birth, dependents, etc.), KSAO information (application blank, references, test scores,

---

EXHIBIT 14.8   Examples of Survey Items for Assessing Manager's Satisfaction With Staffing Services

---

Communication: How well are you kept informed on the staffing process?

How satisfied are you with:

1. the clarity of instructions and explanation you receive on the staffing process
2. your overall understanding of the steps involved in filling a vacancy
3. the amount of training you receive in order to effectively participate in the total staffing process

Timeliness: How do you feel about the speed of recruitment, examination, and selection services?

How satisfied are you with the time required to:

1. obtain central administrative approval to begin the hiring process
2. score oral and essay exams, achievement history questionnaires, or other procedures involving scoring by a panel of raters
3. hire someone who has been interviewed and selected

Candidate Quality: How do you feel about the quality (required knowledges and skills) of the job candidates?

How satisfied are you with:

1. the number of people you can interview and select from
2. the quality of candidates on new register
3. your involvement in the recruitment process

Test Quality: How do you feel about the quality of civil service exams (tests, work samples, oral board interviews, etc.).

How satisfied are you with:

1. your involvement in exam construction
2. the extent to which the exams assess required KSAOs
3. the extent to which the exams test for new technologies used on the job

Service Focus: To what extent do you believe your personnel/staffing representatives are committed to providing high-quality service?

How satisfied are you with:

1. the accessibility of a staffing person
2. the expertise and competence of the staffing representative
3. responses to your particular work unit's needs

Source: H. G. Heneman, III, D. L. Huett, R. J. Lavigna and D. Ogsten "Assessing Managers' Satisfaction with Staffing Services," *Personnel Psychology*, 1995, 48, pp. 170–173. ©*Personnel Psychology*, 1995. Used by permission.

EXHIBIT 14.9   Selection Fairness Survey: Dimensions and Sample Items for Each Dimension

Job Relatedness
The types of questions asked during the selection process were directly related to the job.

Opportunity to Perform
I was given adequate opportunity to demonstrate my skills and abilities.

Feedback
I received information on the hiring decision in a timely manner.

Selection Information
I was given a reasonable explanation for why the specific selection procedures were used to hire people.

Honesty
I was treated honestly and openly during the selection process.

Interpersonal Treatment
I was treated with warmth, sincerity and thoughtfulness during the selection process.

Two-Way Communication
In a way I was able to conduct my own interview, asking questions about the job and company.

Question Propriety
I was asked questions that I felt were inappropriate or discriminatory.

Consistency Bias
Personal motives or biases appeared to influence the selection process.

Ease of Faking
It would be easy for people to be dishonest when answering questions and make themselves look good.

Equity
Given my past experience looking for a job, I feel I received an appropriate evaluation.

Source: S. W. Gilliland and H. Honig, "Development of the Selection Fairness Survey," paper presented at the Society for Industrial and Organizational Psychology, Nashville, 1994. Used by permission of the authors.

etc.), medical information, performance appraisal and promotability assessments, and changes in employment status (promotion, transfers, etc.). Why should records of such information be created?

Basically, records should be created and maintained for four purposes in staffing. First, they are necessary for legal compliance. Federal, state, and local laws specify what information should be kept, and for how long. Second, the information is often used in staffing decisions, and having it available in centralized records is convenient and efficient. Third, having records allows the organization to provide documentation to justify staffing decisions, or to defend these decisions against legal challenge. For example, performance appraisal and promotability assessments might be used to explain to employees why they were or were not promoted. Or, these same records might be used as evidence in a legal proceeding to show that promotion decisions were job-related and unbiased. Fourth, records may be used to audit staffing practices and conduct staffing research. Investigating staffing processes and results (Exhibit 14.5), and conducting validation studies, are examples of such use.

It is strongly recommended that two sets of records be created. The first set should be the individual employee's personnel file. It should comprise only documents that relate directly to the job and the employee's performance of it. To determine which documents to place in the personnel file, ask if it is a document upon which the organization could legally base an employment decision. If the answer is "no," "probably no," or "unsure," the document should not be placed in the employee's personnel file. The second set of records should contain documents that cannot be used in staffing decisions. Examples include documents pertaining to medical information (both physical and mental), equal employment opportunity (e.g., information about protected characteristics such as age, sex, religion, race, color, national origin, and disability), and information about authorization to work (e.g., I-9 forms).[19]

Any document that is to be placed in an employee's personnel file should be reviewed before it becomes part of that record. Examine the document for incomplete, inaccurate, or misleading information, as well as potentially damaging notations or comments about the employee. All such information should be completed, corrected, explained, and if necessary, eliminated. Remember that any document in the personnel file is a potential court exhibit that may work either for or against the employer's defense of a legal challenge.[20]

Various laws specify record keeping requirements for the organization. Failure to maintain and have available such records may result in substantial liability. Some of the requirements are specific and absolute, meaning that the record must be created and retained for some time period. An example here is that of I-9 immigration form records for employees. Other requirements are not as specific. They indicate only the general types of records that are to be retained, if they are created by the organization. Information created and contained in personnel files, as described above, falls into this category.

Federal EEO/AA laws contain general record keeping requirements. While the laws' requirements vary somewhat from law to law, major subject areas for which records are to be kept (if created) are shown in Exhibit 14.10.

The various laws also have requirements about length of retention of records. As a general rule, most records must be kept for a minimum of one year from the date a document is made or a staffing action is taken, whichever is later. Exceptions to the one-year requirements all provide for even longer retention periods. The

EXHIBIT 14.10   Federal Record Keeping Requirements

Records that should be kept include:

- applications for employment (hire, promote, transfer)
- reasons for refusal to hire, promote, transfer
- tests and test scores, plus other KSAO information
- job orders submitted to labor unions and employment agencies
- medical exam results
- advertisements or other notices to the public or employees about job openings and promotion opportunities
- requests for reasonable accommodation
- impact of staffing decisions on protected groups (adverse impact statistics)
- records related to filing of a discrimination charge

All records should be kept for a minimum of one year.

specific record keeping and retention requirements of each law are readily available and should be consulted for amplification and clarification.[21]

Privacy Concerns

The organization must observe legal requirements governing employees' and others' access to information in personnel files, as well as guard against unwarranted disclosure of the information to third-party (e.g., other employers) requesters of it. Information access and disclosure matters raise privacy concerns under both constitutional and statutory law.

Several (not all) states have laws guaranteeing employees reasonable access to their personnel files.[22] The laws generally allow the employee to review and copy pertinent documents; some documents such as letters of reference or promotion plans for the person may be excluded from access. The employee may also have a right to seek to correct erroneous information in the file. Where there is no state law permitting access, employees are usually allowed access to their personnel file only if the organization has a policy permitting it. Disclosure of information in personnel files to third parties is oftentimes also regulated, requiring such procedures as employees' written consent for disclosure.

At the federal level, numerous laws and regulations restrict access to and disclosure of employee personnel information. An example here is the ADA and its provisions regarding the confidentiality of medical information. There is, however, no general federal privacy law covering private employees. Public employees' privacy rights are protected by the Privacy Act of 1974. It has been recommended that the provisions of the act be voluntarily adopted by private employers.[23]

Reports

Under the Civil Rights Act and Revised Order No. 4, private employers with more than 100 employees (50 for federal contractors) are required to file an annual report with the EEOC. The basis of that report is completion of the EEO-1 form, shown in Exhibit 14.11. It can be seen that the primary purpose of the report is to provide employment data (see section D) on the composition of the organization's workforce. The data is to be provided for each of nine job categories; it should show the number of permanent full-time and part-time employees according to sex, race, and ethnicity. Such information may be gathered from the organization's records or by visual inspection. A detailed instruction booklet is provided to aid in preparation of the report.

Each federal contractor must also prepare a report detailing its affirmative action plan (AAP) according to requirements specified in Revised Order No. 4 (see Appendix B). That report must address a variety of issues including: workforce analysis (EEO-1 form), availability statistics, job categories in which underutilization of women and minorities is occurring relative to their availability, hiring and promotion goals and timetables for eliminating underutilization, detailed recruitment and selection plans, internal auditing to measure effectiveness of affirmative action efforts, and management of the AAP.

Federal contractors are also required to prepare and provide additional affirmative action reports if requested by the OFCCP. These reports may be used as part of a compliance review to determine contractor compliance with Revised Order No. 4, or to support a bid on additional federal contracts.

Audits

It is highly desirable to periodically conduct audits or reviews of the organization's degree of compliance with laws and regulations pertaining to staffing. The audit forces the organization to study and specify what in fact its staffing practices are, and to compare these current practices against legally desirable and required practices. Results can be used to identify potential legal trouble spots, and to map out changes in staffing practices that will serve to minimize potential liability and reduce the risk of lawsuits being filed against the organization. Note that development of affirmative action plans and reports includes a large audit and review component. They do not, however, cover the entire legal spectrum of staffing practices, nor do they require sufficient depth of analysis of staffing practices in some areas. For these reasons, affirmative action plans and reports are not sufficient as legal audits, though they are immensely important and useful inputs to a legal audit.

The audit could be conducted by the organization's own legal counsel. Alternatively, the HR department might first conduct a self-audit, and then review its findings with legal counsel.

EXHIBIT 14.11   Employer Information Report EEO-1 Form

EQUAL EMPLOYMENT OPPORTUNITY

EMPLOYER INFORMATION REPORT EEO—1

Standard Form 100
(Rev. 4–92)
O.M.B. No. 3046–0007
EXPIRES 12/31/93
100–213

Section A—TYPE OF REPORT
Refer to instructions for number and types of reports to be filed.

1. Indicate by marking in the appropriate box the type of reporting unit for which this copy of the form is submitted (MARK ONLY ONE BOX).

   (1) ☐ Single-establishment Employer Report

   Multi-establishment Employer:
   (2) ☐ Consolidated Report (Required)
   (3) ☐ Headquarters Unit Report (Required)
   (4) ☐ Individual Establishment Report (submit one for each establishment with 50 or more employees)
   (5) ☐ Special Report

2. Total number of reports being filed by this Company (Answer on Consolidated Report only) _____

Section B—COMPANY IDENTIFICATION (*To be answered by all employers*)	OFFICE USE ONLY

1. Parent Company
   a. Name of parent company (owns or controls establishment in item 2) omit if same as label

	a.

   Address (Number and street)

	b.

City or town	State	ZIP code	c.

2. Establishment for which this report is filed. (Omit if same as label)
   a. Name of establishment

					d.

Address (Number and street)	City or Town	County	State	ZIP code	e.

   b. Employer Identification No. (IRS 9-DIGIT TAX NUMBER) | | | | | | | | | | f. |

   c. Was an EEO-1 report filed for this establishment last year? ☐ Yes ☐ No

Section C—EMPLOYERS WHO ARE REQUIRED TO FILE (*To be answered by all employers*)

☐ Yes ☐ No   1. Does the entire company have at least 100 employees in the payroll period for which you are reporting?

☐ Yes ☐ No   2. Is your company affiliated through common ownership and/or centralized management with other entities in an enterprise with a total employment of 100 or more?

☐ Yes ☐ No   3. Does the company or any of its establishments (a) have 50 or more employees AND (b) is not exempt as provided by 41 CFR 60–1.5, AND either (1) is a prime government contractor or first-tier subcontractor, and has a contract, subcontract, or purchase order amounting to $50,000 or more, or (2) serves as a depository of Government funds in any amount or is a financial institution which is an issuing and paying agent for U.S. Savings Bonds and Savings Notes?

If the response to question C–3 is yes, please enter your Dun and Bradstreet identification number (if you have one): | | | | | | | | |

NOTE: If the answer is yes to questions 1, 2, or 3, complete the entire form, otherwise skip to Section G.

EXHIBIT 14.11   (Continued)

Section D—EMPLOYMENT DATA

Employment at this establishment—Report all permanent full-time and part-time employees including apprentices and on-the-job trainees unless specifically excluded as set forth in the instructions. Enter the appropriate figures on all lines and in all columns. Blank spaces will be considered as zeros.

JOB CATEGORIES		OVERALL TOTALS (SUM OF COL. B THRU K)	MALE					FEMALE				
			WHITE (NOT OF HISPANIC ORIGIN)	BLACK (NOT OF HISPANIC ORIGIN)	HISPANIC	ASIAN OR PACIFIC ISLANDER	AMERICAN INDIAN OR ALASKAN NATIVE	WHITE (NOT OF HISPANIC ORIGIN)	BLACK (NOT OF HISPANIC ORIGIN)	HISPANIC	ASIAN OR PACIFIC ISLANDER	AMERICAN INDIAN OR ALASKAN NATIVE
		A	B	C	D	E	F	G	H	I	J	K
Officials and Managers	1											
Professionals	2											
Technicians	3											
Sales Workers	4											
Office and Clerical	5											
Craft Workers (Skilled)	6											
Operatives (Semi-Skilled)	7											
Laborers (Unskilled)	8											
Service Workers	9											
TOTAL	10											
Total employment reported in previous EEO-1 report	11											

NOTE: Omit questions 1 and 2 on the Consolidated Report.

1. Date(s) of payroll period used:

2. Does this establishment employ apprentices?
   1 ☐ Yes   2 ☐ No

Section E—ESTABLISHMENT INFORMATION *(Omit on the Consolidated Report)*

1. What is the major activity of this establishment? (Be specific, i.e., manufacturing steel castings, retail grocer, wholesale plumbing supplies. title insurance, etc. Include the specific type of product or type of service provided, as well as the principal business or industrial activity.)

OFFICE USE ONLY

g.

Section F—REMARKS

Use this item to give any identification data appearing on last report which differs from that given above, explain major changes in composition or reporting units and other pertinent information.

Section G—CERTIFICATION *(See Instructions G)*

Check one
1 ☐ All reports are accurate and were prepared in accordance with the instructions (check on consolidated only)
2 ☐ This report is accurate and was prepared in accordance with the instructions.

Name of Certifying Official	Title	Signature	Date
Name of person to contact regarding this report (Type or print)	Address (Number and Street)		
Title	City and State	ZIP Code	Telephone Number (Including Area Code)	Extension

All reports and information obtained from individual reports will be kept confidential as required by Section 709(e) of Title VII.
WILLFULLY FALSE STATEMENTS ON THIS REPORT ARE PUNISHABLE BY LAW. U.S. CODE. TITLE 18. SECTION 1001.

An example of such a self-audit is the Employment Labor Law Audit (ELLA).[24] It has sections covering recruitment, selection, and hiring; application forms; reference checking and responding; immigration law; the ADA; employee handbooks; antidiscrimination; and the drug-free workplace. For each section, a series of audit questions are asked, and each is to be answered "yes" or "no." Examples of these questions for the recruitment area are: "Do you accept unsolicited applications and/or resumes?"; and "Do you use a centralized personnel department to recruit new hires?" Following the questions, a written analysis is provided explaining what the best answer is to each question, along with suggestions and dos and don'ts for guiding permissible practices.

Not only is it desirable that legal audits be conducted, but that they be done on a recurring basis. The appearance of new laws or amendments to them, issuance of new policy guidance and regulations by federal agencies, and changing court interpretations all mean that the line of demarcation between permissible and impermissible staffing practices is fuzzy and in need of periodic reexamination.

Managing Legal Compliance

How should the organization seek to minimize the occurrence of legal problems, and how should the organization handle legal problems that do arise? These are questions of legal prevention and reaction, answers to which form the basis of decisions on how to manage legal compliance. A description of current legal compliance practices is provided first to show the wide range of issues to be addressed and how they are currently handled by organizations. This is followed by some suggested questions to ask for deciding what type of legal compliance system might be best for the organization.

Current Practices

A survey of HR professionals was conducted to determine their opinions on the importance of various topics to the field of HR. Results were used to revise the content of the certification exam constructed and administered by the Human Resource Certification Institute. It was found that, across all functions and fields of HR, legal issues was the most important topic for HR practitioners to know; and the content of the exam has been modified to provide more coverage of legal issues.[25]

Given the importance of legal issues to practitioners, how do they actually manage legal compliance in their organizations? Results of another survey provide an interesting description of current practices among the 630 responding organizations.[26] The findings include the following:

- Virtually all organizations sought legal consultation on HR issues.
- Twenty-six percent had an in-house attorney, and twenty-two percent of those housed the attorney(s) in the HR department.

- Thirty-seven percent specified circumstances in which an attorney must be consulted.
- Seeking legal guidance was prompted primarily by new laws and regulations, complaints from employees and applicants, and changes in HR policies and procedures.
- Legal guidance was not usually sought on pending hiring or promotion decisions; but guidance was sought at the onset of discrimination and negligent hiring complaints.
- Major staffing matters subject to legal review were employee handbooks, personnel forms, EEO/AA plans, and preemployment tests.
- Planned legal audits of the HR department were rare; however, twenty-five percent of organizations conducted legal reviews on a routine, scheduled basis.

Those findings suggest that, on average, legal compliance is managed on a casual, as-needed basis, with an emphasis on reaction to legal issues rather than prevention of legal problems. There is also an emphasis on review of written documents, rather than participating in decisions or otherwise interacting with managers.

Elements of a Legal Compliance System

Provided below are some suggested questions to ask when considering development of a legal compliance system within the organization. They represent key decisions that the organization must address as it seeks to determine the type of system that will be best for it.

First, will the organization have its own in-house attorney(s), or will legal counsel be sought externally on an as-needed basis? If in-house counsel is desired, will the people be located within the HR department or elsewhere, such as the legal department?

Second, to what extent should the organization seek to establish formal compliance systems and routines, as opposed to handling matters on a more ad hoc basis? Given the growing complexity of the law and the growing volume of complaints, the organization might well opt for establishment of more formal compliance systems. By doing so, the organization would be able to assume a more preventive (as opposed to reactive) stance. It might also be less costly in the long run to have in place established policies and procedures to handle legal issues, relative to the ad hoc approach.

A third question is how much will legal compliance become a formal area of responsibility and accountability for individual managers, and how will managers be both helped and motivated to perform these new tasks? The answer to this question involves consideration of several matters. Managers will need to become aware, and accepting, of this new responsibility. This will require changes in job descriptions and performance appraisals to formalize the new responsibility, and to evaluate and reward managers on how well they perform it. Accompanying this will be a need for management training that covers such topics as requirements of the law, organizational policies and procedures for handling legal issues, examples of permissible and impermissible practices, consequences of mistakes, and the roles of the HR department and legal counsel. The HR department will also need to gear up for, and be prepared to deliver, advice to managers when it is sought. The organization should anticipate a strong advisory role for the HR department, given the complexity of the laws and organizational policies and procedures. Managers should be encouraged to seek advice on legal matters, and they should receive it when it is sought.[27]

Another question is how will the organization conduct investigations of employee complaints? Here, it is useful to differentiate between complaints that are filed within the organization and those filed externally to an enforcement agency such as the EEOC. Separate systems will probably be necessary for these two types of complaints, and complaints filed with an agency should probably be handled with a very formal, step-by-step investigation process.[28]

Finally, should the organization set up a dispute resolution process, and if so, what should be its characteristics? For unionized employees, such a process is available in the form of the grievance procedure. For nonunion employees, however, what is referred to as an alternative dispute resolution procedure (ADR) will be needed. Exhibit 14.12 shows the numerous approaches to ADR that might be used. Research shows that most organizations do in fact use one or more of these procedures, with negotiation and fact finding being the most prevalent by far. Peer review and mediation are used substantially less, and arbitration is the least used.[29]

EXHIBIT 14.12   Alternative Dispute Resolution Approaches

Approach	Description
Negotiation	Employer and employee discuss complaint with goal of resolving complaint.
Fact finding	A neutral person, from inside or outside the organization, investigates a complaint and develops findings that may be the basis for resolving the complaint.
Peer review	A panel of employees and managers work together to resolve the complaint.
Mediation	A neutral person (mediator) from within or outside the organization helps the parties negotiate a mutually acceptable agreement. Mediator is trained in mediation methods. Settlement is not imposed.
Arbitration	A neutral person (arbitrator) from within or outside the organization conducts formal hearing and issues a decision that is binding on the parties.

EXHIBIT 14.13 Example of Alternative Dispute Resolution (ADR) Procedure

---

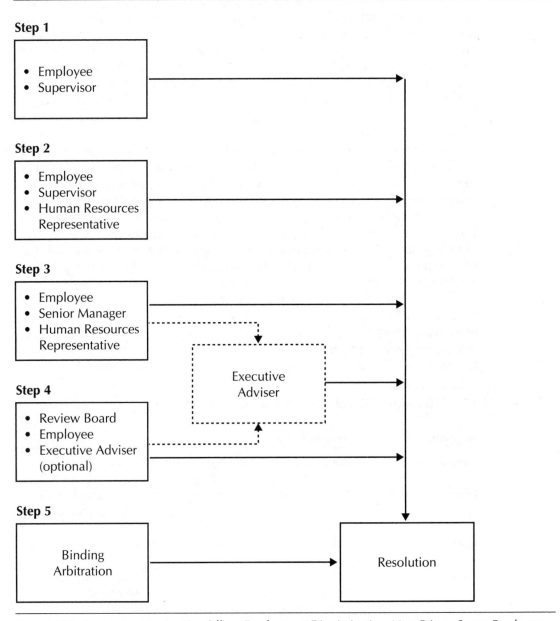

Step 1

- Employee
- Supervisor

Step 2

- Employee
- Supervisor
- Human Resources Representative

Step 3

- Employee
- Senior Manager
- Human Resources Representative

Executive Adviser

Step 4

- Review Board
- Employee
- Executive Adviser (optional)

Step 5

Binding Arbitration

Resolution

Source: U.S. Government Accounting Office, *Employment Discrimination: Most Private Sector Employers Use Alternative Dispute Resolution,* Report 95–150 (Washington, D.C.: author, 1995), p. 9.

Organizations are experimenting with more formal ADR systems that combine elements of all the approaches shown in Exhibit 14.12. An example of such an ADR with five sequential steps is shown in Exhibit 14.13. Step 1 corresponds to negotiation, step 2 to fact finding, steps 3 and 4 to peer review and mediation, and step 5 to arbitration. It should be noted that such ADRs are highly experimental; their effectiveness and legality is open to question. Also, many guidelines are being suggested for their establishment and use.[30]

SUMMARY

The multiple and complex set of activities collectively known as a staffing system must be integrated and coordinated throughout the organization. Such management of the staffing system requires both careful administration and evaluation, as well as compliance with legal mandates.

To manage the staffing system, the usual organizational arrangement in all but very small organizations is to create an identifiable staffing or employment function, and to place it within the HR department. That function then manages the staffing system at the corporate and/or plant and office level. Numerous types of jobs, both specialist and generalist, are found within the staffing function. Entry into these jobs, and movement among them, is very fluid and does not follow any set career mobility path.

The myriad staffing activities require staffing policies to establish general staffing principles, and procedures to guide the conduct of those activities. Lack of clear policies and procedures can lead to misguided and inconsistent staffing practices, as well as potentially illegal ones. Information systems can help achieve these consistencies and aid in improving staffing system efficiency. Electronic systems are increasingly being used to conduct a wide range of staffing tasks. Outsourcing of some staffing activities is also being experimented with as a way of improving staffing system efficiency.

Evaluation of the effectiveness of the staffing system should proceed along several fronts. First is investigation of the validity of selection procedures to determine the quality of person/job matches that are occurring. Second is assessment of the staffing system from a process perspective. Here, it is desirable to examine the degree of standardization (consistency) of the process, and the results of the process according to indicators such as yield ratios and time lapse (cycle time). Costs of staffing system operation should also be estimated. Finally, the organization should consider assessing the satisfaction of staffing system users, such as managers and job applicants.

Considerable attention should be devoted to legal issues. Various laws require maintenance of numerous records and compilation of reports, especially as pertains to EEO/AA. Care must be taken to guard privacy rights and access to information maintained in files. It is desirable to periodically conduct an actual legal audit of all the organization's staffing activities. This will help identify potential legal troublespots that require attention. Finally, consideration should be given to the best mechanism for managing the overall legal compliance of staffing and other HR activities. This will require attention to both the staffing system and to the individual line managers.

DISCUSSION QUESTIONS

1. What are the advantages of having a centralized staffing function, as opposed to letting each manager be totally responsible for all staffing activities in his or her unit?
2. What are examples of staffing tasks and activities that cannot or should not be simply delegated to a staffing information system for their conduct?
3. What arguments would you make in attempting to persuade an organization that it should periodically assess the validity of its selection procedures?
4. In developing a report on the effectiveness of the staffing process being conducted for entry-level jobs, what factors would you address and why?
5. How would you try to get individual managers to be more aware of the legal requirements of staffing systems and to take steps to ensure that they themselves engage in legal staffing actions?

APPLICATIONS

Learning About Jobs in Staffing

The purpose of this application is to have you learn in detail about a particular job in staffing currently being performed by an individual. The individual could be a staffing jobholder in the HR department of a company or public agency (state or local government), a nonprofit agency, a temporary help agency, an employment agency, a consulting firm, or the state employment (job) service. The individual may perform staffing tasks full-time, such as a recruiter, interviewer, counsellor, employment representative, or employment manager. Or, the individual may perform staffing duties as part of the job, such as the HR manager in a small company or an HR generalist in a specific plant or site.

Contact the job holder and arrange for an interview with that person. Explain that the purpose of the interview is for you to learn about the person's job in terms of job requirements (tasks and KSAOs) and job rewards (both extrinsic and intrinsic). To prepare for the interview, review the examples of job descriptions for staffing jobs in Exhibit 14.2, obtain any information you can about the organization, and then develop a set of questions that you will ask the jobholder. Either before or at the interview, be sure to obtain a copy of the jobholder's job description if one is available.

(continued)

Based on the written and interview information, prepare a report of your investigation. The report should cover:

1. the organization's products and services, size, and staffing (employment) function
2. the jobholder's job title, and why you chose that person's job to study
3. a summary of the tasks performed by the jobholder, and the KSAOs necessary for the job
4. a summary of the extrinsic and intrinsic rewards received by the jobholder
5. unique characteristics of the job that you did not expect to be a part of the job

Evaluating Staffing Process Results

The Keepon Trucking Company (KTC) is a manufacturer of custom-built trucks. It does not manufacture any particular truck lines, styles, or models. Rather, it builds trucks to customers' specifications; these trucks are used for specialty purposes, such as snow removal, log hauling, and military cargo hauling. One year ago KTC received a new, large order that would take three years to complete and require the external hiring of 100 new assemblers. To staff this particular job, the HR department manager of nonexempt employment hurriedly developed and implemented a special staffing process for filling these new vacancies. Applicants were recruited from three different sources: newspaper ads, employee referrals, and a local employment agency. All applicants generated by these methods were subjected to a common selection and decision-making process. All offer receivers were given the same terms and conditions in their job offer letters and told there was no room for any negotiation. All vacancies were eventually filled.

After the first year of the contract, the manager of nonexempt employment, Dexter Williams, decided to pull together some data in an attempt to determine how well the staffing process for the assembler jobs had worked. Since he had not originally planned on doing any evaluation, Dexter was able to retrieve only the following data to help him with his evaluation:

(continued)

Exhibit
Staffing Data for Filling the Job of Assembler

Method	Applicants	Offer receivers	Start as new hires	Remaining at six months
Newspaper ads				
No. apps.	300	70	50	35
Avg. no. days	30	30	10	
Employee referral				
No. apps.	60	30	30	27
Avg. no. days	20	10	10	
Employment agency				
No. apps.	400	20	20	8
Avg. no. days	40	20	10	

1. Determine the yield ratios (offer receivers/applicants, new hires/applicants), time lapse or cycle times (days to offer, days to start), and retention rates associated with each recruitment source.

2. What is the relative effectiveness of the three sources in terms of yield ratios, cycle times, and retention rates?

3. What are possible reasons for the fact that the three sources differ in their relative effectiveness?

4. How do these data compare to national data (Exhibit 14.6)?

5. What would you recommend that Dexter do differently in the future to improve his evaluation of the staffing process?

ENDNOTES

1. Bureau of National Affairs, "The Personnel/Human Resources Function," *Personnel Management* (Washington, DC: author, periodically updated), p. 251:15.

2. Society for Human Resource Management, *Human Resource Practices and Job Satisfaction,* (Alexandria, VA: author, 1993).

3. S. Candron, "Team Staffing Requires New HR Role," *Personnel Journal*, May 1994, pp. 88–94.

4. Bureau of National Affairs, "A Profile of Human Resource Executives," *Bulletin to Management*, June 22, 1995.

5. P. Wamser, "How Does Your Pay Stack Up?," *HR Magazine*, Nov. 1995, pp. 38–41.

6. Bureau of National Affairs, "Human Resource Information Systems," *Personnel Management* (Washington, DC: author, periodically updated), pp. 251:501 to 251:531; V. Ceriello, *Human*

Resource Management Systems (New York: Lexington, 1991), pp. 327–435, 551–585; A. Bargerstock, G. Swanson, and J. Mandarino, "Opportunities and Barriers for Computerizing Recruitment Information Systems," *Employment Management Association Journal*, Spring 1995, pp. 2–11.

7. Resumix, *Reengineering the Workforce With Human Skills Management* (Santa Clara, CA: author, 1995).

8. P. J. Harkins, S. M. Brown, and R. Sullivan, "Shining New Light on a Growing Trend," *HR Magazine*, Dec. 1995, pp. 75–79.

9. W. J. Kucker, "Outsourcing Trends in the Employment Arena," *Employment Management Association Journal*, Spring 1995, pp. 20–25.

10. W. J. Kucker, "Outsourcing: The Wave of the Future in Employment?," *Employment Management Association Journal*, Winter 1994, pp. 2–7.

11. D. E. Terpstra and E. J. Rozell, "The Relationship of Staffing Practices to Organizational Level Measures of Performance," *Personnel Psychology*, 1993, 46, pp. 27–48.

12. C. Ostroff, "Best HR Practices," *1995 SHRM/CCH Survey* (Chicago: Commerce Clearing House, June 21, 1995).

13. Exhibits 9.10, 10.17, 11.7 and 11.13 in this book.

14. L. W. Seberhagen, "How Difficult Is It to Conduct a Validation Study?," *The Industrial-Organizational Psychologist*, 1990, 28, pp. 41–46.

15. Employment Management Association, *1994 National Cost Per Hire Survey Report* (Raleigh, NC: author, 1995).

16. Employment Management Association, *1994 National Cost Per Hire Survey Report.*

17. H. G. Heneman III, D. L. Huett, R. J. Lavigna, and D. Ogsten, "Assessing Managers' Satisfaction with Staffing Service," *Personnel Psychology*, 1995, 48, pp. 163–172.

18. S. W. Gilliland, "Development of the Selection Fairness Survey," paper presented at the *Society for Industrial and Organizational Psychology* meeting, Nashville, 1994.

19. H. P. Coxson, "The Double-Edged Sword of Personnel Files and Employee Records," *Legal Report* (Alexandria, VA: Society for Human Resource Management, 1992); Warren Gorham Lamont, *How Long Do We Have to Keep These Records?* (Boston: author, 1993).

20. H. P. Coxson, "The Double-Edged Sword of Personnel Files and Employee Records."

21. Bureau of National Affairs, "Federal Record Keeping Requirements," *Personnel Management* (Washington, DC: author, periodically updated), p. 251:751.

22. Bureau of National Affairs, "Employee Information and Record Keeping," *Personnel Management* (Washington, DC: author, periodically updated), pp. 251:651 to 251:671; A. G. Feliu, *Primer on Individual Employee Rights*, (Washington, DC: Bureau of National Affairs, 1992), pp. 71–86.

23. Bureau of National Affairs, "Employee Information and Record Keeping."

24. R. L. Adler and F. T. Coleman, *Employment Labor Law Audit* (Washington, DC: Bureau of National Affairs, 1995).

25. D. Cherrington, "Study Shows Legal Issues Are HR Profession's Hottest Topic," *HR News*, March 1994, p. 23.

26. Bureau of National Affairs, "Legal Oversight of the HR Department," *Bulletin to Management* (Washington, DC: author, Feb. 2, 1995).

27. C. Palmer, "Avoiding the Courtroom," *HR Magazine*, Oct. 1995, pp. 32–37.

28. E. D. Cooke Jr. and J. R. Altes, "Eleven Tips for Effectively Handling and Responding to a Charge of Discrimination," *Legal Report* (Alexandria, VA: Society for Human Resource Management, Summer 1995).

29. U.S. Government Printing Office, *Employment Discrimination: Most Private Sector Employers Use Alternative Dispute Resolution* (Washington, DC: author, 1995).

30. U.S. Government Printing Office, *Employment Discrimination: Most Private Sector Employers Use Alternative Dispute Resolution.*

APPENDIX
A

Uniform Guidelines on Employee Selection
Procedures (EEOC)

GENERAL PRINCIPLES

§1607.1 *Statement of purpose.*

A. *Need for uniformity–Issuing agencies.* The Federal government's need for a uniform set of principles on the question of the use of tests and other selection procedures has long been recognized. The Equal Employment Opportunity Commission, the Civil Service Commission, the Department of Labor, and the Department of Justice jointly have adopted these uniform guidelines to meet that need, and to apply the same principles to the Federal Government as are applied to other employers.

B. *Purpose of guidelines.* These guidelines incorporate a single set of principles which are designed to assist employers, labor organizations, employment agencies, and licensing and certification boards to comply with requirements of Federal law prohibiting employment practices which discriminate on grounds of race, color, religion, sex, and national origin. They are designed to provide a framework for determining the proper use of tests and other selection procedures. These guidelines do not require a user to conduct validity studies of selection procedures where no adverse impact results. However, all users are encouraged to use selection procedures which are valid, especially users operating under merit principles.

C. *Relation to prior guidelines.* These guidelines are based upon and supersede previously issued guidelines on employee selection procedures. These guidelines have been built upon court decisions, the previously issued guidelines of the agencies, and the practical experience of the agencies, as well as the standards of the psychological profession. These guidelines are intended to be consistent with existing law.

§1607.2 *Scope.*

A. *Application of guidelines.* These guidelines will be applied by the Equal Employment Opportunity Commission in the enforcement of title VII of the Civil Rights Act of 1964, as amended by the Equal Employment Opportunity Act of 1972 (hereinafter "Title VII"); by the Department of Labor, and the contract compliance agencies until the transfer of authority contemplated by the President's Reorganization Plan No. 1 of 1978, in the administration and enforcement of Executive Order 11246, as amended by Executive Order 11375 (hereinafter "Executive Order 11246"); by the Civil Service Commission and other Federal agencies subject to section 717 of Title VII; by the Civil Service Commission in exercising its responsibilities toward State and local governments under section 208(b)(1) of the Intergovernmental-Personnel Act; by the Department of Justice in exercising its responsibilities under Federal law; by the Office of Revenue Sharing of the Department of the Treasury under the State and Local Fiscal Assistance Act of 1972, as amended; and by any other Federal agency which adopts them.

B. *Employment decisions.* These guidelines apply to tests and other selection procedures which are used as a basis for any employment decision. Employment decisions include but are not limited to hiring, promotion, demotion, membership (for example, in a labor organization), referral, retention, and licensing and certification, to the extent that licensing and certification may be covered by Federal equal employment opportunity law. Other selection decisions, such as selection for training or transfer, may also be considered employment decisions if they lead to any of the decisions listed above.

C. *Selection procedures.* These guidelines apply only to selection procedures which are used as a basis for making employment decisions. For example, the use of selection procedures designed to attract members of a particular race, sex, or ethnic group, which were previously denied employment opportunities or which are currently underutilized, may be necessary to bring an employer into compliance with Federal law, and is frequently an essential element of any effective affirmative action program; but recruitment practices are not considered by these guidelines to be selection procedures. Similarly, these guidelines do not pertain to the question of the lawfulness of a seniority system within the meaning of section 703(h), Executive Order 11246 or other provisions of Federal law or regulation, except to the extent that such systems utilize selection procedures to determine qualifications or abilities to perform the job. Nothing in these guidelines is intended or should be interpreted as discouraging the use of a selection procedure for the purpose of determining qualifications or for the purpose of selection on the basis of relative qualifications, if the selection procedure had been validated in accord with these guidelines for each such purpose for which it is to be used.

D. *Limitations.* These guidelines apply only to persons subject to Title VII, Executive Order 11246, or other equal employment opportunity requirements of Federal law. These guidelines do not apply to responsibilities under the Age Discrimination in Employment Act of 1967, as amended, not to discriminate on the basis of age, or under sections 501, 503, and 504 of the Rehabilitation Act of 1973, not to discriminate on the basis of handicap.

E. *Indian preference not affected.* These guidelines do not restrict any obligation imposed or right granted by Federal law to users to extend a preference in employment to Indians living on or near an Indian reservation in connection with employment opportunities on or near an Indian reservation.

§1607.3 *Discrimination defined: Relationship between use of selection procedures and discrimination.*

A. *Procedure having adverse impact constitutes discrimination unless justified.* The use of any selection procedure which has an adverse impact on the hiring, promotion, or other employment or membership opportunities of members of any race, sex, or ethnic group will be considered to be discriminatory and inconsistent with these guidelines, unless the procedure has been validated in accordance with these guidelines, or the provisions of section 6 below are satisfied.

B. *Consideration of suitable alternative selection procedures.* Where two or more selection procedures are available which serve the user's legitimate interest in efficient and trustworthy workmanship, and which are substantially equally valid for a given purpose, the user should use the procedure which has been demonstrated to have the lesser adverse impact. Accordingly, whenever a validity study is called for by these guidelines, the user should include, as a part of the validity study, an investigation of suitable alternative selection procedures and suitable alternative methods of using the selection procedure which have as little adverse impact as possible to determine the appropriateness of using or validating them in accord with these guidelines. If a user has made a reasonable effort to become aware of such alternative procedures and validity has been demonstrated in accord with these guidelines, the use of the test or other selection procedure may continue until such time as it should reasonably be reviewed for currency. Whenever the user is shown an alternative selection procedure with evidence of less adverse impact and substantial evidence of validity for the same job in similar circumstances, the user should investigate it to determine the appropriateness of using or validating it in accord with these guidelines. This subsection is not intended to preclude the combination of procedures into a significantly more valid procedure, if the use of such a combination has been shown to be in compliance with the guidelines.

§1607.4 *Information on impact.*

A. *Records concerning impact.* Each user should maintain and have available for inspection records or other information which will disclose the impact which its tests and other selection procedures have upon employment opportunities of persons by identifiable race, sex, or ethnic group as set forth in subparagraph B below in order to determine compliance with these guidelines. Where there are large numbers of applicants and procedures are administered frequently, such information may be retained on a sample basis, provided that the sample is appropriate in terms of the applicant population and adequate in size.

B. *Applicable race, sex, and ethnic groups for recordkeeping.* The records called for by this section are to be maintained by sex, and the following races and ethnic groups: Blacks (Negroes), American Indians (including Alaskan Natives), Asians (including Pacific Islanders), Hispanic (including persons of Mexican, Puerto Rican, Cuban, Central or South American, or other Spanish origin or culture regardless of race), whites (Caucasians) other than Hispanic, and totals. The race, sex, and ethnic classifications called for by this section are consistent with the Equal Employment Opportunity Standard Form 100, Employer Information Report EEO-1 series of reports. The user should adopt safeguards to ensure that the records required by this paragraph are used for appropriate purposes such as determining adverse impact, or (where required) for developing and monitoring affirmative action programs, and that such records are not used improperly. See sections 4E and 17(4), below.

C. *Evaluation of selection rates. The "bottom line."* If the information called for by sections 4A and B above shows that the total selection process for a job has an adverse impact, the individual components of the selection process should be evaluated for adverse impact. If this information shows that the total selection process does not have an adverse impact, the Federal enforcement agencies, in the exercise of their administrative and prosecutorial discretion, in usual circumstances, will not expect a user to evaluate the individual components for adverse impact, or to validate such individual components, and will not take enforcement action based upon adverse impact of any component of that process, including the separate parts of a multipart selection procedure or any separate procedure that is used as an alternative method of selection. However, in the following circumstances, the Federal enforcement agencies will expect a user to evaluate the individual components for adverse impact and may, where appropriate, take enforcement action with respect to the individual components: (1) where the selection procedure is a significant factor in the continuation of patterns of assignments of incumbent employees caused by prior discriminatory employment practices; (2) where the weight of court decisions or administrative interpretations hold that a specific procedure (such as height or weight requirements or no-arrest records) is not job related in the same or similar circumstances. In unusual circumstances, other than those listed in (1) and (2) above, the Federal enforcement agencies may request a user to evaluate the individual components for adverse impact and may, where appropriate, take enforcement action with respect to the individual component.

D. *Adverse impact and the "four-fifths rule."* A selection rate for any race, sex, or ethnic group which is less than four-fifths (4/5) (or eighty percent) of the rate for the group with the highest rate will generally be required by the Federal enforcement agencies as evidence of adverse impact, while a greater than four-fifths rate will generally not be regarded by Federal enforcement agencies as evidence of adverse impact. Smaller differences in selection rate may nevertheless constitute adverse impact, where they are significant in both statistical and practical terms or where a user's actions have discouraged applicants disproportionately on grounds of race, sex, or ethnic group. Greater differences in selection rate may not constitute adverse impact where the differences are based on small numbers and are not statistically significant, or where special recruiting or other programs cause the pool of minority or female candidates to be atypical of the normal pool of applicants from that group. Where the user's evidence concerning the impact of a selection procedure indicates adverse impact but is based upon numbers which are too small to be reliable, evidence concerning the impact of the procedure over a longer period of time and/or evidence concerning the impact which the selection procedure had when used in the same manner in similar circumstances elsewhere may be considered in determining adverse impact. Where the user has not maintained data on adverse impact as required by the documentation section of applicable guidelines, the Federal enforcement agencies may draw an inference of adverse impact of the selection process from the failure of the user to maintain such data, if the user has an underutilization of a group in the job category, as compared to the group's representation in the relevant labor market or, in the case of jobs filled from within, the applicable workforce.

E. *Consideration of user's equal employment opportunity posture.* In carrying out their obligations, the Federal enforcement agencies will consider the general posture of the user with respect to equal employment opportunities for the job or group of jobs in question. Where a user has adopted an affirmative action program, the Federal enforcement agencies will consider the provisions of that program, including the goals and timetables which the user has adopted and the progress which the user has made in carrying out that program and in meeting the goals and timetables. While such affirmative action programs may in design and execution be race, color, sex, or ethnic conscious, selection procedures under such programs should be based upon the ability or relative ability to do the work.

§1607.5 *General standards for validity studies.*

A. *Acceptable types of validity studies.* For the purposes of satisfying these guidelines, users may rely upon criterion-related validity studies, content validity studies or construct validity studies, in accordance with the standards set forth in the technical standards of these guidelines, section 14 below. New strategies for showing the validity of selection procedures will be evaluated as they become accepted by the psychological profession.

B. *Criterion-related, content, and construct validity.* Evidence of the validity of a test or other selection procedure by a criterion-related validity study should consist of empirical data demonstrating that the selection procedure is predictive of or significantly correlated with important elements of job performance. See section 14B below. Evidence of the validity of a test or other selection procedure by a content validity study should consist of data showing that the content of the selection procedure is representative of important aspects of performance on the job for which the candidates are to be evaluated. See section 14C below. Evidence of the validity of a test or other selection procedure through a construct validity study should consist of data showing that the procedure measures the degree to which candidates have identifiable characteristics which have been determined to be important in successful performance in the job for which the candidates are to be evaluated. See section 14D below.

C. *Guidelines are consistent with professional standards.* The provisions of these guidelines relating to validation of selection procedures are intended to be consistent with generally accepted professional standards for evaluating standardized tests and other selection procedures, such as those described in the Standards for Educational and Psychological Tests prepared by a joint committee of the American Psychological Association, the American Educational Research Association, and the National Council on Measurement in Education (American Psychological Association, Washington, D.C., 1974) (hereinafter "A.P.A. Standards") and standard textbooks and journals in the field of personnel selection.

D. *Need for documentation of validity.* For any selection procedure which is part of a selection process which has an adverse impact each user should maintain and have available such documentation as is described in section 15 below.

E. *Accuracy and standardization.* Validity studies should be carried out under conditions which assure insofar as possible the adequacy and accuracy of the research and the report. Selection procedures should be administered and scored under standardized conditions.

F. *Caution against selection on basis of knowledges, skills, or ability learned in brief orientation period.* In general, users should avoid making employment decisions on the basis of measures of knowledges, skills, or abilities which are normally learned in a brief orientation period, and which have an adverse impact.

G. *Method of use of selection procedures.* The evidence of both the validity and utility of a selection procedure should support the method the user chooses for operational use of the procedure, if that method of use has a greater adverse impact than another method of use. Evidence which may be sufficient to support the use of a selection procedure on a pass/fail (screening) basis may be insufficient to support the use of the same procedure on a ranking basis under these guidelines. Thus, if a user decides to use a selection procedure on a ranking basis, and that method of use has a greater adverse impact than use on an appropriate pass/fail basis (see section 5H below), the user should have sufficient evidence of validity and utility to support the use on a ranking basis. See sections 3B, 14B (5) and (6), 14C (8) and (9).

H. *Cutoff scores.* Where cutoff scores are used, they should normally be set so as to be reasonable and consistent with normal expectations of acceptable proficiency within the workforce. Where applicants are ranked on the basis of properly validated selection procedures and those applicants scoring below a higher cutoff score than appropriate in light of such expectations have little or no chance of being selected for employment, the higher cutoff score may be appropriate, but the degree of adverse impact should be considered.

I. *Use of selection procedures for higher-level jobs.* If job progression structures are so established that employees will probably, within a reasonable period of time and in a majority of cases, progress to a higher level, it may be considered that the applicants are being evaluated for a job or jobs at the higher level. However, where job progression is not so nearly automatic, or the time span is such that higher level jobs or employees' potential may be expected to change in significant ways, it should be considered that applicants are being evaluated for a job at or near the entry level. A "reasonable period of time" will vary for different jobs and employment situations but will seldom be more than 5 years. Use of selection procedures to evaluate applicants for a higher level job would not be appropriate:

(1) If the majority of those remaining employed do not progress to the higher level job;

(2) If there is a reason to doubt that the higher level job will continue to require essentially similar skills during the progression period; or

(3) If the selection procedures measure knowledges, skills, or abilities required for advancement which would be expected to develop principally from the training or experience on the job.

J. *Interim use of selection procedures.* Users may continue the use of a selection procedure which is not at the moment fully supported by the required evidence of validity, provided: (1) the user has available substantial evidence of validity, and (2) the user has in progress, when technically feasible, a study which is designed to produce the additional evidence required by these guidelines within a reasonable time. If such a study is not technically feasible, see section 6B. If the study does not demonstrate validity, this provision of these guidelines for interim use shall not constitute a defense in any action, nor shall it relieve the user of any obligations arising under Federal law.

K. *Review of validity studies for currency.* Whenever validity has been shown in accord with these guidelines for the use of a particular selection procedure for a job or group of jobs, additional studies need not be performed until such time as the validity study is subject to review as provided in section 3B above. There are no absolutes in the area of determining the currency of a validity study. All circumstances concerning the study, including the validation strategy used, and changes in the relevant labor market and the job should be considered in the determination of when a validity study is outdated.

§1607.6 *Use of selection procedures which have not been validated.*

A. *Use of alternate selection procedures to eliminate adverse impact.* A user may choose to utilize alternative selection procedures in order to eliminate adverse impact or as part of an affirmative action program. See section 13 below. Such alternative procedures should eliminate the adverse impact in the total selection process, should be lawful, and should be as job related as possible.

B. *Where validity studies cannot or need not be performed.* There are circumstances in which a user cannot or need not utilize the validation techniques contemplated by these guidelines. In such circumstances, the user should utilize selection procedures which are as job related as possible and which will minimize or eliminate adverse impact, as set forth below.

(1) *Where informal or unscored procedures are used.* When an informal or unscored selection procedure which has an adverse impact is utilized, the user should eliminate the adverse impact, or modify the procedure to one which is a formal, scored or quantified measure or combination of measures and then validate the procedure in accord with these guidelines, or otherwise justify continued use of the procedure in accord with Federal law.

(2) *Where formal and scored procedures are used.* When a formal and scored selection procedure is used which has an adverse impact, the validation techniques contemplated by these guidelines usually should be followed if technically feasible. Where the user cannot or need not follow the validation techniques anticipated by these guidelines, the user should either modify the procedure to eliminate adverse impact or otherwise justify continued use of the procedure in accord with Federal law.

§1607.7 *Use of other validity studies.*

A. *Validity studies not conducted by the user.* Users may, under certain circumstances, support the use of selection procedures by validity studies conducted by other users or conducted by test publishers or distributors and described in test manuals. While publishers of selection procedures have a professional obligation to provide evidence of validity which meets generally accepted professional standards (see section 5C above), users are cautioned that they are responsible for compliance with these guidelines. Accordingly, users seeking to obtain selection procedures from publishers and distributors should be careful to determine that, in the event the user becomes subject to the validity requirements of these guidelines, the necessary information to support validity has been determined and will be made available to the user.

B. *Use of criterion-related validity evidence from other sources.* Criterion-related validity studies conducted by one test user, or described in test manuals and the professional literature, will be considered acceptable for use by another user when the following requirements are met:

(1) *Validity evidence.* Evidence from the available studies meeting the standards of section 14B below clearly demonstrates that the selection procedure is valid;

(2) *Job similarity.* The incumbents in the user's job and the incumbents in the job or group of jobs on which the validity study was conducted perform substantially the same major work behaviors, as shown by appropriate job analyses both on the job or group of jobs on which the validity study was performed and on the job for which the selection procedure is to be used; and

(3) *Fairness evidence.* The studies include a study of test fairness for each race, sex, and ethnic group which constitutes a significant factor in the borrowing user's relevant labor market for the job or jobs in question. If the studies under consideration satisfy (1) and (2) above but do not contain an investigation of test fairness, and it is not technically feasible for the borrowing user to conduct an internal study of test fairness, the borrowing user may utilize the study until studies conducted elsewhere meeting the requirements of these guidelines show test unfairness, or until such time as it becomes technically feasible to conduct an internal study of test fairness and the results of that study can be acted upon. Users obtaining selection procedures from publishers should consider, as one factor in the decision to purchase a particular selection procedure, the availability of evidence concerning test fairness.

C. *Validity evidence from multiunit study.* If validity evidence from a study covering more than one unit within an organization satisfies the requirements of section 14B below, evidence of validity specific to each unit will not be required unless there are variables which are likely to affect validity significantly.

D. *Other significant variables.* If there are variables in the other studies which are likely to affect validity significantly, the user may not rely upon such studies, but will be expected either to conduct an internal validity study or to comply with section 6 above.

§1607.8 *Cooperative studies.*

A. *Encouragement of cooperative studies.* The agencies issuing these guidelines encourage employers, labor organizations, and employment agencies to cooperate in research, development, search for lawful alternatives, and validity studies in order to achieve procedures which are consistent with these guidelines.

B. *Standards for use of cooperative studies.* If validity evidence from a cooperative study satisfies the requirements of section 14 below, evidence of validity specific to each user will not be required unless there are variables in the user's situation which are likely to affect validity significantly.

§1607.9 *No assumption of validity.*

A. *Unacceptable substitutes for evidence of validity.* Under no circumstances will the general reputation of a test or other selection procedures, its author or its publisher, or casual reports of its validity be accepted in lieu of evidence of validity. Specifically ruled out are: assumptions of validity based on a procedure's name or descriptive labels; all forms of promotional literature; data bearing on the frequency of a procedure's usage; testimonial statements and credentials of sellers, users, or consultants; and other nonempirical or anecdotal accounts of selection practices or selection outcomes.

B. *Encouragement of professional supervision.* Professional supervision of selection activities is encouraged but is not a substitute for documented evidence of validity. The enforcement agencies will take into account the fact that a thorough job analysis was conducted and that careful development and use of a selection procedure in accordance with professional standards enhance the probability that the selection procedure is valid for the job.

§1607.10 *Employment agencies and employment services.*

A. *Where selection procedures are devised by agency.* An employment agency, including private employment agencies and State employment agencies, which agrees to a request by an employer or labor organization to devise and utilize a selection procedure should follow the standards in these guidelines for determining adverse impact. If adverse impact exists, the agency should comply with these guidelines. An employment agency is not relieved of its obligation herein because the user did not request such validation or has requested the use of some lesser standard of validation than is provided in these guidelines. The use of an employment agency does not relieve an employer or labor organization or other user of its responsibilities under Federal law to provide equal employment opportunity or its obligations as a user under these guidelines.

B. *Where selection procedures are devised elsewhere.* Where an employment agency or service is requested to administer a selection procedure which has been devised elsewhere and to make referrals pursuant to the results, the employment agency or service should maintain and have available evidence of the impact of the selection and referral procedures which it administers. If adverse impact results the agency or service should comply with these guidelines. If the agency or service seeks to comply with these guidelines by reliance upon validity studies or other data in the possession of the employer, it should obtain and have available such information.

§1607.11 *Disparate treatment.*

The principles of disparate or unequal treatment must be distinguished from the concepts of validation. A selection procedure—even though validated against job performance in accordance with these guidelines—cannot be imposed upon members of a race, sex, or ethnic group where other employees, applicants, or members have not been subjected to that standard. Disparate treatment occurs where members of a race, sex, or ethnic group have been denied the same employment, promotion, membership, or other employment opportunities as have been available to other employees or applicants. Those employees or applicants who have been denied equal treatment, because of prior discriminatory practices or policies, must at least be afforded the same opportunities as had existed for other employees or applicants during the period of discrimination. Thus, the persons who were in the class of persons discriminated against during the period the user followed the discriminatory practices should be allowed the opportunity to qualify under the less stringent selection procedures previously followed, unless the user demonstrates that the increased standards are required by business necessity. This section does not prohibit a user who has not previously followed merit standards from adopting merit standards which are in compliance with these guidelines; nor does it preclude a user who has previously used invalid or unvalidated selection procedures from developing and using procedures which are in accord with these guidelines.

§1607.12 *Retesting of applicants.*

Users should provide a reasonable opportunity for retesting and reconsideration. Where examinations are administered periodically with public notice, such reasonable opportunity exists, unless persons who have previously been tested are precluded from retesting. The user may however take reasonable steps to preserve the security of its procedures.

§1607.13 *Affirmative action.*

A. *Affirmative action obligations.* The use of selection procedures which have been validated pursuant to these guidelines does not relieve users of any obligations they have to undertake affirmative action to assure equal employment opportunity. Nothing in these guidelines is intended to preclude the use of lawful selection procedures which assist in remedying the effects of prior discriminatory practices, or the achievement of affirmative action objectives.

B. *Encouragement of voluntary affirmative action programs.* These guidelines are also intended to encourage the adoption and implementation of voluntary affirmative action programs by users who have no obligation under Federal law to adopt them; but are not intended to impose any new obligations in that regard. The agencies issuing and endorsing these guidelines endorse for all private employers and reaffirm for all governmental employers the Equal Employment Opportunity Coordinating Council's "Policy Statement on Affirmative Action Programs for State and Local Government Agencies" (41 FR 38814, September 13, 1976). That policy statement is attached hereto as appendix, section 17.

TECHNICAL STANDARDS

§1607.14 *Technical standards for validity studies.*
The following minimum standards, as applicable, should be met in conducting a validity study. Nothing in these guidelines is intended to preclude the development and use of other professionally acceptable techniques with respect to validation of selection procedures. Where it is not technically feasible for a user to conduct a validity study, the user has the obligation otherwise to comply with these guidelines. See sections 6 and 7 above.

A. *Validity studies should be based on review of information about the job.* Any validity study should be based upon a review of information about the job for which the selection procedure is to be used. The review should include a job analysis except as provided in section 14B(3) below with respect to criterion-related validity. Any method of job analysis may be used if it provides the information required for the specific validation strategy used.

B. *Technical standards for criterion-related validity studies.*

(1) *Technical feasibility.* Users choosing to validate a selection procedure by a criterion-related validity strategy should determine whether it is technically feasible (as defined in section 16) to conduct such a study in the particular employment context. The determination of the number of persons necessary to permit the conduct of a meaningful criterion-related study should be made by the user on the basis of all relevant information concerning the selection procedure, the potential sample and the employment situation. Where appropriate, jobs with substantially the same major work behaviors may be grouped together for validity studies, in order to obtain an adequate sample. These guidelines do not require a user to hire or promote persons for the purpose of making it possible to conduct a criterion-related study.

(2) *Analysis of the job.* There should be a review of job information to determine measures of work behavior(s) or performance that are relevant to the job or group of jobs in question. These measures or criteria are relevant to the extent that they represent critical or important job duties, work behaviors or work outcomes as developed from the review of job information. The possibility of bias should be considered both in selection of the criterion measures and their application. In view of the possibility of bias in subjective evaluations, supervisory rating techniques and instructions to raters should be carefully developed. All criterion measures and the methods for gathering data need to be examined for freedom from factors which would unfairly alter scores of members of any group. The relevance of criteria and their freedom from bias are of particular concern when there are significant differences in measures of job performance for different groups.

(3) *Criterion measures.* Proper safeguards should be taken to ensure that scores on selection procedures do not enter into any judgments of employee adequacy that are to be used as criterion measures. Whatever criteria are used should represent important or critical work behavior(s) or work outcomes. Certain criteria may be used without a full job analysis if the user can show the importance of the criteria to the particular employment context. These criteria include but are not limited to production rate, error rate, tardiness, absenteeism, and length of service. A standardized rating of overall work performance may be used where a study of the job shows that it is an appropriate criterion. Where performance in training is used as a criterion, success in training should be properly

measured and the relevance of the training should be shown either through a comparison of the content of the training program with the critical or important work behavior(s) of the job(s), or through a demonstration of the relationship between measures of performance in training and measures of job performance. Measures of relative success in training include but are not limited to instructor evaluations, performance samples, or tests. Criterion measures consisting of paper and pencil tests will be closely reviewed for job relevance.

(4) *Representativeness of the sample.* Whether the study is predictive or concurrent, the sample subjects should insofar as feasible be representative of the candidates normally available in the relevant labor market for the job or group of jobs in question, and should insofar as feasible include the races, sexes, and ethnic groups normally available in the relevant job market. In determining the representativeness of the sample in a concurrent validity study, the user should take into account the extent to which the specific knowledges or skills which are the primary focus of the test are those which employees learn on the job.

Where samples are combined or compared, attention should be given to see that such samples are comparable in terms of the actual job they perform, the length of time on the job where time on the job is likely to affect performance, and other relevant factors likely to affect validity differences; or that these factors are included in the design of the study and their effects identified.

(5) *Statistical relationships.* The degree of relationship between selection procedure scores and criterion measures should be examined and computed, using professionally acceptable statistical procedures. Generally, a selection procedure is considered related to the criterion, for the purposes of these guidelines, when the relationship between performance on the procedure and performance on the criterion measure is statistically significant at the 0.05 level of significance, which means that it is sufficiently high as to have a probability of no more than one (1) in twenty (20) to have occurred by chance. Absence of a statistically significant relationship between a selection procedure and job performance should not necessarily discourage other investigations of the validity of that selection procedure.

(6) *Operational use of selection procedures.* Users should evaluate each selection procedure to assure that it is appropriate for operational use, including establishment of cutoff scores or rank ordering. Generally, if other factors remain the same, the greater the magnitude of the relationship (e.g., correlation coefficient) between performance on a selection procedure and one or more criteria of performance on the job, and the greater the importance and number of aspects of job performance covered by the criteria, the more likely it is that the procedure will be appropriate for use. Reliance upon a selection procedure which is significantly related to a criterion measure, but which is based upon a study involving a large number of subjects and has a low correlation coefficient will be subject to close review if it has a large adverse impact. Sole reliance upon a single selection instrument which is related to only one of many job duties or aspects of job performance will also be subject to close review. The appropriateness of a selection procedure is best evaluated in each particular situation and there are no minimum correlation coefficients applicable to all employment situations. In determining whether a selection procedure is appropriate for operational use, the following considerations should also be taken into account: The degree of adverse impact of the procedure, the availability of other selection procedures of greater or substantially equal validity.

(7) *Overstatement of validity findings.* Users should avoid reliance upon techniques which tend to overestimate validity findings as a result of capitalization on chance unless an appropriate safeguard is taken. Reliance upon a few selection procedures or criteria of successful job performance when many selection procedures or criteria of performance have been studied, or the use of optimal statistical weights for selection procedures computed in one sample, are techniques which tend to inflate validity estimates as a result of chance. Use of a large sample is one safeguard; cross-validation is another.

(8) *Fairness.* This section generally calls for studies of unfairness where technically feasible. The concept of fairness or unfairness of selection procedures is a developing concept. In addition, fairness studies generally require substantial numbers of employees in the job or group of jobs being studied. For these reasons, the Federal enforcement agencies recognize that the obligation to conduct studies of fairness imposed by the guidelines generally will be upon users or groups of users with a large number of persons in a job class, or test developers; and that small users utilizing their own selection

procedures will generally not be obligated to conduct such studies because it will be technically infeasible for them to do so.

(a) *Unfairness defined.* When members of one race, sex, or ethnic group characteristically obtain lower scores on a selection procedure than members of another group, and the differences in scores are not reflected in differences in a measure of job performance, use of the selection procedure may unfairly deny opportunities to members of the group that obtains the lower scores.

(b) *Investigation of fairness.* Where a selection procedure results in an adverse impact on a race, sex, or ethnic group, identified in accordance with the classifications set forth in section 4 above, and that group is a significant factor in the relevant labor market, the user generally should investigate the possible existence of unfairness for that group if it is technically feasible to do so. The greater the severity of the adverse impact on a group, the greater the need to investigate the possible existence of unfairness. Where the weight of evidence from other studies shows that the selection procedure predicts fairly for the group in question and for the same or similar jobs, such evidence may be relied on in connection with the selection procedure at issue.

(c) *General considerations in fairness investigations.* Users conducting a study of fairness should review the A.P.A. Standards regarding investigation of possible bias in testing. An investigation of fairness of a selection procedure depends on both evidence of validity and the manner in which the selection procedure is to be used in a particular employment context. Fairness of a selection procedure cannot necessarily be specified in advance without investigating these factors. Investigation of fairness of a selection procedure in samples where the range of scores on selection procedures or criterion measures is severely restricted for any subgroup sample (as compared to other subgroup samples) may produce misleading evidence of unfairness. That factor should accordingly be taken into account in conducting such studies and before reliance is placed on the results.

(d) *When unfairness is shown.* If unfairness is demonstrated through a showing that members of a particular group perform better or more poorly on the job than their scores on the selection procedure would indicate through comparison with members of other groups, the user may either revise or replace the selection instrument in accordance with these guidelines, or may continue to use the selection instrument operationally with appropriate revisions in its use to assure compatibility between the probability of successful job performance and the probability of being selected.

(e) *Technical feasibility of fairness studies.* In addition to the general conditions needed for technical feasibility for the conduct of a criterion-related study (see section 16, below) an investigation of fairness requires the following:

(i) An adequate sample of persons in each group available for the study to achieve findings of statistical significance. Guidelines do not require a user to hire or promote persons on the basis of group classifications for the purpose of making it possible to conduct a study of fairness; but the user has the obligation otherwise to comply with these guidelines.

(ii) The samples for each group should be comparable in terms of the actual job they perform, length of time on the job where time on the job is likely to affect performance, and other relevant factors likely to affect validity differences; or such factors should be included in the design of the study and their effects identified.

(f) *Continued use of selection procedures when fairness studies not feasible.* If a study of fairness should otherwise be performed, but is not technically feasible, a selection procedure may be used which has otherwise met the validity standards of these guidelines, unless the technical infeasibility resulted from discriminatory employment practices which are demonstrated by facts other than past failure to conform with requirements for validation of selection procedures. However, when it becomes technically feasible for the user to perform a study of fairness and such a study is otherwise called for, the user should conduct the study of fairness.

C. *Technical standards for content validity studies.*

(1) *Appropriateness of content validity studies.* Users choosing to validate a selection procedure by a content validity strategy should determine whether it is appropriate to conduct such a study in the particular employment context. A selection procedure can be supported by a content validity strategy to the extent that it is a representative sample of the content of the job. Selection procedures which purport to measure knowledges, skills, or abilities may in certain circumstances be justified by content validity, although they may not be representative samples, if the knowledge, skill, or

ability measured by the selection procedure can be operationally defined as provided in section 14C(4) below, and if that knowledge, skill, or ability is a necessary prerequisite to successful job performance. A selection procedure based upon inferences about mental processes cannot be supported solely or primarily on the basis of content validity. Thus, a content strategy is not appropriate for demonstrating the validity of selection procedures which purport to measure traits or constructs, such as intelligence, aptitude, personality, common sense, judgment, leadership, and spatial ability. Content validity is also not an appropriate strategy when the selection procedure involves knowledges, skills, or abilities which an employee will be expected to learn on the job.

(2) *Job analysis for content validity.* There should be a job analysis which includes an analysis of the important work behavior(s) required for successful performance and their relative importance and, if the behavior results in work product(s), an analysis of the work product(s). Any job analysis should focus on the work behavior(s) and the tasks associated with them. If work behavior(s) are not observable, the job analysis should identify and analyze those aspects of the behavior(s) that can be observed and the observed work products. The work behavior(s) selected for measurement should be critical work behavior(s) and/or important work behavior(s) constituting most of the job.

(3) *Development of selection procedures.* A selection procedure designed to measure the work behavior may be developed specifically from the job and job analysis in question, or may have been previously developed by the user, or by other users or by a test publisher.

(4) *Standards for demonstrating content validity.* To demonstrate the content validity of a selection procedure, a user should show that the behavior(s) demonstrated in the selection procedure are a representative sample of the behavior(s) of the job in question or that the selection procedure provides a representative sample of the work product of the job. In the case of a selection procedure measuring a knowledge, skill, or ability, the knowledge, skill, or ability being measured should be operationally defined. In the case of a selection procedure measuring a knowledge, the knowledge being measured should be operationally defined as that body of learned information which is used in and is a necessary prerequisite for observable aspects of work behavior of the job. In the case of skills or abilities, the skill or ability being measured should be operationally defined in terms of observable aspects of work behavior of the job. For any selection procedure measuring a knowledge, skill, or ability, the user should show that (a) the selection procedure measures and is a representative sample of that knowledge, skill, or ability; and (b) that knowledge, skill, or ability is used in and is a necessary prerequisite to performance of critical or important work behavior(s). In addition, to be content valid, a selection procedure measuring a skill or ability should either closely approximate an observable work behavior, or its product should closely approximate an observable work product. If a test purports to sample a work behavior or to provide a sample of a work product, the manner and setting of the selection procedure and its level and complexity should closely approximate the work situation. The closer the content and the context of the selection procedure are to work samples or work behaviors, the stronger is the basis for showing content validity. As the content of the selection procedure less resembles a work behavior, or the setting and manner of the administration of the selection procedure less resemble the work situation, or the result less resembles a work product, the less likely the selection procedure is to be content valid, and the greater the need for other evidence of validity.

(5) *Reliability.* The reliability of selection procedures justified on the basis of content validity should be a matter of concern to the user. Whenever it is feasible, appropriate statistical estimates should be made of the reliability of the selection procedure.

(6) *Prior training or experience.* A requirement for or evaluation of specific prior training or experience based on content validity, including a specification of level or amount of training or experience, should be justified on the basis of the relationship between the content of the training or experience and the content of the job for which the training or experience is to be required or evaluated. The critical consideration is the resemblance between the specific behaviors, products, knowledges, skills, or abilities in the experience or training and the specific behaviors, products, knowledges, skills, or abilities required on the job, whether or not there is close resemblance between the experience or training as a whole and the job as a whole.

(7) *Content validity of training success.* Where a measure of success in a training program is used as a selection procedure and the content of a training program is justified on the basis of content

validity, the use should be justified on the relationship between the content of the training program and the content of the job.

(8) *Operational use.* A selection procedure which is supported on the basis of content validity may be used for a job if it represents a critical work behavior (i.e., a behavior which is necessary for performance of the job) or work behaviors which constitute most of the important parts of the job.

(9) *Ranking based on content validity studies.* If a user can show, by a job analysis or otherwise, that a higher score on a content valid selection procedure is likely to result in better job performance, the results may be used to rank persons who score above minimum levels. Where a selection procedure supported solely or primarily by content validity is used to rank job candidates, the selection procedure should measure those aspects of performance which differentiate among levels of job performance.

D. *Technical standards for construct validity studies.*

(1) *Appropriateness of construct validity studies.* Construct validity is a more complex strategy than either criterion-related or content validity. Construct validation is a relatively new and developing procedure in the employment field, and there is at present a lack of substantial literature extending the concept to employment practices. The user should be aware that the effort to obtain sufficient empirical support for construct validity is both an extensive and arduous effort involving a series of research studies, which include criterion-related validity studies and which may include content validity studies. Users choosing to justify use of a selection procedure by this strategy should therefore take particular care to assure that the validity study meets the standards set forth below.

(2) *Job analysis for construct validity studies.* There should be a job analysis. This job analysis should show the work behavior(s) required for successful performance of the job, or the groups of jobs being studied, the critical or important work behavior(s) in the job or group of jobs being studied, and an identification of the construct(s) believed to underlie successful performance of these critical or important work behaviors in the job or jobs in question. Each construct should be named and defined, so as to distinguish it from other constructs. If a group of jobs is being studied, the jobs should have in common one or more critical or important work behaviors at a comparable level of complexity.

(3) *Relationship to the job.* A selection procedure should then be identified or developed which measures the construct identified in accord with subparagraph (2) above. The user should show by empirical evidence that the selection procedure is validly related to the construct and that the construct is validly related to the performance of critical or important work behavior(s). The relationship between the construct as measured by the selection procedure and the related work behavior(s) should be supported by empirical evidence from one or more criterion-related studies involving the job or jobs in question which satisfy the provisions of section 14B above.

(4) *Use of construct validity study without new criterion-related evidence.* (a) *Standards for use.* Until such time as professional literature provides more guidance on the use of construct validity in employment situations, the Federal agencies will accept a claim of construct validity without a criterion-related study which satisfies section 14B above only when the selection procedure has been used elsewhere in a situation in which a criterion-related study has been conducted and the use of a criterion-related validity study in this context meets the standards for transportability of criterion-related validity studies as set forth above in section 7. However, if a study pertains to a number of jobs having common critical or important work behaviors at a comparable level of complexity, and the evidence satisfies subparagraphs 14B (2) and (3) above for those jobs with criterion-related validity evidence for those jobs, the selection procedure may be used for all the jobs to which the study pertains. If construct validity is to be generalized to other jobs or groups of jobs not in the group studied, the Federal enforcement agencies will expect at a minimum additional empirical research evidence meeting the standards of subparagraphs section 14B (2) and (3) above for the additional jobs or groups of jobs.

(b) *Determination of common work behaviors.* In determining whether two or more jobs have one or more work behavior(s) in common, the user should compare the observed work behavior(s) in each of the jobs and should compare the observed work product(s) in each of the jobs. If neither the observed work behavior(s) in each of the jobs nor the observed work product(s) in each of the jobs are the same, the Federal enforcement agencies will presume that the work behavior(s) in each job are different. If the work behaviors are not observable, then evidence of similarity of work products and any other relevant research evidence will be considered in determining whether the work behavior(s) in the two jobs are the same.

DOCUMENTATION OF IMPACT AND VALIDITY EVIDENCE

§1607.15   *Documentation of impact and validity evidence.*

A. *Required information.* Users of selection procedures other than those users complying with section 15A(1) below should maintain and have available for each job information on adverse impact of the selection process for that job and, where it is determined a selection process has an adverse impact, evidence of validity as set forth below.

(1) *Simplified recordkeeping for users with less than 100 employees.* In order to minimize recordkeeping burdens on employers who employ one hundred (100) or fewer employees, and other users not required to file EEO-1, et seq., reports, such users may satisfy the requirements of this section 15 if they maintain and have available records showing, for each year:

(a) The number of persons hired, promoted, and terminated for each job, by sex, and where appropriate by race and national origin;

(b) The number of applicants for hire and promotion by sex and where appropriate by race and national origin; and

(c) The selection procedures utilized (either standardized or not standardized).

These records should be maintained for each race or national origin group (see section 4 above) constituting more than two percent (2%) of the labor force in the relevant labor area. However, it is not necessary to maintain records by race and/or national origin (see § 4 above) if one race or national origin group in the relevant labor area constitutes more than ninety-eight percent (98%) of the labor force in the area. If the user has reason to believe that a selection procedure has an adverse impact, the user should maintain any available evidence of validity for that procedure (see sections 7A and 8).

(2) *Information on impact.* (a) *Collection of information on impact.* Users of selection procedures other than those complying with section 15A(1) above should maintain and have available for each job records or other information showing whether the total selection process for that job has an adverse impact on any of the groups for which records are called for by sections 4B above. Adverse impact determinations should be made at least annually for each such group which constitutes at least 2 percent of the labor force in the relevant labor area or 2 percent of the applicable workforce. Where a total selection process for a job has an adverse impact, the user should maintain and have available records or other information showing which components have an adverse impact. Where the total selection process for a job does not have an adverse impact, information need not be maintained for individual components except in circumstances set forth in subsection 15A(2)(b) below. If the determination of adverse impact is made using a procedure other than the "four-fifths rule," as defined in the first sentence of section 4D above, a justification, consistent with section 4D above, for the procedure used to determine adverse impact should be available.

(b) *When adverse impact has been eliminated in the total selection process.* Whenever the total selection process for a particular job has had an adverse impact, as defined in section 4 above, in any year, but no longer has an adverse impact, the user should maintain and have available the information on individual components of the selection process required in the preceding paragraph for the period in which there was adverse impact. In addition, the user should continue to collect such information for at least two (2) years after the adverse impact has been eliminated.

(c) *When data insufficient to determine impact.* Where there has been an insufficient number of selections to determine whether there is an adverse impact of the total selection process for a particular job, the user should continue to collect, maintain, and have available the information on individual components of the selection process required in section 15(A)(2)(a) above until the information is sufficient to determine that the overall selection process does not have an adverse impact as defined in section 4 above, or until the job has changed substantially.

(3) *Documentation of validity evidence.* (a) *Types of evidence.* Where a total selection process has an adverse impact (see section 4 above) the user should maintain and have available for each component of that process which has an adverse impact, one or more of the following types of documentation evidence:

(i) Documentation evidence showing criterion-related validity of the selection procedure (see section 15B, below).

(ii) Documentation evidence showing content validity of the selection process (see section 15C, below).

(iii) Documentation evidence showing construct validity of the selection procedure (see section 15D, below).

(iv) Documentation evidence from other studies showing validity of the selection procedure in the user's facility (see section 15E, below).

(v) Documentation evidence showing why a validity study cannot or need not be performed and why continued use of the procedure is consistent with Federal law.

(b) *Form of report.* This evidence should be compiled in a reasonably complete and organized manner to permit direct evaluation of the validity of the selection procedure. Previously written employer or consultant reports of validity, or reports describing validity studies completed before the issuance of these guidelines are acceptable if they are complete in regard to the documentation requirements contained in this section, or if they satisfied requirements of guidelines which were in effect when the validity study was completed. If they are not complete, the required additional documentation should be appended. If necessary information is not available, the report of the validity study may still be used as documentation, but its adequacy will be evaluated in terms of compliance with the requirements of these guidelines.

(c) *Completeness.* In the event that evidence of validity is reviewed by an enforcement agency, the validation reports completed after the effective date of these guidelines are expected to contain the information set forth below. Evidence denoted by use of the word "essential" is considered critical. If information denoted essential is not included, the report will be considered incomplete unless the user affirmatively demonstrates either its unavailability due to circumstances beyond the user's control or special circumstances of the user's study which make the information irrelevant. Evidence not so denoted is desirable, but its absence will not be a basis for considering a report incomplete. The user should maintain and have available the information called for under the heading "Source Data" in sections 15B(11) and 15D(11). While it is a necessary part of the study, it need not be submitted with the report. All statistical results should be organized and presented in tabular or graphic form to the extent feasible.

B. *Criterion-related validity studies.* Reports of criterion-related validity for a selection procedure should include the following information:

(1) *User(s), location(s), and date(s) of study.* Dates and location(s) of the job analysis or review of job information, the date(s) and location(s) of the administration of the selection procedures and collection of criterion data, and the time between collection of data on selection procedures and criterion measures should be provided (essential). If the study was conducted at several locations, the address of each location, including city and State, should be shown.

(2) *Problem and setting.* An explicit definition of the purpose(s) of the study and the circumstances in which the study was conducted should be provided. A description of existing selection procedures and cutoff scores, if any, should be provided.

(3) *Job analysis or review of job information.* A description of the procedure used to analyze the job or group of jobs, or to review the job information should be provided (essential). Where a review of job information results in criteria which may be used without a full job analysis (see section 14B(3)), the basis for the selection of these criteria should be reported (essential). Where a job analysis is required, a complete description of the work behavior(s) or work outcome(s), and measures of their criticality or importance should be provided (essential). The report should describe the basis on which the behavior(s) or outcome(s) were determined to be critical or important, such as the proportion of

time spent on the respective behaviors, their level of difficulty, their frequency of performance, the consequences of error, or other appropriate factors (essential). Where two or more jobs are grouped for a validity study, the information called for in this subsection should be provided for each of the jobs, and the justification for the grouping (see section 14B(1)) should be provided (essential).

(4) *Job titles and codes.* It is desirable to provide the user's job title(s) for the job(s) in question and the corresponding job title(s) and code(s) from U.S. Employment Service's Dictionary of Occupational Titles.

(5) *Criterion measures.* The bases for the selection of the criterion measures should be provided, together with references to the evidence considered in making the selection of criterion measures (essential). A full description of all criteria on which data were collected, and means by which they were observed, recorded, evaluated, and quantified, should be provided (essential). If rating techniques are used as criterion measures, the appraisal form(s) and instructions to the rater(s) should be included as part of the validation evidence, or should be explicitly described and available (essential). All steps taken to insure that criterion measures are free from factors which would unfairly alter the scores of members of any group should be described (essential).

(6) *Sample description.* A description of how the research sample was identified and selected should be included (essential). The race, sex, and ethnic composition of the sample, including those groups set forth in section 4A above, should be described (essential). This description should include the size of each subgroup (essential). A description of how the research sample compares with the relevant labor market or workforce, the method by which the relevant labor market or workforce was defined, and a discussion of the likely effects on validity of differences between the sample and the relevant labor market or workforce, are also desirable. Descriptions of educational levels, length of service, and age are also desirable.

(7) *Description of selection procedures.* Any measure, combination of measures, or procedure studied should be completely and explicitly described or attached (essential). If commercially available selection procedures are studied, they should be described by title, form, and publisher (essential). Reports of reliability estimates and how they were established are desirable.

(8) *Techniques and results.* Methods used in analyzing data should be described (essential). Measures of central tendency (e.g., means) and measures of dispersion (e.g., standard deviations and ranges) for all selection procedures and all criteria should be reported for each race, sex, and ethnic group which constitutes a significant factor in the relevant labor market (essential). The magnitude and direction of all relationships between selection procedures and criterion measures investigated should be reported for each relevant race, sex, and ethnic group and for the total group (essential). Where groups are too small to obtain reliable evidence, the magnitude of the relationship need not be reported separately. Statements regarding the statistical significance of results should be made (essential). Any statistical adjustments, such as for less than perfect reliability or for restriction of score range in the selection procedure or criterion, should be described and explained; and uncorrected correlation coefficients should also be shown (essential). Where the statistical technique categorizes continuous data, such as biserial correlation and the phi coefficient, the categories and the bases on which they were determined should be described and explained (essential). Studies of test fairness should be included where called for by the requirements of section 14B(8) (essential). These studies should include the rationale by which a selection procedure was determined to be fair to the group(s) in question. Where test fairness or unfairness has been demonstrated on the basis of other studies, a bibliography of the relevant studies should be included (essential). If the bibliography includes unpublished studies, copies of these studies, or adequate abstracts or summaries, should be attached (essential). Where revisions have been made in a selection procedure to assure compatibility between successful job performance and the probability of being selected, the studies underlying such revisions should be included (essential). All statistical results should be organized and presented by relevant race, sex, and ethnic group (essential).

(9) *Alternative procedures investigated.* The selection procedures investigated and available evidence of their impact should be identified (essential). The scope, method, and findings of the investigation, and the conclusions reached in light of the findings, should be fully described (essential).

(10) *Uses and applications.* The methods considered for use of the selection procedure (e.g., as

a screening device with a cutoff score, for grouping or ranking, or combined with other procedures in a battery) and available evidence of their impact should be described (essential). This description should include the rationale for choosing the method for operational use, and the evidence of the validity and utility of the procedure as it is to be used (essential). The purpose for which the procedure is to be used (e.g., hiring, transfer, promotion) should be described (essential). If weights are assigned to different parts of the selection procedure, these weights and the validity of the weighted composite should be reported (essential). If the selection procedure is used with a cutoff score, the user should describe the way in which normal expectations of proficiency within the workforce were determined and the way in which the cutoff score was determined (essential).

(11) *Source data.* Each user should maintain records showing all pertinent information about individual sample members and raters where they are used, in studies involving the validation of selection procedures. These records should be made available upon request of a compliance agency. In the case of individual sample members, these data should include scores on selection procedure(s), scores on criterion measures, age, sex, race, or ethnic group status, and experience on the specific job on which the validation study was conducted, and may also include such things as education, training, and prior job experience, but should not include names and social security numbers. Records should be maintained which show the ratings given to each sample member by each rater.

(12) *Contact person.* The name, mailing address, and telephone number of the person who may be contacted for further information about the validity study should be provided (essential).

(13) *Accuracy and completeness.* The report should describe the steps taken to assure the accuracy and completeness of the collection, analysis, and report of data and results.

C. *Content validity studies.* Reports of content validity for a selection procedure should include the following information:

(1) *User(s), location(s) and date(s) of study.* Dates and location(s) of the job analysis should be shown (essential).

(2) *Problem and setting.* An explicit definition of the purpose(s) of the study and the circumstances in which the study was conducted should be provided. A description of existing selection procedures and cutoff scores, if any, should be provided.

(3) *Job analysis—Content of the job.* A description of the method used to analyze the job should be provided (essential). The work behavior(s), the associated tasks, and, if the behavior results in a work product, the work products should be completely described (essential). Measures of criticality and/or importance of the work behavior(s) and the method of determining these measures should be provided (essential). Where the job analysis also identified the knowledges, skills, and abilities used in work behavior(s), an operational definition for each knowledge in terms of a body of learned information, and for each skill and ability in terms of observable behaviors and outcomes, and the relationship between each knowledge, skill, or ability and each work behavior, as well as the method used to determine this relationship, should be provided (essential). The work situation should be described, including the setting in which work behavior(s) are performed, and where appropriate, the manner in which knowledges, skills, or abilities are used, and the complexity and difficulty of the knowledge, skill, or ability as used in the work behavior(s).

(4) *Selection procedure and its content.* Selection procedures, including those constructed by or for the user, specific training requirements, composites of selection procedures, and any other procedure supported by content validity, should be completely and explicitly described or attached (essential). If commercially available selection procedures are used, they should be described by title, form, and publisher (essential). The behaviors measured or sampled by the selection procedure should be explicitly described (essential). Where the selection procedure purports to measure a knowledge, skill, or ability, evidence that the selection procedure measures and is a representative sample of the knowledge, skill, or ability should be provided (essential).

(5) *Relationship between the selection procedures and the job.* The evidence demonstrating that the selection procedure is a representative work sample, a representative sample of the work behavior(s), or a representative sample of a knowledge, skill, or ability as used as a part of a work behavior and necessary for that behavior should be provided (essential). The user should identify the work behavior(s) which each item or part of the selection procedure is intended to sample or

measure (essential). Where the selection procedure purports to sample a work behavior or to provide a sample of a work product, a comparison should be provided of the manner, setting, and the level of complexity of the selection procedure with those of the work situation (essential). If any steps were taken to reduce adverse impact on a race, sex, or ethnic group in the content of the procedure or in its administration, these steps should be described. Establishment of time limits, if any, and how these limits are related to the speed with which duties must be performed on the job, should be explained. Measures of central tendency (e.g., means) and measures of dispersion (e.g., standard deviations) and estimates of reliability should be reported for all selection procedures if available. Such reports should be made for relevant race, sex, and ethnic subgroups, at least on a statistically reliable sample basis.

(6) *Alternative procedures investigated.* The alternative selection procedures investigated and available evidence of their impact should be identified (essential). The scope, method, and findings of the investigation, and the conclusions reached in light of the findings, should be fully described (essential).

(7) *Uses and applications.* The methods considered for use of the selection procedure (e.g., as a screening device with a cutoff score, for grouping or ranking, or combined with other procedures in a battery) and available evidence of their impact should be described (essential). This description should include the rationale for choosing the method of operational use, and the evidence of the validity and utility of the procedure as it is to be used (essential). The purpose for which the procedure is to be used (e.g., hiring, transfer, promotion) should be described (essential). If the selection procedure is used with a cutoff score, the user should describe the way in which normal expectations of proficiency within the workforce were determined and the way in which the cutoff score was determined (essential). In addition, if the selection procedure is to be used for ranking, the user should specify the evidence showing that a higher score on the selection procedure is likely to result in better job performance.

(8) *Contact person.* The name, mailing address, and telephone number of the person who may be contacted for further information about the validity study should be provided (essential).

(9) *Accuracy and completeness.* The report should describe the steps taken to assure the accuracy and completeness of the collection, analysis, and report of data and results.

D. *Construct validity studies.* Reports of construct validity for a selection procedure should include the following information:

(1) *User(s), location(s), and date(s) of study.* Date(s) and location(s) of the job analysis and the gathering of other evidence called for by these guidelines should be provided (essential).

(2) *Problem and setting.* An explicit definition of the purpose(s) of the study and the circumstances in which the study was conducted should be provided. A description of existing selection procedures and cutoff scores, if any, should be provided.

(3) *Construct definition.* A clear definition of the construct(s) which are believed to underlie successful performance of the critical or important work behavior(s) should be provided (essential). This definition should include the levels of construct performance relevant to the job(s) for which the selection procedure is to be used (essential). There should be a summary of the position of the construct in the psychological literature, or in the absence of such a position, a description of the way in which the definition and measurement of the construct was developed and the psychological theory underlying it (essential). Any quantitative data which identify or define the job constructs, such as factor analyses, should be provided (essential).

(4) *Job analysis.* A description of the method used to analyze the job should be provided (essential). A complete description of the work behavior(s) and, to the extent appropriate, work outcomes and measures of their criticality and/or importance should be provided (essential). The report should also describe the basis on which the behavior(s) or outcomes were determined to be important, such as their level of difficulty, their frequency of performance, the consequences of error or other appropriate factors (essential). Where jobs are grouped or compared for the purposes of generalizing validity evidence, the work behavior(s) and work product(s) for each of the jobs should be described, and conclusions concerning the similarity of the jobs in terms of observable work behaviors or work products should be made (essential).

(5) *Job titles and codes.* It is desirable to provide the selection procedure user's job title(s) for the job(s) in question and the corresponding job title(s) and code(s) from the United States Employment Service's dictionary of occupational titles.

(6) *Selection procedure.* The selection procedure used as a measure of the construct should be completed and explicitly described or attached (essential). If commercially available selection procedures are used, they should be identified by title, form and publisher (essential). The research evidence of the relationship between the selection procedure and the construct, such as factor structure, should be included (essential). Measures of central tendency, variability and reliability of the selection procedure should be provided (essential). Whenever feasible, these measures should be provided separately for each relevant race, sex, and ethnic group.

(7) *Relationship to job performance.* The criterion-related study(ies) and other empirical evidence of the relationship between the construct measured by the selection procedure and the related work behavior(s) for the job or jobs in question should be provided (essential). Documentation of the criterion-related study(ies) should satisfy the provisions of section 15B above or section 15E(1) below, except for studies conducted prior to the effective date of these guidelines (essential). Where a study pertains to a group of jobs, and, on the basis of the study, validity is asserted for a job in the group, the observed work behaviors and the observed work products for each of the jobs should be described (essential). Any other evidence used in determining whether the work behavior(s) in each of the jobs is the same should be fully described (essential).

(8) *Alternative procedures investigated.* The alternative selection procedures investigated and available evidence of their impact should be identified (essential). The scope, method, and findings of the investigation, and the conclusions reached in light of the findings should be fully described (essential).

(9) *Uses and applications.* The methods considered for use of the selection procedure (e.g., as a screening device with a cutoff score, for grouping or ranking, or combined with other procedures in a battery) and available evidence of their impact should be described (essential). This description should include the rationale for choosing the method for operational use, and the evidence of the validity and utility of the procedure as it is to be used (essential). The purpose for which the procedure is to be used (e.g., hiring, transfer, promotion) should be described (essential). If weights are assigned to different parts of the selection procedure, these weights and the validity of the weighted composite should be reported (essential). If the selection procedure is used with a cutoff score, the user should describe the way in which normal expectations of proficiency within the workforce were determined and the way in which the cutoff score was determined (essential).

(10) *Accuracy and completeness.* The report should describe the steps taken to assure the accuracy and completeness of the collection, analysis, and report of data and results.

(11) *Source data.* Each user should maintain records showing all pertinent information relating to its study of construct validity.

(12) *Contact person.* The name, mailing address, and telephone number of the individual who may be contacted for further information about the validity study should be provided (essential).

E. *Evidence of validity from other studies.* When validity of a selection procedure is supported by studies not done by the user, the evidence from the original study or studies should be compiled in a manner similar to that required in the appropriate section of this section 15 above. In addition, the following evidence should be supplied:

(1) *Evidence from criterion-related validity studies.*—a. *Job information.* A description of the important job behavior(s) of the user's job and the basis on which the behaviors were determined to be important should be provided (essential). A full description of the basis for determining that these important work behaviors are the same as those of the job in the original study (or studies) should be provided (essential).

(b) *Relevance of criteria.* A full description of the basis on which the criteria used in the original studies are determined to be relevant for the user should be provided (essential).

(c) *Other variables.* The similarity of important applicant pool or sample characteristics reported in the original studies to those of the user should be described (essential). A description of the comparison between the race, sex and ethnic composition of the user's relevant labor market and the sample in the original validity studies should be provided (essential).

(d) *Use of the selection procedures.* A full description should be provided showing that the use to be made of the selection procedure is consistent with the findings of the original validity studies (essential).

(e) *Bibliography.* A bibliography of reports of validity of the selection procedure for the job or jobs in question should be provided (essential). Where any of the studies included an investigation of test fairness, the results of this investigation should be provided (essential). Copies of reports published in journals that are not commonly available should be described in detail or attached (essential). Where a user is relying upon unpublished studies, a reasonable effort should be made to obtain these studies. If these unpublished studies are the sole source of validity evidence, they should be described in detail or attached (essential). If these studies are not available, the name and address of the source, an adequate abstract or summary of the validity study and data, and a contact person in the source organization should be provided (essential).

(2) *Evidence from content validity studies.* See section 14C(3) and section 15C above.

(3) *Evidence from construct validity studies.* See sections 14D(2) and 15D above.

F. *Evidence of validity from cooperative studies.* Where a selection procedure has been validated through a cooperative study, evidence that the study satisfies the requirements of sections 7, 8 and 15E should be provided (essential).

G. *Selection for higher-level job.* If a selection procedure is used to evaluate candidates for jobs at a higher level than those for which they will initially be employed, the validity evidence should satisfy the documentation provisions of this section 15 for the higher-level job or jobs, and in addition, the user should provide: (1) a description of the job progression structure, formal or informal; (2) the data showing how many employees progress to the higher-level job and the length of time needed to make this progression; and (3) an identification of any anticipated changes in the higher-level job. In addition, if the test measures a knowledge, skill, or ability, the user should provide evidence that the knowledge, skill, or ability is required for the higher-level job and the basis for the conclusion that the knowledge, skill, or ability is not expected to develop from the training or experience on the job.

H. *Interim use of selection procedures.* If a selection procedure is being used on an interim basis because the procedure is not fully supported by the required evidence of validity, the user should maintain and have available (1) substantial evidence of validity for the procedure, and (2) a report showing the date on which the study to gather the additional evidence commenced, the estimated completion date of the study, and a description of the data to be collected (essential).

DEFINITIONS

§1607.16 *Definitions.*

The following definitions shall apply throughout these guidelines:

A. *Ability.* A present competence to perform an observable behavior or a behavior which results in an observable product.

B. *Adverse impact.* A substantially different rate of selection in hiring, promotion, or other employment decision which works to the disadvantage of members of a race, sex, or ethnic group. See section 4 of these guidelines.

C. *Compliance with these guidelines.* Use of a selection procedure is in compliance with these guidelines if such use has been validated in accord with these guidelines (as defined below), or if such use does not result in adverse impact on any race, sex, or ethnic group (see section 4, above), or, in unusual circumstances, if use of the procedure is otherwise justified in accord with Federal law. See section 6B, above.

D. *Content validity.* Demonstrated by data showing that the content of a selection procedure is representative of important aspects of performance on the job. See section 5B and section 14C.

E. *Construct validity.* Demonstrated by data showing that the selection procedure measures the degree to which candidates have identifiable characteristics which have been determined to be important for successful job performance. See section 5B and section 14D.

F. *Criterion-related validity.* Demonstrated by empirical data showing that the selection procedure is predictive of or significantly correlated with important elements of work behavior. See sections 5B and 14B.

G. *Employer.* Any employer subject to the provisions of the Civil Rights Act of 1964, as amended, including State or local governments and any Federal agency subject to the provisions of section 717 of the Civil Rights Act of 1964, as amended, and any Federal contractor or subcontractor or federally assisted construction contractor or subcontractor covered by Executive Order 11246, as amended.

H. *Employment agency.* Any employment agency subject to the provisions of the Civil Rights Act of 1964, as amended.

I. *Enforcement action.* For the purposes of section 4, a proceeding by a Federal enforcement agency such as a lawsuit or an administrative proceeding leading to debarment from or withholding, suspension, or termination of Federal Government contracts or the suspension or withholding of Federal Government funds; but not a finding of reasonable cause or a conciliation process or the issuance of right to sue letters under title VII or under Executive Order 11246 where such finding, conciliation, or issuance of notice of right to sue is based upon an individual complaint.

J. *Enforcement agency.* Any agency of the executive branch of the Federal Government which adopts these guidelines for purposes of the enforcement of the equal employment opportunity laws or which has responsibility for securing compliance with them.

K. *Job analysis.* A detailed statement of work behaviors and other information relevant to the job.

L. *Job description.* A general statement of job duties and responsibilities.

M. *Knowledge.* A body of information applied directly to the performance of a function.

N. *Labor organization.* Any labor organization subject to the provisions of the Civil Rights Act of 1964, as amended, and any committee subject thereto controlling apprenticeship or other training.

O. *Observable.* Able to be seen, heard, or otherwise perceived by a person other than the person performing the action.

P. *Race, sex, or ethnic group.* Any group of persons identifiable on the grounds of rate, color, religion, sex, or national origin.

Q. *Selection procedure.* Any measure, combination of measures, or procedure used as a basis for any employment decision. Selection procedures include the full range of assessment techniques from traditional paper and pencil tests, performance tests, training programs, or probationary periods and physical, educational, and work experience requirements through informal or casual interviews and unscored application forms.

R. *Selection rate.* The proportion of applicants or candidates who are hired, promoted, or otherwise selected.

S. *Should.* The term "should" as used in these guidelines is intended to connote action which is necessary to achieve compliance with the guidelines, while recognizing that there are circumstances where alternative courses of action are open to users.

T. *Skill.* A present, observable competence to perform a learned psychomotor act.

U. *Technical feasibility.* The existence of conditions permitting the conduct of meaningful criterion-related validity studies. These conditions include: (1) An adequate sample of persons available for the study to achieve findings of statistical significance; (2) having or being able to obtain a sufficient range of scores on the selection procedure and job performance measures to produce validity results which can be expected to be representative of the results if the ranges normally expected were utilized; and (3) having or being able to devise unbiased, reliable, and relevant measures of job performance or other criteria of employee adequacy. See section 14B(2). With respect to investigation of possible unfairness, the same considerations are applicable to each group for which the study is made. See section 14B(8).

V. *Unfairness of selection procedure.* A condition in which members of one race, sex, or ethnic group characteristically obtain lower scores on a selection procedure than members of another group, and the differences are not reflected in differences in measures of job performance. See section 14B(7).

W. *User.* Any employer, labor organization, employment agency, or licensing or certification board, to the extent it may be covered by Federal equal employment opportunity law, which uses a selection procedure as a basis for any employment decision. Whenever an employer, labor organization, or employment agency is required by law to restrict recruitment for any occupation to those applicants who have met licensing or certification requirements, the licensing or certifying authority to the extent it may be covered by Federal equal employment opportunity law will be considered the user with respect to those licensing or certification requirements. Whenever a State employment agency or service does no more than administer or monitor a procedure as permitted by Department of Labor regulations, and does so without making referrals or taking any other action on the basis of the results, the State employment agency will not be deemed to be a user.

X. *Validated in accord with these guidelines or properly validated.* A demonstration that one or more validity study or studies meeting the standards of these guidelines has been conducted, including investigation and where appropriate, use of suitable alternative selection procedures as contemplated by section 3B, and has produced evidence of validity sufficient to warrant use of the procedure for the intended purpose under the standards of these guidelines.

Y. *Work behavior.* An activity performed to achieve the objectives of the job. Work behaviors involve observable (physical) components and unobservable (mental) components. A work behavior consists of the performance of one or more tasks. Knowledge, skills, and abilities are not behaviors, although they may be applied in work behaviors.

APPENDIX

§1607.17 *Policy statement on affirmative action* (see section 13B).

The Equal Employment Opportunity Coordinating Council was established by act of Congress in 1972, and charged with responsibility for developing and implementing agreements and policies designed, among other things, to eliminate conflict and inconsistency among the agencies of the Federal Government responsible for administering Federal law prohibiting discrimination on grounds of race, color, sex, religion, and national origin. This statement is issued as an initial response to the requests of a number of State and local officials for clarification of the Government's policies concerning the role of affirmative action in the overall equal employment opportunity program. While the Coordinating Council's adoption of this statement expresses only the views of the signatory agencies concerning this important subject, the principles set forth below should serve as policy guidance for other Federal agencies as well.

(1) Equal employment opportunity is the law of the land. In the public sector of our society, this means that all persons, regardless of race, color, religion, sex, or national origin shall have equal access to positions in the public service limited only by their ability to do the job. There is ample evidence in all sectors of our society that such equal access frequently has been denied to members of certain groups because of their sex, racial, or ethnic characteristics. The remedy for such past and present discrimination is twofold.

On the other hand, vigorous enforcement of the laws against discrimination is essential. But equally, and perhaps even more important are affirmative, voluntary efforts on the part of public employers to assure that positions in the public service are genuinely and equally accessible to qualified persons, without regard to their sex, racial, or ethnic characteristics. Without such efforts equal employment opportunity is no more than a wish. The importance of voluntary affirmative action on the part of employers is underscored by title VII of the Civil Rights Act of 1964, Executive Order 11246, and related laws and regulations—all of which emphasize voluntary action to achieve equal employment opportunity.

As with most management objectives, a systematic plan based on sound organizational analysis and problem identification is crucial to the accomplishment of affirmative action objectives. For this reason, the Council urges all State and local governments to develop and implement results-oriented affirmative action plans which deal with the problems so identified.

The following paragraphs are intended to assist State and local governments by illustrating the kinds of analyses and activities which may be appropriate for a public employer's voluntary affirmative action plan. This statement does not address remedies imposed after a finding of unlawful discrimination.

(2) Voluntary affirmative action to assure equal employment opportunity is appropriate at any stage of the employment process. The first step in the construction of any affirmative action plan should be an analysis of the employer's workforce to determine whether percentages of sex, race, or ethnic groups in individual job classifications are substantially similar to the percentages of those groups available in the relevant job market who possess the basic job-related qualifications.

When substantial disparities are found through such analyses, each element of the overall selection process should be examined to determine which elements operate to exclude persons on the basis of sex, race, or ethnic group. Such elements include, but are not limited to, recruitment, testing, ranking certification, interview, recommendations for selection, hiring, promotion, etc. The examination of each element of the selection process should at a minimum include a determination of its validity in predicting job performance.

(3) When an employer has reason to believe that its selection procedures have the exclusionary effect described in paragraph 2 above, it should initiate affirmative steps to remedy the situation. Such steps, which in design and execution may be race, color, sex, or ethnic "conscious," include, but are not limited to, the following:

(a) The establishment of a long-term goal, and short-range, interim goals and timetables for the specific job classifications, all of which should take into account the availability of basically qualified persons in the relevant job market;

(b) A recruitment program designed to attract qualified members of the group in question;

(c) A systematic effort to organize work and redesign jobs in ways that provide opportunities for persons lacking "journeyman" level knowledge or skills to enter and, with appropriate training, to progress in a career field;

(d) Revamping selection instruments or procedures which have not yet been validated in order to reduce or eliminate exclusionary effects on particular groups in particular job classifications;

(e) The initiation of measures designed to assure that members of the affected group who are qualified to perform the job are included within the pool of persons from which the selecting official makes the selection;

(f) A systematic effort to provide career advancement training, both classroom and on-the-job, to employees locked into dead end jobs; and

(g) The establishment of a system for regularly monitoring the effectiveness of the particular affirmative action program, and procedures for making timely adjustments in this program where effectiveness is not demonstrated.

(4) The goal of any affirmative action plan should be achievement of genuine equal employment opportunity for all qualified persons. Selection under such plans should be based upon the ability of the applicant(s) to do the work. Such plans should not require the selection of the unqualified, or the unneeded, nor should they require the selection of persons on the basis of race, color, sex, religion, or national origin. Moreover, while the Council believes that this statement should serve to assist State and local employers, as well as Federal agencies, it recognizes that affirmative action cannot be viewed as a standardized program which must be accomplished in the same way at all times in all places.

Accordingly, the Council has not attempted to set forth here either the minimum or maximum voluntary steps that employers may take to deal with their respective situations. Rather, the Council recognizes that under applicable authorities, State and local employers have flexibility to formulate affirmative action plans that are best suited to their particular situations. In this manner, the Council believes that affirmative action programs will best serve the goal of equal employment opportunity.

APPENDIX B

Affirmative Action Guidelines—Revised Order No. 4 (OFCCP)

PART 60-2—AFFIRMATIVE ACTION PROGRAMS

Subpart A—General

Subpart B—Required Contents of Affirmative Action Programs

Subpart C—Methods of Implementing the Requirements of Subpart B

Subpart D—Miscellaneous
    AUTHORITY: 5 U.S.C. 553(a)(3)(B); 29 CFR 2.7; Section 201, E.O. 11246, 30 FR 12319, and E.O. 11375, 32 FR 14303, as amended by E.O. 12086.

SUBPART A—GENERAL

§60-2.1. Title, Purpose and Scope
(a) This part shall also be known as "Revised Order No. 4" and shall cover nonconstruction contractors. Section 60-1.40 of this chapter, affirmative action compliance programs, requires that within 120 days from the commencement of a contract each prime contractor or subcontractor with 50 or more employees and (1) a contract of $50,000 or more; or (2) Government bills of lading which, in any 12-month period, total or can reasonably be expected to total $50,000 or more; or (3) who serves as a depository of Government funds in any amount; or (4) who is a financial institution which is an issuing and paying agent for U.S. savings bonds and savings notes in any amount, develop a written affirmative action compliance program for each of its establishments. A review of compliance surveys indicates that many contractors do not have affirmative action programs on file at the time an establishment is visited by a compliance investigator. This part details the review procedure and the results of a contractor's failure to develop and maintain an affirmative action program and then sets forth detailed guidelines to be used by the contractors and Government in developing and judging these programs as well as the good faith effort required to transform the programs from paper commitments to equal employment opportunity. Subparts B and C of this part are concerned with affirmative action plans only.

(b) Relief, including back pay where appropriate, for members of an affected class who by virtue of past discrimination continue to suffer the present effects of that discrimination, shall be provided in the conciliation agreement entered into pursuant to §60-60.6 of this title. An "affected class" problem must be remedied in order for a contractor to be considered in compliance. Section 60-2.2 herein pertaining to an acceptable affirmative action program is also applicable to the failure to remedy discrimination against members of an "affected class."

§60-2.2. Agency Action

(a) Any contractor required by §60-1.40 of this chapter to develop an affirmative action program at each of its establishments who has not complied fully with that section is not in compliance with Executive Order 11246, as amended (30 FR 12319). Until such programs are developed and found to be acceptable in accordance with the standards and guidelines set forth in §§60-2.10 through 60-2.32, the contractor is unable to comply with the equal employment opportunity clause. An affirmative action plan shall be deemed to have been accepted by the Government at the time the appropriate OFCCP field, area, regional, or national office has accepted such plan unless within 45 days thereafter the Director has disapproved such plan.

(b) If, in determining such contractor's responsibility for an award of a contract it comes to the contracting officer's attention, through sources within his agency or through the Office of Federal Contract Compliance Programs or other Government agencies, that the contractor has no affirmative action program at each of its establishments, or has substantially deviated from such an approved affirmative action program, or has failed to develop or implement an affirmative action program which complies with the regulations in this chapter, the contracting officer shall declare the contractor/bidder nonresponsible and so notify the contractor, and the Director, unless he can otherwise affirmatively determine that the contractor is able to comply with its equal employment obligations. Any contractor/bidder which has been declared nonresponsible in accordance with the provisions of this section may request the Director to determine that the responsibility of the contractor/bidder raises substantial issues of law or fact to the extent that a hearing is required. Such request shall set forth the basis upon which the contractor/bidder seeks such a determination. If the Director, in his/her sole discretion, determines that substantial issues of law or fact exist, an administrative or judicial proceeding may be commenced in accordance with the regulations contained in §60-1.26; or the Director may require the investigation or compliance review be developed further or additional conciliation be conducted: *Provided,* That during any preaward conferences, every effort shall be made through the processes of conciliation, mediation and persuasion to develop an acceptable affirmative action program meeting the standards and guidelines set forth in §§60-2.10 through 60-2.32 so that, in the performance of its contract, the contractor is able to meet its equal employment obligations in accordance with the equal employment clause and applicable rules, regulations, and orders: *Provided further,* That a contractor/bidder may not be declared nonresponsible more than twice due to past noncompliance with the equal employment clause at a particular establishment or facility without receiving prior notice and an opportunity for a hearing.

(c)(1) Immediately upon finding that a contractor has no affirmative action program, or has deviated substantially from an approved affirmative action program, or has failed to develop or implement an affirmative action program which complies with the requirements of the regulations in this chapter, that fact shall be recorded in the investigation file. Whenever administrative enforcement is contemplated, the notice to the contractor shall be issued giving him 30 days to show cause why enforcement proceedings under section 209(a) of Executive Order 11246, as amended, should not be instituted. The notice to show cause should contain:

(i) An itemization of the sections of the Executive Order and of the regulations with which the contractor has been found in apparent violation, and a summary of the conditions, practices, facts or circumstances which give rise to each apparent violation;

(ii) The corrective actions necessary to achieve compliance or, as may be appropriate, the concepts and principles of an acceptable remedy and/or the corrective action results anticipated;

(iii) A request for a written response to the findings, including commitments to corrective action or the presentation or opposing facts and evidence; and

(iv) A suggested date for the conciliation conference.

(2) If the contractor fails to show good cause for his failure or fails to remedy that failure by developing and implementing an acceptable affirmative action program within 30 days, the case file shall be processed for enforcement proceedings pursuant to §60-1.26 of this chapter. If an administrative complaint is filed, the contractor shall have 20 days to request a hearing. If a request for hearing has not been received within 20 days from the filing of the administrative complaint, the matter shall proceed in accordance with Part 60-30 of this chapter.

(3) During the "show cause" period of 30 days, every effort will be made through conciliation, mediation, and persuasion to resolve the deficiencies which led to the determination of nonresponsibility. If satisfactory adjustments designed to bring the contractor into compliance are not concluded, the case shall be processed for enforcement proceedings pursuant to §60-1.26 of this chapter.

(d) During the "show cause" period and formal proceedings, each contracting agency must continue to determine the contractor's responsibility in considering whether or not to award a new or additional contract.

SUBPART B—REQUIRED CONTENTS OF AFFIRMATIVE ACTION PROGRAMS

§60-2.10. Purpose of Affirmative Action Program

An affirmative action program is a set of specific and result-oriented procedures to which a contractor commits itself to apply every good faith effort. The objective of those procedures plus such efforts is equal employment opportunity. Procedures without effort to make them work are meaningless; and effort, undirected by specific and meaningful procedures, is inadequate. An acceptable affirmative action program must include an analysis of areas within which the contractor is deficient in the utilization of minority groups and women, and further, goals and timetables to which the contractor's good faith efforts must be directed to correct the deficiencies and, thus to achieve prompt and full utilization of minorities and women, at all levels and in all segments of its workforce where deficiencies exist.

§60-2.11. Required Utilization Analysis

Based upon the Government's experience with compliance reviews under the Executive order program and the contractor reporting system, minority groups are most likely to be underutilized in departments and jobs within departments that fall within the following Employer's Information Report (EEO-1) designations: officials and managers, professionals, technicians, sales workers, office and clerical and craftsmen (skilled). As categorized by the EEO-1 designations, women are likely to be underutilized in departments and jobs within departments as follows: officials and managers, professionals, technicians, sales workers (except over-the-counter sales in certain retail establishments), craftsmen (skilled and semiskilled). Therefore, the contractor shall direct special attention to such jobs in its analysis and goal setting for minorities and women. Affirmative action programs must contain the following information:

(a) Workforce analysis which is defined as a listing of each job title as appears in applicable collective bargaining agreements or payroll records (not job group) ranked from the lowest paid to the highest paid within each department or other similar organizational unit including departmental or unit supervision. If there are separate work units or lines of progression within a department, a separate list must be provided for each such work unit, or line, including unit supervisors. For lines of progression, there must be indicated the order of jobs in the line through which an employee could move to the top of the line. Where there are no formal progression lines or usual promotional sequences, job titles should be listed by department, job families, or disciplines, in order of wage rates or salary ranges. For each job title, the total number of incumbents, the total number of male and female incumbents, and the total number of male and female incumbents in each of the following groups must be given: Blacks, Spanish-surnamed Americans, American Indians, and Orientals. The wage rate or salary range for each job title must be given. All job titles, including all managerial job titles, must be listed.

(b) An analysis of all major job groups at the facility, with explanation if minorities or women are currently being underutilized in any one or more job groups ("job groups" herein meaning one or a group of jobs having similar content, wage rates and opportunities). "Underutilization" is defined as having fewer minorities or women in a particular job group than would reasonably be expected by their availability. In making the utilization analysis, the contractor shall conduct such analysis separately for minorities and women.

(1) In determining whether minorities are being underutilized in any job group, the contractor will consider at least all of the following factors:

(i) The minority population of the labor area surrounding the facility;

(ii) The size of the minority unemployment force in the labor area surrounding the facility;

(iii) The percentage of the minority workforce as compared with the total workforce in the immediate labor area;

(iv) The general availability of minorities having requisite skills in the immediate labor area;

(v) The availability of minorities having requisite skills in an area in which the contractor can reasonably recruit;

(vi) The availability of promotable and transferable minorities within the contractor's organization;

(vii) The existence of training institutions capable of training persons in the requisite skills; and

(viii) The degree of training which the contractor is reasonably able to undertake as a means of making all job classes available to minorities.

(2) In determining whether women are being underutilized in any job group, the contractor will consider at least all of the following factors:

(i) The size of the female unemployment force in the labor area surrounding the facility;

(ii) The percentage of the female workforce as compared with the total workforce in the immediate labor area;

(iii) The general availability of women having requisite skills in the immediate labor area;

(iv) The availability of women having requisite skills in an area in which the contractor can reasonably recruit;

(v) The availability of women seeking employment in the labor or recruitment area of the contractor;

(vi) The availability of promotable and transferable female employees within the contractor's organization;

(vii) The existence of training institutions capable of training persons in the requisite skills; and

(viii) The degree of training which the contractor is reasonably able to undertake as a means of making all job classes available to women.

§ 60-2.12. Establishment of Goals and Timetables

(a) The goals and timetables developed by the contractor should be attainable in terms of the contractor's analysis of its deficiencies and its entire affirmative action program. Thus, in establishing the size of its goals and the length of its timetables, the contractor should consider the results which could reasonably be expected from its putting forth every good faith effort to make its overall affirmative action program work. In determining levels of goals, the contractor should consider at least the factors listed in §60-2.11.

(b) Involve personnel relations staff, department and division heads, and local and unit managers in the goal setting process.

(c) Goals should be significant, measurable, and attainable.

(d) Goals should be specific for planned results, with timetables for completion.

(e) Goals may not be rigid and inflexible quotas which must be met, but must be targets reasonably attainable by means of applying every good faith effort to make all aspects of the entire affirmative action program work.

(f) In establishing timetables to meet goals and commitments, the contractor will consider the anticipated expansion, contraction, and turnover of and in the workforce.

(g) Goals, timetables and affirmative action commitments must be designed to correct any identifiable deficiencies.

(h) Where deficiencies exist and where numbers or percentages are relevant in developing corrective action, the contractor shall establish and set forth specific goals and timetables separately for minorities and women.

(i) Such goals and timetables, with supporting data and the analysis thereof shall be a part of the contractor's written affirmative action program and shall be maintained at each establishment of the contractor.

(j) A contractor or subcontractor extending a publicly announced preference for Indians as authorized in 41 CFR 60-1.5(a)(6) may reflect in its goals and timetables the permissive employment preference for Indians living on or near an Indian reservation.

(k) Where a contractor has not established a goal, his written affirmative action program must specifically analyze each of the factors listed in 60-2.11 and must detail its reason for a lack of a goal.

(l) In the event it comes to the attention of the Office of Federal Contract Compliance Programs that there is a substantial disparity in the utilization of a particular minority group or men or women of a particular minority group, OFCCP may require separate goals and timetables for such minority group and may further require, where appropriate, such goals and timetables by sex for such group for such job classifications and organizational units specified by the OFCCP.

(m) Support data for the required analysis and program shall be compiled and maintained as part of the contractor's affirmative action program. This data will include but not be limited to progression line charts, seniority rosters, applicant flow data, and applicant rejection ratios indicating minority and sex status.

(n) Copies of affirmative action programs and/or copies of support data shall be made available to the Office of Federal Contract Compliance Programs, upon request, for such purposes as may be appropriate to the fulfillment of its responsibilities under Executive Order 11246, as amended.

§60-2.13. Additional Required Ingredients of Affirmative Action Programs

Effective affirmative action programs shall contain, but not necessarily be limited to, the following ingredients:

(a) Development of reaffirmation of the contractor's equal employment opportunity policy in all personnel actions.

(b) Formal internal and external dissemination of the contractor's policy.

(c) Establishment of responsibilities for implementation of the contractor's affirmative action program.

(d) Identification of problem areas (deficiencies) by organizational units and job group.

(e) Establishment of goals and objectives by organizational units and job groups, including timetables for completion.

(f) Development and execution of action oriented programs designed to eliminate programs and further designed to attain established goals and objectives.

(g) Design and implementation of internal audit and reporting systems to measure effectiveness of the total program.

(h) Compliance or personnel policies and practices with the Sex Discrimination Guidelines (41 CFR Part 60-20).

(i) Active support of local and national community action programs and community service programs, designed to improve the employment opportunities of minorities and women.

(j) Consideration of minorities and women not currently in the workforce having requisite skills who can be recruited through affirmative action measures.

§60-2.14. Program Summary

The affirmative action program shall be summarized and updated annually. The program summary shall be prepared in a format which shall be prescribed by the Director and published in the FEDERAL REGISTER as a notice before becoming effective. Contractors and subcontractors shall submit the program summary to OFCCP each year on the anniversary date of the affirmative action program (Added, eff. Jan. 28, 1980).

§60-2.15. Compliance Status

No contractor's compliance status shall be judged alone by whether or not it reaches its goals and meets its timetables. Rather, each contractor's compliance posture shall be reviewed and determined by reviewing the contents of its program, the extent of its adherence to this program, and its good faith efforts to make its program work toward the realization of the program's goals within the timetable set for completion. There follows an outline of examples of procedures that contractors and federal agencies should use as a guideline for establishing, implementing, and judging an acceptable affirmative action program (Sec. 60-2.15 was renumbered from old Sec. 60-2.14, eff. Jan. 28, 1980).

SUBPART C—METHODS OF IMPLEMENTING THE REQUIREMENTS OF SUBPART B

§60-2.20. Development or Reaffirmation of the Equal Employment Opportunity Policy

(a) The contractor's policy statement should indicate the chief executive officer's attitude on the subject matter, assign overall responsibility, and provide for a reporting and monitoring procedure. Specific items to be mentioned should include, but are not limited to:

(1) Recruit, hire, train, and promote persons in all job titles, without regard to race, color, religion, sex, or national origin, except where sex is a bona fide occupational qualification. (The term "bona fide occupational qualification" has been construed very narrowly under the Civil Rights Act of 1964. Under Executive Order 11246 as amended and this part, this term will be construed in the same manner.)

(2) Base decisions on employment so as to further the principle of equal employment opportunity.

(3) Ensure that promotion decisions are in accord with principles of equal employment opportunity by imposing only valid requirements for promotional opportunities.

(4) Ensure that all personnel actions such as compensation, benefits, transfers, layoffs, return from layoff, company sponsored training, education, tuition assistance, social and recreation programs, will be administered without regard to race, color, religion, sex, or national origin.

§60-2.21. Dissemination of the Policy

(a) The contractor should disseminate his policy internally as follows:

(1) Include it in contractor's policy manual.

(2) Publicize it in company newspaper, magazine, annual report, and other media.

(3) Conduct special meetings with executive, management, and supervisory personnel to explain intent of policy and individual responsibility for effective implementation, making clear the chief executive officer's attitude.

(4) Schedule special meetings with all other employees to discuss policy and explain individual employee responsibilities.

(5) Discuss the policy thoroughly in both employee orientation and management training programs.

(6) Meet with union officials to inform them of policy, and request their cooperation.

(7) Include nondiscrimination clauses in all union agreements, and review all contractual provisions to ensure they are nondiscriminatory.

(8) Publish articles covering EEO programs, progress reports, promotions, etc., of minority and female employees, in company publications.

(9) Post the policy on company bulletin boards.

(10) When employees are featured in product or consumer advertising, employee handbooks or similar publications, both minority and nonminority men and women should be pictured.

(11) Communicate to employees the existence of the contractor's affirmative action program and make available such elements of its program as will enable such employees to know of and avail themselves of its benefits.

(b) The contractor should disseminate its policy externally as follows:

(1) Inform all recruiting sources verbally and in writing of company policy, stipulating that these sources actively recruit and refer minorities and women for all positions listed.

(2) Incorporate the equal opportunity clause in all purchase orders, leases, contracts, etc., covered by Executive Order 11246, as amended, and its implementing regulations.

(3) Notify minority and women's organizations, community agencies, community leaders, secondary schools and colleges of company policy, preferably in writing.

(4) Communicate to prospective employees the existence of the contractor's affirmative action program and make available such elements of its program as will enable such prospective employees to know of and avail themselves of its benefits.

(5) When employees are pictured in consumer or help wanted advertising, both minority and nonminority men and women should be shown.

(6) Send written notification of company policy to all subcontractors, vendors and suppliers requesting appropriate action on their part.

§60-2.22. Responsibility for Implementation

(a) An executive of the contractor should be appointed as director or manager of company equal opportunity programs. Depending upon the size and geographical alignment of the company, this may be his or her sole responsibility. He or she should be given the necessary top management support and staffing to execute the assignment. His or her identity should appear on all internal and external communications on the company's equal opportunity programs. His or her responsibilities should include, but not necessarily be limited to:

(1) Developing policy statements, affirmative action programs, internal and external communication techniques.

(2) Assisting in the identification of problem areas.

(3) Assisting line management in arriving at solutions to problems.

(4) Designing and implementing audit and reporting systems that will:

(i) Measure effectiveness of the contractor's programs.

(ii) Indicate need for remedial action.

(iii) Determine the degree to which the contractor's goals and objectives have been attained.

(5) Serve as liaison between the contractor and enforcement agencies.

(6) Serve as liaison between the contractor and minority organizations, women's organizations, and community action groups concerned with employment opportunities of minorities and women.

(7) Keep management informed of latest developments in the entire equal opportunity area.

(b) Line responsibilities should include, but not be limited to the following:

(1) Assistance in the identification of problem areas and establishment of local and unit goals and objectives.

(2) Active involvement with local minority organizations, women's organizations, community action groups, and community service programs.

(3) Periodic audit of training programs, hiring and promotion patterns to remove impediments to the attainment of goals and objectives.

(4) Regular discussions with local managers, supervisors, and employees to be certain the contractor's policies are being followed.

(5) Review of the qualifications of all employees to ensure that minorities and women are given full opportunities for transfers and promotions.

(6) Career counseling for all employees.

(7) Periodic audit to ensure that each location is in compliance in areas such as:

(i) Posters are properly displayed.

(ii) All facilities, including company housing, which the contractor maintains for the use and benefit of his employees, are in fact desegregated, both in policy and use. If the contractor provides facilities such as dormitories, locker rooms, and rest rooms, they must be comparable for both sexes.

(iii) Minority and female employees are afforded a full opportunity and are encouraged to participate in all company sponsored educational, training, recreational and social activities.

(8) Supervisors should be made to understand that their work performance is being evaluated on the basis of their equal employment opportunity efforts and results, as well as other criteria.

(9) It shall be a responsibility of supervisors to take actions to prevent harassment of employees placed through affirmative action efforts.

§60-2.23. Identification of Problem Areas by Organizational Units and Job Groups

(a) An in-depth analysis of the following should be made, paying particular attention to trainees and those categories listed in §60-2.11(b).

(1) Composition of the workforce by minority group status and sex.

(2) Composition of applicant flow by minority group status and sex.

(3) The total selection process including position descriptions, position titles, worker specifications, application forms, interview procedures, test administration, test validity, referral procedures, final selection process, and similar factors.

(4) Transfer and promotion practices.

(5) Facilities, company sponsored recreation and social events, and special programs such as educational assistance.

(6) Seniority practices and seniority provisions of union contracts.

(7) Apprenticeship programs.

(8) All company training programs, formal and informal.

(9) Workforce attitude.

(10) Technical phases of compliance, such as poster and notification to labor unions, retention of applications, notification to subcontractors, etc.

(b) If any of the following items are found in the analysis, special corrective action should be appropriate.

(1) An "underutilization" of minorities and women in specific job groups.

(2) Lateral and/or vertical movement of minority or female employees occurring at a lesser rate (compared to workforce mix) than that of nonminority or male employees.

(3) The selection process eliminates a significantly higher percentage of minorities or women than nonminorities or men.

(4) Application and related preemployment forms not in compliance with Federal legislation.

(5) Position descriptions inaccurate in relation to actual functions and duties.

(6) Formal or scored selection procedures not validated as required by the OFCCP Uniform Guidelines on Employee Selection procedures.

(7) Test forms not validated by location, work performance and inclusion of minorities and women in sample.

(8) Referral ratio of minorities or women to the hiring supervisor or manager indicates a significantly higher percentage are being rejected as compared to nonminority and male applicants.

(9) Minorities or women are excluded from or are not participating in company sponsored activities or programs.

(10) De facto segregation still exists at some facilities.

(11) Seniority provisions contribute to overt or inadvertent discrimination, i.e., a disparity by minority group status or sex exists between length of service and types of job held.

(12) Nonsupport of company policy by managers, supervisors, or employees.

(13) Minorities or women underutilized or significantly underrepresented in training or career improvement programs.

(14) No formal techniques established for evaluating effectiveness of EEO programs.

(15) Lack of access to suitable housing inhibits recruitment efforts and employment of qualified minorities.

(16) Lack of suitable transportation (public or private) to the work place inhibits minority employment.

(17) Labor unions and subcontractors not notified of their responsibilities.

(18) Purchase orders do not contain EEO clause.

(19) Posters not on display.

§60-2.24. Development and Execution of Programs

(a) The contractor should conduct detailed analyses of position descriptions to ensure that they accurately reflect position functions, and are consistent for the same position from one location to another.

(b) The contractor should validate worker specifications by division, department, location, or other organizational unit, and by job title, using job performance criteria. Special attention should be given to academic, experience, and skill requirements to ensure that the requirements in themselves do not constitute inadvertent discrimination. Specifications should be consistent for the same job title in all locations and should be free from bias as regards to race, color, religion, sex, or national origin, except where sex is a bona fide occupational qualification. Where requirements screen out a disproportionate number of minorities or women, such requirements should be professionally validated to job performance.

(c) Approved position descriptions and worker specifications, when used by the contractor, should be made available to all members of management involved in the recruiting, screening, selection, and promotion process. Copies should also be distributed to all recruiting sources.

(d) The contractor should evaluate the total selection process to ensure freedom from bias and, thus, aid the attainment of goals and objectives.

(1) All personnel involved in the recruiting, screening, selection, promotion, disciplinary, and related processes should be carefully selected and trained to ensure elimination of bias in all personnel actions.

(2) The contractor shall observe the requirements of the OFCCP *Uniform Guidelines on Employee Selection Procedures.* (*See 401:2231.*)

(3) Selection techniques other than tests may also be improperly used so as to have the effect of discriminating against minority groups and women. Such techniques include, but are not restricted to, unscored interviews, unscored or casual application forms, arrest records, credit checks, considerations of marital status or dependency or minor children. Where there exist data suggesting that such unfair discrimination or exclusion of minorities or women exists, the contractor should analyze his unscored procedures and eliminate them if they are not objectively valid.

(e) Suggested techniques to improve recruitment and increase the flow of minority or female applicants follow:

(1) Certain organizations such as the Urban League, Job Corps, Equal Opportunity Programs, Inc., Concentrated Employment programs, Neighborhood Youth Corps, Secondary Schools, Colleges, and City Colleges with high minority enrollment, the State Employment Service, specialized employment agencies, Aspira, LULAC, SER, the G.I. Forum, the Commonwealth of Puerto Rico are normally prepared to refer minority applicants. Organizations prepared to refer women with specific skills are: National Organization for Women, Welfare Rights organizations, Women's Equity Action League, Talent Bank from Business and Professional Women (including 26 women's organizations), Professional Women's Caucus, Intercollegiate Association of University Women, Negro Women's sororities and service groups such as Delta Sigma Theta, Alpha Kappa Alpha, and Zeta Phi Beta; National Council of Negro Women, American Association of University Women, YWCA,

and sectarian groups such as Jewish Women's Groups, Catholic Women's Groups, and Protestant Women's Groups, and women's colleges. In addition, community leaders as individuals shall be added to recruiting sources.

(2) Formal briefing sessions should be held, preferably on company premises, with representatives from these recruiting sources. Plant tours, presentations by minority and female employees, clear and concise explanations of current and future job openings, position descriptions, worker specifications, explanations of the company's selection process, and recruiting literature should be an integral part of the briefings. Formal arrangements should be made for referral of applicants, follow-up with sources, and feedback on disposition of applicants.

(3) Minority and female employees, using procedures similar to subparagraph (2) of this paragraph, should be actively encouraged to refer applicants.

(4) A special effort should be made to include minorities and women on the Personnel Relations staff.

(5) Minority and female employees should be made available for participation in Career Days, Youth Motivation Programs, and related activities in their communities.

(6) Active participation in "Job Fairs" is desirable. Company representatives so participating should be given authority to make on-the-spot commitments.

(7) Active recruiting programs should be carried out at secondary schools, junior colleges, and colleges with predominant minority or female enrollments.

(8) Recruiting efforts at all schools should incorporate special efforts to reach minorities and women.

(9) Special employment programs should be undertaken whenever possible. Some possible programs are:

(i) Technical and nontechnical coop programs with predominantly Negro and women's colleges.

(ii) "After school" and/or workstudy jobs for minority youths, male and female.

(iii) Summer jobs for underprivileged youth, male and female.

(iv) Summer work-study programs for male and female faculty members of the predominantly minority schools and colleges.

(v) Motivation, training and employment programs for the hard-core unemployed, male and female.

(10) When recruiting brochures pictorially present work situations, the minority and female members of the workforce should be included, especially when such brochures are used in school and career programs.

(11) Help wanted advertising should be expanded to include the minority news media and women's interest media on a regular basis.

(f) The contractor should ensure that minority and female employees are given equal opportunity for promotion. Suggestions for achieving this result include:

(1) Post or otherwise announce promotional opportunities.

(2) Make an inventory of current minority and female employees to determine academic, skill and experience level of individual employees.

(3) Initiate necessary remedial, job training and workstudy programs.

(4) Develop and implement formal employee evaluation programs.

(5) Make certain "worker specifications" have been validated on job performance related criteria. (Neither minority nor female employees should be required to possess higher qualifications than those of the lowest qualified incumbent.)

(6) When apparently qualified minority or female employees are passed over for upgrading, require supervisory personnel to submit written justification.

(7) Establish formal career counseling programs to include attitude development, education aid, job rotation, buddy system, and similar programs.

(8) Review seniority practices and seniority clauses in union contracts to ensure such practices or clauses are nondiscriminatory and do not have a discriminatory effect.

(g) Make certain facilities and company-sponsored social and recreation activities are desegregated. Actively encourage all employees to participate.

(h) Encourage child care, housing and transportation programs appropriately designed to improve the employment opportunities for minorities and women.

§60-2.25. Internal Audit and Reporting Systems

(a) The contractor should monitor records of referrals, placements, transfers, promotions, and terminations at all levels to ensure nondiscriminatory policy is carried out.

(b) The contractor should require formal reports from unit managers on a scheduled basis as to degree to which corporate or unit goals are attained and timetables met.

(c) The contractor should review report results with all levels of management.

(d) The contractor should advise top management of program effectiveness and submit recommendations to improve unsatisfactory performance.

§60-2.26. Support of Action Programs

(a) The contractor should appoint key members of management to serve on merit employment councils, community relations boards, and similar organizations.

(b) The contractor should encourage minority and female employees to participate actively in National Alliance of Businessmen programs for youth motivation.

(c) The contractor should support vocational guidance institutes, vestibule training programs and similar activities.

(d) The contractor should assist secondary schools and colleges in programs designed to enable minority and female graduates of these institutions to compete in the open employment market on a more equitable basis.

(e) The contractor should publicize achievements of minority and female employees in local and minority news media.

(f) The contractor should support programs developed by such organizations as National Alliance of Business, the Urban Coalition and other organizations concerned with employment opportunities for minorities or women.

SUBPART D—MISCELLANEOUS

§60-2.30. Use of Goals

The purpose of a contractor's establishment and use of goals is to ensure that it meets its affirmative action obligation. It is not intended and should not be used to discriminate against any applicant or employee because of race, color, religion, sex, or national origin.

§60-2.31. Preemption

To the extent that any State or local laws, regulations or ordinances, including those which grant special benefits to persons on account of sex, are in conflict with Executive Order 11246, as amended, or with requirements of this part, we will regard them as preempted under the Executive Order.

§60-2.32. Supersedure

All orders, instructions, regulations, and memoranda of the Secretary of Labor, other officials of the Department of Labor and contracting agencies are hereby superseded to the extent that they are inconsistent herewith, including a previous "Order No. 4" from this office dated January 30, 1970. Nothing in this part is intended to amend 41 CFR 60-3 or 41 CFR 60-20.

APPENDIX C

Employment Regulations for the Americans With Disabilities Act (EEOC)

PART 1630—REGULATIONS TO IMPLEMENT THE EQUAL EMPLOYMENT PROVISIONS OF THE AMERICANS WITH DISABILITIES ACT

Appendix to Part 1630—Interpretive Guidance on Title I of the Americans with Disabilities Act

Authority: 42 U.S.C. 12116.

§1630.1 Purpose, applicability, and construction.

(a) *Purpose.* The purpose of this part is to implement title I of the Americans with Disabilities Act (42 U.S.C. 12101, *et seq.* (ADA), requiring equal employment opportunities for qualified individuals with disabilities, and sections 3(2), 3(3), 501, 503, 506(e), 508, 510, and 511 of the ADA as those sections pertain to the employment of qualified individuals with disabilities.

(b) *Applicability.* This part applies to "covered entities" as defined at §1630.2(b).

(c) *Construction.*—(1) *In general.* Except as otherwise provided in this part, this part does not apply a lesser standard than the standards applied under title V of the Rehabilitation Act of 1973 (29 U.S.C. 790-794a), or the regulations issued by Federal agencies pursuant to that title.

(2) *Relationship to other laws.* This part does not invalidate or limit the remedies, rights, and procedures of any Federal law or law of any State or jurisdiction that provides greater or equal protection for the rights of individuals with disabilities than are afforded by this part.

§1630.2 Definitions.

(a) *Commission* means the Equal Employment Opportunity Commission established by section 705 of the Civil Rights Act of 1964 (42 U.S.C. 2000e-4).

(b) *Covered Entity* means an employer, employment agency, labor organization, or joint labor management committee.

(c) *Person, labor organization, employment agency, commerce, and industry affecting commerce* shall have the same meaning given those terms in section 701 of the Civil Rights Act of 1964 (42 U.S.C. 2000e).

(d) *State* means each of the several States, the District of Columbia, the Commonwealth of Puerto Rico, Guam, American Samoa, the Virgin Islands, the Trust Territory of the Pacific Islands, and the Commonwealth of the Northern Mariana Islands.

(e) *Employer.*—(1) *In general.* The term employer means a person engaged in an industry affecting commerce who has 15 or more employees for each working day in each of 20 or more calendar weeks in the current or preceding calendar year, and any agent of such person, except that, from July 26, 1992 through July 25, 1994, an employer means a person engaged in an industry affecting commerce who has 25 or more employees for each working day in each of 20 or more calendar weeks in the current or preceding year and any agent of such person.

(2) *Exceptions.* The term employer does not include—

(i) The United States, a corporation wholly owned by the government of the United States, or an Indian tribe; or

(ii) A bona fide private membership club (other than a labor organization) that is exempt from taxation under section 501(c) of the Internal Revenue Code of 1986.

(f) *Employee* means an individual employed by an employer.

(g) *Disability* means, with respect to an individual—

(1) A physical or mental impairment that substantially limits one or more of the major life activities of such individual;

(2) A record of such an impairment; or

(3) being regarded as having such an impairment.

(See §1630.3 for exceptions to this definition.)

(h) *Physical or mental impairment* means:

(1) Any physiological disorder, or condition, cosmetic disfigurement, or anatomical loss affecting one or more of the following body systems: neurological, musculoskeletal, special sense organs, respiratory (including speech organs), cardiovascular, reproductive, digestive, genito-urinary, hemic and lymphatic, skin, and endocrine; or

(2) Any mental or psychological disorder, such as mental retardation, organic brain syndrome, emotional or mental illness, and specific learning disabilities.

(i) *Major Life Activities* means functions such as caring for oneself, performing manual tasks, walking, seeing, hearing, speaking, breathing, learning, and working.

(j) *Substantially limits*—(1) The term *substantially limits* means:

(i) Unable to perform a major life activity that the average person in the general population can perform; or

(ii) Significantly restricted as to the condition, manner, or duration under which an individual can perform a particular major life activity as compared to the condition, manner, or duration under which the average person in the general population can perform that same major life activity.

(2) The following factors should be considered in determining whether an individual is substantially limited in a major life activity:

(i) The nature and severity of the impairment;

(ii) The duration or expected duration of the impairment; and

(iii) The permanent or long term impact, or the expected permanent or long term impact of or resulting from the impairment.

(3) With respect to the major life activity of *working*—

(i) The term *substantially limits* means significantly restricted in the ability to perform either a class of jobs or a broad range of jobs in various classes as compared to the average person having comparable training, skills, and abilities. The inability to perform a single, particular job does not constitute a substantial limitation in the major life activity of working.

(ii) In addition to the factors listed in paragraph (j)(2) of this section, the following factors may be considered in determining whether an individual is substantially limited in the major life activity of "working":

(A) The geographical area to which the individual has reasonable access;

(B) The job from which the individual has been disqualified because of an impairment, and the number and types of jobs utilizing similar training, knowledge, skills, or abilities, within that geographical area, from which the individual is also disqualified because of the impairment (class of jobs); and/or

(C) The job from which the individual has been disqualified because of an impairment, and the number and types of other jobs not utilizing similar training, knowledge, skills, or abilities, within that geographical area, from which the individual is also disqualified because of the impairment (broad range of jobs in various classes).

(k) *Has a record of such impairment* means has a history of, or has been misclassified as having, a mental or physical impairment that substantially limits one or more major life activities.

(l) *Is regarded as having such an impairment* means:

(1) Has a physical or mental impairment that does not substantially limit major life activities but is treated by a covered entity as constituting such limitation;

(2) Has a physical or mental impairment that substantially limits major life activities only as a result of the attitudes of others toward such impairment; or

(3) Has none of the impairments defined in paragraphs (h) (1) or (2) of this section but is treated by a covered entity as having a substantially limiting impairment.

(m) *Qualified individual with a disability* means an individual with a disability who satisfies the requisite skill, experience, education, and other job related requirements of the employment position such individual holds or desires, and who, with or without reasonable accommodation, can perform the essential functions of such position. (See §1630.3 for exceptions to this definition.)

(n) *Essential functions.*—(1) *In general.* The term *essential functions* means the fundamental job duties of the employment position the individual with a disability holds or desires. The term "essential functions" does not include the marginal functions of the position.

(2) A job function may be considered essential for any of several reasons, including but not limited to the following:

(i) The function may be essential because the reason the position exists is to perform that function;

(ii) The function may be essential because of the limited number of employees available among whom the performance of that job function can be distributed; and/or

(iii) The function may be highly specialized so that the incumbent in the position is hired for his or her expertise or ability to perform the particular function.

(3) Evidence of whether a particular function is essential includes, but is not limited to:

(i) The employer's judgment as to which functions are essential;

(ii) Written job descriptions prepared before advertising or interviewing applicants for the job;

(iii) The amount of time spent on the job performing the function;

(iv) The consequences of not requiring the incumbent to perform the function;

(v) The terms of a collective bargaining agreement;

(vi) The work experience of past incumbents in the job; and/or

(vii) The current work experience of incumbents in similar jobs.

(o) *Reasonable accommodation.*—(1) The term *reasonable accommodation* means:

(i) Modifications or adjustments to a job application process that enable a qualified applicant with a disability to be considered for the position such qualified applicant desires; or

(ii) Modifications or adjustments to the work environment, or to the manner or circumstances under which the position held or desired is customarily performed, that enable a qualified individual with a disability to perform the essential functions of that position; or

(iii) Modifications or adjustments that enable a covered entity's employee with a disability to enjoy equal benefits and privileges of employment that are enjoyed by its other similarly situated employees without disabilities.

(2) *Reasonable accommodation* may include but is not limited to:

(i) Making existing facilities used by employees readily accessible to and usable by individuals with disabilities; and

(ii) Job restructuring; part-time or modified work schedules; reassignment to a vacant position; acquisition or modifications of equipment or devices; appropriate adjustment or modifications of examinations, training materials, or policies; the provision of qualified readers or interpreters; and other similar accommodations for individuals with disabilities.

(3) To determine the appropriate reasonable accommodation it may be necessary for the covered entity to initiate an informal, interactive process with the qualified individual with a disability in need of the accommodation. This process should identify the precise limitations resulting from the disability and potential reasonable accommodations that could overcome those limitations.

(p) *Undue hardship*—(1) *In general. Undue hardship* means, with respect to the provision of an accommodation, significant difficulty or expense incurred by a covered entity, when considered in light of the factors set forth in paragraph (p)(2) of this section.

(2) *Factors to be considered.* In determining whether an accommodation would impose an undue hardship on a covered entity, factors to be considered include:

(i) The nature and net cost of the accommodation needed under this part, taking into consideration the availability of tax credits and deductions, and/or outside funding;

(ii) The overall financial resources of the facility or facilities involved in the provision of the reasonable accommodation, the number of persons employed at such facility, and the effect on expenses and resources;

(iii) The overall financial resources of the covered entity; the overall size of the business of the covered entity with respect to the number of its employees; and the number, type, and location of its facilities;

(iv) The type of operation or operations of the covered entity, including the composition, structure, and functions of the workforce of such entity, and the geographic separateness and administrative or fiscal relationship of the facility or facilities in question to the covered entity; and

(v) The impact of the accommodation upon the operation of the facility, including the impact on the ability of other employees to perform their duties and the impact on the facility's ability to conduct business.

(q) *Qualification standards* means the personal and professional attributes including the skill, experience, education, physical, medical, safety and other requirements established by a covered entity as requirements which an individual must meet in order to be eligible for the position held or desired.

(r) *Direct threat* means a significant risk of substantial harm or the health or safety of the individual or others that cannot be eliminated or reduced by reasonable accommodation. The determination that an individual poses a "direct threat" shall be based on an individualized assessment of the individual's present ability to safely perform the essential functions of the job. This assessment shall be based on a reasonable medical judgment that relies on the most current medical knowledge and/or on the best available objective evidence. In determining whether an individual would pose a direct threat, the factors to be considered include:

(1) The duration of the risk;

(2) The nature and severity of the potential harm;

(3) The likelihood that the potential harm will occur; and

(4) The imminence of the potential harm.

§1630.3   Exceptions to the definitions of "Disability" and "Qualified Individual with a Disability."

(a) The terms *disability* and *qualified individual with a disability* do not include individuals currently engaging in the illegal use of drugs, when the covered entity acts on the basis of such use.

(1) *Drug* means a controlled substance, as defined in schedules I through V of Section 202 of the Controlled Substances Act (21 U.S.C. 812).

(2) *Illegal use of drugs* means the use of drugs, the possession or distribution of which is unlawful under the Controlled Substances Act, as periodically updated by the Food and Drug Administration. This term does not include the use of a drug taken under the supervision of a licensed health care professional, or other uses authorized by the Controlled Substances Act or other provisions of Federal law.

(b) However, the terms *disability* and *qualified* individual with a disability may not exclude an individual who:

(1) Has successfully completed a supervised drug rehabilitation program and is no longer engaging in the illegal use of drugs, or has otherwise been rehabilitated successfully and is no longer engaging in the illegal use of drugs; or

(2) Is participating in a supervised rehabilitation program and is no longer engaging in such use; or

(3) Is erroneously regarded as engaging in such use, but is not engaging in such use.

(c) It shall not be a violation of this part for a covered entity to adopt or administer reasonable policies or procedures, including but not limited to drug testing, designed to ensure that an individual described in paragraph (b)(1) or (2) of this section is no longer engaging in the illegal use of drugs. (See §1630.16(c) Drug testing).

(d) *Disability* does not include:

(1) Transvestism, transsexualism, pedophilia, exhibitionism, voyeurism, gender identity disorders not resulting from physical impairments, or other sexual behavior disorders;

(2) Compulsive gambling, kleptomania, or pyromania; or

(3) Psychoactive substance use disorders resulting from current illegal use of drugs.

(e) *Homosexuality and bisexuality* are not impairments and so are not disabilities as defined in this part.

§1630.4 Discrimination prohibited.

It is unlawful for a covered entity to discriminate on the basis of disability against a qualified individual with a disability in regard to:

(a) Recruitment, advertising, and job application procedures;

(b) Hiring, upgrading, promotion, award of tenure, demotion, transfer, layoff, termination, right of return from layoff, and rehiring;

(c) Rates of pay or any other form of compensation and changes in compensation;

(d) Job assignments, job classifications, organizational structures, position descriptions, lines of progression, and seniority lists;

(e) Leaves of absence, sick leave, or any other leave;

(f) Fringe benefits available by virtue of employment, whether or not administered by the covered entity;

(g) Selection and financial support for training, including: apprenticeships, professional meetings, conferences and other related activities, and selection for leaves of absence to pursue training;

(h) Activities sponsored by a covered entity including social and recreational programs; and

(i) Any other term, condition, or privilege of employment.

The term *discrimination* includes, but is not limited to, the acts described in §§1630.5 through 1630.13 of this part.

§1630.5 Limiting, segregating, and classifying.

It is unlawful for a covered entity to limit, segregate, or classify a job applicant or employee in a way that adversely affects his or her employment opportunities or status on the basis of disability.

§1630.6 Contractual or other arrangements.

(a) *In general.* It is unlawful for a covered entity to participate in a contractual or other arrangement or relationship that has the effect of subjecting the covered entity's own qualified applicant or employee with a disability to the discrimination prohibited by this part.

(b) *Contractual or other arrangement defined.* The phrase *contractual or other arrangement or relationship* includes, but is not limited to, a relationship with an employment or referral agency; labor union, including collective bargaining agreements; an organization providing fringe benefits to an employee of the covered entity; or an organization providing training and apprenticeship programs.

(c) *Application.* This section applies to a covered entity, with respect to its own applicants or employees, whether the entity offered the contract or initiated the relationship, or whether the entity accepted the contract or acceded to the relationship. A covered entity is not liable for the actions of the other party or parties to the contract which only affect that other party's employees or applicants.

§1630.7 Standards, criteria, or methods of administration.

It is unlawful for a covered entity to use standards, criteria, or methods of administration, which are not job related and consistent with business necessity, and;

(a) That have the effect of discriminating on the basis of disability; or

(b) That perpetuate the discrimination of others who are subject to common administrative control.

§1630.8 Relationship or association with an individual with a disability.

It is unlawful for a covered entity to exclude or deny equal jobs or benefits to, or otherwise discriminate against, a qualified individual because of the known disability of an individual with whom the qualified individual is known to have a family, business, social, or other relationship or association.

§1630.9 Not making reasonable accommodation.

(a) It is unlawful for a covered entity not to make reasonable accommodation to the known physical or mental limitations of an otherwise qualified applicant or employee with a disability, unless such covered entity can demonstrate that the accommodation would impose an undue hardship on the operation of its business.

(b) It is unlawful for a covered entity to deny employment opportunities to an otherwise qualified job applicant or employee with a disability based on the need of such covered entity to make reasonable accommodation to such individual's physical or mental impairments.

(c) A covered entity shall not be excused from the requirements of this part because of any failure to receive technical assistance authorized by section 506 of the ADA, including any failure in the development or dissemination of any technical assistance manual authorized by that act.

(d) A qualified individual with a disability is not required to accept an accommodation, aid, service, opportunity, or benefit which such qualified individual chooses not to accept. However, if such individual rejects a reasonable accommodation, aid, service, opportunity or benefit that is necessary to enable the individual to perform the essential functions of the position held or desired, and cannot, as a result of that rejection, perform the essential functions of the position, the individual will not be considered a qualified individual with a disability.

§1630.10 Qualification standards, tests, and other selection criteria.

It is unlawful for a covered entity to use qualification standards, employment tests or other selection criteria that screen out or tend to screen out an individual with a disability or a class of individuals with disabilities, on the basis of disability, unless the standard, test, or other selection criteria, as used by the covered entity, is shown to be job related for the position in question and is consistent with business necessity.

§1630.11 Administration of tests.

It is unlawful for a covered entity to fail to select and administer tests concerning employment in the most effective manner to ensure that, when a test is administered to a job applicant or employee who has a disability that impairs sensory, manual, or speaking skills, the test results accurately reflect the skills, aptitude, or whatever other factor of the applicant or employee that the test purports to measure, rather than reflecting the impaired sensory, manual, or speaking skills of such employee or applicant (except where such skills are the factors that the test purports to measure).

§1630.12 Retaliation and coercion.

(a) *Retaliation.* It is unlawful to discriminate against any individual because that individual has opposed any act or practice made unlawful by this part or because that individual made a charge, testified, assisted, or participated in any manner in an investigation, proceeding, or hearing to enforce any provision contained in this part.

(b) *Coercion, interference or intimidation.* It is unlawful to coerce, intimidate, threaten, harass or interfere with any individual in the exercise or enjoyment of, or because that individual aided or encouraged any other individual in the exercise of, any right granted or protected by this part.

§1630.13 Prohibited medical examinations and inquiries.

(a) *Pre-employment examination or inquiry.* Except as permitted by §1630.14, it is unlawful for a covered entity to conduct a medical examination of an applicant or to make inquiries as to whether an applicant is an individual with a disability or as to the nature or severity of such disability.

(b) *Examination or inquiry of employees.* Except as permitted by §1630.14, it is unlawful for a covered entity to require a medical examination of an employee or to make inquiries as to whether an employee is an individual with a disability or as to the nature of severity of such disability.

§1630.14 Medical examinations and inquiries specifically permitted.

(a) *Acceptable pre-employment inquiry.* A covered entity may make pre-employment inquiries into the ability of an applicant to perform job related functions, and/or may ask an applicant to describe or to demonstrate how, with or without reasonable accommodation, the applicant will be able to perform job related functions.

(b) *Employment entrance examination.* A covered entity may require a medical examination (and/or inquiry) after making an offer of employment to a job applicant and before the applicant begins his or her employment duties, and may condition an offer of employment on the results of such examination (and/or inquiry), if all entering employees in the same job category are subjected to such an examination (and/or inquiry) regardless of disability.

(1) Information obtained under paragraph (b) of this section regarding the medical condition or history of the applicant shall be collected and maintained on separate forms and in separate medical files and be treated as a confidential medical record, except that:

(i) Supervisors and managers may be informed regarding necessary restrictions on the work or duties of the employee and necessary accommodations;

(ii) First aid and safety personnel may be informed, when appropriate, if the disability might require emergency treatment; and

(iii) Government officials investigating compliance with this part shall be provided relevant information on request.

(2) The results of such examination shall not be used for any purpose inconsistent with this part.

(3) Medical examinations conducted in accordance with this section do not have to be job related and consistent with business necessity. However, if certain criteria are used to screen out an employee or employees with disabilities as a result of such an examination or inquiry, the exclusionary criteria must be job related and consistent with business necessity, and performance of the essential job functions cannot be accomplished with reasonable accommodation as required in this part. (See §1630.15(b) Defenses to charges of discriminatory application of selection criteria.)

(c) *Examination of employees.* A covered entity may require a medical examination (and/or inquiry) of an employee that is job related and consistent with business necessity. A covered entity may make inquiries into the ability of an employee to perform job related functions.

(1) Information obtained under paragraph (c) of this section regarding the medical condition or history of any employee shall be collected and maintained on separate forms and in separate medical files and be treated as a confidential medical record, except that:

(i) Supervisors and managers may be informed regarding necessary restrictions on the work or duties of the employee and necessary accommodations;

(ii) First aid and safety personnel may be informed, when appropriate, if the disability might require emergency treatment; and

(iii) Government officials investigating compliance with this part shall be provided relevant information on request.

(2) Information obtained under paragraph (c) of this section regarding the medical condition or history of any employee shall not be used for any purpose inconsistent with this part.

(d) *Other acceptable examinations and inquiries.* A covered entity may conduct voluntary medical examinations and activities, including voluntary medical histories, which are part of an employee health program available to employees at the work site.

(1) Information obtained under paragraph (d) of this section regarding the medical condition or history of any employee shall be collected and maintained on separate forms and in separate medical files and be treated as a confidential medical record, except that:

(i) Supervisors and managers may be informed regarding necessary restrictions on the work or duties of the employee and necessary accommodations;

(ii) First aid and safety personnel may be informed, when appropriate, if the disability might require emergency treatment; and

(iii) Government officials investigating compliance with this part shall be provided relevant information on request.

(2) Information obtained under paragraph (d) of this section regarding the medical condition or history of any employee shall not be used for any purpose inconsistent with this part.

§1630.15 Defenses.

Defenses to an allegation of discrimination under this part may include, but are not limited to, the following:

(a) *Disparate treatment charges.* It may be a defense to a charge of disparate treatment brought under §§1630.4 through 1630.8 and 1630.11 through 1630.12 that the challenged action is justified by a legitimate, nondiscriminatory reason.

(b) *Charges of discriminatory application of selection criteria—*(1) *In general.* It may be a defense to a charge of discrimination, as described in §1630.10, that an alleged application of qualification standards, tests, or selection criteria that screens out or tends to screen out or otherwise denies a job or benefit to an individual with a disability has been shown to be job related and consistent with business necessity, and such performance cannot be accomplished with reasonable accommodation, as required in this part.

(2) *Direct threat as a qualification standard.* The term "qualification standard" may include a requirement that an individual shall not pose a direct threat to the health or safety of the individual or others in the workplace. (See §1630.2(r) defining direct threat.)

(c) *Other disparate impact charges.* It may be a defense to a charge of discrimination brought under this part that a uniformly applied standard, criterion, or policy has a disparate impact on an individual with a disability or a class of individuals with disabilities that the challenged standard, criterion, or policy has been shown to be job related and consistent with business necessity, and such performance cannot be accomplished with reasonable accommodation, as required in this part.

(d) *Charges of not making reasonable accommodation.* It may be a defense to a charge of discrimination, as described in §1630.9, that a requested or necessary accommodation would impose an undue hardship on the operation of the covered entity's business.

(e) *Conflict with other Federal laws.* It may be a defense to a charge of discrimination under this part that a challenged action is required or necessitated by another Federal law or regulation, or that another Federal law or regulation prohibits an action (including the provision of a particular reasonable accommodation) that would otherwise be required by this part.

(f) *Additional defenses.* It may be a defense to a charge of discrimination under this part that the alleged discriminatory action is specifically permitted by §§1630.14 or 1630.16.

§1630.16 Specific activities permitted.

(a) *Religious entities.* A religious corporation, association, educational institution, or society is permitted to give preference in employment to individuals of a particular religion to perform work connected with the carrying on by that corporation, association, educational institution, or society of its activities. A religious entity may require that all applicants and employees conform to the religious tenets of such organization. However, a religious entity may not discriminate against a qualified individual, who satisfies the permitted religious criteria, because of his or her disability.

(b) *Regulation of alcohol and drugs.* A covered entity:

(1) May prohibit the illegal use of drugs and the use of alcohol at the workplace by all employees;

(2) May require that employees not be under the influence of alcohol or be engaging in the illegal use of drugs at the workplace;

(3) May require that all employees behave in conformance with the requirements established under the Drug-Free Workplace Act of 1988 (41 U.S.C. 701 et seq.);

(4) May hold an employee who engages in the illegal use of drugs or who is an alcoholic to the same qualification standards for employment or job performance and behavior to which the entity holds its other employees, even if any unsatisfactory performance or behavior is related to the employee's drug use or alcoholism;

(5) May require that its employees employed in an industry subject to such regulations comply with the standards established in the regulations (if any) of the Departments of Defense and Transportation, and of the Nuclear Regulatory Commission, regarding alcohol and the illegal use of drugs; and

(6) May require that employees employed in sensitive positions comply with the regulations (if any) of the Departments of Defense and Transportation and of the Nuclear Regulatory Commission that apply to employment in sensitive positions subject to such regulations.

(c) *Drug testing*—(1) *General policy.* For purposes of this part, a test to determine the illegal use of drugs is not considered a medical examination. Thus, the administration of such drug tests by a covered entity to its job applicants or employees is not a violation of §1630.13 of this part. However, this part does not encourage, prohibit, or authorize a covered entity to conduct drug tests of job applicants or employees to determine the illegal use of drugs or to make employment decisions based on such test results.

(2) *Transportation Employees.* This part does not encourage, prohibit, or authorize the otherwise lawful exercise by entities subject to the jurisdiction of the Department of Transportation of authority to:

(i) Test employees of entities in, and applicants for, positions involving safety sensitive duties for the illegal use of drugs or for on-duty impairment by alcohol; and

(ii) Remove from safety-sensitive positions persons who test positive for illegal use of drugs or on-duty impairment by alcohol pursuant to paragraph (c)(2)(i) of this section.

(3) *Confidentiality.* Any information regarding the medical condition or history of any employee or applicant obtained from a test to determine the illegal use of drugs, except information regarding the illegal use of drugs, is subject to the requirements of §1630.14(b) (2) and (3) of this part.

(d) *Regulation of smoking.* A covered entity may prohibit or impose restrictions on smoking in places of employment. Such restrictions do not violate any provision of this part.

(e) *Infectious and communicable diseases; food handling jobs*—(1) *In general.* Under title I of the ADA, section 103(d)(1), the Secretary of Health and Human Services is to prepare a list, to be updated annually, of infectious and communicable diseases which are transmitted through the handling of food. (Copies may be obtained from Center for Infectious Diseases, Centers for Disease Control, 1600 Clifton Road, NE., Mailstop C09, Atlanta, GA 30333.) If an individual with a disability is disabled by one of the infectious or communicable diseases included on this list, and if the risk of transmitting the disease associated with the handling of food cannot be eliminated by reasonable accommodation, a covered entity may refuse to assign or continue to assign such individual to a job involving food handling. However, if the individual with a disability is a current employee, the employer must consider whether he or she can be accommodated by reassignment to a vacant position not involving food handling.

(2) *Effect on State or other laws.* This part does not preempt, modify, or amend any state, county, or local law, ordinance, or regulation applicable to food handling which:

(i) Is in accordance with the list, referred to in paragraph (e)(1) of this section, of infectious or communicable diseases and the modes of transmissibility published by the Secretary of Health and Human Services; and

(ii) Is designed to protect the public health from individuals who pose a significant risk to the health or safety of others, where that risk cannot be eliminated by reasonable accommodation.

(f) *Health insurance, life insurance, and other benefit plans*—(1) An insurer, hospital, or medical service company, health maintenance organization, or any agent or entity that administers benefit plans, or similar organizations may underwrite risks, classify risks, or administer such risks that are based on or not inconsistent with State law.

(2) A covered entity may establish, sponsor, observe or administer the terms of a bona fide benefit plan that are based on underwriting risks, classifying risks, or administering such risks that are based on or not inconsistent with State law.

(3) A covered entity may establish, sponsor, observe, or administer the terms of a bona fide benefit plan that is not subject to State laws that regulate insurance.

(4) The activities described in paragraphs (f) (1), (2), and (3) of this section are permitted unless these activities are being used as a subterfuge to evade the purposes of this part.

NAME INDEX

SUBJECT INDEX